I

The

Religion und Biographie
Religion and Biography

herausgegeben von/edited by

Prof. Dr. Detlev Dormeyer (Dortmund)
Prof. Dr. Ruard Ganzevoort (Amsterdam)
Prof. Dr. Linus Hauser (Gießen)
Prof. Dr. Friedhelm Munzel (Dortmund)

Band/Volume 15

LIT

Ineke de Feijter

The Art of Dialogue

Religion, Communication and Global Media Culture

LIT

Cover illustration: H. N. Werkman, *The Hasidic Legends*, a suite
By courtesy of Collection Groninger Museum, photo John Stoel
(with permision of the Stichting H. N. Werkman).
© Groninger Museum, www.groningermuseum.nl

Bibliographic information published by the Deutsche Nationalbibliothek
The Deutsche Nationalbibliothek lists this publication in the Deutsche
Nationalbibliografie; detailed bibliographic data are available in the Internet at
http://dnb.d-nb.de.

ISBN 978-3-8258-0050-5
Zugl.: Amsterdam, Univ., Diss., 2006

A catalogue record for this book is available from the British Library

© LIT VERLAG Berlin 2007
Auslieferung/Verlagskontakt:
Fresnostr. 2   48159 Münster
Tel. +49 (0)251–62 03 20   Fax +49 (0)251–23 19 72
e-Mail: lit@lit-verlag.de   http://www.lit-verlag.de

Distributed in the UK by: Global Book Marketing, 99B Wallis Rd, London, E9 5LN
Phone: +44 (0) 20 8533 5800 – Fax: +44 (0) 1600 775 663
http://www.centralbooks.co.uk/acatalog/search.html

Distributed in North America by:

Transaction Publishers
New Brunswick (U.S.A.) and London (U.K.)

Transaction Publishers
Rutgers University
35 Berrue Circle
Piscataway, NJ 08854

Phone: +1 (732) 445 - 2280
Fax: + 1 (732) 445 - 3138
for orders (U. S. only):
toll free (888) 999 - 6778
e-mail:
orders@transactionspub.com

Of all affairs, communication is the most wonderful

John Dewey

To Naomi,

Lieven, Amabelle and Jiāo Lín

The 'lovelies' of my life

Contents

Preface

'Of all affairs, communication is the most beautiful', John Dewey said. He is right. There is no greater joy than the feeling of being deeply and mutually related to one another in dialogue, an endless discovery of amazement.

During the formation of this volume, I have been fortunate to experience this joy and amazement many times, in an academic, professional and personal sense. This has occurred during discussions with colleagues in international conferences about media, religion and culture, with students and colleagues in the faculty, and with experienced and admirable scholars, who were willing to share their wisdom. But it has also happened in meeting people who dared to open up in both the most beautiful as well as the most difficult times of their life, sharing deep concerns, far beyond talk. I'm very grateful to all of them.

Communicative joy and amazement however, also can turn into its counterpoint. It was brutally disturbed on September 17, 2004, the day my whole family was involved in a car accident. The day of the loss of one of our four children, my dearest Naomi….

She is sheer amazement. Full of life, enjoying, discovering, playing, blossoming out, teeming with new games and plans. But also mischievous and tender, courageous and shy, a ringleader and sweet and caring, all at the same time. Every time I look at her pictures on my desk -her bright twinkling eyes, the dimples in her cheeks and her generous laugh- I realize over and over again how she lives entirely up to her name: Naomi - the Hebrew word for lovely.

Encouraging she is as well. After her passing away I was not able to continue this volume for a long time. Until that day when I found her little letter again, with those precious childlike written words wishing me luck on presenting my first paper at an international conference. It was boxed in by sweet red hearts, and both our names written all over.

This volume is wholeheartedly dedicated to her - with whom communicating will never come to an end. And to her brave and caring brother, Lieven, her little sister, Amabelle, who is trying so hard to be big now, and to her small and cheerful sissy, Jiao Lin. All three of them live up to their names as well - each also means lovely in Flemish, in French, and in Chinese. Those names deeply relate all four of them forever. They encourage me in innumerable many ways with their little gestures, their many hugs, drawings and conversations, and their loyalty and love. I admire the way they picked up their lives again, their patience, endurance and lovely support for this undertaking. How proud I am of them is far beyond my ability to communicate. If it were not for the love of those four, I am not sure whether I would ever have been able to finish this book, and it fills me with great pride and joy that Lieven participated in the PhD graduation ceremony as my very special *paranimf*.

In a way this book is dedicated to my parents as well, who have seen its progression, but never its completion. Losing both the generation before me as well as part of the generation after me in such a short period of time, is hard to cope with. I remember both of them with love, having dedicated their lives to raise their eight children on a small farm.

Many people -in one way or another- have contributed to this volume. I wish to express my gratitude to all of them. At the risk of incompleteness, however, I would like to mention the names of some of them in special - in which all are included.

I am extremely grateful to Prof. Dr. Cees Hamelink, who taught me more (and still does) than he probably realizes. I joyfully remember our many dialogues, of which the amazement continued to increase even a long time afterwards. I also remember his gentle encouragement months after Naomi died. And his classes that I attended, in order to prepare myself to become his successor at the Vrije Universiteit Amsterdam - which still fills me with pride.

His many publications and contributions to conferences, in which this rare combination of both profound scientific and excellent communicative quality converge.

As well as the way he involves his audiences during his presentations, revealing his other creative competences - being a professional musician as well. Another form of communication through a variety of instruments that are each given their due, and still harmonize in dialogue, up to the point that communication is able to transcend itself.

I cherish our warm friendship that has grown over the years.

I also would like to express my extreme gratitude to another highly-estimated, long-term teacher and now my colleague: Dr. Hanneke Meulink. I came to know her important scientific contributions to pastoral theology as a student 15 years ago. In the past two years her excellent, professional pastoral skills, her warm friendship, and her loving care helped me through those extremely difficult moments when communication seems beyond reach. Without these hours of dialogue, silence, grief, her patience and careful listening and encouragement, I would not have been able to reach today's point.

I would also like to thank Dr. Eddy Van der Borght for his sympathy with this project, and his thoughtful comments and encouragements during long train journeys when we traveled home together. A long-standing colleague in Belgian ministry, I rejoiced on our collegial reunion in the faculty and the intensifying of our friendship.

I could not have wished for two better *paranifms* who are that close to me.

A number of colleagues in the field either shared their knowledge about communication and theology or commented on earlier parts or drafts of this thesis. In random order I wish to thank: Prof. Dr. Franz-Josef Eilers, Prof. Dr. William Fore, Prof. Dr. Paul Soukup, Prof. Dr. Peter Horsfield, Dr. Hans Wolfgang Hessler, Prof. Dr. Robert White, Prof. Dr. Frances Forde Plude, Prof. Dr. Clifford Christians, Dr. Jolyon Mitchell, Prof. Dr. Ruard Ganzevoort, Dr. Wim Noomen, Prof. Dr. Alle Hoekema, Prof. Dr. Birgit Meyer, Prof. Dr. Karel Deurloo, Dr. Jan Greven and Dr. Albert van den Heuvel. I also want to thank my colleagues of the department of practical theology and social sciences at the *Vrije Universiteit* Amsterdam for the valuable, monthly conversations about our work - including this volume- their support and pleasant collegiality. I am also grateful for the help provided by all the representatives of the churches and their institutes who helped me along in the protracted search for policy statements.

Many people helped me out with 'practical', however - very important issues. I would like to thank Annette Mosher for the accuracy with which she corrected my English, her openness and empathy.

I also like to express my deep gratitude to Morris Defeyter, my dearest uncle from Canada, who did (and does) not allow his Parkinson disease to cause him to surrender, nor to keep him from sending his English language comments. After the loss of Naomi he was the first to encourage me to continue, which -as he said- 'would make me very proud'. I therefore dedicate this work also to him, having been an excellent teacher himself, as a present for his 80th birthday. And thank him for his cordiality and wisdom - which is always communicated with humor- for the novel about his life, and his lively and witty poems.

I thank Mrs. Liisa Finch, for translating the Finnish documents and Mr. Harry Onzia for the Swedish translations. Elly de Feijter, who took care of placing all the text in its right lay-out, and Rinus Roepman, who designed the cover, I thank, for putting their energy and creative skills into this book. I also would like to thank sister Johanna -cordial as always- from the abbey 'Onze Lieve Vrouw van Nazareth' in Brecht (Belgium), whose community kindly provided me with the silence I needed and a quiet place to study once a week, during the last year and a half. All computer problems were immediately remedied by Ad, my husband. Part of his wordless, however enduring interest and support to my work - for which I'm grateful.

I hope this volume will inspire theologians, religious scholars and students in this field to reflect on media and communication and to dialogue - regardless of whether they agree with the outcome of this study or not. I also hope it will be a worthy contribution to the interdisciplinary dialogue between scholars in the field of media, religion and culture and to media and communication scholars (becoming) interested in the field of religion.

In the Bible there is this beautiful story of a little boy, the youngest of a family of eight. A nondescript, red-haired, young fellow that dwells in the fields, looking after his father's sheep. His three elder brothers all are at 'the front'. That is to say, they gaze (as does their whole army), everyday at this gigantic terrifying creature who belongs to the adversary Philistines: Goliath. This man-to-man fighter ridicules them day after day, by showing himself every morning and every night, for forty days, on the top of the mountain where both armies are camped. He scoffs their fear and challenges them to pick out and send one man to fight with him.
One day, little David is sent by his father to bring bread and cheese to the leader of his people's army, and to see if his brothers are all right. On his arrival, Goliath climbs the mountain again. After having checked how his brothers are, David looks and listens to Goliath's scoffing. He also notes the fear of his people. They tell him that the man who defeats Goliath will become very fortunate. Whereupon, David asks: 'who for God's sake is this Philistine, this uncircumcised, having been allowed to scoff at the battle arrays of the living God?' And again his people tell him that the man who defeats Goliath will be extremely fortunate. David's eldest brother, overhearing the conversation, flies into a rage, shouting at David: 'why for God's sake did you come? I know your rashness! You just wanted to come and see the war!'.
To which David answers: 'What exactly is it, I've done? It was only just a question'![1]

If this volume might lead to just ask the right questions about (religious) communication, I would be more than pleased.

Shuswap Lake, Canada,
Amsterdam, the Netherlands

Summer 2006

---

[1] In the original Hebrew text it reads: a *dabar*. We will further explain this term in section 4.2 (note 8).

Introduction

On any given Sunday morning, one may surf the local channels to see and hear how churches are using this medium. Typically, a television presentation is related to the liturgical tradition of the congregation (…) but how many religious groups really understand the extensive presence and power of televised rituals and icons? How many have considered how adopting the forms of popular culture will change the shape of their worship life and subtly alter their message? Or comprehend the ways in which ideologies are communicated through commercial television? Unlike America's corporate and advertising institutions, few religious groups seem to grasp the encompassing symbolic function of the medium, either as a means of social integration or as a way to perpetuate a value system[1].

Gregor Goethals

The book of Acts tells us the story of the Apostle Paul's arrival in Athens. Waiting for his companions, Silas and Timothy, he investigates the city. Greatly upset by the abundance of statues of idols, he decides to discuss this subject with other people. Not only with his co-believers in the synagogue, but also with the people in the public square. On a daily basis, he talks with whomever he comes across. Among these individuals are Epicurean and Stoic teachers.

One day, they take him to the *Areopagus*, the place to be for philosophical debate. They ask him to explain his new and strange teachings. Standing before the *Areopagus*, Paul starts -not bluntly by preaching his gospel- but by taking up the way of living and thinking of his audience including their enormous curiosity and excitement for anything new. Paul transports himself mentally to their beliefs, values, truths and practices, before addressing the people of Athens and the many foreigners among them. He acknowledges their beliefs, by saying he 'perceived they are in every way very religious'. For as he passed along, observing the objects of worship, he also found an altar with the inscription 'To the unknown god.' Exactly that is related by Paul to the subject he wants to bring up, and he starts talking about God -who created the world- the Lord of heaven and earth[2].

This small story is, in several ways, a metaphor for the situation of Christianity -and religion in general[3]- that needs to communicate in today's world, which is saturated by electronic media.

---

[1] Goethals, Gregor. 2000. 'The Electronic Golden Calf: Transforming Ritual and Icon' in Forbes, Bruce David and Mahan, Jeffrey H. (eds.) *Religion and Popular Culture in America*. Berkeley and Los Angeles, University of California Press. p. 134.

[2] Acts 17:15-34. See e.g. the English Standard Version http://www.biblegateway.com, *the New International Version*: http://www.ibs.org and the King James Version: http://www.hti.umich.edu

[3] That is one of the reasons why this volume's subtitle is: Religion, *Communication and Global Media Culture* and not *Christianity, Communication and Global Media Culture*. Our research population, as we will illuminate in chapter three, indeed consists of Christian policy statements published by mainstream Churches. However, our interest is explicitly not restricted to institutional forms of Christianity only. All over church history there have been other minor, often suppressed, forms. In contemporary media culture however, focusing merely on institutional Christianity would be a mistake, not to say an impossibility. As we will show in the section on the religious dimensions of media culture, a variety of different forms of religion interact, among which institutional Christianity is but one.

Like Paul, religions have to face the challenge of communicating in a market of ideas, beliefs and practices. It is a competitive market, which is increasingly shaped by media processes themselves.

It is an *Areopagus* in which people find and shape their own views and opinions, their own value systems, their own symbols and icons and rituals, according to their own preferences. Even questions about the meaning of life and ultimate issues have become part of this competitive market. Religious institutes cannot exercise, so to speak 'exclusive' rights anymore, they no longer are the main primary source of religious information. Again, like in the days of Paul, they have to operate from a marginalized position.

But this time, there is more to it. It is not only a matter of declined significance and influence of e.g. the churches, but media, in their own way, offer symbols, rituals, forms of community, etc. According to Peter Horsfield (1997:178), by doing so, the media themselves have become religious by accomplishing a *religious role*. 'The media as the agents of convergence present a significant alternative source of religious information, sentiment, ethical guidance, ritual, and community, not only for the broader population, but also for those who are members of religious institutions. Religious organizations may no longer be the main source of religious information, truth, or practice, even for their own members'[4].

Moreover, it is the media that now set the agenda and put pressure on all social institutions, including the churches.

As Denis McQuail (2000:471) notes: 'As the media have developed, they have, without doubt, achieved two things: diverted time and attention from other activities, and become a channel for reaching more people with more information than was available under 'pre-mass-media' conditions. These facts have implications for any social institution that needs to gain public attention and to communicate to the society at large. Other institutions are under pressure to adapt or respond in some way to the mass media, or to make their own use of mass media channels. In doing so, they are likely to change their own practices, especially by adapting to what has been called a 'media logic' (see page 335). According to Altheide and Snow (1991:ix), 'today all social institutions are media institutions'[5].

Mainstream churches have problems facing this cultural reality and they hardly seem to know how to handle it. Generally speaking their relationship with communication media is problematic.

'Religion does not score on television' was the pregnant statement made by Cardinal Godfried Danneels, head of the Roman Catholic Church in Belgium during a lecture at the Catholic University of Nijmegen in the Netherlands (2002) on his experiences with media.

Although Danneels is a much appreciated and frequently solicited guest of the media, and probably more than any other clerical authority understands -and respects- the logic of media, his criticism is the prototype of the plaintive tone often used by churches when it comes to media.

---

[4] Horsfield, Peter G. 1997. 'Changes in Religion in Periods of Media Convergence', in Stewart M. Hoover and Knut Lundby, (eds.) *Rethinking Media, Religion and Culture*. Thousand Oaks, Sage. p. 78.

[5] McQuail, Denis. 2000. *McQuail's mass communication theory*. 4th edition. London, Sage. p. 471. The book McQuail refers to is: Altheide, D.L. and Snow, R.P. 1991. *Media Worlds in the Post journalism Era*. New York, Aldine/de Gruyter.

Media are 'not interested' in the spiritual message of the churches. They 'use' church leaders only to confront social or ethical issues in order to enliven their programs. Media 'only report church scandals' and are interested in spicy stories. Packaging supplants content and profit demands cause 'hit and run' journalism that is dominated by the never ending pursuit of scoops. Since there is not much to scoop with 'ancient' stories as found in the Bible, and since churches are on the slow side rather than 'quick and fast', they are 'treated step-motherly' by the media.

Whatever the truth of these claims, there is much more to the subject, which is -unfortunately- hardly the focus of enduring, profound, theological research.

Media Culture

We live in a media saturated world. An era amid, as some say, nothing less than a 'communication revolution' is going on. Information and communication technologies spread throughout the universe, linking us all to the 'global village' and beyond.
Downing, Mohammadi and Sreberny-Mohammadi (1995) describe this collective of media as the *'global central nervous system'*.

The impact of this nervous system is immense. It changed the way we work, talk, travel, spend our leisure time, buy and pay, educate our children, vote in elections, perform arts etc.
We can hardly imagine anymore what social, political and economic life was like without radio, television, newspapers and magazines, our mobile telephone and computer, cable, satellite and the internet.

Stock markets -for example- and global financial trading around the clock would be inconceivable without the present state of media.

The same applies to the way wars are fought. A Dutch television news commentator on the second Persian Gulf war called it a "laptop war" since all soldiers of the US and the UK were linked up electronically to each other, which made fast communication and movement possible. There were mesh networks (the same principle the internet is based on) in small mobiles, which eliminated the necessity of masts and exchanges, absent in the Iraqi desert. The soldiers -each provided with a microphone- mutually functioned as such. Combined with the small computer conveyed missiles (which we already knew from the first Persian Gulf war in 1991), we saw network based conduct of war for the first time in history. It was a 'clean' war, at least so the images brought to our television screen wanted us to believe. It was reported by 'embedded' journalists and brought to our homes by satellite as if we were present ourselves. To realize then again we fortunately were not, seeing the other side of mediated reality, in the images of the face of the Iraqi boy who lost both his arms and his parents in the bombing raids.

Mobility would not be at its present level if it were not for information and communication technologies. And what should we think of the global success of music-artists, sportsmen, film actors, televangelists? What about the styles offered to young people on how to dress and behave in the 24-hour -musical- channel MTV in order to be part of any chosen subculture? Or the global knowledge of brand names carefully marketed by advertisers to the farthest corners of the world? Or the influence of media 'images' of candidate members of parliament or candidates running for presidency during elections and in politics in general?

Neither would the growth and fast exchange of information and mobilization in the 'other-globalists-movement'[6] be conceivable without the present state of media. Or the 'Cultural Village' project[7] in which twelve villages throughout Europe formed a grass roots network to counter the effects of globalization and urbanization and as village communities want to contribute to public awareness.

The success of initiatives, like the site 'Religion Online'[8], which provides full scholarly materials on all major religions would also not be possible. Initially built to support third world students and teachers from theological colleges who could not obtain books, now each year more than 1 million visitors throughout the world download more than 3½ million documents.
It was never before so easy for me to be in touch regularly with my old Latin-African university friend Juan Manuel Eko in Brazil, to visit libraries all over the world or to exchange insights on media, religion and culture in list serves[9].

In short, we have come to live in a *media culture*.

Implications

What does this mean to our communication? Or the way we perceive our society, the world, life, time and space, our culture, other cultures and religions, men and women, elderly, blacks and whites, good and bad, success and failure, standards, values, the future, even ourselves, the (O)other and religion?
This is a very important, and at the same time very complex, question to ask for the churches. What does this media culture mean as an assumed context that they are part of? Not only regarding their existence as churches per se that is affected by media culture, but particularly related to the possibilities and restrictions of the public communication of the stories of the bible -which might require, for example, new institutional embodiments-.

The significance of those questions might even become more pregnant if we realize the link between the inventions of new communication media and large cultural, historical transitions. The shift for example from speech being central in oral culture to written communication deeply impacted Christian religion. The Book of Acts shows marks of this shift, in the transition of the early Christian Church, rooted in the Jewish culture, into the Hellenistic culture. This transition, according to Horsfield (1997:173) was 'not just a simple process of organizational expansion', but, 'a movement from a largely oral context into a manuscript context. The dynamic process of adjustment that followed took centuries, resulting in the redefinition of faith from a particular into a universal context, the shift of authority from an apostolic to a hierarchical Episcopal base, the establishment of a written canon, and the stabilizing of orthodoxy through ecumenical creeds'.
The new technology of writing thus meant more than just a means of communication and it was difficult and complex for Christian communities to adapt themselves and their religious thought to it, and integrate it.

---

[6] The 'non-globalist movement', as it is termed in the media, in fact should be termed the 'other' globalist movement, since it strives for a different form of globalization, which includes e.g. social justice etc. instead of merely market driven economic globalization.
[7] http://www.cultural-village-.com retrieved May, 20, 2003.
[8] http://www.religion-online.org retrieved March, 20, 2003.
[9] http://monaro.adc.rmit.edu.au/mailman/listinfo/media.faith retrieved March, 20, 2003.

The same applies to the implications of the print era, which also transcends mere instrumentality.
Annabelle Sreberny-Mohammadi (1995) identifies important social, cultural, economical and political effects. These are due to the impact of print, which mechanized the production of information. These effects vary from new forms of linguistic development (linear, logical and progressive) to symbolic language fostering abstract thinking instead of concrete, oral memory. They also vary from literacy and secular education to the rapid spread of vernaculars and the advent of national identities, the rise of new social authorities and new jobs, -such as authors-.

In regard to communication and religion, the impact of the printing press was profound. Decontextualization of messages, due to the possibility to transport them, accounted for less control and more flexibility. Newspapers were created with new forms of communication -like prose fiction and serialized novels- since the poetic rhyme that served memory in oral culture was no longer the only necessary form. The increase of books -detached from the monopoly of papal authority - stimulated religious debate and secular ideologies. English and vernacular Bibles became bestsellers. Churches' dominance over knowledge and interpretation decreased.
Luther's dissident voice probably would not have had the impact it had without the printing press. It was, according to him, 'the best of God's inventions' and it spread his ideas and pamphlets like wildfire and fuelled the Reformation. Coffeehouses, pubs and salons became new spaces of public sphere. New secular social authorities came to the fore and dissident voices mobilized public opinion, pushing for political democracy and social justice.

On the other hand the printing press also extended the possibilities of control. James Carey (1992) argues that before decentralizing tendencies, centralizing ones enlarged "the domain of empire". In this respect there is an analogy in any new invention of communication whether it is writing, print, electronic or computer mediated communication.
In the Gospel of Luke, Joseph and Mary are forced to come to Bethlehem shortly before Jesus is born due to a command of the emperor to 'register the entire empire'. It is hardly accidental that the invention and application of many information and communication technologies are often closely related to military. Followed by governmental and commercial and -in the past- religious authorities. The archives of the Roman inquisition (established in 1542) and the index of forbidden books (the first one was published in 1559 and they were released for scientific research only in 1998) are examples that show how the printing press was not only an enormous opportunity for writings and ideas, but also for censorship[10].

Sreberny-Mohammadi (1995) underlines the importance of taking into account the way media technology is adopted and institutionalized in society when considering the impact of media. Communication issues are embedded in a broader sociological, political, economic and cultural context.
Bordewijk and Van Kaam (1982) developed a new conception with respect to the traffic of information in society[11]. They pointed out how patterns of information flows also express power relationships. In chapter one and two, we will elaborate on their concept.

---

[10] Godman, Peter. 2003. *Het geheim van de inquisitie. Uit de verborgen archieven van het Vaticaan.* Baarn, Tirion. Reviewed by Gie van den Berghe in Trouw, 26-08-2003. p. 10.
[11] Bordewijk, J.L. and van Kaam, Ben. 1982. *Allocutie, enkele gedachten over communicatievrijheid in een bekabeld land.* Baarn, Bosch&Keuning.

The point at issue for now is that media technology; patterns of communication and culture mutually interact.

Following the invention of print, Carey (1992) identifies two other 'communications revolutions' with impacts at least comparable, if not more fundamental, to that of the printing press.

The first has to do with the separation of 'transportation' and 'communication'. Whereas in print (and before), production and transportation of information belonged together in order to make communication happen, electricity made it possible to discern production and, transmission of messages. Inventions -like the telegraph, the telephone, radio and television- are based on this principle.

In his essay on the history of the telegraph, Carey shows how deeply American society was affected and changed by this new invention.
Understanding this impact is important because the essay (though devoted to the telegraph), at the same time, surpasses this device by serving as a model of interpretation for later (and future), major developments in communications.
As such the telegraph is one in a long line of new information and communication technologies that, however different they may be, seem to develop time and again within and according to similar economic, technological, political, socio/cultural, media theoretical and religious discourses.

Carey, in this respect, identifies four recurring developments regarding the invention of new communication media beginning with the telegraph: (1) being dominated by industrial monopolies, (2) being a product of the electrical goods industry and thus of the science- and engineering-based industries. (3) bringing about changes in language, ordinary knowledge and structures of awareness, and (4) being a watershed in communication.

By telegraph it was possible to have information travel independently and faster than any other transportation medium. It was also possible for the first time to control physical processes, for example, railroad signaling.
In economic terms this meant a wide range of opportunities -especially in combination with the railroad- and had profound impacts. Personal relationships of trade were substituted by impersonal contacts of buyers and sellers. Prices were no longer subject to local supply and demand, but became dependent on decontextualized national markets. New forms of production, management and administration appeared, organizational structures changed, and credit business and mail order houses emerged. Products needed standardization to meet similar categories of quality. A new, national, commercial, middle class arose. Colonial relationships altered, -e.g. the power of the domestic governor declined-, and imperialism by capital took their place. Urban imperialism did the same on a national level. The telegraph also played a substantial role militarily, and in the offspring of new laws.

In communication, the telegraph signaled a turning point. It took only twelve years after Samuel Morse invented the telegraph for the first news agency or wire service to form, The Associated Press (1848). It pushed towards 'objectivity', nationally standardized (and more) 'scientific' language, routine criteria for news, and efficient organization. The reporter displaced the editor, and the correspondent -who once had the 'luxury' of providing background information and analysis- now had to keep to the 'bare facts'. News became a commodity and traditional forms like humor and tall stories disappeared.

The telegraph not only meant a 'technical' change with respect to communication and transportation, but it altered communication itself and the ways it was viewed. According to Carey, a 'transmission' model -aimed at the extension of messages in space- pushed out older religious views of communication that aimed at the maintenance of society in time by representing shared beliefs. This even changed the very structures of awareness. The telegraph was, in Carey's words, not only a "new tool of commerce," but also a "thing to think with". He shows how it deeply altered consciousness of space and time and e.g. led to the grid of time zones (1894) as we still know them. All for the sake of control and coordination of (economic) activity. Resulting in a profound change of the praxis of rhythms and ideas of temporality and 'sacred' time (think e.g. of ritual time).

The impact of the new communication technology thus was far beyond economics that found its power base in communication. As Sreberny-Mohammadi suggests, we need to look at the institutionalization of the telegraph to understand the full range of its impact.

Institutionalization

Carey's essay offers a clear and interesting insight in this respect about the surrounding ideology that guided and legitimized the telegraph.
"(...) these new and unprecedented relations of communication and contact had themselves to be explained, justified, and made effective. What we innocently describe as theory, law, common sense, religion were means by which these new relations were carried through to explicit consciousness and "naturalized" – made to seem merely of the order of things" (1992:206).

Carey states three interrelated connections between the telegraph and ideology: monopoly capitalism, the "rhetoric of the electrical sublime" (which qualified the telegraph in popular imagery as an almost mythical device with possibilities literally even not limited anymore by the sky) and the ideal of universalism and progress, which found its way deep into popular consciousness.

Within the scope of our study, it is important to take a closer look at the role of religion in the introduction of the telegraph. Carey (1992:207) cites revealing statements of preachers at that time about the mysterious invisible forces of electricity newly "under our control" and the "spiritual harvest" to come because "thought now travels by magnetic wires". As Carey comments: "This new technology enters American discussions not as a mundane fact but as divinely inspired for the purposes of spreading the Christian message farther and faster, eclipsing time and transcending space, saving the heathen, bringing closer and making more probable the day of salvation".

In this respect, both the printing press and the telegraph proved to be the first in a long line of recurrent religious views on communication technologies and the role of communication -including communication models- as the deliverers of humanity and progress, of the brotherhood of men, and of the Kingdom of God.
Yet the point is that these views perfectly match with the scientific, commercial and political ideological rationales (power, profit, productivity, progress) mentioned above and help establish not only the uncritical acceptance of this new communication device, with all its profound implications and social and moral effects, but also rooted this ideology in popular consciousness.

That in itself is questionable and verifies the need to include this as an important topic when reflecting on the relationship between churches and contemporary media culture.

But even if we narrow down the question to what new communication technologies mean regarding 'possibilities' for the public communication of churches, a problem arises.
If Carey is right that the 'transmission' model pushed out older religious views of communication, there seems to be a *contradictio in terminis* in this establishing, lyrical religious view towards the telegraph (and its successors).
If one remembers the lament of Cardinal Godfried Danneels mentioned above, it might be sincerely asked whether media developments have turned out to be the churches' Pandora's Box.

However, as Carey summarizes, the telegraph brought forth mass press, new social interactions, new conceptual systems, new forms of language, new structures of social relationships, a national commercial middle class, the extension of spatial boundaries and new conceptions of time[12].

Regarding this last aspect Carey (1992:228) points out the line from the telegraph to the computer: 'The penetration of time, the use of time as a mechanism of control, the opening of time to commerce and politics has been radically extended by advances in computer technology. Time has been redefined as an ecological niche to be filled down to the microsecond, nanosecond and picosecond – down to a level at which time can be pictured but not experienced. This process and the parallel reconstruction of practical consciousness and practical activity begins in those capacities of the telegraph which prefigure the computer (...) Today, computer time, computer space, and computer memory, notions we dimly understand, are reworking practical consciousness coordinating and controlling life in what we glibly call the post-industrial society'.

The third 'communications revolution' that Carey identifies is the linking up of time-shared computers, television and telephone, which produces new systems of communication.

This brings us to contemporary issues of our so called 'information society', 'network society', 'media era', information age', 'digital era' 'multimedia age' with its 'information highways', 'global networks', 'virtual reality', 'cyber space' and 'communication revolutions' to mention but a few of the glossy, uncritically assumed terms, which all seem to share a common problem: they are hard to define, hard to prove and it is difficult to come to grips with their effects, especially in the long run.
The same holds for the impact of electronic public media. Television penetrated most deeply into society and into people's lives. Even to the extent that terms like a 'television society' or 'television era' became common in the 1980's.

Similarities

Looking at the institutionalization of public media, and television in particular, striking similarities between the earlier and later information and communication technological developments show up.

---

[12] As identified by communication scholars Harold Innis and Marshal McLuhan, space and time are two essential aspects for any analysis of media.

To mention but a few, television also altered our perceptions of time and space. We only need to think of a term like *prime-time-television*. According to Sreberny-Mohammadi (1995) electronic media in postindustrial societies are "powerful timekeepers", since television programming schedules put tight time demands on the audience. They do not only support how we divide work and leisure, they also reinforce family life patterns and gender interests. Think for example of the scheduling of soap opera's (a genre said to be attractive especially to women) during daytime. The close relationship between advertisements and program scheduling does not leave much room for flexibility. In this respect even the VCR did not substantially alter anything[13].

The fact that television programs are aired 24 hours a day is another example of what Carey called the 'penetration of time'. The penetration of space even became extra-terrestrial. Carey points out the link between the printing press and the navigation, between the telegraph and the railroad and between the electronic media and the spacecraft.

Other similarities concern monopolistic tendencies and the mythical rhetoric celebration of the 'electronic media revolution'. This was to turn our world into a 'global village' and leading automatically towards democratization, social harmony and peace, decentralization, the enlargement of freedom, ecological balance, massive diffusion of knowledge, universal understanding and unity, and equal chances for anyone to participate in this thrilling new Eden.

The fact that electronic media, one way or another, change social interactions and relationships, and influence new conceptual systems and new forms of language may be beyond dispute (though far from consensus with respect to extent and direction).

According to Sreberny-Mohammadi, television -for example- undermines abstract language and rational analysis and discussion because of its focus on fragmentation, speed, images and celebrities. Joshua Meyrowitz (1995), on the other hand, makes a plea to look at the underlying dynamic of television as an empowering medium, which changed -for example- child/adult, male/female and leader/follower experiences.

Although we do not want to pursue this point for now, the cultural and social impact is obvious.

We only need to think of the presence of a television set in every family member's bedroom or what the exact identification of a word like 'authenticity' in contemporary media environment means. Or simply watch the creation of a totally new binary alphabet used in computer based communication, or imagine the impact of a Western

---

[13] In this respect the newer developments of the so called *'pull media'* (instead of the older 'push media') like 'programs on demand' 'pay per view' might offer interesting developments, due to the opportunity for the audience to skip commercials. Leading advertising companies, however, look for new ways to get their commercials across e.g. by putting them into content. It has become usual already to involve marketing editors in the phase of script writing, so that place and time of the commercials or the way products or services will be 'placed' can be determined exactly and program formats can be adjusted accordingly. Other new 'interactive' ways of reaching people are not restricted to mass media but invade the whole of society. The newest technique in this respect is the 'wizmark'. A 'talking pee-mat' in men's lavatories, introduced by PinkEye in the Netherlands. As soon as men come into the lavatory, the thing starts to speak. 'Hey you...yeah you! I know what you really want'. According to PinkEye it is the best way to attract attention to typical male products and services. A female (digital screen) version is afoot. As well as the *'Hypertag'* , an electronic chip in advertisement and film posters in bus shelters, inviting people to join and play. By activating their infrared function of their cell phone and aim at the poster, they can download a movie trailer or a discount coupon. Unlike sms, this is free, since no telephone line is needed. Some say communicating with these kinds of 'inanimate objects' might be the future of advertising. Source: 'Pratende plasmat als nieuwste adverteertruc' in Trouw, 16/09/05, p.13.

media program diet on the culture and language of a child in a small town village in one of the so called 'developing' countries.

Religion

To observe the impact on religion, we can identify the relevance of highly mediated symbols, subcultures and communities to adolescents - including religious youth - in searching for their way of life and role in society and in their internalization of matters of ultimate meaning, values and beliefs.

In her dissertation, Identity, Discourse, and Media Audiences: A Critical Ethnography of the Role of Visual Media in Religious Identity Construction among U.S. Adolescents[14], Lynn Schofield Clark identifies three distinctive elements of religious identity construction among contemporary teenagers.
Religious symbols, which were formerly -by definition- authoritative and fixed to formal religious institutions, are "flattened" into autonomous symbols that must be made useful just as any other commodified symbol.
In determining religious identities -a matter of personal autonomy and privatized religion- adolescents embrace a variety of publicly available religious discourses. The mediated realm is very important in this respect.
Interpretation of media texts (within the framing of different cultural, social, political and economical discourses and contexts) has a regenerating effect. This means that the interpretation that an individual makes also informs -and thus slightly changes- his/her larger system of beliefs.

Gregor Goethals (2000) in her essay, The Electronic Golden Calf transforming Ritual and Icon, describes the reshaping by electronic media -especially television- of symbolism from a religious to a secular realm. Especially in their function of social integration and expressing, shaping and maintaining community beliefs, values and loyalties, there is, according to Goethals, an analogy between secular media ceremonies and sacred rituals and liturgy. Electronic ritual presence in large events and manifestations -sports, political or entertainment that are set apart in ritual space and ritual time- provides many with a sense of community. It also reinforces the values of e.g. nationality or consumption.
An important issue for churches in this respect is the question, what this means to the icons and symbols of religious belief? What happens to (in Goethals' terms) 'the electronic transformation of the word'? Television evangelism, with its religious commodities and celebrity preachers (who become the new holy images themselves) promoted what Goethals calls a 'technological sacramentalism'.
As she (Goethals 2000: 142/43) demonstrates, the psychological power of conversion involved, finds its match in advertising media. 'Disdained though it may be, the television commercial may be the most significant example of a fortuitous interaction of media and "religion" in contemporary American society. Television advertisement draws upon the "born-again" philosophy of evangelical denominations, since the dynamics of a religious heritage -namely, an emphasis on salvation and choice- are embedded in the structure of many advertisements. Echoing the passionate pleas of the preacher, advertising images evoke in us both fear and desire; products now offer salvation, and the consumer's decision, whether about a new car or a can of beer, marks a turning point that makes life excitingly fresh and different. Thus the conversionist religious motif itself is refurbished in a consumer society. Furthermore, commercials do more than advertise individual products; taken collectively, they promote an encompassing faith in the

---

[14] 1998, Center for Mass Media Research, University of Colorado.

American Way. In buying products and services, we become members incorporated in the mystical body of those who have been redeemed through consuming'.

One might object that this statement is about the U.S. and, therefore, is not applicable to the situation in Europe, with its different media systems and religious realms. There is no doubt that they make things different.
Even so, the point that we have tried to indicate in this introduction is that the impact of media is not only restricted to economic, political, social or cultural aspects, but also applies to religion. Profound changes are happening seemingly unnoticed. If the revolutionary claims of an 'information and communication society' are to be materialized, then -at the very least- it is a 'revolution without revolt' in several respects.

Interdisciplinary

One would expect the interrelation between media, culture and religion to be a much-debated hot issue in churches and among theologians. But the opposite seems to be the case.
Increasingly, churches have come to pay attention to cultural issues, especially relating to the enculturation of the gospel and 'post-modernity'. Curiously enough, they do not take the media sphere into account.

But as media scholars, Hoover and Lundby (1997:10), state: 'It seems impossible to reach a complete understanding of the relationship between religion and culture today without incorporating a theory of media and communication'.
The term 'media' in this respect not only refers to technology, but to a wider context and process of the cultural practice of communication, called mediation[15].

How then is the relationship between media, culture and religion to be approached? Hoover and Lundby strongly urge the necessity of a cross disciplinary enterprise in which cultural studies, media studies and religious studies meet and cross fertilize. This is the only way to grasp the complexity of the relationship and the possible convergence of religion and media within contemporary culture.
Theology is invited and challenged to contribute to, -and to my opinion benefit from-, this interdisciplinary enterprise. This is a challenge theologians and churches cannot and should not be willing to refuse.
For too long, the media sphere has been a blind spot (as is religion in media studies). Both theology and churches minimize the media issue to either lament or opportunism (in which the media are viewed as new missionary tools, used however in old communication patterns). These visions may be part of the discussion, but reflection should go further than these.

The media context as such -that is the contemporary surrounding environment and culture in which people live and make meaning from- should be an important and enduring issue on churches' agenda.
In my own context of the Netherlands it is not. Unfortunately, in the last decade nearly all the institutions working in this field have been discontinued by churches for lack of

---

[15] The term 'mediation' in communication studies, which we will consider in chapter one, is said to stem from the Latin American media scholar Jésus Martín Barbero. 1985. *De los medios a las mediaciones*. México, Ediciones G. Gilli, S.A. de C.V. Also published in English (1993) as *Communication, culture and hegemony: From the media to mediations*. London, Sage. However, as Franz-Josef Eilers pointed out to me (personal conversation, September 3, 2004) Gaston Roberge, in 1980 wrote his book entitled *Mediation: the action of the media in our society*. It was published by Manohar, ASIN: B0006E4BKK.

money and interest. For example, these include the Catholic Media Centre, the Interdenominational Media Institute, the Media Committee of the Netherlands Missionary Council, and the media study group of the Dutch Council of Churches.
In faculties of theology, media are hardly a subject and, if so, are of subordinate and occasional interest[16].

Aim and structure

The general intention of this study is to support theology and mainstream Christianity to understand and relate to contemporary media culture in a more profound way. As well as to contribute to the interdisciplinary field of media, culture and religion.

Mainstream Christianity and religion in general, are profoundly challenged by contemporary global mass media culture. Not only with respect to their public communication, but also in their very existence, their being and public relevance. Mainstream churches in the North-Western context are having problems in relating to the realities of media culture and public communication and dealing with the challenges involved.
Solving these problems is often merely thought of as a matter of praxis, e.g. on the level of improving public relations, restructuring communication departments or even applying marketing techniques.
To our opinion, however, there is a preceding level that initially should be researched and is often missed out: the location of these problems at the level of policy outlines. Exactly at this level insights are to be found on the views of media context and culture and related to issues of Christian identity, theological presuppositions in communication, and responsibilities and priorities in public communication. Moreover insights may be gained on churches' definitions and views on communication and communication models. It might well be that problems in the praxis of churches' public communication, are rooted in this level.

To my knowledge no theological studies exist, which reflect on churches' policy-views in this field -and the ways these policies ground their communication praxis- related to the way (and extent to which) media culture affects churches' communication and being. This is even more compelling as present media culture, to a large extent, is conditioned by digital media and information and communication technologies, and meditated 'interactive' forms of communication. Moreover, this media culture appears to involve religious dimensions. Mainstream institutional churches on the other hand, find themselves in a crisis, which is related to the shift in dominant media in society, from writing and print to digital interactive forms of communication. Churches, having a longstanding tradition of proclaiming, linear forms of communication, in which media are merely instruments of dissemination, hardly seem capable of handling this crisis.

The main aim of this research, then, is (1) to analyze and evaluate recent policies on communication and media by mainstream churches in North-Western Europe and their (global) communication institutes, (2) in view of identifying the main problems in their understanding of contemporary media context and media culture and (3) relate those to the concept of dialogue (and the public sphere being its prerequisite) as the main form of communication suited to -and needed by- contemporary digital, interactive global media culture.

---

[16] Since 2002 the theological department of the Vrije Universiteit Amsterdam holds the only chair on religion and communication in the Netherlands.

Derived from this setting of objectives, our research topic is to be summarized as: what are the challenges of contemporary global media culture to the public communication and being of mainstream churches in North-Western Europe and what are the main problems at the level of policy views on media and communication, as well as the opportunities for mainstream churches in relating to contemporary realities of media culture and public communication?

Policy statements offer a good research population to analyze views at the level of policies. Our research therefore focuses on recent policy statements by mainstream Christian (inter) national churches, councils of churches and related media institutes in the Western-European context, that, since the 1990's, have published official statements on communication and media. The choice of this focus partly stems from the fact that my own (theological) background is from these churches. But it is also the mainstream churches in the North-Western European context that seem to be most profoundly affected by the reality of contemporary media culture[17].

The period of time is chosen for several reasons. In the 1960's and 70's, four, at that time authoritative, official policy-documents on media were published by the Roman Catholic Church, the World Council of Churches and the Lutheran World Federation[18].
In the following years, important new developments took place in the mass-media context and in communication sciences, for which the 1990's appear to be a key turning point. The globalization of media-institutes, the rise of commercial media, the impact of global advertising, the digitization of media, the rise of internet and the expansion of the World Wide Web are but a few of the changes with large implications.
In communication studies, the focus shifted from empirical research on media effects to the complex subjects of media culture and mediation, with an increasing focus on the perception and role of audiences.

The question that arises is to what extent these new developments, insights and changes -of both realms mentioned- are reflected in church policy statements on mass media, and in the way churches deal with media. Another issue is whether the churches acknowledge the profoundness of the impact of electronic media culture, affecting them in their very existence and institutional being?

Our research topics are structured in five chapters. Departing from (1) an analysis of media context and media culture (phenomenological level) and (2) a recent communication theoretical overview (epistemological level) we arrive at (3) the content analysis of the policy statements and the inventory of the main problems in churches' views on media and communication (empirical analytical level). Finally (4) we relate the outcomes to the concept of dialogue and its implications (the level of praxis and

---

[17] Moreover, I researched popular forms of communication in a non western context for my master thesis (1992) *Comunicación popular in Argentinië: aanknopingspunten voor kerkelijk mediawerk (Comunicación popular en Argentina, puntos de referencia para el trabajo eclesiástico de medios).* This thesis focused on popular communication as point of reference for the public communication by churches in Latin America.
[18] *Inter Mirifica,* Decretum de instrumentis communicationis socialis. Decree of the Second Vatican Council on the Means of Social Communication. Rome December 4, 1963
The Church and the Media of Mass Communication. Appendix XI of the Report of the IVth Assembly of the World Council of Churches. Uppsala 1968.
Communio et Progressio, Pastoral Instruction on the Means of Social Communication. Written by the Pontifical *Commission for the Means of Social Communication,* by order of the Second Vatican Council. Rome, May 23, 1971.
Joint Report of the Task Force on Mass Communication and the Task Force on Publication Strategy. Lutheran World Federation. Geneva, 1973.

application) and, (5) in our concluding remarks, we review our option for dialogue throughout the study and share some of the issues that merit further reflection and research (evaluation level).

The first chapter of this volume focuses on media structures and technological developments, media trends -like digitization, globalization, privatization and commercialization-, new media, patterns of communication and the concept of interactivity. We will also identify the social cultural role of media in defining social reality and expressing the shared cultural environment and shared identity. Related to this is the role of the media as a central hermeneutic key of culture, their 'religious' dimension and the media use by people as part of their everyday symbolic interaction and religious meaning making. We will also analyze how media culture affects a social institute like the church.

In the second chapter we turn to recent insights in communication studies with respect to the perception of audiences. We will briefly describe the historical shifts in communication research that can be summarized by a shift in emphasis from sender to audience. This leads us to the audience research tradition, which includes structural, behavioral and cultural reception analysis. Then we turn to recent interpretative rethinking in audience research. Finally we discuss how the choice of paradigm matters not only to corresponding communication models, but also involves implications for churches' attitudes in communication.

The third chapter brings to the stage the policy statements on communication and media, published by the mainstream churches, their world organizations and related communication institutes in the last 15 years[19]. We will explore the views of the Church of England (UK), the Roman Catholic Church (UK, Germany), the Lutheran Church (Sweden, Finland) and the Protestant Church (Germany), the World Council of Churches, the Lutheran World Federation, the Vatican, the World Association of Christian Communication (WACC) and the World Catholic Association for Communication (Signis), -unifying since 2001 Roman Catholic media and communication institutes UNDA (radio and television) and OCIC (cinema and audio visual)-.

Particular attention is paid to:

•   the way Churches -and their related institutes- look upon the context and impact of
    media developments and churches' social and ethical responsibilities in this matter
•   the relationship between media, religion and culture
•   theologial reflection on communication and awareness of paradigm choices
•   Churches' involvement in public communication and the role of theological
    presuppositions in it
•   the challenges and priorities set by the 'information era' as considered by the
    churches

---

[19] The choice of the research population follows from the wish to work with different regions within Western Europe, different denominational backgrounds, and different church 'levels' (international and national). The policy statements by church related communication institutes are involved because of their assumed influence and impact on policies put forward by the churches in general. We are aware of the fact that institutes like Signis and WACC, - as well as the Vatican, LWF and WCC- of course are not restricted to Western Europe. However, for the sake of this research, it implies that we only included international and/or European regional statements, as published by these institutes.

This leads us to an inventory of main problems in the statements regarding communication context, the outlook on the audience, communication models, ecclesiological identity and implementation and praxis.

In the fourth chapter dialogical communication -and public space as its prerequisite- will be the central issue. We will clarify the perspective of dialogue which we would like to suggest related to religious communication. Social responsibilities and media ethics, inherent to public space and dialogical communication, will be discussed under the same heading. Furthermore insights are given as we relate the art of dialogue to our findings on media culture, audience perceptions, on identity and theology. With respect to the latter we will also discuss the concept of communication theology.

In the final chapter, we try to analyze beyond the problems and, in retrospect, come to concluding considerations. We will go into the challenges (and misunderstandings) of genuine dialogue in a digital mass media context and the importance and relevance of religious involvement in public communication. We will also summarize some of the issues which, to our opinion, merit further reflection, as an invitation to subsequent dialogue. They include the concepts of (Christian) fundamentalism, secularization and religion in relationship to global media and media culture.

One

The Context and Implications of Media Culture: From Broadcasting to Business and Beyond

Thus when we are talking about the media we are in fact dealing with much more than press agencies, journalists, radio, television or newspapers; we are talking about a whole organization of social reality. We could not properly conceive of contemporary society and the world system without the role of the high-technology networks of mass and personal communication that bind people and places together, and are an essential part of business, politics, emotional and public life. (...) Yet in everyday life, most of the time the media are taken as massively given[1].

Pertti Alasuutari

Reading our morning paper, watching or listening to our favorite programs, surfing the World Wide Web or logging in to receive our latest emails has become routine for many in Western European society. Media, along with information and communication technologies, are an essential part of our life. Nevertheless, we are barely conscious of the way they are developed and adopted. We do not notice which interests are involved, which are fought over, or what their impact is on our culture and our social relationships.

In fact, the term media itself is not easy to define. The standard association is of 'mass communications media' (both objects and organizations) such as press, broadcasting, cinema, billboards, computers, satellites etc. But as Ryan and Wentworth (1999) show, it can also be used in a wider sense. Even a Barbie doll can be 'a medium' from the perspective that it is a mass-produced, cultural product bearing shared messages of that culture. So can greeting cards or public education be media[2].

The same is true for the complex term 'culture,' that is related to the contemporary media context. According to McQuail (2000), the primary reference is to the symbolic artifacts of the media industries. A wider reference is related to the mass communication process: customs, practices and meanings in its production and reception. Or it may refer to the 'superstructure' of society in which media operate: the framework of beliefs and ideologies.

In modern society mass communication media are an important key bearer of cultural expression. Media and culture are strongly interconnected. Not as loose variables of different realms affecting one another, but as elements within the same complex. This chapter is about the context and implications of media culture[3].

---

[1] Alasuutari, Pertti. 1999.
[2] This wider conception of a 'medium' stems from the work of the French semiotician, Roland Barthes.
[3] Including a wide range of both mass- and individual communication media. The perception of audiences and audience reception will be the explicit issue in the second chapter.

We will focus on the structures and logic of the *communication media system*[4], its changes and trends such as convergence, concentration and globalization, media policy and the new information and communication technologies (ICT's), or new media.
We will also consider the *cultural role* of media in defining social reality and providing and expressing shared identities and the shared cultural environment.
Then we will discuss the *religious dimension* of mass media and media culture.
The last issue of this chapter concerns the *implications* of the media context and media culture for mainline Christianity in general and its public communication in particular.

1.1   Western European media systems

The 1980's were a decade of profound change for Western Europe. In the political realm the fall of the Berlin Wall in 1989 was the main event that caused large transitions. Not only for the people in the countries of the former 'Eastern Europe', but also to the European and international interplay of forces. The USSR structure collapsed[5], Eastern and Western Germany became united and Eastern European nations called for sovereignty. It meant a thorough re-shuffling of the geographical, political and economical landscape that resulted in ethnic and social tensions on the one hand and a firm process of 'Europeanization' on the other hand. The economical and political goals of the European Community played a central role in this process.

The 1980's were also the decade of important technological changes in the realm of media. The main one was the accelerating innovation of digital information and communication systems with profound impact in nearly every scope of life and society. New developments in the technologies of distribution by cable and satellite solved the problem of channel scarcity and limited terrestrial transmission. It caused a boom of new (commercial) broadcasters and put a heavy pressure on the (then) monopoly of public broadcasting, which was strongly regulated in order to secure variety and choice.

Up until the 1980's broadcasting in Western Europe consisted for the greater part in a public service model in which diversity, informative and special youth programming, public accountability, a national scope (protection of language and culture) and non commercialism were important aspects. Neutralization was another aspect, however in some countries -such as- Italy and France, broadcasting was highly politicized by conservative parties.
The public service system was financed by license fees paid by audiences on the one hand and advertisement (under strict conditions) on the other. Free enterprise and profit driven program making were virtually non-existent. This guaranteed space for social and cultural programming and service to different interests in society, including (religious) minorities. Non-commercialism also counterbalanced standardization and guaranteed variations between countries (see 1.1.1).
After the development of the new broadcasting technologies the political climate -in which the public service broadcasting ideal was always honored- changed. The new information and communication technologies were seen as fundamental for future economical growth and therefore had to be given a clear field. This view converged with the political drive to create an 'integrated Europe'. Meaning not only a common currency and liberalization of markets, but, in the realm of media, the convergence of

---

[4] Primarily, we will discuss the media system(s) and model(s) of Western Europe. Since they are strongly affected by global media trends and logics, these will be taken into account.
[5] On the role of mass communication and mass media in the process of change see: Tomka, Miklós. 1993. 'Eastern Europe: The Media in Transition', in Concilium, 1993/6, pp. 47-54.

broadcasting systems. Following the pattern of the US, deregulation was the new magic and market forces were expected to accomplish the job. Commercial competition made its entry in European broadcasting. Many new commercial, advertising supported stations were aired. Mainly owned by the new media bigwigs and their large international corporations of the 1990's. A dual media system arose and broadcasting became big business.

The combination of technological and political changes in the 1980's and 1990's greatly pressurized the public service system. It had to compete for audience rates (to secure political support) and adapt itself to commercial logic. The increase of co-productions with independent production companies, channel differentiation and the adaptation of popular styles and formats, are but a few of the symptoms of this process that lead to the 'gradual erosion' (McQuail: 1995:163) of public service broadcasting in Europe. This may have profound implications concerning diversity, public interest and communication rights, which we will discuss later. First, we want to sketch the structures and participants in the European media landscape.

1.1.1   Structures and players

Up until the 1990's one could picture media systems in Western Europe in terms of national, regional or local structures. By the turn of the century, it was no longer possible to talk about media in any region or country of the world without referring to the global commercial media system. Increasingly, the logic of this system dominates what the media landscape looks like, whether it is in China, the Netherlands, Yemen, Argentina or Liberia. National media systems are linked with this global structure and forced to deal with its economical logic and its far-reaching consequences. The way media operate, media policy is developed or culture is perceived, is related to the overarching global system. In fact, it is even questionable whether the term 'national' is still an adequate one in the contemporary media situation.

The roots of this global media system are located in media developments in the US. In the 1990's, the US media market became increasingly and quickly controlled by a highly concentrated corporate media industry. McChesney (2000) in his profound and critical analysis, *Rich Media, Poor Democracy*, characterizes the main features of this process: concentration of media ownership by large corporations, conglomeration and hyper commercialization. The corresponding data that McChesney provides are revealing and alarming[6].

---

[6] McChesney, in this volume, offers data on developments in media markets and on US and global media conglomerates during the 1990's. Since this decade has been a turning point, (as stated above in the introduction), and our main aim is to show the process which took place and the developments towards today's media situation (which is for the greater part a continuation of the trends mentioned), we will concentrate on data of this period. For recent figures see a.o. : www.media-monitor.nl and www.cvdm.nl (media monitor and commissioner's office for the media, The Netherlands; the latter together with David Ward 2004 published: A Mapping Study of Media Concentration and Ownership in Ten European Countries.); http://www.mediadesk.co.uk/information/mediaprogramme (UK Media Team Online); http://ec.europa.eu/comm/avpolicy/other_actions/av_observatory/index_en.htm   (European audiovisual observatory, EAO, by the European Commission); http://www.obs.coe.int/oea_publ/index.html.en (print publications of the European audiovisual observatory); Publications by the Euromedia Research Group, London, Sage; http://portal.coe.ge/index.php?lan=en&id=million&sub=8 (Council of Europe); http://www.ifj-europe.org/default.asp?index=2723&Language=EN (European Federation of Journalists, part of the International Federation of Journalists);

In US film production, the six largest firms in 1997 accounted for over 90% of the US theatre revenues. Of the 148 widely distributed films produced in 1997, 132 were their productions and distribution deals were concluded with six of the 16 other producers.
In newspaper industry six major chains with large dailies merged with regional monopolies and secured 25% of the $ 6.2 billion US newspaper transactions in 1997.
In 1998, seven firms dominated US book publishing and the market share of independent book dealers fell from 42% to 20% over a period of six years (1992-1998).
In music production the five largest industries obtained over 87% of the market in 1998.
In cable TV ownership six firms have control over more than 80% of the country, whereas seven firms control nearly 75% of cable channels and programming.
A similar image is shown in radio station ownership. Four giants hold 33% of annual revenues of $ 13.6 billion.
In addition to extending their control in one media sector by concentration, media corporations also followed another strategy - conglomeration. By this, McChesney refers to a process of media ownership across the boundaries of one media sector. In this way media industries are involved in (e.g.) cable channel companies, TV show productions and newspaper publishing. It allows them to not only produce their own content across different media outlets, but also to control the distribution of this content (vertical integration). It is self evident that this capacity generates enormous advantages for market power and large profits. On top of this, there is the possibility to cross promote and cross sell products or brands within the different media sectors of the holding. The 'spin offs' of e.g. the movie 'Lion King' generated $ 1 billion by stretching the Lion King product into a Broadway show, a television series and 186 items of merchandising. The 'X files' showed similar developments with television reruns on 22 Fox television stations and the Fox cable network, X files books, an X files movie version and a traveling X files 'expo promotion' (a rock concert and fan festival).

Brand identities play an extremely important role in the everlasting struggle of seeking and holding audiences that are desired by advertisers. Children, in this respect, are of increasing importance. Besides attracting audiences, brand identities and branded properties open up a prosperous market for retail products. In 1997, Disney merchandise earned the company $ 25 billion and an extra $ 10 billion on licensing revenues. Among the merchandise was a new "Mickey for kids" perfume line which was sold in the 660 retail stores of Disney.

The capacity to control distribution and cross selling and promotion of media fare, according to McChesney, is a *sine qua non* for surviving in contemporary media business. The two most important core unifiers in the process of conglomeration are entertainment content production combined with distribution and cross selling and promotion facilities, and news oriented content combined with facilities for advertising.

This is reflected in the way that media conglomerates are constructed in the US. Of the largest ones -that include General Electric and AT&T- six are connected to the six big film

---

http://lass.calumet.purdue.edu/cca/gmm/ (Global Media Monitor);
http://www.mediachannel.org/ownership/ (Global Network for Democratic Media);
http://www.wacc.org.uk/ (Media and Gender Monitor).
McChesney in his analysis includes a wide range of media: book publishing, magazine publishing, music recording, newspaper publishing, TV show production, TV station and cable channel ownership, cable/satellite TV system ownership, film production, motion picture theater ownership and newspaper publishing. Detailed information can be found in his book, *The Global Media: The New Missionaries of Corporate Capitalism* 1997. (Herman and McChesney, London, Cassell). The data used here are extracted from Rich Media Poor Democracy. See also: Robert W. McChesney. 1998. 'The Political Economy of Global Media' in Media Development 4/1998, pp. 3-8.

studios: Time Warner, Disney, Viacom, Seagram, Rupert Murdoch's News Corporation and Sony. In general by the end of the 1990's, these companies accounted for sales rates between $ 50 - 100 billion each. The accelerating growth of the 1990's, when most conglomerates were constructed, is shown in the enormous rise in revenues. In 1988 Disney, as a cartoon company and amusement park, generated $ 2.9 billion a year. By 1998, and within one decade, the figure rose to $ 25 billion. Time and Warner (in 1988 still separate companies) accounted for $ 4.2 billion and $ 3.4 billion respectively. In 1998, Time Warner achieved a result of $ 28 billion. Viacom's figures rose to $ 14.5 billion from a starting figure of $ 600 million in 1988.
Next to these giants, there are about 15 large newspaper based conglomerates such as Gannett, Knight-Ridder and the New York Times Company. They have no film, television or music production capacities, but each still account for $ 2-7 billion sales.

Middle or small sized media barely exist any longer. 'Merge or be swallowed' is what seals their fate. Some independent media are allowed to 'survive' because giant media industries keep a close watch on their creativity in order to trace new possibilities of low risk profits.

The acceleration of concentration and conglomeration of the 1990's resulted in (in McChesney's terms) a media *cartel* or media *oligopoly* of merely seven media conglomerates. The potential of the new technological possibilities of the 1980's and 1990's -paradoxically- did not result in more diversity, competition or an open market. The corporate media system neither is competitive, not even in an economic sense, since numerous joint ventures, overlaps in ownership and cross membership of boards of directors turned it into a closed, collaborating bastion of the happy few. It is a system that is extremely difficult to enter by new players.
The conglomerates also moved into other areas of social life such as leisure and recreation and spectator sports. As an example, Disney -in 1998- started twenty Disney Quest 'virtual reality' mall entertainment centers that capitalized on Disney brands. Now sport leagues are controlled by media companies. Time Warner, Disney and News Corporation, among others, own their own sports teams in order to secure sports content, broadcasting rights and -soared- advertisement revenues. Leisure and sports -the most lucrative content area- became commercialized.

The consequences according to McChesney, at least in the US, are devastating: a media and communication system, which is dominantly commercial, hyper commercialization of culture, the collapse of public service broadcasting, the silencing of public debate, a crisis in public life and democracy and a depoliticized society, inadequate media policy, a loss of investigative journalism and journalistic degradation in general.

Media and communication have developed into very important business sectors that rank at the top of economic drivers. Needless to say, this process did not confine itself to US borders. The new digital, satellite and cable technologies made it possible to expand worldwide and penetrate national markets. Backed by the neo liberal, capitalist, free market wave, deregulation and political support for the interests of transnational corporations, the US system -as McChesney puts it- 'went global' and became the fastest growing export market. It is expected that before 2010 the majority of sales will be non domestic, which means that now is the momentum to capitalize the potential for growth outside the US. In 1998, the major Hollywood studios generated $ 7 billion alone for global television rights. In 2002 they expected to do $ 11 billion. The global music industry, dominated by five firms, already generates 70% of their revenues from outside the US.

The global media market became dominated by nine transnational corporations: General Electric, AT&T, Disney, Time Warner, Sony, News Corporation, Viacom, Seagram and Bertelsmann. Eight of those nine belong to the same eight TNC's that dominate US media. The three most important global players, termed by McChesney as the 'holy trinity of the global media system', are Time Warner, Disney and News Corporation. To picture the global reach of those giants, McChesney provides an enumerative description of their holdings[7].

The next in the line of giants are 50-60 national or regional powerhouses and companies, which hold specialized 'niche' markets such as trade or business publishing. Half of these are US companies, like Dow Jones, the New York Times, the Washington Post, Hearst, CBS, Times-Mirror and Reader's Digest. The other half are mainly Japanese or European, including Kirch, Mediaset, Canal Plus, Reuters, Reed Elsevier, Wolters Kluwer, Axel Springer and CLT.

In national and regional media markets all around the world, a similar boom of mergers and acquisitions followed. It lead to a smaller number of increasingly larger firms. In Britain, (e.g.) 90% of the newspaper circulation became controlled by five firms and British cable by three.
By partnerships with the leading domestic media and complex webs of interrelations, a non-competitive system was established worldwide, in which 60-70 giants control the world's media and assimilates them towards the commercial logic.

Global advertising plays a crucial role in this process. This booming industry became dominated by three TNC's: Omnicom, WPP Group and Interpublic Group. In 1999, $ 435 billion was spent in advertising worldwide; US owned or based industries accounted for nearly half of the amount. Because of sophisticated audience research -which provides vital demographic data- the global advertising industry shows a lucrative growth potential (mainly outside the US market.) This accounts for the rapid rise of commercial television worldwide and in Europe.

European Media Structures

As described, the European media system has been characterized by a strong emphasis on public service. According to McQuail (1995), in the 1980-1990's, several reinforcing technological, economical and political developments accounted for a definitive turning of the tide. Technological breakthroughs of digitization, satellite and cable, the felt necessity of converging broadcasting systems for the sake of European economical integration and a stronger European position against US and Japanese competition, the perception of ict's as an important driver of economic growth, a stronger belief in market forces and deregulation (as in the US), the wish to limit taxpayer support and finally, though not unimportant, commercial pressure by media conglomerates to open up European broadcasting, interconnected.
Opening up was exactly what happened. A gradual process of privatization, internationalization, commercialization and media concentration on a regional/national level followed and pressurized old concepts of public service.

Meier and Trappel (2002) provide facts and figures on media concentration in Europe. The following table shows the ranking:

---

[7] See Appendix one for an overview of this reach. See also: Ryan and Wenthworth 1999:145 -170.

European media firms (Herman and McChesney)		Sales (billion $)		Ranking of European firms on global scale (Hachmeister and Rager)			Ranking top Revenues (billion DM) (1995)	European enterprise in audiovisual sector (EAO)		AV revenues (million ECU) (1995)
First tier										
Bertelsmann	BRD	15	(1996)	2	Bertelsmann	D	20.6	ARD	D	5,170
Polygram (Seagram)	NL	6	(1997)	7	Havas	F	10.4	Polygram	NL	4,230
Second tier				8	ARD	D	9.5	Kirch	D	4,023
CEP	F	8.8	(1996)	10	Lagardère Groupe	F	8.8	Bertelsmann	D	3,929
EMI	GB	5.4	(1996)	11	Polygram	NL	7.9	Thorn EMI	GB	3,643
Reuters	GB	4.1	(1995)	13	Reed Elsevier	GB	7.2	BBC	GB	2,520
Granada Group	GB	3.6	(1996)	17	Reuters	GB	6.1	CLT	LUX	2,446
BBC	GB	3.5	(1995)	20	KirchGruppe	D	5.4	RAI	I	1,917
Axel Springer	BRD	3.0	(1993)	21	BBC	GB	5.0	Carlton	GB	1,903
CLT	LUX	3.0	(1996)	22	EMI	GB	5.0	Canal Plus	F	1,496
Pearson	GB	2.9	(1996)	26	CLT Multi Media	LUX	4.5	TFI	F	1,407
United News and Media	GB	2.9	(1996)	27	United News and Media	GB	4.3	Fininvest	I	1,373
Carlton Comm	GB	2.5	(1996)	28	Axel Springer	D	4.2	BSkyB	GB	1,215
TFI	F	1.8	(1996)	29	Pearson	GB	4.1	ZDF	D	1,149
Kinnevik	S	1.8	(1996)	32	Carlton	GB	3.6	RTL	D	1,137
Bauer	BRD	1.7	(1993)	33	RAI	I	3.5	Rank	GB	920
Wolters Kluwer	NL	1.7	(1994)	35	Fininvest	I	3.5	SATI	D	868
RCS	I	1.6	(1993)	41	WAZ	D	3.1	France 2	F	842
VNU	NL	1.4	(1994)	42	Canal Plus	F	2.9	France 3	F	808
CEP	F	k.A.		43	Bauer	D	2.9	Pro7	D	749
Prisa Group	E	k.A.		44	Holtzbrinck	D	2.8	ORF	A	743
Antenna 3	E	k.A.		45	VNU	NL	2.7	SRG	CH	739
				46	TFI	F	2.6	Nethold	NL	733
				49	Rizzoli	I	2.3	Granada	GB	626
				50	ZDF	D	2.1	RTVE	E	624

Sources: European Audiovisual Observatory, 1997; Hachmeister and Rager, 1997; Herman and McChesney, 1997

Figure 1.1 The largest European private media corporations (Meier and Trappel 2002 (1998): 49)

Bertelsmann and Polygram (after having been taken over by Seagram in 1998) belong to the top ten media conglomerates in the global market. In sum, 25 European firms are among the global top 50. Most of them are involved in more than one media industry (newspapers, magazines, books, TV, radio, film, music and video, on-line and multimedia). The majority also operates in one or more related branches such as book clubs, advertising, rights/licenses, fairs and exhibitions, leisure parks and sports clubs.

Of the 50 leading European firms within the audiovisual sector, eleven are British, eight are German, seven are French, five are Turkish, three are Spanish and three are Dutch. Most of them operate in only one national market. CLT and Canal Plus are the only two big European televisions multinationals. CLT (Bruxelles Lambert/Bertelsmann) holds major positions in the national markets of the Benelux, Germany and France. Canal Plus (owner of Nethold) is a top pay TV operator throughout Europe (except for Great Britain, Spain and Germany.) In Germany, Bertelsmann and Kirch hold a dominant position. Rupert Murdoch's News Corporation has European ventures in Great Britain (where he controls a third of the press) and in Germany (Vox TV). In Italy, Berlusconi's Fininvest controls the market.

Television in Europe is still very much a national and European affair, as far as general interest TV channel ownership is concerned. But American presence is increasing in the thematic cable and satellite sector -especially in children's channels- music video and television documentaries. The Scandinavian countries, Benelux and Germany are saturated by cable and satellite that offer a broad selection of channels which establishes a barrier for pay TV. The same is true for Italy and Greece (although direct broadcasting satellite systems penetration is very low there.) In the UK, France and Spain (where a limited amount of channels is offered by terrestrial TV), pay TV companies have far less competition. Therefore, Canal Plus in France and BskyB in the UK are successful and lucrative.

The major actor in satellite systems is Astra. An American enterprise in origin, it is now owned by the Société Européenne des Satellites (SES). Because of its large capacity of television transponders and coverage of all of Europe, Astra was able to establish a near hegemony by pushing out European direct broadcasting satellite initiatives like TV-Sat in Germany and TDF in France. Astra dominates over 90% of the European DBS market[8]. Its only competitor -next to a number of national/regional satellite systems- is Eutelsat, the European organization of the national telecom companies, which offers continental coverage but mainly serves the Southern European countries.

The newspaper market and periodical press in most European countries is owned by major national press holdings. Smaller newspapers have been taken over. De Bens and Østbye (1998) conclude an increasing concentration of ownership, strong competition[9], the disappearance of editorial identity, a decline of political opinion press and investigative journalism and integration of the newspaper industry with different other media. There are few new entries and the market is no longer open.
Nevertheless, 'In Western Europe, in general, newspapers are still important agenda-setters for the big political issues and newspapers are still considered to be the watchdogs of democracy' (De Bens and Østbye 2002:16). And there are differences within nations and regions with respect to the extent of the process. Newspaper reading, for example, is much higher in northern Europe where there is a subscription system than in the South where newspapers are on free sale. In most countries, newspapers are still directly or indirectly subsidized, which is essential because of the drop of circulation figures and advertising revenues (the main source of income for newspapers). Since the entry (on a large scale) of commercial television, advertising flow patterns changed in most countries - sometimes gradually, sometimes dramatically[10]. In Belgium, for example, the newspaper share of advertising dropped from 42.7 to 23.3% between 1980 and 1995. Conversely, television advertising rose from 8.1 to 35.2% (De Bens and Østbye 2002:19). Whether the impact of concentration on content is to be regarded positive (more resources for quality journalism) or negative (commercialization, sensationalism, and trivialization), De Bens and Østbye claim there is no evidence for either point of view, although ideological pluralism runs a risk. Fact is that, next to the increase of inserts on editorial pages, many new special pages and supplements were created by newspapers for the sake of corresponding advertisements.

Structural changes in European broadcasting were more radical in the 1990's. In a nutshell, the national public service system based on public accountability, public finance/advertising revenues, entrance and content regulation and a general pluralistic service, shifted towards a dual system (public/private) in which the public monopoly disappeared.
In 1980 in Belgium, Denmark, Norway and Sweden, the public broadcasting system was still financed by license fee only. The majority of the countries accounted for mixed revenues (licenses and taxes), with the exception of Luxembourg that always had -and

---

[8] Kleinsteuber, Hans J. 2002. 'The Digital Future' in McQuail and Siune, 2002. 1998, *Media Policy*, Euromedia Research Group, London Sage, pp. 60-4.
[9] In the UK, (e.g.) next to the backdrop in advertising revenues and price wars, the Internet and free papers (both the most popular as news providers among young people) threaten quality papers and lead them to publish tabloid versions (e.g. the Independent and the Times). A paper like the Daily Star, on the other hand, annually attracts thousands of extra readers, with its formula of 'celebrity focussing' and little news. Source: de Vries, Bas, 'Krant krimpt mee met de markt' in *Trouw*, 26 -11- 03, p. 6.
[10] Nowadays there is a shift from television advertising to internet advertising, changing the flow pattern once again. Pay television, or television on demand, in this respect, is another problem for advertisers. Creating difficulties of reaching viewers.

still holds- a private monopoly (advertising only) and Italy and the UK with a dual system of public and private broadcasting. In 1990, the 'license fee only' systems had disappeared and the majority of the countries now had a dual system that consisted of public and commercial national channels. Austria, Denmark, Iceland, Ireland, the Netherlands, Portugal and Switzerland still held a public monopoly/mixed revenue system. In 1997 only Austria, Ireland and Switzerland managed to continue the public monopoly. The dual system clearly prevailed[11].

Cable and satellite brought in many new and/or foreign channels and accounted for a sharp increase in the volume of broadcasted hours. Between 1993 and 1996, 125 channels were launched in Western Europe, 30 of them being subscription channels.

Competition increased, which drew -and draws- heavily on public service broadcasters. In the struggle for viewing time percentages, audience shares, ratings, advertising money and market sectors, public service broadcasters sought salvation either in adaptation, the introduction of thematic channels (culture, documentation, children) or reinforcing their tradition. The latter option prevailed in North-Western Europe where public broadcasters -in the 1990's- increased news, current affairs, domestic fiction and culture.

According to Siune and Hultén (2002), after a decade of competition, empirical evidence supports divergence over convergence. This means that commercial and public broadcasters each focus on different content segments. Private stations mainly offer sports, entertainment, popular culture, US fiction, and news -important to establish a prestigious image-, and public broadcasters supply 'quality' news, current affairs, domestic fiction and culture.

Whichever way you look at it, public broadcasting is affected by competition, which is visible in the shift towards more target group oriented schedules and new styles and formats like infotainment and contemporary fictional series. Besides the battle for audience-ratings and advertising income, this has to do with reducing costs. Sports rights, for example, boomed due to commercialization and competition. Prices for US films and series also went up because they are much sought after as 'schedule' fillers in the increased volume of broadcasted hours.

Siune and Hultén conclude that by the turn of the century European media structure had changed drastically.

In the short term (until 2005), they expected that the growth of distribution channels will continue and that the international integration of program production and distribution will increase. Pay TV will expand enormously and -by diversification- will further fragment audiences.

---

[11] Data in this section are extracted from Siune, Karen and Hultén, Olof 2002, 23 - 37. 'Does Public Broadcasting Have a Future?' in McQauil, Denis and Siune, Karen (eds.) 2002. 1998 *Media Policy*. Euro Media Research Group. London, Sage.

	Old media structure	New media structure
Broadcasting	Monopoly	Competition
Goals	Democracy	Survival/success/profit
Means	Programme production/ selection of material	Selection of material/ programme mix
Logic	Responsibility	Market/economic
Criteria for selection	Political relevance	Sale
Reference group	Citizens	Consumers
Focus on	Decisions taken/ power structure	Processes of policy-making/ new conflict dimension
Perspective	Nation/system	Individual and global

Figure 1.2 Old and new media structure (Siune and Hultén 2002 (1998): 36).

Needless to say, serious implications are involved for the future of public broadcasting, public debate and pluralism, culture, media policy and patterns of communication in society. To examine them, we need to take a closer look at some of the main, technological, political and economical trends and changes going on: a. *digitization* and *convergence*, b. *deregulation*, *liberalization* and *privatization* and c. *concentration*, *globalization* and *commercialization*.

1.1.2   Trends and changes

1.1.2.1 Digitization and convergence

Technological innovation is an important aspect of structural changes in the realm of media and their impact in wider society. The development of digital information and communication technologies (ICT's) may be considered as the main development of the last decades. Hamelink (1997:3) defines ICT's as: 'all those technologies that enable the handling of information and facilitate different forms of communication among human actors, between human beings and electronic systems, and among electronic systems' to be subdivided in: capturing technologies (e.g. mice, image scanners, voice recognition systems or bar code readers); storage technologies (like disks, CD-ROMs and smart cards); processing technologies; communication technologies (e.g. digital broadcasting, local and wide area networks as the internet, modems, fiber optics and cellular telephones) and display technologies (like digital television sets, set-top boxes for video-on-demand, digital video discs and virtual reality helmets).

Digitization is the process by which different sorts of informational texts can be reduced to a binary code - the language shared by computers. By texts, we do not only refer to written documents, but to any encoded or recorded symbolic meaning, whether it is sound, text, voice or image. Because they can all be converted into the same language of digital bits, one process is sufficient to produce, distribute, and store or handle information.

This possibility blurs the lines between different (formerly analogue) media. Computers, telecommunications and audiovisual consumer electronics, which used to be separated areas, now converge. Telecommunications services (e.g.) are no longer the 'property' of telecommunication operators, but can be delivered by television cable networks, whereas telecommunication operators can offer television signals. Other examples involve radio news reports, which can be heard through mobile telephone networks, or the recording and sending of moving pictures by a mobile telephone.

According to Hamelink, multi-functionality, convergence, intelligence and ubiquity are the main features of digital technology, leading to a digital wireless future of information exchange through light waves. The computer -as we know it- will no longer be a separated device, but a built in processor in our shoes, clothing, glasses or even our bodies. This will enable us to handle information and communication in entirely new multifunctional ways. Personal digital assistants, digital agencies and knowledge robots (knowbots) will be needed to help us make our way on the so called 'information highway'.

One of the perceptible developments of this process, so far, are handheld multimedia stations by which we can surf the internet, make our telephone calls, send and receive email, SMS, (moving) pictures, watch the latest news, organize our agenda, make translations, work on our computer, participate in a worldwide teleconference meeting, arrange financial affairs or order groceries via tele-shopping.

In the field of media structures and media players, the outcome of digitization and convergence is visible -not only in mergers and acquisitions- but also in new alliances between media, computer, telecom, chip, and software industries. They all hunt for the best profitable position in the huge market potential of 'cyberspace'. Whose applications will be used or become (worldwide) standards is of extreme interest. Tremendous competition on this level furthers concentration because the huge high risk investments that are necessary to take part in the development of a (global) digital network, its apparatus and content, are only affordable to giant business corporations.
The struggle for the development and introduction of digital television in Europe clearly shows the hallmarks of this process[12]. Kleinsteuber (2002:61-74) demonstrates how after harsh conflicts, rivalries, deals, shifting alliances and political interference, a small number of large media actors controlled the European market in this field by the end of 1997. Canal Plus (active in France, Italy and Spain and in the smaller countries through Nethold), Murdoch (BskyB, Britain), Bertelsmann (CLT/UFA) and Kirch (Germany) divided the 'European cake'. Public broadcasters like ARD (Germany), RTVE (Spain) and RAI (Italy) experimenting with free digital television, and telecom companies like Deutsche Telekom, STET and Telefonica (who also tried to get a piece), could whistle for it.

Kleinsteuber (2002) is convinced that another major shift in the history of European television will take place with the arrival of digital television and will succeed the phase of public broadcasting monopolies and dual systems.
Crucial in the transition to digital television is digital transmission of compressed television images by satellite transponders, cable channel or terrestrial television frequencies. This type of transmission allows for a tremendous increase in capacity of television channels and -at the same time- a decrease of transmission costs.

---

[12] For details on the development of digital television in the US see McChesney 2000:119 - 185.

The major actor in Europe is SES. This global company[13] controls the Astra direct broadcasting satellites. When Astra launched its first satellite in 1988, it consisted of 16 analog transponders. The first digitally equipped one followed in 1995 with 18 digital transponders. Each was capable of transmitting 10-15 television channels. With the launch of the 1998 satellite (32 digital transponders), the Astra system could provide between 500 and 1000 additional digital TV channels for Europe. Eutelsat, with its Hot Bird satellites, reached a similar digital transponder capacity in the same year. In 2000 the availability of digital TV channels expanded to 3,000-4,000. Frequency scarcity finally has become a problem of the past and new opportunities for television appear on the scene.

By digital television it is possible to differentiate packages of content, to deliver time shifted or pay-per-view programs and to offer interactive services like home shopping. It is also possible to survey peoples' media consumption.
TV households receive commercial or topical channels by subscription for a monthly fee, such as cartoons or sports. Attractive popular programs such as new movies or main sports events, which rights increasingly are bought by the large media companies, make good merchandise and have to be purchased per view. This can be done via a telephone back channel or by chip card. The subscription and pay per view system will become the new financial foundation of television programming and complement the current saturated system of advertising revenues.
Subscriptions and payments per view are registered by the same set-top box that decodes the TV signal entering the television set. This box is of extreme importance. It is not only the entrance gate for all channels (including public broadcasters), but also the potential multimedia terminal for -future- digital services and the registrant of bought content, payments and consumption patterns. On top of that, its electronic program guide (EPG) -showing which programs are available- is not a 'neutral' tool. Certain programs may be highlighted over others, or get special advertisements. The determination of the order of programs is another influential aspect.

To be in control of the set top box means controlling power over much more than a link in a chain. In the first place, it decides which and whose channels enter the households. Although other broadcasters are promised access without discrimination this is not without problems because the conditions of the access system itself may constitute obstacles. Besides that there is no equal participation of all parties concerned in the development and provision of the set-top box. This became clear in the case of ARD and ZDF, Germany's public broadcasters, who were interested in a decoder without pay facilities to be used for free digital TV.

Because of the huge commercial potential involved, competition over the set-top box was harsh. Different systems are now used by different players. In Germany, Kirch's d-box (developed by Nokia) won the battle. In France, it was Mediabox, which was developed by Bertelsmann and Canal Plus, the leader in European digital and pay TV. In Britain, BSkyB and British Interactive Broadcasting BIB (venture of BskyB, British Telecom, the Midland Bank and Matsushita) dominate non-terrestrial digital television that is based on their own decoder system, which is co-developed by Matsushita. British Digital Broadcasting, BDB (Carlton Communications and the Granada Group), which is active in terrestrial digital TV and came to an agreement with the public broadcaster BBC, negotiated cooperation with BIB over a joint set-top box (among other things).

---

[13] See http://www.ses-global.com/ses-global/siteSections/SES_The_Group/group-structure/index.php
retrieved 19/10/2006.

All of these systems are only partly compatible. Technically connection to the Internet is possible, but broadcasters are reluctant, afraid of losing audiences to a sector dominated by other players with different power relationships. 'Interactive' in digital television companies' publicity terms (in practice) means no more than pay per view, home banking, on line games, or downloading of software, etc. In Kleinsteubers terms, the information and communication pattern remains 'mainly one-directional' and 'under control of a few technical and economical centers' (2002:73).

To make pay TV successful, much depends on the readiness of households to pay for the decoder and for programming. In a situation with a short supply of free channels, this willingness might be expected to be larger. To push for success and profitability in the long run, companies might subsidize decoders.
Pay TV has been most successful in France, the UK, and Spain; but the European situation is still much diversified and depends heavily on national and language markets.

De Bens and Mazzoleni (2002:170) doubt whether the 'new' digital programs and the multiplication of channels really make a profound difference. Audience research in several European countries shows that people are still very loyal to national broadcasters, even in situations of high cable penetration and a wide range of offered programs. Channel loyalty may be slowing down the impact of digital transition on on-demand television. Readiness to abandon the program schedules of the broadcasting companies and exchange them for a search menu system, in which the audience itself has to be far more active to find its way in the forest of programs available, might turn out to be another obstacle; however, the situation is different in the case of thematic sports, children, films, and news channels.

Television and computer are still 'separated' areas in household media use. But even that might change when a multi media terminal replaces both.

"Make your own radio news" headed a Dutch daily[14] reporting on the new opportunity to select news items from the Dutch press agency ANP from the website of the Internet Service Provider Planet Internet (market leader in the Netherlands). While listening to individually chosen news facts on the media player, one can continue surfing, chatting or emailing. According to the editor in chief of ANP radio, news-on-demand is an 'indisputable trend' that is desired by news consumers who want to assert influence on the news supply. Involved media companies have high hopes for this trend.

Views differ and range from a transition of broadcasting to narrow bit-casting (in which a fragmented audience actively assembles its own television-on-demand diet) to a more complicated adoption process (in which many factors play a role.) Kelly (2002) identifies broader structural factors: class, income, education; age and gender; household type; lifestyle; domestic context and practices; economic factors (production and marketing of media products) and cultural identity with respect to media use in the European household. These all play their role in how media are used.

Whatever its future, Kleinsteuber (2002) might be right in saying that digital television will herald a new era in European television. The race for additional programs (which is visible in the purchasing of all available film materials or exclusive rights on -sports-events) already marks the media landscape and impacts the national public broadcasters. 'To recover the heavy investment in exclusive rights, attractive content will increasingly move from free television to pay TV. The conventional free programs may be

---

[14] *Trouw*, 16-10-2003, p. 2.

'cannibalized' to provide the necessary material for the new pay packages. It seems that television will never be as cheap as it was for the consumer in the old days' (2002:73). This raises urgent questions about media policy on subjects of public service and about equal access of all people to media reach.

Østergaard (2002:95-106) points out digitization and convergence involve specific legislative dilemmas. With transmission prospects of any content in any electronic transport mode, legislation can no longer be based merely on transport mode, as was the case with traditional mass media. Convergence entails a shift from *legislation,* based on the social function of media, to *regulation* of technical and industry policy industries. Especially since the control of the whole process of the outset of content to delivery is involved, leading to media concentration. 'However, convergence creates fundamental differences of interest between users and converged industries. Political decision-making must define and ensure the openness of the national electronic infrastructure, as today's carriers move into content and broadcasting' (Østergaard 2002:95).
This takes us to the next trend, which has to do with media regulation.

1.1.2.2 Deregulation, liberalization and privatization

In 2003, the US government planned a drastic reform in media regulation. In fact, it was the 'most significant relaxation of media ownership rules in decades' as the Guardian stated[15]. Broadcasters were now allowed to own three instead of two stations in the largest markets and to own a newspaper and a television station in all markets (except for the smallest ones). On top of that the upper limit of national television ownership was stretched up to 45% of the nation's viewers. It had previously been limited to 35%. This created the possibility for national broadcasters, through the ownership of a network of local stations, to reach 9 out of 10 US viewers. The relaxing of the rules privileged networks like News Corp's Fox, Viacom's UPN and AOL Time Warner's WB and enabled them to reach 90% of the population.

Although this was a drastic reform, the changes are part of the US deregulation process of telecommunications and broadcasting, taking place since the 1980's. Demac and Sung (1995:277-292) show how in several years (1981-1984) radio and television were deregulated, the fairness doctrine was eliminated, multiple ownership rules for radio and television were loosened and the time limit to re-sell broadcast stations was reduced (from three years to one year), which favored concentration and decreased continuity in community interest.
The impact on radio and television was devastating for community programming needs. Guidelines to secure a minimum of news, public affairs, local programming and public inspection were eliminated, while the way was cleared for advertising by lifting limits on advertising time.
Given the dominant position of the US in the global communication and media sector, it was to be expected that the deregulation trend would not stop at the US border. The 2003 plans of the US governmental Federal Communications Commission to take another major step in deregulation coincided (e.g.) with a similar bill on cross media ownership laws by the UK government.
Demac and Sung consider three developments constitutive of the deregulation policy: the rise of the transnational corporate economy over the last 50 years, the 'computer-telecommunications hookup' (convergence leading to mergers) and the renewed

---

[15] Owen Gibson, May 13, 2003, 'US Plans Radical Revamp of Media Ownership Rules' in *MediaGuardian.co.uk.*

corporate and -neo-liberal- political belief in market forces, which is assumed to automatically outline policy in telecommunications and broadcasting. This accounts for declining government intervention in communications in general, and the restraint in developing new policies to guide and regulate new technology systems.

On the international level there is a similar discrepancy. The increasing internationalization of media companies and conglomerates is not accompanied by media regulation at an international level. In fact, exactly the reverse is happening. The tendency of deregulation, strongly pushed for by the main media actors, affects international, national and regional levels. One of the recurring arguments of McChesney (2000) is that the international corporate media system -made possible itself by international deregulation treaties like GATT and NAFTA- is so deeply entangled with the global capitalist economy that it 'necessarily generates a depoliticized society' (2000:xxxi).

In the case of European policy, the deregulation trend is clearly noticeable; however particularities and variations within the European situation and different European levels (European Union, European Commission, European Parliament, particular nations and regions all with their own governmental structures) must be taken into account.
As we noted, European media historically were strongly oriented towards public service. Heavily regulated public broadcasting traditions, based on governmental subsidies and policies, assessed the media landscape and protected national culture and language.
Transnational corporate economy, cross border ict developments and convergence of media, neo-liberal market forces, global trade deals (WTO) and commercial media lobbies (inside Europe as well) pressurized the European continent to open up their markets. The main discourse of this lobby was that subsidizing media and preserving trade barriers advantaged domestic production, obstructed competition, and harmed consumers.

McChesney (2000:82) concludes that the policy of the market oriented European Union and the European Commission clearly moves toward a 'pro-commercial' stand. Main elements in this policy are the creation of a single European competitive open market, in which European media firms hold strong positions. For the sake of competition -not for public interest- mergers therefore are sometimes opposed by the EU Competition Commission, under pressure of the dominant European players. This (e.g.) was the case with the Bertelsmann - Kirch deal in digital television in 1998.
Other examples of shifting policy are the qualifying of regulations to protect European content -strongly lobbied for by European media giants affiliated with US firms and US media merchandise- and verdicts by the European Court of Justice that overruled national legislation of member states that prevented advertising aimed at children, thereby allowing cable television channels to penetrate this profitable 'market'. Other cases taken to court even more directly impact the position of public service broadcasters. They question (e.g.) the license fee system as being anti-competitive and the 'violation' of competition rules by the European Broadcasting Union (EBU) as they collectively tried to buy sport events rights.

Hirsch and Petersen (2002) also state that European media policy has increasingly become a matter of economics and industrial policies for the sake of the single market. Cultural aspects -such as national values, language, freedom of speech, and information and editorial independence- are of minor importance.

The main issues in the EU directives of the European Commission[16] were: quota of European content (to oppose US programming dominance); media concentration; competition legislation and the planning of the future information society.

The quota issue -right from the start- was a matter of dispute, because of its debatable addition 'where practicable'. It was fought over (again) in the process of revising the 1989 EU directive 'Television without Frontiers' (1996). In a nutshell, the European Council did not attach more restrictions and wanted continuation of the existing clause, whereas the media industry favored more stringent quotas. The European Commission (1995) followed this line by proposing stricter compliance with the quota regulation and deletion of the words 'where practicable', to overcome different national quota regulations which it regarded an obstacle to free trade. The European Parliament, for its part, supported this stand to change the rules. Important in the directive (passed in 1997) is, that broadcasting companies are bound to legislation of the country where they are located and not to the laws of the countries they broadcast to, to secure 'free flow' of programs.

The related fields of media concentration, competition legislation and the steering of the future information society, as Hirsch and Petersen (2002) show, are part of a complex and sometimes contradictory process, with European singularities and problems and a variety of players' interests.

One of the main complications is the difficulty to establish and regulate one unified 'open' market. The attempts to do so -on the one hand- conflict with national self interests, national legislations, national cultures and languages, national historically developed media systems and different national needs and -on the other hand- with global commercial pressures and the rapid development of new digital technological possibilities with expanding impact. The positions taken diverged even within the European Commission itself. One current argued a case for competition policy and regulation (EC Commissioner Van Miert), the other one for industrial policy and \ (EC Commissioner Bangemann). The latter current is likely to be the mainstream, however some 'old order' arrangements -like quota regulation- are still maintained for the time being.

In the interplay of forces, several elements interfere with the regulation view and reinforce the liberalization trend:

- industrial and technological convergence is far from being in step with a 'regulation convergence' and -by definition- favors commercial logic and deregulation, because of the needs of strong global competitive telecommunications and media players;
- fast expanding, new, technological developments hamper a regulatory approach -in general- and urge the need for flexibility and common agreement in regulation. Europe has proved incapable of both considering the failure to develop a common HDTV and digitization policy and to agree on a common standard for decoders. In other cases, Europe simply seems to bring up the rear, as Hirsch and Petersen

---

[16] 1992: 'Pluralism and Media Concentration in the Internal Market – An Assessment of the Need for Community Action, COM(92)480; 1994: 'Europe's Way to the Information Society: An Action Plan' , COM (94)347 and: 'Strategy Options to Strengthen the European Program Industry in the Context of the Audiovisual Policy of the European Union' COM(94)96; 1995: 'Report on Application of Directive 89/552/EEC and Proposal for a European Parliament and Council Directive Amending Council Directive 89/552/EEC on the Coordination of Certain Provisions Laid Down by Law, Regulation or Administrative Action in Member States Concerning the Pursuit of Television Broadcasting Activities' COM(95)86; 1996: 'Communication from the Commission to the Council and the European Parliament on the Application of Articles 4 and 5 of Directive 89/552/EEC "Television Without Frontiers"' COM(96)302.

(2002:215) show in the case of satellites. 'Unlike cable or digital terrestrial television, satellites have developed in an extra-regulatory way. They have been the primary drivers of dramatic media changes in Europe. This had considerable bearing on attempts by regulators to keep track of developments. It would now seem that the main task of regulation is to assure that network operators cannot raise discriminatory barriers to access. These realities also explain why regulation at the European and national level tends increasingly to be guided by considerations of efficiency, enabling operators to optimize their activities by the full exploitation of economies of scale and scope, rather than by the all-encompassing regulatory approach which somehow does not seem to work anymore'.

• Europe's competition and anti-trust policy (its main instrument for regulation so far) is considered a threat for further development of broadband networks and multimedia services by the industrial policy advocates. In the global competition for market shares in the future digital information society, this makes the European media sector lag behind. On top of that, there are intrinsic problems of competition policy raised by globalization trends. They concern issues of definitions and criteria of (e.g.) the market, ownership/behavior and the cultural grounds for exceptions to be made.

• due to globalization, convergence and digitization, it is questionable in the long run whether national or -even- European regulation policy is possible at all. In addition, European policy has been territorially oriented towards a unified market and focused mainly on broadcasting and television, not on the current digital situation and new media like video-on-demand. The telecom market, for example, is much more deregulated, privatized and unified.

• information, communication and media are primarily regarded in terms of their super potential for future economic growth of the European industries and the safeguarding of a strong, competitive and profitable position in the global 'information-society'; not in terms of cultural or social impact or public interest. Crucial in this new 'gold rush' is the free movement of audiovisual services, in spite of public concerns on (e.g.) the flow of pornography or racism on the internet.

Hirsch and Petersen (2002) conclude growing concentration, a shift from policy on a national level to increasing industry oriented initiatives by the EU level, harmonization, regulation in function of establishing a European market and a more business-like approach of cultural industries. Looking at the future, they expect an even more radical liberalization in line with global trends, non-sector specific regulation, and new complicating issues on the agenda like intellectual property, privacy and data protection. 'Digitalization, coupled with satellite TV and the Internet, is likely to make it increasingly difficult to define who the producer and who the consumer are. Present legislation and regulation are based on a territorial concept which the digital environment puts into question. In all of these instances the global availability of the content raises anyway the issue of the practicality of the territorial application of national or European regulations' (2002:217).

According to Bustamante (1997:23), the local and regional administrations might come to play a more essential role as regulator, promoter and coordinator in an increasingly 'regional-international dynamic in which nation-states are becoming both larger and smaller at the same time'. EU policy, in Bustamante's view, disregards the risk of inequality and exclusion of the least developed countries and regions. More attention should be given to small and medium enterprises, which are essential for regional development. On the condition of being protagonists, the regions might be able to successfully absorb this enormous and tricky challenge, since 'cross-border interregional co-operation in itself becomes a symbol of the new instances of sovereignty and power in the service of development, transcending the barriers established by nation-states' (1997:26).

1.1.2.3 Concentration, globalization and commercialization

Within the majority of the European media systems, media diversity, for the sake of political and cultural pluralism, has always been a major concern. In fact, the strict regulation in the old order of public service media was based on this concern. Media concentration is not just an economic affair. The trends mentioned so far, of digitization, technical convergence, privatization, competition, globalization -especially of advertising- and deregulation intensify (in an unparalleled way) the issue of increasing media concentration and its fierce impact all over Europe.

Meier and Trappel (2002:41) define media concentration as: 'an increase in the presence of one (monopoly) or a few media companies (oligopoly) in any market as a result of acquisitions and mergers or the disappearance of competitors'. They distinguish between *horizontal* or *mono-media* concentration (within the same media industry sector); *vertical* media concentration (control of production and distribution of a medium); *cross-media* concentration (control of different media in different markets); *diagonal* or *conglomerate* concentration (control in a media market by an external non media economic industry sector) and *international* concentration (possible in all four types mentioned).

In section 1.1.1 on media structures and players, we presented figures concerning media concentration in Europe. But how are they to be interpreted? As shown by Meier and Trappel (2002:38-59), this is a complicated question due to different conflicting discourses and arguments.

Arguments in favor of monopoly or oligopolistic competition include (among others): cost reduction of products and services to consumers; the high costs of developing media (products services, technology and infrastructure), which can only be sustained by large companies; regulatory barriers preventing competition; the need for (European) integration to secure a market share in the global arena; and, a better guarantee of editorial independence and investigative journalism within strong and large media groups. According to this discourse pluralism, content diversity and quality can be taken care of very well by monopoly or olygopolistic competition, especially since there is no scientific, nor empirical proof of declining editorial quality or media performance.

Arguments against media concentration emphasize the reduction of information sources, the decline of local/regional political news, the increase of content uniformity, the increase of the role of profitability, higher prices for consumers and financial power to push competitors out and a loss of quality and diversity due to cross media monopolies. The arguments in this discourse stress competition as a driving force for editorial independence, accountability, public interest and societal legitimatization.

Results of research so far, are confusing. This has to do with an economic stand assuming a competition policy concept, whereas a social scientific stand assumes a political and cultural public policy concept. However, the former concept prevails, both in public discourse and in media policy.

As the following table by Meier and Trappel (2002:51), shows, the situation in most European countries is characterized by rather strong mono-media concentration[17].

Country	Circulation share of top 5 publishing companies	Circulation share of top 5 titles	Audience market share of top 2 TV channels	Share of US film (fiction) in top 2 TV channels	Share of top channel genre	Share of US film in movie theatres
Austria	45	69	68	6 1	46 (ORF)	-
Belgium (fr)	77	55	47	58	24 (RTBF)	-
Belgium (fl)	-	-	58	-	40 (BRTN)	70*
Denmark	50	49	78	65	41 (TV2)	81
Finland	42	39	71	69	31 (MTV3)	77
France	-	-	60	39	36 (TFI)	54
Germany	-	23	31	69	34 (RTL)	87
Ireland	-	-	60	-	42 (RTE)	91
Italy	-	-	47	63	38 (Canale 5)	63
Luxembourg	100	-	-	-	-	82
The Netherlands	95	-	39	72	24 (Ned 1,2,3)	82
Norway	53	38	80	-	23 (NRK)	74
Portugal	55	91	88	-	37 (RTP)	70
Spain	-	-	51	70	48 (TV3)	72
Sweden	49	33	55	-	28 (SVT)	66
Switzerland (d)	-	-	45	-	28 (SF DRS)	75*
Switzerland (fr)	-	-	49	-	36 (TSR)	-
U K	95	-	68	79	31 (ITV)	82

* = All regions.

Sources: Committee of Experts, 1997: European Audiovisual Observatory, 1997

Figure 1.3 Monomedia concentration ratios in Western Europe (Meier and Trappel 2002 (1998): 51)

They further conclude (2002:39-40) a 'media concentration policy in favor of big, highly integrated media corporations', a 'lack of public debate on media concentration', and, 'market power expanding to political power' -as in the case of the media giant and former Italian president, Berlusconi-.

But they also point out that evaluating the issue of media concentration in Western Europe and its effects on economic competition, pluralism, diversity and quality remains complex. Data are incomplete and media research lacks a paradigm which is capable of relating adequately not only capital and ownership structures to editorial independence/quality and content diversity, but also of taking into account other factors involved, such as policy matters or media logic (see 1.2).

On top of that, effects are dependent on -and vary with- the different positions and levels of actors involved. It is necessary to discriminate between (e.g.) the individual users, the media giant or media policy when 'measuring' the effects of concentration processes. According to Meier and Trappel, a similar distinction must be made between the different types of media concentration as mentioned above. They also underline the urgent necessity of empirical validity with respect to all discourses, for the sake of citizenship needs and public interest.

However, their stand seems to be closer to the view of those expressing concerns with respect to media concentration processes.

---

[17] A dominant market position means a market share of 30-35% by one supplier, 50% or more by two or three players, or over 60% by four or five suppliers.

'(...) competition does not automatically mean content diversity. There is evidence that even the contrary is true as regards quality. So-called competitive newspapers and television stations are often re-writes and re-broadcasts of the same material. (...) In particular, *diagonal concentration* might convert profitable media in monopolistic markets into cash cows to the detriment of further enhancement of journalistic and program quality. (...) The more media become exposed to profit-generating objectives (a serious concern in the cases of diagonal and multimedia concentration), the more *normative journalism* will be replaced by *market journalism*. Advertisers do not pay for high-level quality journalism, but for the requested 'quality' of the sector of society to be reached. Market journalism, however, provides for a different construction of reality in the media and for a substantially different media reality. Its first and foremost objective is not to inform but to satisfy the targeted sector of society' (2002:56-57).

McChesney (2000:86) also concludes 'increased advertising influence over media operations'. Global concentration of both the media sector itself and of advertising, - which is part of a large industry of market research, public relations and marketing- coincide. Since marketing their global brands is of vital importance to the largest transnational corporations, they require global expertise, which is offered by highly concentrated advertising agencies that are able to negotiate the most favorable terms with global commercial media. The top ten among the hundred largest global advertising agencies in 1997 accounted for 75% of the advertising market spent by those hundred ($ 36 billion). The 1990's showed a rapid growth of advertising especially in Europe, Latin America and East Asia-with (e.g.) Chinese annual growth rates of 40-50%.

Ryan and Wentworth (1999:201-215) examining the different relationships between advertising and mass media content, provide figures, which show the huge stakes that are involved, for both advertisers and media.
In 1996, every hour broadcasted on prime time network television in the US consisted of 15 (during daytime 20) minutes of advertisements. In a three-month period of 1997 (second quarter), $ 3.77 billion was spent on television advertising. The expanding market of children's television advertising -limited to 10-12 minutes per hour- included almost $ 900 million the year before. Leading advertisers, like Burger King or Proctor & Gamble, can reach up to 503.2 million households in one week. The costs of one commercial, depend on the ratings of a program. Hit programs, such as main sports events, contain more, and more expensive advertisements -up to $ 400,000 for a 30-second spot-. They compensate for the huge costs of rights involved that the networks pay. If the promised ratings are not made, advertisers are compensated with free airtime -and in many cases the demise of the program is sealed-.

A more 'subtle' way of entanglement of media content and advertising is product placement: payments to use certain products on the screen. Philip Morris (e.g.) paid $ 350,000 to have James Bond smoke a certain cigarette in the movie 'License to Kill'. BMW spent up to $ 12 million linked to another James Bond movie: 'Tomorrow Never Dies'. After Coca Cola purchased a 49% stake in Columbia Pictures, Coca Cola products and slogans appeared in the dialogues of Columbia movies. Screening of scripts by marketing specialists for scenes suitable for product placement is usual and advertisements increasingly take over movie styles, such as more complex story lines.

Other examples of entanglement mentioned by Ryan and Wentworth involve:
direct pressure on programmers (by withholding adds in case of unfavorable stories);
interest group pressure as in the case of the Roman Catholic protest against the program 'Nothing Sacred' -leading companies to the withdrawal of advertising- and US

conservatives' protest against the mini series about the Reagan's to be broadcasted by CBS (Viacom) in November 2003. Conservative lobby actually appealed to advertisers not to buy commercial time and CBS succumbed to the protest and the threatened boycott by advertisers. They withdrew the program. It was relocated to a pay channel owned by Viacom as well. Entanglements are visible also in advertisers' preference for 'non-disturbing' entertaining content, and disapproval of strong content which might reduce attention for commercials or disturb targeted viewers. As in the creation of formats adjusted to advertisers' needs (TV time outs and playoffs in sports to get the most out of TV revenues, or limitation of length of songs to facilitate the amount of advertisements per hour).

A new trend in the same line is target marketing and narrowcasting. Targeted audiences are attracted by specialized content that is focused on their lifestyle and interests. The purpose of this content is to serve as a vehicle for advertising specific products aimed at this group. New technologies make it possible not only to supply ever more sophisticated classifications of audiences according to lifestyles and values, but also to insert even different advertisements into commercial breaks in the same program which are specifically aimed at a neighborhood or even a household.
As Ryan and Wentworth note (1999:214-215) concerns have been raised about individualism, decline in community, fragmentation and polarization. 'If we think of the mass media as the central nervous system of a complex society, and if the mass media are individualized and no longer mass, then we may be losing our means of producing and sharing a common core of culture. Technology, advertisers, and programmers have come together in an effort to cater to and exploit differences. Turow believes that what may result is the creation of "image tribes" in which we will be able to insulate ourselves from ideas we do not agree with and images we do not want to see'[18].

Again, McChesney -as well as Ryan and Wentworth- discuss the US situation and we need to take into account distinctions in the European case. Nevertheless, as media increasingly become a global affair, stamped (to a large extent) by US developments, it is important to include the processes that happen in the US and evaluate the global impact on the different regions.
In the European region, there are large differences between the former Eastern countries[19] where media are flooded by commerce and the position of public broadcasting is severely subverted and Western Europe. Evaluating the impact of media concentration in Western Europe, as stated above by Meier and Trappel (2002), is a complex matter.

The same holds true for the impact of commercialization, as McQuail (2000:159) demonstrates in his conclusions: 'Moreover the evidence for decline in standards of media performance as a result of commercialization is not very strong, at least not in a number of European countries'.

This does not mean McQuail (2002) disagrees upon ongoing commercializing trends which are enormously advanced by the privatization of telecom industries. He recognizes that commercial motives and private investments currently are the main drive for media

---

[18] The book referred to by Ryan and Wentworth is Turow, Joseph. 1997. *Breaking up America*. Chicago, University of Chicago Press.
[19] See (e.g.): Tomka, Miklós. 1993. ''Changing Perspectives in Europe Today' theme-issue in *Media Development*, 3/1999, 2-46; 'Post-Authoritarian Communication' in *Communication Research Trends*, volume 16, nr. 4, 1996 and 'Politics and Propaganda: The Media in Eastern Europe Before and After the Fall of the Berlin Wall', discussion text of a workshop at the Politeia Conference, www.kuleuven.ac.be/oce/Politeia , European Centre for Ethics, Leuven, Belgium, May 26, 2000.

developments in Europe. He also recognizes the former unified paradigm of public service has been overruled by commercial logic. There has been an increase in international channels, in the amount of (imported) television programs and viewing-time, and in the advertising share as the main source of income. The audience share of commercial broadcasters slowly -but surely- increased as well. Public service broadcasting is forced to operate in and adapt itself to a highly competitive, market oriented climate, which makes it even more dependent on license fee income. Signs of this adaptation include the adoption of commercial broadcasting styles, entertainments, horizontal time formats and marginalization of minority programming. According to McQuail, the digital future is more likely to reinforce commercialization trends, pressurizing public broadcasting even further and quietly adapting the cultural climate to ubiquitous commercial values, which qualify whatever programming chosen.

However, changes in media performance are gradual and there is still 'a good deal of stability' when it comes to structures of programming and content, as McQuail (2002:121-124) demonstrates in providing data on the Netherlands, Finland, Norway, Italy, Germany, Flanders and France. In general, public service broadcasters maintained percentages of informational/educational, fiction and news programming -although they also schedule popular programming in order to survive-. Private channels broadcast more news programming, although sometimes it is reduced on prime time. They largely increased advertising time. Some research claims a convergence in style and content of private and public channels.

When it comes to diversity and quality, McQuail's impression is that expansion and competition have not increased program diversity. Viewers do have more choice, but it is 'more choice of the same type.' In general, the audience in Europe has not increased its viewing time dramatically as a result of program abundance; neither did it completely break up as a national audience, although public broadcasting lost its hold. More then 50% of the audience in two thirds of the countries watch the top two channels, of which -in the majority of the cases- one is a public channel. The pattern of media use is more multiform and there is an increasing shift towards watching entertainment and fiction. Most of the hypotheses about the effects of commercialization remain hypotheses. It is a complex matter. Percentages alone are not all there is to it, and it is difficult to account for the interaction of structural changes, means of finance, programming changes, societal changes, and changes in public taste and differing national circumstances. McQuail (2002:126) concludes that the criterion of commercialization -as such- is not useful anymore, since there is no fundamental, functional contrast between public and commercial systems.

Commercialization and concentration are closely related to globalization, which is referred to as 'the overall process whereby the location of production, transmission and reception of media content ceases to be geographically fixed, partly as a result of technology, but also through international media structure and organization' (McQuail 2000:496).

Perhaps the most widely known connotation of the term, global, with respect to media is McLuhan's 'global village'[20] (1964). The roots of the process go back though to the 1850's with the first news agency/wire services, later succeeded by worldwide national radio services and the distribution of American films. Television pushed the globalization process forward enormously due to the fact that its transmission and visual communication can easily cross national borders and language barriers.

---

[20] McLuhan, M. 1964.

According to McQuail (2000:215-240), technology and money -particularly money- are the new driving forces of accelerating internationalization and affect all forms of media. Advertising is a main component of international mass communication and is linked to the globalization of products.

Media content also became a product - especially feature films, television serials, popular music and news. TV news, popular music and advertising show a very high rate of internationalization and concentration.

The three main television news agencies that generate most of the international news that is used by the world's broadcasters are Reuters, World Television News (WTN) and Associated Press Television News (APTV); followed by Agence France Press (AFP), Deutsche Presse Agentur (DPA) and Spanish Agencia EFE.
Five large international media conglomerates dominate the popular music industry: Columbia (owned by Sony Japan), Time-Warner, RCA (owned by Bertelsmann), EMI (Thorn Electronics Britain) and Polygram (Dutch Philips and German Siemens).

As McQuail (2000:220) demonstrates, global mass communication can take different forms: direct transmission or distribution; international media (MTV Europe, CNN International, BBC World); import of content (varying from complete sporting events to TV programs or different content items); the adaptation of formats and genres, and international news.

The main concern with global mass communication has to do with the assumed effects of 'media imperialism' such as westernization, dependency, infringement of cultural autonomy, national identity -including self-image- cultural homogenization and the domination of western values such as individualism and materialism. The ultimate goal of globalization -according to this viewpoint- is not the substantiated 'modernization' of the world, but global market control.
According to Hamelink (1997), global transnational information and culture producers have turned the world into a shopping mall and although a 'global culture' has not yet been achieved, a process of cultural globalization is definitively underway.

McQuail (2000:215-240) states that the concept of globalization -now framing the issues of media imperialism- has grown much more complex in recent (postmodern) decades. Audiences prefer 'own language - own culture' content and, as new cultural theory has shown, actively participate in the negotiating of meaning, thus resisting globalization effects. The 'transmission' model cannot be taken for granted any longer.
The majority of the international media flow comes through nationally based media in a roundabout way. Only a small part is bilateral (cross border transmission and reception) or multilateral (international media channels). Language and culture, national media systems, selective perception and the adaptation of content act like 'filters', and interfere with possible cultural effects.

Servaes and Lie (2001) state that most global linkages only consider OECD and G8 member countries. In their opinion, the term 'global media industry' is used too restrictedly and refers mainly to the extent of coverage without including facts on penetration, actual consumption, significance, meaning or response. Business and marketable, standardized, cultural products are only one feature of media. The other, equally important one, is media's cultural being. Viewing television (e.g.) involves a complex process of decoding cultural meanings, and is more then a simple act of consuming. Local culture and place are still important in people's sense of belonging and interpretations are locally constructed, which makes the concepts of globalization and localization interlinked (*'glocalization'*). All intercultural communication spaces, media or otherwise, are constantly transformed and the globalizing/localizing identities involved need to be studied as complex human socio-cultural processes.

The main trend -according to Servaes and Lie- is globalization through localization. Two strategies followed in this process are the 'cultural striptease' of products -which means doing away with cultural aspects and values, in order to make the product suitable (marketable) for many different cultural contexts (e.g. 'de-Japanizing' *Pokemon*)- and the involvement of local producers for the sake of a 'local dressing'.

Nevertheless, to Servaes' and Lie's opinion (2001:22), plury-cultural products are still embedded and interpreted in local cultures, without profound effects on culture. *'Pokemon* is the latest in a series of fad toy preferences for children. These fads are the result of transnational communication through advertising, the linking of cultures through globalization, the penetration of local markets through localization, and the targeting of children by advertising. These fad toy preferences probably have little long-term effects on culture or society'.

Large brands increasingly operate through multi local global marketing and even media themselves have regional variations (Time magazine, CNN, MTV). This means the concept of globalization as such is not adequate. Servaes and Lie suggest an integrated research approach of globalization, consumption and identity, since the most important development in the communications industry is the 'emergence of cultural-linguistic media (mainly television) markets' (2001:23).

Mattelart (1999) argues the term 'globalization' has lost all substance since it is contaminated by ideologies of the 'global free democratic marketplace' and of 'techno-globalism'. Both are presented as the 'inevitable' paths towards the future.

To his opinion the globalization of communication should be restored as a social construction which is centered at citizenship and 'democratic cosmopolitism'. In this process, 'locality' plays an important and necessary role.

'The planet is not a global society or 'global village' which places all individuals on an equal footing as spectators of 'global events', sports events, television serials and great disasters, but a diverse archipelago with its technologically advanced areas and security ghettos on the one hand, and its immense groups of marginalized people on the other. (...) This obvious fact forces even market-oriented geostrategists to leave aside the globalitarian myth and adopt a segmented approach to markets. Starting with the premise that the factor of life-styles and standards of living is more important than geographic proximity or common national traditions, they seek to construct broad transnational 'consumption communities' whose members share the same 'socio-styles', the same cultural practices, and the same modes of consumption and levels of solvency. (...) none of this implies that we are witnessing the birth of a new 'international civil society'. (...) Contrary to the myth of 'the end of the state', which jives perfectly with the populism of the 'global democratic marketplace', national territories remain the place where citizenship and social constructs are forged. They are also the place where organized civil society (...) can defy the movement toward the 'retreat' of the state leading to full-fledged market liberalism. It is also true that the unification of the world economic sphere requires social organizations, necessarily rooted in a historically situated territory, to learn to broaden their horizon beyond national boundaries' (1999:5/6).

Whatever dissimilarities, -or (better) differences in degree- in the discourses on cultural effects by globalization and global media, there is no argument about the existence of domination in global trade of news, fiction, entertainment, (however production outside the US, e.g. *Bollywood* India, is expanding). Even the Internet -the international medium par excellence- in content and access, is dominated in a western way. Global telecommunications and media infrastructure, which connect with people at an increasingly individualized level, might initiate a new phase in which older models of different media centers and peripheries no longer meet reality.

'In the emerging and still unclear 'system' of global communication flows, it is probable that the nation state will be less significant as a unit of analysis. It is more difficult to assign information and culture to a country of origin. Multinational production and marketing in the control of large corporations and multilateral media flows will establish their own patterns of dominance and dependency' (McQuail 2000:228/229).

The US maintains an advantage, especially because of the increased demand of 'fill-content'. This increase holds true also for Europe, due to channel multiplication and its privatization and deregulation policy for the sake of the EU internal market -which (ironically) advanced US exporters-. There still is a large trade deficit. During the world free trade GATT (now WTO) negotiations of 1993, this led to an intense disagreement between the US and Europe on the issue of whether audio-visual and cultural products were to be excluded from 'free-trade' agreements.

But transnational ownership is limited in Europe. Transnational satellite channels are not very successful and there is limited cross border reception of television in spite of the fact that European member states (according to EU directives) have to allow access to their reciprocal television channels. Most content is nationally produced and viewed. The protection of national culture and identity has always been an important feature in the historical European orientation towards public service broadcasting.

Concerning the European state of affairs, the cultural 'damage' by internationalization is 'exaggerated', according to McQuail. Media culture may have added internationally shared cultural elements, but national, regional and local cultural identity in Europe survived. The situation is different in the case of the so called 'Third World' cultures, although McQuail contends that media (by itself) are 'a necessary but insufficient condition for cultural resistance or submission (2000:238).

He does acknowledge, as does Hamelink, the rise of a globalized media culture in itself, possibly leading to 'cultural synchronization'. This culture -'contextless, timeless and widely diffused in space'- corresponds with (or even promotes) 'postmodern culture'. However, even though it is not fixed to time, place or moral standpoint, this culture is far from being value free either and is stamped by western values.

In the next section we will examine if -and to what extent- this also holds true for the so-called 'new' media.

1.1.3   New Media

The term 'new media' refers to electronic media involved in digital data communication. Those media include computers, computer networks, chips, cable, satellites, fiber optics, broadband technologies, digital television and mobile personal communication.

Digitization and convergence, as discussed before, are the main features in the contemporary development of new information and communication technologies. There is much speculation (or hype) on their 'revolutionary' impact and the 'global information society' that they are expected to bring about.

We will focus on the computer and the Internet to examine whether these speculations have materialized or remain merely rhetoric.

Sinha and Stone (1995:255-276) show how the development of the modern computer[21], from its first versions during World War II to recent varieties -including computer games[22]-, has been closely related to military needs and origin. The need to crack enemy coded communication and calculate firing tables in World War II (leading to the prototype ENIAC: electrical numerical integrator and calculator); the need for new missiles, nuclear and laser weapons systems and the race to conquer space during the subsequent Cold War between the West and the Soviet Union; and the cruise missiles, computerized precision bombs and mesh networks for fast communication and movements during the wars in the Persian Gulf, pushed forward computer technology. The same military origin was the genesis for the computer network, which initially was a network to provide the US defense department with a safe communication system in case of a nuclear strike (ARPAnet).

In the 1970's and 1980's, universities and research labs were attracted to the idea of a network and started building interconnected, informal, open networks that were founded on the same principle of linking all users by many different exchange routes. The first Internet Protocols (IP) and inter- and intra-university e-mail traffic were introduced. The 1980's were the decade in which the home -or personal computer- and the Internet -the global network of networks as we now know it- developed.

The Internet is the first truly global, decentralized, digital two-way personal/mass communication medium. It raises a whole range of new and complex questions about regulation, ownership, ethical issues and the future of 'cyberspace'. Its potential to contribute to a new structure of communication patterns, social change, democratic participation, development, progress and integration on a global scale theoretically exists, but actual practice is different and complicated.

As with many new developments in communication media, the pioneers of this new technology consisted of people in the non-profit public sector. According to McChesney (2000:78-185) the pattern of development of new media in the US after the rise of radio broadcasting in the 1920's, shows similarities and is predictable. Non-commercial applications that forward the initial development are subsequently engulfed by commercial interests (without much public debate) due to strong lobby's and claims equating 'commercial' with 'democratic'. The corresponding discourse is as follows: due to competition and a free market, people are given what they want for the best price. By exercising their right to buy - not buy, use - not use, watch - not watch etc., they, as consumers, decide what is a fair and democratic state of affairs.

The Internet met the same fate as preceding media did during the 1990's, as it was regarded as a very important aspect of -if not the key to- future economic growth. The rise and popularity of the World Wide Web[23] reinforced this belief. But it was the strong

---

[21] The invention of predecessors of the computer, such as the earliest calculating machines are connected to the names of Blaise Pascal 1623 -1662 and Gottfried Wilhelm von Leibniz 1646 - 1716; the latter was the first important European thinker who highly valued and tried to interchange Chinese philosophies and culture, in which -2000 years ago- instruments like the abacus were already developed.

[22] In 2002, in the US alone, the annual turnover of computer games was $ 10.3 billion; estimations of Europe and Asia provide similar figures. Next to the sex industry, the market for computer games is the fastest growing market. Source: Sturm, Edo and Zuidervaart, Bart 'Games, iedereen doe het' in Trouw, 30-07-2003, p. 2.

[23] The Web was developed in 1990 at the European Organization for Nuclear Research (CERN) for the sharing of documents by scientists. It became very popular and within five years it was the fastest growing feature of the Internet. It allows users to navigate the Internet by using browsers

promotion by the Clinton administration to commercialize the net and the accompanying deregulation and privatization policy (1993) that changed the purpose and control of the Internet in an unparalleled way.

It became part of the profit driven setting of the private sector that seems to swallow the development and infrastructure of all modern media and communication technologies. The future of the Internet no longer is based (as it was in the initial development by scientists) in its potential of forcing new decentralized, more equal and participatory communication patterns and a globally accessible pluralistic public service, but in its potential for E-commerce and E-advertising. And the fights over this potential -who in the long run, will net the profits- are brutal and harsh and are visible (e.g.) in the 'war' on the crucial access portals. The wave of mergers, acquisitions and business convergence in the media landscape, according to McChesney (2000:163), is the consequence of the commercial development and the future convergence of digital television and the Internet. This drives global telecommunication, computer and media moguls to synergy instead of competition in order to capture a future dominant position in the highly profitable 'information highway' and 'cyberspace'.

The ultimate shape of the Internet is still in progress, but tendencies (for example, technical standards) strongly support corporate governance and commercial dominance that is made possible by a close coalition between the few largest business and political players worldwide.

Main players in the global struggle over Internet policy (next to the US administrations) are the Internet Corporation for Assigned Names and Numbers (ICANN) (the largest Internet firms from the US, Europe, Australia and Japan); the EU/EC (promoting one internal market to obtain a strong position in the commercial global Internet and discouraging national Internet regulation) and the Organization for Economic Cooperation and Development (OECD) (the world's 29 richest nations). Paradoxically, 'competitors' have many aims in common, such as a collective lobby before WTO to keep electronic commerce duty free or the 'modernization' of the International Telecom Union (ITU, regulating global telecom).

As McChesney states, the overall goal is to shape the policy framework for the development of the Internet by entrepreneurs so that it will be market driven and led and self-regulated by the industry in order to commercially exploit cyberspace (2000:134-135). This has become the dominant, assumed discourse. Conspicuous by its absence is public debate. Public interest issues like access, the giveaway of the electromagnetic spectrum (public property) to media companies, enormous government subsidies to large commercial corporations for research and development -and even advertising industries- (without public sharing in profits afterwards), or ethical issues like violence, racism or pornography on the web, are not on the agenda (at least not prominent.) If there are any debates, they are restricted to (e.g.) criminal 'terrorist' activities (encryption) or the Microsoft monopolies, but they do not challenge the overall 'natural' commercial framework as such.

There is no doubt that we are in a process towards commercialized cyberspace, but it is difficult to indicate exactly where we are and even harder what projections can be made. Major cable and satellite industries, consumer electronics firms, cable companies,

---

(programs to travel among and explore websites and download data) and creates links among ideas or documents by hypertext. Currently we are in the second phase of the Internet: Web 2.0. The first phase lasted until 2001, when the euphoria of an abundance of internet companies bursted like a bubble. According to Dr. W.G. Noomen, chair of the Press Fund in the Netherlands, Web 2.0 is characterized mainly by becoming a platform of internet applications, which will render the desktop redundant (personal conversation 5/10/2006).

broadcasters, telephone-, computer- and internet firms are all in the converging battlefield for the best positions in the future digital economy. Technological developments occur in rapid succession and it is not clear how the new media will impact the totality of the media landscape or how they will be appropriated and used in households.

For the time being, the battle focuses on what McChesney (2000:159) has labeled: 'the hunt for the killer application'. Crucial issues in this respect are the ownership of wires, Internet access, Internet Service Providing (ISP), portals (organizing and managing links that guide people on the Web) and electronic commercial feasibilities.

Prevailing digital television[24], for now, has a good position to dominate the Internet era, since it is projected to become the only converged (computer and television) digital -and commercial- entertainment/communication medium[25].

Traditional media giants -according to McChesney- may benefit from the advantages they already share. They have digital programming available for the Web; are able to generate audiences by promoting websites by their traditional media holdings; possess the most profitable brands (which will allow them to have the best locations in browsers and portals); are able to invest in Internet media companies; and -by being closely related to the advertising industry- are best suited to locate customers, tailor spots, and rake in Web advertising money.

Telecommunications giants also have advantages, i.e. a large cash flow for investments, mergers on a global scale, ownership of the fiber-optic trunk lines (the backbone of the internet), and the wires into people's homes, which put them in a good position to become Internet Service Providers. On the other hand, the Internet (with its possibilities of digital data networks, including voice) may become a threat to their business of voice telephony. A similar paradox affects cable companies. They developed their own cable based ISP services and are trying to restrict their wires to these services in order not to become outplayed, or overruled by telephone based ISP's.

Cable- as well as telephone companies, by way of their broadband access services (e.g. @Home and Roadrunner), might be a threat to other portals. In the end, they may - conceivably- be a threat to the entire media industry, since production and distribution possibilities and costs might take on a different aspect.

---

[24] In 2000, there were 54.9 million households worldwide with digital TV; in 2008 there are expected to be 374 million. Source: Greenspan, Robyn, 'Competition Heats Up Between DBS, Cable' on CyberAtlas, January, 10, 23, 2003, www.nua.ie. For information on CyberAtlas see note 32.

[25] With respect to mobile internet, the struggle is between Microsoft (Smartphone, a special version of Windows) and Intel on the one hand, and Nokia and Symbian, a software joint venture of mobile telephony industries (Nokia, Motorola, Siemens, Sony-Ericsson, Panasonic and Psion) on the other hand. Microsoft, in its effort to bypass the mobile telephony industry, concluded immediate deals with mobile telephony companies like Orange (mobile telephone division of France Telecom). Vodafone Live!, the counterpart of Orange-services and of i-mode (the system of NTT DoCoMo, AT&T and KPN, offering mobile internet in Japan), is part of Vodafone, the world's largest mobile telephony company. Due to options of promotion, they prefer their own name on the mobile telephones, which would be advantageous to Microsoft software. But the Symbian Group, which still sells half of the mobile telephones in the world and NTT DoCoMo, leader with UMTS (the new standard for fast broadband mobile internet) marketed a first UMTS device with Symbian software in 2003. Microsoft fights back by a tried and tested method: new versions of Windows by which Microsoft internet programs will cooperate better with Smartphone software than with Symbian mobile software. People wanting to consult data, at the personal computer at home or in the office, by mobile phone via Internet (Unified Communication), in that case probably might prefer Microsoft's Smartphone. But even if, according to Vincent Dekker, ('Nog is Bill Gates niet verslagen' in Trouw, 16-12-2002, p. 9), US and EU administrations would prevent Bill Gates from doing so, he still wouldn't be defeated. The $ 40 billion in his bank account would allow him to buy half of all Nokia shares, even without a loan.

Computer firms also have their anxieties. They fear digital computer networks, which threaten software monopolies. Even monopolist, Microsoft, exerts its enormous market strength in order to safeguard its future by supporting every possible development as McChesney (2000:162-163) shows. Whatever the route towards the 'killer application' that will dominate the internet and the information age, Microsoft will be in it through its partner/ownerships in digital cable TV, WebTV, high speed internet-access (via cable modems and telephone lines), cable modem service, long-distance carriers, producers of television sets, web browsers (Internet Explorer, linked to Microsoft's Windows-software), online services, website-cable TV (Microsoft NBC) and portals (start.com).

But even if the media giants seem to be in 'poll position' there still are obstacles that have to be negotiated, according to McChesney. Will digital broadcasting be commercially successful? What will be the future of the set top box? Will broadband capabilities be offered that guarantee quick online services, at least as fast as television signals, and eventually win the race? Will electronic commerce be the killer application and will its security problems of paying on the Internet get solved? Will people accept the Internet as an entertainment medium or will the actual practice of divided television and computer use last? Are people willing to pay for what the media and computer giants have in store for them? And will they reconcile themselves to hyper-commercialism, monitoring and the decrease of accountable, public information and public debate, essential for democracy? Or is the point of no return in this respect passed by already?
The answer cannot be known. What can be concluded for now is that the media giants have strongly entered into web activities and web related strategic alliances (see Appendix two). By 1998 75% of the 31 most visited news- and entertainment websites were already associated with media giants and the remaining 25% were linked with America Online (AOL) or Microsoft. AOL (also owner of CompuServe) is the largest ISP worldwide, with revenues over $ 4 billion in 1999.

No wonder the most popular -and lucrative- web-areas are the same as those in the commercial media sector, i.e. music and sports, next to news, entertainment, kidstargets and financial news. It is less information, than the integration of advertising and electronic commerce in the websites and the traditional media, that is the key for the future.
Software, books, music, video's and tickets (sports and entertainment) are (for the time being) the main categories in electronic commerce. Strategic alliances in this field also are concluded. Disney and bookseller Barnes & Noble (e.g.) agreed to the exclusive right of B & N to sell books over Disney's websites, to promote the Disney merchandise in the B & N bookstores and for mutual publicity on their respective websites.

Interests at stake are staggeringly high. Take only the music industry as example. Sales of music online were expected to 'boom' from $ 87 million to $ 4 billion[26] within seven years (1998-2005). Music moguls like Bertelsmann, Sony, Seagram, Time Warner and EMI, in order to secure the position they hold and expand it online, ally with ISP's and portals and lobby severely for cyberspace copyrights. It remains to be seen whether they will be able to successfully resolve the online piracy problem and tackle new

---

[26] McChesney 2000:178.

'competitors' such as artists selling their music online themselves[27].
The crux of the matter is that in the end the question of who will win, even seems less important. One way or another, cyberspace will be primarily a digital marketplace, even if it takes a long path and includes waves of bankruptcies and -in the end- worthless internet activities.
In the horizon ogles the position of being one of the few leading global super web traders selling (whatever) merchandise from (whatever) trademark through an all purpose portal, including 'news' and 'information'.

What does this mean for our world societies, politics, democracy, social life, and culture? There is no question that the Internet will have a profound impact in the way we communicate and live. Neither is there any doubt that a 'non-commercial' civic part will remain, although it will be marginal and difficult to trace since portals will increasingly lead us by electronic 'information highway' directly to our -commercial- destination.

The processes that are mentioned will continue and lead to the extension from the global media oligopoly to a global communication oligopoly, according to McChesney (2000:164.).

Never before in history we have experienced such an overload of 'information'. But in the end, will this planet be better informed because of the digital era of cyber space? Will the digital era allow genuine global participation?
Or will 'being part of it all' become the 'privilege' of the happy few (information rich) in the economically viable areas (dependent on the condition that they exchange their personal information and potential for consummation) Leaving behind the 'have nots' (the information poor) and ignoring the social consequences, tensions, risks and possible future conflicts?
In sum, what is at stake? The way we would want our 'digital info society' to be[28] is far beyond conglomerate goals and the price to be paid by unidirectional commercial development may be (too) high. Moreover, this choice is rarely discussed.

---

[27] In 2001, the five big recording companies, controlling 90% of the world music market, joined forces in two internet initiatives: AOL Time Warner, BMG and Emi work together in Musicnet; Sony and Vivendi Universal (former Polygram) united in Pressplay. CD shops, united in the Global Entertainment Retail Association, claim that music industries monopolize internet sales by withholding the shops digital music files, in order to prevent them from developing sales of music by the internet, as an additional sales network to their shops. It is questionable though whether this is the real battlefield for recording companies. Next to emailing, downloading music is probably one of the most popular activities on the Internet. By peer-to-peer programs (p2p), audiovisual files can be exchanged on the Internet. The most retrieved p2p programs are: Kazaa, Napster, Morpheus, iMesh, Audiogalaxy, Bearshare, Limewire, Grokster, WinMX, Blubster and Xolox Ultra. Mp3 files, small compressed digital files containing musical items, go over the net by millions. Due to this illegal copying of music, cd sales dropped by 7% in 2003. The music record industry fights back with specially designed programs that are hidden in mp3-files and redirect people who download music illegally to legal sites where one can download legally paid tracks. Examples of such sites are Spanish Weblisten.com and iTunes Music Store (Apple). But illegal music supply is still hundred times larger than the supply in legal catalogues. Moreover it is highly unsure whether people are willing to pay much for music on the Internet. On top of that, the cd is 'out'. In the future, the dvd, MP3 player and/or the mobile telephone may become the main sound recording media. Recording music in your mobile telephone is within the bounds of the possible. Others even claim the future is in multi media experiences, with a far more active role of the listener/viewer. Sources: 'Strijd cd-winkeliers tegen pact platenmaatschappijen' in *Trouw* 17-11-2001; 'Muziek voor miljoenen – van internet' in Trouw, 9-7-2003, p. 2.; and 'De cd is niet meer sexy' in Trouw, 30-12-2002, p 12. 'Junkie XL loopt op de zaak vooruit' in Trouw, 4-6-2003, p. 15. See also: www.trouw.nl/nieuwemedia .

Examining the trends that have been described, the new media are as much affected by them -or maybe even have reinforced them- as are the traditional media. At least, it is questionable whether the new digital ict developments have lived up to the assumed (hyped-up) expectations of a revolution, proclaiming a new era. Maybe in the end this era, in some respects, will turn out to be more 'ultra modern' than 'post-modern'.

Finnemann (1999:147) concludes 'the multi-semantic machine represents a revolution in the technology of knowledge representation, a revolution based on a new alphabet, a new format for written, textualised -sequentially manifested and processed-representation. Since the computer provides new ways to produce, represent and organize knowledge in general as well as new ways of communication, it also provides a change in the societal infrastructure, in so far as society is defined by the methods of knowledge representation and communication'. Interactivity, inherent in the serial substructure of computerized communication, is the core of change in the principles of textual representation. Sender and receiver roles become more active and interchangeable. There is no single non-optional hierarchy of values anymore, either is there a documentation monopoly of the sender. This implies a possible extensive breakdown of one-way transmission and communication.
Nevertheless, he argues the computer is more of an extension of modern discursive culture than of something totally different. 'If, as it has often been argued in media studies, other modern electronic media contribute to a revitalization of visual and oral culture -although in a mediated secondary form, as claimed by Walter J. Ong- at the expense of the hegemonic regime of 'typographic culture', as it was claimed by Marshall McLuhan, the computer can more properly be understood as a medium by which the scope of modern discursive culture is extended to embrace vision and pictorial expressions by the textualisation of electronics, which at the same time allows the representation of other media, but now as optional genres within this medium' (Finneman:1999:152).

Addressing the cultural impact of computerization, Finnemann delineates three main epochs in the media history of modernity.
The first is the epoch of the printed text (orality+script+print) that was dominant from the Renaissance to the Enlightenment (1500-1800). A general framework of ideas of this period includes a static world/nature that is created according to rational, eternal and universally given natural laws which are to be detected by human reason. Truth is objective knowledge of the universal laws that is printed in the texts of philosophers and scientists. Related to this framework are ideas of a linear perspective, the author as an independent creator, sovereignty of human reason (leading to public discourse, enlightenment and democracy) and fragmentation of reason in descriptive (scientific) reason (on nature), normative (ethical) reason (on society) and evaluative (aesthetic) reason (on culture).

The second edition of modernity is the epoch of analog electronic media (speech+script+print+analog electronic media) from 1843 (when the telegraph was invented) until the late twentieth century. Many new dynamic media appear that are revolutionary in pictorial representation and simultaneous global communication.

---

[28] In December 2003 the first meeting of the World Summit on the Information Society (WSIS) took place in Geneva, organized by the International Telecommunication Union and the United Nations (the second one was held in Tunis, 16-18 November 2005). See: http://www.itu.int/wsis/index.html or http://portal.unesco.org/ci . Simultaneously the initiators of the CRIS Communication Rights in the Information Society campaign held a meeting: Communication Rights in the Information Society, NGO's belonging to the media advocacy group Platform for Communication Rights. See: http://cris.comunia.org . We will take up the issue of communication rights in chapter four.

Concepts and paradigms in science, philosophy and culture change accordingly. The focus is now on dynamic processes, development and change. The worldview is no longer one of a static wheel, but a dynamic -though still rule-based- interrelated energy system that integrates even its observers (e.g. the relativity, quantum physics and holistic theories). Pragmatic functionalism is the result. Although a new media matrix appears that consists of old and new media, the printed text remains the 'sacred' means that represents true knowledge.

The third epoch is the epoch of digital electronic media (speech+script+print+analog electric media+digital media), which is dated by Finnemann from 1936 onwards.
'From the notions of the world as a mechanical and reversible machine and as an all-embracing dynamic energy system (leading to pragmatic functionalism) we are now on the way to regarding the world as an ecological information system – a system in which it seems that we need to reinterpret the notion of the self, the observer, the idea of universal knowledge, the notion that rules and laws as being given outside and independently of the systems they regulate, as well as basic ideas on visual representation and perspective' (1999:156).

Instead of homogenous rule based systems, Finnemann argues for the inevitable need of a concept of heterogeneous rule-generating systems. Rules in these kinds of systems result from processes within the system and are influenced by other processes. This implies two important notions regarding truth and knowledge: 1. truth is not to be identified with universally valid laws and 2. our representations of whatever phenomenon are always fragmented and never complete (a notion of former stages of modern thinking). Analogous developments to the fragmented notion of truth and knowledge are visible in new concepts on visual representation and perspective. A fragmented perspective, labelled by Finnemann as a 'scanning perspective', replaces the previous linear perspective that was seen as a model for universal representation. According to Finnemann, this is a logical next step and further elaboration of modern thinking, in which the axioms of the previous epoch are now themselves on the agenda as subject of analysis (from invariance to variability). He names this process: 'modernizing modernity', which is a continuation of the process of 'secularization' of the relationship to nature, but this time of a second order. Concepts of the human mind, human reason, knowledge, symbolic representation, language and the text as the medium of truth, the former (symbolic) means of the secularization process are now included in the process itself.

Regan (2000), on the issue of the information revolution, states that the utopian predictions of liberty and equality[29] -which appear as creeds with each new technology- have taken the shape of a 'digital doctrine'. It promises global equality, cooperation, wealth, economic progress, participation, community and democracy for everybody in the information society through the Global Information Infrastructure[30] of information superhighways -constructed by the free market-, facilitating democracy online, cyber communities, and business chances for everyone etc.

---

[29] According to Regan, along with the concepts of freedom of speech and opinion of the French revolution, the Enlightenment produced the concept of communication, as a complement and the condition of all emancipation (rational progress) and inseparable of the idea of equality and universality.
[30] The term -and corresponding digital creed- stems from Al Gore, US vice president in the Clinton administration, in his speech to the International Telecommunications Union in Buenos Aires in March 1994. The concept is also an important aspect of the agenda of the G8.

But has the 'cyber hype' materialized in real-space and real-time world, or did it remain merely doctrinal wishful thinking?

The figures that Regan (2000) provides confirm the latter. According to her estimations, 11 percent of the world population is online. 88 % of the Internet users belong to the industrialized countries (15% of the world population). The majority of internet users consists of young, urban based (white) English speaking men, who are highly educated and have a high income level -however young, well educated women and early retirees are increasing- among the internet users.
At the same time, two billion people on the planet lack electricity and a telephone, which are basic needs to 'travel' the 'digital highway' that is claimed to be open for everybody. Only 15% of the world population has 75% of all telephone lines (Manhattan e.g. has more than all of sub Saharan Africa[31]).

In Europe, the divide between rich and poor countries is visible as well. Compared to the four poorest countries, twice as many households own computers[32] in the six richest countries. (See appendix two: facts and figures on the Internet).

People either go to the websites by direct navigation, or -increasingly- by search engines[33], whose 'referring' role is becoming more important. Search engines have deals with ISP's in order to be the first one people will see when going online. After working one's way through advertisements, pop up banners and buttons, the search engine is expected to deliver the user to sites of the topic required. According to Regan (2000:16), in practice this will be to commercial, highly trafficked, US based sites that belong to the 10% of the web which is indexed by the biggest search engines. This means 90% of the web is not indexed. The reason for that is simple. It is not viable from a commercial point of view.

It is no wonder that the role of search engines is getting more important with respect to e-commerce as well. In the U.S. and the U.K. 'pay-for-performance search listings' already exist. And although -in general- people are reluctant[34] to pay for online content and feel the Internet should be free, nevertheless, they will be habituated to the trend of paid online streaming video and audio content.

On top of that they will be heavily tracked. Favorite websites put 'cookies' on people's computers when they visit their sites. Personal information of people online -even if they don't register- is collected, extracted, manipulated and appended into profiles, which are

---

[31] For an update of figures and statistics on culture and communication (press, libraries, book production, films and cinemas and broadcasting) and science and technology see e.g.: UNESCO Institute for Statistics, www.uis.unesco.org. UNESCO also provides the Observatory of the Information Society, the WebWorld Communication and Information page: http://portal.unesco.org/ci . See also: the United Nations Research Institute for Social Development (UNRISD) www.unrisd.org .
[32] Source: Kelly 1998: 152, (derived from Euromonitor).
[33] The largest search engine in the world is Google, followed by Lycos, Alta Vista and Yahoo. By the end of 2003 Google handled 200 million search orders a day. The site supports 88 languages and has 74 international domains. The profit made by Google is estimated at $ 130 – 200 million (turnover $ 800 million). Income stems from advertising sales and licences for technology. About 100.000 companies advertise on the Google site. Source: redactie economie, '200 miljoen keer per dag effe Googlen', in *Trouw*, 25-10-2003, p. 7.
[34] Source: CyberAtlas staff, 'Users still Resistant to Paid Content' on *CyberAtlas*, April 11, 2003, www.nua.ie based on the RampRate/Synovate survey and the Jupiter research report on payment willingness.

shared or sold to make money from advertising[35]. This is another topic of public reluctance and ignorance and regulatory *'laissez aller'* at the same time, despite social civic and political concerns on online information privacy.

What the global information and world telecommunications infrastructure, -including its content and services- has turned into, then, under the 'patronage' of the private sector, is one of the largest *markets* of the world economy. It is highly privatized and deregulated and 85% is dominated by six international coalitions from North America, Western Europe and Asia/Pacific. Communication and information are increasingly merchandise and decreasingly a public property, service and right.
'The 'information highway' is a toll road. Most of its on-ramps are in a handful of countries and most of its travelers are privileged. Many of its 'public spaces' are 'invitation-only' or they require an additional fee, subscription, or personal information. The vast majority of material that is accessible through the 'highway' comes from commercial, profit-oriented suppliers' (Regan 2000:17).

To answer the question whether the 'cyber hype' with its communication utopia of global participation, democracy and progress has materialized, it is also important to look at another very important aspect as identified by Bordewijk and Van Kaam (1982): *patterns of communication* -including the concept of *interactivity*-.

1.1.3.1 Patterns of communication and interactivity

Bordewijk and van Kaam (1982) developed a new conception of the traffic of information. This transfer happens in a complex communication network, with all kinds of connections, which can be visualized like a wheel with spokes connected to a rim and a centre.

They distinguish different patterns of information flows, which also express power relationships. Bordewijk and Van Kaam ask, 'who decides subject, time and pace of the reception of information (questions of control and access) and whose compilation of information is drawn from (about the storage of information)?' They distinguish four different patterns of information flows, each carrying a different role for the audience: *allocution, registration, consultation* and *conversation*.

Allocution stems from the Latin word *'allocutio'*, which refers to the one-way communication pattern of a Roman general addressing his soldiers. *Allocutio* is the opposite of *'collocutio'* or dialogue. Later the word, *allocutio*, became the name of a papal address to cardinals, who -like the soldiers- were not supposed to react. In the allocutive pattern of information transfer, power is concentrated at the sender. Bordewijk and Van Kaam point to the fact that in common language and in communication science, concepts and words derived from pure technical developments are used to interpret phenomena (apparently in a 'neutral' way.) On further consideration, they are not neutral, but reveal power relationships as well. An example in common language is 'sit at the controls'. In communication science terms like 'sender' or 'receiver' apparently are pure technical descriptions of patterns of information flow, but

---

[35] 'When a person 'participates' in different Web sites, he or she is usually being catalogued -by age, nationality, items purchased, sites visited, etc.- and all of that information goes into databases that are bought and sold by 'e-merchants'. Internet users thus often unwittingly are trading personal and private information in exchange for access to a certain database. That information will be used later by firms which, far from toeing the ideologues' line of 'universalism', use the demographics for micro-targeting their marketing efforts' (Regan: 2000:19).

according to Bordewijk and Van Kaam they also tell us something about power relationships involved in communication processes. Characteristic of allocution patterns is that the centre decides the content, time and consumption tempo of the information. Examples of allocution are a ballet or movie performance, broadcasting or a preaching minister or imam on the pulpit.

Registration refers to the collection of information by the centre (on conditions of the centre); examples are the referendum or an exam. But one could also think of the ever-increasing possibilities of (electronic) surveillance and control.
In consultative patterns, the receiver has an active role, to select from the information supply and decide on content, time and tempo, for example the world wide web
Conversation patterns require an equal position of the partners in the communication process, who send and receive both. The information stems from both sources and is shared according to agreed terms of time and tempo. An example of this pattern is a mutual exchange between computers. In communication studies, personal communication is valued to have the strongest possibilities of influence -stronger than any mass media. A similar view is largely held in churches, where this pattern of personal or private communication is valued higher than other (mediated) forms.

Each pattern has its own view of the audience[36], either passive (in allocution and registration patterns) or (inter)active (in consultation and conversation patterns).
With respect to new media developments, non-mass medial typologies of the audience are needed. They are not based on a centre-peripheral form of communication, but on mixed forms of mass and personal -interactive- communication - in which production, distribution and consumption can be mixed. Compared to 'traditional' mass media, it is striking how former distinctions between sender/receiver, production/consumption, individual/mass and private/public have blurred.

Exactly at this point the question of underlying power relationships (identified by Bordewijk and Van Kaam) is a very important one. Although communication patterns are transforming due to interactive media, remodelling (e.g.) allocutive communication, registration patterns have increased as well. Questions about storage of information, control, access, management (which information is used, or even offered to us?) and monitoring maintain relevant issues.
With respect to communication patterns then, it is also questionable whether one can speak of a 'communication revolution'.

The impact of new digital media on the way we communicate and on traditional media is profound. Often this impact is centered on the concept of *interactivity*. According to Jensen (1999:161) -building on Bordewijk and Van Kaam-interactivity is one of the most used media-hype 'buzzwords'. It is a 'watered down' term and at the same time has been a blind spot in media and communication studies. In this field the concept was related to audience-action with respect to media content -the relationship between text and reader-, based on traditional one-way media and not on user input or two-way-communication.

Regarding the defining of concepts of interactivity in media studies and computer science, Jensen discerns three ways: (1) as a *prototype*, (2) as a *criterion* or (3) as a *continuum*. All types refer to consultative and conversational media patterns.

---

[36] See also sections 2.2.4 and 2.3 on the perception of audiences in communication theory.

A problem with prototype references is whether media for interpersonal communication, like the telephone or e-mail, are to be considered 'interactive'. Face-to-face communication is considered ideal. Forms that come closest to this ideal are supposed to have the highest degree of interactivity. For example a conversational medium as video conferencing is more 'interactive' than a consultative medium as a computer based online service.
Criteria definitions have a similar including/excluding problem. They exclude services like teletext, which are interactive, but without user's input. Both prototype and criteria definitions cannot differentiate forms and levels of interactivity.

Continuum definitions can. They define interactivity as a variable with diverging multidimensional interactive degrees. They are more flexible and better suited to deal with fast technological developments. A problem with these concepts, however, is the arbitrary classification of media technologies on the continuum and the forcing into the same dimension and scale of different types of interactivity, referring to different communication patterns. Is e.g. a telephone conversation -involving another type of communication traffic (conversation)- more interactive than searching data in a database, -which refers to another communication pattern (consultation)-? Or is a video game more interactive than home shopping or pay per view? Another problem is the definition of the (sometimes overlapping) dimensions and degrees of interactivity (e.g. choices available, degree of modifiability and linearity, the potential to monitor, add information by users, or facilitate interpersonal communication).

To overcome the problems of the prototype, criteria, and continuum definitions mentioned, Jensen offers a new description of forms of interactivity that is focused on patterns of information flow. He argues in favor of distinguishing between the concept of *interactivity* (referring to media use and mediated communication) and the (sociological) concept of *interaction* (referring to non mediated communication.)
He defines interactivity as 'a measure of a media's potential ability to let the user exert an influence on the content and/or form of the mediated communication' (Jensen 1999:183). Interactivity is to be divided in four sub concepts: *'transmissional* interactivity' (choice without return, e.g. teletext, multi-channel systems); *'consultational* interactivity' (choice from an existing selection in a two-way-media channel (e.g.) video-on-demand, online information services, WWW); *'conversational* interactivity' (production and input by the user in a two-way-media system, (e.g.) video-conferencing, e-mail, mailing lists); *'registrational* interactivity' (registration of information from a user, response to his actions/needs, (e.g.) surveillance systems or intelligent agents/guides/interfaces). All four types of interactivity come together in the 'interactivity cube', a 3-dimensional graphic model and result in 12 different types of interactive media[37].

---

[37] Note that in relating the communication traffic patterns as identified by Bordewijk and Van Kaam (allocution, registration, consultation and conversation) to the forms of interactivity given by Jensen, three out of the four terms used are congruent (registrational, consultational and conversational). The fourth one, 'allocution', in Jensen's terms is 'transmissional'.
To Jensen's goal, identifying the manifold dimensions and levels of interactivity, a three dimensional representation is most suited. A tree diagram e.g. lacks the possibility to exactly discern positions and levels of interactivity. The choice by Jensen to represent transmissional and consultational interactivity in the same dimension of selection has to do with the fact that both are about the availability of choice, with and without a request. (See also above on choice with and without return).
Jensen departs from conversational interactivity (vertical axes) as opposed to registrational interactivity (diagonals). Moving up and down the vertical axis, or back and forth along the diagonal axis, implies higher or lower levels of conversational or registrational interactivity. The poles of each axis show the highest level of conversational or registrational interactivity or, at the opposite, the lowest or so to speak 'non-conversational' and 'non-registrational' interactivity (indicated by the -).

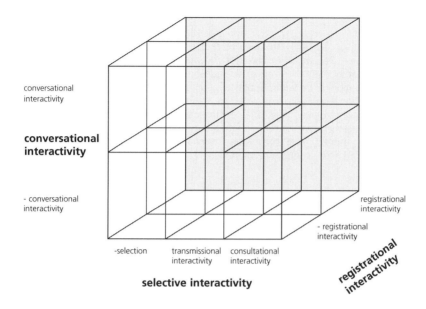

conversational
interactivity

**conversational
interactivity**

- conversational
interactivity

registrational
interactivity

- registrational
interactivity

-selection   transmissional   consultational
                    interactivity   interactivity

selective interactivity

*registrational
interactivity*

Figure 1.4 The 'cube of interactivity': a 3-dimensional representation of the dimensions of interactivity (Jensen 1999:184).

Although Jensen doesn't claim to offer the ultimate definition of interactivity, his concept contributes to a better understanding of its complexity; and, in relation to our subject, to a more appropriate answer to the issue of the 'media revolution' and the 'communication utopia' of our information society. The least we can say is that it remains to be seen whether information and communication flow patterns have changed in a revolutionary way with the arrival of the digital interactive media. Or, with the current state of affairs and architecture of the 'information highway', even will change more dramatically.

McQuail (2000:131), next to the new patterns of dominance and dependency in multilateral media flows -as discussed in the section on concentration and globalization- observes a 'redistribution of information traffic from allocutory to conversational and consultative patterns' and at the same time an 'extension of surveillance' and a 'growth of registration' in the digital age. The allocution pattern (of old mass communication media and the transmission model) still exists but now in a new form of 'narrow casting' for segmented audiences.

But again, does this 'redistribution' lead to the revolutionary rhetoric that is claimed with respect to the new media? The technical potential is probably there, but the predictions

On the base axes, selective interactivity is located, which can likewise consist of different levels of selective interactivity, varying from consultational interactivity (in different degrees as well), transmissional interactivity (also in different degrees) up to low levels of selective interactivity, resulting in the pole of 'non-selective' interactivity. By locating different 'media' (e.g. PC-tools or Registration-systems) as well as interactive communication 'behaviour' (e.g. taking a virtual reality tour, or chatting), in the cube, Jensen can distinguish their stand related to conversational, registrational and selective interactivity. In this way Jensen is able to pin-point every form and every level of interactivity, in a non-static way.

of 'utopia' were not reached, -as was neither the case with earlier communication innovations-.

According to Splichal (1999:5), 'the idea of *radical diversity* pertaining to the electronic media is delusive. Despite the changes brought about by new communication technologies, traditional or 'modern' questions and processes of influence, consensuality, opinion expression, (political) competence, identity, freedom, equality, access and media regulation continue to have fundamental importance for the development of communication in the 'postmodern' society. Changes brought about during the centuries are evolutionary rather than revolutionary. New communication technologies may, indeed, have a revolutionary character in the technological sense, but its social consequences cannot revolutionize the *cultural, political and economic continuity*'.

Hamelink (1995, 1997), with regard to the relationship between digital technologies and social development (in contrast with the utopian digital expectations), demonstrates a global information and communication imbalance. This imbalance involves much more than the flow of media products, such as television programs. It also concerns (e.g.) the development of and access to hardware and software, data networks[38], scientific and technical information, financial and trade information, environmental information, military intelligence information (satellites), political information (propaganda during war) and news. Production, distribution and access are unequally distributed. In Hamelink's words, there is a 'digital disparity' and an 'ICT gap', which is ever increasing[39] and it is questionable whether 'developing' countries -and the information poor in the rich countries- can bridge this financial and technical gap. In his opinion, it is too early to predict a 'revolution' in the case of digital innovation. Technological processes are seldom revolutionary and mostly gradual. There is no real discontinuity of a 'post industrial' era based on a service economy, neither is there a 'global information society'.

---

[38] In his article 'Digital Cohabitations: The Social Consequences of Convergent Technologies', Pradip Thomas discusses the 'informationalisation' of production in contemporary society, the management and control of knowledge via informational networks -being the source of social, economic and political power- and the increasing convergence between separate technologies like information technologies and biotechnologies. He claims that the informational logic of cybernetics has become the basis for productive processes in many different sectors, bringing along its own logic of understanding everything, including living organisms (bio informatics), in terms of information systems.
Crucial issues in these developments are the ownership of global knowledge and resources and patents in the new knowledge economy. 'The ownership of information is already a critical and contentious area in global cultural, economic and trade policy. Databanks on biological and physical information along with archives on culture and society are increasingly being privatised. Global intellectual property regimes support the creation of enclosures via archives and databases. Together they can be used to create formidable fortifications around knowledge that are only made available for a fee. Even the large public databanks in the USA that ostensibly are public repositories of knowledge cannot be accessed by the ordinary citizen (...)'.
Studying communications, according to Thomas, then can no longer be confined to traditional structures, processes, politics and systems, but has to include the new sources of global cultural, economic and political power: 'In other words, the lessons of the AOL-Time Warner merger and the decline of that partnership may, in the long run, be of less significance than IBM's massive investments in the life sciences. And rather than deal with communication policy issues per se, it is imperative that we interrogate the source of property power in the knowledge economy – the structures, systems and instruments of intellectual property that have become the means of maintaining corporate dominance in the new economy'. Thomas' article can be found on the website of the World Association for Christian Communication, www.wacc.org.uk and was published in Media Development, 2/2003, p. 3-12.
[39] See e.g. the UNDP development reports.

ICT may have a revolutionary power, but it never develops in an economic-social vacuum, neither does technology as such create the progress promised by the claims of visionary predictions.

The concept of digital democratic participation[40] (e.g.) thus is problematic. Direct electronic fora and referenda are technically possible, even on a world scale, but how will results impact representative democratic systems and institutions as we now know them? And how democratic will the results be if the largest part of the world population is uninformed and unwired, and e-mail voting privacy cannot be guaranteed? Besides, if commercial exploitation of the digital highway prevails, where does this leave public service, public property and public information?

In the end, it may be possible that the 'technological revolution' is not accompanied by a 'social revolution'.

Instead of unfruitful debates between utopian and dystopian perspectives, Hamelink urges the necessity of pro-active scenario's that depart from a desired future -local and global-, social relationships -which are economically and environmentally viable- and the social and institutional changes needed in a country in order to reach this future. Only when those scenarios are clear, discussed democratically, and implemented, the potential of digital technology to contribute to what is claimed by the digital doctrine, might occur.

But even as far as the European context is concerned, is European media policy at all heading for this direction? The trends of media deregulation, liberalization and privatization, -even stronger in the case of new media- as described in 1.1.2, seem to provide evidence to the contrary. The development of the European part of the 'digital highway' and the European Union's concept of the 'information society' are no exception to the framework of free movement of audiovisual services within the single market, European harmonization, and the facilitation of globally competitive players[41].

1.1.4   Evaluation

In spite of similar trends, it is complicated to evaluate 'European' media developments. Results are dependent on national and regional media systems, distribution and access, policies, funding, culture, media use, size, geography and social factors.

Nevertheless, as McQuail (2004) comments, there are some common features in Europe with respect to media, i.e. basics in law, human rights and democracy; the mixed model of public and private broadcasting; a tradition of possible intervention for the sake of public interest; political party competition, which shapes the outlook and role of media; and the regulatory role of the European Union and the Council of Europe with respect to access, diversity and cultural goals, and cultural identification.

McQuail (2004) also identifies five general common main issues that dominate today's European media spectrum: (1.) the struggle over deregulation and commercialization, that resulted in a new, mixed model without public monopoly and growing extension for commercial enterprise and private ownership; (2.) the new technologies, digitization and the growing role of the Internet along with the connected problems of regulation and

---

[40] See e.g. 'UK Citizens Online Democracy' http://www.democracy.org.uk or in the Netherlands: http://www.democratie-digitaal.nl

[41] See e.g. the 1994 European Commission's Green Paper 'Europe's way to the information society'. Brussels: EU Commission, or the 1995 EU Commission's Green Paper 'Liberalization of Telecom Infrastructure and Cable TV Networks'. Brussels: EU Commission.

conflicts between private and public forces; (3.) structures of (transnational and cross) media ownership, and issues of openness and diversity; (4.) the economic and policymaking integration of Europe, accepted in national policy making and less focus on cultural protectionism from 'Americanization' than in former days; (5.) the issue of overall control and accountability of media problems such as declining information standards, harmful content, cyber crime, privacy, human rights, and standards of decency without much possibility of supervising (at the national as well as the European level) or effective self-regulation.

All of these issues are current issues. This, next to regional and national particularities, is another important reason why it is difficult to draw conclusions about the transformation of the European media landscape.

With respect to the indicated structures, a new European mixed public/private model of electronic media has already been established. Although the end of its monopoly (in 1990) didn't mean the end of public service broadcasting as such in Europe, it is still under pressure and vulnerable, because it is based on a fragile political and public consensus. Despite important system changes, public broadcasting principles such as debate and information, access rights, diversity, protection of national culture and language and public accountability still hold and viewers' loyalty to national public broadcasters is more tenacious than perhaps was expected. On the other hand, adaptation to commercially oriented formats, style, content and policies by public broadcasters, the press and the audience is a reality as well. The cultural, social and language differentiation -and national and regional economical and political self interest- within the European continent will be a preserving power for national broadcasting. But will public service broadcasting (in the long run) turn out to be an indispensable aspect as well? Or will Europe successively let go of its 'European' media tradition and media culture in order to keep pace with the global commercial developments? In that case, what will be the consequences involved for public information and public debate, diversity and the needs of democracy?
Or will the digital interactive media technologies of the future (once they have been fully established) make public service broadcasting into a superseded concept anyway?

McQuail (2002:218-224), assessing the changes in an adequate and balanced way with a view to the future, expects the present mixed model will continue and include the continuation of public broadcasting, however, due to harsh competition for audiences it 'approached a condition of implosion' (2002:220) in McQuail's words. The continuation thus will be a continuation in reduced size (one national public channel, viable in terms of audience shares and finance). Funding will be supplied by program or channel subscription, which will replace the system of license fees, advertising or sponsorship. 'It is still unclear what the typical form of a national media (TV) structure will look like, in terms of balance of content provision, but the safest bet for quite a long time is a continuation of approximately the present system, with any major changes or additions to the 'national' system, whatever the means of distribution, requiring political sanction and fitting into some system of accountability. There will continue to be rather few popular general news/entertainment channels (still broadcast or cabled), coupled with a range of specialist channels and many other services provided by a variety of distribution technologies, including multimedia and the Internet' (2002:220).

He also expects greater oligopoly in the future private sector, although the impact of participation by the national telecom monopolies -and of increasing American participation- is unclear.

As far as the described trends are concerned, there is considerable concentration and commercialization of media and a more commercial electronic media sector on the way. According to McQuail, media expansion and the new order enlarged the freedom of the market, competition and convergence, but it did not increase freedom of expression or lead to fundamental changes with respect to the social and cultural role of media. Nevertheless, the European media situation is not as commercialized as in the US. And even though the framework is loose, media are regulated and accounted for in Europe. There is economic and regulatory convergence -at the same time countered by (e.g.) restrictions on cross-ownership-, and system (television and related services) convergence in Europe in spite of the lack of technological convergence, especially when it comes to competing distribution technologies.

McQuail finds no proof of more cosmopolitan or American media experience[42], although there is an impact of international media culture with respect to formats and standards. Media experience in general, -print media in particular- is still very national, although there is a trend towards 'tabloidization' and de-politicization of content and control. The European regulatory and transnational bodies, however, do pressurize towards similar standards, norms, policies and practices; globally identical media innovations and media industrial trends will only reinforce this. But there is also the audience that resists cultural convergence, which makes the need for cultural policy differences an enduring matter.

Media policy, says McQuail, is entering a new era. The days of strong national regulation that was based on limited permission and direct control are over. 'The new era of policy will be characterized by more internationalism, market realism, technical and administrative complexity and large components of media industry self-regulation designed to reconcile public, private and commercial interests' (2002:224).

Issues, values and fora may have changed, but political and public concern and debate on media have remained - if not enlarged; not the least about media behavior.

1.1.5   Summarizing remarks

The 1990's appeared to be a turning point in the context of media and media culture. The main technological innovation was digitalization and the arrival of new multifunctional information and communication technologies (ICT's). This development profoundly impacted communication structures and communication traffic patterns as well as the position of public broadcasting. Global, national, regional and local levels became intertwined, not only with respect to structures, but also to media regulation and media players. Increasingly the media context became global.

The main trends involved the commercialization of media output, the domination of the global media market by transnational media industries, and the rise of commercial media and dual systems. The convergence of technologies and media conglomerates, as well as commercialization and privatization, went hand in hand with liberalization and deregulation in the political realm. Media policy in this respect enters a new era. For the

---

[42] Opinions on this differ though, as demonstrated in the following conclusion drawn by Jeremy Tunstall, (2004:271). 'The United Kingdom' in The Media in Europe. London, Sage, 262-274. 'The BBC will certainly survive beyond the year 2010. But both the BBC and British television will have absorbed additional doses of American material and influences. With so much cash going into peak-time British programming, there will be an irresistible urge to put yet more cheap US material into 'fringe' time (early evening and late night) and into daytime. Also by 2009-10 the BBC will be asking, yet again, whether it can survive solely on a license fee which represents a still dwindling share of total broadcast expenditure. It is also highly probable that American ownership will have spread from satellite and cable into one or more of ITV and Channels 4 and 5'.

sake of the market and economic potential on a global scale, EU policies as well as national policies have become increasingly pro-commercial. Marketing and advertising of (global) brands play an important part in this process. They outweigh issues of media diversity, pluralism in supply, quality, public interest and accountability.

With respect to new media, especially the internet and the World Wide Web, similar drives and trends showed up. The 'cyber hype' has not materialized its potential for globally accessible equal communication. Notwithstanding an 'overload' of information, there is a digital imbalance and divide, and millions of people lack even basic infrastructure to participate. Regarding communication traffic patterns, there is a redistribution from allocutory to conversational and consultational patterns, as well as to registrational ones. Interactivity in this respect appears to be a buzzword, and difficult to define. Prototype, criterion and continuum definitions are inadequate. Based on patterns of communication traffic, sub concepts of transmissional, consultational and registrational interactivity are more satisfactory.

Evaluating the impact of all the trends and of European media developments is complicated. Within Europe there are many national and regional differences in the media realm concerning systems, distribution, access, policies, funding, media use, geography and social factors. However, there are general common main issues. Towards the future, a larger private oligopoly, a more commercial media sector and a widespread international media culture are on the way.

1.2   The social cultural role of media

Interviewed on television by a political journalist about her policy concerning the expulsion of immigrants who had been waiting for more than five years for a decision on their request for asylum, and asked whether she was able to do something about the poignant cases such as families with children born in the Netherlands, the Dutch minister for integration and immigration answered that this was an example of 'emotion-democracy'[43].
What she actually meant by this was that to her opinion by the coverage of the media, focusing on commotion and protests in the country (refusing mayors and aldermen to implement government policy to expel people), and showing concretely what the policy meant to individual people by putting them on the screen, the facts about immigration law and judicial sentences that confirmed her policy had disappeared from view.

This is only one of the examples of debate about the role and impact of media in society. Deacon, Pickering, Golding and Murdock (1999) identify a range of connections between communications and contemporary life, in which media play a central organizing role. Communications companies provide information and communication links necessary for around the clock financial trade and global production. They are also pivotal to consumption by selling not only their own services and products but also by being the conduit for advertising that underlies the consumer system. They play an important role in the organization of politics (being the major public space in society[44]),

---

[43] Ferry Mingelen interviewing minister Verdonk in *Nova*, 9-2-2004.
[44] The European Centre for Ethics at the Catholic University of Leuven, Belgium, every two year organizes the *Politeia Conference,* -alternated with the *Multatuli lectures-.* Topics among others were: 'Courageous or Indifferent Individualism' (Robert Bellah, 1998), 'Modern Media and Social Dialogue' (Elihu Katz on multiplication of media and social segmentation, and Zygmunt Bauman on the social political effects of television, 2000), and 'Lifestyle Politics' (Pippa Norris, John Gray and

and they play a role in constituting cultural systems and commonly held imaginative spaces. They also offer generalized world views and images of self, which are continually renegotiated within people's experiences of understanding and of identities. Finally they organize routines and rituals of everyday life.

McQuail (2000:4) addressing the significance of mass communication (near universal reach, great popularity and public character) points to the impact on two important realms: political organization and cultural life.

With respect to the latter, he states that mass media constitute 'a primary source of definitions and images of social reality', the 'most ubiquitous expression of shared identity', and they provide -more than any other institution- the 'shared cultural environment'. We might add to this tripartition the 'ritual - religious function' of mass media.

So far, we have emphasized the structural and technological aspects of the media.

In the present section, we will consider the broad and complex issue of *socio-cultural* aspects of media. To discuss this issue in extension is beyond the scope of this volume and our subject. Therefore, we will focus on the relationship between electronic/digital media and culture, since television and internet are the main information media for the majority of people in contemporary 'information era'. Based on McQuail's tripartition as mentioned above, superadded by the religious dimension.

1.2.1   Defining social reality

On the first day of March 2004, the long awaited 'Dutroux' trial in Belgium finally started. It was eight years after his arrest for kidnapping and sexually abusing children, which put the whole country in a state of shock. It pushed the politics and justice system of Belgium into crises. The television news that evening showed some of the hectic fuss of the hundreds of radio and television reporters from all over the world. They had invaded the city of Aarlen, where the trial was held, on the weekend before. One of them stated that this was a 'global' story. Another one felt a little disappointed because she had expected more tumult and riots on this first day. A third was angry about the 'blurred pictures only' of the main suspect that had been issued by the court, and a fourth one declared that this was a very complicated story to explain abroad with its extensive dossier of 450,000 pages -impossible to read completely- and many changes in prosecutors and attorneys over the years.

In fact, the first day of the trial was not interesting at all. The only thing that happened was that the jury was seated[45] and one of the defense attorneys demanded that the charges be read out loud, which took hours the next day. By then, many outside broadcast units and journalists had disappeared from the spot -in spite of the fact that the third day was a crucial one in the trial, with the foreman of the district court cross examining the four suspects-.

Whatever the foreign journalists reported that first night in their home countries -it would make an interesting case study- they provided their viewers with a glimpse of a

---

Christina Holtz-Bacha, 2002). We will get back to the content of the addresses in chapter four. www.kuleuven.ac.be/oce/Politeia.

[45] The Belgian Assise Court's system is composed of a jury of 12 laypersons, chosen on the first day of the trial (from a larger group of especially for that trial by lot appointed candidates), assisted by magistrates of the district court; the foreperson of the Assise Court at the same time acts like examining magistrate during the trial. The laypersons define the verdict; thereupon the Assise Court, together with the laypersons, defines the sentence.

'world news event'. But what made it noteworthy to so many of them? How did this 'world news', 'live' from the spot come about? Going by the reactions mentioned above, one might immediately deduce some features: 'live' news is something that is, in the majority of cases, planned; it is about -dramatized- stories; images play an important role, as does personalization; news is not about complex issues, but on matters that can be simplified and explained in a few statements; news is where the majority of the journalists decide to go; and news is above all 'fast': hit and run.

Van Ginneken (1999), provides a clear insight into the construction of world news and news values. This construction turns out to develop according to a specific selection, interpretation and representation of world affairs. Or, to put it in Van Ginneken's words: 'the creation of the world in the news' (1999:19).
'Views of the world', -which in contemporary society for most people are mediated views- and 'world views' are much closer interconnected than we presume or even are aware of. According to Van Ginneken, we are all, both individually and societal, guided by 'mental maps': cultural, ethnocentric 'frames', which determine our perception and representation of the world. This also holds true for journalists and media.

Media are often considered our -neutral- 'window to the world'. A window, by necessity though, offers us a focused and fragmented view. Certain issues in everyday media reality are 'news' while others are not. The tragic death of one celebrity or the hundreds of deaths of a plane crash might become a main item in the evening's television news, whereas 30.000 children dying daily due to lack of health programs and (cheap) medication[46], are not 'noteworthy', as Van Ginneken states.

Citing two classical studies in this realm[47], he points out that news is more about -known- individuals (mainly formal political leaders) than on groups or social processes. Unknowns come in only when they break conventions (victims, strikers, violators etc). Types of activities that dominate news are: government conflicts; government decisions and ceremonies; government personnel changes; protests; crimes, scandals and investigations; disasters; innovation and tradition and national ceremonies.

Factors which determine an event as newsworthy include: time span (short and within the deadlines and frequency of programming or publication); scale and intensity; clarity (fit in a clear category); meaningfulness (familiar culture or relevant in contrast to it); consonance (correspondence to what is expected to happen); unexpectedness (within the meaningful and the consonant); continuity (a news item must hold for some time); composition (balance of categories represented in the news); authority (elite nations and persons, authorities, experts); personification (concrete, possible to identify with) and negativity.

If we look at the Dutroux trial, we can immediately notice a 'high' score on the 'scale of feasibility' to become world news. The story contains much of the criteria mentioned: Dutroux -by locking little girls in his basement, abusing them and letting them die of starvation- is breaking conventions. Although an unknown individual, he is a violator in an extreme sense. The story is not only about his crime and scandal, but also about the scandal of the law and the police that were unable to prevent the facts due to mutual conflicts and rivalry. The decisions and failures of the government to interfere (reaching the depths of misery in the short term escape of the main suspect in the fourth year of his detention, forcing ministers of justice and the department of the interior to resign),

---

[46] See Memisa Cordaid: http://www.memisa.nl/Over_ons/English/Default.aspx?mId=10261&rId=140
[47] Gans, Herbert J. 1980. Galtung, Johan and Ruge, Mari Holmboe. 1965.

and all the investigations during eight years are another set of 'positive' criterions. Next to the funerals of the victims which grew into national ceremonies of mourning and the protest of hundreds of thousands of Belgians in the streets of Brussels some time after that on October 20, 1996.

Scale and intensity of the story are high. It fits clearly into a category. It is meaningful in both recognition and contrast to culture; it is unexpected and it will certainly hold for some time. The question whether Dutroux acted on his own behalf or in the interest of a network in which political and even royal elite was said to be involved, grew into a nearly mythical issue that split camps into 'believers' and 'non-believers'. Finally and perhaps most important, it is a story which holds multiple possibilities for personification. There are concrete suspects (contrast-identification) and the victims and their parents to identify with. Negativity is obvious.

Most of the criteria for news that are mentioned above are interrelated and form a firm frame or grid by which the world is mediated to us. This holds for selection as well as interpretation. Van Ginneken shows that such a frame is not without ideology. Focusing (e.g.) to a high degree on individuals, negativity or the extraordinary might make structural background information, positive actions or developments, or the 'normal' disappear from view. This is especially true when it comes to culturally distant issues, nations or people (the so called 'third world countries' e.g. only make it to the news if in crisis).

An example given by Van Ginneken concerns the issue of drugs. Alcohol and tobacco - traditional western drugs- that are produced by Western companies are labeled 'legal', but non-Western drugs are 'illegal'. The negative effects of the latter are highly emphasized, but the pubic health risks of the former (which cause many deaths) are much less prominent in media attention. The focus is on city drugs-scenes, which are only one of the scenes of drug consumer's -including celebrities-. The frame used is criminalization.

In the Netherlands (e.g.), in 2003 media attention about the issue of drugs was almost entirely focused on the Antilles' smugglers who swallow little cocaine balls and take a plane to Amsterdam to deliver their fare. It was also focused on the Antilles' authorities, which 'did not take appropriate measures'. The Dutch minister of justice issued severe policy and safety measures and cleared corresponding budgets. Special prisons were equipped and people were scanned, physically examined and/or refused admittance to planes departing the Antilles, heading for Amsterdam. There was little attention about the fact that the majority of the drugs in the Netherlands comes in through containers via the harbors of Rotterdam and Amsterdam, which are much more difficult to control, at the expense of high economic costs and risks. Neither was questioned whether the Dutch consumers were to blame or the Dutch authorities, who are unable to tackle the problem of drugs consuming by their own population.

The problem, according to Van Ginneken, is not so much media selection as such, but the fact that the biased underlying criteria in doing so are not explicit. They are taken for granted as natural common sense, based on consensus. News however is selectively articulated. Certain facts and relationships are emphasized, while others are left out. Van Ginneken (1999:32) in this respect labels evening TV news not so much in terms of 'main important events', but as 'a form of collective therapy'. 'Possible threats to our world order and our world-views are evoked, identified, labeled, categorized, dealt with and dispatched again. For this purpose, anchormen or women summon a daily parade of authorities and experts. They put our minds at rest, so that we can go to bed reassured. But it is the concerns and values of the First World which remain central, those of the Second and Third Worlds remain marginal'.

90% of the transcontinental flows of media material come from G-8 (major industrialized) countries through highly concentrated global news agencies such as Reuters, AP and AFP. Since only 10% of the world population lives in these countries, a minority shapes the news and views of a large majority (the world's three prime 'newsmakers' are the White House, the US State Department and the Pentagon).

Within this minority it is another minority that gets to speak in the world news. Not eyewitnesses, but officials of -mainly Western- governments, major corporations and established institutions. This selection is based on their assumed authority and credibility, and above all: institutional availability (all three measured to Western standards). Journalists are highly dependent on information by those officials, which means they set the media -and public- agenda to a considerable extent. Increasingly, 'spin doctors' (public relations strategists) plan and manipulate this process by 'organizing' and 'managing' the news. Providing for the ideal quote is only one of the options that range to complete campaigns of propaganda and media manipulation as was the case in both the Gulf wars.

This is not to say that media cannot and will not represent 'other-side-stories'. They do, but as Van Ginneken (1999:91) states, 'not outside the overall framework'. Prime definition of a news event (defined by the large news agencies who report it first) plays a key role in 'labeling' a certain conceptual framework on this event. Once this framework has been set, it will continue and perpetuate itself. Mutual access of officials and media elites plays an important role not only in setting the news agenda, but also in maintaining frameworks.

According to Hamelink (2002) in his inaugural lecture on lies and delusion in the information society, lying in the media takes three forms: deliberately lying, passing on lies by others and concealing. Deliberate lying, says Hamelink, was the case in the television report made by ITN's Penny Marshall in Trnopolje, Bosnia. This report showed a very skinny man 'behind barbed wire' suggesting concentration camps instead of the storage depot it in reality was. The man deliberately was picked out and asked to step forward to the fence. He was the conclusive evidence and the 'perfect' picture of what the reporter was looking for: the story of concentration camps in Europe once again. In the interview with him -and others surrounding him-, questions were deliberately guided in that direction in spite of the fact that they stated they were treated well and cared for. The material was manipulated and provided with 'neutral' translations and comments. Nevertheless, the images were spread worldwide and played an important role in the propaganda war against the Bosnian Serbs. The image of this man is still used frequently in media, as a kind of 'icon' of that period. It is a 'one in all' concluding, powerful image that tells us the simple truth in what was, in fact, a very complex conflict. Especially in television news though, this complexity cannot be dealt with and results in stereotypical replays.

Although there are more examples of this kind of lying, also among 'quality media' -The New York Times reporter Jayson Blair in 2003 made the feathers fly with hise confession of at least 35 faked (some of them front page) stories[48]-, most of the time, says Hamelink, media do not deliberately lie. Although serious research journalism is under pressure, reporters do uncover and reveal. More frequently, though, they accept without question -and spread- the lies of civil service's spin doctors, especially in times of conflict

---

[48] Source: www.nrc.nl/buitenland.

and war[49]. Or they withhold important facts and developments from the public, for reasons of alleged 'national security'. Media also uncritically accept and adopt certain frames or specific interpretations of reality. What fits the frame is perceived; what doesn't fit, -or cannot be made fit-, stands a good chance of being overlooked or ignored. Who gets to speak in the news then has a lot to do with the power to establish the dominant frame.

Next to the official sources, the authoritative experts speak in the world news (mainly white, male officials and professionals). Ordinary people (if belonging to upper or middle class of a Western capital) may have a chance to become a news source, but an illiterate's chances in the rural area's or slums of a third world country are next to non existent -even if the news item is about his or her life conditions-.
The hierarchy in sources is also pursued in the way sources are quoted (in extenso, in bits, or paraphrased) and labeled (qualification, status, political conviction or role, gender). Value judgments thus are subtly added to persons and statements. In the invisible process of cutting and editing techniques, parts of quotes, comments, sub-introductions and sub-conclusions may completely alter an interview. Sometimes those are deliberately recorded for this purpose on another location at a different time.

Time frames and geography are also important aspects in the selective articulation of news. 'Live' news in the majority of cases turns out to be planned coverage of expected or even announced events. This holds for news in general: it is planned and staged according to political processes such as run-ups to elections, international political meetings etc.

According to Van Ginneken (1999:122), the significance of certain events only relates to their 'planned media effect'. These include pseudo-events like current commemorations, which serve rather political significance and the socialization of ideology by making them into mythical events, than the purpose of informing. The commemorations are reported by a Western bias and without much historical perspective. An example of this is the 500th anniversary of the 'discovery' of the Americas (1492-1992).
When I lived in Argentina in 1990, the people of Latin America prepared for their 'celebration' of what they labeled as the 'discovery by the people of Latin America of Columbus' (and the according European occupation which was to impact their continent without precedent[50]). In the news-reports on the festivities in Western Europe, for example, it was hardly mentioned that millions of Indian inhabitants died as a consequence of diseases and violence of the 'discoverers'[51]. The 'celebrations' in Latin America were ignored, as usual with commemorations by third world countries.

The focus of world news is on short-lived events. Historical context or long-term processes disappear from sight. Western civilization is overemphasized in terms of

---

[49] On the eve of the first Gulf war, Iraq invaded Kuwait. A crying nurse in front of the camera told she saw Iraqi soldiers taking babies out of incubators and let them die on the ground. It was a faked story; the nurse appeared to be the daughter of the Kuwaiti ambassador in the US. Other examples involve stories on the son of Saddam Hussein killing political opponents in a snipping machine (on the eve of the second gulf war) and on US soldier Jessica Lynch, as leading lady in an Iraqi heroic epic 2003. All of these stories were part of the news flow all over the world.
[50] See: Galeano, Eduardo. 1982-1986. *Memoria del fuego* [Memory of Fire] (trilogy). Madrid/Mexico, Siglo Veintiuno Editores. And *Las venas abiertas de América Latina* (1971) [Open Veins of Latin America]. Siglo Veintiuno Editores.
[51] Central American and northern Andean Indian. 2006. In *Encyclopedia Brittanica*. Retrieved November 1, 2006 from *Encyclopædia Britannica* Online: http://www.britannica.com/eb/article-57760

progress, modernity, enlightenment, civilization, freedom and wealth. Other civilizations are portrayed in opposite terms as uncivilized, authoritarian, extremist, poor etc. In spite of the fact that every medal has its reverse, the historical roots of Western wealth and progress, and the tremendous harm caused (e.g. by crusades, slave trade, the robbery of raw materials, colonization, armed interventions, unequal trade conditions etc. which impact conditions of the present state of world affairs) is no regular news item in 'hit and run' news.

News rhythms also determine world news. News comes in cycles. Production and consumption by the major audiences follow time patterns and working hours of the Western world.

In the same way time frames and historical perspectives interact with selective news articulations, so do spatial and (social) geographical bias. Major news process centers are located in the major Western nations and language areas. The majority of the correspondents, spokesmen, commentators etc. are Western. Two thirds of the foreign correspondents are located in the US and Europe. They cater primarily to their home - due to commercial pressure greatest common denominator- audiences, bringing about little background and/or analysis and much stereotyping. Due to the high costs, foreign correspondence posts are discontinued and increasingly media items formerly produced by foreign correspondents are now purchased from global news agencies. In places where foreign correspondents are remained, they tend to professionally rely on mutual contacts, contacts with other natives from their own countries and other international media. Especially in situations of crises when journalists are 'dropped' to report from unfamiliar cultures and language areas without longstanding local contacts, the 'recycling of information' is common.

Much debate (and controversy) has been spent on the unequal direction of global news flows and the geographical and topical one-sidedness of news. The most famous perhaps is UNESCO's New World Information and Communication Order, or NWICO debate that was initiated by the non-aligned countries. It eventually led to the UK's and US's withdrawal and non-compliance with financial obligations, a crisis in UNESCO and the petering out of the debate.
A major study by the International Association for Mass Communication Research, under the authority of UNESCO, already in 1984 concluded the near universality of selection criteria; the US and Europe being the main newsmakers in all regions; the prevailing of US and European stories, followed by 'hot spot' stories; and national agencies or own correspondents being the main source for international news, followed by international news agencies. Third world countries remain underreported and are increasingly losing out to what Van Ginneken names the 'American news soap operas', such as the O.J. Simpson trial.

The dominating media system as such, as Van Ginneken shows, has its own set of core values: free enterprise and free market (economic values); individualism and social mobility (social values); pragmatism and moderation (political values); materialism and autonomy (lifestyle values); and 'we have no ideology' (ideological values). These values, as well as the functioning of the media system according to these values have become the 'natural' commons sense state of affairs.

What is 'relevant' in world news then is what is important to the relevant audience groups in Western countries and their values and standards since they are the ones that the news agencies cater to.

'Objectivity,' according to Van Ginneken (42-44), is not so much a notion, which tells us something about neutrality or impartiality, but an economic one. Complete objectivity is not possible at all, to his opinion. Reports are always situated and shaped socio-historically. Journalists -reporting the 'facts'- are, as we all are, socialized by their own specific (sub) culture, -which is mostly white and male- (primary socialization). But they are also socialized by their professional (sub) culture -education, licensing, professional organizations and codes of ethics, 'public service' role etc.- (secondary socialization). And finally by the mores of the medium/company they work for (tertiary socialization). In their profession, they are led by social patterns and mental frames, internalized worldviews and cultural grids that include (e.g.) enemy images or images towards other religions that may easily lead to stereotypes or categorization.

Annabelle Sreberny-Mohammadi, in a revealing case study on international news coverage of Iran (1995:428-443) argues that severe cultural mythology and ethnocentrism are displayed in the verbal and visual languages and codes of television. 'News language, whether international or domestic, supplies subtle and not so subtle value-laden terms that constitute an interpretive framework for the audience. Thus it is important to examine media use of such terms as *terrorist and fanaticism*, which can be contrasted with *freedom fighter and commitment* The terminology often derives from the prevailing political atlas, especially as articulated by the president of the day' (1995:435/6). Her conclusion is that the need is not for more 'good news', but for more debate about what 'good news coverage' is.

The formulation of messages and the editing of images are another key factor in the process of selection and selective articulation. Language, sentence formulation, and narrative constructions are not merely unambiguous instruments as Van Ginneken shows. They are related to sign systems and cultural grids (denotations, connotations, and associations), mega-stories and central myths and ideologies in society. A choice of words can be legitimating, while another choice can be de-legitimating. Apparently it doesn't make much difference whether in the news reports on the Dutroux-trial we hear the 'suspect' or the 'accused'; 'Dutroux' ex-wife' (also one of the suspects) or 'Michelle Martin'; the 'businessman' or the 'drugs dealer' Nihoul. And yet it does make a difference. As it does make a difference whether we get to see a picture of Nihoul, apparently taken by the police shortly after he was arrested and/or questioned (unshaven, shady, pouches under the eyes, handcuffed), a picture of Nihoul in a wheel chair (after he was released on bail) or one in suit and with tie when entering the court.

The structure of news formats (organization and style) is, in Van Ginneken's words, another 'organizing' perspective that is usually in line with common sense -dominant-views in a society.

Images, even more than words, seem to provide us with 'what really happened'. What we see before our eyes appears to be 'true' and makes us live witnesses of world history even though it is mediated by a camera. Camera's do not simply 'register' though. Visual stories are highly constructed. Location and orientation of the camera (prearranged during events), distance (close up's and medium shots stressing individuality and intimacy and personal relationship, panoramic or long shots stressing anonymity and thus different identification) and vertical angles (higher -angle down- or lower -angle up-vantage points stressing power and authority respectively weakness and smallness) involve implicit issues of meaning. Every image is just a miniscule fragment out of a range of possibilities to picture reality. It is a choice, a representation of a point of view. By editing, highlighting or cropping, correcting (e.g. color; film sensitivity and lighting-standards are based on white skin), retouches etc., images of the real cannot only be 'manipulated', but the editor may also put a preferred 'reading' in it. If images 'mirror' anything at all, it is the underlying view of reality.

Evening television news, for many still the primary and most credited informant, involves similar processes led by arbitrary decisions and staging rules. According to Van Ginneken (1999: 176-188), television news is staged as a little 'morality play' to 'recycle' the dominant worldview of a society that follows a particular 'ritual'.

The actors in the play are the anchormen and women (behind desks, stressing authority, factual knowledge and credibility), correspondents and reporters (against the backdrop of famous buildings with specific connotations and symbolic values in order to stress the 'eye-witness' impression and status of 'verified reality').
The play carefully follows the preordained script. Trailer and leader 'raise the curtain' by a hybrid complex of various news symbols and dramatic music that are followed by the opening piece: the major item (similar in nearly all television channels and highly dependent on the availability of good visuals). The following items are grouped together (foreign news, domestic items, political, economical, social affairs etc., stressing the impression of non-arbitrariness) in typical frames and story lines. The tailpiece offers something positive and optimistic, whereupon the ritual of leave-taking by the anchorperson follows. Even the weather report, used as a kind of cliffhanger that stresses scientific prediction and control, is not as neutral as assumed as demonstrated by Van Ginneken (1999: 1-21) (e.g. in the use of concentric maps with our own region in the centre and world maps with Northern and Western bias).

The play is also carefully staged according to certain rules. Full front camera position is the privilege of the professionals: the anchor person, the correspondent or reporter. Accessed voices are not allowed to look right into the camera. The reason for this has far more to do with direct relationships and claims of objectivity and truth, than with the mentioned claim of an 'unnatural' look of things. Interviews are also 'technically' staged. But where to stand, chosen background and how to look and speak (short, no complications or nuances) reveals something about the role that must be played according to the journalist's perception. A businessman is usually filmed in suit and tie, behind the desk in his office, or behind the table addressing the shareholders meeting. A farmer is filmed in overalls in front of his farm, or between the cows or the crops and a drugsdealer poorly clothed in a city-scene. It reflects what Van Ginneken labels as the 'hidden scripts' in television news.

Quoting Fiske and Hartley,[52] he concludes that the overall ideological function of television news is not so much about neutral objective information, but about the maintenance of cultural consensus about reality, cultural identity and membership, and dominant value systems.

Fore (1997) also holds this vision of news as ideology (we/they, good/bad), but next to the need of society to reinforce its basic cultural worldview, he adds the need of the communication industry to hold the largest possible audience. News, says Fore, portrays society in three spheres of activity: private, public and state. Although the public sphere and public welfare is said to be central, private business and economic considerations prevail. According to Fore, the economic marketplace shapes the press to produce profit and reproduce the status quo of economic, social and political powers. This leads to distortion, bias, oversimplification and problems in the search for meaning in mediated reality. In the political realm (e.g.) the accentuation of slogans, the personalization, the

---

[52] Fiske, John and Hartley, John. 1992. *Reading Television*. London and New York: Routledge.

triumph of pictures over ideas, the reliance on polling etc. undermines true dialogical conversation and free and open communication, which is the base of democracy. Christians, therefore, says Fore, have to insist on regulation and public service obligation -as a key moral issue- and critically 'test' news[53].

Television news is embedded in a continuous flux of drama, entertainment, talk shows, documentaries, fictional movies etc. In the increasingly commercial environment that television operates in, the most popular formats affect other types of programs. 'Infotainment' is but one example of this. Another one is the style of advertising, modeled after miniature film scripts, or clips.

But the issue at stake is beyond format. Television, in its totality, shares and mediates a common outlook on and provides a common experience of reality.
Fore (1990) analyzes television as signs and symbols, as economics and as psychology.
As psychology, television is a 'factory of dreams' (1990:69). It involves emotions beyond seeing, feeling, thinking and rationality. In this respect, Fore discerns 21 needs or 'uses/gratifications': reasons why television is psychologically appealing to people: to be amused; see authority figures, experience the beautiful, have shared experiences (community), satisfy curiosity, identify with deity, find distraction or diversion, experience empathy, experience extreme emotions (in a controlled and guilt free situation), find models to imitate, gain identity, gain information, reinforce the belief in justice, believe in romantic love, believe in magic and the marvelous, see others mistake, participate in history (without risks), be purged of unpleasant emotions, obtain outlets (sexual drives in a guilt free context), explore taboos safely, and to affirm moral, spiritual and cultural values.

Television thus has seven socially useful functions, as described by Fore (1987:19-20): providing relaxation, psychological compensation, a sense of security and stability, information, help to cope with life, providing a sense of belonging and a fantasy world.
In the realm of signs and symbols, television offers us signifying concepts, by its images, spoken words, fantasy, camera shots, editing techniques etc. Signs and symbols have a strong appeal. They relate to levels of communication beyond the cognitive level. People use different -socialized- cultural codes (e.g. association, non-verbal codes) to deal with signs and symbols. In fact, cultures are systems of codes. The whole medium of television, according to Fore (1987:21), 'reflects and expresses the myths[54] by which we live'.

Media then, in defining social reality simultaneously impact the cultural realm. Examining this process and its implications will be the subject of the next section. We will focus on - and briefly discuss- the work of Antonio Gramsci (the concept of *hegemony*), Jesús

---

[53] A way this could be done is provided for by Deacon, Pickering, Golding and Murdock 1999:162-207. They describe five stages of analysis related to position, composition and immediate inter-textual relations in staging the news; the thematic structure of the text; the discourse schematization (sequencing structure, sources -quantity and quality-, framing procedures); lexical choice and finally the text in the light of broader ideological concepts.
Van Ginneken 1999 offers an appendix: *Studying Global Media*, in which he provides for a 'course' in critical media analysis. It is not only suited for communication students, but would also make an excellent case study for theological students and/or churches' young and adult education programs.
[54] The central myths and values of the worldview of television, according to Fore 1987:63-68, are: the fittest survive; power and decision occur at the centre and then move out; happiness consists of limitless material acquisition, consumption and property; wealth and power are more important than people; progress is an inherent good; and -finally- there is a free flow of information. The underlying values are those of power, wealth, property, consumption, narcissism, immediate gratification of wants and creature comforts.

Martín Barbero (the concept of *mediation*) and George Gerbner (*cultivation* theory). Those concepts provide the broad outline of the process as such. We then will consider what the relationship between media technology, patterns of communication and culture means in terms of personal identity. Finally we will discuss the role of visuals in culture, shaping identity and the perception of reality.

1.2.2   Shared cultural environment and shared identity

The work of the Italian Marxist Antonio Gramsci, (1891-1937), who was killed by the fascist Mussolini regime, deeply influenced the understanding of 'culture' in cultural studies -and critical media studies based on them-. In particular his concepts of *'hegemony'* and *'social reproduction'* played an important role. Gramsci criticized the Marxist view of culture as just a residual product of economics. Culture, in his view, is an instrument of social reproduction in the struggle for hegemony in society. Between economical power and repressive power, cultural power plays a key-role by imposing cultural-ideological standards for the sake of consensus. Cultural power reproduces social-cultural bias that is represented as necessary and natural ('the general interest', 'public opinion'). It hides, and at the same time maintains, underlying power structures. This cultural power explains how non-repressive, liberal societies are able to permit free debate and oppositional subcultures and at the same time build a dominant ideological consensus.

In Latin America, Gramsci's range of thought became widespread in the 1960's and 1970's in spite of the fact that during the military dictatorships his work was forbidden.
In the 1960's a massive awakening process took place that questioned neo colonial suppressive structures[55] among the peoples of Latin America (and third world countries in general). This led to the organization of small scale popular movements: co-operations in the slums, centers for education and 'cultura popular', organizations of women, youth, farmers, indigenes, Christian 'base-communities', human rights groups etc. by which people struggled for economical, political and cultural freedom.

In the maintenance of suppressing structures, mass media were found to play an important role. Ownership, control, formats, language and mediated reality all reflected the vertical authoritarian structure of communication, from which the popular movements were not only excluded, but neither found space to express their 'cultura popular'. People, therefore, started alternative, participative grass roots media like radio popular, 'prensa comunitaria', community theatre, cassette forums like Radios Mineros in the tin mines in Bolivia, etc. One of the first experiences (1969) with cassette forums were (religious) drama-series for group use like 'Un tal Jesús', that dealt with daily reality of the people in six different nations of Latin America. The same model was later used for the development of radio popular that resulted in a network of popular educative radio channels, which were united in the Asociación Latinoamericana de Educación Radiofónica (ALER).

In my Master's thesis (1992) on the development and practice of 'comunicación popular' in Argentina as a lead for ecclesiastical communication, I summarized the main features of comunicación popular. It is a participative form of communication that departs from the social context, priorities and needs of the people, which are based on the reality of their daily life experiences. It cannot be defined in terms of functional technology, but is

---

[55] In Latin America the work of Paulo Freire, *Pedagogy of the Oppressed* and his concept of 'educación popular' played a key role in this process of 'concientización'.

a dialectical and sometimes paradox process that is embedded in the struggle against processes of dominance. It has many different expressions, but common references are: participation, openness, dialogue, plurality, solidarity and accessibility. It 'demythologizes' mass media because it questions not only their content but also the concept of communication itself. It breaks out of the scheme of sender-receiver, rejects one-way communication and is a cultural expression that respects artistic traditional production.

This praxis of social communication helped engaged media and communication scholars to release the linear instrumental models and concepts that communication was considered in. In doing so they became aware of the plurality of forms and the active role of the receiver. It led to the reconsideration of media use and of structures of communication. New models arose that departed from the perception of reality of life by the audience itself, exchange and dialogue. Communication started to be considered as a dynamic process.

Another factor contributing to this insight was the reflection on the felt increasing trans-nationalization of communication. National governments played a dubious role in this process. They disposed of comunicación popular as folklore and failed to realize -as did the majority of scientific communication scholars- the deeper dimensions of these processes. They overlooked their function as a social space of transformation, facilitating the awareness (on the basis of understanding one's own daily reality) of dominance, disinformation and socio-cultural transformation.
In the early history of comunicación popular, its function was primarily focused on educational support: a tool for education and organization, for consciousness-raising and for dialogue. Later on, the autonomous power of communication processes themselves became another primary focus. Followed by new challenges in recognizing the complex relationship between comunicación popular and mass communication.

It is against this background that one of the most influential media scholars in Latin America, Jesús Martín Barbero, in 1985 wrote his book De los medios a las mediaciones, Comunicación, cultura y hegemonia,[56] building on Gramsci. The essence of his book is that media research should not focus on the media, and their assumed hegemonic control over passive recipients, -reflecting a behaviorist effects perspective-, but on the process of mediation, i.e. media production on the one hand and daily media use by people in their family lives and context (political, social, cultural, geographical, national/global/local) on the other hand -a structuralist, cultural studies approach-.

The locus of study was the 'barrio', or the urban neighborhood, where millions of migrated people -through cooperation- tried to survive during the repressive military regimes. Through their own communities, movements and communication strategies, they also began taking a new sort of political action in the cultural realm. What social development and identity meant to them was defined within the context of their everyday life and oppression. This included what was mediated to them through the mass media. The 'telenovela', a Latin American commercially produced soap series genre, (e.g.) was very popular among the popular classes. They identified the melodrama of the telenovela with the melodrama of their own daily life, their humor and narrative memory and tradition. According to Martín Barbero, telenovelas are a point of interaction between commercial mass influences on the one hand and experiences of recognizing cultural identity and forming interpretations that resist dominant ideologies -

---

[56] In 1993 an English translation was published: From the Media to Mediations: Communication, Culture and Hegemony, by Sage (London). See also note 14 of the Introduction.

mediated by transnational media culture- on the other hand. Interactions with media thus can help people to construct their own culture[57] and the way media are appropriated is at least as important as media structures and media technologies.

To appropriate the new mass culture of television, the mediation process -as Martín Barbero points out- is supporting at three levels: the level of the family (facilitating emotional unity and linking the family to the larger cultural world); the level of the temporal rhythms (sentiments associated with seasons, sports and holidays of the year, a song, a TV-character, or synchronization with real life drama) and the level of genres (the interaction of mass commercial television and the pleasure of recognizing cultural identity and/or resistant interpretations).

George Gerbner (specifically interested in long term media impact on culture) was one of the first to combine content analysis and audience study. The main point of his *cultivation theory*[58] and his *Cultural Indicators Paradigm* is that mass media, in a long-term accumulating process, cultivate views and values in culture.
According to Gerbner, mass media, -especially television- are so common and central in people's lives that they have the power to dominate -stronger than any other source of information or personal experience- the way people perceive the world.
Not by direct stimulus-response though. In a gradual cumulating process, 'televised' reality becomes dominant and offers a selective, distorted picture of the world. In this process mass media bring along or *cultivate* views, attitudes and values in culture. These cultivated views, attitudes and values become common and are strengthened within society by consensus. They help the dominant culture to maintain -and if necessary adapt- itself. This process is referred to by Gerbner as the process of *cultivation and acculturation* in which televised reality as a perpetual motion machine deeply penetrates culture and society.

What then does this process as outlined by the three concepts mentioned above, mean in terms of 'media-culture' and personal identity?

Media technology, patterns of communication and culture mutually condition and influence each other. Technologies always develop in a historical context, which facilitates their development, adaptation and application. As they -for their part- shape the cultural environment. As once the printing press and the telegraph stamped 16th and 19th century society far beyond communication and information instrumentality, we may presume in contemporary 'information era' there is a relationship between current electronic media and ict's and contemporary 'post-modern' media culture.

Staudenmaier (1989) traces the roots of this culture to the development of Western industrial capitalism in which scientific-technological rationality became normative, not

---

[57] See also: Vink, Nico. 1990. *The telenovela and emancipation*, a study on tv and social change in Brasil. Amsterdam, Royal Tropical Institute. Vink disapproves the notion of the telenovela as a product of the television industry leading to alienation. To his opinion this is a leftist intellectual prejudice. Telenovelas ofer the popular class images which may contribute to break out of the natural and obvious. Martín Barbero, noting the same point, in this respect states that political motivations often first are expressed in e.g. comedy and satire, popular music, legends and portrayals of conflict and injustice in daily life.
In chapter two we will discuss audiences' interpretations, including the work of John Fiske on television culture.
[58] Gerbner, G. 1973. pp. 553-73. See also section 2.2.2. Gerbner was criticized for his cultivation theory as well. See e.g. de Boer en Brennecke, 2004. 1995: 159-184.

only in production modes, but in all areas of life. This fostered individualism, standardization, conformity and fragmentation of human discourse.

The private inner *self* became divided from the public exterior *persona*, the news item from its context and the producers of public messages became divided from their direct contact with the audience and vice versa.

In the village, life public identity and behavior rooted in storytelling. In the anonymity of the large cities, for the sake of standardized behavior and conformity, the function of surveillance, control and discipline, was taken over by e.g. etiquette literature. Individual self-expression was to fit into the standards of conformed behavior.

This new technological ideal and style led to a radical shift in social ordering and values in society. Standardization called for precision design and centralized authority. The railroad, the telegraph, the telephone and electric utilities became major features of the technological progress. But scientific rationality, the new social order and the technological style in all areas of life, at the same time eroded the interactive creativity of people as a source for national self-identity and political cohesion. The negotiation of different values, perspectives or engagements and participation became only possible within the boundaries of the technological system's conformity, says Staudenmaier.

The standardization ideal and the new media of communication in society connected with each other perfectly. Electric immediacy and the precision of communication networks at the speed of light (wire services) led to the standardization of a continuous flow of news in fragments, called items', divided from their context of origin and without much nuances or background as well. Due to speed, directness, immediacy and competition, interpretation, according to Staudenmaier, was lost out to sensationalism. With the arrival of radio, the audience could even instantaneously 'participate' in an event. Passively though, without much possibility to interact or actively engage in public discourse.

In Staudenmaier's opinion the electronic discourse, by its technological design leads to an extraordinary new concentration of economic and political power that favors a single message spread from a central point to reach as many as possible. In the context of industrial expansion and mass production, this message increasingly became related to the ideal of consumption. Advertising underwent a revolutionary style change and in Staudenmaier's words (1989:40) became 'the programmed self'. Whereas early 20th century advertising aimed at a rational dialogue on product qualities, in later 20th century advertising, reason was replaced by emotion as the preferred rhetorical style. To keep the mass production system going, a continuous stream of ongoing consumption was necessary. Cyclic dissatisfaction with formerly purchased products was to stimulate this turnover buying. This meant the focus on product information and the perception of a product as a tool, was no longer sufficient. Emotions became attached to products.

What a product meant in terms of personal identity[59], -e.g. social status, individualistic freedom, and sexuality- offered a whole new and nearly inexhaustible source of advertising, promoting the 'new = better' idea. Whereas in the village culture personal identity was formed by interaction with lifetime stories of the wider community, individualistic identity now became reflected, through media interaction, by personal achievement measured in terms of purchases.

Kellner (1995:336) in this respect speaks of a 'fake individuality' or 'commodity self': products communicating aspects of personalities. He considers advertisements as part of contemporary promotional culture (marketing, telecommunications, packaging, display and an environment of stores, malls and shopping) important and complex cultural texts. Texts that offer symbolic gratifications[60] to people, associated with socially desired values (happiness, eternal youth, success etc.), aimed at the adoption of values, role models and lifestyles. Identity, according to Kellner, becomes a passive matter that separates public from private life. Individuality and freedom consist of the right to choose between products and styles; not of autonomy in terms of thought, action or dissent.

According to Staudenmaier (1989), advertising and economic pressures increasingly shape and drive functioning and content of the media. Advertising is not only about the sale of products, but also about selling affective bonds between audience and products, about networks selling ratings and about ratings influencing program decisions. This leads to fragmented and 'least-common-denominator' style discourse and the decrease of challenging content being a 'high risk'.
Next to this impact on public discourse, says Staudenmaier, media -especially television- teach passivity. They also teach ambivalence about the capacity for intimacy and talk that matters, and break up the narrative context into atomized information fragments without sequence.
Since the interaction with electronic media happens on an emotional level, media style influences the affective core of our being and our development of human personality and the perception and interpretation of personal history.

---

[59] An intriguing documentary in this respect was aired in April 2004 by one of the Dutch public broadcasters: Sneakers. Director Femke Wolting tries to answer the question how the 'poor black man's shoe' grew into a globally worn article which became a major icon of identity. Originated in the popular subculture of skateboarding and hiphop, -in which young people wore shelltoes without shoelaces in imitation of black prisoners leaving prison-, Wolting shows how the sneaker, in an interaction between sub-cultural popularity and commercial exploitation by brands like Nike and Puma, using 20.000 'correspondents' worldwide to go after the newest trends in the streets, photographing how young people wear and decorate their sneakers, made it from the street to the catwalk. Videoclips ("Walk this way" by Run DMC who made a hit with 'My Adidas'), films ('Fast Times at Richmond High', Sean Penn and 'Do the right thing' by Spike Lee), tours (Vans Warped Tour) and commercials (Michael Jordan) plaid an important role in this development. 'Now I know I can reach something in life', says a young black guy asked what Sneakers mean to him.
At present the sneaker is at the centre of fashion. It became a cultural icon, aimed not to run with, but to be seen with. Expressing people's image, identity and individuality. Sneakers as 'a way of life', or in the words of a Japanese fan and obsessive collector -owning 500 pairs-: 'it is not just lifestyle anymore, it is just life'.
Femke Wolting, 'Sneakers', in Het uur van de wolf, VPRO, 23-04-04.
See also: www.submarinechannel.com/sneakers
[60] Belgian philosopher Herman de Dijn and sociologist Walter van Herck (eds. 2002) offer essays on holy places. Next to Jerusalem and Lourdes, sociologist Walter Weyns, in one of the essays also analyses shopping malls as 'holy spots'. According to Weyns, shopping malls might be the most adequate expression of contemporary culture, -like the cathedral for ages was the symbol of traditional religion- representing the religious longing for renewal of the world. The saints in this culture are the stars of publicity and advertising.

Warren (1997) shows how this interpretation increasingly passes off via images. He discerns two kinds: *iconic* or *representational* images and *metaphoric* or *perceptual* images. Iconic images are the pictures we see. They consist of (1.) Graphic representations in a single frame (our taken for granted visual horizon of billboards, magazines etc.); (2.) Graphic representations in sequential internally coherent frames, linked to form a narrative (film, television-ads, news- talk- and game shows) and (3.) Graphic representations in sequential internally incoherent, but externally coherent frames. An example of the latter are the music video clips: non-associated sequences of images that do not form a narrative, but get their coherence from outside, (e.g.) by text.

According to Warren, with the arrival of television, a huge cultural shift took place. People now had unlimited access from within the home to graphic representations and filmed and televised narratives that shaped the world of signification. Increasingly the boundaries between the representations in coherent frames and those in incoherent frames blur. By the interruption (e.g.) of television advertisements, with different emotional keys, people become conditioned to accept incoherence, which might in the long run affect the way human consciousness functions. The constant sequence of unrelated image-'flashes' might for example complicate the historical or antecedent perception of issues.

But the crucial thing to understand about iconic images, according to Warren, is their (latent) power to trigger a way of imagining ourselves and move us to imitations. This is nothing new as such. Religious medieval imagery (e.g.) invited imitation of the icon as well. In electronic narratives, however, we are not only invited to mimesis of another kind of 'saints'[61]: synthetic celebrities, famed for their 'image'; moving images also exert greater mimetic power and patterns of images can 'code' our way of seeing. Pornographic images (e.g.) not just 'present reality', but also can construct a world of meaning in which rape, sexual abuse or prostitution is sexualized, authorized and legitimized. Depictions then are culturally significant.

Most of the media images, especially because of their overload and the fact that they are so much part of our daily life and thus become 'lived', are taken for granted and remain unexamined. Visuals, however, are not only about physical aspects; they also involve moral and spiritual aspects. According to Warren the constant bombardment of images for commercial and entertainment reasons makes modern people think of themselves as 'disengaged voyeurs'. This might lead to 'cultural pollution' that despoils human processes of understanding, signifying, and valuing.

The problem stated by Warren, transcends the issue of content. Images -as products- function in different kinds of contexts: the immediate context (sales); the intermediate context (the nature of the visual, to please, inform or portray) and the distant context (the culture of origin, setting the possibilities of expression). A similar division can be

---

[61] In the Netherlands, the annual 'month -and night- of the Philosophy' in 2004, was dedicated to the topic of idols. Connie Palmen, Dutch writer and philosopher, wrote the accompanying essay: lets wat niet bloeden kan' in which she analyses the motives of fans, stalkers and killers of famous people like Kennedy, Versace and Lennon, by connecting writer and killer, fiction and reality, real and unreal.
In a column on the very popular television program *Idols*, Daan Roovers, general editor of *Filosofie Magazine*, states that with the rise of mass media, the meaning of the idol, stemming from the Greek 'eidolon', was turned upside down. The idol no longer is a humanised god, but an idolized human. According to Roovers the immense and worldwide popularity of 'Idols' is to be explained by the paradox of a public seeking a role model to identify with, which at the same time can be admired infinitely. Daan Roovers. *Idolen*, in Trouw, 01-04-04, p. 14.

made with regard to our context of seeing. The immediate context has to do with our purpose for watching (e.g. to relax); the intermediate context concerns our physical environment (do we watch at home alone, or in a noisy bar); the distant context stems from our personal life structure.

The way visuals affect us, then, is a complex matter. Visuals differ from written or spoken discourse because of their indirectness. They literally 'mean' in a different way. They do not assert, but present versions. And the context in which they are arranged frames their understanding indirectly at the level of connotations or metaphors.

Television, according to Warren, plays a major role in providing the 'matrix of thought' in society: implicit structures and patterns of perception and conceptualization. The images through which we see affect the iconic images we actually see. These *metaphoric images* concern the function of imagination. They help us understand and name reality by way of analogies and metaphors. Images entail pre-conscious chains of associations and expectations that are tied to feelings. They act like a type of lenses, which arrange and evaluate the significance of what we see or experience. Underlying these lens images, comprehensive metaphors act that provide and organize coherence in our matrix of thought (for example the winner-looser, good-bad, North-South metaphor). Though not conceptualized, they shape our perception and interpretation of reality. Iconic images receive coherent power from the context in a wider metaphoric image system.

What is new in the 'time of the sign', according to Warren, is the proliferation of iconic images. In the image culture, we are immersed in metaphors by which we (in a process of negotiation) explain ourselves and view reality. He, therefore, urges for a special skill of cultural awareness and agency with regard to visuals, narrative images and metaphors by examining the conditions that shape the context of television production and consumption[62]. He also urges for the evaluation of its narrative basics beyond style, pace and performance.

These narrative iconic basics of our -visual- media culture increasingly involve religious dimensions, which we will examine in the next section.

1.2.3   Summarizing remarks

Media and mediated communication have become an intrinsic part of social cultural life, in which they play a central and organizing role. They fulfill a central constituting function in culture and public space. They not only define social reality, they also express shared identity and provide our shared cultural environment. People renegotiate the views and perceptions of the world and the images of self offered by the media in their daily lives, for which media organize routine and ritual.

---

[62] Negus 1995, discussing popular music as one of the most important components of mass communications also urges to look at either side of production and consumption. His concept of *articulation* shows how performers, texts, audiences, industry and their symbols articulate with one another. '(…) focusing on processes of articulation and the mediations that link production and consumption can help us to raise critical questions about popular music. Meanings are not simply imposed by production or appropriated in the act of consumption. Meanings are created, constraints are imposed, and possibilities are continually opened up through the processes that connect artists, industry, audiences, and texts' (Negus, 1995: 390).

World news and news values are constructed according to specific (Western) selection, interpretation and representation. 'Framing' plays an important role in this process. Underlying criteria are not explicit and taken for granted. Especially in times of conflict or crises this may lead to the uncritical recycling of biased and/or stereotyped interpretations. Objectivity is an economic notion rather than one of neutrality. Television news -for many the most credited informant- is important in the maintenance of cultural consensus, cultural identity and dominant value systems. Together with drama, entertainment, documentaries, fictional movies etc. television, in its totality, mediates a common outlook on and experience of reality.

In defining social reality media impact the cultural environment. The concepts of hegemony and social reproduction, mediation and cultivation and acculturation explain this process.
What this means in terms of personal identity is discussed by exploring the mutual impact of media technology, patterns of communication and contemporary media culture. Role models and life style are important features in this respect. In a media environment, which is under increasingly commercial pressure, this not only impacts public discourse, but also the perception of human personality.
Images play a central role in this interpretation. Their impact goes beyond content as such. They are understood indirectly, involving levels of connotations and metaphors. Iconic images trigger imagination and imitation. In media culture patterns of images may code our way of seeing and our perception of reality, whereas visuals may shape identity.

1.3   The religious dimensions of media culture

'In earlier days, God rested after six days of work, nowadays God dances at the seventh day. And why not? Religion can be fun', says Winfried Gebhardt, sociologist at the University of Koblenz, researching *scenes*[63].
One doesn't become a 'member' of scenes, they are not alike parties or churches (in scenes any kind of member administration is considered altogether wrong anyway). Scenes are to be experienced and enjoyed with a congenial group, and with all your senses during large well organized aesthetic events that vary from dance events to the Pope's pray-in (Madrid, April 2003), from Taize-gatherings to Gothics- or techno parties. According to Gebhardt, there is a lot of religiosity going on in scenes. It only looks quite different from organized religious belief and its contours are much less visible. In scenes, people search their own (continuously shifting) way of dealing with ultimate questions and being, which is based on their own experiences. They experience unity and wholeness based on unwritten and temporary -non-institutional- rules. Their diffuse spirituality is not build on intellectualism, institutionalized religion, and university-theology. It is about their own religious competence to find one's way to God. And although scenes might be questioned on e.g. media technique enhancing modern ecstasy, the moneymaking aspects of mega-dance-parties, or on the temporality of unity, Gebhardt rejects the opinion that scenes are superficial. In his opinion, these 'part-time-communities' offer a 'counter-world of ecstatic border-land experiences'.

A similar observation is made by Jesús Martín Barbero (1997) while studying new popular urban religious culture from a Latin-American perspective, in which

---

[63] Gebhardt was one of the speakers during the conference: 'Longing for enchantment', about the religious aspect of youth-cultures at Berlin's Evangelische Akademie, February 2003. Source: Van Loenen, Gerbert, 'Geloven voor even, en dan weer verder' in *Trouw*, February 6, 2003.

secularization -not as atheism but as liberation and autonomy from the church- and popular religiosity as a source of resistance to modernity play an important role. He describes youth as 'nomadic tribes' that rapidly move from one temporal cultural identity to another. The global cultures of media (especially popular music) play an important role in discovering and experimenting with new identities. 'The patch of soil, the native village, the consecrated church and temple have ceased to have power of enchantment. Instead, the mass media create symbols of the sacred; and the youthful nomadic tribes, identifying with these totems, have learned how to make holy and enchanted any place they decide to inhabit' (1997:116)[64].

Media, says Martín Barbero, are not to be considered just in terms of economics, commerce, politics, ideological manipulation or technology. Media are a 'site of resacralization of contemporary cultures'. They are the locus where cultural identities are created, communities are configured, and social actors are constituted.
Media offer a possibility to people to 'meet' and deal with the central questions of life. A place where people increasingly construct their meaning of life. Media thus offer ritual and communitarian celebration[65]. They articulate the integrating myths of society and provide possibilities of identification.

Television drama, according to Martín Barbero, is especially important because it is a basic form of ritual. The telenovela is so popular in Latin Amercia because it offers people an opportunity to ritualize fears, joys and burdens of daily life. To experience moments of re-enchantment amidst the instrumental rationality of modernity, which 'banned' (so to speak) the magic and the mystery and -according to the earliest secularization theories- was to mark the 'end' of religion. Instead, says Martín Barbero 'Religion has shown itself capable of eating modernity alive and making modernity an important ingredient for its own purposes. What we are witnessing, then, is not the conflict of religion and modernity, but the transformation of modernity into enchantment by linking new communication technologies to the logic of popular religiosity' (1997:112).
The significance of the electronic church, (including its success in Latin America), is far beyond the use of a new medium to reach many, according to Martín Barbero. The electronic church transformed media into a new mediation of the religious experience with ritual and celebration as the focal points. In tune, not only with the popular sectors and the new tribal cults, but also with the re-enchantment of the world as a basic human need.

Media -with their melodrama, the star system, the idols, gigantic contests, spectacle etc.- are mysterious, magic, and exciting to many people. 'Somehow' says Martín Barbero (1997:111) 'they have eliminated the distance between the sacred and the profane[66].

[64] In this respect the global craze of 'flash mobs' among the internet-audience is an intriguing phenomenon: through internet a time and place to meet is agreed upon; people en mass pop up, e.g. in a park, a shop, a hotel or whatever, do something together for a few minutes like applauding, imitating bird sounds etc. and disappear again. On the weblog Cheesebikini www.Cheesebikini.com, one can find information about flash mobs around the world, including self recorded movies of mobsters. Source: *Trouw*, August 1, 2003.
[65] Knut Lundby 1997 in this respect has researched the televised opening ceremony of the Olympic winter games in Lillehammer 1994. He concludes that media, playing with symbols and images, are crucial in establishing, maintaining and changing collective representations, amongst which are common myths, beliefs etc. In contemporary society, based on individual reflexivity, media, religion and culture, says Lundby, are linked through an interrelated web of collective representations.
[66] The increasing use of explicit -and implicit- religious terms and images in television commercials are revealing texts in this respect. Ola (Unilever) promoted seven new ice creams with the names of the seven sins from Roman Catholic belief; a Belgian beer company advertised its beer related to

(…) Television, especially, has introduced magic into the realm of the profane and has made secular what once was sacred'.
White (1997), conceptualizing religion and media in the construction of cultures, argues that the sacred and the secular -as well as other modernist oppositions such as imagination/rationality, subjective/objective, individual/society- are better understood as dualities. Autonomously but interdependently, they operate within a multiplicity of categories of meaning that continually facilitate, evoke and affirm each other mutually.

In 19th century modernist conceptions of both public religious discourse and media were reduced to a function of social integration for industrial progress in the new nation-state. With the postmodernist movements of the 1960s and 70s, the worldview of instrumental rationality -and accompanying steady secularization- became questioned. The focus shifted to the many subcultures based on ethnicity, race, language, gender religion etc. as actors creating cultural meaning in the forum of the media. As well as to audiences defining their identities and values in interaction with this global and pluralistic context.

The religious and the mass media, according to White (1997), touch common ground as reflexive discourses on culture. He conceptualizes culture in terms of a mutual interaction of prefiguring and configuring areas in which core symbols and symbolism of meaning play a crucial role. In communicative processes, symbols -both sacred and secular- are created and recreated, articulating meaning for one moment that is challenged and changed the following moment in order to be revitalized. Thus, in the dialectic of paradox, a ritual process of constant cultural renewal takes place in which the sacred and the secular mutually address each other. Together, religious and media studies can identify this process of renewal and the resacralization of the cultural environment.

Cultural revitalization and the confrontation between sacred and secular can take place at different levels (existential, cultural, the level of denomination and the level of individual movements) with different discursive symbols. Think (e.g.) of societal secularization on the one hand and religious revitalization at the other. Only if all levels have an intense sacred-secular dialogue at the same time, this might imply profound changes in religious or cultural paradigms, says White (1997).

White does not identify the sacred with explicitly religious institutions and the secular with non-religious ones. Both are aspects of all institutions; the revitalization of the Church by the Second Vatican Council (e.g.) was toward a more open and secularized definition. 'The central question is not whether our societies are becoming more or less sacred or secular, much less whether church activity is growing or diminishing, but rather

'the eleventh commandment: thou salt enjoy'. And a cheese spread was advertised by male angels on motorbikes.
In 1993 the slogan 'gsus are coming' was used by gsus industries (global company based in Amsterdam) to introduce their new gsus clothing collection. In their website it says: 'Gsus: what's in a name? A lot, the name gsus was a big help in the success of the brand. The letter 'G' became hyped up in the early nineties. Gangsta rap was rulin', G Love came out with his first record. Gsus symbolizes global individuality. An always positive view on fashion soaked with humour. There's a lot of affection with the skate- and snowboard-scene, where a slick stock of words is common. Some examples of typical Gsus expressions: 'Welcome to heavens playground', 'gsus ramp lords' and 'gsubelle'. More than a religious interpretation, the company wants to give it more a rebellious, controversial touch'. Advertisements involved 'closer to gsus', 'gsus the way' and 'gsus saves'. Or: 'Become a disciple, be the first to receive the latest news from our heavenly playground and other neat stuff…', 'every 13th new gsus disciple wins a F.C Yeti fanclub scarf … www.g-sus.com ", retrieved September 5, 2003 and October 21, 2006.

how the discourses of sacred and secular are addressing each other at this moment'
(White 1997:51).
The meaning of the sacred and the secular is that they call each other into dialogue and
reform. Revitalization generates new symbols of both and new interactions and
discourses of dialogue, as White (1997) shows in his analysis of revitalization
movements. They each involve different levels: the countercultural movements of the
1960's-1970's marking a new religious consciousness (existential level); the civil religion
of the populist nation state (1830-1970) (cultural level); the sectarian revitalization of
Evangelical fundamentalism (denominational level) and the postmodern cults of symbolic
liminality (level of individual and small group). In the latter, the conscious creation and
use of an artificial symbolic liminal state to 'inhabit' and to quickly move from again as
soon as it becomes rational, has become a site of the sacred, which is always 'beyond'.

White (1997:47/48) discerns three areas in which media (especially genres of mass
popular communication) are 'the site for the dialogue between the sacred and the
secular': (1.) the search for ultimate meaning (the integration of the unexplainable into
commonsense cultural consensus); (2.) the search for perfect community; and (3.) the
search for authentic personal identity. The public's involvement in this dialogue includes
several moments which White summarizes in five central points: (1.) context (the 'time
out' or festive dimension of leisure where one can explore one's identity beyond daily
routines); (2.) the articulation of a sense of the sacred in dramatic symbols (by stars,
artists and media professionals); (3.) the creation of a text (a formulaic genre, to facilitate
return and interpretation of the communicative moment); (4.) the negotiation and
recreation of the text (from one's personal and cultural identity) and (5.) the struggle
over the symbolism of media texts (cf. fandom or sub-cultural identity).

Media, in White's opinion, then, are of key importance as public cultural rituals and a
process of cultural negotiation. A ritual space, where sacred symbols are dramatized by
various actors.
'Increasingly, we are overcoming the high-culture/low-culture dichotomy and are willing
to see the "popular" as the common language of all. The media invite all cultural fronts
to be present in a time-out context when our dogmatic, purist identities are most
permeable and we are in festive mood, ready to discover something of our common
sacred archetypes in the sacred symbols of all. The media experience is a moment more
open to the immense variety of sacred symbols being generated, and audiences are less
ready to dichotomize the sacred and the secular. Thus, both media studies and religious
studies are coming together to create a new understanding of the media as cultural
negotiation' (White1997: 62).
Goethals (1989) in this respect speaks of the church and the mass media as 'competing
architects of our dominant symbols, rituals and myths'. Visual arts, she says, have always
been part of ritual and symbolic worlds that were aimed at legitimizing and maintaining
beliefs, values and worldviews. In today's pluralistic culture, there is no unified
framework of interpreting and ordering anymore. This does not imply, though, that
symbolic structuring of experience and visualization of faith are absent. According to
Goethals, the imaging of shared worlds has moved to contemporary visual arts of
popular culture, especially television. Mass media now construct public symbols of
authority -political, informational and mythic- and values, and fulfill ritual functions
analogous to religious rituals.

Elements of this religious ritual, as identified by Goethals in her essay, *Myth and ritual in
Cyberspace* include: entry into special zones of time and space; attentive, dynamic
engagement and participation; the formation of community and a renewal of spirit
(Goethals: 2003:257-269).

Examples of the electronic transformations of ritual space and time are televised large popular (sports) events or (inter)national grief and mourning such as after the death of Princess Diana, Band Aid concerts (Bob Geldof) or the memorial services to the victims of the 11-03-2004 Madrid train bombings or the Tsunami. But they are not restricted to television alone. Participation on web sites also offers ritualistic experience and holds 'ritual-like' components that are based on shared symbols for formation and maintaining community. Goethals, in this respect, speaks of 'cyber myth' and 'cyber ritual'. Discussing several websites[67], she finds gathering places of recasting and recreation of ancient myths and mysteries for people to identify with as well as a ritual space for Word centered sacramental or contemplative religious communication.

Goethals' definition of myth and ritual regards ritual as the embodied enactment of myth and engagement with a transcendent order of being. She finds analytical advantages in adopting a broad functionalist view on religion as a critical tool. Her central aim is to understand the symbolic forms on the Web and in popular media and to identify the latent role of religion in cultural symbols.

According to Goethals, mass media in their symbolic and ritual role have taken over the latent role of religion of legitimatizing and integrating, just as the high arts used to compete with religion's saving dimension. 'From commercials, as well as from entertainment shows, come popular mythologies and dogmas that represent social norms and expectations. These programs combine with TV's political and informational images to form a comprehensive and complex environment of symbols' (Goethals 1989:65). This challenges the religious and aesthetic imagination, as 'under this giant canopy of images all denominations and religious traditions are exposed to the same framing of reality' (Goethals: 1989:58).

Hoover (1997, 1998, 2001, 2002), involved in US research on religion and meaning making in the media age[68], signals a 'parallel evolution of 'postmodern' religious and media cultures' which resulted in an 'unprecedented convergence of religion and media as they meet in the cultural marketplace' (2001:10). The point of convergence is: meaning and identity in contemporary culture. Increasingly, individual religious 'seeker-culture', active meaning making by media-audiences and a diverse media-marketplace providing religious and spiritual material, products and services, come together. In this 'commodified popular culture', people seek and find meaning in a self-consciousness and autonomous way for which media provide the resources in the form of symbols and artifacts.

'Looking at the cultural landscape from the standpoint of everyday life, we are bound to see that media and religion are not as separate as once thought. More and more commodified, mediated, religious material is circulating. Autonomous, religiously questing individuals increasingly turn to those sources for material meaningful to their construction of self. Further, what they are constructing is what I call 'plausible narratives of the self'. These are self-descriptions that 'make sense' in profound and important ways; that embed people in social life and at the same time describe their social and cultural aspirations, providing grounding in space, time, experience, and history. Media practices, symbols, and artifacts become touchstones, decorations and illustrations for

---

[67] The Millennium Matters www.mm2000.nu/intro/html ; Star Wars www.starwars.com ; The New Media Bible www.newmediabible.org ; Christworld: www.christworld.com and The Monastery of Christ in the Desert www.christdesert.org/pax.html .

[68] The Resource Center for Media, Religion and Culture at the School of Journalism and Mass Communication University of Colorado, Boulder, USA directs several 'New Media at Home Projects', on the intersection of religious and media-related practices in the everyday lives of contemporary adults and their families: Symbolism, Media and the Lifecourse Project; Symbolism, Meaning and the New Media @ Home Project; Teens and the New Media @ Home Project; Teens and the Supernatural. http://www.colorado.edu/journalism/mcm/research.htm.

these narratives. They provide many of the symbols, metaphors, and terms of reference out of which these meaningful accounts of the self are constructed. They must be assumed, therefore, to be at least potentially involved in projects and quests that are profoundly religious' (Hoover 2001:12).

Instead of separating a 'secular' media realm from a 'sacred' religious realm, Hoover urges conceptualizing religion as religious practice (experience, participation) that inhabits the 'religious-symbolic marketplace'. Objects, the visual, rituals, experience and body play an important role in this practice. Modes of expression, which are, says Hoover, repressed in institutional Christianity in the West, but amply present within media. The realm we used to think of as religion (practices, symbols, meaning) comes into play in these constructions. Religion of the future, according to Hoover, no longer finds its symbols and values in tradition, history, doctrine or institution, but is a 'religion a la carte' or 'cafeteria Catholicism' (1997:4). This transitional religion gradually will dominate and change traditional religious practice by shifting its centre from tradition to the symbolic marketplace, from private to public, from belonging to doing. People turn to this new context of symbols offered by media not just to find information or seek, but to experience religious identity and piety or shared patterns of life, (e.g.) in new created rituals or elements of culture (iconic leaders, images of leadership, distinctive language, decorations, sounds), and the use of paraphernalia. It is a praxis of popular, material and commodity-based religiosity that is centered on the symbolic resources of the public sphere.
An important effect of these developments, as identified by Hoover (1998), is the 'flattening of symbols'. Religious symbols become submerged in the universe of symbols of the media sphere and no longer hierarchically relate to other cultural symbols. Instead they are forced to compete and sometimes are simply appropriated by (e.g.) commerce; which questions their authenticity.

In this respect, it is important to question which narratives, symbols, icons and stories are established in the media and which ones are absent or simply 'left out'.

1.4   Implications for mainline religion

For a long time telling stories, experiencing the mystical and mythical, taking part in rituals, practicing faith, ethics, perceiving reality, and developing identity and community has been the private realm of religion.
Moreover, mainline religion -especially in the cultures in which writing and print were the dominant media of communication- was at the center of the mediation process constructing cultural and religious reality, strongly connected with the hegemonic structures, institutions and modes of mediated communication.

The invention and development of electrical/electronic media, however, meant a radical shift in the social structures of mediated communication, and turned the tide. A turning, which is only partly understood if restricted only to technology as a new communication tool, or a business.

Horsfield (1997, 2002) points out the significant role of media changes and changes in the patterns of social communication on cultural transformation in terms of 'communication-cultural-convergence'. Any culture, according to Horsfield, in the way it is organized, interacts and thinks, is conditioned by its dominant media of communication, whether they are oral, written, printed, or electronic. When the dominant media and patterns of communication change, the web which mediates the culture to itself is changed, which effects correlated changes in a culture's self-perception, organization, meaning and value system[69].

Moreover, every medium has its own characteristics, which are part of the meanings communicated (McLuhan). These involve the different use of memory and different physical senses, the preferences of kinds of information over others, the requirement of skills and resources (establishing status and power), patterns of social relationship, and the fill and meaning of space and time.

The current cultural ferment, says Horsfield (1997:168/169), is to be understood within 'a major paradigm shift from largely nation-based cultures in which print was the dominant medium, to world-linked cultures in which electronic-based means of communication have become dominant'. The crisis of modernity and the search for re-enchantment, which was the result of it, created a convergence in which the symbolic marketplace of the electronic media became the dominant spot of this re-enchantment process in terms of information, ritual, experience and praxis.

Television, according to Fore (1997), plays a key role in this process due to its capacity of combining formerly separated attractive features of other electronic media such as immediacy, reach into the home environment, its capacity to picture events, its ability to tell stories at any time and anywhere, its flexibility, its magic and excitement, its capacity to build our dreams, fantasies and myths and influence the way we perceive reality and human identity.

Horsfield (1997) claims media are ideally suited and even more effective and influential in ritualistic practice and meaning construction than any other institution -including religious ones- because of their easy accessibility, their location within leisure time, their life-relatedness, their strong mythic construct and dramatic form, their constancy and rhythm (habit and order) and their attractiveness and entertainment appeal.

Media, then, seem to have grasped much of the role of religion since they are a major source of religious information, universal myth and ethics, a centre of religious ritual, and a site of religious experience and practical re-enchantment for people, as discussed in the former section.

Identifying and summarizing, in this section, some of the major implications of the electronic media context and culture as described in sections 1.1 - 1.3 for mainline institutional religion, an immediate overarching conclusion which surfaces, regards the profoundness of what is happening. In a number of ways, mainstream institutional religion and the postmodern electronic media culture don't seem to 'match'. The implications are more profound than one might realize at first thought and go beyond the level of a 'communication problem'. They involve a broad spectrum of issues which call for serious and critical reflection, such as: '*locus standi*' and power, authority, ideology and truth, spirituality, ritual and religious experience and expression, worship, identity, participation and community, institutional organization, ecumenism, ministry, core activities and theology, education, moral and ethics and last but not least: religious communication.

One of the disenchantments with modernity, as identified by Horsfield (1997a), next to the loss of faith in progress, the failure of consumerism and an intensified sense of social meaninglessness, is a growing suspicion about modern institutions, whether political, corporate or religious. Mainstream churches, as one of the traditional western sources of

---

[69] In this respect I find Rosengren's (2000:54-58) 'Image of the great wheel of culture in society' very helpful.

religion, are very deeply embedded in modernity's structures and Enlightenment culture whether it concerns their organization (central bureaucratic, authoritative), their ideas, practice and spirituality (controlling, intellectual, abstract, universal, objective, routine, disenchanting) or their media and communication models (print, books, linear instrumentality).

In the re-energizing of religious interest that is happening now in the realm of the media, allowing for a pluralist variety of possibilities and alternatives -with respect to content as well as experiences and senses- churches no longer hold social or political privileges. Their institutions are distrusted and have declined in authority. Instead, they have to cope with a new, totally different cultural situation in which the institutional appears to be more of a handicap than a benefit. Increasingly, people find meaning, act and express themselves individually within a loosely connected network society. They do so through the use of and interaction with electronic media. Churches, are not at the center of the cultural mediation-process anymore. Media are. Not just as communication tools, but also as, in Horsfield's (1997:169) words, 'the central hermeneutic dimension of culture' to which all other social institutions have to adapt themselves. Rather than possessing the power to communicate their reality into the media, says Horsfield, they are placed and even constructed by the media on the web of culture. There, religiosity is re-mediated within a symbolic material marketplace. Think (e.g.) of pastoral functions and services formerly attached to religious institutions that are now commercialized into the secular therapy industry. This re-mediation of religiosity impels churches not only to compete -even over their 'own' symbols, functions, services and heritance-, but moreover, media, as the central hermeneutic dimension of culture, function as a matrix for values and meaning and as a lens or framework through which we see and experience any other social collective.

The electronic media culture affects (e.g.) our understanding of truth and reality, the past, ethics and moral, identity and community. Building on Ong's concept of electronic media culture as 'secondary orality', Horsfield notes a shift from the understanding of truth as an externalized, abstract, historically objective -and eternal- logic, as experienced in print culture, towards an internal, participatory and consequential notion (which are features of an oral culture). Abstract, universal and objective faith frameworks, totalizing interpretations, absolute claims or central ideologies -usual in mainline religion-, thus become pressurized. Moreover, the concept of 'virtual reality' -and digitized convergence- questions any notion of reality anyhow.

A similar shift happens in the notion of identity and community., Mediation offers the locus for both in contemporary culture. If we think back of the fluid, fugitive, non-geographical 'nomadic tribes' formed by adolescents in popular media culture as identified by Jesús Martín Barbero, or the popularity of 'chatting' sites on the internet -in which we can be any-one at any time- the notion of church communities, grounded in personal loyalty, long term devotion and commitment, seems not to correspond anymore.

Another aspect concerns the method and style of communicating. Electronic media culture involves all our senses. It is stimulating, attractive, exciting, participatory and engaging. If we take this style as a hermeneutical lens focusing back on the communication culture of the churches, which is very much word, text, book and print based (especially in the mainline protestant environment), it questions the churches' way of action.

These are only three examples, but picture all the shifts as identified by Hoover[70] in contemporary radical pluralistic postmodern media culture; from the hegemony of print to electronic media, from cognitive to affective multi-sensory piety, from the civic public level (authority) to the individual level (autonomy), from belonging to doing religion (praxis) and from the cosmopolitan (ecumenical) level to the local particular (globally related) level. To which might be added that in this culture, in which the boundaries between the secular and the sacred have faded, ritual has been reshaped and the spiritual has been commodified, media and mediation are *the* central hermeneutic. Then one may conclude what we experience is a matter of a major cultural paradigm shift and a media context which challenges mainstream religion in unprecedented ways.

The crisis it finds itself in is not a just a crisis of secularization or institution. In essence, it is about meaning -and control-. And about the relevance and visibility of religious meaning and faith in the public sphere.

This compels mainline religious institutions to profound, accurate, critical and proper analysis of the media context and media culture.
There are urgent issues at stake concerning the concentration and commercialization of our media environment at the cost of being a community good; the erosion of the public realm and public discourse; the visualization of the world by television and computer mediated communication in individual terms, blurring social or historical backdrops; issues of media-cultural ecology and pollution; the role of technology in reshaping the mediation process and the cultural web; the impact of media to construct and segment audiences.
There is a range of other media ethical issues to consider, regarding access, human communication rights, privacy[71], cyber decency, media logic, neutrality etc.
There are also critical questions to be asked with respect to the commodification of nearly everything in the world -and even beyond- including spirituality, and the role of advertising and commercials as the most prominent icons of our culture promising salvation by a product.
As there are questions that have to be raised with respect to the alignment of mainline religion with the dominant media of a culture. Or mainline religion's entering - deliberately and voluntarily or otherwise- of the 'media sphere'.

But a profound, accurate, critical and proper analysis cannot be restricted any longer to the vision of a media sphere apart from a religious sphere. This implies that the views that the mainline religious institutions hold themselves with respect to media, culture, religion/faith, church, communication and the role of believers/the audience cannot be kept out of range. Neither can their own communication praxis, their media- and other ministries, nor their theological reflection. In sum, this analysis necessarily involves the whole being and essence of mainline religion and its institutions.

From this chapter on media context and media culture we may already deduce five main issues for this challenging and provocative reflection:

---

[70] Building on Marty, M.E., & Appleby, S. 1992. *The glory and the power: The fundamentalist challenge to the modern world*. Boston, Beacon.
[71] In 2004 the European Bureau for data-protection was founded in Brussels. The average Dutchman, without realizing it, is met with in 700 files, varying from company files, tax files, medical files, financial files, assurance files, internet provider files, telephone company files etc. These data are attractive to a variety of institutes as insuring companies, advertisers and employmentbureaus. Source: Malika el Ayadi 'Privacy van de Europeaan beschermen' in *Trouw*, 25-03-2004, p. 5.

-    Is it possible to hold a linear instrumental transportation view of media and
     communication or is it necessary to abandon this vision and replace it by a
     cultural notion?
-    Is it adequate to hold a dualistic vision between secular and sacred, religion and
     culture, high legitimate culture and popular/material culture, mainstream and
     marginal praxis, private and public, direct and mediated experience; and is it
     advisable to hold a separate category of 'religious media'?
-    Is it feasible to hold the understanding of church as an (authoritative)
     institution in which faith and faith praxis is grounded?
-    Is it adequate to see communication in terms of sending and preferred readings
     or is it necessary to look in the opposite direction: relate -popular- contextual
     faith praxis to mainline religion, and abandon 'print culture'?
-    Is it possible to hold a view of the believers/the audience as rather passive and
     (separate) 'receiving' collectivities?

In chapter three we will turn to views of the mainline religious institutions as expressed
in their policy statements. The issues we listed in this chapter on media context and
media culture will be our point of departure, including issues on the role of the audience
listed from recent paradigm shifts in communication and media studies, which we will
address in the next chapter.

1.5   Conclusion

Returning to the opening quote of this chapter, about the fundamental role of media in
society yet taken as massively given, at the end of this chapter we may conclude it is only
too true. Media and mediated communication may be the most essential features of this
era, since they are important bearers of cultural expression and yet are, comparatively,
reflected upon surprisingly little.
In mainline religion the absence of serious theological reflection on media -and the
practical consequences of it- astonishes all the more, since it is affected to the very
kernel by current cultural transitions in which the media are a key factor. The crisis is
deep and cannot, in our opinion, be tackled without highlighting the media issue in the
analysis of culture.

In this chapter we have identified the context of the media in terms of its structures,
players, developments and trends.
We discussed digitization and convergence in the technological realm, interrelated with
concentration, globalization and commercialization in the economical realm and
deregulation, liberalization and privatization in the political realm.

We also pictured the so-called 'new media', the myths of the 'information revolution',
and identified the patterns of communication including the concept of interactivity.

We discussed the social-cultural role of media, the way they act in defining our social
reality, expressing our shared identity and providing our shared cultural environment.

Finally we paid attention to the religious dimensions of media culture and listed the
implications and challenges for mainline religion and its institutions and the main issues
for -theological- reflection.

Mainline religion now has to act in a totally new cultural situation and context, defined
by the electronic media. Mainstream Christian institutions, one of the main definers and

storytellers in Western European history, have mislaid their position to the media. Media not only have taken over the function of ritual and sacred symbolism, shaped by the process of mediation, but also define social and personal ethical issues, in a discourse churches cannot control. In fact, they are hardly even part of it. Mainline religion now has to compete over its own 'core business', with media determining its position in the web of culture, seemingly fulfilling its role in a much more appealing way.

This puts an unprecedented challenge to mainline religion, affecting not only its relevance and public presence and representation, but every part of its being.

Two

The Perception of Audiences:
Recent Changes in Communication Theory

There is no doubt that the audience concept is in many ways outdated and its traditional role in communication theory, models and research has been called into question. We can (and largely do) go on behaving as if the audience still exists "out there" somewhere, but we may be largely deceiving ourselves.[1]

Denis McQuail

Despite its jazzy name the 'church of fools', the 'world's first 3D online church', is a serious online religious project[2]. It is an extension of 'Ship of fools', the magazine of Christian unrest'. It is about so to speak 'non denominational' Christianity (and sponsored by the Methodist church in the UK).
The 'First Church of Cyberspace', nowadays 'GodWeb', is a sophisticated online religious congregation[3]. It was set up in 1994, by Presbyterian minister Charles Henderson, as the first congregation to be organized entirely on the internet. It aims at 'spiritual surfers', and is not restricted to Christianity. The large world religious are present as well.

Henderson thinks the Internet will have an impact on religion that is equal to, or greater than, Gutenberg's invention of the printing press. He points out that the printing press removed the Bible out of the control of the church hierarchy by allowing individual worshipers direct access to the text. It effectively ended the 'monopoly' that church officials had over the truth, and led to the splintering of religious organizations into denominations.

"Now we are seeing a collapse of the denominational structures", he says. "Religion is becoming much more highly individualized. It is a sort of a 'supermarket' approach where people come in with their own shopping carts and pick a bit of this and a bit of that. They basically reconstruct on an ad hoc basis their own personal faith'.[4]
In common language both the 'spiritual surfer' and the 'individualized religious supermarket shopper,' as well as the 'men of Athens' Paul addressed himself to at the *Areopagus*, all belong to 'the audience'. Also included are the people attending a concert, or people watching opening ceremonies of large events on television. As well as contemporary viewers of a serial soap; the reader of a glossy woman's magazine; or the young man watching his favorite music program on MTV, downloading the latest hit record from internet, and producing his own remix of music styles, participate in the dynamic. They are all part of 'the audience out there'.
Looking at this brief summary, it is obvious that the concept of audience is quite an ambiguous one. Is it, for instance, to be defined by lively presence? Does the 'spiritual

---

[1] Denis McQuail. 1997.
[2] See: www.churchoffools.com
[3] See: www.godweb.org
[4] Reported by William Dowell at the Website of *Time*, www.time.com/godcom, retrieved 24/02/2002. See also: Joshua Cooper Ramo. 1996. 'Finding God on the Web' in *Time*, December 16, 1996, pp. 44-51.

surfer' belong to an audience, if it is only a virtual one? What about the person present in a room where a television set is turned on, who is reading a book? Does he/she belong to the statistics of the audience ratings just by being present when the set is switched on? Or is he/she part of the book medium audience because that is his/her focus of attention? Are the people watching a videotape of an opening ceremony, two weeks after the event, still part of the audience? To which audience does the young man who expresses his personal lifestyle by downloading and remixing the latest hit, belong? And what about the girl that 'hangs out' in a virtual gathering place and participates in a MUD: a multi user domain/dungeon/dimension[5]. To which audience do they belong, if any at all?

Audience, then, is an ambiguous concept used in an unambiguous way. This is true not only in common language, but also in social institutions, whether it is political parties, civil authorities, public service and commercial broadcasters, or churches. 'The audience' is referred to as voters, citizens, the public, rated figures of people attending a television program, viewer ship, consumers, clients, special interest segments, the market, a loosely aggregated mass, (passive or active), or, as written in one of the church policy statements on communication: 'people at the receiving end' or 'recipients'[6].

In communication theory, the concept of audience and its role in the communication process became subject of increased attention, causing paradigm shifts. In this chapter, we will briefly look at the historical shifts of communication theory, which will lead us to the audience research tradition and the recently emerged rethinking of the media audience. The insights of this rethinking involve important implications for any contemporary mass communication theory or model and, thus, for communication processes in general -including public communication by religious institutions-.

2.1   Communication research: from sender to audience

Though it remains questionable whether we can refer to contemporary society by speaking of an 'information and communication revolution' (see 1.1), communication

---

[5] In computer gaming a MUD (Multi-User Dungeon or Domain or Dimension) is a multi-player that combines elements of role playing games, hack and slash style computer games and social chat rooms. Typically running on a bulletin board system or Internet server, the game is usually text driven, where players read descriptions of rooms, objects, events, other characters, and computer-controlled creatures or non-player characters (NPCs) in a virtual world. Traditional MUDs implement a fantasy world populated by elves, goblins, dwarves, halflings, and other mythical or fantasy-based races with players being able to take on any number of classes, including warriors, mages, priests, thieves, druids, etc., in order to gain specific skills or powers. The object of the game is to slay monsters, explore a rich fantasy world, to complete quests, go on adventures, create a story by role-playing, and/or advance the created character. Many MUDs were fashioned around the dice rolling rules of the Dungeons & Dragons (D&D) series of games. MUDs often have a fantasy setting, while many others are set in a science fiction based universe or themed on popular books, movies, animations, history, etc. Still others, especially those, which are often referred to as MOOs, are used in distance education or to allow for virtual conferences. Most MUDs are run as hobbies and are free to players; some may accept donations or allow players to "purchase" in-game items. There are also many professionally developed MUDs which charge a monthly subscription fee. Source: Wikipedia. http://nl.wikipedia.org/wiki/MUD_%28computergames retrieved 19/10/2006. See also: P. Curtis 1996 'Mudding: social phenomena in text-based virtual realities', in M. Stefik (ed.), *Internet Dreams. Archetypes, Myths and Metaphors.* Cambridge, MA, and London: The MIT Press.
[6] The term 'people at the receiving end' is used in the Vatican Decree *Inter Mirifica*, (1963) nr 227; recipient in the pastoral instruction *Communio et Progressio*, 1971: 256, published by the Pontifical Commission for the Means of Social Communication of the Vatican.

has grown out to *the* key feature of society at the start of the third millennium. But as 'easy' as it is to make up for a chronology of communications media[7] -from prehistoric cave paintings and clay tablets to satellites, camcorders and hand palms- as difficult it is to account for a historical overview of communication theories or communication studies. Without doubt, this has to do with the elusiveness of communication[8]. The multiplicity and diversity of disciplines involved in communication processes is large. It varies from biology, mathematics and linguistics to sociology, ethnology, psychology, political science and cybernetics. It reflects different 'schools' and approaches. Only in the last decades of the twentieth century communication studies emerged as a new autonomous academic discipline, including specialized institutes and university departments.

Rebel (2000) distinguishes seven types of communication theories:

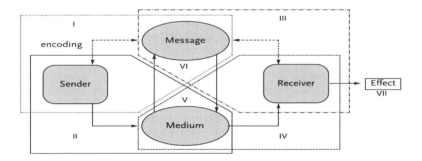

Figure 2.1 Types of communication theories. (Rebel 2000:44)

I   Language production theories (e.g. rhetoric)
II   Sociological theories (e.g. power and conflict theories)
III   Psychological theories (e.g. selectivity theory)
IV   Communication theories (e.g. uses and gratifications approach)
V   Media landscape, media history and media technology
VI   Semantic theory (e.g. semiotics)
VII   Social psychological and sociological effect theories (e.g. cultural effect theory).

The upper half of the scheme contains semantic models, which are about meaning. The lower part covers syntactical or process models that look upon communication as a

---

[7] See for example Downing, John, Mohammadi Ali, Sreberny-Mohammadi, Annabelle. 1995.
[8] The term communication has manifold definitions. Fiske (1989:2) refers to communication in a general sense as 'social interaction through messages'. McQuail (2000:492-493) also states sending and receiving of 'messages' central to communication in a process of increased commonality or sharing between participants. However, he also points out theoretical disagreements. These disagreements concern feedback or interactivity being essential to communication and the issue of a communication relationship that is by definition a social one. Especially the so-called 'new' technologies, like Internet and the World Wide Web, show possibilities of communication processes less bound by social basis.
Due to the elusiveness of communication, it can be studied at many levels and in many forms. Rosengren (2000) distinguishes e.g. verbal and non-verbal communication, mediated communication, intrapersonal, interpersonal and group communication, organizational communication, societal communication, mass communication, international and intercultural communication. For the sake of our subject, the public communication of mainstream religion, we will focus mainly on mass communication.

(linear) process. What is carried out from the scheme is pragmatic: the behavioral effects (effect models of communication).

Another classification or arrangement given by Rebel (2000:45) is a horizontal one. It contains supply theories on the one hand and demand and effect theories on the other hand. Supply theories are about production of messages and ownership relationships in the media world. Demand and effect theories cover user theories and the *audience cum content*' approaches[9].

Accounting for the development of communication theory historically instead of following a systematic approach is possible, according to Rebel, although sometimes it causes confusion about continuity. This has to do with fluctuating interest in models and approaches, which come and go.

Literature about theories of mass communication offer few chronological surveys. The closest volume probably is A. and M. Mattelart's, *Theories of Communication*[10]. However, they emphasize the circularity of approaches and not linear development.

Fiske (1989) also gives some sort of historical overview in describing 'process school' and 'semiotic school' models and methods, although this is neither strictly chronological.

Other communication scientists follow alternative approaches by describing mass communication theories according to the elements involved in the communication process, such as sender, message, medium, effects or audience (Windahl, Signitzer and Olson, 1998). Denis McQuail (2000), in his elaborated *McQuail's Mass Communication Theory*, uses theories, structures, organizations, content, audiences and effects as entries. Rosengren (2000) describes communication according to its forms, functions and levels, while Cobley (1996) conforms to signification, linguistic and visual meaning, speech acts, inscription of the audience in the message and readers' meanings.
Our aim, in the context of churches' public communication through the mass media, is not to elaborate a broad historical overview (if at all possible) of communication theory, but to discuss the principal representatives of the main communication theories and models in order to indicate paradigm shifts. We will indicate those shifts by focusing on the position of the 'receiver'. The main theories that will be considered are: *functionalist sociology* and *information theory*, *semiotics* and *critical theory*.

2.1.1   Functionalist sociology and information theory

Communication visions have always been closely related to views of society and/or media. In the 19th century, many technical systems of communication such as the telegraph (Samuel Morse 1836), the telephone (Alexander Graham Bell 1876), the Kodak camera (Eastman 1888), the kinetoscope (Edison 1892), radio telegraphy (Guglielmo Marconi 1895) and the motion picture camera (Lumière Brothers 1896) were invented. As free trade emerged, and the large scale urban industrial society emerged, the need for integration was felt.

---

[9] See de Boer and Brennecke 2004:157-236.
[10] Mattelart, Armand and Michèle. 1998. Originally published as *Histoire des theories de la communication*. Paris, Éditions La Découverte.

'Mass'[11] society had to be managed and communication was to fulfill the function of community organization for the sake of social cohesion and integration as well as the continuation of society and the progress of human kind[12]. It is not surprising therefore, that communication as a theme for the first time was paid attention to by the advent of the empirical social sciences.

The functionalist paradigm originates from the U.S. political scientist, Harold D. Laswell (1902-1978). Deeply concerned with questions of propaganda techniques used in World War I, Laswell developed the first conceptual framework of mass communication research[13]. This framework consisted of Laswell's famous "five w's formula": who says what in which channel to whom with what effect? "Who" refers to a sender. "What" refers to a message. "Channel" refers to a medium. "Whom" refers to a receiver and "effect" refers to outcome.

His was an impact-oriented scope of analysis (in which the concerns about media effects on the young can be traced back to the time before World War I), which resulted in a long tradition of research on media and violence (behaviorist theory) beginning in the 1930s. The impact-oriented scope was (also in the 1930s) reinforced by commercial demand.

According to McQuail (2000), the *effect research tradition* is to be distinguished in four phases. The first phase was when media were thought to be 'all powerful' and able to shape opinions and beliefs in society (1900-1930). In the second phase, research that was concerned about the harmful influence of media -especially on children- lead to the insight that social and psychological factors, personal contact and social environment also played their role. It was thought that media only had a minimal effect and there was certainly no direct link between media stimulus and audience response (1930-1960). Joseph Klapper (1960) in his book, *The Effects of Mass Communication*[14], highly influenced this view. The types of media effect that Klapper described were conversion, minor change and reinforcement. The 'minimal effect' theory was heavily criticized in the third phase (1960-1980), which was the stage of television. The criticism charged that this theory merely concentrated on short term, non-social and non-institutional effects. In the fourth phase (since the 1980's), 'negotiated' media influence came to the forefront: the interaction between media that construct frames of reality and the audience that constructs its own views of social reality by 'negotiating' the symbolic constructions offered by the media. In this negotiation process, the social/cultural context plays an important role.

Though attention is given to mass media and the audience, functionalist sociology of the media focuses its analysis mainly on content and effect (behavior, attitudes, emotions,

---

[11] The term 'mass' in its origins had fairly negative connotations like: large, undifferentiated, without order. Mass society is identified by elites' control over the -manipulated- mass. Mass media are a sine qua non in this process. Mass communication processes are characterized by large scale, impersonality, anonymity, calculation and one directional flow of standardized content. The produced 'mass culture' is a non-elite, mass produced, commercial, homogenized culture. The mass audience, a new type of social formation, is mainly looked upon as dispersed, anonymous, heterogeneous and not self-acting. This view was criticized later because of audience experiences research (see 2.2. and 2.3). The more recent -far less negative- term used is: popular culture.
[12] The ambivalence towards the new society (emancipation-disintegration) also marked the general vision on mass media, which were paradoxically seen as 'cause of - remedy for' the loss of social community. See for example Mattelart 1998.
[13] Laswell H. 1948. 'The structure and function of communication in society' in L. Bryson (ed.), *The communication of Ideas,* New York, Harper, pp. 32-51.
[14] Klapper J. 1960. *The Effects of Mass Communication.* New York: Free Press.

opinions, actions) of messages. This is done by an empirical approach of content analysis and the so-called 'semantic differential'.

Content is 'measured' by quantitative, 'objective', systematic description. It identifies and counts chosen units in a communication system, for example, the use of the words 'democracy' or 'public security' in political television campaigns. Other examples include the frequency in which women in upper-level political, university, or industrial occupations are invited to comment on current events in fact-finding programs; or the number of records of ethnicity in crime coverage in daily newspapers. Such analyses produce statistical data. At the same time, however, they reveal something about culture and media bias.

Semantic differential, the other method of functionalist media sociological analysis, was developed by Charles Osgood[15] to study people's attitudes and emotions with respect to media content. The method consists of three stages. It starts with the identification of values. This is done by a pilot sample in which people freely discuss and react to e.g. television shots or newspapers' images. The main ratings that are found are then plotted on a 5-7 point binary opposed scale. Subsequently, the research sample is asked to react on each scale. Final results are averaged.

By focusing on effects of media output, functionalist sociology revealed its view of both society and media. Society is seen as consisting of an undifferentiated mass and a small 'elite'. Important information in society flows directly from medium to mass. Media are all powerful instruments with an undifferentiated impact; the mass audience is totally powerless, passive and uncritical. In this view, communication is a one-way, linear process that directly affects the audience. From this view, theories like the 'magical bullet' or the 'hypodermic needle' resulted, in which the audience is equated to a victim or a patient who is passively waiting for the 'media-needle' to inject him/her with a message. These models are known as *stimulus-response theory*.

According to Laswell, by acting in this way, mass media fulfill three functions in society: they safeguard the dominant value system in society, they make different sections of society respond in the right way to their environment and they act as a cultural transmitter by passing the social heritage from one generation to the next.

Information Theory

Apart from functionalist sociology, there was another 'school' at the dawn of 'communication studies'[16]. The study that is widely mentioned as the main initial impetus of communication studies, is Shannon and Weaver's, *Mathematical Theory of Communication* (1949). This study emerged from information theory. As exact scientists of Bell Telephone Laboratories, Shannon and Weaver's main interest was the efficient transmission of messages in order to reach an optimum action of channels such as telephone cables or radio waves. Their line of approach was purely technical.

They developed a straight-line transmission model in which communication was seen as a linear process by which an information source via a transmitter sent a signal to a receiver. What counted were the accuracy of the transmission and the effectiveness of symbols, which were meant to produce the appropriate conduct by the receiver. Meaning was supposed to be an immanent element of the message.

---

[15] Osgood C. 1967. *The measurement of Meaning*. Illinois, University of Illinois Press.
[16] On the interpretation of communication, this school has the linear process view in common with functionalist sociological theories.

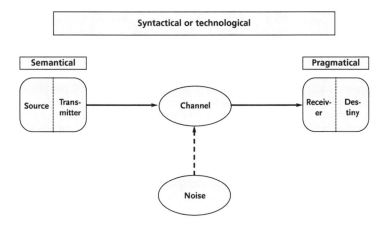

Figure 2.2 The communication model by Shannon and Weaver (Rebel 2000:37)

Unlike Laswell, Shannon and Weaver were not equally interested in source, receiver or effect, as they were in the accuracy of technical processes. Their model, therefore, is known as the Sender-Channel-Receiver scheme. They did not pay attention to content (the message) or processes of meaning. The sender determines the message and what the destination has to do is literally 'receive' the message. In other words, to 'consume' the cut-and-dried information from the receiver as bite size chunks. Thus, the image of the audience is a rather passive one.

Nevertheless, the transmission model -with its instrumental vision- became the dominant paradigm. It was, and still is, frequently used in standard definitions. Applied by Laswell to mass media, it was extended and challenged by others. The 1950's in this respect may be regarded as a turning point.

According to Fiske (1989), the triangular communication model by Newcomb[17] broke with the linear transmission model by introducing the role of communication in societal relationships. Communicator (A), receiver (B) and social environment (X) are the points of the triangle. Their internal relationships are interdependent. If one changes, the others do as well. If one relationship alters, this affects other relationships. In this way, the role of communication is to keep the social system's balance.

Westley and MacLean[18] applied Newcomb's model to mass media and extended it by two fundamental changes. The editorial function (C) -positioned between A and B- and the fragmentation of X in X[1], X[2], X[3] etc. underlined the multiplicity of the social environment that was caused by mass society. B, therefore, needs more information and

[17] Newcomb T. 1953. 'An approach to the study of communication acts' in Psychological Review, 60 pp. 393-40 and in Smith A.G. (ed.) 1966 Communication and Culture. New York, Holt, Rinehart & Winston.
[18] Westley, B. and MacLean M. 1957. 'A conceptual model for communication research' in Journalism Quarterly, 34, pp. 31-80.

orientation, which makes him dependent on mass media. A and C, then, become more dominant.

According to McQuail (2000), Westley and MacLean offer the most complete early model of mass communication in line with the linear transmission thinking. By emphasizing a new 'communicator' role, mass communicators act as a go-between among society and audience by selecting events to report on (according to what interests the audience) or giving access to voices. Mass media do not have the task of improving society or to educate people, but are 'neutral' service institutions. What the audience demands is evident by their selection of what is offered.[19] Feedback from the audience is important. In this regard, Westley and MacLean's model is no longer strictly linear. Instead of the sender-message-channel-receivers scheme the sequence is: events and voices in society-channel/communicator role-messages-receiver.

By bringing 'events' to the forefront there is some similarity with the model of George Gerbner (see below), however his model is more complex than the model of Westley and MacLean, which holds a far less active role for the audience. It still is about the transmission of messages.

According to Mattelart & Mattelart (1998), the first innovation in the history of functionalist sociology of media was caused by the discovery of the intermediary. Paul F. Lazarsfeld and Elihu Katz are the names affiliated with the 'two step flow of communication' theory. They co-authored a book in which they presented the results of research showing the behavior of consumers in the process of choosing films to watch[20]. By asking a sample how decisions are taken, they discovered the importance of the 'primary group'. Communication did not flow directly through a linear process having a direct impact on mass society, but through an intermediate step: the opinion leader. This means that information from mass media first flows to people who are in direct media contact and subsequently, through their role of opinion leader to people with less media contact, 'less informed' and/or dependent on information from others. In this way, people in their decision making process are influenced by the judgments of opinion leaders. This was a novelty in functional analysis. Laswell's view that 'omnipotent' mass media had an almost mechanistic direct mass effect on society and receivers was challenged. The underlying instrumental view, however, remained.

Lazarsfeld added a fourth function of communication processes -entertainment- to Laswell's three mentioned above. Together with F. Stanton, Lazarsfeld in the 1940's researched why radio listeners were so attracted to soap operas and quizzes on radio[21]. Those 'satisfaction studies' that analyzed the reason why people use media and what they use them for, were perfectly in line with the functional analysis, which assumed that media fulfill the role of watchdog of the ruling value system, cultural transmitter and maintainer of cohesion in society. Along with fulfilling societal 'needs', media were also to fulfill individual needs of the people who used them, according to this line of reasoning. Not only for information, but also for personal guidance or entertainment, for example.

---

[19] In contemporary media debates on public service and commercial broadcasters, traces of this view appear as well. Commercial broadcasters claim they 'give people what they want', being the main 'raison d'être' for any media company. It is no coincidence in this respect that the model of Westley and MacLean is current for commercial media, since it was based on the American system of free market media.
[20] Katz E. and Lazarsfeld P.F. 1955. Personal Influence: The Part Played by People in the Flow of Mass Communication. Glencoe, Ill. Free Press 1970.
21 Lazarsfeld, P.F. and Stanton F. Radio Research, 1942-3. New York: Duell, Sloan and Pearce.

This type of research became known as the *uses and gratifications approach*. In the 1970's, it was revitalized as a consequence of ethnographic studies on audience and reception. (See 2.2.2 and 2.2.3).

The two-step flow of communication theory (and its subsequent version of 'multi step flow') was later applied to the distribution and adoption of (technological) innovations. Different stages of awareness, interest, evaluation, trial, adoption or refusal were identified and converged with marketing models, and played an important role in consumer behavior research. This also had its impact on (western) views of development and modernization, which were seen as a linear process towards modern society in which technology and mobility were indispensable for progress. Media, in this respect, fulfilled a mobilizing function. Developmental communication e.g. followed the two-step flow pattern through western opinion leaders and predicted the 'development stages'.

Mattelart and Mattelart identify another turn -or perhaps more a break- from the linear communication model towards a circular model. A group of US scholars, representing different disciplines, convened at the 'Palo Alto School' or 'The Invisible College' in San Francisco. The driving force was Gregory Bateson, an anthropologist. Together with Edward T. Hall[22], who was interested in intercultural communication by his experience as an officer in an African-American regiment in World War II, they may be considered as the main representatives of this school.
They took the work of Norbert Wiener, a former professor of Shannon, as their point of departure. Wiener had published a book on cybernetics[23] in which he saw future society as an 'information society', which he called a 'new utopia'. This information society, according to Wiener, had to be based on the circulation of information.

Bateson and Hall felt it was necessary to study communication within social sciences, and that it needed models of its own. Communication was such a complex phenomenon that it was impossible to 'reduce' it to three linear variables. In the circular vision of communication, the role of the receiver was as important as the role of the transmitter. The essence of communication was to be found in relational and interactive processes. All acts of human behavior -not just deliberate verbal acts- had communicative value. Communication was looked upon as an ongoing social process. Therefore, it was not the analysis of content that had to be emphasized, but the analysis of context. Hall's work was related to different languages and codes that were characteristic to various cultures.

This guides us in the direction of both semiotics and critical theory, which is the focus of the following paragraphs.

According to Fiske (1989), the 'bridging' theories between the linear process models and semiotics stem from the work of George Gerbner and from the linguist, R. Jakobson.
Gerbner, in 1956 wrote an article entitled: 'Toward a general model of communication'[24].
Like Shannon and Weaver, Gerbner's view of communication was a transmission of messages (process model) view. Not in the straight linear way of sender-channel-receiver, but rather in horizontal and vertical dimensions consisting of several elements: event (E), the percept of the event (E1) by M (human person or machine like a camera),

---

[22] In 1959 Hall published a book called The Silent Language, on the silent languages and codes characteristic of every culture. New York, Doubleday.
23 Wiener, N. 1948. Cybernetics or Control and Communication in the Animal and the Machine. Paris, Hermann.
[24] Gerbner, G. 1956. 'Toward a general model of communication' in Audio Visual Communication Review. IV: 3, pp. 171-99.

the conversion of the percept into a signal about the event (SE) (the message) and percept of the statement about the event (SE1) by the receiver (M2).

The great difference with Shannon and Weaver's model is that Gerbner adds E, the event. By doing this, he relates the message to reality and offers the possibility of bringing questions of meaning and perceptivity into the communication model.

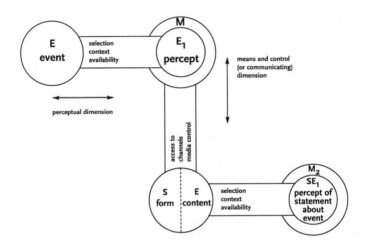

Figure 2.3 Gerbner's model (modified). (Fiske 1989:26).

To explain the model, we will summarize Fiske's (1989:26-31) description of it.
What happens in communication processes is that an event is perceived by M. E1 is the perception of the event made by M (in S&W's model this is called the source). In this perception, process selection and availability are involved. M cannot perceive the entire totality of E and, therefore, makes a selection. The communicator does likewise by selecting how the event will be made available. In the selection and perception process context plays its part. The way people form perceptions is by 'making meaning' of what they perceive. Not by simple 'stimulus-response', as assumed in the hypodermic needle theory, but by matching new information (external stimuli) to already existing and internalized ideas and concepts, which depend on culture. By doing so, people interact actively from the beginning of the communication process.

Next, the percept E1 is made into a signal or message about E. Gerbner calls this SE, which consists of closely related form and content. In S&W's model, with its emphasis on the technical process of communication, the message was thought to be detached. As an isolated pre-existing package that was ready to be transported (encoded), subsequently unwrapped (decoded) and understood as it was originally meant. Gerbner argues that there is no content pre-existent to form. In the very articulating of the message itself (encoding as well as decoding), it is put into existence. Form and content interact in a creative, non-static way.
In the process of making the percept into a message, selections are made of communication means (medium and channel) as well as of content and form. As E1 never can be a totally exhaustive picture of E, neither can SE be a totally complete message of E1.

There are two other important 'selection features': media control and access to channels. By selection of the messages transmitted, and the way they are transmitted, it is shown where power and social control in society is settled and exercised.

Finally what is 'meaningful' for M2, the receiver, is not E -the event itself- or even SE -the message- but the interactively negotiated perception, SE1. The same processes of selection, context and availability as between E and M/E1, take place on this level. Once again meaning is not 'in' the message, but arises from interaction between the (sub) culturally determined needs and concepts of the receiver (M2) and the message (SE). Only if those needs can be related to SE will the message have 'meaning'. In the interaction itself, the potential meanings of a message are constituted into perceived meaning (SE1).

Gerbner thus describes communication as a process in which two dimensions alternate: the horizontal level -which is the perceptual dimension- and the vertical level -which is the means and control dimension-. Gerbner later extended the model, however, the transmission view of communication remained. Especially semiotic scholars especially criticized him therefore, because he did not pay enough attention to forms and codes that generate meaning. Fiske (1989:31), nevertheless, describes Gerbner as 'the one major authority whose work comes closest to combining the two approaches to the study of communication'. (We will return to the work of Gerbner, especially his *cultivation theory'* in section 2.2.2).

According to Fiske (1989), the linguist Jakobson[25] eventually bridges the gap between the process school that we discussed and semiotic theory. Jakobson, as a linguist interested in meaning and internal structures of messages, created a double model.

His point of departure was modeling the constitutive factors of any act of communication. He discerns six factors that are related to each other in a triangular form: the *addresser* sending a *message*, referring to a *context*, and to an *addressee*. Then he adds two 'new' factors: *contact*, the physical channel and psychological connections between addresser and addressee, and *code*, consisting of a shared meaning system, to structure a message. In this way, he 'combines' the 'linear process' part of the communication model with a 'meaning' or semiotic part.

Each of the mentioned six factors determines different functions of language. Jakobson links the factors and functions of communication as follows: addresser and the emotive function (this is the relationship between message and addresser, the expressive function); addressee and the cognitive function (the effect of the message on the addressee). Context is linked to a referential function. This is the reality orientation of the message, which is important in factual communication. Message is linked to a poetic function, which means the relationship of a message to itself. Contact is linked with a phatic function which includes keeping the channels open and maintaining a relationship between addresser and addressee. And code, to conclude, is associated with the metalingual function, which identifies the codes or frames being used.

This brings us to semiotic theory.

---

[25] Jakobson, R. and Halle, M. 1956. *The Fundamentals of Language.* The Hague: Mouton. Jakobson, R. 1960. 'Closing statement: linguistics and poetics' in Sebeok, T. (ed.) *Style and Language.* Cambridge, MIT Press. Also in de George, R. and de George F. (eds.) 1972. *The Structuralists from Marx to Levi-Strauss.* New York, Doubleday, Anchor Books.

2.1.2   Semiotics

The process models of communication, with their instrumental view of media, equalize communication to the transfer of information from a sender to a receiver. Message, 'that what is transmitted', is supposed to contain meaning in itself. Not *a* meaning, but *the* meaning, independent from the receiver's use of it, or from factors inside or outside the message, dependent on context or culture. There's no distinction between an intended message, a sent message, or a received or perceived message.

Exactly at the point of message and *meaning* the process models are diametrically opposed to semiotic models, although both, of course, are bothered with the process in which a sender, a receiver and a 'message' are involved. But the essence of communication, in a semiotic view, is not about transmission, but about the production and exchange of meanings.

These meanings are not given with messages, as isolated units per se, but constructed in languages by the combined action of signs, codes, myths and metaphors. This implies that socio-cultural factors play their part. And so do receivers, because meaning is also constructed in a process of interaction between 'reader' and 'text'[26]. This implies that the receiver of a message plays at least as important a role as the sender and, therefore, is far from the passive victim as was assumed in the early transmission models. In fact, the sender becomes less important and the emphasis shifts to texts and how they are 'read'. Producer, reader of a text, 'message' and external reality (such as social factors or how 'reading' is learned in a culture) all are involved in a dynamic structural relationship. In this view the communication models are not *process* models, but *structural* models.

In terms of meaning, the study of communication processes result from linguistic and logic/mathematical studies and go back to late 19th and early 20th century. Accounting for an historical development of theories -because of diversity- is complex. Insights from a variety of disciplines are incorporated (linguistics, semiology, philosophy and literary theory) and different geographical areas (France, US, UK and Russia) had their own sometimes separated, sometimes cross-fertilizing influence. Paul Cobley, editor of the *Communication Theory Reader* (1996) in which the 'grand names' of 'theories of the sign' are reviewed, speaks of an 'uneven development of communication theory' (1996:22). It is discussed e.g. whether the origins of structuralism were dominated by certain regions and thinkers. The work of other theorists, like Charles Saunders Peirce and Valentin Vološinov e.g., was not included in these discussions.

Moreover, the time spectrum in which theories appeared does not always follow chronological lines[27] and terms are not always used in the same sense.

In his introduction, Cobley gives a brief history of the breadth of theory. It includes *Saussurean Linguistics and Its Influence* (on Claude Lévi-Strauss, Roland Barthes); *Post-structuralism* (Jacques Lacan, Jacques Derrida); its British version, *Speech-act Theory and Reader-response* (J.L. Austin, John Searle, Stanley Fish, David Morley, Ien Ang, Janice Radway); and *Social Theory of Language* (Valentin Vološinov/Mikhail Bakhtin, Basil Bernstein, M.A.K. Halliday, Gunther Kress, Theo van Leeuwen) and Peirce's, *emiotic Theory and Its Influence* (Umberto Eco, John Fiske, J.K. Sherrif).

---

[26] The terms 'reader' and 'text' are not to be restricted to writing. A text can refer to writing, audio, audio-visual etc. An advertisement, soap, a composition, an SMS, a speech, a movie, a ballet or a billboard for example all are 'texts'.
[27] According to Paul Cobley 1996:8 for example post structuralism questions in fact preceded structuralist thinking.

In this paragraph, we will restrict ourselves to identifying the two main models of meaning and their basic thinkers. Successively, we will consider semiotics and semiology.

The term, *semiotics*, can be shortly defined as 'the science of signs and meanings'[28] (Umberto Eco). It is related to the work of the US logician/mathematician, Charles Sanders Peirce (1839-1914). Peirce was one of the 'founding fathers' of (the American tradition of) semiotics.

The term, *semiology,* -'the science to study the life of signs within society'-[29] is from the Swiss linguist, Ferdinand de Saussure (1857-1913). He is the other most influential scientist in this area. De Saussure mainly studied language and was interested in the mutual relationships of signs[30].

Semiotics: C.S. Peirce

In semiotic theory, a message is not an isolated package to be transferred (meaning included), but is made up of signs. Peirce defined a sign as 'something, which stands to somebody for something in some respect or capacity'[31]. A sign, then, is not only related to something -an object- but also stands for something. Or we might say in common language, it 'means' something.

For example, when my 5-year-old daughter is playing outside and gets stuck with her boots in thawing soil, and yells 'Mama!' I perceive a sign upon hearing this sound. This sign relates to a child crying (object). But it also 'causes' something in my mind, i.e. it stands for something: trouble.

In Peirce's terms, this 'causing something in my mind' or 'standing for something' is an *interpretant*[32] - the sign is a *representamen*. Together with the object, he models them in a triangular shape:

---

[28] Fiske 1989:2. Fiske claims the equality of both terms semiology and semiotics, though uses the term semiotics as a general term for structural models 1989:43. McQuail 2000 defines semiology as the 'science of sign systems' or 'signification'; semiology is 'a more specific version of the general structuralist approach' 2000:311. McQuail refers to the term 'semiotic' only in relation to the 'semiotic power' of people in the cultural economy, namely the power 'to shape meanings to their own desires' 2000:103. Cobley 1996 points to the usage of the term semiotics as opposed to semiology, being the study of signs other than in literature (e.g. in biology). Semiology according to Cobley should strictly be associated with the European tradition; but due to Umberto Eco's influence 'semiotics' is frequently used to refer to any theoretical interest in signs on either side of the Atlantic 1996:27. We therefore will use the term semiotics.

[29] De Saussure, F. 1974. 1915. *Course in General Linguistics*. Translation W. Baskin, London, Fontana.

[30] For the main analogies and differences between Peirce and de Saussure and their respective influence see: Fiske 1989: 42-67 and Cobley 1996.

[31] Quoted from Mattelart & Mattelart 1998:23 and Fiske 1989:45.

[32] Fiske 1989 appropriately draws attention to the fact that the interpretant is not the same as the user of a sign, but a mental concept based on sign and experience together.

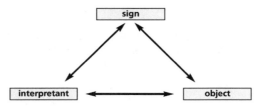

Figure 2.4 Peirce's elements of meaning (Fiske 1989: 45).

The interpretant is the effect caused by the sign. What the interpretant actually does, is to set off an additional set of sign-object-interpretant, in which it becomes a sign itself. This set, which brings along its own interpretant, in its turn sets off another set of three and so on.

So sign, object, and interpretant are related to each other in a triad. And all three of them make up for 'meaning' in the above-mentioned process. In itself, sign and object mean nothing. It is not until they cause an effect in my mind, and are related to a mental concept of trouble -which is based on experience-, that they mean what they mean. This experience is learned. If my culture, language, and social environment had not in one way or another 'taught' me that this kind of yelling implies danger, I probably would not have reacted in the way that I did -running outside- simply because I might have interpreted the sign differently.
This means that interpretants depend on their user's experience and concepts. They act like mediators of reality.

Meaning is not, as thought in the process models, something definite that can be transferred as a little parcel encoded by the sender, and opened up by the receiver who then decodes it according to the encoded meaning. Meaning is a process. It is something that is produced by the interplay of sign, object and interpretant which continuously furthers sign triads. Peirce called this process: *semiosis*, the act of signifying[33]. The distinction between an active encoder and a passive decoder is not relevant anymore. In the process of semiosis both fulfill an active and creative role.
Three kinds of signs, related to Peirce, are often mentioned in literature: *icon*, *index* and *symbol*. An icon is a sign that resembles an object, e.g. a photograph. In an index there is a direct link between sign and object, e.g. shadow is an index of sunshine. A symbol has no connection between sign and object, but is a matter of agreement. For example: Maria as a symbol of the devoted virgin or the whore. Peirce spent a lifetime working to characterize sign types[34]. The results of the combination of sign types are manifold. This points to Peirce's significance for the relationship of communication to reality. His importance was immense, however, not recognized until the 1980-1990's. In fact, his work played no role in early literary analysis. We will turn to that analysis now.

Semiology: F. de Saussure

Because de Saussure was a linguist, the sign itself was the main object of study in his basic model. A sign is part of a meaning system, which is dependent on language and culture. De Saussure's basic model consists of a *signifier* and a *signified*.

---

[33] Fiske 1989 therefore proposes to use the term *semiosis* (active) instead of meaning (passive).
[34] According to Cobley 1996:29, he estimated 59,049 different types.

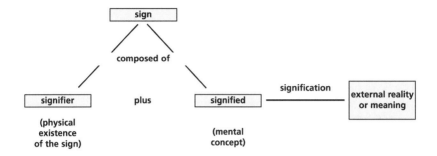

Figure 2.5 Saussure's elements of meaning (Fiske 1989:47).

The signifier is the physical element in a message. Examples include a photograph that we see, a whistle that we hear or a word that we read. In order to gain control of this reality, we make categorizations in our mind. The signified is the mental concept we make when we see, hear, taste or touch a physical element. For example, a road sign consisting of a red circle and white inside -in my culture- refers to a prohibited area for cars. Seeing the physical signpost, we refer to it mentally as a road sign. We even know what it means: no entrance for cars. Our language and culture taught us this. So signifier and signified are not naturally linked, but (sub) culturally linked, and thus arbitrarily produced. Together they make up for the signification, which is the external reality.

As a linguist, what interested de Saussure most, was not so much the signification part - the external meaning- but how one sign is related to another in the same system. He believed that it was the differentiation from other signs that counted for the meaning of a sign.

To communicate, signs are combined and organized in sign systems or codes. De Saussure distinguishes *'paradigmatic'*, or 'associative' relations or sets of signs (e.g. synonym, vocabulary) and *syntagmatic* relations or sets, which combine signs into a message (for example the linear connections between words in a sentence).

To make a message, one chooses the desired signs (selection) from the paradigm and then shapes them into a *syntagm* (combination). Not haphazardly, but by 'rules' or conventions (i.e. a grammar). Once chosen signs are put in place in the syntagm, they are affected by the relationship to others. For de Saussure, this structural relationship of signs was the key to understanding them.

'So, then, the area of reality or experience to which any one signified refers, that is the signification of the sign, is determined not by the nature of that reality/experience, but by the boundaries of the related signifieds in the system. Meaning is therefore better defined by the relationships of one sign to another, than by the relationship of that sign to an external reality. This relationship of signs to others in its system is what Saussure calls *'value'*. And for Saussure *value* is what primarily determines meaning'[35].

---

[35] Fiske 1989:49.

This became the dominant concern in European semiotics. In the 1950's the French anthropologist Claude Lévi-Strauss, belonging to the structuralist movement, in his famous studies on myths owed to de Saussure. His main aim was to reconstruct a master code, or universal 'langue', that 'programmed' human thought.

Roland Barthes, another follower of de Saussure, who -like Lévi-Strauss- believed in a 'science of signs', wrote a series of essays called *Mythologies* in 1957. The most important concepts in this work are myth, connotation and denotation. Myths are large, secret, cultural systems of meaning that are passed on from one generation to another. They carry certain beliefs and values and 'co-determine' the signification of signs. The relationship between signifier and signified is the first order of signification, or *denotation*. *Connotation* relates to a second order of associated meaning. In this respect, signs are able to signify a master code of values and beliefs. What appears as 'natural' in culture is, in fact, constructed (cf. de Saussure's arbitrariness of the relationship between signified and signifier). It is not neutral, but ideological. In his later work on visual signification (early 1960's), second order connotative codes play an important role. This causes him to speak of the *readerly* and the *writerly* text. The reader is characterized respectively as a consumer and a producer who produces by himself what is presented to him by selecting from a profusion of meanings (see 2.2).

By then post-structuralists -like Benveniste[36], Lacan and Derrida- had already criticized structuralism for being concerned only with isolated signs structured by culture, cut off from context. They mainly pointed to the subjectivity of human language.

The further theories developed, the more complicated the question of meaning became. Text played a role in meaning, but context and conventions did as well. So did the use of the text. By the mid 1960's the role of the reader in communications is introduced in the *reader-response theory*. Readers make their own interpretation of texts and decide what contributes to the meaning of a text. Others point to the fact that readers are 'implied' in texts by authors, which guides textual meaning. In the 1980's, a range of ethnographic studies followed, to analyze reader's responses to media texts (see 2.2.3.1).

During the same period (1970's – 1980's), socio linguist M.A.K. Halliday worked on theory from another scope: the way signs and language are related to the social framework. This subject had (much) earlier been the focus of the Soviet theorist, Valentin Vološinov, in his book, *Marxism and the Philosophy of Language* (1929). But it took until the 1970's -even in Russia, where it was published- before it got attention.

Halliday's was a sociological model of language. He extended text-reader interactions to social relationships. His research on the development of children's language showed the patterns in which 'meaning is learnt', and how general relationships in society and situational variables build up language.
Besides structuralism, social relationships also played an important role in critical theory, which we will discuss in the following section.

---

[36] Strictly speaking chronologically, Benveniste was a 'pre-post-structuralist'; he formulated his *post structural* questions already in the 1940's, before the structuralism of Lévi-Strauss; see about this paradox also note 24.

2.1.3   Critical Theory

The linear transmission models, as mentioned before, became the mainstream dominant paradigm in communication studies. But its focus on direct effects and its view of all-powerful media, as humanizing technologies for regulation and progress of society, were criticized for not being related to social and cultural factors and human experience. In fact, it became heavily attacked by Marxist inspired theory, political economy of communication studies, cultural studies, including 'new' approaches that brought forth daily experiences of the audience.

Also in the realm of functional analysis, C. Wright Mills'[37] dissident voice raised questions on culture and power. He contended that contemporary mass culture was commercial and caused alienation in society. He also criticized the neutrality of functional analysis and is regarded as one of the founders of American cultural studies.

The origins of an alternative social *critical theory* are situated in the *Frankfurter Schule*. Connected to this school are the names of Walter Benjamin, Theodor Adorno and Max Horkheimer, Leo Löwenthal and Herbert Marcuse.

Adorno and Horkheimer, exiles of the nazi regime, developed the concept of *culture industry*[38] while working at New York's Columbia University in the 1940's. In their opinion, culture in mass society -which was primarily culture produced and reflected by mass media- degenerated to a commodity of mass produced, profitable, cultural goods that produced false escapist needs. The capitalist ideology of technical rationality, with its standardized production, was the cause of alienation. Culture was no longer able to be a source of critical or even revolutionary thinking. On the contrary, it caused domination and social control and conformed people to the state and economic order by turning them into mass consumers. Adorno and Horkheimer rejected the 'neutrality' of media as being unbiased transmitters, and the model by functional sociology.

Marcuse in his *One Dimensional Man*[39], which was published in 1964, offered a more comprehensive version of the same theme. He sketched a world shaped by a science of technology, which was narrowed to one dimension, not only politically, but even in consciousness and speech. It was a world in which the one-dimensional man looks upon technological rationality as the 'natural' and logical way of things. Moreover, it was the best way of things. By the time this one-dimensional philosophy is not only assumed -but even sustained- man, according to Marcuse, is turned into a servile 'instrument'.

In 1962, the German philosopher Jürgen Habermas had drawn attention to the decline of the public sphere that resulted from the processes caused by technical rationality. In his book, *Strukturwandel der Öffentlichkeit,*[40] he drew attention to the influence of market laws that turned public communication into what he called 'the manufacturing of opinion', and the citizen into a 'consumer', who was an isolated receiver of stereotyped attitudes. In 1968, he published his theory of technical rationality, *Technik und Wissenschaft als Ideologie*[41], and it was followed in the 1980's by his *Theorie des Kommunikativen Handelns*, (Theory of Communicative Action). This theory addressed the communicative relations and networks of interaction in society.

---

[37] Mills, C. Wright. 1956. *The Power Elite*. New York: Oxford University Press.
[38] The same issue was addressed before, in 1933, by Walter Benjamin.
[39] Marcuse, Herbert. 1964. *One Dimensional Man*. Boston: Beacon Press.
[40] Habermas J. 1962. Darmstadt: Hermann Luchterhand Verlag. English translation by Burger T. and Lawrence F. 1989. *The Structural Transformation of the Public Sphere: An Inquiry into a Category of Bourgeois Society*. Cambridge, Mass.: MIT Press.
[41] Habermas, J. 1968. *Technik und Wissenschaft als Ideologie*. Frankfurt: Suhrkamp Verlag.

As critical theory highlighted the cultural industry, the *political economy of communication*, in the 1960s, began questioning the unequal exchange of cultural activities/products and flows of information. Cultural dependency and cultural imperialism were the main themes. In the US, Herbert Schiller showed the strong ties between the military industrial complex and the communication industry, which caused the privatization of the public sphere[42]. George Gerbner, by that time head of the Journal of Communication, focused his attention on the worldwide imbalance of communication. In Europe Peter Golding (UK), Cees Hamelink (the Netherlands), and Kaarle Nordenstreng (Finland) did the same, publishing about media imperialism and the myths cultivated by it. A radical critique of the modernization theories came from Latin America, especially by Helmut Schmuckler, Armand Mattelart and -later- Mario Kaplun, Jesús Martín Barbero and Néstor García Canclini. They focused on the relationship between 'cultura transnacional' and 'culturas populares'. They were influenced by the pioneering work of Paulo Freire, who published *Pedagogia do Opremido* in 1970[43]. Freire's pedagogic practice in Brazil led him to discover 'a culture of silence' in Latin American masses in the 1960's. They had internalized their oppressors to the extent that they were unable to raise consciousness and preferred security with a lack of freedom to the uncertainty of freedom. Another way of education was necessary. Not the 'deposit' method by which knowledge was transferred as a kind of 'feeding' process that the receiver had to comply with. This, in fact, was the 'education of silence' by the myth of an uncomplicated world, which maintained the status quo and alienated people and made them passive. Instead Freire developed a form of education based on the concrete existential situation, experiences and needs of the people themselves. The contrasts within that situation made the context problematical to them and helped them not only to develop consciousness about reality, but also to react to it and thus eliminate isolation and regain self-esteem. Freire's method was profoundly dialogical. It was more of a process of mutual education and communication without any strict roles for 'teacher' or 'student'. The implicit criticism of the dominant linear transmission model of communication is obvious.

In the 1970's, the process of cultural equalization led to discussions on a New World Information and Communication Order (NWICO). It resulted -in 1978- in the first major international report on this issue published by UNESCO[44] (see also 1.2.1).
Marxist texts that had led to critical theory also influenced the neo Marxist structuralists[45], who opposed the dominant American sociological theory of media as well. The French philosopher, Louis Althusser, indicated the ideological domination of civil society, which was effected by school, church, media, family etc. Bourdieu indicated the codes of dominant representation and Michel Foucault indicated the mechanism of internalization of surveillance techniques in which television, to his opinion, played a prominent, manipulative role. The 1970's put the structuralist view of the consciousness industry under scrutiny. It was found to be the overture to user theories and increasing attention to the emancipatory potential of media.

---

[42] Schiller H. 1969. *Mass Communications and American Empire*. Boston: Beacon Press.
[43] Freire, Paulo. 1970. *Pedagogia do Oprimido*. Translation: M.B. Ramos. 1974 New York, Seabury Press.
[44] UNESCO. 28-11-1978. Declaration on Fundamental Principles Concerning the Contribution of the Mass Media to Strengthening Peace and International Understanding, to the Promotion of Human Rights and to Countering Racialism, Apartheid and Incitement to War. Paris, UNESCO. Also known as the 'MacBride Report', named after Sean MacBride, president of the international commission.
[45] In Paris, France, it was the Centre for the Study of Mass Communication (CECMAS) that analyzed the relationships between society and mass communication and in Italy the A. Gemelli Institute in Milan, of which Umberto Eco was one of the prominent thinkers.

The first work in this direction of *cultural studies* stems from Stuart Hall, director of the Birmingham Centre for Contemporary Cultural Studies. The centre was influenced by the thinking of Antonio Gramsci. In particular, his concepts of hegemony and social reproduction[46]. And by contemporary feminist studies, which put forth the questions of gender and subculture. Hall, interested as he was in popular culture and the way people 'read' ideology in media texts, wrote an article on encoding and decoding of television programs in 1973. He recognized four phases: production, circulation, distribution/consumption and reproduction. The audience was not just a receiver from messages, but also a 'source' because of the role it plays in encoding. After all, media professionals have a certain view of their audience, which influences their messages. But audiences also had opportunities of being active in the decoding phase. According to Hall, there were three types of decoding: *dominant* decoding (the prevailing, common sense, and 'natural' view of things), *oppositional* decoding (a resistant reading frame) and *negotiated* decoding (being a contradictory mixture of opposition and adaptation)[47].

Hall's theories started a new form of critical media research that seriously questioned the theories of ideology and reproduction of dominant meanings and functional analysis. It resulted in a series of television inquiries in the late 1970's and 1980's of which the most 'famous' -and cited- is *Every Day Television: Nationwide* by Charlotte Brunsdon and David Morley[48].

The 1970's meant a turning point in media studies and indicated the shift towards the study of the audience and popular culture.

2.2   The audience research tradition

McQuail (1997, 2000) distinguishes three main approaches in audience research: *structural, behavioral (or functionalist)* and *social-cultural (or contextual)*.

The structural tradition focuses on *audience measurement* and typologies of audiences. The behavioral tradition employs a twofold orientation towards *effects* (stimulus response theories) and, in reply to this orientation, towards *media use* that includes its derived 'gratifications and uses' theory.
The social cultural tradition, also called cultural reception analysis or reception research, is about the social cultural use of media and the use of media related to everyday life.

---

[46] Antonio Gramsci 1891-1937 Secretary General of the P.C.I. (the socialist party of Italy) was arrested in 1926 under the fascist dictatorship of Mussolini and kept in isolation for almost a year before he was sentenced to 20 years of prison. In 1929, despite illness and deplorable circumstances, he started writing his prison diaries that were smuggled to Moscow after his death. In his reflections on culture the concepts of hegemony (ruling ideology) and cultural reproduction played a prominent role. Gramsci interpreted culture as an instrument of social reproduction in the struggle for hegemony, thereby criticizing the Marxist view of culture as being just a spin-off from economy. Hegemony, the ruling ideology in a society, acts in such a way that it appears 'natural', and, therefore, is unquestioned. Moreover, people unconsciously reproduce this ideology and legitimize and maintain it. Cf. the theory of Paulo Freire's *Pedagogy of the Oppressed*.
[47] Alasuutari 1999 attributes four 'ideal-type' positions, from which decodings can be made, to Hall. Next to dominant, negotiated and oppositional codes there is the *professional code*, which is employed by professional broadcasters in transmitting messages that are already signified in a hegemonic way.
[48] Brunsdon C. and Morley D. 1978. *Every Day Television: Nationwide*. London: BFI.

In this tradition, Alasuutari (1999) mentions three generations of reception studies: *reception research* (encoding/decoding); *audience ethnography* and the most recent emerging trend of the *constructionist view* with a broadened focus on *media culture*.

In this section, we will discuss the different approaches mentioned and describe the process in which a shift took place from attention fixed on effects and use of mass media to the insights of media culture as part of social reality.

2.2.1   The structural approach

Structural research is the earliest -and largest- version of audience studies. It is directed at insights about structural statistics of the audience, such as size and composition. Media industries, on commercial grounds, need to 'know' -as exactly as possible- their actual or potential audience. In the daily competition for subscriptions and ratings, by these statistics they hope to safeguard their main source of income, which is paid advertising. Currently, it is not only the commercial media that are concerned with these statistical research results, public broadcasters are as well. (See 1.1).

Because of the huge commercial interests, structural audience research became intertwined with an even larger advertising and market research apparatus. It developed over time and often operates internationally, crossing geographical, political, and cultural borders.

Next to measuring reach (which is important to advertising), McQuail (2000) identifies manipulation and channeling of audience choice behavior and the identification of audience markets as one of the main goals of audience research.

Mattelart & Mattelart (1998:126) point to the fact that: '(...) contemporary cybernetic rationality requires knowledge to manage not just production, but consumption as well. The consumer, once *terra incognita*, indeed becomes both the subject and object of research, as demonstrated by the sharp rise in the use of techniques to measure consumer 'targets' and life styles – techniques that are constantly refined through computerized production technologies and the storage of data on individuals and groups. The action informed by knowledge exercised on consumers, attempts to decompose their movements and sound out their needs and desires. The knowledge of these movements and desires informs and feeds the circular movement of programming, production and consumption, which, though always unstable, tends none the less towards the functional and affective integration of the consumer into the mechanisms of the market economy'.

It goes without saying that critical theory berated structural audience research for suppressing, exploiting and violating the audience, which to their opinion was an innocent victim of capitalist, consumerist forces.

Interesting in this respect is the provocative theory of the Canadian scholar Dallas Smythe,[49] who claims that audiences are produced by television, sold to advertisers as a kind of commodity, and -to top it all- literally pay the price. In this way, they 'work' for advertisers. The process begins as people watch television. The fact that they are watching -unpaid- is then sold in the form of ratings to advertisers. Subsequently, the

---

[49] Smythe, D.W. 1977. 'Communications: blind spot of Western Marxism' in *Canadian Journal of Political and Social Theory* I: 120-7.

audience has to pay the price. Marketing and advertisement costs are added to products, which they are -by the same advertisers-prompted to buy. Not only this working for free -but also even paying for it- is the absolute definition of economic exploitation. This type of audience research, is an implement of control and manipulation.

The feminist communication scientist, Ien Ang, in her book, *Desperately Seeking the Audience,* makes this point as well[50]. She argues that mainstream audience research tradition is only interested in the audience as far as it is commercially relevant (which goes no further than proving its existence.)

Nevertheless, according to McQuail (1997), the structural approach theoretically remains important for its contribution, among other things, to effects research (when data on opinion, attitude or behavior are related to demographic and media use data); to research that studies the flow of an audience over channels and content types; to determine audience typologies, and to relate media use to social background.

And however the bulk of audience analysis may be about control, even structural audience theory progressively shifted its focus on the perspective of the receiver. 'Despite this overall imbalance and general disconnection of research effort, the clearest line of development in audience theory has been a move away from the perspective of the media communicator and towards that of the receiver. It seems as if media industry has also accepted this as a pragmatic trend as a result of the steadily increasing competition for audience attention', (McQuail 2000:365).

2.2.2   The behavioral approach

The vast amount of inquiries on television and violence -and even greater disagreement- perhaps made effect studies the most extensively researched part of media analysis.

The history of effects research (see 2.1.1) shows a development from a fairly 'uncomplicated' view of media impact on the audience to an increasingly complicated one. Starting from direct 'stimulus-response' theories, media impact successively was found to be related to: psychological factors, personal contacts, social environment, media structure, institutional and historical conditions, audience needs, motives for media choice and media use, socialization, questions of gender and ethnicity, lifestyle and everyday life.

The role of the audience changed, accordingly, from a (manipulated) passive victim over a negotiator/decoder to an active powerful interpreter. Even this would appear to be too narrow of a framework, as the audience, in most recent theory, is linked to a complex web of media culture (see 2.2.4).

The phenomenon of 'effects' also became subject to more sophisticated descriptions, varying from levels (individual, group, social institution, the whole society, culture) to kinds of effects (cognitive, affective or behavioral) or types of effects, such as Klapper's conversion, minor change and reinforcement (see 2.1.1).
McQuail (2000:424) identifies six main types of media-induced change, which are: intended change, unintended change, and minor change, facilitate change, reinforce

---

[50] Ang, Ien. 1991. *Desperately Seeking the* Audience. London, Routledge.

what exists and prevent change, each feasible to occur at any of the levels mentioned above.
Even this does not exhaust the distinctions. Effects can also be opposite to what was intended such as 'boomerang' effects, or (turning up much later), 'sleeper' effects, third party effects (they may be thought to influence others, but not me), or 'reciprocal' effects (effects that occur as a consequence of the fact that somebody or something is covered by media.)

This brings McQuail to map out the main media effect processes according to intention and time co-ordinates.

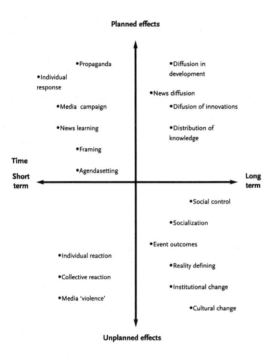

Figure 2.6 A typology of media effects. (McQuail 2000:426)

Media do not 'just' disseminate messages or news. They go beyond that in both 'impact' and in time scale. In the late 1960's and 1970's, theories appeared on *agenda setting, the spiral of silence,* and *the cultivation theory.*
Agenda setting is the process by which the media, by selecting issues, 'decide' what is 'on the agenda' and thus determine public debate and public opinion in society. The agenda setting theory was criticized in the 1980's and 1990's. The final conclusion according to McQuail seems to be 'likely, but not convincingly proven'[51].

---

[51] The agenda setting theory originates from McCombs, M.E. and Shaw, D.L. 1972. 'The agenda-setting function of the press' in *Public Opinion Quarterly*, 36:176-87. For main criticisms on the theory see: McQuail 2000:455-457.

Elisabeth Noelle-Neumann[52] developed the hypothesis of the spiral of silence, in which mass media 'guide' people to what they presume are the dominant meanings in society. Because people do not wish to become isolated, they will be sensitive to the climate of what is 'correct' and avoid overt expression of deviating opinions. In this way these alternatives become increasingly 'silenced', in a descending spiral.

George Gerbner's cultivation theory[53] (which we discussed in 1.2.2), is another theory on long-term media effects. He refers to the same process, but developed it in another direction, by identifying the role of media in maintaining dominant culture in a process of cultivation and acculturation.

Cultivation analysis, a combination of content and audience analysis, traces the televised view of reality -in fictional and factual programs- and compares it to views of the audience and the degree of television exposure.

Content analysis not only identifies units in a communication system, it also reveals embedded values. If for example women are rendered according to features concerning their appearance, family or personal circumstances during a report on their business or political career, this tells us something about underlying gender roles and cultivated views of women[54].

Gerbner combined content analysis (to examine embedded values in culture) to semantic differential audience analysis in order to analyze the cultivation of the mediated values in the audience.

His cultivation theory -and the Cultural Indicators Paradigm in general- was much debated. Issues concerned the assumed accumulation, socialization, active construction of meaning by the viewer, the causality between television use and values and opinions, and the complexity of interrelated symbolic structures, views and attitudes.

The behavioral tradition was not only oriented toward effects, but also toward *media use*, which of course co-conditions any effects of media. The first studies in this direction, 'satisfaction' studies among radio listeners, appeared in the 1940's and were conducted by Lazarsfeld and Stanton (see 2.1.1).

In the 1960's and 1970's, the approach was regenerated, especially in studies on media use by children. After functionalist sociology had been severely criticized by semiotic as well as critical theory and audience ethnographic studies (see 2.2.3.1) began to emerge, which underlined the criticism of the 'passive' receiver, studies on media use flourished. This time the effects of 'all powerful media' and the underlying instrumental view of Laswell's theory were relativized. Therefore, Mattelart & Mattelart (1998) identify this as a next phase in media research.

---

[52] Noelle-Neumann, E. 1984. *The Spiral of Silence.* Chicago, University of Chicago Press. In 1974 she published a first article on this subject: 'The spiral of Silence: a theory of public opinion' in: *Journal of Communication,* 24:24-51.

[53] Gerbner, G. 1973. 'Cultural indicators – the third voice' in Gerbner G., Gross L. and Melody. W. (eds.) *Communications Technology and Social Policy.* New York: Wiley, 553-573.

[54] Interesting in this regard are the research results of the Swedish Media Panel Program, a longitudinal study of media use by children and adolescents conducted at the University of Lund. According to these studies, television viewing (and the foundations of media habits are formed at early age) effects self-esteem. This is not only restricted to childhood, but is found in adulthood as well. For boys, television viewing and self-esteem are positively related in spirals of mutual influence. For girls and young women, there is a negative relationship. Television 'helps' to locate young people at different positions within societal structure (women at lower positions) and to maintain gender roles. For an extensive description of the media Panel Program and a list of (English) publications from it, see Rosengren 2000:152-169.

The broad stream of this kind of research became known as the *uses and gratifications* approach. The first ones to publish in this area were E. Katz and J. G. Blumler, who edited *The Uses of Mass Communications* [55] in 1974.

The uses and gratifications approach focuses on motives for choices that people make in selecting certain media or media content. It assumes an audience, which actively, rationally, and intentionally chooses its media use based on its needs. To Blumler and Katz these needs are social by origin. As media fulfill societal needs, like cohesion or transferring culture, people satisfy their needs e.g. for information or relaxation by their media use. In this sense, media use offers 'gratifications' to its users. However not only on a cognitive level by providing information. People use media for multiple reasons: relaxation, diversion, companionship, to 'ease' social contacts (media as a subject to talk about), social belonging (fandom or lifestyle), to escape daily burden of life, or simply habit. Media can also be used to structure people's everyday practices or patterns.

With respect to audience motivations, McQuail, Blumler and Brown[56] and McQuire[57] (respectively in 1972 and 1974) identified a typology of media person interactions based on people's needs of diversion (escape, emotional release), personal relationships (companionship, social utility), personal identity (self reference, reality exploration, value reinforcement), surveillance (information seeking) (McQuail et al.), and cognitive/affective needs related to an active/passive, external/internal, growth/stability orientation (McGuire), which lead to 16 different types of motivation.

The research method applied by the uses and gratifications approach is similar to semantic differential analysis. Starting from an unstructured sample discussion, motives for (e.g.) watching television are traced and randomly noted in a questionnaire to which the research population is asked to express their approval or disapproval. McQuail Blumler and Brown, in their study on the use of quizzes[58], found four main gratifications: *self-rating, social interaction, excitement* and *education*.

In the 1980's, attempts were made to develop a non-functionalist approach to account for media use. The functionalist thesis was found to be difficult to prove. The motivation of the audience was far more complicated, subjective, inconsistent, less rational, less conscious, and weaker than had been assumed. Age proved to be an important factor. A.S. Babrow[59] pointed to reflexive media choice (habit) and the existence of general concepts of interpretation that guide media choice.

McQuail brings the dual spring of audience choice together by integrating 'media side' factors and 'audience side' factors in one model. Media factors include: the media system (availability), structures of media provision (patterns), available content options (formats and genres), media publicity (advertising, marketing), and timing and presentation (competition strategies). Audience factors concern: social cultural background (milieu, personal attributes like gender, lifestyle, level of income etc.),

---

[55] Beverly Hills, CA: Sage. In 1955 Lazarsfeld and Katz already published a study on people's choice of films: *Personal Influence: The Part Played by People in the Flow of Mass Communication* based on surveys from 1945. Glencoe, Ill. Free Press, 1970. See also 2.1.1 on the two-step flow of communication theory.

[56] McQuail D., Blumler J.G., & Brown, J. W. 1972. 'The television audience, a revised perspective' in D. McQuail (ed.), *Sociology of mass communications*. Harmondsworth, UK: Penguin, 135 –164. See McQuail 1997, 2000.

[57] McQuire, W.J. (1974). 'Psychological motives and communication gratifications' in J.G. Blumler & E. Katz (eds.) *The uses of Mass Communications*. Beverly Hills, CA: Sage, 167 - 196. See McQuail 1997, 2000.

[58] See note 53.

[59] Babrow A.S. (1988). 'Theory and method in research on audience motives' in *Journal of Broadcasting and Electronic Media*, 32 (4), 471-87.

media-related needs, personal tastes and preferences, general habits of leisure-time media use (of which economic potential is a part), awareness (of availability of choices and information), specific context of use (sociability and location), and chance (media exposure).

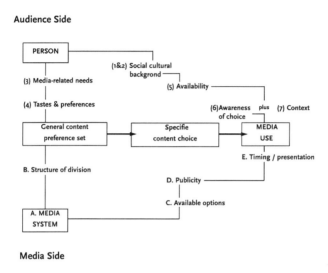

Audience Side

Media Side

Figure 2.7 An Integrated Model of the Process of Media Choice (McQuail 1997:77)

The process by which people actually choose, according to McQuail, has to do with '*a general content preference set*', formed at early age and remaining fairly consistent. Audience 'roles' and 'mental' sets, to which we will get back in 2.2.4. when we turn to media culture and the related constructionist view, also impact their choice.

2.2.3   The social cultural approach

By breaking with the paradigm of media effects and underlining the activity of the audience by choosing and using media to gratify needs, the uses and gratifications approach -notwithstanding appropriate criticism- brought about greater attention to the role of the audience.
In semiotics and critical theory -especially cultural studies- this role was an important theme as well. Especially in *cultural reception analysis*, which pursued the questions that were raised in the uses and gratifications paradigm.
The cultural reception approach -that bears a resemblance with semiotics- builds on Stuart Hall's concept of encoding and decoding (see 2.1.3) and grants the audience the possibility of *reading*[60] media texts differently, according to personal experiences and culture. Instead of the behaviorist view, in which communication is seen as a process that involves effects, uses and gratifications, this analysis focuses on the interpretation

---

[60] Mattelart and Mattelart 1998 and Alasuutari (1999) both point to the influence of German literary studies -especially the work of Hans Robert Jauss-, which in the 1960's introduced the question of reader and reception; the subject had earlier been mentioned by Jean Paul Sartre (*Qu'est-ce que la literature?* 1947) and by Umberto Eco (*The Open Work*, original Italian version 1962).

that people derive from messages when they 'co-determine' content and effects. Reception, in this way, is not just a 'technical thing' as it was in the linear view of communication, but a 'semiotic' thing; people actively make meaning of the message they get. Hall pointed out they could even do this in an oppositional way and resist the intention of the communicator. Received messages are not necessarily the same as sent messages. Neither are received messages equal to internalized messages. Furthermore, people decode differently, which leaves room for different interpretations of the same message.

To John Fiske, this line of thinking was a source for developing the concepts of *semiotic power*, *intertextuality* and *polysemity*. Even if people are economically and socially subordinated, they still have the cultural power to resist preferred perceptions or subliminal dominant meanings within messages or programs. In the end, they decide the meaning since they 'produce' the text. The term 'text' in Fiske's usage does not refer to the common language use of text as a message, but to the moment in which the receiver interacts with content and by reading and interpreting the message, 'produces' its meaning. Only then a message becomes a 'text'. Production is not just a matter of communicator, but also -or even more perhaps- of the receiver. Since different interpretations are possible, any text in principle is polysemic, i.e. can bear a *'prosumer'* variety of meanings.

Intertextuality has to do with the interconnectedness of meanings of different media outlets or genres. Fictional programs, for example, may influence our perception of news information or factual programs on a similar subject. In this respect, the strict distinction between elite culture and popular culture could no longer be held. Whereas earlier in media research *'mass'* culture always had been viewed as a denigrated form produced by mass media in a mass society, now *popular* culture became a subject of increasing attention and valuation. Especially due to the work of Fiske. It also meant a shift from research on 'serious' factual content, like news programs, towards popular fictional content like soap opera's. According to Fiske, especially the latter category of popular media culture is by necessity inherently *polysemic* in order to be able to be 'popular,' i.e. of the people, liked by the people and dependent on their semiotic power.

An example of early television decoding studies is D. Morley's, *The Nationwide Audience: Structure and Decoding*[61]. Its title reveals how much it derived from and rested on Hall's differential decoding and the assumption of the audience as an interpretative community.
Another example, of decoding popular content, is Tamar Liebes' and Elihu Katz's research of the television series, 'Dallas'[62]. However this study strictly is to be situated within the uses and gratifications flow in the 1980's, this approach also addressed receiver's activity and developed its own notion of meaning. That notion was generated in 'interaction' by the concept of 'negotiated reading'. (Interaction between text and audience or receiver *roles* that are determined by culture and by personal experience).

---

[61] Morley. D. 1980. London: British Film Institute. In his later work Morley is much more critical of the interpretative capacity of the audience to resist hegemonic meanings. Morley D. 1997. 'Theoretical orthodoxies: textualism, constructivism and the "new ethnography" in cultural studies' in M. Ferguson and P. Golding (eds.) *Cultural Studies in Question*. London: Sage, pp. 121-37. In an article on the third generation of reception studies he points tot the fact that in his own development of thinking and his shift of paradigm he did not 'abandon' the analysis of program interpretations, but rather 'reframed' the decoding paradigm within the new focus of the domestic context. Morley 1999:197.
[62] Liebes T. and Katz E. 1990. *The Export of Meaning: Cross-Cultural Readings of 'Dallas'*. Oxford: Oxford University Press.

Since 'Dallas' was broadcasted all over the world, Liebes and Katz researched cross-cultural 'readings' of Dallas in Israeli society (Russian Israeli, Arab citizens, Moroccan Jews and Israeli born *kibbutzniks*), Americans in Los Angeles (second generation) and Japanese in Japan. The idea was that membership within different national and ethnic communities might account for differential decoding of the program. Analyzing the discussion of groups after they watched a sample episode of 'Dallas', Liebes and Katz counted the amount of *referential* reading statements (the program and the characters are related to and meaningful in real life) and *critical* reading statements (the program is seen as a fictional construction). They found significant group/ethnic differences in the reading of the program.

Alasuutari (1999:15) criticizes Liebes' and Katz's approach for methodological problems. 'Although codes such as 'referential' and 'critical' can quite reliably be identified in interview texts, a major problem in Liebes and Katz's study is that they equate the two types of discourse with two kinds of perceiving or 'reading' *Dallas* as a programme. It is simply assumed that individuals who predominantly speak about the episode by referential utterances take the programme as real.
This hasty equation of interview talk with a decoding of a programme or with cognitive structures inherent in a culture or 'interpretive community' is challenged in present-day media research, influenced by different trends of discourse analyses'.

Except for its methodology and being insufficient in its results, first generation reception studies were also criticized for overestimating the potential power of the audience to resist dominant meanings in media texts. For concentrating too much on the psychological moment of decoding, for relating reception only to an interpretative individual/community and neglecting the social aspect of media use and reception in daily life.

The second generation of the social cultural approach, *audience ethnography*, made up for this deficiency.

2.2.3.1 Audience ethnography

Two works of David Morley might best illustrate the shift towards a new paradigm. In his study on *The Nationwide Audience* (1980), he focused on the interpretation of a television programme by a decoding audience. Emphasis was on the interaction between a viewer and the content of the programme.
Six years later, he published *Family Television: Cultural Power and Domestic Leisure* [63] on the reception and consumption of media within the domestic context. In a qualitative, in-depth study among eighteen (white) working class families in London, Morley explored the interaction of family members with television. The focus of this study did not ask what the viewer does with the content offered, and if he/she is capable of resisting the preferred meaning the communicator wants him to adopt. Instead it asked: what is the role of the social use of television within the natural context and practice of family viewing? And does this social use or social context of viewing influence reception? If so, meaning would not be only a matter of individual interpretation, but -also- would have to do with contextual factors.

Morley's findings did point in this direction. His study showed when people watched, the role television played in their leisure time, and the many unwritten rules that guided

---

[63] Morley, D. 1986. *Family television: Cultural Power and Domestic Leisure*. London, Comedia

family viewing. It also revealed the differentiation in media use and receiving practices, and the existence of unequal power relationships between men and women when it came to the question of who was in charge of choosing the programs to watch.

This illustration is an exact map of the transition from cultural reception research to audience ethnography.

By Morley's approach, it became clear that the first generation of reception studies (which were focused on effects and interpretations) was framed too narrowly. Gradually, the reception paradigm shifted to a new *audience ethnography paradigm*.
Central to this paradigm, according to Alasuutari (1999), are three points:
media use and reception are part of social reality. A reality that cultural media studies had neglected. The functioning of a medium and the social use made of it, therefore, need more attention, whereas programme content deserves less;
research has to start from the audience 'end' i.e. everyday life to which the use of media is related, instead of taking reception in an interpretative community as point of departure;
a growing interest is shown in identity politics (gender, race and ethnicity) and fictional programs.

Morley (1999:195-205), with respect to the changes from the first to the second generation of media studies, notes a simultaneous shift from factual to fictional media forms; questions of knowledge to questions of pleasure; programme contents to media functions; conventional to identity politics; and matters of class to race, ethnicity, and gender.

With regard to the relationship that he was interested in between media use/reception and power roles within the family, Morley owed inspiration and insights to contemporary feminist media studies.
British feminist, film critic had published an article on the masculine identification of pleasure in Hollywood films[64] (1975), thereby stimulating new research and reflection on the interaction of media text, context and female audience.

Though not restricted to those, media genres that were specifically produced for or aimed at women -e.g. woman's magazines, romance fiction and soap opera's- became the subject of feminist media research. Scholars did pioneering work in feminist media studies, such as Janice Radway, Ann Kaplan and Tania Modleski in the US; Charlotte Brunsdon and Marjorie Ferguson in Great Britain; and Ien Ang, Joke Hermes and Liesbeth van Zoonen in the Netherlands[65]. So did Jacqueline Bobo and Ellen Seiter in their research among colored woman and they criticized the whiteness of feminist and cultural media studies[66].

---

[64] Mulvey L. 1975. 'Visual Pleasure and Narrative Cinema' in *Screen*, vol. 16, no. 3.
[65] Brunsdon C. (1981). 'Crossroads: Notes on a Soap Opera' in *Screen* vol. 22, no. 4; Modleski, T. (1982). *Loving with a Vengeance: Mass-Produced Fantasies for* Women. London: Methuen; Ferguson, M. (1983). *Forever Feminine: Women's Magazines and the Cult of Femininity*. London, Heinemann; Radway, J. (1984). *Reading the Romance*. Cpale Hill, NC: University of North Carolina Press; Ang I. 1985. *Watching 'Dallas': Soap Opera and the Melodramatic Imagination*. London Methuen; Zoonen L. van, 1988. 'Rethinking women and the news' in *European Journal of Communication* 3 (1): 35-52 and (1994) *Feminist Media Studies*, London: Sage; Kaplan, E.A. 1992. 'Feminist critiques and television' in Allen, R.C. (ed.), *Channels of Discourse Reassembled*, pp. 247-83. London, Routledge; Hermes J. 1995. *Reading Women's' Magazines*. Cambridge, Polity;
[66] Bobo, J. 1988. 'The Colour Purple: Black Women as Cultural Readers' in Pibram, E.D (ed.), *Female Spectators: Looking at Film and Television*. London: Verso; Seiter, E. (ed.) (1989). *Remote Control*.

Those studies directed attention to the gendered differentiation of media production and media use, the social construction of gender and its influence on media choice, and the emancipatory potential of popular media culture and the pleasure of media reception.

Ethnographic research examined the use of romance fiction, women's magazines and soap opera's and pointed out a wide range of motives. These genres, according to women themselves, (e.g.) offered privacy (time and space for themselves), emotional comfort (ideal romance), support (images and role models), personal reflection, and sociability (topic for conversation).

But research also highlighted socially and culturally held judgmental repertoires on media use; for example, the notion that television viewing is such an 'idle waste of time' that women feel guilty sitting and watching and therefore combine viewing with household work (men on the other hand after a 'hard days work' deserve some relaxing viewing). The soap opera genre with its narrative continuity appears to be 'born' for women, fitting smoothly into their fragmented 'domestic daily round'. Another example of this repertoire is the valuation of factual news programs over fiction, or 'serious' women's magazines over gossip rags, which include respective feelings of 'duty' and 'guilt'.

Female audience hood   -or one might say gendered audience hood in general-, appeared to be co-determined by an intermingled jumble of daily routines, a certain offer of content, and social structures of patriarchal society.

McQuail (1997) points out the early acquirement of audience hood in social/cultural practice. Identification, reinforced by media, plays an important role in this process. Family, peer groups, social contacts and gender, socialize media use -including normative frames-.
How people assess and use media depends on complex -mostly unarticulated- social and situational factors that shape routine practices.

Reception and meaning of content, therefore, are far more dependent on experiences, perceptions and social location of audience members than previously assumed by early reception research. Decoding is not merely a matter of oppositional or dominant reading, but also of shared perspectives within a community.

Summarizing the main features of the culturalist (reception) tradition of audience research[67], McQuail arrives at the following six points:

- 'the media text has to be "read" through the perceptions of its audience, which constructs meanings and pleasures from the media texts offered (and these are never fixed or predictable);
- the very process of media use, and the way in which it unfolds in a particular context, are central objects of interest;
- media use is typically situation-specific and oriented to social tasks that evolve out of participation in "interpretative communities";

London: Routledge; Bobo J. and Seiter E. 1991. 'Black Feminism and Media Criticism: "The Women of Brewster Place" in Screen, 32 (3); Bobo J. 1994. Black Women as Cultural Readers. New York: Columbia University Press.
[67] According to McQuail (1997:19, 2000:367) reception analysis is no independent tradition, but 'the audience research arm of modern cultural studies'.

- audiences for particular media genres often comprise separate "interpretative communities" that share much the same forms of discourse and frameworks for making sense of media;
- audiences are never passive, nor are all their members equal since some will be more experienced or more active than others;
- methods have to be "qualitative" and deep, often ethnographic, recognizing content, act of reception, and context together (Lindlof, 1991)'. (McQuail:1997:19; 2000:367).

Since the interrelationship between media and social cultural experience is obvious, the need to reorient to audience-hood, as part of common social, gendered experience and interaction is self-evident.

According to Ann Gray (1999), the contribution of feminist scholarship to the study of audiences is that it forced this new paradigm to be placed on the agenda. The existing male, white, academic, dominant paradigm of the 'public knowledge project', with its 'neutral' focus on factual media and its naturalization of hierarchical and gendered division, which was simply accepted, no longer holds the exclusive right.

The new audience studies of the 'popular culture knowledge project' understand media reception and meaning in terms of social/cultural conditions, actual viewing and reading contexts, power relations, the role of media use in daily life, access, gender, race, ethnicity and the role of media technologies in constructing gendered and classed identities.

Thus macrostructures of media and microstructures of viewing are related. These structures have to do with power. Media use and meaning are part of a complex process in which a variety of public and private discourses play their role. Studying audiences is no longer a 'simplified' matter, for it must take all these currents into account, also methodologically.

This enormous task is to be done by the emergent third generation of reception research that recently tries to examine and contour this gigantic new landscape.

2.2.4   Media culture and the discursive audience construct

Whether or not the changes one witnesses in his or her lifetime are of decisive historical importance always remains a question to be answered definitely by the future. The same applies for shifts in scientific approaches. Nevertheless, there is a reasonable expectation that the third generation of audience studies will be a shift with serious impact.
Since it emerged recently (by the end of the 1980's and during the 1990's), there is no well-rounded paradigm to describe the novelty of it. But in the process of taking shape, there are some points to recognize.

Sketched in broad outlines, the most central point seems to be that of *media culture* and media *discourse*. Because of the increasing importance of media and information and communication technologies (and of mediation and communication) in contemporary society and their intertwinement with culture, (see 1.2) we might speak of media culture. In this media culture, there is a 'go-round' of a variety of media and audience 'discourses'.
Among media professionals (e.g.) there is a discourse about the audience members to whom they broadcast their programs. This discourse may well interfere with programme

policymaking and the producing of content that makes this discourse important to reception research and audience ethnography.

Audiences, themselves, share visions of media in general and of their media use in particular. Often these have to do with moral stances. This discourse is likely to influence (e.g.) their media choice and perception of content. So the discourse on media also concerns reception research.

Media scholars have their own analytical outlook when researching audience behavior, which may well influence the outcome of their research or the development of theories and models. The position of research in this respect not only matters to ethnographic reception studies, but it is also at stake, since it is one of the discourses itself.

And media industries, trying to track down the audience as accurate as possible, put its discourse 'on the market' which is likely to interfere with other discourses as well.

The novelty of the third generation of reception and audience ethnography studies is twofold. First, it recognizes the self-perception of the audience -the notion audience members have of themselves as being in the audience- as a discourse. And this discourse is one among others in media culture. Second, it broadens its frame of audience reception to the wide context of this media culture, or better media cultures that have different discourses on media and audiences. This means that it relates (e.g.) questions of meaning not only to decoding capabilities or to domestic viewing practices, but also to the role that media play in the daily life of media culture and its different discourses. I.e. it relates its issues to a broad and complex context of different discourses that each 'construct' the audience according to their own views and/or needs.

That is why audience research cannot be restricted to decoding studies, or in-depth qualitative ethnographic analysis, but must be a 'multidimensional' undertaking, which includes a central role for discourse analysis.

It then follows that, when it comes to theory and methodology, -and perhaps this might be seen as the third novelty- a complementary approach is needed, which exists of qualitative and quantitative methods. (We will get back to this later).

A good example of a discursive layer between individuals and media culture on the role of media figures in identity construction, is given by Joke Hermes (1999). She argues that popular media figures fulfill an intermediating function by linking the 'abstract' of the media text to the concrete daily reality and viewing practice of the audience. This is not a 'neutral' happening. Involved are production routines and ideologies on the one side and everyday repertoires in media reception by the audience on the other side. One of those production routines is 'personalization'. Two objectives are met in this routine. It meets the audience interest in stories -which need a central character to tell them- and at the same time it gives the audience an opportunity to identification, which is very important in the process of meaning making. Therefore, Identification is not just an individual achievement, but part of a process that motivates formation of meaning. In this process, popular media figures are 'anchors'.

Hermes 1999 stresses that practices of identification and meaning making are gendered at different levels, both in the praxis of everyday life and in the abstract and theoretical level. Media figures link those levels and give the viewer entrance to the intermediate level of
-gendered- meaning production. Hermes criticizes both the modern production ideology of quality news and the post-modern production ideology of commercial media production, because both discourses have strongly sexist connotations.

Popular media figures not only play a role in individual identification and meaning making, but also in the creation of collective community identity. Hermes 1999 takes tabloid reading as an example and identifies two 'repertoires'. By reading gossip on popular media figures, people extend their private life by drawing those figures into an imaginary enlarged community (the extended family repertoire). But the gossip also tells them something about the 'meaning' of life by making the misery, happiness and drama of the media figures public. These events compare to their everyday life with its ambiguities, frustrations, ambitions, complexity of relations, etc. (the melodrama repertoire). Especially after 'shocking' events -for example, the death of a royal or celebrity- this repertoire creates community. But also in 'normal' circumstances, reading and talking about gossip with others creates a sense of belonging and shared moral values.

So media figures, audiences, identity construction and meaning formation are connected. How the audience relates to a mass media text is embedded in specific social relations as well as in the discursive role played by media figures. Meaning production is not just a matter of media production and audience practice. Every media genre has its own sets of repertoires and so does the audience. Third generation research has to deal with the intersection of all of them and, in addition, with repertoires outside the scope of audience and production.

Hermes' book, *Reading Women's Magazines*[68], is an example of a 'third generation' study.
Research on meaning production in this type of study is not necessarily focused only on content, but includes (e.g.) interview texts as a research object in its own right, because it provides information about the different discourses that interfere in the process of meaning making.

As mentioned before, this inclusive -or multi-dimensional approach- calls for a methodology that is capable of simultaneously considering the broad range of aspects indicated in third generation reception studies and audience ethnography.
Kim Christian Schrøder (1999), therefore, argues in favor of one research design in which quantitative and qualitative traditions are brought together and requirements of validity, reliability and generalization are met.
Due to the rivalry of both paradigms, this is not an easy task.
The quantitative method of the uses and gratifications approach was criticized by cultural ethnography not only for ignoring the everyday social context of media use, but also on methodological grounds since survey questionnaires and statistical measurement were low in validity.

The qualitative method used by media ethnography was criticized for not being representative. Critics doubted the reliability of qualitative in-depth research results that were most likely valid as far as the studied object concerned, but that in no way were -or could be- generalized.

Therefore, the best feasibility when it comes to a combination of the two seemed to be the creation of a type of 'inter-paradigm' in which both models mutually supplemented each other.

Schrøder 1999 rejects this 'junction by triangulation' because of epistemological issues. Quantitative methods prevail in functional, administrative research, while qualitative

---

[68] Hermes, J. 1995. *Reading Women's Magazines.* Cambridge: Polity.

methods dominate phenomenological, hermeneutical, critical research. Shaping them in a triangle does not resolve the tension from underlying premises. According to Schrøder, only a truly integrated model can overcome rivalry problems and account for the challenges posited by third generation reception and audience ethnography studies. Needed is a theoretical framework, which specifies how both methods approach the same object.

Schrøder performed such an integrated approach in his case study of media use in Denmark.[69] He related media use in everyday life to participation in democratic processes. This research departs from validity, but combines qualitative data collection and analysis with procedures that try to ensure reliability and generalization. Reliability, according to Schrøder, can be met by a very systematic and consistent description of steps in analysis and procedures followed in measurement and interpretation (including underlying assumptions). This is to be checked upon by the observation of others. Therefore, (e.g.) extensive quotations of interview transcripts must be available. All data and processes of analysis must be allowed for in order to facilitate scrutiny; either by different members of the research team, who independently redo the same analysis, or by 'external auditing' from scholarly peers. By generalizing data into categories according to a similar procedure, one can try to meet demands of representativeness.

Morley (1999) endorses Schrøder's view by making a plea for the use of a range of different methodological perspectives instead of the superiority of one over others.

But as mentioned in the beginning of this section, no well-rounded paradigm has yet occurred. Rosengren (2000:23) points to the *essential* interplay of theory, formal models and empirical data for any communication research current to develop.

'(...) it does not seem far-fetched to predict that in the near future an enterprising group of communication scholars will concentrate on the highly strategic variables to be found in the substantive theories of so-called qualitative reception analysis. Aiming at empirical and theoretical generalization, they will start the laborious work of
relating the substantive theories to relevant formal models;
translating the variables into empirical measurements, applicable in studies of representative samples drawn from carefully defined populations under carefully defined circumstances and
analyzing the empirical data in terms of both substantive theories and formal models'.

As with these methodological questions, third generation reception and audience ethnography research in general, according to Morley (1999:197), has to reframe emphases of earlier approaches rather than abandon them. In summarizing the shift from first to second and from second to third generation studies, he states this 'reframing' is crucial.

'(...) to attempt to move towards a model of media consumption capable of dealing simultaneously with the transmission of programmes/contents/ideologies (the vertical dimension of power) and with their inscription in the everyday practices through which media content is incorporated into daily life (the horizontal dimension of ritual and participation). (...) similarly, the transition (if such there be) from a second to a third generation of reception studies should be one in which that emphasis on viewing

---

[69] Schrøder, K.C. *Danskerne og Medierne: Dagligdag og Demokrati* (The Danes and the Media: Daily Life and Democracy), Report for the Commission on the Media. Copenhagen, The prime Minister's Office.

practices, rather than itself being abandoned, should now be reframed within the new focus on the broader discourses within which media audiences are themselves constructed and inscribed'.

To the extent that this reframing process and the question of methodology are successfully accomplished by the third generation approach, it will prove whether it is to be a consistent and enduring paradigm of decisive importance. And whether it is capable of parrying criticism of 'depoliticizing' media studies.

Whatever its future may be, reception and audience ethnography paradigms definitely increased the reflection on the perception of audiences.

2.2.4.1 Views on the audience

The many different discourses on media and media culture hold -explicitly or implicitly- as many different perceptions of 'the audience'. Third generation reception and audience ethnography research -for the first time- highlighted the cognition the audience holds of itself, being one of the discourses.

This cognition is interrelated to their perception of media and conversely cannot be dissociated from the perception that media (professionals) hold on audiences. Their view of the audience (e.g.) is part of the discourse on media policy strategies and determines the way media professionals 'inscribe' the audience in media content.

Ingunn Hagen (1999) in regard to media images of the general public -researched in (television) news production studies- qualifies the perception by media professionals as subjective, intuitive and stereotypical. According to Hagen, they simply do not know their audience -except for being a figure in measurement ratings- and lack interest in its opinion on their work, which is disposed of as not being representative. Professionals also lack interest in audience demands, which are regarded to be a threat to professional autonomy. As far as standards, norms, questions of quality and diversity, morals and feedback are concerned, professional peers and institutional customs and traditions provide the model for the way things are done. Otherwise, only external reviews, broadcasting councils and parliamentary debates on media, matter to them as sources of knowledge on the relationship with the audience.

Due to the increase of competition and deregulation however, there is an enormous pressure in all media sectors and genres to reach and hold quantity and, as a consequence, a growing necessity to take the audience into account[70].

The 1990's show the growth of an extensive, technically sophisticated, measurement apparatus, for which excessive amounts of money have been appropriated. Ratings -or 'people meters'- have become dominant criteria (see 2.2.1). Hagen, with regard to this, refers to the position of producers and journalists as 'slaves of the ratings tyranny'.

This ratings tyranny is an important aspect of media policy discourse. Both in commercial as well as in public service broadcasting, which -in the current market situation- is also liable to economic logic.

---

[70] This tendency is accelerated by new interactive media possibilities. The moment Dutch filmmaker The van Gogh was murdered e.g. was pictured by people using their cell phones; within a couple of minutes the images reached the Dutch national press bureau ANP and the national news programs, by e-mail. Broadcasters and editors of newspapers also adjust themselves by creating possibilities for phoning in, taking part in internet polls, sending sms etc. The general editorship of one Dutch daily even established an office hour in the evening, for people to react.

In the former discourse arguments of consumer sovereignty ('give the people what they want') are stressed. High ratings stand for popularity and are considered equal to quality. The view of the audience is that of an individual consumer. This consumer is valuable in terms of the need of attention both to be sold to advertisers and for the sale of products. Programming must be done carefully therefore, i.e. in a least objectionable way, in order to not even lose one viewer.
In the latter discourse, based on what the audience needs (or should want), ratings are used to legitimate the license.

According to Hellman (1999), there are signs of discursive convergence in the argumentations of programme policy by commercial and public service broadcasters that are based on pragmatic considerations. He summarizes this convergence in four points: (1) popularity rules (the share of viewing has to be protected and ratings are generally accepted); (2) money buys (greater exposure to economics); (3) variety is popular (diversity as an economic concept, by competition, and diversity as a cultural pluralist concept converge); (4) duties are shared (commercial broadcasters use public service justifications for prestige and legitimation and public service broadcasters cannot escape popularity (see also 1.4).

Hagen points out that the increase of audience measurement impacts not only programme policy, but also redefines the relationship to the audience. Social or political identification of the audience has become less important. Instead, the individualized and privatized viewer is spotlighted. Because this private individual 'consumer' is not easy to trace -in spite of very sophisticated measurements, which the composers spare no effort to prove the 'scientific reliability'- and the increasing complexity of the audience concept, media and media professionals tend to conform and keep the beaten track in order to make up for uncertainty. They turn to routine programme concepts and specialization in known audience groups, which impedes professional maturation as well as the development of new concepts in both content and audiences.

In this everyday 'routine' programming and production, one of the strategies is to 'inscribe' existing discursive views of the audience and viewing in programme production. This is called *audiencing*. It is an essential part of production habits.

An example of how this is done is given by John Tulloch (1999), who conducted a third generation *ethnographic production* study by researching the everyday work practices (including discourses, frames, rhetoric, schemes and mythologies) of the producers of the Australian soap opera, 'A Country Practice'. Tulloch describes different frames for implying audiences to secure high ratings. Medical and social issues frame the narratives. A broad range of audience is secured by different story lines and sub plots. A serial formula in which romances, daily events and social issues are interwoven in an open-ended way must 'keep the audience hanging in'. Stories and inter-texts (e.g. myths and memories) are carefully balanced, so that different audiences can be 'inscribed'. Directing strategies on the framing of scenes, actors positions, camera use, music etc. 'lead' the audience emotionally, as where careful editing and driving forward the 'momentum' must guide viewers to accept 'heavy' messages or be ready for 'reality'.

Tulloch advocates that we should rethink television communication in terms of *processes* by 'reading the text at the production 'implied audience' moment rather than at the actual audience level'.
His conclusion is that television production works according to a whole range of concepts of its audience. Even within the same production process, audience is not something 'out there' but a plural discursive construct.

Audience measurement is mainly a matter of quantification. Background information such as audience experience, selection, interpretation, use, identification, motivation, attention, appreciation or satisfaction is simply not considered. Thus it produces a fairly limited view of the audience. McQuail (1997, 2000) even doubts the possibility of measuring the audience. He believes it is reconstructed at best. And even then ambiguities remain. Does the measurement of the newspaper audience, for example, refer to the number of subscribers, households reached, or readers? And are casual readers to be included?

Nevertheless, program policies -as well as production routines- are built on this restricted and narrow view. According to Hagen however, 'figures' measurement is not sufficient for this purpose. She argues that a genuine care of audience needs (not the constructed audience as a market, but the real social audience) and communication rights is needed. This compels the more in contemporary media state of affairs, in which public debate and plurality and communication rights are in danger of being overridden by commercial logic. Beyond audience measurement, insights from the new reception research and audience ethnography, should be taken into account and have their implications in institutional practice. Including the image of the audience itself.

2.2.4.2 Views from the audience

In media discourses, the audience remains an institutional construct. It is a measured 'abstract', whether as a commodity to be sold or as a rated figure. It is an object of analysis, but what about the actual audience of flesh and blood?
Third generation reception research and audience ethnography, which delved deeply into the social cultural use of media related to everyday life, also revealed the audience as a subject.

Birgitta Höijer (1999) shows that audience hood -in daily practice of Western society- is often experienced in a complex, ambivalent and contradictory way. This has to do with the fact that audience members in their perception of being part of an audience- referred to by Höijer as *metacognitions*- consider various kinds of social-cultural ideologies, norms and moral codes that are generally held. A striking amount of morality -also based on gender- thus enters into metacognitions and revolves around the concept of activity-passivity.

The first that has to be mentioned is the 'television viewing as an unproductive, passive waste of time' view (see also 2.2.3.1). -According to Höijer 1999, this is a fruit of the Lutheran inheritance with its morality of 'do your duty and work hard'-[71].

The second related topic is the value hierarchy of genres. News and factual programmes are highly valued in society. It is a social duty to be an 'informed citizen'. Behind this is the ideology of news as a political genre. Höijer points out that this ideology is not put into political practice though. Viewing the news is a complex and ambivalent matter. This is especially noticeable with respect to expressed violence in the news. Watching it on the one hand is a necessary social duty of being informed ('that's reality'), and on the

---

[71] A recent striking example of the persistence of this ideology -even in research- is the way in which research bureau, O&S, conducted a survey of 800 Amsterdam young people between 12 – 18.They were asked whether they indeed feel they are "too busy" as the television spots of SIRE (a Dutch foundation which produces charity advertisements) claim. In the research, 'passive occupations such as television viewing and relaxing are not included. Examples that were included are museum visits, sports, and nights out'. Quoted from *Trouw*, 6-02-2003, p. 2.

other hand causes distress. Besides being felt as a duty, people also watch news by daily habit, as a ritual behavior or simply to broaden their knowledge.

Soaps, as an alternative example, are valued as a 'second sort'. Watching this type of programmes is passive, immature and of 'low taste'. Again, this does not withhold people from watching, since behavior does not always follow defined morality. But people are aware of and even hold these moral judgments. They (e.g.) tend to apologize for their viewing or reading of gossip, whereas they have no objection at all about being noticed when reading a 'quality' magazine. A historical example -in my context- of how these ideologies work, is the transposition of popular magazines to the bottom of the pile in protestant culture, when the deacon or minister was to pay his yearly visit. (Which were -of course- cheerfully read afterwards). Just as people read gossip-magazines only 'at the hairdresser's'.
Obviously, this value hierarchy reflects collectively adopted moral codes independent of programmes. An interesting question is what will be the consequence of the convergence of the different media discourses previously mentioned on moral codes and ideologies.

Viewers also apply different viewing strategies to different genres and differ their role as audience. Fiction and entertainment require less mental effort, and allow for more relaxation and physical comfort. News -on the contrary- is more demanding and requires an active attitude, -best in an upright position, as the hard pew of olden days-. Perhaps the lines blur here as well. Höijer 1999 notes e.g. that social realistic fiction activates processes of recognition and identification, resulting in a higher emotional engagement and 'learning'.

The complexity of audience hood and metacognitions is also demonstrated by the *'third person effects'*. This has to do with the opinion that others are influenced by mass media far more than oneself. Therefore, criteria may differ considerably, according to whom they apply.

McQuail (1997) offers another example of the judgmental framework held by audiences when it comes to media: the general view, also held by religious institutes, that high media use is harmful and that media behavior needs to be subject of regulation (parental and/or societal). Content norms are another topic within the same framework. Public opinion holds judgments on matters like good taste, morality, bad language, violence and sex on the screen; but also on media behavior in general which has to be fair, impartial, reliable, complete and accurate. McQuail, like Höijer, notes the paradox of a critical public attitude and a normatively inconsequent use. Again private and public norms do not correspond and they appear to be more socially desirable than actually internalized.

But in general, according to McQuail (1997, 2000), the audience does not experience its relationship with media as problematic. People make their own choices according to what they like, or what seems interesting and relevant to their taste, needs, preferences and social cultural identities. Although there maybe (e.g.) annoyance about unsolicited media outlets or different levels of loyalty, involvement, intention, attachment, interaction or identification (fandom e.g.), media routines are so much a part of familiar environment that they are even associated -unconsciously- with personal identity and lifestyle. Normative framing still remains strong. Schrøder (1999), from his case study of media use in Denmark (see note 69), focuses the public concern about 'devastating' television. He argues that 'television is not different in 'doing to modern culture' from what other media have done, and they were less criticized and feared'.

Höijer (1999:189) concludes: 'The picture that has been presented here show that people have some audience identity, partly in the form of collective ideals about being an audience and partly in the form of ideas about one's own and about other people's audience hood. Metacognitions on audience hood are as much stamped by culture and ideologies, as are other practices and social roles'. She, therefore, pleads a deepened understanding of the concepts of active/passive without presuming *a priori* what is best for the audience.

Probably one could say that all the contradictions, ambiguities and underlying ideologies and morals make the perspective *from* the audience as much of a 'construct' as are the other discourses.

Or, to put it in Hagen's (1999:145) words: 'The point is that audience images are always inscribed: the institutional according to institutional goals; the academic according to methodological and other scientific (theoretical) discourses; and the audience's image according to cultural codes for good taste and decent lifestyles, that is, according to moral hierarchies in the culture'.

No wonder then, many typologies exist regarding the audience.

2.3   'The audience is dead; long live the audience'

There are various ways to distinguish audience typologies. McQuail (1997, 2000) differentiates according to media audience formation, models of the mass communication process, or the relation to 'traditional' mass media or 'new' interactive media. Partly overlapping typologies are the result.

Media audience formation can be viewed as happening from within media, or from within society. Each on two levels: macro society: *the audience as group/public*; micro society: *the gratification set as audience*; macro media: *the medium or channel audience* and micro media: *the audience of particular media content.*
A typology related to mass communication models results in three different views on audiences: the transmission model, aimed at cognitive processing, leads to a view of the audience as a *target* for the transfer of meaning; the expressive or ritual model, aimed at sharing and commitment, considers the audience as *participants*; the attention model, looking for attention, regardless of the communicative effect, regards the audience to be a *spectator*. This view applies especially within commercial circles with its emphasis on ratings and time spent[72].
Bordewijk and van Kaam (1982) in their concept with respect to the traffic of information -as described in 1.1.3.1- distinguish four different patterns of information flows. Those patterns -*allocution, registration, consultation* and *conversation*- express

---

[72] The same terminologies are used sometimes in different and therefore confusing ways, judging by the next quotation: 'According to Ang (1991: 26-32), the two paradigms of the audience stem from two diverse theoretical models of mass communication. The first, the idea of the *audience as a public,* fits the so-called 'transmission' model of communication. Implied in this model is the conception of audiences as 'receivers' of messages sent and meanings transferred. The other, the *audience as a market,* is related to an attention model of communication. Here transfer of meaning is of secondary importance, while communication is considered effective as soon as attention is given to it by audiences (see also McQuail, 1987)'. Heikki Hellman. 1999. 'Legitimations of television programme policies: patterns of argumentation and discursive convergences in a multichannel age' in Pertti Alasuutari (ed.) 1999 *Rethinking the Media Audience.* London, Sage. p. 106.

power relationships (with respect to control, access and storage of information) and, at the same time each of them carries a different role for the audience.

In allocutive communication patterns, the audience role is passive as in the traditional mass audience. In consultation, the audience is an active, individual searcher without any shared audience experience. In conversation patterns, control is shared by both sides through interaction, involvement and feedback. Due to partnership in the communication process, the distinction between sender or receiver roles blurs. This is very important with respect to new media developments in order to develop non-mass medial typologies of the audience. In mass media communication production, distribution and consumption is separated. It is a centre - peripheral form of communication. But the new interactive technology makes mixed forms of mass and personal communication possible in which production, distribution and consumption can be mixed ('prosumer'). This leads to new audience behavior and media use.

McQuail (2000:132), with regard to this, urges the reconsideration of the relevance of media-effects-theories. Since they apply only to allocution patterns (transmission model), and the trend is from allocutory to consultative or conversational modes, there is a need for 'interactive', 'ritual' or 'user-determined' models.

The terms 'audience' and 'receivers' have long been associated with each other in mass communication discourses as well as in common language. One can (e.g.) speak of a 'live' or 'national' audience.
One of the earliest typologies -owed to the insights of functionalist sociology (see 2.1.1)- was that of *audience as a mass*; a large, anonymous and heterogeneous entity, which is on the -passive- receiving end of a one directional flow of media messages (like the early national television audience).

In the 1940's -1950's, the audience concept was related to networks of social relationships that were based on (e.g.) locality or common interest: *the audience as group*[73]. Examples of such an audience are the local newspaper audience, or a church magazine audience. After the rise of the effect research tradition, the influence of the social environment on media experiences was recognized. Today, due to competition and concentration, the identification of the audience as a group becomes more difficult because media tend to 'serve' the largest possible heterogeneous audience. This leads to 'neutral' and common denominator based news and other programming.

Media industry gave rise to *the audience as market*. McQuail (1997) indicates that the ever-increasing pressure to consume reinforces this view of the audience, which consists of 'buyers and users of technology as much as of receivers of messages'.
Highly segmented audience interests are served as *consumers* - not only by the commercial system, but also by alternative media (think (e.g.) of ethnic, linguistic or religious minorities, or of professional scientific journals). In this respect, the *gratification set as audience* -originally formed on media related interests, needs and preferences by the audience-changed as well. Religious and political commitment declined and due to

---

[73] In the Netherlands the *audience as a social group* until recently was an exceptional reality, because of the unique existence of non-commercial broadcasting associations on the basis of voluntary membership by audience members. Compartmentalized groups, belonging e.g. to the socialist, protestant or Roman Catholic segments, each became member of their "own" association, which led to different divisions in our broadcasting system. However, contemporary reality foreshows the end of this 'pillarized' system of public broadcasting. Channel coordinated programming based on predictable formats decided upon by 'network coordinators', are the first signs of this development.

the increase of commercialization the growth of (e.g.) lifestyle magazines led to the development of 'taste cultures' and sets of similar media products to 'gratify' its audience. Increasingly these taste cultures are promoted universally (think of the music station MTV) and lead to a *transnational audience*, which contains all the related issues of cultural autonomy etc.

McQuail (1997, 2000) concludes that there are many different meanings of 'the audience' concept. They depend on media, content, the purpose of sending and receiving, social cultural circumstances and experience and different discourses. The audience as consumer of media products, 'revealed' through ratings, is the most dominant meaning in contemporary society since media business runs on it. And an important part of 'audience research' is about 'keeping the figures' on content or channel.

Apart from the doubts about measurement that was mentioned before, this view is also related to a partly superseded, 'purely' mass medial situation, which is susceptible to many economical, technical and social changes.

In an economic sense, increased transnationalization -with its flow of international events and global marketing- posits the problem of transnational homogenization and cultural synchronization (see 1.2) and questions the consequences on the audience and its ability to resist. Will this lead to new audiences and, consequently, to new conceptualizations of the audience?

Technologically speaking, huge and accelerating changes are occurring concerning delivery, recording possibilities, the convergence of information and communication technologies, and interactive capacity.

On the one hand, this shifts control to the audience (from allocutive communication patterns to conversational patterns) and leads to new audience roles (sender/receiver). It will indeed be more difficult to trace a continuously fleeing fragmented and segmented individualized audience. But does interactivity necessarily mean greater diversity and participation? Will it generate new (cyber) community formation? Does it really empower the audience? Will people prefer a fully decentralized network to collective identities and community interests?

McQuail (1997, 2000) doubts whether the concept of interactivity -if possible to speak of one- is as 'revolutionary' as is generally assumed. In his opinion, technical possibilities extend patterns of audience behavior instead of replacing them. Since audiences are as much the 'products' of technology as of social life, social forces, such as the need of social formation and structures and habits of media use, must be considered as well. Those forces are still strong and deeply rooted. New media forms did not yet prove to be an alternative to mass media. An interactive audience did not replace spectatorship. And despite of technological convergence McQuail thinks it's even questionable if old and new media forms will merge. The old, allocutive media order is still in charge. Society itself has not changed dramatically in the mass communication era, and new media forms are hedged in old power relationships and used for traditional purposes, such as the reinforcement of advertising, that has to achieve an ever-increasing effort to reach the audience(s).

This implies many uncertainties about the 'end' of mass society and mass audience.

Beyond doubt the concept is challenged. It cannot be denied that new types of audiences arise that have new patterns of media use and that the image of a passive receiver and the distinction between sender and receiver are no longer valid. But at the same time mass audience realities are 'alive and kicking'.

McQuail refers to audience fragmentation in terms of four succeeding stages: the *unitary* model of the early beginnings of television with a single homogeneous audience; secondly the *pluralism* model of diversity in unity (more options but still within the same unitary framework); the *core-periphery* model of the third phase shows the break out of the unitary framework, by unity in diversity. The final stage is that of the *break-up* model in which there is no shared audience experience left, nor a central core. According to McQuail the third phase of the core periphery model is reached; the break up phase though has not yet dawned.

Nevertheless, McQuail -recognizing a diversity of possibilities of audience formation and a multiplication of audience meanings- concludes that old definitions can no longer be held. New terms will be needed, and no single typology does justice to reality.
'The classic meaning of the audience term has always been *message related*, while theory and experience have come to recognize the near-equal significance of *behavioral* and also the *social, emotional, and affective* aspects of media use – the intrinsic pleasures and satisfactions of the process of using media in various contexts. (…) We can no longer use the term without giving a clear indication of what we mean by it in a given instance, and any 'measure' of audience will have to be understood in a specific way' (1997:149-50).

The main dimensions of contemporary audience interpretation, as given by McQuail are: degree of activity or passivity; degree of interactivity and interchangeability; size and duration; locatedness in space; group character (social/cultural identity); simultaneity of contact with source; heterogeneity of composition; social relations between sender and receiver; message vs. social/behavioral definition of situation; degree of 'social presence' and sociability of context of use.

Therefore, we cannot continue to speak easily and innocently of 'the audience'.

And due to the (highly) central position the audience has become to hold in communication studies, this insight inevitably impacts upon the choice of communication models.

2.4   The choice of paradigm

So far we have identified main approaches, models, views and theories regarding mass communication. All of them -in one way or another- involve senders/receivers, messages, media, effects and meaning. But there are serious differences in comparing those elements and defining their content. Moreover, they interact with societal relationships, social cultural factors, economical forces, technological developments and research focuses. These are expressed in different discourses, which -in a particular way- 'construct' their own conceptions. Not only wit regard to the role of the audience, but also e.g. concerning views on society and culture, public interest, mass media and human progress.

In this section, we will integrate those views with the approaches mentioned before in order to identify the features of the different primary paradigms.

From its early beginnings, mass media have been closely related to societal and cultural views (see 2.1.1). In agreement, as well as in conflicting ways. The main issues were concerned with power and inequality, social (dis) integration and identity, and social change.
We will list the main theories in this respect, as given by two respected communication scholars: Denis McQuail and Karle Nordenstreng.

McQuail (2000) discerns seven different media society theories, which contrast critical and consensual views of society (conflict/consensus), and media centric and society centric views.

1. The characteristics of *mass society theory* are: a large scale society with centralized dominant media, a one way transmission of information and an atomized mass audience of consumers, markets and electorates which depend on media for their identity.

2. In *Marxist theory,* media are owned by a bourgeois class. They secure their interests and cause false consciousness among the working class. Political opposition is denied access.

3. In *functionalist theory,* mass media are essential to society for integration, co-operation, order, control, stability and continuity of culture and values.

4. *Critical political economy* focuses on economic control of the media and its logic, media concentration, global integration, the commodification of content and audiences, the subordination of public to private interests, the decrease of diversity and the marginalizing of alternative voices.

5. In *modernization and development theory,* media act as agents of development toward the (Western) 'blessings' of democracy, literacy, education, individual change and mobility, public health, technical progress and consumerism.

6. *Theories of communication technology determinism* view communication technology as fundamental to society, which will influence social change. Communication revolutions will lead to social revolutions.

7. *Information society theory* defines society -based on new media technology- by: predominance of information; a great volume of information flow; interactivity of relations; integrations and convergence of activities; growth and interconnection of networks; globalizing tendencies and post-modern culture.

On the same subject, Kaarle Nordenstreng (1997) identifies five different normative theory paradigms:

1. *the liberal-pluralist paradigm* with a central role for the market, which provides according to the interest of the individual consumer (which is equated to the public interest);
2. *the social responsibility paradigm*, which focuses on a wider responsibility to society (cf. public service broadcasting);
3. *the critical paradigm* which shows similarities with McQuail's description of Marxist theory, by assigning mass media a strategic position between the hegemony of dominant industrial/state control and oppressed masses;

4. *the administrative paradigm,* bureaucratic and technocratic and an elite press with an emphasis on 'objective informing';
5. *the cultural negotiation paradigm* with its attention to subcultures, mutual understanding and respect and community (stemming from liberation theology, grass root movements and cultural studies).

Next to the outlooks and theories on society and culture, there are also different outlooks on media. In describing different cultural images of media, which have become routine in daily practice, Alasuutari (1999) comes to three different (metaphorical) sets, resulting in two key images of media:

- the first is the metaphor of media as a *channel or window,* which offers us a 'view of the world';
- the second metaphor -the metaphor of the *square*- considers media either as an agora, which offers us a public forum for debate or as the *market,* which leads to different views of the audience as either the informed citizen or the voter/customer;
- the third image encompasses the *personal relationship* that people maintain with media, which is very dependent on context and personal factors and, therefore, very heterogeneous.

The two key images of media relate either to:

- the metaphor of media as a *link* in which media are the world or news itself (a self-evident extension of ourselves) and the audience is regarded as informed citizens.
- the *representation* metaphor, which includes a view of media portraying a biased view of reality as a result of which the audience is hardly able anymore to be critical.

On the same issue McQuail (2000) identifies different *mediation roles* of media. They fulfill functions of: a window, a mirror, a filter or gatekeeper, a guide or interpreter, a forum or platform or an interlocutor. The question concerning the 'new media' is whether *'intermediation'* will replace 'mediation', according to McQuail.
If we now relate this abundance of society/media/mediation theories to the approaches of mass communication we described earlier -functionalist sociology and information theory, semiotics and critical theories inspired by Marx, political economy of communication, cultural studies and audience research- we may derive *two main paradigms.*

By uniting theories this way, we aim at three goals: the sake of survey; underlining the importance of the choice of paradigms in (churches') communication; and identifying a theoretical tool to be used in the analysis of policy statements on the outlook of communication (chapter three). Our own construction, then, distinguishes (1) a *dominant* and (2) an *alternative* paradigm:

1. the *dominant* paradigm holds a *liberal pluralist* view and a *functionalist* perspective of a *large-scale mass* society. *Technology* serves *progress* of society and humankind and the influence of the *market* is essential. *Media* are seen as *powerful* instruments that are essential to maintain *stability* and *cultural continuity.* They follow and -confirm- the *logic* of the *market.* Beyond that they have *no wider responsibilities* to society. They *link* people to the world in an objective and neutral way. The *audience* is a *mass* public of *individual consumers* (market), who exercise power by choosing and buying. Public interest is consumer interest. Culture is to be divided into *elite* and *mass* culture; the latter is evidence of *lower quality. Communication* follows the *process* model of *linear transmission.* Power in this process is concentrated on the

sender's side. A *message* is a 'take away,' 'meaning filled' package ready to be *received* by a fairly *passive* consumer. *Attention* may prevail against being informed or genuine communication.*Research* and *analysis* is by nature *quantitative* and focuses on *numerical measurement* whether it is content, effect or audience.

2.   the *alternative social cultural critical* paradigm is critical of mass society and concerned with questions of power and inequality. *Technology* is not an automatic guarantee for progress, but can be *dehumanizing*. The *market* reflects *power relationships* and must be controlled. *Media* are instruments of *power* and *control* and carry and maintain ruling *ideologies*. They are in *no* respect *neutral* or objective. The *audience* is not a passive consumer, but *active,* which means it can be *critical.* It is able to *interpret* and *co-determine meaning. Public interest* far *exceeds* consumer interest. *Culture* is a contested area of powers and relationships in society. Human experience is of great importance. There is a strong interest in *popular culture*, which is *not* at all *inferior. Communication* is not to be described in terms of *linear effect process* models. *Transmission* is rejected. What a *message* means is eventually *decided* upon by the *receiver*, who has the power to *resist. Genuine communication* has to do with *sharing* and *community*. Research and analysis are by nature qualitative and in depth. They recognize the interaction between media experiences and social cultural experiences and take into account the different discourses of media culture.

Since mass media are -on the one hand- part of economic and social structures and -on the other hand (in their mediating role)- strongly intertwined with culture, the choice of a mass communication paradigm is not value free.
It is not just an 'option' for one communication scientific model over others, but implies one's position with respect to society, media, culture, communication, humanity and, last but far from least, the audience.

2.5   Implications for Christian communication

'However, for politicians, advertisers, pressure groups, campaigners, and advocates of all kinds who want to influence behavior and opinion, the emerging media situation does represent a potential problem. Much greater ingenuity is now required to catch attention and engage an audience' (McQuail 1997: 136).

There is no reason to assume that this situation, applied to other groups in society, would differ for religious institutions. Since churches claim a never-ending mission -by divine order- to preach the Gospel to 'the world', perhaps McQuail's statement is even more compelling to their situation.

We, therefore, have to sort out what exactly the implications of our findings are for the public communication of the churches. We will identify them in the form of six issues -in random order- that deserve attention.

The first considers what a *message* is. The view of a ready-made parcel containing an 'instant' meaning has been severely criticized. Meaning is negotiated in a complex process in which personal factors, socialization, culture, media experiences, generally held conventions and (media) discourses are included.
This immediately raises the fundamental question whether 'The Message' -the Gospel- is 'a message'?

We have dealt with the *audience* concept at great length. Simple remarks no longer hold. The audience is continuously reforming. Religious institutions, therefore, need to revise and refine audience definitions and look for new, adequate terms suited for the present media situation and the new types of audiences (sender-receiver) that emerge.
They also need to take into account a variety of contradictory and overlapping typologies and audience discourses and indicate the main dimensions of audience as identified by McQuail.
In this respect, it seems to be a legitimate question to ask churches what type of 'audience' do they consider 'the world' is?

Regarding *communication* as a one way, linear transmission process from a sender to a receiver is, as different insights of communication theory have shown, a view that is no longer valid.
What does this mean for the public communication and the dissemination of information by religious institutions?

The different generations of cultural reception research and audience ethnography have drawn attention to the social cultural use and reception of media; the interaction with daily life; the identity politics of gender, race and ethnicity; the perception of the audience; the existence of 'interpretative communities'; the shift from factual to fictional media outlets; and the fact that media use and meaning are part of a complex web of media culture, with many discourses.
Have mainline churches -one way or another- taken notice of those new insights and are there traces to be sensed of impact on communication policies by the churches?
A legitimate question (e.g.), related to the insights on popular culture and 'learning' and the judgmental views on factual programmes seen as a 'duty', could be whether more attention should be given to *fictional forms* of communicating instead of putting an emphasis on factual forms such as the dissemination of information?

The selection of a communication *model* (as we have seen) is not just an easy and innocent choice of a 'tool'. Bordewijk and Van Kaam emphasized power relationships and different audience roles in four patterns of information flows: allocution, registration, consultation and conversation.
McQuail (2000) points out the 'redistribution of information traffic from allocutory to conversational and consultative patterns'. The audience role is no longer restricted to 'traditional' descriptions of a passive receiver, consumer or target. There are new roles to play, as a seeker, consultant, browser, respondent, interlocutor and conversationalist. Allocutory patterns, according to McQuail, perform less well. They still exist, but in new 'small scale' forms that are aimed at special-interest- audience segments (narrow-casting).

This raises two questions:

1. Are *allocutary* patterns, aiming at cognitive processing and 'transfer of meaning', still feasible and/or useful if they shift to a small-scale form? Do they still serve the purpose of the churches to 'reach the world'?
2. (B) In their choices of models, do churches account for the implications of the paradigms mentioned above and are they aware of the fact that different paradigm choices include a different positioning of the churches themselves?

The last issue we want to consider is the matter of *media culture* and *new media*. The concept of media culture that is outlined by third generation reception research and audience ethnography questions how churches handle their public communication and whether it is appropriate for this new situation. Would it (e.g.) be advisable to focus more on the expressive or ritual communication model, which seems better suited for sharing and commitment and seems better placed to guarantee participation of the audience?

Another question concerns new (interactive) media. Although experiences with those are still quite recent and research in this area only can provide provisional results, they may turn out to be of profound impact on communication patterns.
Churches have 'embraced' the new media, as they formerly did with radio and television, because of the 'new possibilities' they bring.
But the question is whether churches feel challenged to develop policies and strategies of use that are specifically oriented towards the communication singularities of those new media, or are they 'embedded' in already existing communication policy views, communication paradigms and communication habits stamped by modernity?

Whether or not churches, in their communication policies, have made allowance for historical and more recent insights from communication theory, is a pivotal question we will turn to in the next chapter.

2.6   Conclusion

The position of the audience has been subjected to increasing attention in mass communication theory and its conceptualization has been proven to be of crucial importance.

Early mass communication research viewed communication as the linear transmission of information and the audience as a mass of passive receivers, who are -literally- at the end of the line.
Most recent insights from reception research and audience ethnography put the audience in the front line by underlining their active role in the use of media in daily life and their capability to resist media influence. Those insights have drawn attention to the interaction of media use and the social cultural context of the audience. As well as to contemporary media culture in which audiences are also constructed and multiple media- and audience discourses, go about. Communication is no longer an instrumental matter, but in essence characterized by consultation, participation and interactivity.

Unambiguous views of the audience are no longer valid. There is a continual change; a variety of typologies and an emergence of new types call for new terms. An 'innocent' choice of communication paradigms cannot be sustained since outlooks involve power relationships. This becomes even more important with the arrival of new media that involve new communication patterns.

The insights of communication theory and research hold important implications for any institute engaged in public communication. Including religious ones.

Three

The Policy Statements of the Churches

Das Mandat der evangelischen Publizistik verpflichtet sie, die Vielfalt des Protestantismus, die volksreligiöse Distanz vieler Menschen zur „fremden Heimat Kirche" und die Phänomene einer postmodernen Religiosität wahrzunehmen und den Versuch zu machen, die Menschen in diesen Lebensbezügen und die Kirche als Ort der Gemeinschaft füreinander kommunikationsfähiger zu machen.

Den Adressaten (Leser, Zuschauer, Zuhörer, Empfänger) muß die publizistische Aufmerksamkeit und unternehmerische Bemühung gelten, wenn der Kommunikator (die Kirche im weitesten Sinne) nicht bei sich selbst bleiben will. Nicht eine von institutionellen Interessen gelenkte kirchliche Publizistik kann sich erfolgreich vermitteln, sondern eine kundenorientierte, den Menschen zugewandte Publizistik, die sich konsequent auf den Adressaten ausrichtet.

Damit werden Strukturen und Angebote der evangelischen Publizistik weder den Erfordernissen des gegenwärtigen Medienmarktes gerecht, noch sind sie auf die Herausforderungen eingerichtet, die sich durch die Medienentwicklung ankündigen. Sie sind zu stark an die kirchlichen Organisationsformen gebunden, zu deutlich absenderorientiert und zu wenig am Publikum ausgerichtet[1].

3.1   A brief historical overview

The history of church documents about modern electronic mass media of communication dates to 1936 when Pope Pius XI published his encyclical letter on motion pictures, *Vigilanti Cura*. It consisted of a doctrinal section, (the importance of film, the power of motion pictures, the popularity and impact of film and the necessity of vigilance), and a section about practical consequences (standards for production, moral obligations and concrete proposals, among others things film classification)[2].

The 1950's show a burgeoning interest in mass media within ecumenical circles. Against the background of the Second World War, the process of regeneration and the founding of the World Council of Churches in Amsterdam in 1948, European Christian communicators shared their concern for religious broadcasting in an international conference on the theme in 1950 (Informal International Conference on Religious Broadcasting). Three years later an international group of radio and television leaders established the World Committee for Christian Broadcasting (one of the predecessors of

---

[1] Quoted from: Mandat und Markt, Perspektiven evangelischer Publizistik. 1997. Evangelische Kirche in Deutschland. Frankfurt am Main. (Mandate and Market, Perspectives of protestant publicity).
[2] The (second) Catholic Film and (first) Broadcasting Conference, however, took place already in June, (17-20), 1929. It resulted in a 432 page book, which includes all the reports from the meeting, both in German and French. Ernst, Georg, Marschall Bernhard (Eds.) 1929. *Film und Rundfunk. Zweiter Internationaler Katholischer Filmkongress/ Erster Internationaler Katholischer Rundfunkkongress. Gesamtbericht.* Muenchen, Verlag Leohaus.

the later World Association for Christian Communication, WACC). The World Council of Churches published its first policy statement on mass media during its assembly in Evanston in 1954: *The Media of Mass Communication*, followed by *Sound and Image* in 1956. On the Roman Catholic side in 1957 pope Pius XII devoted an encyclical letter to electronic media (film, radio and television): *Miranda Prorsus*.

The main documents -with authoritative status- of the 1960's and 1970's include *Inter Mirifica*, the Second Vatican Council's Decree on the Means of Social Communication (1963); *The Church and the Media of Mass Communication*, Appendix of the Report of the 4th Assembly of the World Council of Churches in Uppsala in 1968; *Communio et Progressio*, the Pastoral Instruction on the Means of Social Communication written by the Pontifical Commission for the Means of Social Communication by order of the Second Vatican Council (1971), and the *Joint Report of the Task Force on Mass Communication and the Task Force on Publication Strategy*, published by the Lutheran World Federation in 1973. Two main reports published by UNESCO in the same period - the *New World Information Order* (NWICO, 1978) and *Many Voices, One World* (1980)- also influenced the ecumenical discussion.

The Churches and New Communication Technologies (LWF, 1982), *Credible Christian Communication* (WCC, Vancouver assembly, 1983) and *Communication and Community* (WACC, Manila 1989) belong to the main documents published in the 1980's.

In the 1990's *Aetatis Novae* (Vatican, 1992*), Communication for Human Dignity* (WACC, New Mexico, 1995), and *Value, Power and the Information Society* (LWF, Hong Kong, 1997) have similar status. It might be concluded they are the last main 'overall' documents in a long row. The first five years of the new millennium seem to predict a shift from basic overall documents towards specialized statements, focusing on different issues regarding (mass) media and new information technologies. Examples of this trend include *Ethics in Advertising* (1997), *Ethics in Communication* (2000), *Ethics in Internet* (2002) and *Church and Internet* (2002) all published by the Vatican[3].

Haikarainen (2002) discussing the evolution of the ecumenical debate on communication from 1948-2000 discerns three periods, each with a different emphasis regarding media and communication and different theological assumptions underlying the views and attitudes.
The first period (1948-1972) is characterized by a positive outlook on mass media -and technology, in general- especially for their hermeneutic relevance.
In the next years (1972-1984), disappointment about the positive expectations of mass communication and a less 'naïve' view towards 'technological progress' turned the tide. The UNESCO debate on the New World Information and Communication order (NWICO) and communication technological criticism (Freire, Ellull) made the churches turn towards a greater commitment to alternative media.
In the last period (1985-2000), discussions focused on the concept of *communio* and universal ethical values in reaction to value relativism of post modernity. The cultural-ritualistic theory of James Carey (1989), regarding communication not merely as transportation of information but about building and maintaining culture, influenced this thinking.

---

[3] The most recent document on communication by the Vatican *The rapid development* 2005 might be the exception to the rule since it discusses a general perspective on media developments. However, being an 'Apostolic letter of the Holy Father John Paul II to those responsible for communications' it has a slightly different status and is directed towards specific addressees. Moreover, the document basically repeats views and insights expressed in former main basic documents by the Vatican.

The theological assumptions shifted from Christological emphasis in the first and second period to Trinitarian and communion concepts in the third period.

Haikarainen's conclusion is that the ecumenical discussion on communication and media is characterized by the tension between technology and transmission of information, on the one hand, and communication and community, on the other.

In the next section we will outline our examination of recent statements on communication and media by mainstream Christianity in north western Europe.

3.2   Outline of the research

Our goal is to examine the implications of contemporary media culture for public communication -and linked with that: the role and being- of mainstream Christianity in western Europe. Our research focuses on policy statements about media and communication that were published by mainstream churches -from different denominations- their world organizations, and related communications institutions. We will analyze those statements against the background of developments in the global media context, the implications of global media culture and recent insights by communication and media studies.

This enables us to identify the churches' current understanding of (a) the digital cultural context that they are part of and in which they have to communicate, (b) the impact of media culture upon institutional self analysis and change, (c) their view of communication -and related paradigm choices- and, (d) the relevance of their involvement and social responsibility in the realm of media and public communication.

This identification makes it possible to trace whether or not the churches are up to date in their understanding of communication and the challenges raised by media culture.

This is not only a prerequisite for the successful implementation of any media policy and communication praxis; it is also a matter of major concern across the width of all church policy. At stake is whether mainline religion is capable of relating in a fruitful way to a changing, new media culture and 'information' society.

To what extent she will be able to deal with the challenges of the digital media culture will turn out to be of overriding importance for the public communication and the presence of mainline Christianity in western Europe.

In this section we will present the findings from the content analysis of church policy documents on media and communication.

A first inventory -made in 2001- of statements[4] about media and communication, published by mainstream churches, their world organizations, councils of churches and

---

[4] The definition of documents to be regarded as main policy statements of the churches and their institutions is, of course, always an arbitrary decision (on the side of the researcher as well as on the side of the church/ institution representative requested). Our purpose is not to offer an exhaustive listing of every report or document that has been published. In the request for policy statements, we defined some criteria by asking for: separate basic main documents, which focus on the issue of communication and media (which excluded for example overall church strategy documents or annual reports) that express the churches' policy views on the subject (or are to be considered to have impacted and represent these views) and that were recently published (at least since the 1960's-1970's) by the (central) church leadership.

Christian communication institutes (in western Europe[5]) since the 1960/1970's[6], resulted in the identification of over 150 titles[7]. They differed in status, size, scope and region. Included in this first inventory were Roman Catholic, Anglican, Lutheran and Protestant churches and their communication institutions in the UK, Scotland, Finland, Norway, Sweden, Denmark, Italy, Spain, France, Germany, Switzerland, Belgium and The Netherlands.

On the international and European level, the World Council of Churches (WCC), the Vatican (Pontifical Commission for Social Communications), the Conference of European Churches (CEC), the Lutheran World Federation (LWF), the World Association for Christian Communication (WACC), UNDA (the International Catholic Association for Radio and Television -now Signis), the Catholic Media Council (CAMECO), the *Comité Episcopal Europeen pour les Medias* (CEEM), the Commission of the Bishops' Conferences of the European Community (COMECE) and the Central Religious Advisory Committee (UK) were approached as well.

Not all of the churches and institutes that responded had published separate policy documents about media and communication[8]. Fifteen different churches and institutions did however: the Vatican, the WCC, the LWF, WACC, the ecumenical working group of UNDA/WACC, CEEM, COMECE, the Church of England, the Bishops' Conference of England, Wales and Scotland, the Central Religious Advisory Committee (UK), the *Evangelische Kirche Deutschland* (Germany), the *Deutsche Bischofskonferenz* (Germany), *Svenska Kyrkan* (Sweden), the Evangelical Lutheran Church of Finland and the *Norske Kirke* (Norway).

A first selection of documents to be included in the research was based upon the range of media discussed (with a focus on audio-visual and new media) and on the criterion of period of time. The 1990's proved to be a key turning point with respect to global media developments, structures and policies, and global media culture, as well as to new insights by communication and media studies -especially with reference to reception research and audience ethnography-. The changes in both fields were profound. We therefore restricted our analysis to statements that were published since this time. This resulted in narrowing the list from over 150 to 68 documents.

A second criterion was based on the status of the policy statement within its church or organization. An annual pontifical message for world communications day for example is

---

[5] In referring to 'Western Europe', we only want to indicate that we focused on statements that were published in this part of Europe and apply to this context (that is also the reason why we did not include the many and important statements made and published in other parts of the world. Latin America and Asia, for example, are regions in which specialists are very active in this field). However, in the case of, for example, WACC, the LWF, Signis and the Vatican, the reference to 'Western Europe' is not fully applicable, since they are global institutes. Moreover, people from other parts of the world may well have contributed to these statements. In the case of WACC, for example, this is obvious; but it is more than likely this also applies to the other three institutes mentioned. By underlining this issue, we explicitly want to give due to these contributions that also impacted the final statements.

[6] The period of time in which this initial inventory was taken, was broader than the one defined in the research (from the 1990's onwards) in order to be able to gain understanding of historical developments and possible trends since the publication of the first four authoritative documents in the 1960/1970's.

[7] For an extensive overview of documents identified see appendix four.

[8] This did not always mean, however, that media and communication were not on the churches' agenda; some churches (or church departments), for example, published on the subject in their national church magazine.

not on the same level as a pastoral instruction like *Aetatis Novae* (Vatican), or an assembly document or statements published by general synods or bishops conferences. Identifying the basic policy statements for each church or organization, either on a general global level or with a focus on the situation in north-western Europe, resulted in a further reduction of the list of 68 to 39 documents.

Subsequently, an inventory was made regarding the content of the main focal points of these 39 documents. This resulted in the identification of the following five main categories of statements:

- Basic overall documents about church, media and communication
- Communication and media ethics
- New media and information society
- Church communication strategy, involvement, education and theology
- Churches' official reactions on media policy

The final selection then of documents to be included in the research, was based upon six criteria:

1. Recentness (published since the 1990's)
2. Focus (audio-visual and new media)
3. Status (main basic statements within the church or organization)
4. Representation of the main five categories mentioned above
5. A variety of denomination, institutional background and level (national, European, international, church or media professional), and:
6. A variety of region and ecumenical cooperation

This resulted in the following final selection[9] of statements:

Basic Overall Documents

Communication and Community	1989	WACC
Aetatis Novae	1992	Vatican
The Lutheran World Federation, a Communicative Communion	2002	LWF
The Rapid Development	2005	Vatican

Ethics

Communication for Human Dignity, the Mexico Declaration	1995	WACC
Ethics in Advertising	1997	Vatican
Ethics in Communication	2000	Vatican
Ethics in Internet	2002	Vatican

---

[9] The final selection does not claim representativeness in the strict sense of a sample being representative for the whole of a research population; it may, however, be considered to cover the variety of policy statements that were published by churches and/or their communication organizations on the subject of media and communication in north-western Europe.

New Media and Information Society

Multimedia, der Wandel zur Informationsgesellschaft	1995	German Bishops Conference
Chancen und Risiken der Mediengesellschaft	1997	Protestant/RC Church Germany
Value, Power and the Information Society	1997	LWF
Cybernauts Awake!	1999	Church of England

Church Communication Strategy, Involvement, Education, Theology

Kommunikoivaan Kirkkoon	1992	Lutheran Church of Finland
Audiovisual Media Education, an Urgent Pastoral and Social Concern	1994	UNDA/WACC
L'ímportance du travail médiatique de l' église Appel du Comité Episcopal Européen des Médias (CEEM) aux Conférences Episcopales en Europe	1995	CEEM
Mandat und Markt Perspektiven Evangelischer Publizistik	1997	Evangelische Kirche in Deutschland
Identities and Communities	1999	UNDA/WACC
Evangelio, Iglesia y Sociedad de la Información Congreso de Obispos Europeos de Medios de Comunicación Social	1999	CEEM
Medien und Kommunikationskompetenz	2000	Deutsche Bischofskonferenz
Kommunicera Mera	2000	Church of Sweden
Church and Internet	2002	Vatican
A Communicative Church	2004	Lutheran Church of Finland

Churches' Official Reactions on Media Policy

Comments on the Green Paper of the European Commission concerning the Convergence of the Telecommunications, Media and Information Technology Sectors and their Effects on Regulatory Policy. A Step towards the Information Society	1998	COMECE
The Future of EU Media Policy in the Information Society	2001	COMECE
Television Without Frontiers, Public Consultation	2003	COMECE
Submission to the BBC Charter Review	2004	Bishops' Conference of England and Wales

Table 3.1 Selection of statements

To identify the understandings -as presented in the statements- of 1) the digital media context, and media culture and its impact and challenges, 2) the views on media and communication and 3) the relevance of involvement in media and public communication, we researched the documents by the following method.

First, we identified all relevant issues in a selection of recent literature in the realm of communication, mass media, communication theory, audience analysis and theories of culture[10]. The issues found (53) were clustered into 22 topics. They functioned as provisional trial topics and were tested in the close reading process of several policy statements. As a result of the testing, we reduced the topics to nine final key issues which constitute a grid for comparison and guarantee consistency. They are:

1. *Document* (includes: kind of document, goal, target group, and references made to other statements)
2. *Analysis media context: media structures and media culture*[11] (includes: definitions of the 'information' society, its trends -such as commercialization, globalization, digitization and convergence-; its challenges and implications -including media effects on social institutes-; media logic; matters of   public interest and the cultural/religious dimension of mass communication media and, finally, media use as part of everyday social life and interaction)
3. *Media studies: Audience research* (includes: the perception of/from 'the audience'; the underlying audience theory that is assumed; the inclusion of recent insights in reception studies and audience ethnography; audience behavior or use of media and the effect of new technologies on audiences -interactivity- and the implications of a shift in paradigm from sender to receiver for church communication goals)
4. *View of Christian culture/identity* (includes: the challenges presented by the digital media culture to issues of identity, authority, community, authenticity, truth, institutional position, tradition and theology)
5. *Views on media roles and communication models*
6. *Theological presuppositions* (includes: theological implications in churches' communication views)
7. *Church involvement in communication/media* (includes: churches' consideration of the main goals of involvement in and/or contribution to public communication and media)
8. *Social responsibility* (includes: ethics, communication rights, structure and legislation, access, public debate, language and culture), and
9. *Challenges and priorities* (includes: communication strategy, planning, research, media literacy, education, theological curriculum, support, experiments, alternative media and finances).

Based on these issues, we will now turn to our analysis.

---

[10] Van Ginneken, Jaap. 1999. *Understanding Global News. A Critical Introduction*. London, Sage.
McChesney, Robert W. 2000. *Rich Media, Poor Democracy*. New York, the New Press.
Rebel, Henk Jan. 2000. *Communicatiebeleid en Communicatiestrategie*. Amsterdam, Boom.
McQuail, Denis. 1997. *Audience Analysis*. London, Sage.
McQuail, Denis. 2000. *McQuail's Mass Communication Theory*. London, Sage.
Tanner, Kathryn. 1997. *Theories of Culture, a New Agenda for Theology*. Minneapolis, Fortress Press.
Hoover, Stewart M. and Knut Lundby (Eds). 1997. *Rethinking Media, Religion, and Culture*. Thousand Oaks,   Sage.
Hoover, Stewart M. and Schofield Clark, Lynn (Eds). 2002. *Practicing Religion in the Age of the Media*. New York, Columbia University Press.
[11] The term 'media culture' refers to the inextricable relationship between media and culture (as explained in chapter one) in contemporary globalized society and not to a 'culture of the media' in the sense of habits or logic.

3.3   Content analysis

We will present the results of the content analysis according to the nine key issues identified in each document. Due to the fact that some pronouncements in the statements refer to more than one key issue, there might be some overlap. However, to enable the reader insight to both the nine issues within each document, and an overview of all pronouncements on one key issue, as well as to trace the results per institute or denomination or geographically, we decided to offer this detailed elaboration, which moreover does justice to each statement and institute. For the sake of clarity and accessibility of the materials, we will compile summarized conclusions on each issue after the identification of all results, before turning to the main problems in the statements. This should be helpful to the reader both as a final overview and to better grasp the identification and the resulting conclusions that are drawn regarding the main problems in the subsequent section.

3.3.1   Documents

The 26 selected documents vary from:

(AD) Assembly documents and/or statements by an international congress on a specialized theme (e.g. WACC's statements *Communication for Community; Communication for Human Dignity; Values Power and the Information Society* by the Lutheran World Federation) to:

(PI) Pastoral instructions and Apostolic Letters (e.g. *Aetatis Novae* by the Vatican; *The Rapid Development* by Pope John Paul II)

(CS) Church Communication Strategies and Policy Programs (e.g. *A Communicative Communion* by the LWF; *The Communicating Church* by the Finnish Evangelical Lutheran Church of Finland; *Mandat und Markt, Perspektiven Evangelischer Publizistik* by the German Protestant Churches; *Medien und Kommunikationskompetenz. Die Zukunft der AV-Medienstellen in der Informationsgesellschaft* by the German Bishops Conference; *Kommunicera Mera – med flera* by the Church of Sweden; *The Communicative Church* by the Finnish Evangelical Lutheran Church of Finland)

(ST) Statements on special themes/issues (e.g. *Ethics in Advertising, Ethics in Communication, Ethics in Internet and Church and Internet* by the Vatican Pontifical Council for Social Communications; *Multimedia, Der Wandel Zur Informationsgesellschaft* by the German Bishops' Conference)

(CD) Common declarations (e.g. *Chancen und Risiken der Mediengesellschaft* by the German Bishops' Conference and the Protestant Churches in Germany)

(DS) Contributions to church-internal and societal debate to encourage informed awareness and reflection on media development implications (e.g. *Cybernauts Awake* by the Church of England; *Identities and Communities : What kind of Communication?* by UNDA/WACC's European Ecumenical Working Group on Media, Culture and Society)

(AR) Appeals and/or recommendations to authorities of European Churches by communication specialists (e.g. *Audiovisual Media Education an Urgent Pastoral and Social Concern* by UNDA/WACC's Working Party Television, Culture and European Society; *L'importance du travail médiatique de l' Eglise. Appel du Comité Episcopal*

Européen des Medias (CEEM) aux Conférences Episcopales en Europe; *Evangelio, Iglesia y Sociedad de la Información. Recommendacion dirigidas a las Conferencias Episcopales* by CEEM)

(CP) Comments and Reflection on Media Policy: (e.g. *Comments of the Secretary General of the Commission of the Bishops' Conferences of the European Community (COMECE) on the Green Paper of the European Commission; The Future of EU Media Policy in the Information Society; Television Without Frontiers* by COMECE; *Submission to the BBC Charter Review* by the Catholic Bishops' Conferences of England and Wales).

Addressee and Purpose

The addressee and purpose of the documents is not always explicitly stated. In the cases it is (of the 26 documents there are 20 with references to addressee and 23 with references to purpose) the main focus of the majority of the statements is church-internal (10 documents). Explicitly outward bound are 4 statements and another 6 are directed to an internal as well as an external target group.
When the purpose of the document is explicitly mentioned, the main references are towards:

(a)   reflection and discussion on the pastoral implications of technological changes and the impact of media developments in general and for religion and the church (including providing resource materials)
(b)   provide a working tool, guiding principles, manual, and media/communication policy program (principles and applications)
(c)   encourage and support professionals and people engaged in church work
(d)   fulfill (renew) communication vocation
(e)   start the communication process within the church
(f)   foster and engage in dialogue and public debate on media developments and the formation of media society (with religious groups, policy makers, professionals and all interested within society)
(g)   set out church/Christian views of (new) media
(h)   provide orientation (ethical responsibilities, moral and spiritual issues, proclaim truth)
(i)   contribute to free communication by responsible people in a responsible society
(j)   encourage informed awareness
(k)   strengthen community, gospel inspired publicity in the media and information society
(l)   recommendation/appeal to church authorities - underline critical issue of identity and community
(m)   face challenges to media society
(n)   contribute to public consultations; monitor and promote political philosophy at service to the common good (EU media policy, regulation, public service broadcasting).

Provide principles and applications for a media communication policy program (b)[12] and reflection on the implications of media developments (a) are referred to most frequently: respective 8 and 7 times. This is followed by engagement in dialogue / public debate (f) and the provision of ethical and spiritual orientation (h): both 5 times.

---

[12] This may be due to the fact that a proportionally larger number of church communication strategy documents are included in the research population. However, it is not until we have drawn conclusions on all key issues (especially the findings with respect to church involvement and challenges and priorities) that we can give a decisive answer to whether this is the case.

References to other documents

Out of the 26 documents, 20 refer to other statements. In nearly all cases (17) this reference includes documents that were formerly published by the supporting church or institute. The Roman Catholic documents especially draw heavily on former documents published by the Vatican[13]. The Lutheran churches (Swedish and Finnish), the LWF and institutions like WACC also tend to refer basically to their own statements. The only exceptions are the statements that were written and published with an explicitly ecumenical focus such as the German document, *Chancen und Risiken der Mediengesellschaft* (Roman Catholic and Protestant Churches), and the statements published by communication specialists (UNDA/WACC). Other exceptions are the statements contributing to public consultations (like T*he BBC Charter Review* or *Television without Frontiers*, by respectively The Bishops' Conference of England and Wales and COMECE*)* or the comments on EU media policy (COMECE). They basically refer to other EU documents or documents on the BBC.

The identification of the main key issues of the different documents (in terms of frequency and quantity) show that what appears most frequently, is:

(9) challenges and priorities for the church towards communication / media
(2) the analysis of the media context (structures and culture)
(8) social responsibility of the churches
(5) church's views on media roles and communication models

This is followed by (7) church involvement and (4) view of Christian culture/identity. Strikingly absent among the main key issues is (3) audience research.

In table 3.2 we summarized the main features with respect to documents[14.]

	Sort of Document	Addressee internal	Addressee external	Main Purpose	Own reference	Other reference	Main key issue
1.1	AD	-	-	-	-	-	5 8 9
1.2	PI	x	-	a,b,c	x (13)	-	2 5 7 8 9
1.3	CS	x	-	b,d,e	x (1)	-	4 5 9
1.4	PI	x	-	a,m	x (8)	-	5 7 9

---

[13] Apparently, the Vatican's policy with regard to its official documents is that it never refers to 'non-Vatican' documents, as was indicated to me by Alle Hoekema, and confirmed by Franz-Josef Eilers (personal email respectively, 24-10-2006 and 1-11-2006.

[14] The numbers 1.1 – 5.4 point to the research population of documents mentioned in section 3.2 (final selection of statements). The order is continued. 1.1. *Communication and Community*; 1.2 *Aetatis Novae*; 1.3 *The LWF, a Communicative Communion*; 1.4 *The Rapid Development*; 2.1 *Communication for Human Dignity*; 2.2 *Ethics in Advertising*; 2.3 *Ethics in Communication*; 2.4 *Ethics in Internet*; 3.1. *Multimedia, der Wandel zur Informationsgesellschaft*; 3.2 *Chancen und Risiken der Mediengesellschaft*; 3.3 *Value, Power and the Information Society*; 3.4 *Cybernauts Awake!*; 4.1 *Kommunikoivaan Kirkkoon*; 4.2 *Audiovisual Media Education, an urgent pastoral and social concern*; 4.3 *L' importance du travail médiatique de l' Eglise*; 4.4 *Mandat und Markt*; 4.5 *Identities and Communities*; 4.6 *Evangelio, Iglesia y Sociedad de la Informacíon*; 4.7 *Medien und Kommunikationskompetenz*; 4.8 *Kommunicera Mera*; 4.9 *Church and Internet*; 4.10 *A Communicative Church*; 5.1 *Comments on the Green Paper of the European Commission*; 5.2 *The Future of EU Media Policy in the Information Society*; 5.3 *Television without frontiers, Public Consultation*; 5.4 *Submission to the BBC Charter Review*.
'Sort of document', 'addressees', 'purpose' and 'references to other documents' are based upon explicit main references on these issues -or their absence- provided for by the documents themselves.

	Sort of Document	Addressee internal	Addressee external	Main Purpose	Own reference		Other reference	Main key issue
2.1	AD	-	x	-	x	(2)	-	5 8 9
2.2	ST	x	x	a, b	x	(10)	-	2 5 8
2.3	ST	x	x	a,c,f,h	x	(5)	-	2 5 8 9
2.4	ST	-	-	f,g	x	(11)	-	2 8
3.1	ST	-	-	-	x	(1)	-	2 8
3.2	CD	x	x	f,h,i	-		-	2 5 8
3.3	AD	x	-	a	-		-	2 9
3.4	DS	x	x	f,h,j	-		-	2 8
4.1	CS	x	-	b	x	(2)	-	7 9
4.2	AR	x	-	l	-		x (1)	2 8 9
4.3	AR	x	-	l	x	(3)	x (1)	4 9
4.4	CS	x	-	b,h,k	x	(2)	x (1)	2 7 9
4.5	DS	x	x	a,f,h,i,l	-		-	2 4 5 8 9
4.6	AR	x	-	l,m	x	(1)	-	9
4.7	CS	-	-	b,h	x	(3)	x (1)	2 9
4.8	CS	-	-	b,d	x	(5)	-	2 4 9
4.9	ST	x	x	a	x	(14)	-	7 9
4.10	CS	x	-	b,c	x	(2)	-	4 9
5.1	CP	-	x	n	-		x (2)	2 5 8 9
5.2	CP	-	-	n	x	(6)	x (9)	2 7 8
5.3	CP	-	x	n	-		-	8
5.4	CP	-	x	n	-		x (4)	5

Table 3.2: Sort of documents

3.3.2   Media context, structures and media culture

In this section, we will identify how the media context is analyzed in the statements with respect to media structures as well as media culture. What definitions are given (e.g. on the 'information society')? Which trends (concentration, globalization and commercialization; digitization and convergence; deregulation, liberalization and privatization) are identified? Which are considered to be the main implications and challenges? Are media logic and matters of public interest a subject? Is the cultural and religious dimension of media recognized and are any references made to effects on social institutions or media use as part of everyday social life and interaction?

When it comes to describing media developments, the statements refer to: a 'revolution', ''radical changes impacting all areas of life' (geography, culture, nationality, ownership and production of information, life options perspectives and models, ideas, values in science, commerce, education, politics, arts, religion), 'unprecedented developments', the 'global village', the 'information or media or network or knowledge society', 'hyper-mediated society', 'media-culture' the 'age of mass or global communication', 'increasing complexity', 'computer-age', the 'information age', internet, the 'web', 'multimedia', cyberspace and cybernetics, 'common info space', and communication. In the majority of cases, however, there are *no definitions* given about what is exactly meant. Exceptions are given in four documents: 3.1 (on multimedia and cyberspace), 3.3 (mass media and new media), 5.1 (communication) and 3.4 (internet and www).

The issues of analysis of the media context referred to most frequently in the statements include: *trends, implications* of media developments, the *cultural/religious dimension* of and in media and *public interest* issues.

In describing the main trends the statements signal:

*   the explosive growth and rapid development of *communication technology*, (new media, the multiplicity of channels and transmission, technical convergence, a declining division of production and distribution, increase in speed, data sound image in one device, increasing overlap of traditional audio-visual media and internet, and the explosive growth of programs
*   *digitization and convergence*, not only technical but also with reference to utilization, markets and services, contents (new content universe)
*   the increase in *monopolization*, international horizontal and vertical concentration, mergers, acquisitions, media 'empires' and international conglomerates, and mass media and information industries as structures of power intertwined with national political economic and military power, and the internationalization of media markets
*   *commercialization and the increase of advertising and marketing*: economy being the most important aspect of new ICT, media as business (financed by advertising), merchandise, (information, entertainment and advertising more interwoven than ever)
*   *increasing market competition* (the selling of viewers to advertisers; attracting maximum audiences, ratings as sole criterion, and places of sociability such as sports and music are now part of the marketplace
*   *deregulation and privatization* (neo-liberalism, profit and law of the market only parameters, market as main regulator social relations), and greater reliance on self regulation
*   the remit of *public service broadcasting*, its function and financing in the digital age
*   *imbalance in communication structures* (gap of information between rich and poor, communication flow in one direction, and global communication following the division of economic, social powers)
*   *globally linkage* (same series, news, fewer sources, cultural colonization)
*   *audience and consumerism* (client instead of citizen, rising audience for local media in Europe, more time spent with media, citizens as provider, and fragmentation)
*   *content* (the increase in the circulation of data, information as weapon in war, vulgarization of content, less variation, and increasing mix of domains e.g. formation/commercials, edutainment, etc.)
*   the *shift* from communication *to information* (denoting the linear sender receiver model of mass communication) and from print to *imagery*, and growing importance of (fragmented) media in modern globalized society

The *implications and challenges* of media trends and developments, especially in the cultural realm, is the subject that receives the most attention by the statements. They speak of a 'new reality' that is fundamentally reshaping our comprehension of the world.
One statement (3.1) even describes multimedia as an 'universal think tool', which - beyond digitization or interactivity- alters the human informational environment in all areas of life.

What is signaled is how media affect our perception of world views, ideologies, values, place and time, identity, life, meaning, etc. Media modify learning processes and affect the quality of human relationships. The constant availability of images and ideas, and the ever wider range of media, impact lifestyles and the way we judge, choose or behave. Space and time worlds are simulated and experienced, pressurizing one to maximize any experience and short term commitment.

The consequences of those revolutionary changes are profound. Identities are no longer given by geography, age or sex, but by global 'tribalism'. The same holds true for the formation of (Christian) values. In the age of what is labeled as 'traditional communication', values were passed on through personal interaction within the family, community, school and the church. Now ideologies present themselves, in an entertaining and attractive form as life styles that are focused on the image and seeing. Cultural nomadic behavior and zapping predominate, and according to a majority of the statements communication is replaced by a mediated, virtual variety.

Because of the central place of media in culture and the orientation in life, the statements show concern that, increasingly, media are only steered by technical and economic interests.

They value developments towards the information society in terms of chances and risks within all areas of life. They acknowledge economic growth possibilities, tele-cooperation and decentralized employment possibilities, access and interactivity and worldwide data transfer, and the possibility of electronic publication. But also do they point to the danger of information as a production factor, the cause of unemployment or isolation, the danger of data secure problems, of infringing information rights, of central registration and control, and of user profiles for marketing goals. As well, they point to the problem of the overload of information and the new information- and knowledge gap, both worldwide and within societies.

In the area of culture, arts and entertainment, they acknowledge new expression possibilities at lower costs, the opportunities of scene cultures, and the stimulation of traditional media. However, the commercialization, the trivialization of entertainment, the excitement intensity, and the cultural fragmentation -hampering common cultural identity- are valued negatively. So is the individualistic value orientation, ways of finding meaning, and the minimizing of the role of institutions (family, church).

With respect to public space and politics, the statements stress the risks of commercial pressures, the race for topicality and the increase of selection criteria towards drama, negativity, sensation, conflict, and voyeurism. They fear for the function of media as a forum for exchange, the forming of public opinion and consensus, and societal integration.

The implications of new media, especially the internet, are also valued in terms of 'opportunities and drawbacks' (3.4). They provide more information but, at the same time, reduce it to uniform items without intrinsic values. They habituate to interactive communication but discourage interpersonal relationships. They eliminated time and space in communication, offering immediate, worldwide, decentralized and endlessly expandable content outreach, but the benefits are shared unequally. New media can be powerful tools for education, cultural enrichment, political participation and intercultural dialogue, but they can also exploit, manipulate, dominate or corrupt. Regulation is needed for pluralism and public responsibility and to curb exaggerated individualism and liberty.

Just like other media, new media are not neutral; they bring about changes not only in the media landscape but in all areas of life, also spiritual. Human life is represented in virtual worlds (games, chats, muds, virtual reality immersion without physical limits or geography) in which information can be easily manipulated. This questions e.g. concepts of truth, human life, thinking, presence, relationship, body, space and time. Thus the new media environment creates a more complex social space. This also challenges the public presence of the churches; on the one hand, there are increased possibilities for social communication, but, at the same time, the public presence of the churches decreases in importance. Religiosity increases, but piety and devotion decrease (4.4).

Communication is 'at a crossroads' (from communication to information) and one of the 'major ethical challenges to the churches' (3.3).

These include:

• the prevalence of commercial criteria and the global impact of advertising (stimulating artificial needs and consumption)
• public interest, pluralism and social cohesion (the aggravation of social discourse and the undermining of communities)
• navigation and valuation of the overload of information (equal 'items' of info without intrinsic value)
• public accountability on media content and media regulation in favor of public service, common good and cultural identities
• media literacy and media skills
• ethical, spiritual and moral issues (privacy, freedom, free speech, security, data shadows, copyright and intellectual property, pornography, racism, hate sites, encryption technology, implants, and inequality) and
• information and communication justice (digital divide).

With respect to the view of the *cultural/religious dimension* in and of media offered by the statements, they show awareness of the intertwinement of media and culture. The degree of relationship is valued to different extents though. Media are 'signs of the time reflecting culture' (3.1), a 'central area of culture' (3.2); 'affected by culture as much as media affect culture' (3.3) or the 'main carrier of culture' (4.5). But other statements acknowledge a deeper intertwinement (e.g. 1.2, 2.2, 4.2, 4.6, 4.9, 5.1, 5.2). Media are the 'privileged way for the creation and transmission of culture' (1.2); they 'not simply mirror, but help shape the reality they reflect' (2.2); they are 'the main agent of cultural processes, forming culture while at the same time being part of it' (4.6); 'culture and media are inextricably interconnected: media are not just an instrument to organize culture, they reflect the culture they create' (5.1, 5.2).

Media are considered to be the main means not only of information and education, but also of guidance, personal and social orientation, and the construction of identity. As one statement puts it: 'Human experience itself is an experience of media' (1.2). This also implicates the religious realm and the perception of churches. Reality is what media recognize as real. In this sense, it is felt by some statements (e.g. 1.2), that media have the power of overriding the traditional reference points of religion and culture and -in the worst scenario- might 'reduce the gospel to silence' (1.2). If a community is not visible in the media, there is a danger it might disappear from conscious and reality (4.1). The tendency to privatize religion is counterbalanced by the tendency of media to enter in all aspects of human life, including the intimate; increasingly religion has thus become a media issue (4.6).

Since socialization (also religious) is, in a new sense, also socialization by media, faith has to prove its plausibility and the possibility to be experienced, and its practical meaning in a world and life stamped by media communication (4.7). The pluralism of meaning supply in a market of possibilities and opinions forces traditional meaning monopolies into competition. They are weakened in their integration power, and can no longer impose right or wrong by canon, but must win respect (4.7). This holds especially true for the proclamation of the church. It should be connected to the changed faith experience of people in daily life (from theoretical to a concrete approach), the situation of diversity and the new spiritual search (4.8).

There is a climate of religion in and outside the churches in which fundamental issues of human purpose and destiny have become matters for probing speculation rather than easy affirmation or denial (5.4).

On the other hand, documents show concern towards the 'climate of absence of meaning' (1.4) in which certainties belong to the past, and meaning has become provisional and fleeting. Media culture is mosaic and dynamic and touches upon emotions before intellect (4.2). The impression of possession leading to happiness can mislead and frustrate. Vulgarity, the morally degrading depiction of sexuality (pornography) and violence, the appeal to envy, status and lust, and seeking to shock are judged negatively. The exploitation of religious themes or persons for the selling of products (2.2), superficiality and bad taste entertainment and the internationalization of 'values of the secularized society' (2.3) are equally, negatively judged.

The various interpretations of the relationship between media and culture, and the absence of definitions of religion, spirituality and secularization, question whether the documents accurately analyze the religious implications of media culture. Whether they do or not will become more explicit in the sections about (Christian) identity (3.3.4), the view on media roles (3.3.5), church involvement (3.3.7) and the challenges and priorities (3.3.8).

Public interest is another important issue in the statements. The concept refers to a variety of related issues. It includes: access, participation, public accountability, regulation, ethical standards, communication rights, plurality and media and communication competence.

Public service broadcasting is felt to be 'more important than ever' (5.4). It has a major role to play in democracy, and in the guarantee of cohesion in community, pluralism and cultural diversity. The radical changes in the media landscape question the role of public service broadcasting and its principles and media regulation. The shift from linear to network media -without borders-, the unclear identification of media organizations, the abundance and commercialization of supply, and the unknown business model (pay for access or for content and interaction services) impact the role and development of public service broadcasting. So do the lessened distinction between editorial and commercial information, the fragmentation of the public, and the way it uses media.

A broad discussion is needed in the public arena on values and objectives of future communication systems -not only in an economic or technical sense- but in service of public interest. This discussion also includes the role of public service broadcasting in a multi channel digital universe.

Media regulation (which is increasingly self-regulation) should aim at the safeguarding of general availability and access for all and enable people to actively participate in the communication process, not merely as consumers, but as informed citizens. Values and standards should play a central role as basis for regulation criteria and which role is to ensure the objectives of public interest. Regulation should take into account, the plurality of content and providers, free opinion forming, commitment to universal services (digital divide), the protection of private life data, cultural diversity (minorities), and the protection of minors and user's needs. The paradigm for orientation should not be commercial pressure but human service, community and progress.

The immersion in a virtual world in which libertarianism is the absolute value instead of truth, sincerity, community and solidarity can, in this sense, be a threat to traditional values of freedom of expression and exchange of ideas. Knowing the truth, for example, is a communication right, and the distortion of truth, propaganda or spin are a violation of communication rights.

(Visual) media literacy and communication competence is considered to be one of the key qualifications in the information and communication future. Since the responsibility of viewers is increasing, media education is fundamentally important at all levels of the education system - so are associations of users.

Media logic, media use as part of everyday social interaction, and *media effects on social institutions* are issues mentioned but not elaborated upon extensively by all documents.
It is recognized that media have their own 'laws' (4.3), but concern is felt about professional standards and quality in journalism (the preoccupation with the mighty, sensationalism, the merging of news/advertising/entertainment, the decline of serious reporting and commentary, and the rise of a whole 'apparatus' for public opinion -spin, lobby, PR). In the field of religion and church, the 'treatment according to usual news criteria' (4.8), as stated in some documents, leads to problems which worsen conflicts and impacts the public image of the church in society. What is needed is a greater expertise in the coverage of religion in news and current affairs and in editorial policy (5.4).
The special character of internet as a direct, immediate, interactive, and participatory medium (4.9) is also touched upon as a new environment impacting journalism (2.4).

Media use as part of everyday social interaction is impacted by the advent of new media. The cultural benefits (especially with regard to access to literature, drama, entertainment) are recognized. However, depending on their media use, people can become 'more compassioned or isolated in a self referential world of stimuli with near narcotic effects' (2.3). And the replacement of human interaction by media use is felt to be a source of social problems (1.2). People are more involved in computer leisure away from reality and 'find transcendence through cyberspace more interesting than the message of the church of God' (3.1). However others feel that if the church wants to be of some influence in the life of all, it should exactly participate actively in media (4.1). It cannot exist in a social sense without media visibility (4.5).

Classical socialization institutions are all questioned and challenged by computerized society.
There is a shift towards info/edu(cation)-tainment at a more individualized level. There is a lack of participation in community life, and the position of membership has changed. Geographical community and physical presence are 'out', (virtual) specialist individualized interest groups are 'in' (3.4). This challenges for example the self perception of the church as fellowship, the Christian doctrine of incarnation and the valuableness of group norms.
There is also a shift from the socially oriented democracy ideal and its values towards individualism, materialism, free moral and ethics, and individual self realization. Institutions (and their values) are under criticism, idea systems are doubted and the complexity of the world makes people focus more on the 'small' world.
Institutes such as the churches can no longer rely on hierarchy, are forced to competition, and have to prove their 'relevance'. 'This significantly impacts church structures and modes of functioning' (1.2) as one statement puts it (unfortunately, without getting into elaboration regarding extent or direction). One document (4.8)

explicitly relates the church to the heritage of structures of the industrial uniform society and concludes there is now a 'very different field'.

Before turning to audience research, we will present a table about media context and media culture. Tallies can provide only a certain insight in the complex, extensive analysis statements make on the contemporary media context and need to be accompanied by remarks in regard to the content as given above. However, they can be helpful in providing us with an insight into the foci in the field of media context by each statement.

	trends	definitions	implications	logic	use	cultu / reli dimension	public interest	effects institutions
1.1	x	-	-	x	-	x	x	-
1.2	x	-	x	-	x	x	x	x
1.3	x	-	-	-	-	-	x	-
1.4	x	-	x	-	-	x	-	-
2.1	x	-	x	-	-	-	-	-
2.2	x	-	x	x	x	x	x	-
2.3	x	-	x	x	x	x	x	-
2.4	x	-	x	x	x	x	x	-
3.1	x	x	x	-	x	x	x	x
3.2	x	-	x	x	-	x	x	x
3.3	x	x	x	-	-	x	x	x
3.4	x	x	x	-	-	x	x	x
4.1	-	-	-	-	x	x	-	x
4.2	x	-	x	x	-	x	x	-
4.3	x	-	x	x	-	x	-	-
4.4	x	-	x	x	x	x	x	-
4.5	x	-	x	-	-	-	x	x
4.6	x	-	x	-	-	x	x	-
4.7	x	-	x	x	-	x	-	x
4.8	x	-	x	x	-	x	-	x
4.9	x	-	x	x	x	x	-	-
4.10	x	-	x	-	x	-	x	x
5.1	x	x	-	-	-	x	x	-
5.2	x	-	x	-	x	x	x	-
5.3	x	-	-	-	-	x	x	-
5.4	x	-	x	x	-	x	x	-

Table 3.3 Media context and media culture

3.3.3   Audience research[15]

The first striking feature with respect to the audience is the relative little attention given to it in the statements. There are astonishingly few elaborations made to the position

[15] In this section we will focus on tracing possible references made to recent insights by media and communication studies, especially in the field of reception research and audience ethnography as described in chapter two. The audience in a wider sense and audience in the sense of church membership are not to be separated -church members are immersed in media culture just like anybody else-. However, for the sake of clarity: in this section we do not elaborate upon the position of church membership and internal communication (within the church). This will, however, be included in section 3.3.4 on identity and 3.3.8 on challenges and priorities in church communication.

and role of the audience. This is all the more amazing since, in the analysis of the media context, the far reaching changes in the media landscape are recognized. Moreover the implications of media developments are a major issue that include interactivity, audience fragmentation, media socialization and the autonomy in the perception of identity, values, spiritual search and faith experiences. The need for an attitude of listening and dialogue for example is also recognized; next to the need to be relevant to people. At the same time however media use as part of the daily social interaction is not an explicit issue in itself, and the concept of for example interactivity is neither defined nor elaborated upon. This questions what the view of the audience exactly is and might account for the total absence of references to the field of audience research.

Whenever the position of the audience is mentioned in the statements, the references are varied and sometimes contradictory. 'Victims', 'objects', 'subjects', 'receivers /recipients', 'users', 'target groups', 'public', 'citizen', and 'client' are but some of the qualifications that are reviewed, whether or not accompanied adjectively by: 'passive', 'isolated', 'responsible' or 'excluded'.

Ordinary people are 'victims of media power' and treated more as objects than as subjects (1.1). Or, in the opposite direction: 'the public has more critical freedom than is believed; the impact of television on the public is an illusion' (4.5). Changes are mainly technical and do 'not involve the conditions of the communication partners' (sic) which brings the risk that people are excluded from information (4.8). Since people are 'immersed in media culture', all content must be adapted to the needs of different groups; the goal must always be to make people aware of the ethical and moral dimension of information (1.4). Others claim that the means of social communication 'can give rise to 'passivity among users', who should practice 'moderation and discipline' in their approach to media (2.2). By their media use, people can 'grow in sympathy and compassion' or become 'isolated self-referential individuals' instead of a 'global community', and solidarity media developments can lead to a 'fragmented network of audiences of one' (2.3, 2.4). 'Recipients' must be 'self-disciplined' since the immersion in the virtual world of cyberspace may be damaging to psychological health (2.4). And the overwhelming quantity of information is 'a problem to many' (2.4). People should choose the position of responsible citizen instead of client/consumer (3.3, 4.1, 5.4). It is therefore of 'capital importance to 'help the public make more free and more responsible choices', which demands formation. Instead of 'despair because of the passivity of the public, or shutting off in refusal or censure -as Christians often do-, it is better to appeal to the responsibility of the public by giving it means of taking action' (4.2). Regulation should meet 'the needs of users' (balancing individual and general public interest) and not restrict them to the role of consumers (5.1, 5.2).

On the other hand, there are also statements which go beyond an ethical and formational appeal. They recognize the electronic media 'brought us into a global context with intercultural symbols and messages' that 'contain as many meanings as there are receivers'. And since 'the social context of receivers has greater impact on the interpretation of the message than the intent of the sender', the issue is raised whether 'we can create a Christian culture of communication which focuses on recipients' (3.3). In a communicative culture, the attitude must be towards 'subjects in an ongoing dialogue' and 'receiver oriented communication' instead of an object or a target group (1.3).

Direct references to audience analysis are rarely made (4.8 e.g. does). One document refers to 'reader's analysis' (4.4), but in the context of 'marketing'. It claims that if the communicator (the church) does not want 'to stay in itself', the addressee must be the most important. 'A customer oriented publicity, dedicated to people and consistently oriented towards the addressee can be successful' but 'the church publicity led by institutional interest' cannot. 'Market capable' means 'group oriented'. Needed, therefore, is market- and reader's analysis. The former division in church members and worldly addressees decreases. Social scientific analysis shows an 'undivided receiver', communicating in multiple ways, who 'can be made an offer which finds his interest' (4.4).

The same document, however, also claims 'it belongs to the mandate of protestant publicity to orient the journalistic work to the Word and tradition of biblical faith and take seriously the interests and life-situations of people'. The tension between 'communication adapted to receivers' and 'communication on terms of the sender', between a view of 'objects to be informed' and 'subjects who need to be listened to and dialogued with', is highlighted (4.8) to which is added that the 'task of the church to proclaim the divine message is often the cause of aggravating conflict'. Nevertheless, theological changes in history show development of the gospel, to which dialoguing with people made its contribution. Therefore, people should be accepted as subjects, (4.8) and messages should be related to the circumstances of the hearers (4.10), like Paul did when he called himself a 'Greek to the Greeks'.

Summarizing, there appears to be two different positions from which the audience is viewed and both vary in graduation.

The first position is the view of the audience in the context of media developments and media culture. The graduation varies from a victim of media power, over a rather passive, unknowing object that needs to be helped in critical awareness, moderation and discipline to a critical subject and responsible citizen refusing to be degraded to a consumer. Formation in this view is critically important.

The second position -however, related to the media context as well- focuses more on the position of the audience in its social context and its role as addressee and recipient in meaning making. This position more directly implicates church communication, since the audience is viewed in terms of subjects in dialogue, which demands receiver oriented communication.

3.3.4   Christian identity

Social cohesion is deeply impacted by contemporary media culture. That is one reason to identify Christian identity as one of the key issues. Another one is that the view of one's own identity is an important aspect of one's view and praxis of communication. In this section, we will identify the statements' perception of self/Christian identity. This is not an issue in all documents. In particular the statements with a focus on ethics, audiovisual media education and media policy take no notice of it. (There are no explicit references in 2.2, 2.4, 3.1, 4.2, 5.2 and 5.3).

Christian identity is a broad concept. Within the scope of our research it specifically refers to the institutional position related to communication and contemporary communication culture. In particular, we researched five related issues:

- the view of authority (the power dimension of being and meaning)
- the cultural 'style' in relating to the audience and media culture;
- the view towards plurality;
- the outlook on tradition (viewed as an unassailable 'package' ready to be delivered, or a temporarily construct impacted by culture) and
- the outlook on cultural materials in social practice being a subject for theology.

Because each reference in itself might include various positions, it is less useful to present a table in regard to identity, which may only reveal whether or not a subject is addressed. When constructing one, however, it is immediately clear that a view of cultural materials in social practice as a subject of theology is totally absent. The issue of tradition as a temporarily construct is also rarely mentioned.

The views of identity strongly vary. They appear to be denomination related. Distinction in church institutional belonging or communication expertise also accounts for differences. Positions given by the statements may resemble in terminology (e.g. the issue of communion/community), but differ in elaboration. Sometimes there is also an overlap of (contradictory) positions that complicates the understanding of the exact outlook.

Therefore we first will present the views according to denomination/organization before extrapolating a more generalizing categorization.

The identity of WACC[16] is rooted in 'a community of communicators' in solidarity with 'the poor, the oppressed and the marginalized, who bear the hallmark of God's communication' (1.1). Attention must be given to the reinterpretation of the contents of Christian discourse as based on the 'deposit of faith'. Christian communicators must consider both the biblical text as well as the cultural context in their work (2.1). And democratize their own media (1.1).

The *Vatican's* identity is positioned in being a church which is to bring all in 'full union with Christ' (1.2) and called to 'announce to all the message of salvation' (1.4). The church, therefore, must take advantage of the opportunities of media as 'pathways given by God to 'intensify communion and the penetration of the proclamation of the Word' (1.4.). Everything possible must be done to make the gospel permeate society so that people 'listen and embrace its message' (1.4). Media culture must be taken into account; pastoral and cultural revision is needed to deal adequately with the times (1.4). The church must 'maintain an active listening presence in relation to the world' and 'communicate suited to media culture' (1.2).

The church is a communion 'mirroring the community of the Trinity'; communication, therefore, is of essence to the church. Its communication practice should be exemplary, and fulfill the highest standards of truthfulness, accountability, and sensitivity to human rights, principles and norms (4.9). Since God 'continues to communicate with humanity through the church', the church is the 'bearer and custodian of the revelation, to whose living teaching office alone He has entrusted the task of authentically interpreting his word' (4.9). It has a 'long tradition of moral wisdom' (2.3).

COMECE's duty related to communication is to observe and react to economical and political developments in the EU and to contribute to the process of European integration. Examining culture 'implies studying media and its structures' (5.1).

CEEM views itself as a church that is part of the 'developing info space' and 'amidst media culture'. Communication is essential and related to communion, which is a concern of a 'church charged with preaching the Gospel'. Dealing with media often leads to negative experiences (one sided criticism, scandal orientation, destruction of values and the simplification of the complex reality of church life). Refusal and defense, therefore, are easier than seizing the opportunities of media culture and the acceptance

---

[16] The work and mission of Christians in communication is set out by WACC in its document, *Christian Principles of Communication* (which is not included in our research). It describes communication from a Christian perspective. Communication is marked by: creating community, being participatory, liberating, supporting and developing cultures, and being prophetic. London, WACC, 1986.

of its challenges. However, a church secluding in isolation, in the end talks only to itself and is unable to fulfill its mission to preach the gospel to all. The church is oriented to 'communion with God and human beings'. As a 'community of faithful, the church, in the nature of sacrament, is a sign and instrument of communion with God and unity among all men' (Quote from *Lumen Gentium*). 'Communication between members of the church has to serve the promotion and cultivation of communion, as well as the exchange of the variety existing within church'. The quality of the church as communion 'can be measured by the quality of communication between its members', which is a 'prerequisite for authentic communication with the world'. Free exchange must therefore be promoted and secrecy restricted (4.3). The challenge of contemporary language is to provide 'spirituality for media culture'. The discussion of media issues is a vital challenge for the 'enculturation' of Christian faith (4.6).

The *LWF*[17] is identified as a 'community of believers' that 'informs to challenge response', 'enriches and is enriched' and 'creates communication to promote communion'. Meaning is created together in a two way process of communication. Information is shared in advance, and it is ensured that everybody is included as a subject and active participant. Cultural diversity is affirmed and solidarity is felt to be an important message in itself in a context of economic and political dominance, and cultural homogenization. Views are to be 'communicated clearly', but there is readiness to be changed ('we no longer have to be the ones who know'). Thus, all thus become partners in an ongoing dialogue (1.3).
The LWF wants to be a 'communicative communion' of churches, 'confessing the triune God, agreeing in the proclamation of the word of God and united in pulpit and altar fellowship'. It wants to 'create a Christian culture of communication focused on recipients' according to their history, language, skills and abilities (3.3).

The *Lutheran Church of Finland* in its 1992 document (4.1) signals that after the break up of 'the common culture' (formerly ensured by state, church and school), 'many expect the church to ensure the common basis in values and moral'. It feels that 'when the authority and influence of the church is weakened, one of the fundaments of western culture is damaged'. Communication of the gospel is best reached 'when people increase in mutual listening and sharing their experiences, views and needs'. The focus of the church therefore moved to 'the real questions of the time' (4.1).
In the 2004 statement (4.10) this line is pursued in accordance with the overall church operational strategy *The Church that is present*. The church's mission is 'the great commission given by Christ to his church'. As a 'community of God's presence', the Lutheran folk church is present in Finnish life and in contact with the people where they live. In today's context this means amid an urban culture with social conflicts, a multi-faith situation, and changes in family life. The vision and the operational idea of the church that is present is a communicative church that is engaged in dialogue (meaning both the church's internal and public debate). The church is by its nature, mission and activities a 'communicating community'. The hallmark of the strategy of the church that is present is 'that the presence of another world can be sensed' (the voice of the gospel). The Church 'conveys' the message of the gospel (grace, faith, hope and love). 'Preaching the gospel' is its 'non-relinguishable' task. The '*communio sanctorum*' is called to communicate in word and deed 'so that the world might believe'. Since the Lutheran church is a folk church, -part of Finnish society and culture-, it is to be there for the whole people. It 'depends on the recipients and the matter to be communicated what best serves the message'. The marks of the communicative church are: 'dignity (every

---

[17] The focus of the 2002 LWF statement *The Lutheran World Federation, a Communicative Communion*, is mainly towards communication within the federation worldwide.

human is respected); people listen and ask; interaction is encouraged; diversity is appreciated; fellowship is built up; people communicate with consideration for he other party; people communicate their convictions clearly and intelligibly; people are bold in expressing their opinions; people are prepared to change; people take initiative and react; information is provided openly and in advance and people encounter the church in the media they use'. The way members live as a church and practice their faith is important in how 'the truth about the church and its faith' is experienced. The way in which internal communication works, tells people the basic truth about church. The communicative church listens to people and to the contemporary world. This means: 'being present, walking alongside, and giving space'. On the other hand: 'communication is sharing convictions, including the mystery of faith'. Only 'if all parties open up, communication is reached', and everyone is enriched. The communicative church creates an 'atmosphere' in which there is room for different languages: speech, music, drama, dance and images. The gospel can be conveyed by all; 'all have the right to be heard and to express' (the priesthood of all through baptism). In the communicative church 'communications takes into consideration the other party in dialogue'. It is accepted that different groups or members have different expectations of the church and its communication. Unless the church 'recognizes and takes seriously' the circumstances and questions of its members, what it says will be ignored and rejected. In that case, there is no living interaction. In the communicative church, communications (and things like language) changes with the persons involved. Communication tools and channels are chosen according to the communications the receiving group is accustomed to. Being communicative is an 'attitude' that can be realized in bilateral encounters, internet communications, writing, etc. Every message is 'a contribution to an ongoing discussion'. In the communicative church, communication is 'a resource and an opportunity'. By supporting dialogue in the church and society, progress is made towards 'the goals set' (4.10).

For the *Church of* Sweden (4.8) it is important that the community experiences the church as 'an organization you can easily communicate with'. A clearer division of responsibilities and church competences must lead to better functioning communication. Due to globalization, local communities stand in a larger connection; local community life must be developed in openness for the world that includes concrete renewals in church service, music and meetings. Communication by the Swedish church (with members and society) must be connected with questions of meaning. In this way the church contributes, in cooperation with co-citizens, to the development of local communities. Rather than 'owning the truth', it 'practices the role of truth seeker'. This attitude does not imply, however, 'the church floats over the goal of its own opinion'. To strengthen the role and identity of the church, it needs 'to multiply the number of persons going to church, keep up Sunday school and raise the number of baptisms and confirmation candidates'. Professional expertise in public opinion is needed. 'Listening more carefully to the needs of the people and getting a better insight in the points of departure and contact, will improve the conditions for success'. In the 21st century, the church has to work in a pluralistic, multi ethnic and multi religious and global society. Values and standards are individualized, without conformity. 'Truth is what an individual understands as truth', not what is identified as such by authority. Secularization, however, is not just a negative feature; 'the interest in the church and an honest search for meaning of life' is positive. Secularization is more about freeing oneself from church collectives, than from fundamental metaphysical issues. The privatization of religion may lead to 'a church which meets the spiritual needs of people on their own conditions'. The church, therefore, must be 'open as well as faithful to its confession'. Silence, prayer and meditation attract people. But 'symbolic deeds and words are able to mystify without entering into divine truth'. Being clear in profile must not be tightening though;

it includes being positive, solid, and taking part in dialogues. The church, as an independent folk church, must 'adapt its rules to strengthen the fellowship of all who belong to the church and supplement an offensive pastoral program'. 'Both continuity as well as identity must be preserved'. The task of the church 'is still the same: honor the sacraments, proclaim Gods word and help the poor'. To hold and increase membership, it is important, that people associate the Swedish church with what she stands for: 'bring the glad tidings of liberation and salvation, the rehabilitation of the oppressed, hope of eternal life, be part of global community and live and work in a spiritual culture stamped by the values of Jesus and by the knowledge God is love'.

There is an increasing interest in religion and questions of meaning 'if let go of the traditional definitions of religious activities'. If people's views are taken seriously, there are 'enough possibilities for communication'. The church 'cooperates in the ecumenical and world religions dialogue', as an 'institution seeking truth, but not owning it'. People are no 'objects to be informed', but subjects to listen to and dialogue with. The task of the church to proclaim the divine message, 'often is the cause of aggravating conflict'. Theological changes in history however show 'the gospel developed'. Dialoguing with people contributed to this development. According to the Lutheran theology, the Swedish church cannot 'speak in the name of the whole church. Not even its archbishop'.

The *Protestant Church and the Roman Catholic Church in Germany* are the only churches that produced an ecumenical document (3.2). Whether or not this means there is some sort of 'common identity' will have to become clearer when analyzing their individual documents as well (see below). But in this document there is some common denominators. Apparently, asking how 'to bring their offer of life interpretation in the societal discussion' is regarded to be one of their tasks and thus reveals something about their identity. They strongly agree about the 'never to be abandoned relationship between personal contact and the passing on of faith within the congregation' for church and religion. Against the rise of media offerings and media use, 'the private, not mediated experience increases in value'. It is a major task to provide opportunities for 'direct interpersonal meeting and primary religious experiences'.

The *EKD* (Protestant Church in Germany) claims 'the changing media and info society does not alter the obligation of the church to proclaim the entrusted gospel as a public message directed at the whole of society'. In the light of the gospel it 'dedicates itself to truth and freedom in living communication'. It understands itself, according to bible and reformation, as 'a unity of people, created by God and justified by Christ'. The changed position of the church (decrease in bindings and income) could 'in a beneficial crisis lead to a church in search of finding new ways to people'. This might help the church to change from 'an alien felt organization' to an 'inviting community'. Furthermore, 'it belongs to the mandate of protestant publicity to orient journalistic work to the Word and tradition of biblical faith and to take seriously the interests and life situations of people' (4.4).

According to the *German Bishops' Conference*, 'specific religious questions nowadays are taken up in the respective fields of culture, publicity and media'. Church media bureaus therefore need to accomplish 'religiously founded formational and cultural work'. Their supplies are 'a contribution to evangelization in a secular world'. Media developments change all domains of life and place new challenges to church proclamation and socialization. Faith has to 'prove its plausibility, its possibility to be experienced and its practical meaning in life, in a world stamped by media communication'. The church must extend its initiatives for church communication pedagogy, put them into praxis more broadly, and systemize them in a theologically founded communication theory. Formation must be aimed at the development of the fullness of human communication competence (4.7).

In its submission to the BBC charter review, the *Bishops' Conference of England and Wales* (5.4) does not elaborate upon issues of identity. It does acknowledge, however, 'there is a climate of religion inside and outside the churches, in which the fundamental issues of human purpose and destiny have become matters for probing speculation rather than for easy affirmation or denial'. It therefore agrees with the Central Religious Advisory Committee that 'there should be even greater variety, more exposition, more speculation and more experiment'.

Like the German churches, the *Church of England*, in its document on the challenges of new media and the information society (3.4), , stresses the importance of 'real communities'. 'The church is a real community for the 21 century, gathering people in real communities, which become an increasing human necessity'. It also argues that it is necessary to 'rewrite the church as a place of truth -individual and social- for what is happening in society'. Moreover, it should 'speak up for those who can't'.

The ecumenical document by the communication specialists from *UNDA/WACC* explicitly deals with identities and communities (4.5) related to communication in today's global media world. The more openness, they argue, the greater the problem of identity is. The diversity of references, the confrontation with the other, and anxiety can result in a withdrawal into the individual sphere. The dilemma of identity and openness 'too often is resolved in centralizing uniformity in the name of -badly understood- universalism, wiping out differences. Every political or social entity should ask itself whether it wishes to be 'a collective bringing co- existing individuals together', or 'a participative community'. This applies in the first place to churches. More often they are 'institutions providing services' instead of 'communities,   inviting members'. What is needed is a 'renewal of the community spirit' in order to become 'living communities' similar to the first Christians. Resolving the dilemma of identity and openness by a centralizing uniformity 'gives up on real communication'. Identity is 'a multiple, living and developing reality'. The more aware a community is of its own culture, 'the more capable it is of dialoguing'. Identity is 'not an obstacle to openness, it is its condition' (if not manipulated towards aggression, or xenophobic violence). It is necessary to 'help people see we deny the basis of our own humanity, if we fail to accept people in their difference'. In churches and religions, believers think of identity as 'a fortress to be defended' more than as 'a conviction to be affirmed in the midst of a debate'. Community supposes that 'each has the effective right to speak'. 'Without mutual listening and communication, community is not possible'.

The focus on administrative reorganization policies is not helpful in this respect. Offering services is impersonal and will not increase a feeling of belonging. 'More deeply our churches should ask themselves if their members are truly able to have a say at the heart of the institution'. They should move away from 'turning their internal communication into an instrument in the interest of selling the views of their leaders' to a view 'in which communication serves to express the views of their members'. Thus they can 'help keeping identities from dissolving and maintain a belief in human and religious universalism (which is neither westernization nor globalization) based upon the universal fatherhood of God'. As Pentecost (speaking to all languages) shows, 'universalism is not uniformity', but a 'symphonic unity in which each culture expresses something of the mystery of being human and of the goodness of God'.

Identity, then, appears to be a concept with a broad variety of meaning. Identity is found in: solidarity with the poor; in proclamation; in communion (theologically founded); in being a communicative community oriented at the needs of recipients towards dialogue and interaction; in enculturation; in being a custodian of tradition; in providing the common basis of values and moral; in offering life orientation in the societal debate; in being a place of truth for what is happening in society; in 'real' community of interpersonal contact; in passing on faith in the congregation; in primary religious experiences; in formational work to contribute to evangelization or in a theologically grounded communication theory.

Generalizing categorizations are difficult to make. It is more adequate to speak of variables on a line than of clear cut positions. The extremes of the line are, on the one hand, constituted by a church community grounded in the communion of the Trinity and charged with proclamation and safeguarding of the revelation and tradition. Sacraments and the passing on of faith in real communities are emphasized. The other extreme appears to be characterized more by openness towards today's media culture, recipient orientation, dialogue and living interaction, plurality and a common search of meaning and truth.
However, the first variable, of which the Roman Catholic Church (especially the Vatican) is an example, also bears features of the second one. The Vatican documents also stress the importance of an 'active listening presence in relation to the world' and communication 'suited to media culture'. And the Lutheran churches, clearly representing the second variable, state for example, 'preaching the gospel is its non-relinguisable task'. The Swedish church claims 'continuity and identity must be preserved'; 'the task of the church is still the same: honor the sacraments, proclaim Gods Word and help the poor'. And to strengthen its role and identity, it focuses on 'increasing church attendance, Sunday school and baptism and confirmation'.
Nevertheless, there is a difference in attitude in both positions.

The statements discussed in this section vary. The fact that they describe their identity in overlapping and sometimes contradictory ways, -without clearly defining what is meant by terms like proclamation, openness, sharing convictions or communication-, aggravates the identification of identity. It might be concluded, however, that the adherents of the first position mentioned appear to include far much less institutional change due to media culture than the ones closer to the second variable. The also appear to hold a more constant view of tradition, whereas the second variable holds an inconstant outlook.

3.3.5   Views on communication and media roles

In this section, we will consider the views about media roles and communication as presented in the different statements. One of the key questions will be whether a different outlook on identity, as researched in the section above, results in a different outlook on communication and the role of media (instrumental or otherwise). There are only two documents which have no explicit references towards the outlook on communication and the role of media (4.6 and 5.3). The Submission to the BBC charter review by the Catholic Bishops' Conference of England and Wales (5.4) is notable for its extensive elaboration on the subject.
WACC strongly relates communication to humanity, social cohesion/community and human dignity. It identifies communication as 'a unique gift of God', 'crucial for humankind', and for peace and international understanding. Communication is to serve society as a whole and the entirety of humankind. Commitment to democratic communication is the responsibility of all. A new phase of dialogue is needed to achieve a common understanding of communication 'in the service of free, just and peaceful communities'. Just like the 'natural environment' needs to be nurtured and cultivated, so

must be the 'communication environment'. Thus, the role of media thus is to work for peace and international understanding (1.1). Media should encourage the creative use of symbols, images and other folk expressions by which people's identities are strengthened and cultural traditions and diversities are recognized. Communication technology should be a tool to aid interactivity and not be exploited. Christian churches and organizations should recognize and respond to the challenges of the media age by developing an 'organic' rather than 'instrumental' understanding of media. Christian communicators should engage in consciousness raising with respect to communication in pursuit of religious tolerance, justice and peace (2.1).

The Vatican, in Aetatis Novae (1.2), defines communication (quoting Communio et Progressio) as 'a way toward communion' -rooted in the communion of the Trinity-. 'More than the expression of ideas or emotion, communication is the giving of self in love'. 'Social communications', the term consistently used in Vatican documents, is theologically founded and oriented towards 'the benefit of humanity'.
Media are 'instruments of unity and understanding', 'Gifts of God that, in accordance with his providential design, unite men in brotherhood' and 'so help them cooperate with his plan for their salvation'. They are also 'instruments in the Church' program of re- and new evangelization'. They cannot, however, 'take the place of immediate personal contact and interaction'.
It is 'imperative that media respect and contribute to the integral development of the person and the cultural, transcendent and religious dimensions of man and society'. Media are 'at the service of persons and cultures, the dialogue with the world, human community and progress, ecclesial communion and new evangelization'. The Spirit helps the church to interpret the signs of the times and carry out its prophetic task among which 'the study, the evaluation and the right use of communications technology and the media of social communications are now fundamental'18. Media are a mixed blessing; at times they exacerbate problems in the way of human solidarity and integral development (secularism, consumerism, materialism, and dehumanization, and lack of concern for the poor and neglected). The church has a 'special urgency to bring all to full union with Christ', to which the media of social communications can make 'an important contribution'. Under God's providence they can 'promote communication and communion among human beings' and contribute to the diminishing of conflict and division. They can also be used for the 'fundamental right of dialogue and information within the church' (1.2).

Basically, this instrumental view of communication, in which social and theological arguments are intrinsically intertwined, is pursued in the other Vatican statements, whether they have an overall orientation (1.4), an ethical focus, (2.2, 2.3, 2.4) or discuss new media (4.9).

The most recent document -the apostolic letter The Rapid Development, by pope John Paul II that was published in January 2005 shortly before his death- explicitly refers to 'the appropriateness to reflect on the challenges of media for the church, 'since the more than forty years of the publication of Inter Mirifica' (1963). Inter Mirifica was the first Council document on communications. The Pontifical Commission for the 'Instruments of Social Communication' was a direct outcome of it. This commission was responsible for Communio et Progressio (1971) which, next to Aetatis Novae (1992), might be considered to be the main documents on communication by the Vatican. The Rapid Development, then, might be expected to provide us with a sort of 'recapitulation'

---

[18] In the appendix to Aetatis Novae on a plan for social communications, the exercise of this prophetic role involves 'the moral dimensions of significant public issues'.

of views, all the more since it consists for a great part of quotes from and references to previous statements.

There is no explicit definition on communication theory given in The Rapid Development. The instrumental vision is carried on. Media are 'powerful means' (quote from Evangelio Nuntiandi); they 'provide the providential opportunity to reach people everywhere, overcoming the barriers of time, space and language'. The content of faith can be 'presented in the most varied ways imaginable' and 'offered to all who search the possibility of entering into dialogue with the mystery of God, revealed in Jesus Christ'. Media, if used by believers with faith and in docility to the light of the Holy Spirit, can 'facilitate the communication of the gospel and render bonds of communion among ecclesial communities more effective'.   The document acknowledges the need for a 'change of mentality and pastoral renewal' without elaborating on the subject or clarifying what exactly is meant. 'In communication media the church finds an aid for spreading the gospel and religious values, for promoting dialogue, for ecumenical and inter-religious cooperation and for the defense of principles of a society respecting human dignity and the common good'. The church 'employs media to furnish information about itself and expand the boundaries of evangelization, catechesis and formation'. It considers the use of media as a response to the command of the Lord 'to proclaim the Gospel to the whole world and every creature (MK 16:15)'.

In the contemporary climate of absence of meaning, media 'can be used to proclaim the Gospel, or to reduce it to silence' (Quote from AN). With respect to new media, it is stated that the internet has the potential to 'assist evangelization, education, internal communication, administration and governance'. New technologies 'further the opportunities for communication understood as service to pastoral government and the organization of different tasks of the Christian community'. The internet e.g. provides resources for more information and 'habituates persons to interactive communication'. (This issue is not further elaborated upon either). New and traditional media must be used. Without proper formation, there is a risk of media 'manipulating and heavily conditioning, rather than serving people'. Modern technologies 'increase the speed, quantity and accessibility of communication', but 'above all, do not favor the delicate exchange between mind and mind, heart and heart, which should characterize any communication at the service of solidarity and love'. 'The mass media can and must promote justice and solidarity according to an organic and correct vision of human development, by reporting events accurately and truthfully, analyzing situations and problems completely and providing a forum for different opinions'. 'An authentically ethical approach to using the powerful communication media must be situated within the context of a mature exercise of freedom and responsibility that is founded upon the supreme criteria of truth and justice'.

The ethical documents Ethics in Advertising (2.2), Ethics in Communication (2.3) and Ethics in Internet (2.4), all share a common focus on community, common good, human dignity, mutual responsibility, and solidarity and growth in the capacity of dialogue. They emphasize the 'missionary' aspects less. However, Ethics in Communication (2.3) summarizing the 'religious benefits', states that media can 'enrich, give information about huge events and about persons, are vehicles for evangelization and catechesis inspiration, encouragement, worship and spiritual enrichment'. They have a duty to 'uplift popular standards'. With respect to ethics in internet (2.4, common good and solidarity also are the cornerstones: 'In regard to the message, the process of communication, structural and systematic issues, the fundamental ethical principle is: the human person and community are the end and the measure of the use of media'. 'Communication should be by persons, to persons for the integral development of persons'.

New media are evaluated along the same lines as mentioned before. In Church and Internet (4.9), the view of media as gifts of God to unite men and involve them in the plan of salvation still remains. Modern media are acknowledged as cultural factors, but also 'offer new ways of confronting people with the Gospel'. In media, the church finds 'a modern and effective version of the pulpit' (Paul VI in Evangelii Nuntiandi 1975:45), but, they are also the 'first Areopagus of the modern age' (John Paul II in his Encyclical letter on Mission Redemptoris Missio 1990: 37c) and 'it is not enough to use the media simply to spread the message and the Church's teaching'. It is also necessary to 'integrate the message into the new culture created by modern communications' with its 'new ways of communicating... new languages, new techniques and a new psychology' (ibidem). This is even more important since human experience itself is an experience of media. The internet offers 'direct and immediate access to religious and spiritual resources, libraries, places of worship, teaching documents of the magisterium and the religious wisdom of ages'. It has the capacity to 'overcome distance and isolation and join people in virtual communities of faith'. The church can offer an 'important service to Catholics and non-Catholics by the selection and transmission of useful data'. The internet is also a 'tool for internal communications' and an 'instrument for administration and governance, a channel for expressing public opinion, education and training'.

The outlook on media and communication then appears to be multi interpretable. The instrumental vision focused on social development -which is theologically founded- and proclamation prevails. New insights on media culture, integration of the gospel, interactivity, and dialogue are touched upon. But tensions in what exactly is meant, or what implications are involved, remain unsolved.

The LWF documents appear to be much clearer with regard to their view of communication. 'Communication is a two way process of giving and receiving information via all senses, followed by mutual deliberations and the creation of common meanings and new insights' (1.3). Personal communication 'in the Lutheran communion comes first and last'. It is the 'most important mode of communication in the Church'. In face to face communication people are 'apt to change their perceptions of reality and their opinions'. Communication at a distance reinforces existing opinions. Communication is 'intrinsically human', a 'creative life giving force through social relationships' (belonging and communion). It defines, develops and maintains social reality. The Latin term *communicare* refers to 'share, to make common'. Communication involves all senses; music drama and visual arts 'may be more effective than speech'. To communicate is to 'speak to the eyes of the listeners', telling stories which they 'visualize and contextualize'. Listeners, then, are 'active participants' in communication. Sharing information is 'basic', but does not 'ensure communication'. Sharing information without discussion is 'one way communication' without readiness to change'. This is *informare*, which means to engrave or carve into. Information in the church by necessity is a 'two way process of communication, which involves mutual enrichment, the creation of meaning together and the building up of the congregation'.
Radio and television are 'excellent to nurture believers', but 'not necessarily the best mission tools'. People are. Communication at a distance may have 'decisive impact' when opinions are not involved. Alternative media, however, and happenings that bring people together, will always be the main channels of communication for Christian faith, except for highly personal communication. Media are 'a means to an end' and the church has its own contribution to make to foster cohesion in communion (1.3).
However, in the Hong Kong assembly statement on the information society (3.3) -which focus is more outward bound instead of within the Lutheran communion as is 1.3- the outlook on communication and media is not that unambiguous as it seemed at first. An

instrumental vision seems to sneak in when it is asked for example 'what kind of media usage is appropriate for the Christian message and for the churches in their witness to the world'. Or in statements like: 'Christians use many ways and means to spread the gospel, now including the internet' (3.3).

The German Bishops Conference, in its statement on multimedia and information society (3.1), strongly resembles the Vatican outlook. Multimedia 'belong to the instruments of social communication'. Engagement by the church is important to 'examine whether media serve man and humanity'. The goal of social communication is 'unity and the advance of human society' (3.1).
The same outlook is propounded in Media and Communication Competence (4.7). 'Central in all engagement in media, is that they are 'to serve as instruments of social communication'. But at the same time, the outlook is also slightly extended. Communication is on the one hand the 'key to understand media structured reality' and on the other hand, also the 'hinge between the theological tradition and a new theological draft which tries to open up the present day in faith'. Communication is understood as 'the centre of all human reality'. Media are 'phenomena of expression' and 'to be analyzed in relationship to individual life stories and collective interpretation models'. Media are 'tools of interpretation', they 'serve mutual exchange' and are 'of dialogical nature'. A medium does not transport meaning in itself, but 'obtains meaning in the process of communication'. Media and communication pedagogic competence is seen by the church as a 'key qualification'. Not merely technically, since there is 'a deep connection of media communication and human existence in the light of faith'. Communication is the 'essence of life'. Media 'can build essential elements in the construction of a tolerant and human culture', but also run the risk of 'contrast experiences'. Media are to be understood as 'crossroads', 'entries to history, the world, liaisons to the immediate and global context' and 'builders of bridges between reality, the persons, and others'.

Mandate and Market (4.4), the statement by the Protestant German churches, shows a similar though individual combination of social integration and theological foundations with respect to media. It is asked 'what should be done to get to the goal of gospel inspired publicity in media and in the information society'. The answer is given in the trinity of communion, communication and community: 'strengthen the community of Christians and people of good will' and 'bring into life serving relationships elements of communication with God and fellow man'. In this way, God is glorified and the worth and freedom of people is served 'through information and a proclaiming orientation of truth'.
Media must contribute to 'inform, orient and entertain'. They 'contribute to understanding and condition responsible social acting'. In 'responsible independence and commitment to human dignity and justice they contribute to social integration within an informed democratic communality'.

It is not surprising, then, that the ecumenical (RC/Protestant) German statement, *Chances and Risks of Media Society*, pursues the lines as described above. Communication is a 'human necessity' and necessary for 'societal living together'. Social communication is stamped by media. Media are 'instruments of social communication', and, at the same time, 'the expression of human communication,' and the reflection of individual and social self understanding. For the churches, it is decisive whether life possibilities, critical account and global living together are served by media. 'From the basic orientation of the churches, media are to be understood as instruments of social communication, in service of people, human dignity and living together'. In design and use they are to 'serve life and the free communication of independent people in a responsible society'. Media need to 'bring people together'. Central issues for the church with respect to the development of mass media are not, in the first place, technical, political or financial ones. They 'follow from the question whether media advance or obstruct the realization of human existence in all its dimensions'. Whether they 'serve communication in service of people and societal living together'. The Christian outlook on man is connected with freedom, worth, self destiny and living in relationships - in the first place with God-. Communication is to build up relationships. Through communication, community gets its deeper meaning. Solidarity and community are the 'main objective of all communication'.

Cybernauts Awake! is the challenging title of the statement by the Church of England on new media. The view on media, however, is the traditional one of an instrumental outlook. 'Historically, every new advance in communication has been a means of proclaiming the gospel, and cyberspace is no exception; it can be used in service of the gospel' (e.g. for social justice and evangelization). Christians should take an active role in the shaping process of cyberspace that is based upon 'a chosen end for the social system'. They should 'add helpful content and participate in online debates to make Christian voices heard'. Churches should be 'very pro-active, since cyberspace is the most important source of information about organizations'. Cyberspace may offer a 'rich new store of analogies and parables' and 'intelligent agents may seem like angels'. But: 'the gospel is bigger than cyberspace; many people are kept away from the Christian faith'. 'As cybernauts awake, we will continue to rejoice in the amazing news of the Word made flesh. Heaven, earth and cyberspace are full of His glory'. Cyberspace, according to this statement, is one of the places to use for friendship and neighborhood and to encourage each others faith. Aspects of it reflect 'the call to respond to God, who spoke and created, and to Jesus, the incarnated Word'. But it has its limitations. Humanness is related to our existence as physical beings. It is the basis for relationships, community and fellowship. 'Physicality is an essential aspect of the human being, bound up with location in space and time'. Cyberspace is relevant for sharing, but there is concern about 'events and relationships in cyberspace'. It is 'a common good, and a strong force for social change and social justice'. But 'expressing in words is essential' and 'participation in worship is physical'. Cyberspace 'may be helpful in providing other ways of communicating about faith; e.g. send questions by email'.

Both documents by the Evangelical Lutheran Church of Finland (4.1 and 4.10) relate communication to 'listening and being listened to, giving and receiving and active participation'. Communication is 'a basic need and right'.
Personal encounter is said to be 'the most effective and convincing form of communication'. The verbal aspect is only one part of it. Personal communication provides the possibility 'for the seeker as well as members' to 'clarify one's own situation and to receive and give support and strength'. 'Distant communication' can 'inform and activate and arouse interest'. Just like the LWF documents, the Latin term *communicare* is used (make common) and defined as interaction. The model of communication is 'a two way model based on inclusiveness and interactivity'. It is the opposite of 'a one way model based on exclusiveness and authority'. Informative communication 'works on the terms of the sender'. It is 'transfer' and 'the given information is final'. The basic condition for 'communicative communication' is that 'as many people as possible have the opportunity to receive open and adequate information'. 'Communicativeness in all forms of communication within the church' is felt as important. 'By nature' this includes 'raising questions, encouraging conversation and challenging people'. Participation -via members- in the public debate and influencing the social development of media is another issue that is paid attention to. The church needs to be visible and participate in media to 'serve all Finnish' (4.1).

This line is pursued in the 2004 document (4.10) which provides us with a more detailed insight into the exact outlook on communication. 'Traditionally, it has been thought that the basic task of communications is to help organizations to reach their goals. Because, for instance, preaching the gospel is by nature human communication, the Church is justified in regarding communications both as a support measure and as part of the Church's main activities' . Communication is basically a 'social activity'. Interpersonal relations are created, developed and changed by communication. For the church, communication is 'a vital necessity'. Community disintegrates if communication is distorted.

Communication, says the statement, is 'a broad concept'. Information is only one (crucial) part. Communication includes not only the verbal, but all senses: hear, see, smell, taste and feel. A person, as well as an organization, is 'always communicating'. Communication is based on the 'exchange of information'. The basic meaning of *communicare* is: to make common. It has the same root in Latin as *communio,* communion and community. One of the basic principles is that communication is 'a force for creation and change'. 'How we communicate cannot be separated from what is communicated'. Personal encounters take a key position. 'To ensure all feel valued, it is necessary to speak of the validity of a person in God's eyes'. Appreciation encourages 'active interaction' instead of being 'a passive object'. With respect to the 'communicative church', communicative is defined as 'equal dialogue'. 'Genuine dialogue is always equal in the sense that all participants have the right to express themselves and be heard'. The communicative church 'listens to people and to the contemporary world'. This means: 'being present, walk alongside, and give space'. On the other hand it is stated that communication is: 'sharing convictions, including the mystery of faith'. 'Only if all parties open up, communication is reached' and 'everyone is enriched'. In the church communication is 'a resource and an opportunity'. By supporting dialogue in church and society, 'progress is made towards the goals set'. Remote communication can 'promote dialogue, but not substitute personal communication'. It can act as 'an introduction or continuation of personal dialogue'. It 'depends on the recipients and the matter to be communicated, what best serves the message'. Church communication will 'support the sense of community, respect human worth, and promote a good life for all'. Openness is another important aspect of it. Via church internet-communication, it is possible to 'give 'information about the church, as well as spiritual support'.

The document by the Lutheran Church of Sweden elaborates the subject of communication and media roles less extensively, but nevertheless offers an interesting outlook. They e.g. enter into 'professional public relations' which is not 'manipulation', but 'putting together information in a way it is 'understandable and initiates communication'. Internet is said to be 'a practical medium for communication with youth'. It 'brings about relationships and knowledge'. In communication people are no 'object to be informed', but a 'subject, to be listened to and dialogue with'. The task of the church 'to proclaim the divine message, often is the cause of aggravating conflict'. The theological changes in history show the gospel 'developed'. Dialoguing with people, is a contribution to this development.

Most clearly of all documents, the ecumenical statements by communication specialists of UNDA/WACC reject the instrumental view of media and communication. In the document on media education (4.2), there are no explicit references, although it is made clear that media communication is regarded as public service. In its *Identities and Communities* (4.5) this view is elaborated upon. Communication is said to be 'a fundamental human need' that makes the role of media and cultural goods 'not commercial like any other'. Culture and education should not be left to commercial logic. The market 'cannot by itself ensure pluralism, privacy, and the right to information or general interest'. The argument that media offer what people want is rejected. 'Not everything that interests the public is in the public interest'. Competition offers no benefit for the public. The political-economic censorship by big press agencies (not on moral or political, but economic grounds) and the turn of information into entertainment are viewed negatively. 'What sells, determines what is moral'. Instead of 'instrumentalizing' communication in the interest of 'selling their project', social institutions and churches should 'serve communication as a value in itself'. They should 'promote intermediate communities' between big social institutions and groups people choose to identify with. 'Social groups, institutions and churches have to move from 'instrumentalizing' their internal communication in the interests of selling the views of their leaders to one in which communication serves to express the views of their members'. New technologies 'can be ways of reorienting communication in this manner'.

With respect to the role of media, it is stated that media should balance providing a focus for social identity, on the one hand and communicating between groups with diverse identities, on the other hand. In situations of conflict they especially have 'a great responsibility'. The 'communicability of identities' is regarded as one of the 'keys to peace in Europe', which should be 'prioritized' by media. Their impact and responsibility commensurate with the common interest and not merely the particular interest. Media are 'at the service of everyone and society as a whole'. This should also be the goal of media regulation. 'Communication between people' must be the 'first political and social objective, as well as the priority in media and communication'. Interpersonal communication is a fundamental need; 'fully human' can only be reached in communication with others. The statement calls for a 'fundamental shift in orientation in the area of mediated communication: it needs to be centered anew in the capacity to live with another'. In an open society, with urgent problems of social fragmentation, general interest channels and public service channels are an 'important meeting place'.

Only in the first document CEEM (4.3, 4.6) refers to communication - following the Vatican outlook: 'By nature the church is oriented towards communication leading to communion with God and human beings'.

COMECE (5.1) agrees with the ecumenical communication experts that 'communication is more than consumption'. The 'primary understanding of communication as transaction' is 'limited to the consumer's freedom of choice'. The Christian social doctrine, however, departs from 'the reciprocal relation between communication, community and freedom'. The freedom for political, economic or cultural activity 'can only evolve in a context of community and communication'. Freedom obliges to serve. The main shortcoming of the *Green Paper* in this respect is its 'one sided understanding of communication from the perspective of the consumer'. Communication may not be 'reduced to consumption'; neither should it become the 'exclusive object of the market'. Mass media and the internet open up other opportunities than the 'market logic determination': not 'to supply service to a consumer', but 'to open up a forum for encounter, exchange and communication'. The outlook on the market is not a 'supermarket supplying consumption', but the 'market as a public forum'. Instead of the 'laws of supply, demand and competition', the opportunity of 'free encounter, discussion, play and communication'. A public area, 'free of the compulsion to consume', is 'essential for social life and democracy'. Citizens should not 'be reduced to consumers'. It is 'contradictory to leave securing such an area (public, open to all) exclusively to market forces'. Since media are not just instruments to organize culture, they reflect the culture they create themselves. Broadcasting is a 'medium for formation, public opinion, social and cultural integration, education and the guarantee of diversity of opinion'. Human dignity should be respected; minorities and the young protected.

The classical objectives of media in democracies -information, formation of opinion, criticism and control- remain important. The same holds true for specific objectives of classic media areas relevant to journalism; they need 'particular care' and are to be 'preserved in the future in a democratic Europe dependent on responsible citizens'. Media are to 'promote social cultural cohesion and integration'. Pluralistic societies, in which objectives, behavior, moral concepts and philosophies of life differ greatly, 'require forms of communication which permit understanding via standards and rules of co-existence, and via solutions to central problems to which minorities and socially and financially disadvantaged also have access'. In view of the increasing fragmentation of media on offer -depending on target/interest groups- the 'significance of integration, the forum and the model and functions of public service broadcasting is growing'.

In the statement on the future of media policy in the information society (5.2), COMECE takes a critical stand in the discussion between 'utopians' and 'skeptical'. The key issue, says the statement, is how technical improvements can 'enhance the quality and content of communication'. The internet is 'impressive as technology', but its 'potential to produce social benefits' depend on its use, its regulation and its integration with other modes of communication'. The web is 'commercially dominated'. How people are 'guided' is a key issue. What is needed are 'trusted intermediaries' and 'a strong public interest in the encouragement of such bodies' (as aspired by public broadcasters). The primary concern of the church in the communication and media sector is not technical and economic. The key question is: 'to what extent do technologies and communication services characterize our understanding of ourselves and the world?' Are they primarily oriented towards the purposes of 'communication, interpersonal comprehension and the interests of social co-existence'? The church has 'a distinctive contribution and vision to bring to cyberspace': human dignity human rights, human community, solidarity and the common good of all (Quote from *Ethics in Communication*). 'Imaginative exploitation' is encouraged. The aim must be to 'strengthen the possibilities of real communication and interaction'. Only 'as far as internet is a true medium of communication, it will be a true medium for building communities'.

The Catholic Bishops Conference of England and Wales in its *Submission to the BBC Charter Review* (5.4) summarizes its view in the conclusion that charter renewal 'should result in a strengthened independent and properly financed BBC' which is 'better equipped to its public mission and remains at the very heart of the UK's democratic, social and cultural life'. The BBC's importance as a public service institution 'in an era of fragmenting audiences, increasing competition and convergent technologies' is stressed. Public service broadcasting is 'more important than ever' and needs to be championed by at least one major broadcasting institution dedicated to this goal. In a democracy, it is 'not desirable' that all channels serve private interests. Public service obligations 'might be placed upon commercial channels, but maximizing profit remains their primary goal, not the interest of the audience'. Any broadcaster 'can make innovative quality programs', but only a public service broadcaster is obliged to 'provide a range of programs with the primary aim of serving the public as a whole'. The public service broadcasting ideal 'is good in itself and not just a response to market failure'. The BBC expresses 'a fundamentally social purpose for broadcasting: to serve the interests and needs of the British citizen'. The *Communications Act 2003*, stating that 'broadcasters must meet the needs of audiences in their different roles as citizens and consumers', is still valid. The publicly funded BBC has 'a vital democratic contribution to make, in ensuring that as many people as possible are able to participate fully in the information society'. The BBC then should 'continue to have particular concern to entertain, inform and educate those who otherwise might be marginalized by geographic, linguistic, cultural, social, educational, physical or mental factors'. The BBC is important to 'compensate market failure'. It also plays a major part in 'underpinning the cultural life of the country' (arts, music, opportunities for talent, training academy etc). To fulfill this social function, a 'unified organization is needed, of sufficient size and scope, to offer a wide range of services'. The statement opposes to 'hiving off substantial parts', especially now 'the global trend is merger and consolidation of smaller broadcasters and ITV has become a unified organization'. It is 'important to make majority of the programs in-house, to retain a leading position as innovator -in programming and technologically-. It is also 'vital that the ethos of public service in the production process is nurtured and passed on to the next generation of broadcasters'.

Now that information and communication technologies merge and reshape economy, society and culture, the BBC has to be 'present within the whole range of media platforms'. An online presentation is 'especially significant' so citizens 'have access to the accumulation of information and knowledge freely available in the public domain'. Local radio/web services need to be extended in order to guarantee access to 'underserved' parts of the population. The combination of new and traditional media to meet social needs underlines the importance to 'allow the BBC to enter in the widest range of broadcasting markets'. Especially since commercial stations do not invest in such local levels. The statement then opposes 'any proposals reducing the presence of the BBC in the overall broadcasting market'.

With respect to programming quality and standards, says the statement, the BBC 'must be allowed to compete across the board'. In a 'distinctive way', however, that is characterized by 'thinking in the long term'. This means: nurturing long term projects (giving programs a chance to find their place in schedules) and providing a range of programs to meet the changing needs of the audience over the course of life time. This commitment 'inevitably includes' programming for small audiences also ('scheduling, knowing one will loose the ratings battle'). Based on one's own convictions, one needs to have the courage to 'schedule important documentaries, social current affairs, religion, arts or cultural programs in prime time'. The logic of competition in a digital age makes the concept of prime time a 'more flexible construct', but 'multiple channels and channel surfing cannot be used as an excuse to hide demanding programs in the corners of the schedule or on digital channels where only technologically literates will find them'. BBC 1 and 2 are 'flagship channels', whose 'program mix must reflect the core purposes of the BBC'. As citizens 'we expect excellence, quality, respect for the audience, insight'. If there is no consistency in this, there is a danger 'the audience questions the rationale of a publicly funded BBC'. This does not, however, mean a plea for 'only worthy programs'. Stressed is a 'wide range of quality popular programs in all genres'. The most popular and entertaining programs are 'often the most informative and educational in the broadest sense'. The BBC is a 'standard setter', the benchmark for other broadcasters, and 'helps driving up standards'.

Religious coverage and programming have a 'major contribution to make' and take a 'major part in religious life'. Since the 1990's religion is felt to be 'pushed to the margins'. What is needed is a 'renewed commitment to the BBC's obligations in this area'. Now programs are 'counted' in terms of hours, but no account is taken of amount of money, amount of original programs and scheduling (margins or peak time). In future commitment these should be included. Religion is 'not simply an interest'. Religious broadcasting should 'not be primarily concerned with broadcasting to the converted'. Political and economic subjects, says the document, 'are taken for granted' and religious broadcasting is 'questioned'. It should be taken 'as seriously as other topics', 'intellectually, journalistically, in investment, and with respect to programming making talent'. The Bishops conference 'would like to see religious items more fully treated in news, current affairs and documentaries'. Religion should be treated 'seriously and intelligently' since it is a 'central part of human experience' and 'a major shaper of the world we live in'. The BBC should consider how 'to help the audience understand the diversity and power of religious belief today'. The Catholic community 'experienced insensitivity and poor quality journalism' in this respect. There is 'no objection to a rigorous, well informed and balanced scrutiny of religious beliefs, institutions and conduct'. But 'the systematic anti catholic bias in certain sections BBC' is denounced. The BBC should 'ensure greater understanding and expertise in the coverage of religious topics in its news and current affairs'. 'Appropriate expertise and sympathetic understanding in religious issues' should also be present at the heart of the system for monitoring editorial policy. There should also be an 'increasing sensitivity in multi faith coverage and multi cultural society'. Religious broadcasting should 'encourage and sustain the real exchange of understanding and views between adherents of different traditions'. This requires 'sensitivity, knowledge and experience'.

With respect to funding, the license fee is felt to be the most appropriate. It 'underpins political independence and accountability' and provides for a 'direct link' between the tax payer and the BBC. The use of the license fee to 'subsidize' commercial broadcasters to meet public service obligations is rejected. The statement also opposes BBC services paid for by subscription. It would 'undermine the principle of universal access to BBC services, free at the point of delivery'. Adequate finance should also be guaranteed to the BBC World Service, and its editorial independence from the government should be maintained.

In the EU and the Council of Europe 'there is much debate about the remit of public service broadcasters'. The *Communications Act* attempts to 'clarify the range of programming considered under public service'. The existing BBC Agreement to the Charter, in present circumstances, is 'inadequate'. It specifies a 'minimum set of standards/obligations. The Bishops Conference is 'not opposed to amend the Agreement', but it is felt there is more value in specifying particular objectives for particular BBC services. The danger of a 'too prescriptive approach' is that the 'minimum too easily becomes the maximum, absolving the extension of range'. Being too prescriptive is also 'not helpful in a rapidly changing technological and broadcasting environment' where media must 'seize opportunities as they arise'. In the present situation, the Charter and Agreement set out the broader principles and identify more general goals, while the 'most workable solution' is the BBC 'draws up more specific objectives and targets'. Charter and Agreement are to be rewritten in order to make them more accessible documents. Their merit is in the proposal to 'identify and state general purpose for the BBC's independence and public mission'. Regulatory and governance structures must also 'ensure the continued strength of the BBC's independence and public mission'. The strength of the British broadcasting system is the 'separation of regulation for BBC from regulation for commercial broadcasting'. The commercial sector regulator (OFCOM) should ensure 'commercial broadcasters fulfill specific public service obligations in exchange for the opportunity to make profit'. The primary aim of the BBC regulator is to ensure the BBC's adherence to its core mission: to serve the public. These are 'fundamental different objectives'. The danger of bringing the BBC under OFCOM is that 'the core public mission drifts into becoming a list of specific public service obligations'. The result would be 'a BBC institutional shell, without spirit'. When OFCOM, regulating the commercial market in broadcasting funding from levies and fees on commercial broadcasters, would also regulate the BBC, this would raise conflicts of interest. It is 'essential that the role of governors as trustees in the public interest be clearly distinguished in practice and theory from the executive management of the BBC'.

With respect to accountability and transparency, it is said that the BBC 'improved the quantity and style and quality of informing the public'. 'Genuine consultations' should be further developed. The only 'serious regular on air accountability' is the radio program *Feedback*. The BBC should produce television 'properly dealing with viewers' complaints and concerns and views' and broadcast it in prime time.

With respect to the parliament and accountability, it is stated that proposals to amend the Charter and Agreement 'should be published for pre-legislative scrutiny by the joint committee of both houses of parliament'. There should also be 'no significant change in the Charter and Agreement 'without approval of the parliament'.

3.3.6   Theological presuppositions

Ten out of the 26 documents do not explicitly refer to theological presuppositions in their view of communication and media. This is especially true for the ethical and media policy statements (2.2, 5.1, 5.2, 5.3 and 5.4; the other statements without explicit references are: 3.1, 4.2, 4.3, 4.6 and 4.8).

Both documents by WACC (1.1 and 2.1) offer only few references. The poor, the oppressed and the marginalized are to 'bear the hallmark of God's communication'. Communication is a 'gift of God', and Christian communicators have 'no option but with them' (1.1). Few references, however, do not mean that theological presuppositions are not an issue in WACC's vision. WACC even published a separate basic statement with respect to theological premises called *Christian Principles of Communication*. The general principles of Christian communication are Christology based. He announced the coming of God's Kingdom and was commissioned to 'proclaim the Good News to all people'. Living by the Good News and witnessing to it is 'the basic calling of all Christians'. They do this by the power of the Holy Spirit who can 'change the Babel of confusion into the Pentecost of genuine understanding'. It blows where it pleases (John 2:8), and 'no-one, neither church nor religious group can claim to control it'. Christ's own communication was an 'act of self-giving'. He ministered to all, 'but took up the case of the poor, ill, the outcasts of society, the powerless and the oppressed'. In the same way, Christian communication 'should be an act of love which liberates all who take part in it'. The Gospel -the Good news for the poor- 'needs to be constantly reinterpreted from the perspectives of the poor and oppressed'. 'This challenges church hierarchies to disassociate themselves from the power structures which keep the poor in a position of subservience'. The Good News for the poor, in this sense, 'embodies genuine reconciliation by means of which the dignity of all people can be reaffirmed'. The Christian communicator 'proclaims God's Kingdom rather than our divided churches', which 'do not exist for their own sakes'. Ecumenical communication - Christians of different denominations speaking with one voice and bearing witness to the one body of Christ- is preferred. There is a need to 'rediscover' the early Christian community's understanding of a 'witnessing and communicating church'. The church is defined as a 'community of believers' meant to 'embody and testify to the central values of the Kingdom' (oneness, reconciliation, equality, justice, freedom, harmony, peace and love). Christian communicators are 'conscious of and show respect for God's mysteries, being aware of their inadequacies when speaking of God, or telling the story of God's people'. Finally, the 'glory of God and the joy of people should be the hallmark of all Christian communication, which is challenged to witness to God's transforming power in all areas of human life'.

In the 'context of today's communication problems' these principles lead to four elaborations that refine communication:

1. *Communication creates community* (open and inclusive communication rather than unidirectional and exclusive, rights and justice for all, and acceptance of and commitment to one another regardless of race, color or religious conviction).
2. *Communication is participatory* (mass media are organized along one way lines while communication 'by definition is participatory, a two way process'; people are to become subjects rather than objects of communication; communication is an 'individual and social necessity of fundamental importance, a 'universal human right' that 'adds the concept of access, participation and two-way flow to the freedom of expression and the right to seek, receive and impart information'. Participatory communication may 'challenge authoritarian structures in society, churches and media -and their professional rules-).
3. *Communication liberates* (mass media are structures of power and reinforce status quo; genuine communication is not simply 'imparting information or selling media products'. It presupposes equal worth of all people. People can be subtly silenced. Freedom of communication is 'bound up with the quest for community and the individual and social needs of all'. Communication, therefore, needs to 'liberate and enable people to articulate their own needs, enhance their sense of dignity and underline their right to full participation in the life of society' (this includes bringing about more just structures in society).
4. *Communication supports and develops cultures* (a people's basic culture and need for cultural identity are 'part of the dignity of the human person'. Rediscovering this identity is 'urgent' where culture, language, religion, gender, age, ethnicity or age are under attack. Global communication structures are a 'threat to cultures and priorities of many nations'. The media environment is 'alien and alienating'; Western criteria set global standards, 'often preventing alternative forms of communication'. Communicators now have the responsibility to use and develop indigenous forms of communication. 'They have to cultivate a symbolic environment of mutually shared images and meanings which respect human dignity and the religious and cultural values at the heart of Third World cultures'. 'One of the greatest assets of today's world is its many different cultures, revealing the richness of God's image in all its diversity'.
5. *Communication is prophetic* (in interpreting the signs of the times Christian communicators must listen to God and be led by the Spirit. This is a condition of prophecy. Prophetic communication 'expresses itself in words and deeds'. It serves truth - lies and half truths are a great threat to communication. It stimulates 'critical awareness of the reality constructed by media'. Often it is 'necessary to develop alternative communication, so that prophetic words and deeds can be realized'.

Finally, 'communication must be seen as central to the churches, as the process in which God's love is received and shared, thus establishing communion and community'.

The Vatican partly shares the theological presuppositions put forward by WACC, but appears to differ with respect to their effects with regard to communication and identity. For the Vatican (1.2), 'God's self-communication in Jesus is definitive'. All human relationships exist within this framework. The 'loving self-revelation of God, combined with humanity's response of faith, constitutes a profound dialogue'. It is 'part of the human vocation to contribute by living out the unlimited communication of God's love in creative new ways'. Communication 'must lie at the heart of the Church community'. The meaning of communication in the church 'is based upon the realization that the Word of God communicates Himself'. The church as communion is rooted in the communion of the Trinity. Jesus Christ is 'God's Word made flesh, the image of God'. In and through him God is 'communicated to humanity by the Spirit's action. Christ is

'both the content and the dynamic source of the Church's communications in proclaiming the gospel, for the Church is 'Christ's mystical body'.
This line is pursued in 1.4. God's self revelation, in His act of love, encompasses 'all forms and ways of communication'. By responding in faith man, as the image of God, , may enter in this 'loving and fruitful dialogue. Because of sin, however, the capacity for dialogue at personal and societal level is altered with the result of separation (the history of human communication 'from Babel to Pentecost' is, as stated in 4.9, restored by Jesus). Through redemption, -by sending His Son-, the 'communicative capacity of believers is healed and renewed'. The encounter with Christ 'makes them new creatures, and introduces them into the intimate life of the Trinity'. The communication by the Trinity is 'the continuous and circular communication of the perfect and infinite love among the Father, the Son and the Holy Spirit'. The communication of God with humanity achieves its perfection in 'the Word made flesh'. This gives communication 'its most profound saving meaning'. He explains the Scriptures, expresses in parables, dialogues, and speaks in squares, streets, lakeshores and on mountaintops'. The personal encounter with Him 'does not leave indifferent' and 'stimulates imitation'. The 'culminating moment' in which communication becomes 'full communion' is the 'Eucharistic encounter'. By recognizing Jesus in breaking the bread, 'believers feel urged to announce his death and resurrection and witness the Kingdom'. Christ, the 'communicator of the Father', always 'shows respect for those who listen', 'teaches understanding of situations and needs', is 'moved to compassion for suffering', and is 'resolute in His determination to say only what they need to hear' without 'compromise, deceit or manipulation'. Jesus teaches that 'communication is a moral act'. In the Spirit 'man is given the capacity to receive salvation' and to 'proclaim and give witness before the world'. Paul's message for those engaged in communication is to 'speak the truth, without foul language and with grace to those who hear' (Eph 4: 25-29). To 'analyze processes and value of communications', Scripture can help as 'a code of communication of a non-ephemeral message'.

In *Ethics in Communication* (2.3) the church is said to be the 'communion mirroring the Trinity'. Communication 'in and by the Church' finds its starting point in the communion of love among the Trinity and its communication with humanity'. Jesus Christ, the 'perfect communicator', is the model and standard of human communication, 'communicating God's love and the meaning of life'. He communicated not only in words, but in his 'manner of life'. He spoke from within and adjusted to 'the people's way of talking and their patterns of thought'. (Quote from C&P). He used parables and stories to 'express profound truths in simple everyday truths'. Christian communicators have a 'prophetic task' against 'false gods', 'idols of the day', 'materialism, hedonism, consumerism and narrow nationalism'. To hold up the 'moral truth based on dignity, the option for the poor, the universal destination of goods, the respect for all human life' and 'seeking the Kingdom'. Human communication bears in it 'something of God's creative activity' as 'man shares in His creative power'.
With respect to new media (2.4), it is stated that the world of media 'including the internet' is brought by Christ 'within the boundaries of the Kingdom' and 'placed in service to the Word of salvation'. 'This earth needs to be developed'. The 'expectancy of a new one' spurs people. 'Here the body of the new human family grows', 'foreshadowing the age to come'.
The statement on the *Church and Internet* (4.9) holds the same views as stated in the other Vatican documents. Added to the line of communication in and by the Trinity and through Jesus Christ is the church. 'God continues to communicate with humanity through the Church, the bearer and custodian of the revelation, to whose living teaching office alone He has entrusted the task of authentically interpreting his word'. Since the church 'mirrors the communion of the Trinity', communication is 'of its essence', and its

practice of communication should therefore be 'exemplary'. This means the 'highest standards of truthfulness, accountability and sensitivity of human rights, principles and norms'. Christ, the 'perfect communicator', is the 'norm and model' for the church's approach to communication and the 'content that the church is obliged to communicate'.

The LWF (1.3) grounds its view of communication more in the creation narrative, than in the Christological and Trinitarian presuppositions - as do the Vatican statements. Media are part of the creation. Communication is 'a creative force'. God created through words. The Hebrew term *dabar* refers to 'creativity and dynamic action'. Salvation includes 'the full participation between humans and humans and God'. The Holy Spirit is mentioned with respect to the 'elimination of a language problem'. In 3.3 it is said that what the church 'has to communicate is essentially a mystery'. It is asked 'what the role of the Holy Spirit can be' in this context.

Also in its theological groundings, the ecumenical statement by the German churches (3.2), shows traces of consensus of both denominations. The Christian image of man is one of 'freedom and self determination'. People live in relationships. The anthropological basic statement is to be found in the message of creation: 'man is the image of God'. This is a 'decisive distinguishing mark'. The relationship with God (the 'vertical line') is 'basic to the identity of people'. Solidarity and community are the 'highest goal of all communication, originally rooted and showed in the highest secret of eternal communion between the Father, the Son and the Holy Spirit' (Quoted from *C&P*).
In their separate documents (4.7 by the German Bishops' Conference and 4.4 by the EKD) the same line is generally pursued. 4.7, in its footnotes, points to *C&P* again, naming Christ 'the master of communication' because God 'communicates in Him' and Jesus changes the life of people by that. The EKD statement states the 'mandate of Protestant publicity is grounded in the gospel, which offers not only tasks, but also 'the freedom to seize chances of publicity in a market of possibilities'. It belongs to the mandate of protestant publicity to 'orient the journalistic work to the Word and the tradition of biblical faith and to take seriously the interests and life situations of people'. It is asked what has to be done to 'get to the goal of gospel inspired publicity in the media and in the information society'. The answer is found in 'strengthening the community of Christians and people of god will' and 'bringing into life serving relationships elements of communication with God and fellow man: communion, communication and community'. In this way, 'God is glorified' and the 'worth and freedom of people is served through information and a proclaiming orientation of truth'.

The ecumenical statement by the communication experts of UNDA/WACC (4.5) does not suggest theological presuppositions as a model for communication. Indirectly, there are references to 'the universal fatherhood of God' and to the Holy Spirit. Pentecost shows that 'all cultures each embody part of the mystery of humanity and the goodness of God'. Communication is a 'necessity to be fully human'.

The Church of England (3.4) mainly refers to the Christian doctrine of the Incarnation when speaking of theological presuppositions in its outlook on communication related to cyberspace. Jesus, the 'Word made flesh', is 'not just a projection into the world', but 'fully human'. He entered the 'world of relationships'. He will 'return to reveal the Kingdom', and we will 'relate to Him in the flesh'. The statement also points to the 'bodily nature of resurrection life'. God is the 'creator and origin' and the human - the 'co-creator' with a 'free will and creativity'. After the human 'disruption' and God's 'reconciliation' 'full life' is to be achieved. Cyberspace must be 'offered to God'. To 'discover God's will in it' is needed. The Christian story provides us with 'principles of action'. Since 'nothing is outside God's care or concern', this also applies to cyberspace. We can look at it 'with confidence'. It is a 'duty' to relate it to the 'needs of society and a just and peaceful world'. This means there is no exclusion and 'proper relationships'. Christians are to 'give up false ideas of who is inside and who is outside'. God gave human freedom but the 'misuse of information denies humanity'. Individual autonomy must be 'protected', and we need to 'grow into the fullness of humanity'. God 'lives and acts in and through believers' - which gives 'new power'. The challenges of cyberspace include the situation where 'desires are fulfilled instantly' and 'considerations on the effects towards others are discouraged'. What is needed is to 'rejoice in fellowship and interdependence'. Priority is to be given to 'the interest in the common good of all'. Cyberspace will be 'full of His glory'.

The Lutheran Church of Finland (4.1) states that 'in church life faith and communication cannot be separated'. The 'whole existence of the church' is 'based on the communication between God and man'. Life in church is always 'interaction between Christ and the church and between the church and its members' (Quote form the Church Document, 2000). 'Interaction -often in the form of dialogue- is a precondition for the implementation of joint priesthood'. Based on the Creed of Augsburg, the 'holy community' 'begins by communicating at the level of word and sacrament'. Communication 'in this context is: listening and being listened to, giving and receiving'. The basic condition of 'genuine dialogue is inclusiveness and interactivity and mutual enrichment'.
This line is pursued in 4.10. God created 'by the Word'; the Word 'became flesh' and made God 'visible and real'. The Word 'created the church'. Beginning with Jesus, (asking Bartimeus: what do you want me to do for you?), the 'basic form of conveying the gospel has been personal communication'.

3.3.7   Church involvement in communication

'A church secluding itself in isolation in the end talks only to itself and is unable to fulfill its mission to preach the gospel to all' says the statement by the media committee of the European Bishop's conference (4.3).
All statements, somehow or other, are convinced of the necessity of church involvement in media and communication. They do not, however, share the same outlook on the shape and the content of this commitment. Earlier sections -especially 3.3.4 and 3.3.5- already provided us with a glimpse of various views. Since church identity (the subject of 3.3.4) and the views of media and communication roles (the subject of 3.3.5) are intrinsically related to what churches feel should be their own involvement, the issues at stake here, thus, partly overlap.

In the last three sections that follow, we will scrutinize this involvement. For the sake of clarity, we will distinguish three related issues. In this section we will research the outlook on involvement in media. In 3.3.8 we will focus explicitly on social responsibilities with respect to media, media structures and media ethical issues. What the statements see as the main challenges and priorities for the churches in media and communication is the subject of the last section (3.3.9).

Regarding involvement in media, the statements by the EKD, the German Protestant Church (4.4) and the Vatican documents (1.2, 1.4 and 4.9) are noticeable for extensive elaboration on the issue, as is the COMECE statement on the future of EU media policy in the information society (5.2). The LWF documents, on the other hand, pay little attention to the theme (which underlines again the internal focus of both LWF documents within the world federation).

WACC (1.1, 2.1) feels that Christian churches and organizations should recognize and respond to the challenges of the media age. It underlines the need for an 'organic' outlook instead of an 'instrumental' understanding of media by Christian churches, and for cooperation with 'all of good will'. Attention must be paid to the 'reinterpretation of contents of the Christian discourse, as based on the deposit of faith', by considering both the biblical text and the cultural context in communication work. Christian communicators need serious theological reflection on their work and mission, particularly on the challenges posed by the new ICT's. Education must be strengthened. Christian communicators should engage in consciousness raising with respect to communication in pursuit of religious tolerance, justice and peace.

For the Vatican (1.2), 'communication in and by the church' is essentially 'communication of the good news of Jesus Christ (proclamation, testimony, witness to justice and communion among peoples, nations and cultures). The importance of alternative media is stressed. All means of media are recognized. In evangelization and catechesis the use of media is 'essential'. It is not enough, however, to simply use the media to spread the message. It is also necessary to integrate it into the new culture that is created by modern communications. The church should maintain an 'active sympathetic presence within the world of communications'. At the same time, it should make a 'critical evaluation of mass media and their impact upon culture'. New media 'offer new possibilities' for the mission of the church. It is a 'critically important apostolate'. The church must communicate in a\manner suited to each age and culture. Today, this means communication 'in and to the media culture'. The church must 'seek dialogue with the modern world' and with those responsible for communications media. The church must 'understand the purposes, procedures, the forms, the genres, the internal structures and modalities' and 'offer support'. Relationships of mutual confidence and respect are felt to be important. Christians have the responsibility to 'make their voice heard in all media'. Media of social communications can and should be instruments in the church's program of re- and new evangelization. Social communication has a role in 'every aspect of the church mission'. The church has to 'identify new strategies for evangelization and catechesis through the application of communications technology and mass communication'. Communications should be 'an integral part of every pastoral plan'.
Public relations by the church means 'active communication with the community through both secular and religious media' (communicate gospel values, publicize church programs etc). Public relations offices should be maintained. The production of publications, radio and television programs, and video should be of 'excellent quality'. To encourage media professionals, media awards should be promoted. The celebration of the annual World Communications Day should make people aware of the importance of and support to social communications. The church 'welcomes ecumenical and inter-religious cooperation'. A 'united religious presence in the very heart of mass communications' is 'necessary'. There is a need to 'collaborate with ecumenical organizations, other churches and religious groups' to 'guarantee access to media by religion' and to 'collaborate in recent media (satellite, data banks, cable networks and informatics).

In 1.4 it is stated that the 'use of techniques and technologies of communication is an integral part of the church's mission in the third millennium'. The Christian community should 'use the means of communication for religious information, evangelization and catechesis, the formation of pastoral workers, and education of the users and recipients of media'. New evangelization meets 'many challenges in a world rich of communicative potential'. The world of communication is the 'first *Areopagus* of modern times' (Quote from *Redemptoris Missio*). Communication 'permeates the essential dimensions of the church which is called to announce to all the message of salvation'. It therefore 'takes advantage of the opportunities offered by communications media as pathways given by God to intensify communion and render more penetrating the proclamation of the Word'. In communication media, the church finds 'an aid for spreading the gospel and religious values, promote dialogue, for ecumenical and inter religious cooperation and for the defense of principles of a society that respects human dignity and the common good'. The church 'employs media to furnish information about itself and expand the boundaries of evangelization, catechesis and formation'. It considers the use of media 'a response to the command of the Lord to proclaim the Gospel to every creature and the whole world' (MK16:15). The talents of the church community are 'encouraged with pastoral prudence and wisdom' to become 'professionals capable of dialoguing with the world of media'. Communications media 'take into account aspects of expression of faith; Christians must 'take into account media culture', from liturgy to catechesis which 'cannot prescind from being directed to people immersed in the language and culture of the day'. This impels the church towards a 'pastoral and cultural revision to deal adequately with the times'. In using media pastors and people with charisma have a 'special responsibility' ('help promote quality programs, respectful of moral law and rich in human and Christian values'). The mass media are the 'crossroads of the great social questions'. The church is faced with three fundamental options: formation, participation and dialogue. It also has a role in public opinion.

The statement on ethics in advertising (2.2) pursues the two lines of evangelization and integration of the gospel in media culture. 'Besides using media to evangelize, the Church for her part needs to grasp the full implications of the observation by Pope John Paul II: that media comprise a central part of that great modern 'Areopagus' where ideas are shared and attitudes and values are formed. This points to a deeper reality than 'simply using media to spread the Gospel, important as that is'. It is also necessary to integrate that message into the 'new culture' created by modern communications with its new ways of communicating…new languages, new techniques and a new psychology'. (Quote from *Redemptoris Missio*, no. 37).
Christians have a duty in 'correcting the unethical practices of advertisers'. 'In today's society advertising has a profound impact on how people understand life, the world and themselves, especially in regard to their values of choosing and behaving. 'These are matters about which the Church is and must be deeply and sincerely concerned'. Church involvement in media, 'including advertising, today is a necessary part of a comprehensive pastoral strategy'. Both the use of 'own' media and participation in secular media, should be pursued. Catholic institutions should follow the development and techniques of advertising and 'know how to make opportune use of advertising to spread the Gospel, in a manner which answers the expectations and needs of contemporary man'.

In the document on ethics in communication (2.3), these lines are pursued. Ethical questions are 'acute'. The church's approach must be 'positive and encouraging, not merely judgmental'. Professionals must be supported by 'positive principles', and a dialogue 'must be fostered with all interested parties'. The church 'brings to this conversation: its tradition of moral wisdom and its social teaching, which theological orientation is corrective to the atheistic solution that deprives man of the spiritual dimension and leads towards permissive and consumerist solutions'. Tradition 'offers itself in service to media'. The church's culture of wisdom 'can save the media culture of information from becoming a meaningless accumulation of facts' (Quote from World

Communications Day 1999). The church also 'brings its vision of the dignity of the person revealed in the mystery of the incarnate Word'.

'The church cannot impose answers, but it can and must proclaim the answers she received' says the document on ethics and internet (2.4). The world of media, including the internet, is 'brought by Christ within the boundaries of the Kingdom and placed in service to the word of salvation'. The church needs to 'help people see the meaning of life'. There is a need to 'develop this earth' and the 'expectancy of the new one must spur us on'. 'Here the body of the new human family grows, foreshadowing the age to come'.

The most extensive Vatican elaboration about the involvement of the church in media is given in the statement, *Church and Internet*. (4.9). The internet appears to be incorporated in the outlook on media in general, including the 'proclamation/integration' lines. However, its particularities are also touched upon within the area of church communication.
The world of communications offers 'unique opportunities for proclaiming the saving truth of Christ to the whole human family. The internet has 'positive capacities to carry religious information beyond all barriers'. Such a 'wide audience is beyond the wildest imaginings'. Communication in and by the church is essentially 'proclamation of the Gospel; testimony, in the face of radical secularization, to the divine truth and the transcendent destiny of man; and witness against conflict for the sake of justice and the communion of peoples, nations and cultures'. 'Announcing the Good News to people formed by media culture requires taking into account the characteristics of media'. The church needs to 'understand the internet to communicate effectively'. It can play a role in some forms of pastoral counseling and community building (although it cannot be compared to the community 'of flesh and blood'). The internet can also be relevant to apologetics. The church should 'explore the opportunities for ecumenical and inter-religious cooperation in the use of internet'. In its involvement, the church has a 'twofold aim'. One is to encourage the right development and use of the internet for the sake of human development, justice, peace, society and community in the light of the common good and solidarity'. The church, therefore, needs to 'seek to dialogue with those responsible for shaping media policy'. It also needs to 'understand' purposes, procedures, forms and genres, internal structures and modalities' and 'support professionals' (Quote from AN). Based on this understanding, then, it is possible to 'offer meaningful proposals for removing obstacles to human progress and to the proclamation of the Gospel (Quote from AN). The church's concern is also related to 'communication in and by the church'. It is more than a technique. It finds its starting point in the communion of the Trinity and its communication with man. Since the church is a communion 'mirroring the communion of the Trinity', communication 'is of the essence of the Church'. Its practice in communication should be 'exemplary' (highest standards of truthfulness, accountability, and sensitivity to human rights, principles and norms). The church has an important service to offer to Catholics and non Catholics by 'the selection and transmission of useful data'. The internet is relevant to different church programs: evangelization (re-evangelization, new evangelization, and traditional missionary work *ad gentes*), catechesis and education, news and information, apologetics, governance and administration, some forms of pastoral counseling, and spiritual direction. The virtual reality of cyberspace, however, 'cannot be a substitute for real interpersonal community, for the incarnation reality of the sacraments and liturgy, or for the immediate and direct proclamation of gospel'. But it can 'complement and enrich'. It can also be a 'means for the church to communicate to particular groups'. The church must also 'use the internet as a tool for internal communication'. It must 'keep in view, the special character of the internet as a direct, immediate, interactive and

participatory medium'. Two-way interactivity 'blurs the distinction between communicators and receivers'. It is not the 'one-way, top-down communication of the past'
and 'many are familiar with this characteristic in other areas of their lives and also look
forward to it in regard to religion and the church'. Quoting C&P, it is stated that 'as a
living body, the church needs public opinion to sustain giving and taking among
members'. Although the 'truths of faith do not leave room for arbitrary interpretations',
there is an 'enormous area, where members of church can express their views'. With
Aetatis Novae it is said that the 'two way flow of communication and public opinion is
one of the ways of realizing, in a concrete manner, the church's character as
communio'. Quoting Ethics in Communication, however, it is added that 'in a two way
flow of information and views between pastors and faithful, freedom of expression must
be sensitive to the well being of the community and the role of the magisterium'.
Fostering this sensitivity and a 'responsible' public opinion, both are 'expressions of the
fundamental right of dialogue and information within the church'. Internet, in this
regard, 'provides a means'. It also plays a role in 'another opportunity and need':
continuing media education and training. This is also more than a technique. The church
must help form standards of good taste, truthful moral judgment, and conscience
formation. In pastoral planning it must provide training for personnel, teachers, parents
and students. The young must be taught 'to be good Christians as recipients'. They must
learn how to 'be active in using aids to communication', how to 'function well in the
world of cyberspace', how to make 'judgments based on sound moral criteria' and how
to 'use technology for the integral development and benefit of others'.

The LWF (1.3, 3.3) relates its involvement in media to federation community building.
The use of new media and networking focuses on 'building communities (local to
global), sharing knowledge, make voices heard, strengthening advocacy, empowering
participation and enhancing cultural diversity'. In its public relations 'openness and
trustworthiness' are stressed. Well functioning church media 'increase and enlarge
personal communication'. The churches need to be publicly present, and new media
must be used 'in a communicative way'. Communication is a 'vocation and ongoing
task'. People need to be 'empowered to communicate and participate in communion'.

The German Bishops' Conference, in its document on media and communication
competence (4.7) primarily refers to the position of its catholic media bureaus. Now
central are the 'rental of media, media advice, the opening up of media by catalogue,
help in orientation and media education'. In the information society, 'critical competence
is not enough; people need to be active communication partners'. Communicative skills
and a 'strengthening of the moral-ethical consciousness of the individual and especially
the family' are needed. This means an increasing effort by the churches in media courses
and communication pedagogy. This effort goes beyond church educational formation,
due to 'changes in the target audience'. Since the 'specific religious questions nowadays
are taken up in the respective fields of culture, publicity and media', the church media
bureaus need to 'accomplish religiously founded formational and cultural work'. Their
supplies are a 'contribution to evangelization in a secular world'. The institutional
position and cooperation of media bureaus needs to be better coordinated; resources
are to be combined to 'tackle the challenges of the information society more efficiently'.
Due to massive cut backs, 'urgent tasks in church formation and pastoral work cannot
be done'.
The statement on the information society (3.1) concludes that 'multimedia use is
meaningful' for documentation or scientific work (e.g. CD ROMs for Bible work or
lexicons of international films), for presentations (terminals) or for education of church
personnel. It is 'questionable', however, 'whether the CD ROM is useful as a medium for
religious education', especially because of the 'communicative competence beyond

factual issues'. 'The goal of multimedia work within the religious realm, is in the cultivation of interpersonal communication - beyond technology'.

This view is shared in the ecumenical document published with the German Protestant church (3.2) where it is stated that the 'dominance of one-sided media communication by churches and religion neglects the intrinsic connection between personal contact and passing on of faith within the congregation and hampers pastoral care'. There are, however, also opportunities: 'invite publicly to faith', 'draw attention to Christian life', 'encourage a Christian way of life' and 'creative possibilities to present church proclamation of Christian faith in new forms'. Furthermore, there are 'prospects for interactive, dialogical oriented supplies for target groups'. Interaction stimulates new forms of communication (e.g. discussion panels). The contact with churches is enlarged (e.g. by requests for information), but it is 'not a commitment'; it can only 'lead to further contact'. Local churches should 'use local media' and 'cooperate in the 'construction of a network of social communication'. They should also be 'active in public relations to make known their activities'. Because of the increase in media supply and media use, 'non-mediated' experiences increase in importance, therefore it will be more important to 'offer direct interpersonal encounters and religious primary experiences'. Churches should make their own contributions to the education and formation of journalists, especially with respect to 'consciousness of journalistic responsibilities, quality of journalistic work and ethical issues'. With respect to the latter the church is said to have a 'special responsibility'. It should 'make media logic transparent'. Church media information services have an important role to play in this. The quality of media content should be accentuated. The means needed to this end should be provided for by public and private bodies, and also by the churches.

According to the individual document by the EKD (4.4), it is 'the task of protestant publicity to make public God's concern with people and especially acquire a public for the gospel as well as the life and action of the church in societal publicity'. The changing media and information society 'doesn't alter the obligation of the church to proclaim the entrusted gospel as a public message directed at the whole society, and in the light of it, dedicate itself to truth and freedom in living communication'. The task and mandate of protestant publicity is a 'not to be abandoned elementary form of expression of the protestant church' and of 'central significance in the media and information society'. It facilitates the participation of the church in public debate. Protestant publicity must fulfill the same conditions as general publicity (legal, technical, economical). It offers services to others and contributes with its own offerings. It 'participates in the development and safeguarding of publicity goals, standards and impact with Christian standards for just and social communication'.
To get to its goal of 'gospel inspired publicity in the media and information society', the community of Christians and people of good will must be strengthened 'to bring into a life serving relationship elements of communication with God and fellow man: communion, communication and community'. In this way, 'God is glorified and the worth and freedom of people is served through an informing and proclaiming orientation of truth'.
Challenges can only be met as a common task in the 'tension between mandate and market' and 'the assignment of the gospel and enterprise acting'. New tasks are to be developed. Since the 1980's the folk church has to 'defend its case in a differentiating pluralist culture'. It must 'clarify its message and the meaning and relevance of a church community'. It is the task of Protestant publicity to testify the gospel 'in different forms with different means'. Protestant publicity is only 'obliged to its mandate, not to official instructions'. By its mandate it becomes an institutional part of the church. It helps formulate church positions. But it is not just an instrument of the church. At the same

time its mandate obliges it to independently report about church and Christian life and critical support (the Gospel itself holds critical potential). Protestant publicity can especially contribute to discussion about Christian faith in informing, arguing and dialoguing in competent forms. Its mandate involves missionary, diaconal and social dimensions. These include listening to the oppressed and pointing to physical, psychological, material and creational needs. Protestant publicity is also 'bottom up, in favor of excluded ones'. Its mandate includes 'ecumenical openness and willingness to serve world wide Christian and religious communication'. It 'obliges to observe the multiplicity of Protestantism, the folk religious distance of many to the church and the phenomenon of postmodern religiosity', and to try to make people in these life areas and the church as place of community 'more communicative to each other'.

The praxis of Protestant publicity is characterized by 'market capability and professionalism'. It operates on a 'free market of opinions, stamped by competition'. It needs to make 'market capable' supplies that endure in public communication. Market capability is defined synonymously with acceptance. Its improvement is 'not oppositional to the content and the goals of protestant publicity'. It can, to the contrary, be 'beneficial' to observe more clearly and more seriously the individual and the public. The addressee must be 'the most important, if the communicator (church) does not want to stay to itself'. It is not the 'by institutional interest led church publicity' that will be successful; rather the 'customer oriented publicity', that is dedicated to people and, consequently oriented towards the addressee. Aiming at presence in secular media, this is 'a condition for success'. Protestant publicity can 'only exist because of succeeding'; then its financing is 'justified'. It must to a great extent be self supporting, although it is an 'illusion that it can be completely so'. The gospel is 'too delicate and the market too narrow for that'. 'Market capable' also implies working 'group oriented'. This is only possible with good 'market and reader's analysis'. Former divisions, made between 'church members' and 'worldly addressees', decrease. Social scientific analyses of the EKD show an 'undivided receiver', who communicates in multiple ways and who can be made an offer 'to his interest'. The situation of competition must be used creatively, and without providing church subsidy grants too fast. Market capability includes setting goals and securing efficiency. Means and powers are to be concentrated 'where people can be reached and are willing to be addressed'. Protestant publicity, however, can never be led by economical goals only. Public interest and the well being of society must be taken into account. Economic dominance must be 'opposed by cultural and social balancing'.

Professionalism implies meeting professional standards (handicraft, format, competence, and speaking skills) and ethical rules (obligation of truth, objectivity, respect for human dignity, faithfulness to tasks and orientation to current times and addressees). Conditions for professional work are to be created. Needed are 'qualified' people, who 'bring forward themselves as Christians and practice being a Christian in church'.
On the other hand, it is said that protestant publicity needs to be acknowledged as 'a task of the community'. The common goal in all multiplicity of supplies by the church is the communication of the gospel and the mutual communication of people. Cooperation (e.g. between Protestant journalists and those responsible for publicity in member churches or ecumenical bodies) is a result of professionalism and a 'necessity because of the decreasing public acceptance of Christian values and financial possibilities'.

Protestant publicity in former Eastern German member churches is 'challenged especially'. For a long time, it fulfilled a critical opposition. It was known as trustworthy. It was still a critical opposition after 1989, but it lost its societal meaning. Increasingly, there is a shift to target group publicity, in particular older Christians. Added to the concentration of press services in the regions and dwindling income that is subsidized by the larger churches, the new organized publicity is in 'an existential crisis'.

The multiplicity in protestant publicity mirrors the multiplicity of Protestantism. Different theological regional traditions, independent churches and church groups are involved in media. Within the federal structure, the center of publicity is in the *landeskirchen*. Next to autonomous media, the publishers and the *Evangelische Presse Dienst*, there are private radio, and church media houses. Radio and television are representative in public service broadcasting. On the EKD level, the *Gemeinschaftswerk Evangelischer Publizistik* (GEP) plays a central role (press service, specialist journals, book education materials, training, radio television, public relations, coordination, and conferences).
Public relations, in the whole of society, are 'highly valuated'. The church must 'present itself professionally'. Finances partially come from church tax means. In the statement, concern is expressed about not being sufficiently market oriented; about production which is not sufficiently oriented to addressees; about the worsened position in the competition with secular media, and about internal competition.
Research in the use of church media shows that people close to the church are mostly reached. 'In this time when societal structures and values are more diffuse and a larger part of information, orientation and formation are mediated by media, the church must orient its publicity more strongly outward, so that what the church does, what drives and moves her, becomes public'.
 According to the Church of England (3.4), Christians should have an 'active role in the shaping process of cyberspace' that is based on 'a chosen end for a social system'. Cyberspace may offer a 'rich new store of analogies and parables' and 'opportunities as channels for proclamation'. Christians should add helpful content and participate in online debates to 'make Christian voices heard'. Churches should be very 'pro-active' since cyberspace is the 'most important source of information about organizations'. They should 'seek the common good': social justice and evangelization and 'pray in and for cyberspace'. Concern is felt about events and relationships in cyberspace. The church maintains a real community for the 21 century - 'gathering people in real communities becomes an increasing human necessity'.

The Finnish Church (4.1) considers religious programs as 'public communication' that requires 'generality' in communication structures, content and language. 'Remote communication' is successfully used 'when it leads to improvement in relations'. Ecumenical cooperation, mutual responsibility, and transnational unity of Christians are underlined. The aim of communication of the church is 'to encourage open interactivity and dialogue, to promote genuineness, reality, responsibility and love for the neighbor and to strengthen hope'. *Communicare* (meaning: making common, interaction) is a task of all members. They need to be stimulated to communicate. The church is public in its essence. It is the task of church members to 'carry out its mission and present their interpretation of reality'. People, in the 'chaos of ideas and ideologies', seek values and meaning. The more active church members are in media, the greater possibility to 'find Christian options'. The church needs to be visible in public media. Reasons to communicate publicly include: to reach people and challenge them to form their opinion about the church message; to participate in discussions on values; to support those in difficulties; to bring together creative interactive communities in the middle of loneliness and separation; to offer examples of communicative communication; to support and deepen the faith and life of church members; to help understand structures of the Finnish culture and tradition, and to inform about church matters and Christian faith. The aim of internal communication is to support Christian identity. Every member 'has a basic message to come alive'. The aim is to create a more communicative church. This implies receiving information in advance and to be able to participate in ideas and planning. Communication is a 'common commitment', that asks for 'communicative leadership'. Weak communication relates to the inability of the hierarchic organization to function communicatively. Conformity in non-verbal and verbal communication and internal and public communication is essential for a clear identity. Communication techniques are not enough. What is needed is a change in attitudes. The church needs a wide internal communications net, in order to make it 'more current and relevant'. The church needs to encourage and serve the needs of media. For example, by relating current themes to Christian life that are interesting for readers. Advertising and marketing might be worthwhile in the case of large projects and then 'must meet the requirements'. Commercial advertising in general, however, is stated to be 'seldom communicative'. In sum, the church opts for 'stirring up conversation and a more visible presence' beyond the ones that are 'already reached'.

This line is pursued in 4.10, however, other accents are added. The church is 'by nature, mission and activities a communicating community'. It 'conveys the message of the gospel and God's world (grace, faith, love, hope)'. 'Preaching the gospel is its 'irrelinguishable' task. The *Communio Sanctorum* is called to communicate in word and deed so that the 'world might believe'. Preaching and its traditional form, the sermon, are an 'essential part of the Church's communication'. 'Preaching communicatively' implies 'relating the message to the circumstances of the hearers' (Paul: 'Greek to the Greeks'). Church communication 'must support the sense of community, respect the human worth, be open, and promote the good life for all. Functional internal communication is the 'basic requirement' for functional public communication. Via church internet communication, information about the church and spiritual support can be given. Church communication must be 'professional'. Harmony in the verbal and non-verbal is needed, as well as a good planning and investments. The church should be engaged in internal and public dialogue. In church, 'close range communication traditionally is the most important'. Now remote communication has become dominant, and personal contacts have decreased, the communication environment is 'more challenging'. The church must invest in remote communication and be present in media.

For the UNDA/WACC communication experts (4.2, 4.5), involvement in media education should be ecumenical and in cooperation with secular existing projects. With respect to communication, in general, it is 'a social and pastoral responsibility of churches to re-humanize communications'. Building community and promoting intermediate communities is an important issue. 'Instead of instrumentalising communication in the interest of selling their project, social institutions and churches have to serve communication as a value in itself'. The existence and funding of all broadcasts (including entertainment) that favor sociability and social interaction should be encouraged and supported. Communication should be regarded as a place of sociability and therefore be supported with human and financial means. A production policy that does not succumb to 'the temptation of being quick and flashy' is needed. The main question posed to the churches (as to other political and social institutions) is: is communication, in the first place, a means for own objectives or a value in itself because it contributes to the building of relationships and social ties? Community (in general) presupposes that each has the effective right to speak and that, without mutual listening and communication, community is not possible. Today one cannot exist in a social sense without being visible on television. The churches should participate in media. Not just for themselves, but for the sake of the wider debate. Christian communication bodies like UNDA and WACC should 'link their research in media ethics to the churches and offer a place for ethical debate at the service of media professionals and society as a whole'. The churches should 'not moralize' with regard to media, but ask themselves 'what the implications are with respect to their own way of communicating', and what tasks and consequences are involved for their media organizations like WACC and UNDA. 'Social groups, institutions and churches have to move from instrumentalising their internal communication in the interests of selling the views of their leaders to one in which communication serves to express the views of their members'. New technologies could be 'ways of reorienting communication in this manner'.

CEEM (4.3) concludes that the 'relevance of mass media to pastoral work and society as a whole should be taken into account in all the work areas of bishops' conferences and dioceses. Account should be taken of the 'possibilities and effects of media in the pastoral care of families, youth and in parishes'. Churches should take an 'active part in shaping public opinion', be 'open in their public relations', and 'cultivate contacts with secular media'. Ecumenical and international cooperation, as well as cooperation with secular institutes in media education, is indicated. Catholic media work should be promoted by moral recognition, material assistance and, 'if necessary', financial support. The statement on gospel, church and information society (4.6) underlines the need to 'develop pastoral care for the generations formed in media culture'. The 'tension between individual and community, needs to be confronted'. The church must be 'actively present' in public and private media and develop the 'knowledge of the art of public relations'. There is an 'urgent need' that the voice of the church is 'heard in media and as part of the general moral debate'. Faith needs to be 'seen doing justice'. Discussion of media issues is 'vital in solving the challenge of *inculturating* Christian faith'. Without this discussion, there will be an 'ever widening gap between faith and culture'. The church needs to develop a 'spirituality in and for media culture'.

The Church of Sweden (4.9) argues that communication with members as well as society should be related to 'questions of meaning'. Practicing the role of 'truth seeker' rather than 'truth owner', the church can, in cooperation with citizens, contribute to the development of local communities.

For COMECE (5.1, 5.2) 'examining culture implies studying media and their structures'. With respect to the future of the information society, the statement is anxious that internet and e-mail might 'undermine human relationships'. Virtual community is 'at the service of real communities, it cannot substitute for them'. The church must 'avoid encouraging the polarization between real world and virtual communities'. Its task is to 'assist building up community links'. Church members 'already use internet and email communication and take part in chat forums and news groups'. Some groups 'set up virtual communities'. The existence of virtual communities 'opens up questions' about whether community in the internet context is 'more than the use of a link'? Is internet community possible if there is no face to face interaction and physical presence? A working definition of community is needed. Quoting Lonergan[19] the document states that community means that 'people share a common field of experience, a common or complementary way of understanding people and things and common judgments and aims'. Being a member is 'to recognize and wish to be part of a community as the carrier of a common world mediated by meaning and motivated by values'. Virtual community, in this respect, is 'feasible'. It builds a common world online. The greater the interaction, the greater degree of community cohesion, and the more likely the community encourages attachment and commitment. Virtual community is successful because people can feel part of it and, at the same time, feel free about whether and when to reveal themselves. Personal encounter and freedom and belonging and remaining independent can be a 'blessed anonymity for those in distress'. The Catholic Church, given its place in European history and culture, is obliged to 'participate actively in processes of self reflection and formation'. This duty also entails 'intensive dialogue with the media'. For the church this dialogue means 'analyzing and evaluating the opportunities and risks of developments in the media sector and reconcile them with the

[19] A Third Collection. (ed. F.E. Crowe) New York: Paulist Press, 1985, p. 5-6.

anthropological prerequisites of a Christian philosophy of humanity and the aims of a social community'. The church's primary concern is not technical and economic. A key question is to what extent technologies and communication services characterize our understanding of ourselves and the world. Do they 'primarily contribute to the purpose of communication, interpersonal comprehension and the interests of social co-existence'? The church should have a 'strong commitment and advocate and promote internet/virtual literacy.   The statement fears the 'creation of a world in which intellectual and moral discrimination disappears in an ocean of information'. The church has a responsibility to 'help people navigate'. The 'waters of internet' need to be 'charted'. People need to be helped in discovering the 'monsters of pornography, racism and cults'. They need skills to use and evaluate information 'intellectually and imaginatively enriching'.

The outlook on church involvement in media and public communication will include the churches' view of social responsibilities in this respect. That is what we will consider in the next section.

3.3.8   Social and ethical responsibilities

According to WACC (1.1), 'communication is a social necessity and therefore a responsibility of everyone'. The principles of communication for the 1990's, grounded in the last 15 years, show an imbalance (NWICO). A commitment to the vision of democratic communication that involves 'entering into a new phase of dialogue to achieve a common understanding of communication in service of free, just and peaceful communities' is needed. The growth of technology, the increase in media monopolization and the vulgarization of content make this dialogue even more urgent. Principles of communication should be based on the power of people (beyond formal processes of politics) and on new ways of participation which increase the 'freedom of all people to communicate'. The search for peace and international understanding is the most important issue in this respect. Media should abandon militaristic language and stereotyping of nations and cultures. What is decisive is a 'communication environment which perceives humankind as one family, one world'. This calls for a 'revolution in social values and priorities'. Communication is 'as essential' as food, shelter and healthcare. Ordinary people now are 'victims of media power' and 'objects' (women, children, indigenous, seniors, manual laborers). To reverse this trend, people need to be empowered. Priority should be given to 'media that people can control' and to the development of traditional media rooted in local cultures and the cultivation of grass root communication. The new information and communication technologies offer new possibilities for empowerment and the right to communicate for all.

To be human (2.1. focuses on communication for human dignity) is to relate to others and to communicate. Communication helps the 'struggle against dehumanization, so that the 'oikumene may realize dignity and grace'. People of faith should 'strive to establish fundamental principles of communication ethics on a global, regional and local level. Globally, communication ethics should be 'explicit in international negotiations'. All communicators (private and public) are encouraged to adopt diversity, community, identity, and respect for all peoples, unconditional love, wholeness, and truth as central values. Regional and local alliances should be built with networks of grassroots organizations, communication trainers and program-makers to 'help reflect the central ethical concerns of respect for life, truth and non violence'. Christian communicators are called upon to 'press for the inclusion of human values; to utilize new media creatively and to develop alternative media where possible; to preserve public sphere, media access, and communication rights of all people and to join colleagues in the struggle for a more just new world economic order'. They should advocate for a communication environment that is 'free from manipulation on the global level'.

With respect to communications technology, there is an 'urgent need to understand and demystify the implications of ict'. Technology should be a tool to aid interactivity. In the policy making process of public and private entities controlling technology and media, they should be a 'voice for human dignity, freedom, fairness, diversity and full participation in planning and implementation. Research and studies by/with indigenous citizens on their world views and modes of communication should be given priority and be publicized. The same holds for gender issues. Economic and political contexts of media control, media production, human rights, freedom of expression, media education and communication technologies should be looked at 'through the prism of gender'. Definitions of power, masculinity and male oriented value systems in communication structures should be criticized. Training and empowerment of women in communication should be sustained.

Christian communicators should 'inform themselves about instruments to implement and protect human communication rights' and inform audiences about them. They should 'expose and denounce abuses' and 'mobilize support for victims'. Christian communicators should 'establish networks with human rights activists, support human rights lobbies and participate in public education policies for the promotion of human rights, including communication rights'. Social identity and a sense of belonging are human necessities and presuppose the right to use 'the mother tongue in all media of communication'. Media should encourage the creative use of symbols and images and other folk expressions by which people's identity is strengthened and recognize diversities and new identities. The potential of popular culture to affirm and build human dignity (not as a 'spectacle', but as the creation and dissemination of meanings, experiences and values) should be recognized. Christian communicators have a responsibility to 'strengthen and bring together expressions of popular culture (religious rituals, oratory storytelling, songs and dance, theatre) so they can become authentic expressions of lived experience, rooted in reality, and means of developing human dignity'.

The church must offer a 'critical evaluation of mass media and their impact upon culture' says the Vatican (1.2). Communications technology is a 'mixed blessing' that requires 'sound decisions' (by individuals, private sectors, governments and society). The church must 'not dictate', but be 'of help in indicating ethical and moral criteria'. The church has a 'duty to critical formation' and to 'engage in the defense of liberty, respect for dignity and a firm rejection of monopoly and manipulation'. The essential social role of media is to 'contribute to the human right of information, the promotion of justice and assistance in the search for truth, the exchange of ideas and information among all classes and sectors and to make all voices heard'. In the appendix (pastoral plan), it is stated that it is the task of the church to 'bring gospel values in contemporary media activities, to contribute to international solidarity'. It needs to 'cooperate with secular media' out of concern about religious, moral, ethical, cultural, educational and social issues. It should also exercise a 'prophetic role' 'by pointing to moral dimensions of public issues'.

With respect to human (communication) rights, Christians 'must give voice to the voiceless and information to the deprived'. The right to information is a 'fundamental' right, and the 'right to communicate is the right of all'. This includes the 'church's right of access'. The right to communicate is 'part of the right of religious freedom'. In situations of 'domination', the church must 'urge respect for the right to communicate, including it's own right to access to media, and at same time seek alternative models'.

With respect to media structures, legislation, and steering tools, the document states that the church should be 'actively concerned with secular media, especially in the shaping of media policy'. It signals problems of access and the right to information and domination of media by economic, social and political elites. In the appendix the necessity is argued for the defense of the public interest and the safeguarding of religious access by 'taking position on matters of communication', with respect to media law and media policy and the development of communication systems. The exclusion of groups and classes to access and means of communication is 'unjust'. The 'domination of media by economic, social and political elites is 'a problem'. The poor must have access for their development and also play an effective role in deciding on media content and the determination of structures and policies of their national institutions of social communications. The church 'views with sympathy the desire for more just and equitable systems of communication and information, against domination and manipulation' (affecting developing countries as well as minority groups). People ought to be able to 'participate actively, autonomously and responsibly in the communication process'. The appendix urges the church to 'develop strategies for a more widespread access to media'.

Human cultures should be 'defended'. It is the duty of the church to 'elevate authentic cultures of peoples', by rejecting manipulation and monopoly. The appendix adds the necessity to 'analyze the social impact of communication technology and to help prevent social disruption and cultural destabilization'.

The church as, 'teacher of humanity', has a duty to make its 'own contribution for a better understanding of outlooks and responsibilities in communication developments' says 1.4. Because media influence consciences, form mentality and determine views of things, it is important to 'stress that mass media constitute a patrimony to safeguard and promote'. Regarding media structures, it is stated that media must 'enter into a framework of organically structured rights and duties' (from the point of view of formation, ethical responsibility, reference to laws and institutional codes). The 'positive development of media at the service of common good, is a responsibility of all'. Because of the close connections of media with economics and politics and culture, a 'management system is necessary capable of safeguarding the centrality and dignity of the person and the primacy of the family as the basic unit of society'. Communications media are 'for all humanity'. Ever new means must be found, including legislative measures, for 'true participation in management by all'.

With respect to ethics in advertising (2.2), the church should 'enter into a dialogue with communicators' and, at the same time, 'express moral principles and norms and criticize what is against ethical and moral standards' (truthfulness, completeness, freedom, human dignity and social responsibility). Advertisers, publishers and broadcasters are 'morally responsible for what they seek to move people to do'. It is 'morally wrong to use manipulative, exploitative and corrupt methods of persuasion and motivation'. Indirect advertising is a 'special problem'. People are not fully aware 'when products or behavior is shown in glamorous settings or of 'subliminal messages'. Rhetorical and symbolic exaggeration is allowable - deliberately deceiving is not. Problematic are the violation of human dignity through content and the impact it seeks (manipulation of human weakness), and the deformed outlook on life, family, religion and morality. Elderly, poor, children and culturally disadvantaged people are especially vulnerable because their fears are played upon. With respect to advertising and social responsibility, many issues are involved. One of them is the ecological issue. The lavish lifestyle, as promoted in advertising, wastes resources and despoils the environment - 'have and enjoy' rather than 'be and grow'. Authentic and integral human development is at stake. Advertising that reduces human progress to material goods promotes a 'false vision of humanity' and is harmful to individual and society alike. 'Rigorous respect is needed for the moral, cultural and spiritual requirements, based on the dignity of the person and the proper identity of each community'. Advertisers and communicators have the duty to 'express and foster an authentic vision of human development in its material, cultural and spiritual dimensions'. Then communication is a 'true expression of solidarity'. Quoting the Catechism, 'solidarity is the consequence of genuine and right communication and the free circulation of ideas that further knowledge and respect for others'. Advertisers and communicators must 'ensure ethically responsible practices: avoid abuses, repair harm (correct and compensate), and increase the quantity of public service advertising. Cooperation between self regulatory bodies of the advertising industry, public interest groups and public authorities is needed. Christians should call upon professionals to eliminate harmful aspects and observe high ethical standards. The advertising industry should not just serve the interests of financers, but the rights of the audience and the common good. External structures, voluntary ethical codes and public involvement (including ethicists, church people and consumer groups) are important. Public authorities should not 'control or dictate the advertising industry more than other media sectors'. But regulation should extend beyond 'banning false advertising'. It should 'ensure that public morality and social progress is not endangered through the misuse by media'. Government regulation is needed to control the quantity of advertising (especially in broadcast media), the content of advertising directed at vulnerable groups, and political advertising (amount of spending, how and from whom money is raised etc). For the sake of public debate, media must 'keep the public informed about the world of advertising'. Because of its social impact, it should be 'reviewed and critiqued regularly just as are other groups influencing society'.

Regarding ethics in communication in general (2.3), the 'choices made by receivers and controllers with respect to structures, policy and content' are central. The communication flow in one direction is a 'serious ethical question'. For the church, the main ethical principles are solidarity, justice, equity, accountability in the use of public resources and public trust. Communication must always be truthful. Truth is essential to individual liberty and authentic community. 'The ethical dimension relates not just to the content of communication (the message) and the process of communication (how the communicating is done) but to fundamental structural and systemic issues, often involving large questions of policy bearing upon the distribution of sophisticated technology and products (who shall be information rich and who shall be the information poor?)'. These questions point to other questions with economic and political implications for ownership and control. 'At least in open societies with market economies, the largest ethical question of all is how to balance profit against the service to the public interest understood according to an inclusive conception of the common good'. 'In all three areas –message, process, structural and systemic issues – the fundamental ethical principle is this: the human person and the human community are the end and measure of the use of the media of social communication; communication should be by persons to persons for the integral development of persons'. Integral development includes growing 'physically, intellectually, emotionally, morally and spiritually'. A second principle is complementary: the good of persons cannot be separated from the common good of communities. Solidarity ought to govern all areas social life: economic, political, cultural and religious.

Audiences have ethical duties as well. They must be selective, make responsible, and informed choices, that are based on continuing media education (not only on technique, but also on standards and the formation of conscience). Parents have a duty to 'teach children how to evaluate and use media, how to resist uncritical passivity, peer pressure and commercial exploitation'. Continuing research is needed about the impact of ethics on new media. The new ethic application of principles to new circumstances is a task of everyone. Broad reflection is needed. 'Serving the human person, building up human community grounded in solidarity and justice and love, and speaking the truth about human life and its final fulfillment in God were, are, and will remain at the heart of ethics in the media'.

With respect to human communication rights, 'freedom of expression and exchange is a right and a moral duty' (Quote from C&P). It is not an absolute right, however. Slander, hatred, obscenity, violence and conflict are not part of this right. Free expression should observe truth, fairness, respect and privacy. State control is not a solution to unregulated commercialization and privatization. Regulation according to public service criteria and greater public accountability are. Professional ethical codes made in cooperation with public representatives, in which members of religious bodies should take part, is needed. There is a 'pressing need for equity' at an international level. The 'misdistribution of materials is exacerbated by the misdistribution of communication resources and information technology'. This also holds true for the wealthy countries where people are marginalized. A 'broad participation' in decision making, messages, processes, systemic issues and in the allocation of resources is needed. Decision makers have a 'moral duty' in respect to the interests of 'vulnerable, families, and religious groups'. The international community and communication interests should have an 'inclusive approach to nations and regions'. They share in the 'blame of the perpetuation of poverty, illiteracy, human rights violations, inter-religious conflicts, and the suppression of indigenous cultures'.
Another relevant principle is the public participation in policy decision making. It should be 'organized, systematic and genuinely representative'. 'Especially when media are privately owned, for profit'. Communicators must 'seek communication' and not merely 'address'. They should 'learn peoples needs' and use all forms of communication 'sensitive to human dignity'. Ratings and market research 'represent the market operation', but are not the 'best indicators' of public sentiment. Decisions about content and policy should not be left to the market. Economic factors do not safeguard the public interest as whole, neither do they safeguard the interests of minorities. Diversification and specialization should not be implemented too far. The 'niche' is 'legitimate' up to a point, but media must remain the *Areopagus*, the forum of exchange, which draws people together in solidarity and peace. The church should contribute to the discussion about media with its vision of the human person and human dignity, of inviolable rights (expertise in humanity), and of human community (solidarity and the good of all). This is a pressing need since 'in time there will be an inadequacy of perspectives and crisis with the ephemeral as value and real meaning of life'. The church, therefore, seeks dialogue and collaboration for high ethical standards with others: public officials, people from culture and art, scholars, other churches and religious groups and professionals.

With respect to the internet (2.4, 4.9), again the dignity of persons, the sustaining of communities, solidarity, and the common good of all is central to the ethical evaluation made. The main ethical question is 'whether the revolution in social communications contributes to authentic human development helping to be true to man's transcendent destiny'. In many ways, according 2.4, 'the answer is yes'. Due to deregulation, there is a 'shift of power from the national states to transnational corporations. They should be 'helped to use their power for the common good of humanity within and among nations'. There is a need for more dialogue between them and 'concerned bodies like the churches'. If used in the light of 'sound ethical principles', media can be 'means to integral development and the creation of a world of justice, peace and love'. A 'spirituality of communion' and 'globalization and a new global economy in service of all' is needed. Many have a responsibility in this (corporations, users, parents, schools). People that 'shape structures and contents' have a special duty to 'practice solidarity in the service of common good'.
Again, freedom of expression is a fundamental, however, -non-absolute- right. Internet must 'leave room for authentic community, the common good, and solidarity. Recipients need to be 'self disciplined' due to the danger of 'getting lost in virtual reality, missing real life'. Seeking and knowing the truth is 'a fundamental right, and, provided moral

order and common interest are respected, a cornerstone of democracy'. Being truthfully informed is a public interest. Public authorities that block access or manipulate by propaganda or disinformation (authoritarian regimes as well as liberal democracies that access political expression for the wealthy, violate truthfulness and fairness, or shrink issues to sound bites) are rejected.

Government censorship is not felt to be the solution to problems in cyberspace, but there are to be 'certain laws and regulations' with respect to criminal behavior in cyberspace (hate sites speech, libel, fraud, or pornography). Or, as 4.9 puts it: 'free expression may require some tolerance, but, next to industry self regulation, intervention by public authority to establish and enforce limits is required'. New laws, says 2.4, are needed, for internet crimes like the dissemination of viruses or the theft of personal data. Other issues include privacy, the security and confidentiality of data, copyright and intellectual property law, and the dissemination of rumor and character assassination under the guise of news.

What is preferred is self regulation by the industry along the lines of public service and greater public accountability. Industry codes of ethics are useful. Public representatives should take part in their formulation and enforcement, and they should include penalties for violations (including public censure). State intervention is sometimes useful, e.g. to set up media advisory boards. International cooperation is needed to set standards, protect the international common good and bridge the digital divide. Action in both private and public sectors is needed and should be handled on an international level, including the UN. International consensus is necessary, e.g. to guarantee privacy, for the surveillance of criminals and terrorists, to protect copyright and intellectual property without limiting access to materials in the public domain, and with respect to the issue of how to define the public domain. Other issues that need to be tackled are: how to maintain a broad availability in many languages, how to protect women's rights with respect to internet access and how to close the digital divide in its technical, educational and cultural aspects. International solidarity offers the UN as a meeting place of states and civil societies, a place of 'convergence of interest and needs' (cooperation of international agencies and nongovernmental organizations), and a 'unique opportunity to the globalization of solidarity'. Hope is expressed (2.4) that the WSIS[20] 2003 campaign can make a 'positive contribution to the discussion'.

Cyberspace should be a 'resource of information and services without charge to all, in a wide range of languages'. Public institutions have a 'particular responsibility to maintain sites of this kind'. Dialogue between cultures should be fostered. Cultural domination or imperialism (imposing world views, values or language) is rejected. Respect to other peoples' values and beliefs and cultural sensitivity is 'imperative'. Cultural oppression is 'especially serious' if the dominant culture spreads 'false values'. Internet and media alike spread a 'value laden message of western secular culture to societies ill prepared to evaluate and cope with it'. This is the cause of problems and crisis. Distinctive cultures are to be regarded as 'creative expressions within the unity of the human family'.

Continuing analysis and discussion about the development of cyberspace 'by all concerned' is necessary. 'Religious people', says 4.9 'as concerned members of the internet audience who also have legitimate interests of their own' 'wish to be part of the process that guides the future development of cyberspace' that 'sometimes requires them to adjust their own thinking and practice'.

Compared to the Vatican, the LWF pays remarkably less attention to the issue of social and, particularly, ethical involvement in its statements (1.3 and 3.3). This is especially striking with respect to 3.3, which focuses explicitly on 'value, power and the information society'.

---

[20] The World Summit on the Information Society

LWF urges to 'actively work against the global trend of 'new technology for the few' and the divide between the 'have and have nots'. Participation and access for all must be empowered. Within the LWF the 'top priority' is e-mail and web access for all member churches for a variety of goals: 'speed, connectivity, mission development work, health education, better access to information and to challenge analphabetism'. The LWF wishes to 'share the Lutheran tradition' 'without colonial asymmetries between contexts and cultures and languages'. All should challenge economic, political and cultural forces and work towards the 'decolonization of minds'. Local communication cultures and patterns should be used. 'Sharing a language', according to 3.3, 'means sharing power and worldview'. LWF wishes to empower people to participate in the communion, and by sharing their culture and life experiences to communicate. It also asks 'whether we can create a Christian culture of communication which focuses on recipients, with their history, their language, their skills and abilities'.

The statement by the German Bishops' Conference (3.1), also about the information society, elaborates more extensively on the subject. The contribution of the churches, 'next to political regulation', is related 'in special to the social ethical dimensions of multimedia developments'. These developments 'raise ethical and theological questions and demands' e.g. the blurring of spatial, time and functional borders'. Socio-cultural systems increasingly become 'socio-technical'. The political and ethical criteria for handling multimedia techniques, according to the statement, are 'overlooked'. It identifies (interrogatively) four issues in this respect.

1. The demand for esthetical and dialogical competences. The surety of human existence depends on a 'socially bearable dealing with technique'. The church should offer 'education for responsible dealing with new technique' and for 'existential human competence'. These involve e.g. compassion, personal communication, the skill of observation, encouragement, and creativity in complex issues. It is asked what the 'increasing segmentation of observation means'? The increase in information is 'not by definition a reinforcement of communication competence'. Issues of meaning of information are 'just as important as e.g. issues of transfer speed'.
2. Does multimedia mean the farewell to public discourse? The implications that are signaled are the 'massive segmentation of the media market, the farewell of mass communication characteristics, the danger of de-politicization and the breakdown of public discourse in specialized discussions'. This implies a 'loss of the integrating function of instruments of social communication.
3. Theology and multimedia, church and information society. The question is raised whether theology and pastoral theology 'are involved intensely and critically in the information' technological developments, or do they take them for granted?' Is 'communication, dissolved in digital bits, compatible with the religious Christian speech culture?' How does theology relate to the changing humanity views and worldviews? The 'explosion of information' involves a 'loss of orientation'. Is a 'counterculture, which offers church involved alternative spaces of experience, needed?' Is, 'socio cultural training and culture education, on pastoral grounds, an assignment?'
4. What about communicative and social justice? What about the access of users and underprivileged players? Are we up to a 'social class society' with unequal entry for the poor and the rich? Will the gap between the industrial information society and the third world be deepened? Will the labor market be developed socially? The main criterion in dealing with media should be 'appropriateness and serving humanity'. Since there is 'less regulation by the state and more freedom and self responsibility', an 'energetic activation of ethical powers' is needed.

Nine consequences are listed:

1. Media culture is a reflection and expression of times. Working towards and with media is part of pastoral care.
2. Sensory multiplicity in the passing on of information and the possibility of worldwide connections meet the communication needs of people and therefore are welcomed.
3. Living in fullness (John 4) is something fundamentally different and more extensive than the experience of synthetic reality constructions in virtual spaces. Observation skills must be differentiated and practiced. Helping to find the trace of the other in personal communication must be a normative effort of the church. This includes the attempt to mediate between faith speech and speech of multimedia. Schools have a special task in this. Their formation, however, should not be restricted to technique, but -above all- accomplish psycho-social and communicative competence in dealing with the information society.
4. Computerization can deepen social injustice (gap third world and segmented societies).
5. There is a need for political regulation (protection of communication rights, access without discrimination, monopolies and social and labor policies).
6. A counter world of familiar spaces and personal conversation, in which -in dialogue- the meaning of multimedia technique can be realized, and corresponded with Jesus' word of life in fullness, is indispensable. Open pastoral offerings, like meeting and culture centers, are important in this respect.
7. The church must make clear how she deals with computerization, and how its possibilities can be matched with its conception of media. She should ask whether the involvement of theology in the information super highway must be considered (information, pastoral and social services, news) where it could theoretically reach hundreds of thousands.
8. Because of the introduction of niche programming the church should renew the discussion on its own engagement in electronic media.
9. Personal faith is a benefit of world and God-experience. Multimedia can reduce this experience to a mathematical information-technological quantity. This tension is a 'people friendly' assignment of the church.

In its statement on media and communication competence (4.7), the German Bishops' Conference restricts itself to the tasks of its media bureaus. 'In a commercial information society, they must contribute to information justice (free access of information and media and communication competence for all societal groups)'. They 'represent a view of media which always questions technical issues in relationship to human and societal compatibility'. And they 'support media education in school teaching plans'.

'The church has a responsibility for life and living together and therefore must make an ethical contribution to the development of media'. This is the outlook in the ecumenical statement published by the German churches (3.2). Mass media developments are said to be a 'complex reality'. They are situated in the 'area of tension between technical possibilities, economic necessities, demands of law and ethical issues'. Chances and risks should be 'weighed and connected to the Christian anthropological image of man and the goals of societal living together'.
The development of media society is an 'ethical assignment'. Technical structures should be at the service of humanity. Several recommendations for action are identified. General ethical reflections include: helping orientation and identity building; strengthen media competence; restrict media power and make it transparent; assure free access and self responsible participation; regulate systems ethically; respect dignity and intimacy and

a realistic view of societal living together; and empower international communication justice and understanding between peoples. The design of media and communication techniques is a 'common task of all'. Chances should be used and risks limited. Self-regulation and control should be enlarged. The same holds true for protection rights. Churches should 'contribute to the construction of a democratic media and communication order and use new possibilities in their own publicity work'.

Media competence is a 'life enduring central education assignment'. People must know how to use, to evaluate and to deal with media, understand media logic and be 'skeptical towards manipulated images'. A 'knowledge gap' should be avoided. All should have affordable access. Reading and writing should receive attention. Pedagogic concepts should be developed.

Journalists and communicators should publicly engage in an ethical dialogue about their profession and develop self control between editorial staff. Churches should make their own contribution by offering ethical formation.

Societal self regulation is urgent to strengthen the influence of media users. Human dignity should be protected. What is needed is a broader societal dialogue on communication and media ethics. A 'responsible consciousness' of media users and producers is a 'special responsibility' in church media ethics. Media information services by the churches have the task of making media logic transparent. Independent scientific research about the consequences and risks of media developments is needed. This needs to go beyond 'data' and include for example what is societally tolerable and a multiformity of opinions.

Media are 'constitutive for democracy'. The freedom of forming opinion should, 'also in the digital era and the international media market', be politically and legally retained. All media players 'have a societal duty to serve public opinion forming'. German and European legislators should restrict economic and publicity power by circumscribing market shares and 'persevere rules'. Monopolies (also in rights and licenses) should not be allowed. Media power should be transparent. All licensees should have equal access to digital broadcasting that is free from discrimination. The order of press neutrality should also be applied to electronic services. Regulation should be in favor of the media's cultural function. Digital technique should be obliged to make the manipulations of materials known.

With respect to the organization of broadcasting, all three forms (public, private and public citizen channels) should be further developed. A channel for youth must be safeguarded, and properly financed (no advertising and less sponsoring). Party political influence must be restricted. Private media need to respect a minimum standard of information and multiformity. Self control should be obliged. Non professional programs on public channels should be 'politically ensured'. Local broadcasting should be financed by license fees. In order to 'sharpen' the quality of media content, means should be provided by public and private bodies, 'as well as by churches'.

Protection rights should be strengthened. Protection of data should be taken care of legally and meet European and international minimum standards. Controlling bodies should be adjusted and have the possibility to apply sanctions. The young should be protected from content which is 'negative for their mental, spiritual, emotional, moral and religious development'. Protection rules should be adjusted to new media. In online services the glamorization of violent racism, war, the violence of human dignity and the offerings of pornography should not be permitted. Self-regulation is needed by players, service providers and parents. Programming aimed at children should be restricted in advertising (only at certain times and clearly distinguishable). Due to the development of teleshopping and electronic media services, the protection of users should be strengthened. The mixture of advertising and programming should be resisted. The legal protection of creative work should be further developed.

With respect to development policy, a gap should be resisted. Access to data files is needed for everyone. International efforts must be made. This is also an assignment for churches because of their global connections. Communication should be a factor in (church) development policies. Issues in this respect involve not only hard and software, but also know how, transfer of technology, education, and local media production. Reporting on the Third World should include daily life and background information, connections and development trends. Foreign correspondents should be familiar with local cultures.

The central question for the church in all this is not, in the first place, a technical, political, financial or legal issue. These follow from the main question of whether communication and media, stamping self- and world understanding, serve human dignity, humanity and societal living together. Socially responsible development of media and communication, therefore, is a challenge for the development of international political and legal frameworks and public debate. Since communication opportunities currently take part in deciding about the quality of life, it is necessary to order them in a way, so that everyone can take part and have a say in defining them. Mass media are important in preserving democracy. The assurance of multiplicity and differentiation of information are 'important ethical goals' that should not be sacrificed in spite of market mechanism pressures. The educational assignment of media is not 'contrary to market orientation'.

The church has a 'special responsibility' towards the challenges of media society. Demands and obligations apply to the churches as well. They should give an impulse to the worth of freedom and contribute to the preservation of media as factors of social communication. This includes formation of journalists, media pedagogy, media political engagement oriented towards the common good of all, and start a media, ethical, public debate. In the transition to the information society, these assignments will only increase in importance. Even with more tight finances, the churches still can make a qualified contribution to human justified communication.

The individual statement by the German Protestant churches (4.4) elaborates upon the issue of social involvement by the churches much less. The 'task and mandate' of protestant publicity is to 'facilitate the participation of the church in public debate'. Publicity, therefore, is a 'basic service' for the church. The church should 'participate in the development and the safeguarding of publicity goals and standards' and 'impact them with Christian standards for just and social communication'.

'In each case, the pervasive influence of computers forces us to address moral questions. But since these questions fall outside the territory of our shared consensus we have to figure out right and wrong all over again. That in turn requires us to have a moral framework, and that is where Christians have something to offer', says the *Cybernauts Awake* statement by the Church of England (3.4) Christians should have an 'active role' in the shaping process, the development and the use of cyberspace that is based on a 'chosen end for a social system'. The Christian story (God as creator and origin, community, free will, creativity, human disruption, God's reconciliation and full life) provides 'principles of action'. These include focusing on the needs of society and a just and peaceful world. The church should be motivated by the joy of love and confidence in the future, not by fear of catastrophe. It should give a 'joyful response to love, not a depressing obligation, nor aimed at own salvation'. It should be 'willing to accept help from unlikely sources and to give help wherever needed'. Reconciliation involves forgiving relationships. Cyberspace provides much information to individuals, but its 'moulds are inappropriate to proper relationships'. Christians should 'give up false ideas who is inside and who is outside', and 'worry about being excluded by cyberspace'. Social inclusion means 'access for all at low cost'. Frailties should be recognized. God

gave human freedom, but by the misuse of information 'humanity is denied'. Individual autonomy should be protected by legislation. People should be able to 'grow into the fullness of humanity'. Cyberspace challenges this; desires should be fulfilled 'instantly' and the consideration of effects to others is discouraged. Cyberspace can be used to 'rejoice in fellowship and interdependence' or destroy it. There is not just 'one answer of participation to the responsibility of full humanness in cyberspace, (there are many ways to live in accordance with God's will). The common good of all should be the priority. Technology is part of the continuing human story of which our 'times are but a small part'. Ethical implications of living with cyberspace involve: business and work, property and ownership, justice, content, access, privacy, security, cryptography and the integrity of physical beings (invasion into bodies). Concerns are raised anew. Cyberspace forces people to adopt the speed of business networking. It sustains globalization - weakening local and national links of employees. Wealth power is concentrated (however there are new job opportunities for Third World countries). Electronic commerce leads to inner city deprivation, changing work patterns (from hierarchical structures to flat management and net and team working and local decision making new style). Teleworking makes work more contract driven (freelance, lack of security and stable schooling, and work communities becoming less important - which increases the importance of other communities like the church). With respect to property, cyberspace has 'real social effects on real relationships'. Easy duplication (theft), the power of information (objectification, data records for profit) and the power of ownership and standards (licenses, justice inequality) raise ethical questions. What are the responsibilities in sharing and using information? What is the meaning of property? Ownership, for the church, is always relative to God's call on what is owned. Ownership in cyberspace (medical records, genetic data, copyright software and the right to make public for example) should be object of accountability. New forms of marketing, shareware, public domain software, copyright, authorship, exclusion and exploitation should be held accountable under the command to 'love God and one's neighbor and to build up common life. Justice and accountability in cyberspace involve the protection of consumer computer programs and the responsibility of intermediate operators for carried content. A global solution and international agreement is needed. 'Cyber exclusion' should be resisted: infrastructure, skills and access to information should be available for all (public libraries should become 'cybercentres'. Christians have the duty to 'speak up for who cannot speak', for the excluded and literally mute, who have no means and are excluded from a new language. This situation devalues humanity.
Issues of privacy are another area of concern. Digital information can be easily manipulated, linked and reproduced. Email should be confidential and personal. Its legal status (protection) is unclear. Internet service providers can use it for commercial information. Log in patterns to websites can be tracked and data can be matched. The integration of information sources (credit card, medical, legal and financial records) can be used for 'protection of the state' and digital memory can be 'persistent or disappear without trace'. For the church, there is a connection between privacy and humanity in the 'love and free gift of self disclosure, manifest in the incarnation'. Personhood is of fundamental importance in Christianity. Man is always 'more than the information about him'. Personal information is not a 'freely to manipulate commodity'. Email privacy and web access raise security issues about email interception, (justified by the 'improvement of service') and about the disclosure to third parties, as well as the archiving of information (the identification with data shadow). Christian teaching about forgiveness is appropriate here. Issues of 'secrets and lies' are at stake as well. Cryptography is 'more extensive' than the secret coding of messages. It is about tapping communication, non-forgeable signatures, public key security (to lock messages) and group security. It raises political, moral issues on individual freedom versus the interest of society, on anonymity of electronic cash (payments without any bank knowing), and on audit trails (control by

nations, banks, police or military and secret services). There is a 'difference between a warrant and a blanket mechanism for surveillance'. The question is: 'what outcome do we want?'

Moral issues are also 'pressing' with respect to implants and direct interaction with the human brain. What happens 'if a computerized bit of brain makes moral decisions for us?' Will a 'direct connection to cyberspace, make us get wiser or get lost?' Examples of moral decisions by computers already exist. Examples are credit ratings by head office computers; filters for children's use of computers or electronic tags for prisoners. More complex moral decisions could be delegated to the computer in future. Routinely taken, this could 'demoralize' issues. The whole vision of the ethical is at stake: on what basis do computers decide? They probably calculate consequences better, but is that all? Or are we up to credit rating system inside the head of the banker or a moral filter in a child? There are commercial pressures towards brain implants. 'Whether' and 'under what circumstances' are moral and spiritual issues; can e.g. an implant change one's personality? And what about social justice issues -the 'have nots', the people unconnected to a telephone-, do they get implants? The digital divide might be increased. Implants can become consumer items; nanotechnology even might inject implants. But do technology implants improve human relationships? In the Christian view, the priority is with common life.

Debate is necessary on short and long term issues. With economic and security concerns dominating, liberty, charity and helping the poor are not promoted. Given the examples on climate changes or biodiversity. But there are implications involved for all of us. Good design is a moral issue: for information technologists as 'co creators of a new dimension of being'; for directors, with respect to the interaction with the kind of organization you want to be; for the user, who should make his/her views known about systems, computer dependency, digital deception and netiquette; for parents who should use computer technology with their children, be aware of the potential deception and depravity (free speech culture), help develop safety rules and report harmful material; and for Christians, who should be aware of the difference between analogies and idols with respect to the perception of spiritual reality by experiences in cyberspace. The spiritual is not opposed to physical things. Cyberspace may offer a rich, new store of analogies and parables and intelligent agents may seem like angels, but it remains an analogy. The gospel is bigger than cyberspace. 'Historically, every new advance in communication has been a means of proclaiming the gospel, and cyberspace is no exception; cyberspace can be used in the service of the gospel'. Christians should beware of those hostile to the gospel, -using cyberspace to attempt to prove the gospel is false-. They should add helpful content and participate in online debates in order to make Christian voices heard. Churches should be proactive; cyberspace being the most important source of information about organizations. Cyberspace is a strong force for social change. It should be used to work for social justice, evangelization and proclamation of the gospel. The church, however, remains a real community for the 21st century. Gathering people in communities will become an increasing necessity in a remote fragmented world.

The social and ethical involvement by the Finnish churches (4.1, 4.10) is marked by its wish to 'offer examples of communicative communication'. Communication is the 'basis of human life and a human right'. Global communication, however, 'follows the division of economic social powers'. Global journalism 'changes the communication environment all over the world'. The church should 'participate in a global dialogue' and 'international forums'. Decisions in telecom within the EU that are made now, are 'to be compared with decisions on water and motorways in earlier times'. New communication solutions will 'regulate the cultural and economical development far into the future'. Poorer countries are lagging behind. The church should participate in 'implementing more righteous communication around the world'. Com should be 'included in programs of the church and development work.

In 4.10 it is added that justice for the poorest countries without technology is a 'global challenge to the church'. In accordance with its values, 'it should promote a just and sustainable global media development and support remote communication globally'. This can create the 'conditions for increasing international dialogue, which is essential to world peace'. The church's sense of community across boundaries challenges it to be active in this. It is not active in the media field just as a producer of programs. It should also take part in a discussion about media ethics and ensure communication training is 'one of the main subjects in public and church education'. Greater investments are needed in communication in the church and in government development aid.

According to the ecumenical communication experts of UNDA/WACC, the church's pastoral action should urgently engage in media education. It should launch action to schools, families and media. For schools, a 'concerted plan based on church projects dealing with media and education' should be offered. Churches can make an inventory of existing projects, recognize them officially (without a defensive attitude) and offer training to teachers (who are used to the world of books). They can build on a European coordination of educational institutions dependent on churches. With respect to families, churches could dialogue on the subjects and the programs watched by people. This can 'diminish the impact of powerful images'. Children learn to 'unravel the real and the imagery and compare media values and behavior with family values'. Parents need training and distance to analyze media. It should give children the 'necessary freedom and pleasure of watching'. Parishes should offer 'reflection on the place of television in family life and analysis of media'. A concerted planning of church projects concerned with media and pastoral care for families will result in new initiatives, 'grafted on existing (non church based) projects. Audiovisual media education can also be fostered through press, radio and television; the public 'appreciates help in choosing and judging'. The churches' own media can 'help the public watch intelligently', e.g. by offering questions to discuss about favorite programs or information about how television works (content, forms, the composition of images, etc). They have editorial freedom, but should be sensitive to pastoral concern shown by church authorities. Christian channels should make studies together with church authorities and professionals - not 'to criticize, but for the sake of audiovisual education'. Church projects and Christian inspired media should 'contribute to a world wide policy of media education'.

The statement on identities and communities (4.5) does not restrict itself to media education. Media (and the internet) should not be left being 'dominated by commercial logic solely'. There is a responsibility -also by the churches- for 'the common interest, for the non-profitable public, for not denying ethics of media professionals and for research in media ethics' ('human and financial resources should be provided and results be widely diffused'). As there is a responsibility for 'general channels for the sake of social cohesion and the disadvantaged' and for public service broadcasting, which is not just 'charged with public service mandates which could equally be undertaken by commercial channels'. Public service channels are entrusted with 'serving the common good of society'. The question is 'how to give them, beyond specific mandates, the means to serve the general interest and the ethical values underpinning common life? Another issue for the churches is how to 'promote social cohesion in their own communications and how to keep a presence in public space', and how to 'help generalist channels create a forum in a compartmentalized society'. The more pluralist a society is, the more 'generalist communication' is necessary. Churches should 'commit themselves to open communication and an attitude of dialogue'. They should 'ask themselves whether their own media should focus on the interior Christian community or on presenting a debate in society open to other traditions, social and religious groups. They should 'refuse niche thinking'. With respect to communication rights, it is stated that 'self regulation is not sufficient'. Legal regulation is a 'necessity to ensure freedom of information and expression and the right of communication for all within a democratic framework'. However, this should not 'limit innovation or communication, neither penalize audio visual industry. Priority is the general interest. This 'implies rules governing social and cultural aspects of media and a universal community service'. In an open society, it is vital to have general interest channels and public service channels. The 'future of life together' is at stake. At the European level, the 'current regulation for free competition and protection of rights of authors and minors, are not enough'. Free competition 'does not ensure freedom of expression'. Moreover, the freedom of expression of cultural, religious and linguistic minorities is to be safeguarded (under the condition that they respect democracy). The focus on profitable customers' interests neglect marginalized people. Public authority regulation is needed, next to regulation by industry and professionals or involvement by consumer associations. Regulation must guarantee the democratic character of society. Media are 'not just information pipes, in a technical and economical sense'. There are also social, cultural concerns (especially in Central Europe, where the liberalization pressures by the EC are a threat). Churches must support regulation 'in the name of the right of all to communicate, especially the poorest'. UNDA/WACC should serve churches and public authorities alike by making their reflections available.

Finally, it is urgent to set up a 'universal community service' with access and education for everyone in order to prevent a social divide between information rich and information poor. Churches in this respect can do more than be 'the voice of the voiceless'. They should ask themselves (with all concerned) 'what political and economic conditions would allow the excluded to speak for themselves and find a media place of education, socialization and communication'. Churches should 'encourage and support the existence and funding of all broadcasts which favor sociability and social interaction'. The statement concludes that it is an 'urgent necessity to re-open lines of communication between individuals, citizens and social groups, between different streams of thought, cultures and peoples'. To open new ways of communication in which everyone is involved is a 'force for social cohesion and respect for the person'. 'Change and re-humanize communications, is a priority for cohesion at the heart of the European society'. This is a responsibility of the citizen, the politicians, media-professionals, and 'certainly of churches in their internal dealings as well as in their exercise of social and pastoral responsibilities'.

The church, in the outlook of CEEM (4.3, 4.6), is 'part of the developing info space, and amid media culture, called to co operate in shaping it'. It should take an 'active part in shaping public opinion' by 'open public relations and the cultivation of contacts with secular media'. It should not allow the gap between information poor and information rich to widen. Parishes and church institutions should 'facilitate easy access for everyone'. Deregulation and digitalization 'bring stiff competition from commercial broadcasters to public service broadcasting. Bishop's conferences' should 'be aware of this and take clear positions'. Public service broadcasting should be 'widely used and supported'. It offers services that 'cannot be expected from private broadcasters'. The church should be 'actively present in public and private media and develop the knowledge and art of public relations'.

The Swedish church (4.8) states that the fast growth in electronic media brings with it the risk that 'people are excluded from information'. There is a 'growing need and interest in ethics; church presence is invited frequently in this respect'. The church should 'take part in all societal discussions and be present at all levels in public debates', just like it attended the UN conferences in search for common ethics (the conference on the environment in Rio of 1992; on human rights, Vienna 1993; on population problems, Cairo 1994; and on equal rights, Beijing 1995).

The primary concern of the Catholic Church in developing the communication and media sector is 'not primarily on technical and economic issues', says COMECE (5.1). Cultural perceptions (to what extent do new technologies and communication services characterize our understanding of both ourselves and of the world) and whether media serve the purpose of communication, interpersonal comprehension and the interests of social co-existence are more important. Individual interests and collective well being are 'mutually conditional'.

COMECE's remarks on the Green Paper involve the concept of legislation, the concept of convergence, differentiation of contents and dissemination technology and the role of public service broadcasting.

The concept of regulation in the paper is negatively perceived (restriction of freedom, an obstacle for development, etc). It should be more differentiated and thus 'become more positive if the meaning and function of regulation are defined more accurately'. COMECE agrees with the paper that regulation is not an end in itself. It serves values and aims. It is an 'instrument' in a framework of regulatory policy 'determined by values and standards'. Curiously enough, however, the paper hardly reflects on the central role of values and standards as basis for a framework. This is particularly the case in the regulations referring to the public interest. Individual freedom and collective well being to COMECE are relative. Freedom can only exist if it is determined by values. Regulation serves to secure the freedom of speech, assembly and choice. The aim should be to achieve protection of the well being of public interest and the individual, the promotion of cultural and regional diversity, social coherence and free participation in the communication process. Principles of regulation must protect and promote fundamental values and objectives derived from the equilibrium of individual freedom and collective well being. Fundamental principles involve: transparency of the regulation process and underlying interests, of special features sectors and areas, of subsidiary regulation and of mechanisms and authorities. Concrete policy framework must be deduced from objectives and principles of regulation. The determination of objectives and principles of regulation is the aim of politics, which also have a control function. The directing objective should not only refer to the normative power of technological development and the self regulation of the market, especially when market values are completely different from the values and objectives of the community. Not only economic perspectives should be promoted, but also ethical and regulatory policy dimensions and the advocacy of fundamental human rights. Principles should not be left exclusively to self regulation by the sectors. The latter should be promoted, but independent regulatory bodies socially legitimized are vital as well.

The concept of convergence is not defined and applied very differently. It is applied to technical convergence, to convergence in utilization, in markets and services and in contents. To conclude the necessity for the convergence of legal regulations, according to COMECE, is premature. From a consumer's point of view, convergence in utilization and contents is most specific. The paper 'wrongly ignores those two aspects'. It is 'not decided at all that existing terminal equipment will be replaced by a single global piece'. Probably different features will be used simultaneously. Predictions about changes in the pattern of media use depend on 'the willingness to accept new technology and continue investing' and are 'too uncertain as an argument for revised regulation.

Another point of criticism is the lack of clear differentiation in regulations affecting contents and dissemination technologies. Regulation on infrastructure, which is mainly technological and economical (e.g. standards, free access, no monopolies), might -under circumstances- be left to the market. But regulation of content should be more differentiated. Broadcasting law must 'secure broadcasting as a medium for formation, individual and public opinion, social and cultural integration, as educational factor and as a guarantee for diversity of opinion'. Respect for the person and human dignity and protection of minorities and young must be ensured. Content regulation (especially referring to broadcasting) also has its 'own objectives inherent to classic mass media functions within democracies' (information, the formation of opinion, criticism and control). These should be secured and defended. As great of a diversity of contents possible must, in principle, be upheld. COMECE questions, however, whether diversity of contents, linked in the paper to the demand of further opening of the market, is 'confused with diversity of supplies with basically the same content'. Opening up of the market is understandable for competitive reasons, but improbable as a means increasing diversity. COMECE raises the question about how the objectives of public interest can be secured in an environment of technological innovation, and whether a change in regulation can be reconciled with public interest objectives. To secure the objectives of public interest on the basis of contracts is 'one of the most important tasks of the EC. They should guarantee social and regional cohesion in community; the general commitment to universal services and basic supplies at reasonable prices; the protection of private life and data; cultural diversity; the protection of minors and public law order. These objectives are 'all of major significance for the church'. Public interest in telecommunications and media is 'a decisive issue for the churches'. 'Any new suggestion of regulation must promote effectively the objectives mentioned'. It is 'doubtful whether the proposals for extensive market orientation and self regulation can prevent public interests being undermined by economic priorities'. The allocation of transmission frequencies, e.g., being preferentially treated when there is a greater economic added value, 'contradicts public interest objectives'. It increases the information gap and 'helps exclude cultural, informative, social and educational contents without added value'. This is 'social exclusion instead of social cohesion'. It is also contrary to the EU Media Ministers' conference in Thessaloniki in 1997 that states that 'new ict services should be universally accessible to all at a reasonable fee and irrespective of location'.

The role of public service broadcasting is 'examined by the paper only at a few points'. Its cultural importance is recognized by the protocol in the Treaty of Amsterdam. It is linked to democratic, social, cultural and pluralistic requirements, and member states may finance it adequately in their own way -within the regulations of the EC treaty-. In account of technological convergence, the expansion of the mandate of public service broadcasting institutions is encouraged (new activities and access to media users and new sources of income). Surprisingly, however, the current system of public service broadcasting is extensively challenged. The paper demands to 'check whether regularly objectives can be achieved by normal market activities', whether 'objectives are justified in view of the new communication and media environment', and 'whether other than to date organizations can be entrusted with these obligations'. Moreover, fear is expressed about cross subsidizing new services by 'compulsory' license fees and 'disadvantaging other market parties'. To the opinion of COMECE, however, the importance of public service broadcasting -due to the general trend of commercialization in the ICT sector- is growing. The non-profit character, the mandate of programs, and the importance of broadcasting as cultural asset are vital. In a converging environment, 'the range of cultural, informative, social and educational contents should not be pushed into a ghetto'. Pluralistic societies, with a variety of objectives of behavior in which moral concepts and philosophies of life differ greatly, require forms of communication that permit understanding via standards and rules of co existence and via solutions of central problems - to which minorities and socially and financially disadvantaged also have access. Facing the 'increasing fragmentation of media on offer, depending on target/

interest groups the significance of integration the forum and model functions of public service broadcasting are growing'. Against the danger of media concentration (especially in television), strong public service broadcasting contributes to secure pluralism and freedom of speech. Its preservation should be ensured in all EU media and communication policies. (To which is added that support does not exclude criticism on its manifestation, nor the recognition of the dual broadcasting system). Independent regulatory authorities are of key importance.

The Catholic Church, 'characterized by its European history and cultures', has the 'duty to participate actively in cultural self reflection and formation processes'. This entails intensive dialogue with communication media, analysis and evaluation of the opportunities and risks of developments in the communication sector, and 'reconcile them with the anthropological prerequisites of a Christian philosophy of humanity and the aims of social community'. A broad social dialogue is needed about the values and objectives of the future communication order. Decisions should be taken transparently and in a democratically legitimized manner.

With respect to the future of EU media policy in the information society (5.2), the church 'should be in the forefront' demanding people to be alerted to the social, cultural, political and ethical implications of internet and ict. As 'internet becomes more important for the delivery educational, commercial and government services, will the poor be disadvantaged?' There is a danger of digital divide. The ownership of computers and internet access in the UK depends on income (1998/99: 70% top, 10% lowest income). Another concern is the commercial exploitation internet. How much will users have to pay for the access of information? Sports programs for example shift from free air to cable satellite channels. It is 'important that public sites e.g. from public broadcasters and quality information remains freely available to the widest range of users. The church has an important role to 'ensure that poorer communities in the real world are not excluded by limited access to the virtual world, inequity and discrimination'. It should work together with allies (like UK Communities Online) to create a public space on the internet so that all groups can benefit from ICT. The church should also join other groups and emphasize the wider issue of global inequalities in access, ownership and the use of ICT.

In a commercially dominated web, the question about how people are guided is vital. Trusted intermediaries are needed. There is a strong public interest in the encouragement of such bodies (as aspired by public broadcasters for example). With respect to human (communication) rights, it is the opinion of the church that the right to communicate is the right of all. The task of communication is to bring people together and enrich them, not to isolate or exploit them. The question is raised about how and to what extent the internet can be regulated. There are technical and complex debates on the protection of minors, privacy, personal data, freedom of speech and copyright. The growing consensus of the global nature of internet and the nature of technology, 'make public regulation difficult if not impossible'. Self regulation (depending on the willingness of ISPs), codes of conduct, and blocking access have 'limited effects'. Software filters have limitations. The church's point of view is to support and strengthen public and self regulation, and to encourage parents and children in virtual literacy.

With respect to EU audio visual media policy, it is important to 'develop the social dimension to the information society'. Regulation must 'take account of user's needs without limiting them to role consumer'. Regulation is not an end in itself, but needs to serve objectives and values in the interest of the individual and public good. Broad discussion is needed in the public arena about the values and objectives of our future communication system -beyond economic and technical aspects. Journalism in service of the public interest must be safeguarded in a democratic Europe that is dependent on responsible citizens.

In the statement on *'Television without Frontiers'*, the need for a consistent comprehensive framework for EU audio visual policy is underlined. Here it is said the 'it may be that the best response is not regulation but programs such as MEDIA Plus'. It is agreed with the report of the EU parliament committee on culture, youth, education, media and sport (June 2003) that the 'principles of the Community's audio visual policy should be set down in a package of graduated levels of regulation as an overarching framework for the audio visual sector'. The protection of minors and human dignity requires 'supra national action' in the current media environment (digital satellite TV channels, broadcast from one country to another and streaming Internet). Along with the changing standards of taste and decency, the greater reliance on self regulation and differences in acceptability of cinema, video, television and internet content and classical regulation diminished. Media education, therefore, is fundamentally important. The directive requires a minimal level of consumer information on TV programs. Even though self regulation of the TV provider must be maintained, there is more responsibility on the viewers. It is therefore more important that 'they are equipped properly for informed judgments about content'. The church 'urges the commission to support the ongoing dialogue between national regulators, media producers, educators and viewer's representatives' to share experiences and information about the best practice in media literacy and consumer awareness. At the structural level, it 'urges the commission to support national regulators to promote the implementation of national policies towards the systematic introduction of media literacy programs at all levels of the educational system'.

Cultural diversity is 'one of the main objectives of EU Treaties'. The audio visual sector is the 'key for this'. The church has 'growing concerns about the concentration of media in Europe and possible restrictions on pluralism and cultural diversity'. Changes to the directive should strengthen cultural diversity expressed through audio visual media that 'enables the diverse cultures of Europe and minority cultures to feel recognized in society'. Media enable the appreciation and knowledge of other cultures social groups. It is 'not sufficient cultural diversity is assured by niches and specialized channels, which have limited audiences'. The risk of cultural groups closing in on itself and intolerant behavior is too big. The major challenge for Europe is the integration of people from non-European cultures. Programs e.g. from Asian or African countries should be shown. The expression of cultural diversity in media is an essential condition for social cohesion and democratic life. The church supports the recommendations by the EU Cultural Committee on 'Cultural Diversity and European Awareness'. It urges the commission to support and maintain corresponding articles in the directive. It also urges the commission to encourage further dissemination of high quality European programs aimed at children. With respect to the provisions made in the directive towards religious broadcasting, it is stated that it is 'important to give a privileged position to programs that present an authentically European form of religious practice'. Since 'ways of living and expressing religious convictions are closely linked to local cultures', respect for the broadcasting of religious services should be ensured by 'strict limits on advertising' in order to maintain the dignity of the service and 'prevent unscrupulous advertising forms'. Advertising should respect human dignity and religious beliefs. It is 'important to guarantee social cohesion and tolerance for different religious traditions'.

The Bishops Conference of England and Wales, in its submission to the BBC charter review (5.4), 'wishes to see measures taken to reinforce the BBC's public service values and ethos by strengthening independence, accountability, transparency and by giving it clear incentives to produce the highest quality programming across the board and different platforms, such that it serves all British citizens'. Particular requirements follow from that overarching aim. The coverage of religious programs is seen in the context of 'broadcasting to the common good of society as a whole'. With respect to financing, 'the license fee is the most appropriate, since it underpins political independence and accountability and puts a direct link between the tax payer and the BBC'. The status, governance and funding of the BBC should be 'discussed as widely as possible across all sectors of the community'.

3.3.9   Challenges and priorities

In the former sections, the priorities in communication for the churches have already become implicitly clear. As far as they overlap and have been touched upon, they will not be repeated in this last section. We will focus on concrete outlooks with respect to the place of communication in church policy making, to strategy plans, guidelines and recommendations, to study and research in relation to theology, to internal media educational and pastoral aspects and to alternative media, finances and traces of self criticism.

WACC (1.1) states that churches (and other social institutions) should democratize their own media and empower alternative media. The family capacity to communicate should be restored and extended to neighborhood community. In an increasingly mediated communication environment, the need to develop skills in interpersonal communication is to be prioritized. . Media education should be a part of the curriculum in schools, church related institutions and theological seminars. It should be complemented by media education in the family and to youth and church groups, 'leading to a more constructive relationship between media workers and media consumers'. WACC and its partner institutions should widen the network of 'all people of good will' to 'accelerate the implementation of the right to communicate'. It should work out common principles of international communication to guide debates on the information and communication order. It should also promote the interaction of traditional communication and alternative media. Likewise it should encourage the study and documentation of the social problems and potentials of modern communication technologies. It should strengthen engagement in programs of media education in and across different cultures and promote communication studies in theological education. Priority should be given to the empowerment of women in communication and the use of non-sexist, inclusive language. It should also increase assistance and service to church related institutions and other groups to develop communication policies and programs to meet current challenges.

Media professionals, the 'prophets of our times', deserve respect and solidarity. Journalists, however also are to be criticized for their preoccupation with the mighty and the lack of public communication rooted in the languages and dialects and culture of the peoples - especially in Third World countries. All should be involved in the communication process and cultural integrity and renewal should be promoted. This implies 'advocacy journalism'. Participants in WACC should work towards a new communication environment. Alternative media should be used to empower people, and priority should be given to the development of media that people can control themselves, and which are rooted in local cultures. Grass root communication should be cultivated.

Christian communicators (2.1) need serious theological reflection on their work and mission, particularly on the challenges posed by new ICTs. Education, in this respect, should be strengthened. They should engage in consciences raising with respect to communication in the pursuit of religious tolerance, justice and peace. Wacc calls upon communicators to affirm the richness and power of communication within all cultures that are life enhancing (especially indigenous people); to challenge power structures within media (private or public, secular or religious), in order to incorporate values that enhance human dignity; to support the empowerment of people in all regions of the world struggling for dignity that is denied by media; and to interpret potentials and limitations of new media (Global Information Infrastructure) so people are empowered to determine their own priorities and future. Recommended in this respect are issues of communication ethics, economic issues, human rights, media education, communication and religion, Christian communication, social identity, ecology and environment, indigenous perspectives, popular culture, communication technology and gender issues. With respect to communication and religion, Christian churches and organizations should recognize and respond to the challenges of the media age and develop an organic rather than instrumental understanding of com media. They should give attention to the reinterpretation of contents of Christian discourse that is based on the deposit of faith. Christian communicators should consider both biblical text as well as cultural context in com work.

Recommendations with respect to media education involve that churches and NGOs should encourage people to use media in an innovative and responsible ways. One of the main objectives of media education should be the promotion of critically active audiences and responsible involvement in formation of media policies. Training in media literacy should be integrated in all educational levels, including churches, schools, and theological seminaries and should take into account the specific media and cultural contexts of the North and the South.

'Communication must lie at the heart of the Church community', says *Aetatis Novae* (1.2). Challenges involve critical evaluation, solidarity and integral development, policies and structures, and the right to information and communication. The importance of pastoral planning is underlined. The appendix provides a plan for social communications. Catholic media work should not be 'one more program alongside Church activities'. Social communications should have a role in every aspect of the church's mission. There should not only be a pastoral plan for communications, communications should be an integral part of every pastoral plan. Communications work is a 'high priority' for bishops and others responsible for human and material resources. The contemporary Areopagus of mass media has been 'neglected' by the church until now. It is 'strongly recommended that dioceses and Episcopal conferences or assemblies include a communications component in every pastoral plan, including social service, education and evangelization. They should also develop (and share) specific integrated pastoral plans for social communication, in consultation with Catholic media organizations and professionals. These plans should involve secular media and the church's own organizations. Guidelines given for social communication plans include: vision and strategy; inventory of the media environment; proposed structure in support of evangelization, catechesis and education, social service and ecumenical cooperation, including: PR, press, radio, TV, cinema, cassettes, computer networks, facsimile services and telecommunications; media education with special emphasis on media and values; pastoral outreach to and dialogue with media professionals, particularly with respect to faith development and spiritual growth; and adequate financial support. Every plan should set 'realistic goals and priorities'. The planning process includes two phases: research and design. The research phase concentrates on an assessment of needs, information gathering and alternative models of a pastoral plan. It includes an analysis of the internal communications environment, strengths and weaknesses of the church's current structures, and opportunities and challenges. Planning issues involve: education; spiritual formation and pastoral care; cooperation (with media professionals, in production, marketing and distribution regionally and nationally, with religious congregations in communications, ecumenical bodies, and with secular media); public relations; and research and communications and development of peoples. The church should also be actively concerned with secular media, especially in the field of media policy and dialogue. The challenge is to 'bring Gospel values upon contemporary media activities to contribute to international solidarity'.

Dialogue requires the 'development of an 'anthropology and theology of communication'. Theology itself must be more communicative. In the appendix, Catholic schools and universities are encouraged to offer communications courses. Church communicators, seminarians, religious and clergy should be offered courses, workshops and seminars in technology, management and communication ethics, and policy issues. The church's strategy in social communication must be based on media research and informed analysis and evaluation that is related to the mission of the church in particular nations and regions. Institutes of higher studies, research centers, and universities are encouraged to engage in applied and fundamental research related to communication needs and concerns of church and society. Interpreting current research and applying it to the mission of the church is also needed. Ongoing theological reflection upon processes and instruments of social communication and their role in church and society needs to be supported. Priests and religious should be offered 'training and doctrinal and spiritual formation' as well as critical formation by communication professionals and public. Education and training in communications should be 'an integral part of the formation of pastoral workers and priests'. They should 'at least have a working grasp of the impact of media and technology' and 'know to invite into dialogue'. People who work in media, next to professional skills, need doctrinal and spiritual formation. Education in communications should be offered to 'all persons engaged in the work of the Church'. Programs in media education and media literacy should also be developed for teachers, parents and students. Pastoral care must be given to those professionally involved in secular media work/communication industries, who need to cope with psychological pressures, ethical dilemmas, and the commitment to serve humanity. Ongoing formation is needed to integrate moral norms in work and private life. Professionals should also be assisted in ethical standards, especially fairness, justice, decency and respect for life. Creative artists and writers should be encouraged to reflect gospel values. Alternative community media are to be promoted and folk media preserved for evangelization and catechesis. They can, in particular societies, be 'more effective in spreading the gospel' and facilitate greater personal participation in production and the communication process in general. Grassroots and traditional media are an important forum for local cultural expression and develop the competence of active participation in shaping and using mass media. The church must also develop and maintain its own specifically Catholic instruments and programs for social communications (press, publishing houses, radio and TV, offices of public information and media-relations, training, media research and organizations of communication professionals).

With respect to finances, 'difficulties are arising from the fact of limited resources'.

The lines of *Aetatis Novae* are pursued in subsequent Vatican documents. 'The use of techniques and technologies of communications is an integral part of the mission of the church in the 3rd millennium', says 1.4. Media culture 'impels the church towards a sort of pastoral and cultural revision to deal adequately with times'. Mass media of communication are 'so important' that they must be inserted in pastoral programs (Quote from *Redemptoris Missio*). New technologies further opportunities for communication understood as service to pastoral government and organization of different tasks of the Christian community. Internet has the potential to assist evangelization, education, internal communication, administration, and governance. New and traditional media must be used; Catholic TV, radio and publications remain useful means within the complete panorama church communications. While content must be adapted to the needs of different groups, the goal must always be to make people aware of ethical and moral dimensions of information. Formation, participation and dialogue are recommended. As the church has a role in public opinion, public opinion has a role in the church. The code of canon law recognizes, under conditions, the right to express one's own opinion. Truths of faith, however, are not open to arbitrary interpretations and respect for the rights of others limits expression. Communication within the church community and between the church and the world requires openness and a new approach towards facing questions regarding the world of media. The church has the need and the right to make its activities known and should not be afraid of new technologies. Collaboration between lay and pastors is most needed. Spiritual formation and pastoral attention should be given to media professionals.

'Church involvement in media, including advertising, today is a necessary part of a comprehensive pastoral strategy', says the statement on ethics in advertising' (2.2). Catholic institutions should 'follow the development of the techniques of advertising and know how to make opportune use of advertising to spread the Gospel in a manner which answers the expectations and needs of contemporary man'. Steps to be taken include media education programs as part of pastoral planning.

In the statement on ethics in communication (2.3), it is recommended that the church's own practice of com should be exemplary. Pastors should encourage the use of media to spread the gospel. Those who represent the church in relations with journalists should be honest and straightforward ('even in the case of awkward questions'). No one has the right to speak for the church unless he is properly designated (personal opinions should not to be presented as church teaching). The church should provide media education and use media for personal and community growth. Since media often impose a mentality and a model of life in contrast to the Gospel, formation is needed. Often the church has judged media in a negative way and failed to understand the standards of media practice such as objectivity. Church personnel should be offered training. Media offer Christians a front line in their missionary role. Pastors must offer guidance.

With respect to internet (2.4 and 4.9), 'The Catholic church should have a visible active presence' and be a 'partner in public dialogue on its development'. It should not dictate, but be of help by indicating ethical and moral criteria based on human and Christian values. (quote from AN). The church must 'help people search for self understanding'. It cannot impose answers, but 'can and must proclaim the answers she received'. A positive pastoral planning for the internet is needed. The use of internet, creative projects (church sponsored) and internet presence are encouraged. Exchange of ideas and information is recommended.
The internet also poses special problems to the church. The world of media sometimes is indifferent or hostile to Christian faith and morality. Partly because media culture is deeply imbued with the 'postmodern sense of only one absolute truth, that there are no absolute truths', or that they are irrelevant. Another problem is web sites labeling themselves as 'catholic'. Church related groups should be present on the internet. Well-motivated, well-informed individuals and unofficial groups who take initiative are 'entitled to be there as well'. It is, however, necessary to distinguish 'eccentric doctrinal interpretations, idiosyncratic devotional practices and ideological advocacy bearing a catholic label' from authentic positions of the church.
To be part of the process that guides the internet's future development, to use the internet creatively at all levels to help fulfill the church's mission and to facilitate internal communication, and to use the internet to dialogue with the world around her, thus involving the church more immediately in the common search for solutions to humanity's many pressing problems' (World Com Day 1992) is recommended.

Encouragement needs to be given to church leaders, pastoral personnel, educators, and parents and the young. Church leaders should understand media and apply that understanding in pastoral plans for social communications and concrete policies programs. They should make use of media and receive media education and training. The church is obliged to use the full potential of the computer age to serve the human and transcendent vocation of every person and thus give glory to the Father. The internet should be employed in many different aspects of the church's mission. Opportunities for ecumenical and inter-religious cooperation should be explored. With respect to the confusing proliferation of unofficial web sites labeled catholic, a system of voluntary certification under supervision of the Magisterium might be helpful in regard to material of doctrinal or catechetical nature. Censorship should not be imposed, but a reliable guide should be offered to materials that express the 'authentic position of the church'. Pastoral personnel should have media education and internet training. They should not only understand the impact of social communications on individuals and society, but also 'communicate in a manner that speaks to the sensibilities and interests of people in media culture'. They should profit from websites offering theological updating and pastoral suggestions. Church communicators should have professional training and doctrinal spiritual formation (to witness to Christ, it is necessary to have a personal relationship through prayer, the Eucharist and sacramental reconciliation, to read and reflect upon God's word, study Christian doctrine, and service to others (World com Day 2000). With C&P, the statement underlines the 'urgent duty' of catholic schools to train communicators and recipients in relevant Christian principles, which is even more urgent in the age of internet. Universities, colleges and schools should offer educational programs at all levels and advanced training in technology, management, ethics and policy issues for professionals and decision makers. Parents should be offered skills of discerning viewers, listeners and readers and models of prudent use of media in the home. They are obliged to guide and supervise children. Unsupervised exposure to internet is 'not allowed'. They need to dialogue with children about their experiences and share with other families that have the same values, in order to help children become responsible internet users instead of addicts who neglect contact with peers and nature. Children and the young should be open to formation and resist uncritical passivity, peer pressure or commercial exploitation. They 'owe it to themselves, their friends, family, pastors and teachers and to God to use the internet well'. The internet is not merely a medium of entertainment and consumer gratification. It is a tool for accomplishing useful work and young people should learn to use it as such.

Justice, especially needed to close the digital divide, requires commitment to the international common good and the globalization of solidarity. Continued research and study, including the development of an anthropology and theology of communication as urged for in *Aetatis Novae*, is underlined with specific reference to internet. So is a positive pastoral planning for internet. Areas for research in this respect include the spillover effect of the wide range of consumer products and services and the shopping of 'packages' to personal tastes on religion (consumer approach of faith). Whether and to what extent the internet exacerbates the tendency of 'some Catholics to selective adherence to the church's teaching' needs to be researched. Reflection on the virtual reality cyberspace, which has 'worrisome implications for religions', is also needed. 'Virtual reality is no substitute for the Real Presence of Christ in the Eucharist, the sacramental reality of the other sacraments, and shared worship in a flesh-and-blood human community'. There are no sacraments on the Internet; and even the religious experiences possible there by the grace of God are 'insufficient apart from real world interaction with other persons of faith'. Study and reflection is needed. At the same time, pastoral planning should consider how to 'lead people from cyberspace to true community' and how, 'through teaching and catechesis, the internet might subsequently be used to sustain and enrich them in their Christian commitment'.

The focus on a communicative culture (in attitude, leadership, evangelization, teaching and witnessing) also determines the LWF's (1.3, 3.3) priorities and challenges. 'All fields of theology should also be looked at 'from a communication point of view'. Personal communication skills and media awareness are priorities in this respect. Values embedded in ways of communicating and building community are as important as the choice of media appropriate to the context. Issues and priorities identified are:

1. to promote a communicative culture of communication (features are: a receiver oriented attitude, all are partners in an ongoing dialogue, full participation of the marginalized, communicative leadership, encouraging, use tools of communication in a communicative way in all fields, personal communication skills, and media awareness).
2. Emphasize personal communication (features are: the most important mode of communication in the church, communication skills as a top priority and a necessary prerequisite for external communication, alternative media use, and local culture).
3. Improve the sharing of information (experiences, concerns, and ideas): this is a two way process between member churches and the Geneva office. (features are: inclusiveness, good balance, inform the public at large in full transparency, openness in communication -also negative for the benefits of trustworthiness- and the shortcut of rumors.
4. Utilize new technologies in addition to personal communication (first) and small media. Make use of local communication cultures and patterns. Internet access for all churches is a top priority.
5. General Assemblies for cross cultural communication (features are: sharing, participation, foster direct and interactive communication, communication as an ongoing task, a wide network of communicators and a variety of media use).
6. Strengthen ecumenical cooperation and common witness of public statements in communication.

Communication must be a 'major part of the curriculum of all theological and leadership training'. With respect to finances, the necessity is stated to 'ensure funds for extra communication professionals to communicate the potential of assemblies'.
The statement about value power and the information society (3.3) adds the church must 'pay attention to the complex interaction of biblical text, socio-cultural environment and new technologies'. In this context, a 'reformulation of the Christian message is necessary to make it relevant and able to compete in the information marketplace'. Another challenge to the churches is to 'equip people to critically read media and uncover the values and messages embedded'.

'Open up to new challenges' is identified by the German Bishops' Conference as a priority in their statement on the information society (3.1). Work 'to and with media is a constitutive part of pastoral care'. It is a challenge to the church to make clear that 'only in personal interaction', the trace of the other is to be found. This is one of the normative distinctions between the reality of faith and virtual reality. The European Catholic News Forum (ECNF) (a network of European bishops-conferences, dioceses, and Catholic news agencies) now available online with an electronic archive, makes it clear that 'a new discussion on own media is necessary'.
Media and communication developments, the statement on media and communication competence says (4.7), places 'new challenges to church proclamation'. The assignment of faith is to 'prove its plausibility, its possibility to be experienced and its practical meaning in life in a world which is stamped by media-communication'. Initiatives for church communication pedagogy should be 'systemized in a theologically founded communication theory and in pastoral praxis'. There is need for action and further

development. The development of the information society in the BRD has far reaching consequences for church media work. Communication should be the key concept of church media work. Communication in the center of the faith community establishes itself through the celebration of the Eucharist, the mutual exchange of faith, and through communicative connection with the Bible, the tradition and church history, as well as through dialogue with contemporaries. In church media papers, the central meaning of communication for the design of human living is clear, but 'concrete media work renders not enough account of the meaning of communication yet'. The initial impetus should be developed further and extended in the frame of a theologically grounded communication theory. Therefore, 'conceptualization and institutional measures' are needed.

Conceptual elements from church media and communication pedagogy involve media as well as communicative competence. The goals for users as 'church multipliers' include:

1. Acknowledge media as phenomena of expression and understand every medium as an attempt to open up and interpret reality, and analyze them in relationship to individual life histories and collective interpretation models.
2. Regard and use media as instruments of social communication. Media are tools of self and world interpretation, self becoming and group building. They serve mutual exchange and are of dialogical nature. A medium does not transport meaning in itself, but obtains meaning in the process of communication. Community is the result from mediated communication. Therefore, one can denote communication as essence of life.
3. Understand media as crossroads, as entries to history, to the world, liaisons between the immediate and global context, which build bridges between reality, the person and others. Therefore, they can build essential elements in the construction of a tolerant and humane culture, but also have the risk of contrast experiences (pedagogy and ethics are needed).
4. Obtain the skill to speak in social publicity from one's own position and help build society based on Christian responsibility. Within the church setting, a concrete transform of goals involves: new opening up of traditional church forms of expression, from image symbolism to theological notions; the use of technical possibilities for the construction of church community (network); understand the multiplicity of the media world as a chance for renewal of faith and develop a renewed church communication profile in plural publicity.

Institutional measures include the provision of adequate means, competence and resources needed and strengthen and develop the basis there is. Five points are of importance in this respect:

1. the decisive option for diocese media bureaus (pastoral engagement in a world in which the decisive theme will be communication);
2. The extension of communication pedagogy supply (orientation and navigation);
3. Technical and personnel strengthening of the media bureaus.
4. Cooperation and extension of strategic alliances for the sake of synergy effects;
5. Media politics: contribute to information justice (free access to information, media and communication competence of all societal groups) and humanity and support media education in school teaching plans.

Adequate pastoral concepts must be developed for a changing society. Initiatives already taken include: pedagogy (group discussions on decoding mass media coded reality, religious reflection, non-explicit Christian productions which inspire religious existential reflection, practical use, virtuality and cyberspace issues); new profiles for the audio visual media bureaus as centers for communication (the church as space of experience to promote a culture of meeting, observation, communication, exhibition, video gallery, and children's library); continued training (certification courses on media work); film work (film nights, seminars, the *Augenblicke* Project, to be booked by church media bureaus, and Church and cinema forum); the ecumenical media fair (small media, films, audio visuals, workshops, and conference).

The challenges of media society are a 'special responsibility for the church', says the ecumenical German document (3.2).   It should 'give impulses' towards human worthiness and freedom. It should improve the churches media work and adapt it to technical developments and social demands. Seven assignments are identified.

1.   Church publicity should be measured according to technical and professional quality and conceptually aimed at media society. Necessary finances should be provided for.
2.   Churches should contribute to the preservation of media as factors of social communication (formation of journalists, media pedagogy, and media political engagement towards the common good of all).
3.   In responsibility to its tradition as a 'book religion', churches -in a special way- are 'obliged to word culture'. The relationship between 'letter and spirit' and word and image 'needs intensive attention and care'. Print media should be organized in a way where quality and survival probability is safeguarded and the possibilities of electronic media should be used. 4. New formats in programs should be developed and positioned attuned to the engagement of churches in the dual system and to the general church publicity concept.
4.   Church media work should be adjusted to new generations (use interactive media for the assignment of communication of the gospel).
5.   Existing offerings of media information and media critics should be strengthened.
6.   Churches and church institutions should intensively participate in discussions about media society. The results of information overkill, knowledge gap and loss of orientation should be limited. Media ethical debates should be initiated (be prepared to discuss and make proposals). This statement should be followed up in the near future. The assignment remains to make media, as instruments of social communication, serve to citizens, to restrict the danger of self alienation and the loss of orientation and to limit the curtailment of multiplicity of information and freedom of opinion. Even in the situation of less financial funds, the church should uphold a qualified contribution to dignified communication.

The EKD (4.4), elaborating extensively on the issue[21], states that 'communication and publicity belong to the essence of the church'. A renewal of structures and Protestant publicity strategy is necessary. Recommendations (cooperation and improvement) should be implemented. The 'goal is clear': find new ways to reach people in a pluralist and secular society that are distanced from the church. Because of the key function of media in perception and life orientation, Protestant publicity must do everything to

---

[21] In chapters four to eleven of *Mandat und Markt,* the actual situation and the activities of different work areas of protestant publicity are extensively examined. They include: press and information service, print publicity (church press, magazines), electronic media (radio television and new media broadcasting), pubic relations, formation and education, film and audio visual media work, press associations, GEP, and special areas (documentation, media awards, international contacts). They are not included in this section, whose aim is to identify the general outlook of statements with respect to the challenges of media society and the assignments and priorities of churches in public communication.

'concentrate forces and realize tasks with new ideas in directed multiplicity'. The church must orient its publicity more outward. If necessary, traditional working areas should be given up.
Recommendations with respect to structure include:

1. Strengthen activities towards people on the fringe, (too much insider-oriented).
2. A stronger orientation to the market and users
3. Clarification of finances is needed (common strategy).
4. A better use of federal structures (cooperation, improvement of the decision making process).
5. Increase of scientific research about communication of the church with members, on how people use media, and how people without regular contact church are to be reached.

In its future orientation to Protestant publicity, the point of departure is that the church is 'public in its nature'. Its mandate obliges the church to make the Christian message and its action observable in the world. This obligation is independent from the societal position of the church; it also applies when the church is a minority and generally shared, basic convictions are absent. Especially then, Christian faith and life should be public and brought as a theme in media. It is not easy for traditionally guided institutions like the church to gain attention for the mediation of religious convictions. Media decide what themes to use and how to set the public agenda. They become agencies of meaning mediation themselves. The EKD has long organized its public presence by independent publicity and according to journalistic standards. A publicity strategy is needed which consciously interferes with structures of media society and, in doing so, gives public attentiveness to the voice of the gospel, the action of the church, and the interest of Christian faith. This means professionally addressing itself to the demands of media, and respecting the interests of the public in what is offered. At present, weaknesses include: reach (only a restricted group of church related people, not a broad public), ineffective organizational structures, too many individual products subsidized by churches, ambiguous goals, poor transparency and guidance. Structures and offerings are not arranged by the demands of the media market, nor to the challenges of media developments. They are 'too strongly tied to church organization forms, too much sender oriented and too little to the audience'. New orientation and structuring is unavoidable. This must be oriented to three basic aspects:

1. The changed technical, socio-cultural and economic conditions of media society, which includes proving oneself in competition.
2. The need to conceive and transform into target group oriented publicity (with special attention to the people that are not reached).
3. The obligation to seek publicist success, which makes cooperation, common planning and enterprise action necessary.

Media society offers many chances. There is a broad interest in religious themes and basic fundamental questions of life orientation. Publicity which takes up these trends and themes and connects them to the message of the gospel and the task of the church is necessary. Common action is needed. With respect to target group publicity, 'the development and implementation of models oriented at supporting life phases' would be a 'good step forward'.
In sum, 'clear reforms are needed' that should also be taken up 'regularly' by the church conference and synod. Merely restricting finances is 'the wrong way'.

The Church of England (3.4), with respect to cyberspace, identifies priorities in 'adding helpful content, participate in online debates and make Christian voices heard'. Churches should be proactive, pray 'for and in cyberspace', use it to work for social justice and evangelization, and keep gathering people to real communities.

To the Finnish Church (4.1, 4.10), 'communication is part of the essence and basics of the church'. Challenges and priorities are related to the development and implementation of the 'church communicative communication culture which must be built on the basis of interactivity'. They involve 'a change in attitude', church wide communicative internal and external communication serving the needs of people, communicative leadership, improvement in media relations, the use of language which expresses openness and community, and high quality programs (more communicative worship services and religious programs).

New challenges must be met. Activities that should be prioritized (and properly financed) include: training and research, news article and picture service, supplying theological ecclesiastical background material (databank), the production of radio and TV programs, the production of audiovisual material, marketing, and public relations. Christians must be supported to bring their own view into discussion in general media. Communication needs a curriculum of its own. Local networks should be optimized to multiply communication reserves. They should be activated to communicate at a grassroots' level. Interactive training inside the church is vital. This should strengthen church identity and a communicative attitude, increase co operation and skills, encourage creative ideas and open conversation, and internalize the meaning of close networks and non verbal communication (deeds, visual symbols). Church press should be open to views of the entire church and the surrounding world.

The document about the communicative church (4.10), with respect to the place of communication adds that in the 'next operational strategy, it must be part of the main strategy, for 'communications are a matter of life and death for the Church and its message'.

The goals of the communicative church in 2010 are explicitly set. Church communications will support the sense of community, every person's human worth will be respected and chances of good life are promoted, Church employees, council members and volunteers, with the support of communication training, will have adopted the communicative culture and reinforce it. Openness and a sense of community will have increased in the church. Church members and others in Finland will have a clear information based idea what it means to be a member of the Lutheran Church. The links with young adults will have become stronger. The people in Finland will be able to make contact with the church and its message via the media. By the church's internet communication, people in Finland and elsewhere will be able to find a wide range of information about the church and receive help and spiritual support when they want it. The church's information service and other media activities will be performed with greater professionalism. The verbal and non-verbal communication of the church will be in harmony with its message and the values it represents. Individual churches will produce communications plans as part of the general communications planning and in connection with individual projects and processes. The church will invest in communications because it is realized that everyone is always communicating - even by what is not done or does not happen.

The marks of the communicative church are: people listen and ask; interaction is encouraged; diversity is appreciated; fellowship is built up; people communicate with consideration for the other party; people communicate their convictions clearly and intelligibly; people are bold in expressing their opinions; people are prepared to change;

people take initiative and react; information is provided openly and in advance; and people encounter the church in the media they use.

Basic principles include that the church is present in Finnish life 'where people are'. This implies the church is in the context of urban culture, of a multi-faith situation, and amidst social conflicts and changes within families. It supports justice for children, fights for the weak and disadvantaged, removes dividing walls between people, looks upon the older generation as educators, takes care of its personnel, and defines leadership. It has an active presence in media, but also meets and interacts with people on a genuinely personal level, which is the 'foundation' of church life.

Societal changes and communication developments challenge 'every church member'. Church members should be 'better acquainted with church doctrine and faith'. Knowledge of their own tradition facilitates dialogue. Reinforcing church membership and parish identity are also challenges faced by communications. It challenges the church to communicate the gospel more clearly - taking into account people's circumstances in line with the communicative culture. It should maintain a working dialogue with all sub cultures, including the young. The church should concentrate on the most important strategic challenges. Three main strategic goals are specifically mentioned.

1. Reinforce communicative cultural communication skills in line with the communicative culture (with special emphasis on personal communication, internal communication as a source of strength and remote communications as a promoter of dialogue).
2. Reinforce the meaningfulness of membership (with emphasis on young people and a more recognizable visual image of the church).
3. And reinforce church presence in various media (with emphasis on internet communications, public debate and networking).

Each operational unit should have a communication staff and formulate a communication policy as part of a general plan of action. Parishes should organize communication as a priority (by reorganizing duties). Parishioners are the church's most important conveyors. Promoting a communicative culture can only be taken care of by cooperation of all church levels and sufficient resources in the budget. Assignments must be clearly defined. Open and honest dialogue is needed and is especially important in difficult unpleasant matters.

Ecumenical communication experts of UNDA/WACC (4.2, 4.5), identify priorities in media education and communication as a social responsibility. Churches have a long tradition and competence in education and means for action at their disposal (institutions, media). They should have an active, ecumenical attitude in media education and support existing projects. They also should support media professionals.

With respect to social responsibilities, churches should abandon instrumentalizing their communication. It is urgent for the vitality of communities to 'put in place a real plan for internal communication at all levels'. Churches should favor broadcasting which helps promote communication and opens up real debates. They should promote the vitality of intermediate communities for people to identify with. They should fight for uni-diversity. Communicability of identities in the audiovisual sphere must be a priority which demands urgent reflection, imagination and audiovisual conception. The churches in this respect have an important contribution to make to a crucial social problem. It is an urgent necessity to open new ways of communication individually and socially and to re-humanize communications. Media should be turned into spaces for dialogue which stimulate new community life (local and (inter) national). The development of neighborhood media should be supported. Churches created and financed thematic channels aimed at believers and internal communications. That is not sufficient. They should prioritize social cohesion in their communications and be committed to public service broadcasting. They should commit themselves to open communication and an attitude of dialogue.

To CEEM (4.3, 4.6), the 'relevance of mass media to pastoral work and society as a whole, is to be taken into account in all the work areas of bishops' conferences and dioceses'. It urgently requests attention to five concrete proposals, which are the 'first necessary steps, to prepare for the challenges and to better assume responsibilities in the field of social communications'.

1. Credibility and professional quality of the church's information and media work (respect media's laws; organize information and media work at all church levels consistently and to professional criteria; introduce permanent spokesmen (who are directly informed); promote free exchange of information and ideas at all church levels and restrict secrecy of information in church; promote catholic media work by moral recognition, material assistance and if necessary financial support; take active part in shaping public opinion by open public relations and the cultivation of contacts with secular media).
2. Education, training and ongoing formation of priests and pastoral workers in social communications (media instruction as an integral part of the formation of theologians; workshops on media at the diocesan, national and European level; inform bishops about initiatives and new developments in social communication so they inspire pastoral workers and support media work as broad as possible; and carry out media training courses).
3. Take up church responsibilities in general media education (in church run kindergartens, schools, educational institutions, parishes; increase the use of church media work for a critical approach of media (e.g. film criticism); intensify ecumenical and international cooperation, also with secular institutes, in media education; commitment to organize world communications day);
4. Take into account the relevance of mass media to pastoral work and society as a whole in all work areas of bishops' conferences and dioceses (opportunities and effects of media in the pastoral care of families, youth and parishes; integrate media education in church education; deal with media questions in European church bodies and promote exchange at a European level).
5. Develop pastoral plans of social communication in dioceses and bishops' conferences (analyze current communication and media work, identify goals and challenges; respond appropriately to regional and local situations; cooperate with catholic communications organizations and local media professionals; coordinate media work of dioceses and at European levels, subsidiary and in solidarity; revise plans regularly and equip church media work with adequate material and human resources).

The bishops' co-responsibility for the means of social communication and their use, is emphasized in both pastoral instructions C&P and AN. In wide circles of the church, however, there is still 'insufficient awareness of the importance of communication itself and its social role'. A 'dynamic reception and realization of C&P and AN (including their interpretation in different media contexts within church and society) still is an 'important task, which is far from completed'.

The document on gospel, church and information society (4.6) recommends to 'reflect more on philosophical, theological, political and theoretical aspects and changes of the media landscape. Dialogue and structural interchange is needed between church authorities and academic institutions in the field of media and media ethics. They should be linked to faculties of theology - especially to develop a theology of communication (as begun in C&P) in relation to the changed media landscape. Bishops conferences should initiate special study days on media issues. Ecumenical collaboration in media work is essential and new media should be used to get closer to the generation of young adults. The church also has to face the challenge of contemporary language and develop spirituality in and for the media culture.

Priorities for the church of Sweden (4.8), are varied. One of the problems of communication output by the churches is its overlap, division and costs, and its lack of coordination. A change in attitude and professionalism is needed. Areas of special attention include: the improvement of communication with children and the young, a more effective media policy, improvement of the church's reputation in public opinion and a free, open, autonomous and credible church paper in the public arena. Professional expertise in public opinion is needed. 'Listen more carefully to the needs of people and better insight to points of departure/contact will improve the conditions of success'.
The internet is a practical medium for communication with youth. Target groups should be analyzed and plans made together with the young. Contemporary structures do not 'stimulate people taking own initiatives'. For the future of the church and the place of Christianity in the country, 'continuous improvement and adaptation of the information policy is important'. A common agreement on goals and organization should be prioritized.
The church should provide as much information as possible that can contribute to a correct and varied image of the church (e.g. the church as mediator of a value system; the church as preacher of a Christian philosophy as meaning of life; the church as place of meditation, silence and reflection, or as meeting community; the church in its historical role in society (healthcare, schooling); the church in its social welfare and missionary work; the church as listener/comforter, supporting in crisis and sorrow; and the church as bearer of culture (arts music poetry). Anyone should be allowed access in order to gather all desired information about life, doctrine/teachings and organization of the church. Media will come together, which implies the sender no longer needs to 'decide on the form of information, the receiver does'. 'The sender can concentrate on how and what should be published'. The church should 'seize this golden opportunity' to reform its 'one-way information into a real communication means'. There are 'overwhelming possibilities to dialogue'. There is a large response when the church opens up its website for conversations related to issues of meaning of life. Access to 'net-missionaries' is neccesary.

Strategic considerations are related to 'meeting new demands of communication'. It is questionable whether, in the future, the church in future can count on its place in media and remain supported by social institutions like schools. In the area of media as well as religious education in schools, the church should influence public opinion and be relevant to people. Openness to media is necessary. A better cooperation demands different attitudes and a new way of thinking - a change of priorities and a higher effort by the church. Since non-church media will decide what is to be published, the church has a greater responsibility in opinion forming and needs to clarify the relevance of the church for modern times and human being. It should react faster, have an open attitude on all church levels, and 'all should be confident to participate in public discourse'. All communication workers should be familiar with this strategic thinking, which needs to be part of all education. Church and state are not the authorities anymore. The church should accept people as subjects and accept it has to work in a market of many considerations. The positive aspect of this is that there is an increasing interest for religion and issues of meaning 'if one gives up on a traditional definition of religious activities'. If views are taken seriously, there are 'enough possibilities for communication'.

The church needs to take part in all social public discussions. The wish of the church to communicate with the whole society is based in the gospel. Therefore, channels must always be open. The growing complexity of society increases the need for ethical support. At the national level, the church should offer a dialogue forum for faith and life issues. In societal-cultural debates the church is less present and less theological analyses are offered on what happens in society and cultural life. To tackle the competition of fast daily debates, the church is suggested to start a morning paper on the internet with daily reports and comments on the actuality. Systematical use of research publications by church departments for societal cultural debates could be improved as well. Theological innovations are now stuck in study rooms. Contacts with journalists should be improved. 'Strive for cooperation to communicate, not just to inform'. If the church is not able to solve its problems with media, 'opportunities will be lost'. With respect to international issues meeting halls are important, e.g. contacts with the church can provide reliable knowledge in times of crises. They can also provide 'interesting side effects for journalists, like short seminaries or meetings on actual issues'. Media service in all possible ways could be offered: cultural debate materials, e.g. social ethical reports or text and image materials via electronic search and download systems that are always available.
In the concluding words, it is stated that it is 'not easy to match all levels, but the implementation of media policy is to be realized, in common deliberations.

Comece's (5.1, 5.2), priorities are related to the 'primary importance of principles that are to form the basis for future regulation of the communication sectors'. These include:

1. Universal participation for all and the guarantee of a social dimension of the information society.
2. Future regulation meeting the needs of users as citizens and not merely consumers.
3. Regulation securing values in the interest of the individual and community.
4. Independent regulatory authorities.
5. Differentiation in regulation and values with respect to dissemination techniques or infrastructure and contents.

In 5.2 virtual literacy and media education, internet experiments, study and research are identified as priorities - next to church ethical contributions and strengthening of real communication and interaction.

3.3.10   Summarizing Conclusion

As indicated in section 3.3 we will summarize the content analysis, by shortly referring to each key issue.

Documents

The 26 documents analyzed vary from assembly documents to pastoral instructions, communication strategies and policy programs, statements on special issues (mainly ethical considerations), common ecumenical declarations, contributions to (public) debate, appeals to church authorities, and comments on media regulation and policy.

Addressees and purposes of the statements are not always explicitly stated. The main focus of the majority of the documents is internal. The focuses include: to provide principles for communication policy programs, to reflect on media developmental implications, to engage in dialogue/debate and to provide ethical and spiritual orientation. They appear to be the main goals of the churches. It is remarkable that, judging by the references they make to other statements, churches hardly seem to cross denominational and/or national borders. They mostly refer to statements formerly published by their own church or institute (the statements by in particular the Vatican draw heavily upon formerly published documents).
Ecumenical cooperation is exceptional.
The main key issues (in order) are:

(9) challenges and priorities for the church towards communication / media
(2) the analysis of the media context (structures and culture)
(8) social responsibility of the churches and
(5) church's views on media roles and communication models.
Audience research (3) is given least attention in the documents.

Media context and media culture

All documents are convinced that deep changes are taking place, not only in the field of media technology but impacting all areas of life. These changes are labeled differently and are not clearly defined ('unprecedented developments', 'far reaching change', 'revolution', 'extraordinary transformation of society', 'revolutionary turnover', 'new age of communication', 'evolution'). The tone is not pessimistic or blaming; the media context is valued in terms of chances and risks and positive and negative features. All documents analyze structures and trends such as commercialization, convergence, globalization, etc. (without providing clear definitions, however,) and the way they impact media logic and media regulation. Conspicuous is that, generally, new media appear to be evaluated along the same lines as traditional mass media, which raises the question of plausibility regarding the shift from linear to network structures and media. The concept of interactivity for example is neither defined, nor elaborated upon extensively in its implications beyond journalism impact, ethics and church communication possibilities.
Next to the trends, the main issues in the statements are: the implications of media developments, the cultural/religious dimension and public interest. The implications and challenges of media developments ('from communication to information') are evaluated particularly in the social/cultural realm. Included are: sociability and disintegration, the perception of identity and the meaning of life and the reshaping of values and morality. Statements agree that media fundamentally reshape our comprehension of the world. The degree of intertwinement of media and culture however is valued to different extents.
Media developments also deeply challenge religion, religious attitudes and the perception of the church. Historical meaning monopolies, that are forced into competition must win respect and are weakened in their integration power. Religion is simultaneously privatized and 'mediatized'. Although a changed faith experience, a new spiritual search and a 'climate of religion in and outside the churches' are acknowledged, there is concern about the 'climate of absence of meaning' at the same time.
Since there are various interpretations of the relationship between media and culture, and clear definitions on religion, spirituality and secularization are absent, it is questionable whether the statements accurately analyze the religious implications of media culture. The religious function of media and media culture, as described in sections 1.3 and 1.4, appear to be overlooked. The competition and flattening of

symbols, the shift in the relationship between sacred-secular, the transitional religion changing religion in the historical sense, the positioning of the church by the media in the web of culture, media agenda-setting, and media use as part of the daily symbolic social interaction are hardly elaborated upon. Consequently, the media cultural/religious awareness does not result in a profound, critical analysis in which the being of mainline Christianity and churches is included.

The sections on identity (3.3.4), views of media (3.3.5) church involvement (3.3.7) and challenges and priorities (3.3.8) will have to shed light on the question whether the media's cultural/religious implications are restricted to and focused on ethics and morality, church community and ecclesiastical media work.

The concept of public interest refers to a variety of issues. Public service broadcasting is felt to be more important than ever. Media regulation should be based on values and standards and aim at access for and participation by all. The paradigm for orientation should be human service and community and progress, not commerce. Media literacy and communication competence are regarded as main key qualifications and media education as fundamentally important.

With respect to media logic, there is concern about standards and quality. The coverage of religion and church needs 'greater expertise'. Media use as part of everyday social interaction is related mainly to new media, -especially in an ethical sense-, and not an explicit issue in itself. It appears to be valued more in terms of negative features ('self referential', 'detriment of social interaction' and 'cyberspace transcendence') than in positive ones. The implications of media developments for the church as an institute are realized. This does not, however, lead to an adequate analysis of institutional, structural change or modes of functioning.

Audience research

The role and position of the audience is not an issue widely elaborated upon in the statements and is obviously not a priority. Views with respect to audiences differ. On the one hand, they are objects in need of formation; on the other hand, they are viewed as subjects in dialogue. Church communication must therefore be receiver oriented. The extent and the implications of this orientation, however, is unclear. Although all statements realize that communication on terms of the sender is no longer possible, the tension between informing, proclamation and dialogue remains unresolved. And by that an exact position of the audience is not accounted for. Moreover, there are no views included *from* the audience. References to audience research are absent.

Identity

The views of Christian identity as presented in the statements differ. The Lutheran vision is characterized by a 'communicative community' and a 'comprehensive communication attitude' (openness to the questions of the time, the creation of meaning together, contributing socially to the wellbeing of all). In their statement the Christian media professionals opt for a 'living participative community' instead of a 'collective of individuals'. This vision implies 'symphonic instead of centralized unity', and a Christian identity which is 'not a defensive fortress, but a conviction affirmed in debate and a dialogue of all'. (Communication in this respect serves to express the views of members and to strengthen social cohesion). The Roman Catholic statement presents a more theological and missionary oriented view. Church is 'communio rooted in the communion of the Trinity'. It is Christ's mystical body. Communication and communion, therefore, are closely related. The goal is to 'bring all to union with Christ'. The church should be present in the world in 'active listening presence' and communicate suited to media culture. The statement by the Church of England speaks of a 'fellowship' -as part of wider society- and of 'diversity'. Its definition of church as 'a place of truth - individually and socially- for what is happening in society' and the emphasis on 'gathering in real community', however, questions whether institutional change is at stake and what perception of Christian tradition is involved. Both seem rather untouched by contemporary media culture. The German ecumenical statement looks upon tradition as a medium for orientation (life, world, self, style). Christian identity is by definition relational and founded theologically on the relationship between God and man and man and his neighbor. Direct personal encounter and primary religious experience in the congregation are stressed. An institutional vision of identity and faith seem to prevail (even the commitment to word culture is explicit, since it is a tradition of a Book religion).

Clear cut general categorizations are difficult to distinguish. Identities are variables on a line with higher or lower degrees of openness to media culture, theological grounding, proclamation, safeguarding tradition, emphasis on interpersonal contact within the community of faith, recipient orientation, dialogue, living interaction and a common search for truth. Overlapping and sometimes contradictory features and the absence of clear definitions aggravate the understanding of identity. There are, however, differences in attitude that also account for differences in outlook on institutional change and the consistency of tradition.

Communication and media roles

Communication is a basic human need and right and socially necessary for cohesion. This is agreed upon by all statements when it comes to the views of media roles and communication. A similar agreement holds true for the position of interpersonal communication and encounter that is ranked as most valued (next to personal gatherings and the use of alternative media other than mass media). Encompassing definitions of communication, interactivity, etc. are absent.
The Lutheran statements points to communication as a creative force by relating it to the Hebrew term dabar' in the book of Genesis. Dabar stands for God's creative words which at the same time are deeds (He said … and it was). The concept of 'communicative communication' describes a two way process, i.e. mutual creation of meaning and enrichment that involves all senses and builds community. The statement clearly abandons the one way model of communication and the unilateral emphasis of the word. A distinction is made between 'informare' (carve into, meaning: final, one way communication on the terms of the sender) and 'communicare' (share, make common, meaning; two way communication, encouraging, searching together, involving change). The view of media is less clear, however. An instrumental view seems to prevail in references such as 'not the best mission tools', 'means to an end' and as regards new media - 'unprecedented possibilities for witness'.
Roman Catholic statements consistently use the term 'media of social communication'[22]. They are 'gifts of God' and at the same time 'a mixed blessing' (exacerbating secularism, consumerism, materialism, dehumanization, and concern for the poor). Media are 'instruments in service of unity, understanding and new evangelization'. Communication is closely tied to communion and rooted theologically in the Trinity. It 'cannot take the place of personal communication'. Social and theological arguments are intrinsically

---

[22] For the history on the term social communication see: Eilers, Franz-Josef. 2002. 'Social Communication: The Development of a Concept' in *Communicating in Community, An Introduction to Social Communication*. Manila Logos (Divine Word) Publications. Third Revised and Enlarged Edition. Appendix A pp. 311-318.

intertwined in an instrumental view of media ('assist evangelization', 'facilitate the communication of the gospel', an 'aid for spreading religious values').

On the other hand, media are also said to be an 'aid for promoting dialogue'. Media are 'the first *Areopagus* of modern times' and simply using them to 'spread the message is not enough'. Integration in the new culture created by media is 'necessary'. So is 'a change of mentality and pastoral renewal'. Both issues are not elaborated upon, however. Neither are they dealt with for their consequences towards institutional change. The same holds true for the term 'interactive communication' that people are 'now used to'. Tensions thus remain unsolved.

Both statements by the European Bishops' Conference (COMECE) stress the relationship between communications, social/cultural integration and cohesion, community and freedom and the importance of public service broadcasting, 'real communication' and interaction.

This is also the outlook presented by the Bishops' Conference of England and Wales, which strongly pleas for the public service broadcasting ideal. Free availability in the public domain and the needs of audiences -in their role as citizens and consumers- are also underlined. Interesting is the statement made in 5.4 that 'religious broadcasting should not be primarily concerned with broadcasting to the converted'. Whatever consequences are involved is not elaborated upon, however. Neither are the implications for the church in its public communication.

According to the statement by the Church of England, cyberspace 'like every advance in communication' is 'a means for proclamation of the gospel'. It is a strong force for social change, social justice and social cohesion. It is the most important medium for information about institutions. It can also be helpful in providing 'other ways of communication about faith'. A clear demerit is its limitation as regards physicality, which is essential in the statements' view of Christian identity ('real community gathering') and on communication ('listening with our bodies' is said to account for 60% of human communication). A definition of interactivity is absent and its implications are not considered.

The ecumenical statement by the German churches gives evidence of consensus of Roman Catholic and Protestant views by defining media as 'instruments of social communication and of self-expression' 'at the cross-roads of individuality and sociality'. They offer possibilities for new (dialogue-oriented) forms of proclamation. Media can be helpful in pointing to and encouraging Christian life and as a way of making contact. Interactivity is a concept which is related to the 'communication of the gospel to new generations'.

The instrumental view of media and communication is most clearly renounced by the statement of the (ecumenical) Christian media professionals (UNDA/WACC). The emphasis is on the social cultural role of media and the public common interest. This statement calls for a shift in the orientation of mediated communication. Priority is given to 'serve the communicability of identities' in order to strengthen the capacity to live with one another. Social institutions (among them churches) should not 'instrumentalize' communication in the interest of 'selling their project', but 'serve communication as a value in itself'. This reorientation of communication also involves internal implications. Communication will serve the expression of the views of church members instead of leadership's views (attitude of dialogue). The promotion of social cohesion in communications and the maintenance of presence in the public space are mentioned as priorities for churches.

In summary, the general conclusion may be stated that the one way model of communication and the instrumental view of media are changing slightly, but they still prevail. The statements by the Christian media professionals and the Finnish Lutheran Church (more than the LWF document) break new ground by seeking a different attitude in communication and towards media that necessarily involves the whole being of the church. In general, the cultural role of media is acknowledged, but its implications for the being, role and communication of institutional mainline Christianity are not pursued. Communication in the digital era appears to be more about an extension of forms than a change of thoughts. New media are considered within the same traditional keynotes. In this respect one might ask whether the term 'communication' is used for old ideas parading as new ones, since it remains so strongly related to proclamation. Moreover, the emphasis on personal encounter within the congregation and the secondhand value attached to (mass) mediated communication keeps faith and gospel firmly wrapped up within the institution. This raises questions, not only of power, but also of connecting with the (religious) dimensions of contemporary media culture and with the increasing use of media by the audience for (autonomous) ritual, community and meaning negotiating activities.

Theological presuppositions

The outlook on media and communication praxis remain theologically founded. Different accents are emphasized. Assumptions in this realm include:

*   Christologically based arguments Jesus as the 'Word made flesh' and the 'perfect communicator, model and standard of human communication' (the Christian doctrine of Incarnation-Resurrection grounds the importance of bodily relationships); Jesus in relationship to the poor, the marginalized, and the oppressed who 'bear the hallmark of God's communication (the Gospel as Good News for the poor); beginning with Jesus, (asking Bartimaeus: what do you want me to do for you?), the 'basic form of conveying the gospel has been personal communication'.
*   God's self revelation in Jesus Christ; in Creation through his Word; communication is a creative force *dabar*; the communication between God and man is the basis for the 'whole existence of the church'.
*   Christian anthropological arguments based on the Creation narrative: man as the 'image of God' sharing in the creative power; the Christian image of man is one of 'freedom and self determination'. People live in relationships. The relationship with God is basic to man's identity; communication is a 'necessity to be fully human'.
*   Trinitarian arguments - the communion of the Trinity as a communion of love between Father, Son and Holy Spirit and the communication with humanity; solidarity and community, the 'highest goal of all communication', are rooted in this communion.
*   Pneumatological arguments - the Holy Spirit 'blowing where it pleases', beyond the control of church or religious group; leading to 'genuine understanding' (from Babel to Pentecost); 'giving man the capacity to receive salvation' and to 'proclaim and give witness before the world'; the Pentecost story means all cultures are part of the mystery of humanity and God's goodness, which makes communication a necessity to be fully human.
*   Soteriological arguments - salvation includes 'the full participation between humans and humans and God'.
*   Scripture - as a 'code of communication' to analyze processes and value of communications; to 'orient' journalistic work to the Word and the 'tradition of biblical faith'; as 'principles of action'; biblical communication and communicators

- parables, stories, communication adjusted to the people, not only in words but also in deeds and in 'manner of life', prophetic communication, Paul's message for those engaged in communication to 'speak the truth, without foul language and with grace to those who hear' (Eph 4: 25-29)
- Ecclesiological arguments - God 'continues to communicate with humanity through the church', as the 'bearer and custodian of the revelation to whose living teaching alone He has entrusted the task of authentically interpreting His Word'; the church 'mirroring the communion of the Trinity'; the church as 'Christ's mystical body'; the church as 'community of believers, meant to 'embody the central values of the Kingdom'; the church as a 'holy community' and 'joint priesthood', for which interaction is a precondition - inclusiveness, dialogue, mutual enrichment.
- Ritual concepts - the Eucharist as the 'culminating moment in which communication becomes full communion'.
- Ecumenical arguments - Christians of different denominations speaking with one voice and bearing witness to the one body of Christ.

The Kingdom of God, as a theological presupposition, is not directly referred to in the documents researched (however, it is a main principle for WACC in its *Christian Principles of Communication*). Theological presuppositions refer mainly to the (socio)-ethical realm. For example – with respect to the outlook on the position and approach of the audience – the consequences are not actively pursued. Whether or not theological presuppositions are the best point of departure when it comes to public communication -or whether they might be an obstacle as well-, is not a point of reflection. Either is whether they are accurate in coping with the digital media culture.

Church involvement and social and ethical responsibilities

Church involvement and social/ethical responsibilities are an important issue upon which nearly all statements extensively elaborate. Generally speaking, the outlooks vary from engagement in communication for the sake of the importance and role of communication in society (sociability and social interaction), to a more missionary oriented view. The line of evangelization, however, is complemented by a line of integrating the gospel into media culture.
Active participation in communication is regarded as an ongoing task. All documents underline the importance of professional quality in ecclesial communication. Understanding media logic and dialoguing with people involved in media are felt to be important, as well as improving public relations.

With respect to involvement, the Finnish Lutheran document offers the broadest possible view (challenge to form opinions about the church message, participate in discussions on values, bring together communities, support those in difficulties, be an example of communicative communication, empower participation, serve the needs of the media e.g. by offering a background material databank, support the faith and life of members, present a gospel interpretation of reality and Christian options, be visible, and enhance cultural diversity). Most strongly of all the Roman Catholic statements relate involvement to missionary aspects. It is stated, however, that the church should communicate suited to media culture.
As do the statements by the media professionals and the Lutherans, *Aetatis Novae* explicitly mentions ecumenical and inter-religious cooperation - on the other hand, the Vatican statements also make a strong plea for maintaining their own media across the width of media work. At this point, they disagree with the statement by the media professionals who caution against 'niche' thinking.

Social and ethical responsibility is a main issue in all documents. Churches have a special responsibility towards the challenges and shaping of media society. The ecumenical German statement is particularly extensive and thorough in this respect. The main orientations are to offer an ethical evaluation and framework for media and ICT developments, and praxis aimed at international communication justice, community service, solidarity, and protection of human dignity and communication rights for all - and to stimulate media awareness and education and involvement in social and political regulation for the sake of community, (cultural) diversity, integration and democracy. The Lutheran and media professional documents explicitly include their own being in media involvement and social and ethical responsibilities and do not only direct them towards others.

Challenges and priorities

Challenges and priorities are strongly related to the main focus of each statement.
For WACC this is the democratization of and empowerment in communication.
The Lutheran documents, emphasizing the ideal of communicativeness in general and an internal   communicative culture attitude at all levels, regard skills in personal communication as a top priority and as a prerequisite for external communication. The way of communicating and building community is as important as the right choice of media appropriate to the context. Communication should have a curriculum of its own and all fields of theology should be looked upon from a communication point of view as well.
The Roman Catholic documents stress the importance of pastoral planning (social communication should have a program of its own and be part of every pastoral plan), of upgrading the priority of communication and church presence in media, of media education and communication skills and of theological reflection. The need for an 'anthropology and theology of communication' is stated (without explanation what exactly is meant by it), as well as communication justice.
The German churches focus on the churches' responsibility for media developments and the safeguarding of media as instruments of social communication; for pastoral engagement, communication skills, media formation, participation in public debate and a new church communication profile - including a renewal of communication structures and strategies and market orientation. The identification of the 'contribution to the survival of print media' as a priority is striking.
Ethical contributions and participation in online debates are a priority in the statement on cyberspace by the Church of England.
Media professionals, in their statements, prioritize media education and communication as a social responsibility for the churches. Ecumenical cooperation is a prerequisite. They also prioritize the abandoning of instrumentalizing communication, 'uni-diversity' and an audio visual conception towards the communicability of identities. Finally, they stress the importance of grass root communication, the development of own media into spaces for dialogue and commitment to public service broadcasting.
CEEM underlines credibility and professional quality, media education (internal and external), the development of pastoral plans in communication and theological, philosophical, political and theoretical reflection.
COMECE's priorities are related to the importance attached to principles of universal participation, the needs of users, values in the interest of individual and community, and independent and differentiated regulation.

With this summary of the conclusions of each of the key concepts we finish our content analysis. It provides us with the base for identifying the -according to our opinion- main problems.

3.4   Inventory of main problems

In this section we will outline the main problems in the statements, based on the content analysis described in section 3.3[23].
The focus on problems, by no means, suggests there are no positive remarks to report - as section 3.3 has shown also-. However, if, as is stated in the introduction, one of the aims of this book is to 'contribute to the interdisciplinary field of media, culture and religion in order to support theology and mainline churches to understand and relate to contemporary global media culture in a more profound way', a focus on problems and challenges is legitimate and necessary.

As section 3.3 made clear as well, there are differences in outlook and attitude towards communication that are related to views of identity, ecclesiology, theological presuppositions, denominational and regional background, ecumenical cooperation, and communication expertise. This allows for a variety of problems which do not always apply to all statements, nor in the same degree. Although an extensive final assessment was made of each individual document, it is beyond the scope of this research to go into the evaluation details of each and every document. Our goal in this section is to identify the main, more or less, common and related problems in the churches' statements on communication. They involve:

• the outlook on media, communication context and culture
• the outlook on the audience and related audience research concepts
• communication models and theological presuppositions
• ecclesiological identity and
• implementation and praxis.

A general problem for all of the five issues mentioned is that policy documents by the churches, or related communication institutions, are inaccurate in defining terms that are frequently used or referred to. By this, it is suggested that these terms are univocal in their interpretation[24]. The reality they refer to, however, on further consideration, appears to be more complicated. Consequently, this results in indistinctness -and sometimes even contradictions- which not only affects the reflection of issues but even might procure inadequate analysis. To give but just one example of this, we will examine the issue of globalization[25]. The problem posits itself in a comparable way, however, with respect to for example concepts of information society, information superhighway, age of mass communication, mass media, communication revolution, culture, religion, mission, theology of communication, information, the audience, secularization, technology, interactivity, public interest, cyber space, etc.

Three related general problems include: repetition, the status of related documents and coherence in outlook. Statements often seem to repeat earlier stands and views without

---

[23] The goal of this final section is not to repeat the conclusions given about the topics in each section, but to summarize and relate them to each other in order to try to get to the core of the main problems in the statements.
[24] An exception is document 5.1. by COMECE in its *Comments of the Secretary General of COMECE (Commission of the Bishops' Conferences of the European Community) on the Green Paper of the European Commission concerning the Convergence of Telecommunications, Media and Information Technology Sectors and their Effects on regulatory policy*. The concept of convergence, being the explicit topic of the statement, is considered here in its various applications.
[25] The concept of globalization is chosen because of its extensive use as an unquestioned, overarching premise, both in common parlance as in the documents while being of vital importance to nearly every other issue in the five general problems identified.

really contributing new insights. The amount of quotations from former statements in the Vatican documents is striking; the same applies to the documents published by the Roman Catholic Bishops' Conferences, which very often refer to (and quote) the Vatican statements. This questions whether the new media-cultural developments and their impact are truly incorporated, whether they are judged on their merits, and whether they are contextually applied.

At the same time, it is not at all clear how statements with contradictory views relate to each other. An example of this is the *Instruction on Some Aspects of the Use the Instruments of Social Communication in Promoting the Doctrine of the Faith* published by the Congregation for the Doctrine of the Faith (March 1992)[26]. This instruction is more about disciplinary authority regarding the church's teaching on faith and morals than on anything else. It presents an outlook on communication which is at least 'at odds' with other statements (*Communio et Progressio, Aetatis Novae and Redemptoris Missio*):

'The social communications media surely have to be counted among the most effective instruments available today for spreading the message of the Gospel. Not only does the Church claim the right to use them (cf. Canon 747); she also encourages bishops to take advantage of them in fulfilling their mission (cf. Canon 822.1).' (Introduction no. 545).

'The new Code of Canon Law also deals with the instruments of social communication (Canons 822-832) and entrusts their care and supervision to the bishops. Religious superiors, especially major superiors, also have specific responsibilities in this regard by virtue of their disciplinary authority' (no. 546).

Although the document was not written by the Pontifical Council for Social Communications and people involved in social communication were 'not amused'[27], the Council did not distance itself from it. Its president, Archbishop Foley, considered it "a useful summary of the norms of church law on the subject of books and articles on Catholic doctrinal and moral teaching' (...) meant to guarantee the principle of 'truth in packaging' (...); (...) it does not really enunciate new principles; it gathers existing norms in a brief document in which long valid principles are made more readily accessible' (Eilers, 1997:200)[28].

---

[26] Please note this was one month after the publication of *Aetatis Novae* (February 1992), which in itself repeats much of what was said earlier in *Communio et Progressio* (1971). The prefect of the Congregation for the Doctrine of the Faith at the time was Cardinal Joseph Ratzinger, the present Pope.

[27] Eilers (1997:200) notes that the Catholic International Union of the Press (UCIP) during its world congress in Brazil in 1992 passed a resolution that was quite critical of this document. '(...) The need for approval of certain religious books is understandable. On the other hand, the instruction has a system of prohibitions and limitations, of censorship and threats of punishment woven through it like a red thread. These contradict the rules of mass communication which direct newspapers and magazines and the vocation of baptized and confirmed Catholics to proclaim the Good News. Proclaiming the Good News demands that the proclaimer and the mediator have a strong, authentic faith. Such faith grows from the freedom of a well formed conscience rather than from prohibitions and commands. This document conveys an attitude of mistrust toward journalists which contradicts the spirit of the Second Vatican Council and the documents "*Communio et Progressio*" and "*Aetatis Novae*"'. The UCIP members express their regret "that this document emphasizes legal regulations instead of positive encouragement". Eilers puts the document in the line of the index of forbidden books which became a church institution (The Congregation of the Inquisition) in 1564 after the Council of Trent and was later renamed the Holy Office (1908). Now it is the Congregation for the Doctrine of the Faith. In 1966, after Vaticanum II, the index was abrogated. Other decrees on the censorship of books were to follow, however, (e.g. the *Decretum de Ecclesia Pastorum Vigilantia circa libros*, 1975) to close the legislative gap. (Eilers 1997:201).

[28] Another example of such a contradicting view is given in the documents *Criteria for Ecumenical and Interreligious Cooperation in Communications* published by the Pontifical Council for Social Communications, (1989) and the declaration *Dominus Iesus* on the Unicity and Salvific Universality

The status of documents and coherence in outlook on communication within churches thus appears to be problematic. This probably is not only the case within the Roman Catholic Church, in which it appears to point to a different outlook between Vaticanum II adherents and those who reject Concilliar outcomes. The Lutheran Church of Finland e.g. in its most recent document on communication (2004) explicitly makes a plea for the integration of the communication policy document in the overall strategy statement (2003-2010).

The problems of status and coherence might be considered to be related to the problem of inadequate defining.

The concept of globalization, for example, in the statements -as in common parlance-, appears to refer to a McLuhan sort of vision of a shrinking world: a global village with global communication opportunities for all. In *Redemptoris Missio* Pope John Paul II considers the world of communication 'as unifying humanity and turning it into what is known as 'a global village' (no.37c).
In chapter one (section 1.1.3 p 39), we discussed Regan's (2000) concept of the 'digital doctrine' accompanying every new technology. It promises global equality, cooperation, progress, solidarity, participation, etc. through the *Global Information Infrastructure* (quoting Al Gore in his speech to the International Telecommunications Union in Buenos Aires in 1994)[29]. Although the church statements consider the new breakthroughs to have both good and bad potential, the underlying premise is a global network of instantaneous transmission leading humanity to progress and unification.

Globalization, however, is a very complicated and contested concept. Being one of the defining terms of contemporary society, Scholte (2000:1) points to many blunt, vague, inconsistent and confusing claims about it. '(...) much discussion of globalization is steeped in oversimplification, exaggeration and wishful thinking. In spite of a deluge of publications on the subject, our analyses of globalization tend to remain conceptually inexact, empirically thin, historically and culturally illiterate, normatively shallow and politically naïve'.

Scholte distinguishes five general conceptions: globalization as internalization, as liberalization, as universalization, as westernization or modernization and as de-territorialization. The former four he considers to be redundant.
His core thesis on the subject is that globalization is 'a transformation of social geography marked by the growth of supraterritorial spaces' (2000:8), which coexist and interrelate with territorial spaces. However, appearing earlier, he considers it to be a distinctive and recent phenomenon (its greatest expansion took place since the 1960's) resulting from a combination of four factors. Rationalist knowledge (producing global consciousness); capitalist production; automated technology (especially in communications and data processing) and bureaucratic governance (regulatory frameworks by states and suprastate institutions).
Globalization, however, is to be considered not only as an outcome, but also as a cause. In reorganizing geography, it generated social transformations (think of Carey's analysis on the telegraph described in the introduction). Scholte, in this respect, considers four issues: globalization and production; globalization and governance, globalization and community, and globalization and knowledge.

---

of Jesus Christ and the Church, published by the Congregation for the Doctrine of the Faith (2000). This is of importance with respect to church identity, which in its turn is related to communication models as we will see in this section (problems 3 and 4).
[29] The statement of Al Gore is quoted e.g. in document 3.1 Multimedia Der Wandel Zur Informationsgesellschaft.

According to his view, the predominance of capitalism as the main structure of production is not challenged by globalization. Globalizing capitalism expanded commodification (consumerism, expansion of finance capital and the emergence of information and communication capital) as it caused reorganization (e.g. transborder corporate networks, mergers and acquisitions, the rise of global oligopolies). The globalization processes of surplus accumulation, says Scholte, might harm vulnerable social circles. 'The contemporary growth of transworld capitalism can in this respect be linked: to substantially increased gaps of material welfare within and between countries; to heightened ecological degradation; to weakened social cohesion; and to reduced democratic controls on economic policy' (2000:131).

With respect to globalization and governance, Scholte claims that the position of the state by no means has dissolved and is still central in governance and regulation - though it has been 'reconstructed'. Supraterritoriality caused shifts towards multilayered public governance - putting an end to state sovereignty (e.g. substate transborder governance, regionalization, transworld governance, privatized governance, public agencies and non-official actors like NGOs, etc.). Bureaucratized principles however, - whether in global governance agencies, global corporations or global civic associations- for the larger part remain bureaucratic. Democracy is under threat, according to Scholte, and not the state nor bureaucracy. (Scholte 2000:158). Part of the problem is the state relations with global actors and flows which escape democratic control. And however globalization widened opportunities for democratic activity by unofficial channels, 'consumer democracy' through global markets has in practice allocated voice in proportion to assets; 'shareholder democracy' through global companies has in practice concentrated voice in boardrooms and large investment funds; 'network democracy' through global communications in practice excludes many of the world's people; 'civic democracy' through global civil society has in practice shown many shortfalls in participation, consultation, transparency and public accountability' (Scholte 2000:281).
Scholte concludes that static concepts and practices of democracy have become inadequate in post-territorialist and post-sovereign politics, and new ones are needed to make democracy work.

Also of major interest regarding our subject is Scholte's view on globalization and community. Important changes took place in the shape of nations and the former national position of the state. Nation states now are accompanied by non-state forms of nation such as ethno-nations (e.g. the Kurds), region-nations (e.g. the Pan-African movement) and transworld nations (e.g. Chilean exiles). Albeit nationhood as a primary framework of collective solidarity remained, new non-territorial communities emerged. They are based upon class solidarities, gender, lesbian and gay and racial solidarities, global youth and religious solidarities (revivalist movements).
A third shift includes cosmopolitanism trends, for example humanitarian relief campaigns, human rights promotion, global environmentalism, etc. One might include the 'anti (sic) globalist movement' demonstrating during the G8 conferences as another example.
A fourth and final shift in the construction of communities due to globalization is in Scholte's words the 'increased hybridization at the level of individuals'. '(...) hybrid persons can emphasize several strong aspects of their identity, with the result that, for instance, national loyalties, religious bonds and gender solidarities could compete and conflict. (...) the immediacy of the whole world in contemporary conditions of globalization has greatly multiplied and intensified experiences of being several selves at once. (...) Global relations can in this way decentre the self. (...) globalization has tended to increase the sense of a fluid and fragmented self (...) Hybridity presents significant challenges for the construction of community (...) Moreover, hybridity can hardly be

reconciled with a communitarian approach to social cohesion, where solidarity rests on neat group distinctions and oppositions'. (Scholte 2000: 180-181).

Globalization, he concludes, has not put an end to nationhood, but it did complicate the geography of community. Formerly, the state nation structured community. Now it is replaced by a variety of alternative frameworks of solidarity, making collective identities more multidimensional, fluid and uncertain.

Nevertheless, Scholte identifies one important key continuity: communitarianism. 'All of the national and nonterritorial communities discussed above have arisen and been sustained through processes of othering, that is, by separating groups and setting them in opposition in terms of difference. (...) Insofar as communitarianism builds solidarity through denigration and exclusion of the other, it yields artificial cohesion for the in-group and violence towards the out-group'. (Scholte 2000:183).

Another key social issue is how we understand. So far modern rationality has remained the main epistemology in the social construction of knowledge. Globalization, according to Scholte, has not really altered this. This is not to say that there have been no shifts. Global problems, the conception of 'the world', new fields of study and new approaches to education, local cultures, developments within science, philosophy and religion all contributed. But rationalism, more reflexive as it might be, is persistent and has become more widespread globally. It constructs knowledge in secular, anthropocentric, techno-scientific and instrumental terms.

Counter movements, encouraged by globalization as well, include ecocentrism, postmodernism and religious revivalism (of which some exploit global relations as well). Their impact to rationalism, however, according to Scholte, is marginal. 'True, several religious revival movements have attracted large followings and exerted notable political influence. However, on the whole religious revivalism has enlisted only a small proportion of the world's population and stimulated relatively few major policy changes. (...) Transborder relations have helped to stimulate and sustain some renewals of anti-rationalist faith, but global networks have more usually promoted activities involving rationalist knowledge. (...) Meanwhile today, as during much of the past two centuries, many if not most influential religious thinkers have sought to marry faith and reason, that is, to combine and reconcile experience of the transcendent with scientific and instrumental knowledge' (Scholte 2000: 188,189).

If not epistemology, other forms of knowledge, as Scholte shows, have been influenced by globalization. He points especially to the key issues of ontology (how we define reality): the character of God, life, the self, time and space. With respect to the latter, the concept of virtual reality for example leads to post territorialist definitions of space and thus post territorial ontology (however, many people still equate space and geography with territory). A similar ontological shift happened with respect to time. The connection between time and distance has dissolved. Distance has been displaced by speed. Globalization thus contributed not only to the acceleration of life, but also to the need to experience the fullness of time[30].

Methodology as a third area of knowledge, according to Scholte, has not been impacted by globalization. That is to say core methodological issues in social inquiry (materialist/idealist views, perspectives on the relationship between facts and values, links between theory and practice). However, there have been implications for the role of academic disciplines (multidisciplinary and interdisciplinary research, -albeit old academic divides, including funding, are still strong-) for processes of teaching and learning (transborder textbooks, distance learning and English as the global main

---

[30] In this respect, Scholte notes that it is no coincidence that concepts of supraterritoriality and stress have raised together in current history.

language) and for evidence (global data and research, digital information and the internet changing the character of research).

Nevertheless, Scholte's conclusion is the same as with regard to production, governance and community: '(...) the new post-territorialist geography has on the whole affected the margins more than the core when it comes to structures of knowledge. Rationalist epistemologies have retained primacy in global realms and contemporary social relations generally' (Scholte 2000:202/203).

Overlooking Scholte's view on globalization, the way the subject is treated in church policy documents is very meager. Arthur (1998:7) has a point when stating that it is 'extraordinarily naïve' considering the 'wired' world only in terms of facilitating communication. According to his view, terms like global village, world civilization and information revolution even are 'dangerously cosmetic' and 'obscuring'.

All of the issues raised by Scholte are of importance to the subjects discussed with respect to church statements on communication - whether it concerns their analysis of media culture, their assumptions and expectations of media, their ethical claims and views of regulation, their view of the audience, the premises of their communication models, social cohesion and community, or the notion of religion/faith and their theology. A closer look at the main problems identified is therefore needed.

For two reasons we will do this in an interrogatively way. The first is that the goal of this research, as its title refers to, is to invite dialogue, rather then pretending to provide final answers to the complex intertwined changing realities of media religion and culture (which in itself are complex areas). This would be far beyond the scope and reach of this research (and the capabilities of its author).
The second, referring to the story of David and Goliath (see the preface), is that posing the right question might be considered to be at least of even (if not major) importance than giving the 'right' answers. At least from a biblical theological point of view, as we will discuss in chapter four.

Departing from Scholte's definition of globalization as a transformation of social geography -resulting from, among others, automated technology (communication and data processing) and generating social transformations (e.g. in knowledge and community)-, it is obvious that religion is not unaffected. This requires an accurate understanding of the relationship between communication technology as being one of the facilitators of globalization and media culture, and religion[31].
This understanding is of vital importance and, to my opinion, one of the major underlying problematic issues of the church documents. This is not to say the communication context is not analyzed by the majority of the statements. The problem is in the incoherence and/or partiality of outlooks, and the fact that their impact is not pursued within the topic nor in related topics.

This leads to a number of questions within each of the five issues mentioned, which we will list below.

---

[31] Beyond the scope of this section but not of lesser importance or interest is the relationship between religion and the other three facilitating factors mentioned by Scholte: rationalist knowledge; capitalist production and bureaucratic governance. The same applies to the social transformations mentioned with respect to production, governance, community and knowledge. Some of these issues will be handled either in other sections (3.4.3, 3.4.3) or in chapter four (4.1, 4.1.1).

3.4.1   The outlook on media, communication context and culture

Media are credited with considerable power in the statements. They appear to satisfy each eight of the hallmarks with respect to the 'omnipotent media theory' that was identified by de Boer and Brennecke (2003:17). These features involve: 1. mass media reaching everyone; 2. the influencing process is one way: from sender to receiver; 3. content of the message and impact on its recipient are directly related; 4. the receiver is capable of and willing to take in all messages; 5. the receiver adopts the content of a message passively and without question; 6. the (worst) impact of the media is received without question; 7. there is no filter between sender and receiver and 8. the 'man in the crowd' is more receptive to media impact than is the elite.
Effect research, however, is a complicated and contested area that springs from methodological problems in measuring variables (independent or dependent effects on knowledge or behavior, and short and long term behavior and intervening variables), interpretation, contradicting effects, effects of elements of the communication process itself etc. The omnipotent media theory, therefore, no longer holds. The current paradigm in communication research is the 'limited effect model' by Klapper[32]. This model takes into consideration selective exposure, selective perception and remembering; groups and group norms, interpersonal spread of the content of a message, opinion leadership and the commercial character of media.

This raises a first question: do the statements have an accurate outlook on media and what exactly is their definition of media? An instrumental vision and a traditional concept of 'mass' media (especially traditional television) appear to be prevailing[33]. Technological developments, however, do also change traditional media and interpersonal communication (computer technology for example strongly influenced newspaper and magazine production; television becomes more interactive; people can make their own radio if they want). Moreover, in the outlook of the statements there is a contradiction in the recognition of media being cultural transformers, on the one hand, and an instrumental view of media, on the other. This might also account for an over emphasis on assumed 'effects' (which are treated mainly in moral claims) and of media 'use' for church purposes. It is striking, however, that hardly any media theory is given to ground visions and positions taken, or even to define concepts accurately. Likewise, the relationship between media and culture is not examined thoroughly enough.
A second related question involves new media developments, patterns of information traffic and the concept of interactivity.

With respect to new media developments, even a statement like *Cybernauts Awake!* (3.4), -however analyzing cyberspace for its ethical, moral and spiritual implications- claims that 'historically every new advance in communication has been a means of proclaiming the gospel and cyberspace is no exception' (1999:89). Again the question raises whether an instrumental, moral and institutional preoccupation hinders an accurate outlook on the way the media context is developing. This holds true not only for the integration of conventional media and the computer, but also of virtual reality, application of artificial intelligence, symbiosis of human/machine, application of cybernetics, etc. Whatever the outcome of developments maybe, they seem to be moving beyond ethical control, and flying humanity on automatic pilot into a foggy

---

[32] See 2.1.1 and the typology of media effects by McQuail described in 2.2.2
[33] However, statements note the importance of all forms of communication and of all media 'to be used in church communication'. The focus is on mass media and new media; alternative media are not equally elaborated upon. Even interpersonal communication, which is said to be the most important form, is not elaborated upon or grounded in communication theory.

environment without a final destiny. A dispute about online and physical worship, in this respect -a concern in several statements- is not the height of identifying priorities in the vital need for accurate evaluations, public debates and signposts towards a commonly defined communication future. It is also not helpful in learning to cope with new social-cultural ICT realities. Once they dare to release themselves from inner ecclesiastical survival and power strategies, theology and church statements could make important contributions to this societal debate.

In this respect, it is striking that regarding regulating contemporary and future media policy -a subject which we will treat more fully in the fourth chapter (4.1.1)- general statements mostly keep to moral and ethical responsibilities of audiences and journalists. Whether the same ethical standards (e.g. of honesty and openness, objectivity, and representation of different views) also hold for church internal and external communication praxis is to be argued. Acknowledged on paper, the praxis (especially when there is 'bad news' to report) shows the opposite.

It is also questionable why the statements easily seem to leave the area of media policy to self regulation by media industries and political regulation (which increasingly is more difficult to reach) to safeguard for example public broadcasting. This again questions whether the statements have thoroughly analyzed the impact of contemporary developments beyond their views of traditional mass media - in which new media are incorporated. The contribution that could be made by the churches, in this respect, in the public arena - if the focus was less on moral and more on human communication ethics and values in the so called information society - seems to be underestimated. No matter how important that is, the goal the statements aim at is media education.

Calling to mind the four patterns of information traffic as identified by Bordewijk and Van Kaam (1.1.3.1) -allocution, registration, consultation and conversation-, the documents appear to not distinguish between them. Registration developments, e.g. get little to no attention. The implications of the remodeling of allocutive communication - due to interactivity are also not fully considered with respect to the instrumental vision of media. The same applies for the redistribution in traffic from allocutory to conversational and consultative patterns.

Another overlooked issue is that each pattern has its own view of the audience. This questions whether the statements are aware of the need of non-mass medial typologies of the audience that can no longer remain based on a center-peripheral form of communication. It is even questionable whether the latter can be regarded as communication in its full meaning, and whether the uncritical muddling of terminologies of communication, proclamation, etc. is possible. Even views about communication via new media appear to be considered more as an extension of these forms than as a new form of communication in its own right that asks for different policies.

Just as globalization is a complex issue, so is interactivity.

Compared to the continuum definition of interactivity given by Jensen (1.1.3.1) as a variable with diverging multidimensional interactive degrees, the outlook given by the church statements is feeble and instrumentally restricted. In particular the expectations regarding the possibilities in internal networking and in communication with youth are high. So are the assumed effects. De Boer and Brennecke (2003) state that these assumptions are not always materialized. They refer to studies on the effect of violent videogames on aggression[34] (which appears to be small), and the positive effects of games on children with learning problems in improving concentration, being more aware of what happens in class, and their attitude towards tests[35]. This again questions

---

[34] Sherry, J.L. 2001. 'The effects of violent video games on aggression' in *Human Communication Research* 27 (3), 409-431
[35] Giles D. 2003. *Media psychology.* Mahwah, NJ: Lawrence Erlbaum Associates.

whether the statements in the double outlook of high instrumental expectations, on the one hand, and their emphasis on the moral dangers and 'responsibilities' of parents and young people themselves, on the other hand, are based on media studies. Uses and gratifications studies in the motives of the use of internet[36] for example, point to 'interpersonal use' as the main motive. Being a combination of 'helping others, express myself freely, like to answer questions, know more points of view, take part in discussions, learning what others think and meet new people' (De Boer and Brennecke 2003:147). This also questions the valuation of personal communication as 'best' given in several statements.

With respect to the concept of interactivity, De Boer and Brennecke (2003:149/152) identify six underlying dimensions: 1. reaction or feedback; 2. conversation or mutuality; 3. selectivity; 4. modification; 5. linearity/non linearity (the internet contrary to, for example, a book is structured non-linear) and 6. multimedia. They state that media theories do not allow enough for interactivity. The possibilities of internet change both media and interpersonal communication processes. Considering the latter and the dimensions mentioned above, one might say that neither of the church statements allow enough for interactivity. Putting a 'contact' button on a church web page filled with rationalist and linear oriented messages, in this respect, is but one -and a very limited- dimension.

A general overview of churches and faith organizations on the internet[37] shows that contents on church websites consist of: self-presentation; time tables, agenda's and programs, art and tourist attractions of church buildings; publications; prayers (prayer lines); ecclesial statements, encyclicals; historical and theological studies; education by extension; community access and literacy programs; missionary activities and pastoral counseling and care, all classical church functions. It is the church leaflet of olden days in an electronic coating. A study by Sturgill (2004:165-176) endorses this outcome. Researching the scope and purposes of church websites, she concludes that literature suggests 'churches may see Websites as instruments of evangelism, corporate reputation builders, or community extenders that provide virtual substitutes for relational experiences.' Her content analysis of 251 Southern Baptist church web sites shows that the 'promotion of the church as an organization was quite important and was followed by the evangelistic function of Web sites. (92% of the sites had the schedule for the church services). 'The ideas that communication creates community or that it is participatory did not seem to be developed in the Web sites that were examined. (...) The Pew study found church Web masters primarily wanted to attract visitors to the church, which seemed to be the focus of many sites (Larsen, 2000[38])' (Sturgill 2004:174).

The most vital issue regarding interactivity and the church statements, in our opinion, is whether 'interactivity' includes the core of communication: dialogical conversation, which creates community by the mutual willingness to listen, understand and be changed. Thus it is strongly related to identity.

The third and last issue under this heading, involves the outlook on the social cultural role of media and its religious implications.

---

[36] De Boer and Brennecke 2003:147 point to a study by Papacharissi, Z. and Rubin, A.M. (2000). 'Predictors of internet use'. *Journal of broadcasting & Electronic Media*, 44 (2), 175-196.
[37] Report compiled by Heinz Hunke, Secretary-General of IDOC in Rome, for the international workshop on 'Globalisation and Electronic Communication' in Seoul Korea, 9-14 June 1997 (London, WACC).
[38] Larsen, E. 2000. *Wired churches, wired temples: Taking congregations and missions into cyberspace.* http:www.pewinternet.org.

Regarding the social cultural role, the main focus in the statements is on issues typical of the churches: sociability and disintegration, the perception of identity, the meaning of life, and the reshaping of values and moral.

An analysis of the underlying media logic as given by Van Ginneken (1.2), however, is not elaborated upon. It is acknowledged that media have their own 'rules', but important aspects of media logic such as the (long term) implications of framing, are scarcely considered. Statements do expect, however, that religious or ecclesiastical issues should be considered more accurately. This is not to say that this might not be an appropriate claim (albeit churches themselves in their communication could contribute a lot to this by taking a more subservient communication position towards media instead of an instrumental outlook and moral demands). The point is, however, that claims towards media (e.g. participation by all) do not -by definition- seem to equally apply to church praxis.

The focus on sociability and disintegration questions the position of the church itself within the social cultural realm. It is self evident that the churches position has changed and become more marginal (at least in the Western context). The globalizing issues identified by Scholte (see above), however, at least also question the churches' relationship with and attitude towards rationalist knowledge, capitalist production, technology, bureaucratic governance, the different forms of (nation) state, democracy, and non-territorial communities.

As it questions the churches' outlook on culture. The majority of the statements appears to still dichotomize between culture and media and between church and culture. Apart from being questionable whether this outlook is still possible, it also points to an underlying orientation towards 'high' culture apart from 'popular' (mass media) culture[39].

This brings us to the religious implications of media culture, which we described extensively in 1.3 and 1.4. In analyzing the outlook in the statements (3.3.2), we concluded a contradicting view in the statements' in acknowledging a 'climate of religion in and outside the churches', on the one hand, and concern about a 'climate of absence of meaning', on the other. Definitions about religion, spirituality, secularization, meaning, tradition, truth, etc. are not given and appear to be self evident. However, they no longer are. It is questionable, therefore, whether the profoundness of the religious implications of media culture are fully acknowledged. The focus remains on institutional religion. There is awareness of developments taking place, and at the same time there is an astonishing amount of assumptions that the church and church communication can remain the same. Media cultural developments, however force the church to rethink her identity, societal position and structures; her stand towards culture; the meaning of faith, religion, spirituality, truth and tradition; the position of the people in and outside the church; and the way they use media as part of their symbolic social interaction and religious identity and expression; the way outward bound ethical claims with regard to communication and communication rights can be implemented within the church - the ways the church communicates and the underlying premises of church communication, including their power structures.

It will also be necessary to rethink concepts of rationality, linearity (church and print are still very close) and to understand what the incorporation of a concept of interactivity means.

As it is necessary as well to rethink the main ethical challenge in an era in which communication, in its full sense, is harder to get at and religious fundamentalism and hatred is increasing.

---

[39] We will more extensively consider the views about the relationship between church and culture in section 4.3, when discussing the work of Niebuhr and Tillich.

Recalling Scholte's one important key continuity of communitarism - by which communities sustain themselves through processes of 'othering' (others are 'different'), and group solidarity is built through denigration and exclusion of the other, producing artificial cohesion internally and violence externally, this last issue might be of vital importance.

3.4.2   The view on audience and audience research concepts

In chapter two we discussed the different approaches in audience research, the views on the audience and the views from the audience. With respect to the implications for church communication goals, we concluded that simple remarks of the audience no longer apply. We argued that a revision and refinement of definitions suited for the present media situation and new emerging types of audiences is needed. Those definitions should take overlapping typologies and main dimensions of audience as identified by McQuail (section 2.3), into account.

In the same section, we also pointed to Van Kaam and Bordewijk's concept of the traffic of information (*allocution, registration, consultation and conversation).* Those different patterns of information flow do not only express power relationships with respect to control access and storage, but also hold different audience roles.

In section 2.4 we identified two main paradigms, that relate society/media views, audience views, outlooks on communication models and research and analysis. We argued that the choice of a mass communication paradigm is normative. It is not just an optional choice for one communication scientific model over another, but implies positions with respect to society, media, culture and also the audience.

We argued in 2.5 that the different generations of cultural reception research and audience ethnography have drawn attention to the social cultural use and reception of media, as well as to the interaction within daily life and to the identity politics of gender, race and ethnicity. The perception of the audience and the existence of 'interpretative communities' has also received attention. The same applies to the shift from factual to fictional media outlets and to the fact that media use and meaning are part of a complex web of media culture, with many discourses.

If we relate our findings of chapter two to the outlook of the audience presented in the policy statements (3.3.3), we can identify various problems.
The concept of 'the audience' is taken for granted. References are undefined, varied and sometimes contradictory. They do not include views from the audience and appear to be based on historical 'mass' typologies. The shift in patterns of information, overlooked in the analysis of the media context, consequently results in overlooking the need of differentiating audience concepts.

If we look at the two main paradigms as given in section 2.4, the majority of the documents show features of both, but in overall outlook appear to be closer to the dominant paradigm.
In section 3.3.3 we summarized two positions with respect to the audience. The first position (objects in need of formation) is found more frequent than the latter (subjects in dialogue). However, features of both are again found, sometimes within one and the same document. The concept of the audience thus remains unclear. The implications of either position taken, or of mingling the two, are not explicated.

The reason the audience concept is not adequately treated is twofold. One the one hand, the (religious) implications of media culture are not fully acknowledged as described in section 1.3 and 1.4 . Neither is the concept of interactivity and its implications. On the other hand, the focus on media as instruments to be used for church goals of proclamation and on presumed effects, favors a communications model in which the emphasis is not on the audience and the way they construct meaning in their interaction with media. Audience positions simply do not get much attention.

Even when the audience is viewed in terms of subjects in dialogue, and the need of communication to be receiver oriented is acknowledged, implications of this stand are restricted to the issue of communication an media choice. Moreover, no references are made towards insights of audience research.

The majority of the statements thus appears to rely on a functional, linear transmission model. Its focus on effects, and its view of powerful media as humanizing technologies for regulation and progress of society, however, became criticized - especially for not being related to social and cultural factors and human experience.

This gap is visible in the policy statements. The audience research tradition, as described in section 2.2 – 2.2.4.2, appears to have passed the churches policy statements completely. Therefore audience typologies are not distinguished. In section 2.3 we discussed different typologies leading to different views of the audiences. The transmission model, aimed at cognitive processing, holds a view of the audience as a target for the transfer of meaning. A ritual or expressive model aims at sharing and commitment, considering the audience as participants. The attention model (regardless the communicative effect) regards the audience as a spectator (based on ratings and amount of time spent).

A similar division applies to the communication patterns by van Kaam and Bordewijk (1982). Allocutive communication patterns (center-periphery) contains a passive view of the audience role - as in the traditional mass media audience. In consultation, the audience is an active individual searcher. In conversational patterns, there is interaction, involvement and feedback. With respect to new media developments new non mass medial typologies of audience can develop. New interactive technology makes mixed forms of mass and interpersonal communication possible, in which production, distribution and consumption can be mixed. This leads to new audience behavior and media use. Media effect theories apply only to allocution patterns (transmission model). Moreover, the trend is from allocutary to consultative or conversational modes that urge new interactive, ritual, or user determined models. This again questions the focus on effects by the majority of the statements. The view of the audience remains message related. McQuail (1997), however, has shown a diversity of possibilities of audience formation and audience meanings. He argues that message related views no longer hold. Theory and experience showed the near equal significance of the behavioral, social, emotional and affective aspects of media use.

In this respect, the audience receives far too little attention in the policy statements; the choice of a paradigm, however, is not value free. Neither is the accompanying outlook of audience concepts - which should be clearly revised and defined.

Insights in communication theory and media studies, therefore, are indispensable when churches consider communication and publish communication policies. At least the main theories about media effects and audience research should be taken into account and incorporated[40]. In this respect, it would be helpful to pay attention to the various

---

[40] This not to say that theories about media effects and audience research are the only ones that should be taken into account. Communication theory involves many other aspects of

theories of limited effect-models (media reach, multi-step-flow, impersonal impact and knowledge gap hypotheses, news diffusion and to the spiral of silence theories) and - with respect to the audience-, to the uses and gratifications approaches, media system dependency theories, interactivity and cultivation theories. Theories combining the role of the audience and media content (agenda setting, priming and framing and reception analysis) should also receive analysis. This is not to say that one concluding paradigm can be deduced. Theories are criticized, refined, combined and constantly developing. They could, however, arouse awareness about the complexity of pronouncements about media, the communication concepts and context, the importance of the choice of a paradigm, and the impossibility of naïve outlooks. Moreover, new media developments inevitably imply changes in culture and the use people make of media. Empirical research on the latter, therefore, should also be noticed[41]. The fact that communication theories and audience research are lacking, therefore, is a serious and problematic shortcoming.

Whether these shortcomings are also to be related also to the underlying theological presuppositions of the communication models will be the issue in the identification of the third problem.

3.4.3   Communication models and theological presuppositions

In sections 3.3.5 and 3.3.6 we pointed out the different views of communication and the underlying theological presuppositions. We concluded that an instrumental view of media and linear communication models prevailed in the majority of the statements, notwithstanding references to, for example, dialogue. The Finnish Lutheran statement clearly opts for two way communication; however, their outlook on media shows features of an instrumental view. The statements by communication experts of UNDA and WACC opt for a truly different view, emphasizing the social cultural role of media, public interest, and the serving of communication as a value in itself. This view also involves the position of the church. The latter is also included in the statement of the Lutheran Finnish Church, however, an emphasis on the growth of church membership as one of the top priorities for the coming decade, again questions the exact view of the institutional position of the church, its communication goals and models.

The majority of the statements grounds its view of communication in theological presuppositions (which are not always explicated nor clarified with respect to their application). We identified ten different options in section 3.3.6, including -amongst others- Christological, anthropological, Trinitarian, ecclesiological, ritual and ecumenical arguments, next to the self revelation of God. Remarkably, the kingdom of God as a separate category is absent.
These presuppositions are treated as autonomous categories, apart from any communication context. Albeit the analysis given from the latter, there is no relationship between the theological arguments, communication developments, communication traffic patterns, media structures and culture. Moreover, references to or definitions by communication theory are absent. Consequently, the theological models are not tested

---

communication processes, as shown in chapter one and two. Effects and audience are highlighted here because the policy statements to my opinion overemphasize media effects and at the same time overlook the position of the audience. Moreover, especially in the area of audience theories, recent developments took place.
[41] Stewart M. Hoover and Knut Lundby (eds. 1997); Chris Arthur (ed 1989) ; Jolyon Mitchell and Sophia Marriage (eds.2003); Daniel A. Stout and Judith M. Buddenbaum (eds. 1996); Stewart Hoover and Lynn Schofield Clark (eds.2002); Peter Horsfield, Mary E. Hess and Adán M. Medrano (eds. 2004); Paul A. Soukup and Robert Hodgson (eds. 1997).

against communication models or media studies, nor to communication praxis or audience use. This is another major problem - next to the inadequate understanding of the (religious) implications of contemporary media context and media culture. It is questionable whether (sometimes contradicting) theological arguments can be applied directly to communication, as the majority of the statements assume.

How, for example, are we to derive and apply communication models, which are adequate to the contemporary (mass) communication context, from, for example, Trinitarian arguments as the communication and communion of love between Father, Son and the Holy Spirit? Dulles (1992:37/38, *The Craft of Theology, From Symbol to System*) states that the Trinity is the 'deepest mystery of communication' where: 'Our human eyes are blinded by its surpassing brilliance. The created analogies, while falling immeasurably short, point through their convergence to the communicative character of this exalted mystery. The Trinity is communication in absolute, universal perfection, a totally free and complete sharing among equals. In generating the Son as Word, the Father totally expresses himself ... the Holy Spirit completes the intradivine process of communication' (quoted in Eilers 2003:159/160).

Or how can we derive and apply communication models from pneumatological arguments? Or even from the acts of Jesus, labeled as 'the perfect communicator' (sic)? Or from scripture, which shows many different styles and formats of (non-mass-medial, contextual) communication as a contemporary 'code of communication'? Moreover, applying -for example- a Trinitarian based model of dialogue to a non-dialogical medium, such as, television, causes problems of method.

Soukup (1999: 219-231), on communication models and translation of the Bible in new media with respect to fidelity, shows how within four different perspectives on communication each contain different consequences. A transportation model looks upon fidelity as a message that can be transmitted and measured in likeness and in meaning. In ritualistic models of communication, fidelity becomes more functional and depends on both ritual exchange as well as information (encoded message). Semiotic systems consider fidelity to 'manifest surface changes in a deeper structure'. And in the interactive, conversational outlook of communication, fidelity becomes more an issue of the audience than of the text.

'Each perspective on communication suggests a perspective on the Bible. The transportation or transmission model regards the Bible as valued information that must be delivered from on location to another. The semiotic model also regards the Bible as information, but as encoded information that exists in relation to other codes. Here we become aware of the Bible as part of a larger structure of relations. The ritual model sees the Bible as a container of shared beliefs, as an opportunity for sharing belief, and as a means of maintaining the believing community. The Bible does not exist apart from the community and any use of the Bible presumes the role of the community. Finally, the conversation model situates the Bible as a partner of the believer or the community. It takes life only in the interaction; the Bible manifests the power of the Spirit who acts upon the believer. (...) Multimedia translation focuses our attention not only on the question of fidelity but on the nature of the Bible itself. Does what translators do change the nature of the translated text? Historical studies show that the use of the Bible has changed over the centuries, as has the nature of the Bible – the manuscript Bible functioned differently from the oral tradition. The advent of the Gutenberg Bible (or, more generally, the printed Bible) similarly changed how people regarded the Bible and how people used the Bible. But these changes do not affect the Bible only; they are part of a larger sweep of cultural change marked out in communication patterns. Multimedia work has identified another phase change and can tell us much about the Bible and the Church in our own day, as well as about fidelity' (Soukup 1999:230/231).

In other words: it is of extreme importance that churches clarify their communication models, not merely from a theological point of view, but from a (critical) communication scientific stand. This necessarily involves their own societal position, their outlook on the audience and culture, their view of theology, tradition and Scriptures and communication scientific stands. Moreover, it would help clarifying their perspective and involvement in public communication.

Regarding the latter Hamelink (1975) commends the development of a prior conceptual framework that grounds the perspective for public communication involvement by the churches. Theological motives in this respect, to his opinion, are not adequate. He examines four of them in relationship to the social reality of public communication and meta scientific aspects of communication research. His objection to the *communicatio divina* as basis for human communication is its 'transmission syndrome'. Media, in this model, are seen as inferior to the Divine communication; they are technical instruments, used for one way messages to passive receivers. Moreover, the term *communication* is overloaded with non-realistic assumptions, which are not related to actual processes of communication.
The second theological motive is based on the perspective of the Incarnation. The Christological dogma justifies and shapes communication activities by the churches. This motive again regards media as instruments. Moreover, it does not critically examine the structures and messages from the media. Another objection is that the incarnation motive is not pursued for its consequences with respect to culture. Respecting the incarnation motive fully means being 'in the world', not separating Christ and world into different dimensions. The commission of the church is not to fight for its own position, but to testify.
The third motive is the *kerugma* motive. The mass media's reach offers the church the opportunity to proclaim the *kerugma* publicly a thousandfold. Targeted, however, to an individual believer. Thus the social context and ideology criticism are not included. The church is tolerated as long as she justifies the current order. Dominant values remain untouched. Liberation is out of the question. Used as a model for the public communication of the church, it becomes either a presentation of identity without social political identification, or a social political identification without critical self analysis of prejudices and conditioning. An ideology-critical, public proclamation, says Hamelink, is not the only thing that is needed. Needed as well is a critical public communication within the church. Another problem is that the conceptual framework of the *kerugma* motive is presented in terms of evangelization. Aimed to winning people, is rejected by Hamelink. It is a crucial element in the ideology of oppression and contrary to emancipative self discovery. It does not hold a view of people as subjects of their own choices and passes by issues of communication structures, message content and needs of the audience. It is a market model of proclamation as a product that coincides with commercial media structures. As a result, these structures cannot be valued critically anymore.
The fourth and last model examined by Hamelink is the ecclesiological model - the church as the body of Christ. Within this concept Hamelink identifies a problem of method. Changes are to be achieved by better understanding and reason with logic. This, however, is not helpful with respect to irrational prejudices. Moreover, the social economical context is again disregarded and the 'should be' structure of the ecclesiological model is not realistic. A functional, pragmatic approach -aimed at the actual and potential functions of the church in its praxis and at the analysis of infrastructural factors- would be more appropriate.

Hamelink thus objects to a 'theology of communication'. His alternative conceptual frame is a dialectical, ideology critical analysis. This approach is interested in emancipation and dialogue and views public communication as a common process aimed at public consensus. Moreover, it holds an intrinsic relationship between theological theory and communication praxis. In terms of communication research, this concept breaks with conventional marketing research, which is exchanged for an emancipating research interest.

He motivates his choice for the dialectical concept with theological, ethical and sociological arguments. Theologically, there is the fundamental hermeneutical question about how biblical reality and contemporary reality relate to one another. This involves the social relevance of theology. When information is contextualized, it becomes relevant to the information seeker. In theology, says Hamelink, an application-information model is often used that is based on the 'transport syndrome'. Simple and frequent repetition of the same is supposed to have missionary impact. Contextualization of information, however, remains closer to biblical exegesis and takes the analysis of social reality more seriously. 'The biblical reality does not prescribe the form the here-and-now reality should take, but provides insights enabling us to discover and demythologize the character of the here-and-now reality. The biblical narratives are the hermeneutical framework without which the analysis of the here-and-now reality inevitably remains no more than a description of unalterable factuality. When superimposed on the concepts arrived at by analysis of the social reality, the biblical concepts became strongly demythologizing forces' (Hamelink 1975:105).

He elucidates his point with reference to the key concept of biblical history: *tsedaka*, which is about serious partnership, justice and solidarity. Biblical history shows a multiplicity of contributions that are dialectically united and in which all people participate and are taken serious. From that experience of communication all appear changed.
An ethical argument why the churches should opt for a dialectical perspective is in the debate of the effects of media. When people are not taken seriously with their alternatives in the decision making process which determines their reality and identity, this leads to alienation. Churches should make this identifiable and act towards emancipation as an 'exodus from the powers'.
The sociological argument given by Hamelink is that churches are often blind to social reality - especially in matters of church structures and political functions. Churches are part of existing power relations. Critical self analysis is needed to identify how churches as social institutes are involved in societal and political communication processes, both structural and functional. Traditional research methods should make room for methods oriented to the users of information and involve them in the research. Otherwise, information remains a tool of oppression.

The Roman Catholic statements appear to be most explicit in grounding their view of communication in theological arguments. Roman Catholic theologians/communication specialists are also prominent in the development of a communication theology or theology of communication (Forde Plude, 2001; Bonnot, 2001; Martini, 1994; Dulles, 1989, Eilers 2002, 2003; and White (1992, 2001). White (1992:258) for example states, that 'one of the best syntheses of Catholic Theology of communication is still that found in Part I of CP' (*Communio et Progressio*). On the issue of communication planning, White (1998), discerning six different phases, calls for a 'new theology of communication, to be perfected in all phases' (1998:20). In the same article he notes:
'a Theology of communication provides a justification and explanation of why we must communicate our faith in a particular way. For example, the emphasis on communitarian

communication emerges from our theological tradition and is very much supported by the theology of communication in Communio et Progressio. Virtually every decision we make about how we are to communicate (...) will be determined on the basis of our theological reflection on the communication context in which we live' (White, 1998:38/39). In his article on 'the new communication emerging in the church' (2001), he states: 'Christianity is pre eminently a religion of communication, placing central emphasis on: a divine revelation, the Incarnation and a Church that is continually becoming incarnate in different cultures; the mandate of proclaiming the Word of God; the formal ecclesial community as the context of faith development; the key role of written scriptures; and the teaching of a tradition to succeeding generations. The vitality of the Church has depended very much on adapting its gospel witness to the forms of communication of a particular era' (White 2001:18).

Koole (1981), former director of the ecumenical broadcaster IKON in the Netherlands, and thus speaking from a praxis experience for over 30 years, with Hamelink opposes a relationship between theology and communication science, that is to close, but then the other way around: in applying scientific models of communication to theology. He opts for a dialogue between both - departing from the actual situation of the churches. He agrees with Hamelink that the direct involvement of the churches in the social political spectrum must be continuously under dispute. Media structures reflect power structures and questions the churches' independency. With respect to a more 'communicative' theology[42], Koole makes a plea for the development out of the praxis - not normative, not descriptive but creative[43]. Issues at stake are, for example, how to translate Christian concepts to a media public and the implications of working with images. Finally, he concludes that a move outside always implies a move inside. A key issue, in this respect, is whether churches and theology are prepared to be changed by working with media and learn something new about themselves. If not, they will not be able to critically guide the media or reflect on codes of ethical conduct.

Concluding, we might say that the outlook on communication models reveals more than just the choice of a paradigm. It also includes the role that is allotted to the audience, an outlook on culture and the relationship between theology and culture, and the position of the church in society. Hamelinks criticism, based on four policy statements published before 1975[44], questions whether the documents published after 1990 show a changed outlook. They partly do. The mass media context is widely analyzed, (including media structures), the tone of the churches towards the media is different (more realistic and less demanding), and social and ethical responsibilities by the churches towards the realm of communication are given. However, if we look at the paradigms given in section 2.4, we must conclude that the dominant paradigm prevails in the majority of the churches' outlook on communication and media. This poses major problems with respect to the public communication by the churches. These include the overlooking of the role of the audience, the outlook on culture, and the societal position of the church

---

[42] The concepts of communicative theology, communication theology, and theology of communication will be dealt with in section 4.5.1
[43] Hamelink (2002:6) underlines Koole's view with respect to praxis: He pleas for a shift of the centre of practical theology from 'the accent on the practical application of theoretical-theological knowledge into the communicative praxis, towards the fundamental questioning of the theoretical-theological knowledge from within the praxis of public communication as a process of inclusive dialogue'.
[44] Inter Mirifica, the Vatican, 1963; The Church and the Media of Mass Communication, World Council of Churches, Uppsala 1968; Communio et Progressio, The Vatican, 1971; Joint Report of the Task Force on Mass Communication and the Task Force on Publication Strategy, Lutheran World Federation, 1973.

itself with respect to the media context. Theological presuppositions, as given, do not solve these problems. Therefore, the issue of the relationship between communication and culture and between theology and communication
must be further examined (which we will do in sections 4.2 and 4.5.1), as well as the identity of the church.

3.4.4   Ecclesiological identity

In section 3.3.4 we overviewed the churches' outlooks on their identity. Included are the view of authority, the cultural style in relating to the audience and media culture, the view towards plurality, the outlook on tradition and the outlook on cultural materials in social practice being a subject for theology. Ecclesiological positions differ and are denominationally related. Due to overlapping (and sometimes contradictory) features, clear cut categorizations are difficult to derive. The lack of definitions aggravates the understanding of identity. Identities appear to be variables with higher or lower degrees in respect to media culture, theological grounding, proclamation, safeguarding tradition, emphasis on interpersonal contact within the community of faith, recipient orientation, dialogue, living interaction and a common search of truth. Differences in attitude, however, also account for different outlooks with respect to institutional change and tradition.
Overlooked is the possibility of cultural materials in social practice as a subject for theology. The latter corresponds with the partial analysis given to media culture and the position of the audience.

The identity of the churches, as given in the majority of the statements, appears to be non-problematic to themselves. At least, not problematic enough to redefine issues of identity and societal position - let alone reforming itself. The indistinctness in defining their identity, however, is a problem. The crisis the institutional churches in Western Europe find themselves in, in fact, is a crisis of communication.

Horsfield (2003: 271-282) sees 'many of the current institutional forms of the Christian Church as well past their use-by date' (272). Albeit he is not concerned about the de-institutionalization of religious faith as such, he questions its concept. In his opinion what is going on is not the de-institutionalization but re-institutionalization of religious faith within the institutions of commercial mass media. The maintenance of diversity, however, needs social institutions, which can counteract institutional forms constructed or privileged by those media.

The churches' analyses, both of the crisis they find themselves in as well as of culture, overlook the crucial role of changes in the structures of mediated communication. Those changes impact the forms of mediation in the construction of culture and cultural meaning.

'The method of making faith real by grounding it in a text, interpreted by accredited teachers into ethical actions and re-membering rituals has remained a very effective method for making faith real within Christianity to this point. To a significant extent, the 'reality' of the words of textual faith have been validated by the development of powerful religious institutions aligned with significant political, military and economic forces. Reality was constructed in the words through the churches' political and social power to discipline, socially ostracize or even execute those who ignored them' (Horsfield 2003:281).

Those text based strategies today are no longer valid. Text based mediation has shifted to electronically mediated reality and churches no longer can exercise power over meanings in words and symbols of Christianity. The consequence, according to Horsfield, is that the social and cosmological view which provided meaning to Christian words and rituals has disappeared. Their logic may still have meaning for insiders, but increasingly lacks the power to be meaningful in differently mediated cultures.

Thus, the analysis of the crisis by the churches is inadequate. Consequently, the strategies to cope with it and reposition themselves, according to Horsfield, are 'retrograde – their operating assumptions seems to be a Christendom model of social dominance, political coercion, patriarchal imposition and moral imperialism' (Horsfield 2003:273).

Related to the problem of inadequate analysis by the statements, we pointed out the lack of definition, and sometimes contradictory features with regard to identity. Communicative community, participative community, 'the body of Christ', fellowship, 'bearer and custodian of the revelation', and 'teaching office to authentically interpreting his Word' are all mentioned.

Particularly Roman Catholic volumes have considered the subject of church model related to communication. They all draw upon the work of Avery Dulles; *The Church is communication* (1972), *Models of the Church* (1974) and *Vatican II and communications* (1989). Dulles analyzed the Vatican II documents and derived five different models of a communicating church: the church as institution or hierarchy; the church as herald; the church as sacrament; the church as communion and the church as servant. Each model of the church implicates a different model of communication. Both Soukup (2002:54-56) and Eilers (2002:58-60, 2003:55-58) summarize these models.

In the institutional model, authority and official doctrine are important features. Communication in a theological view begins with God and descends through hierarchy as an authoritative teacher to church members. This model favors print-mass communication for its match of centralized organization with central authority. The faithful thus receive all the same message and are expected to submit.

The herald or *kerugmatik* model is based on the mandate of Jesus to proclaim the gospel to the world, which can be effected by all baptized believers - the entire church. The model of communication is oral, person to person proclamation; its aim is conversion.

In the sacramental model, Christ is the revelatory symbol and sacrament of the covenant of God. The church, in its turn, is the sacrament in which Christ is present. Communication in this model is communication of salvation by God and the church via sacramental action, for example, liturgy that is aimed at sanctification.

The communion (*koinonia*) or community model favors dialogue. It is based in the secular dialogic theology, in which both the church and the world communicate mutual knowledge, fellowship, truth, etc. with the aim of enriching and respecting each other and effectuating communion of the church. Since the world is created and redeemed by God, it can, through the Holy Spirit, be a place where salvation is spoken.

The church as servant, following in the footsteps of Christ, includes the entire church, which serves the world through actions and works for others - more than communication in words.

In Eilers' terms this model is the secular-dialogic model that is based on the Vatican document *Gaudium et Spes*. The world is looked upon not as an object of mission, but as a place where the mystery of God's will is in action. The interpretation of the times and dialogue with cultures (including the world of communications as well as with religions) find a place here. Eilers points out that, according to Dulles, this secular dialogic theology also impacts the kind of dialogue in the church.

Both Soukup and Eilers state that no one model suffices for the communication of the church. Eilers (2003), differentiating between pastoral communication (inner ecclesiastical, ad intra) and evangelizing communication (outside, ad extra), connects the community and sacramental models to the first and the herald and secular-dialogic models to the latter. He also identifies different modes of church discourse: the prophetic mode (related to the hierarchical institutional model), the theological mode (explaining principles), the diplomatic mode (to foster better relations) and the pastoral mode of discourse (combining the three others) (Eilers 2003:58/59).

Soukup concludes that 'Correlating the different models of the Church with various modes of communication invites both a deeper understanding of the Church and a more communicative response by the Church. It also dramatically proposes a communication strategy with multiple prongs so that the Church can be present in the world and to its own members in a variety of ways. Finally it corrects an ecclesiological error that favors only one kind of communication, thus leading people to misunderstand the nature of the Church itself' (Soukup 2002:56).

Thorn (1996:82-106), building on Dulles as well, points to different analytical starting points in both communication and ecclesiology. Communication analysis can begin with the mass media system, the communicator, or the audience. Church analysis can be identified theologically or sociologically. Thus the interdependency between communication and church can take different directions and is a complex phenomenon.

A mass media model oriented to communicators and the medium emphasizes the communicators' control by 'proper manipulation of the instruments'. This model ignores the role of audiences (selective attention and perception according to psychological and sociological needs and gratifications), the fact they use and interpret media within familial and social groups, and the role of interpersonal communication. Churches structuring communication to this instrumentalist view overemphasize the power of the communicator and the message. At the same time, they overlook the frames of reference that audiences and individuals use to interpret a message. If the primary peer groups of a person differ from church like-minded, communication can be unintelligible -due to interpretations from a different perspective- and lead to misunderstanding. Subcultures (which hold different values), therefore, need to be taken into account. Moreover, primary groups (as well as the churches) are related to surrounding social structures.

'The model's [Riley&Riley 1959] emphasis on primary groups should alert Church communicators to another dimension: dialogue as a way of clarifying misperceptions arising from divergent ways of understanding. The vast reach of electronic media multiply the difficulty, particularly as economic pressures reduce the amount of time available for full elaboration and public dialogue' (Thorn 1996:87).

Communio et Progressio, according to Thorn, called for using the media for dialogue and participation in the formation of public opinion, and explanation of the church to the community. Being present in public debate and public policy, however, also increased public scrutiny by the press. It reports on problems and conflicts that are based on diversity of the community, whereas church leaders expect the press to maintain consensus. Since dominant media shape expectations of the audience, they impact religious media that might differ in tone or style, but cannot afford to diverge too much from dominant models, because of the risk of being not feasible, nor accepted.

Thorn, with Dulles, underlines that successful communication is not an absolute criterion. 'Not everything that is congenial to the mass media is consonant with the Gospel of Christ. In the perspectives of theology, therefore, communications, like every other human reality, has to be interpreted and evaluated in the light of the gospel.

Concern with the techniques of communication must always be subordinated to the primacy of the Christian message' (Thorn, 1996:98, quoted in Dulles 1989:546).

Departing from models of church, Thorn states theological analysis prioritizes the relationship between the hierarchy and the faithful and the self-image of the church. Sociologically, ecclesiological models are based on social structures. According to Thorn until Vatican II, the dominant model was a monarchial one. With the Pope as the supreme pontiff over the entire church, this model underlined the juridical structure of the church. This model was contested by a communal model, that stressed the spiritual inner side of the church and the role of the Holy Spirit. Unity in this model is not secured by jurisdiction, doctrines and dogma, but by a view of the faithful as a spiritual community. The monarchial model, with Latin as the global liturgical language, favored top-down communication. This model was also applied to mission.
'In communication terms, the top-down model resembles Lasswell's original formulation with an emphasis on hierarchical stature for credibility and manipulation of the instruments in order to reach the entire audience'. (...) Wit a poorly educated audience and modestly educated clergy, the top down model provides a highly effective means of dissemination. Coupled with an educational system which emphasizes the monarchial model, the system provides solid defense against both secular and heretical assault. The problem is that it has little ability to adapt to changes in the audience and it cannot prepare the faithful for an alternate model without jeopardizing their allegiance to the institution and their very faith' (Thorn, 1996:93/94).

The top down model, closed up dialogue, not only with alienated, educated Catholics (who started their own publications), but also with ecumenical and inter-religious partners, as well as with the world. The church considered itself supreme in the world, but at the same time separated from it. Fitting this ecclesiology, non-dialogical communication was the result.
After Vatican II the dominant ecclesiology shifted and with it the implicit communication models. References were now made to the body of Christ (all the faithful are one in Christ). Authority is with the Pope and the bishops. The latter are also teachers. The laity must testify and make their needs known to their pastor. Thorn shows how this shift in ecclesiology results in a far more complex communication model, including internal and external subsystems. Building on Dulles models of ecclesiology, Thorn develops an expanded model which includes the demands of transmission of authentic teaching, proclamation, and dialogue (with church members, other Christians and non-Christians). Moreover, building on *Aetatis Novae*, the media society -with its multiplicity of sources- needs to be incorporated. As well as legal and economic aspects, account must also be taken of the dominant media styles against which church communication is evaluated. Therefore, Thorn locates the Catholic community within a larger framework of culture and society, stressing communication relationships. The social cultural component includes political and economic systems, social mores and culture. The Catholic community is segmented and includes official church media, other Catholic media and the Catholic population at large. The latter is divided in autogenic, pneumatic and institutional groups that differently define the role of the church and their spirituality. Institutional groups are loyal to the church and rely on its teachings as their primary source of information. Pneumatic groups focus on spiritual growth, which can be nourished by the church. Social and theological issues are secondary to them and they are less interested in media. Autogenic groups consider the church as divinely inspired but fallible. Self responsibility in religious development and church teaching as one source among many others, and parish commitment over commitment to diocese or Rome, are features of this group.

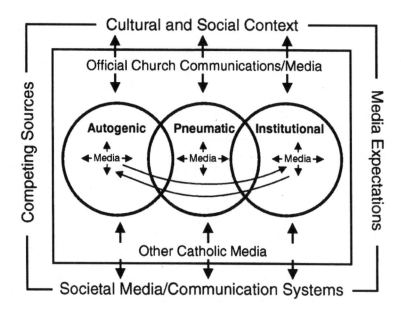

Table 3.4 (Thorn, 1996:195)

With addition of generational differences (older rural and younger urban) and differences in attention to and consumption of Catholic media, Thorn concludes the 'Catholic community is far from a homogeneous audience patiently waiting for the latest official information (...) The profound differences based on the perceived role of the Church and personal religious life demand a sophisticated, multi-pronged approach' (Thorn 1996:104).

Returning to our conclusion about the outlook on communication models and their theological presuppositions in the section above, we might conclude that ecclesiological identity is closely related to both. Likewise, the outlook on communication models is more than just a choice of paradigm, as is the outlook on ecclesiological identity. Different outlooks about identity include different outlooks about communication, the audience and tradition or message. These issues need to be clarified more accurately by the statements.
Both Eilers and Soukup stress that communication by the church, should not be restricted to one model. We agree upon that: however, the question arises whether the church can opt for any model of communication, any model of church, and any possibility to relate the two. In our opinion, it can't. Like Dulles' pronouncement that not everything congenial to the mass media is consonant with the gospel, we might say that not every church model is either. The analysis we have given of the media context and media culture (chapter one) and the insights of audience research (chapter two) force the church to redefine its view of communication, its societal position and, consequently, its identity. In my opinion, both on theological as communication scientific grounds, this implies the exclusion of an instrumental vision of media and communication and of dominant models of church. Departing creatively from contemporary praxis, as Koole urges, and a functional approach, as suggested by Hamelink, seem to be a more appropriate approach.

3.4.5   Implementation and praxis

In section 3.4.3 we treated the methodological problem of theological theory related to communication praxis. In this section we will consider some issues of implementation and praxis. Our goal is not, however, to overview the actual involvement of the churches in communication, -which is context determined-. This is beyond the scope of our research and would be the subject of another thesis. Identifying implementation and praxis as one of the problems, however, can also be looked upon from within the policies of the churches and by relating them to our findings of media context and media culture and audience research. Thus the line of the study will be pursued. Moreover, it will facilitate summarization of various issues that have not so far been addressed.

Eilers (2002) pointing to the consultations and continental meetings that were held in all parts of the world to implement *Communio et Progressio* (1971), concludes that the recommendations of the conferences only had limited effect. 'Generally it seems that the Pastoral Instruction on Social Communication still has to be discovered by many people'. (Eilers 2002:231)

White (1992), evaluating the Roman Catholic Church's thinking about communications comes to a similar conclusion in his considerations on *Aetatis Novae* (1992). 'Indeed, the message is coming through "loud and clear": although *Communio et Progressio* provided us with a beautiful, idealistic vision of communication in our societies and in the church, at the level of the typical diocese and parish there has often been little *action*. The Catholic Church, in comparison with other religious groups, still has not put a new era of communications to work to communicate the gospel both within ecclesial communities and to the society around it' (White:1992:248). Nevertheless, according to White, *Aetatis Novae* is an important document for emphasizing social communication and should be an integral part of pastoral planning. In doing so, it reflects the major shifts of thought about communication among people involved in church communication activities. These shifts include, says White,

1.   the notion of social communication (which is broader than mass media but also involves alternative forms of communication),
2.   the shift from linear models to communion models and the close relationship between communication and cultures,
3.   a growing concern with internal pastoral communication and evangelization,
4.   a more critical stand towards media institutions and
5.   the centrality of theological reflection on communication, media and church communication.

'Surprisingly, however, the communion model of public communication was never picked up, commented on and used to any great extent within Catholic Church circles. In my years of teaching and discussing *CP* in seminars with Catholic communicators, I find that virtually all still tend to work with a linear, transport model of communication. The exceptions are those who come from the "New Churches" and who have an experience of the "Communio" model of church embodied in the basic Christian communities' (White 1992:252).

However, *Aetatis Novae* reflects the new communion and cultural understanding of communication, it does not pursue this outlook in its appendix, "Elements of a Pastoral Plan for Social Communication". In White's words, it 'tends to evaporate and we are back in a more linear, transport and technology dominated conception of communication' (White 1992:253). Moreover, the concern with internal communication and evangelization, due to the crisis the church finds itself in, shows difficulties as well. Communications activities by the church (mostly on the level of a communication office taking care of public relations) are not coordinated or integrated in pastoral planning. They are marginal to both the pastors and the parish.

'The pastoral communication at the diocesan and parish level continue on in its traditional, centuries-old patterns as if the media did not exist at all. At the best, the media are looked on as "just entertainment" that might be vaguely damaging to religious and moral values but still something quite tangential to the spiritual growth of Catholics. Most pastors have had only the vaguest notion of how much their parishioners use film, television, popular music, radio and the press, and there is even less awareness of how this enters into the construction of values of the people. (...) Preparation of future priests and other pastoral personnel is generally carried on with no reference to the arrival of the mass mediated culture that CP has proclaimed. (...) seminarians and young religious are often restricted in their use of mass media with little or no introduction to the cultural and pastoral significance of the media. (...) In fact, with the influence of the recent great systematic theologians, theological education since Vatican II often has tended to become more analytical and even more remote from pastoral communication.' (White 1992:254).

Albeit churches have not yet integrated communication developments and new notions of communication. White appears to expect much of pastoral planning -especially at the local level-, since it has become 'a much more central "language" for evangelization and renewal' (White 192:258). He recommends including spirituality of faith communication and the grounding of the pastoral planning in a process of theological reflection.

Whether his expectations -one and a half decade later- have become true remains questionable, at least in the Western European context. Nevertheless, both Eilers and White point to problems that, by no means, are unique to the Roman Catholic Churches. However - contexts, ecclesiological structures, theological, liturgical and sacramental traditions and the outlook on believers and the wider audience prohibit an easy 'application', similar problems apply to other churches.

Overlooking the statements one might ask, for example, whether the statement on audiovisual media education: 'an urgent pastoral and social concern' by UNDA/WACC (1994) has been broadly implemented. To my knowledge it has not. Or whether communication has been integrated in theological education. It has not. Or whether churches engage themselves in the development of communication structures and communication rights. The recent campaign on Communication Rights in the Information Society (CRIS) alongside the World Summit on the Information Society (WSIS) did not attract much church attention, apart from individual 'critical enthusiasts' and UNDA/WACC.

The many repetitions of the same arguments and similarity in overlooking the same issues in the majority of the statements is not very promising. The lack of financial efforts and manpower to put policies in place (very exceptionally mentioned in but a few of the statements) is another fateful sign. This would require a major restructuring of flow of funds and church personnel.

One might object that the statements by the Lutheran churches opt for a different outlook on communication, which I fully admit they do. As well they as they attempt, as do the German churches, to involve the local level in their policies and offer parishes and congregations assistance in communication. Or, in the case of the Anglican church, provide materials to think through the dawning cyber society.

Nevertheless, I find it hard to avoid the impression that communication from a church perspective is primarily focused on 'surviving' the institutional crisis that the churches find themselves in. Whatever legitimacy one feels this might be, it might also restrict the churches to an inward perspective, avoiding the real challenges that media culture places upon them. Moreover, it hinders ecumenical and interreligious cooperation as well as cooperation with organizations that strive for the same societal goals (e.g. non governmental organizations or pressure groups). However this cooperation is stressed as being important in the majority of the documents.

This impression is likely due to the fact that churches, in their statements, incorporate both church communication as well as communication from a Christian perspective and sometimes intermingle the two. The moral and ethical claims of objectivity, truthfulness, etc. placed on media do not always appear to be unbiased. Moreover, standards of 'highest quality', referred to in terms of their own church communication, -theologically grounded in the perfect Trinitarian and incarnational communication of which the church is the continuation-, cannot always bear the test of implementation and praxis.

3.5   Conclusion

The 26 policy statements vary in sort, scope addressee and purpose, which are not always clearly explicated. References to other documents hardly cross denominational and/or regional borders. Main key issue of the documents are challenges and priorities for the church and its communication - followed by the analysis of media context, social responsibility by the churches and church view's on media roles and communication models. Audience research scarcely receives attention. New media appear to be evaluated and used along traditional patterns of outlook and use of mass media. Concepts used are not adequately defined. The degree of intertwinement of media and culture is valued to different extents and not always clear. The challenges that communication developments offer to religion, religious attitudes and the perception of the church are acknowledged but not fully thought through. The religious component in media culture is overlooked and does not result in an critical analysis, in which the being of mainline Christianity and institutional and structural change is involved (with the exception of the Lutheran churches and the WACC/UNDA specialists' document).
Human service, community and progress constitute the paradigm that media should be oriented to. Media use, as part of everyday social interaction, is mainly related to new media and elaborated upon in a moral and ethical sense. It is no explicit issue in itself.
Audience views differ between a 'subject' and an 'object' outlook. Receiver orientation is acknowledged but not pursued for its implications. The tension between informing, proclamation and dialogue remains unsolved.
Christian and church identities are variables with higher and lower degrees of openness to media culture, theological grounding, proclamation, safe guarding tradition, emphasis on interpersonal contact within the faith community, recipient orientation, dialogue, living interaction and a common search for truth. The outlooks differ from a 'communicative community' to a 'non-centralized living participative community', a *commnio* and 'Christ's mystical body', and a fellowship.
Communication is a basic human right and a necessity for social cohesion. The one way model of communication and the instrumental view of media are under pressure, however, they prevail in the majority of the documents. Communication appears strongly related to proclamation. The emphasis on personal encounter within parish or congregation, interpersonal communication and the second hand value attached to mediated communication shows that faith and the gospel are bound up within the institution. This raises questions of power and of connecting with the religious

dimensions of media culture, as well as to the understanding of media use by the audience for autonomous ritual community and meaning negotiating activities. Public service broadcasting is an important issue in the statements. Definitions about interactivity are not elaborated nor is it analyzed for its implications for the church and its communication. It is mainly related to the communication of the gospel to new generations. The statements by the Lutheran churches and the Christian media professionals break new ground in seeking a different attitude towards media and their own communication praxis, involving the church itself as well.

Theological presuppositions grounding media and communication praxis by the churches are still strong. They involve a variety of arguments. Whether they are the best point of departure or are adequate in coping with digital media culture is not reflected. Neither are methodological problems. Church involvement in communication and social and ethical responsibilities are extensively elaborated. The outlooks vary from engagement for the sake of sociability to mission. Ecumenical and interreligious cooperation are mentioned, but not elaborated upon. Maintaining own religious media is felt to be important, whereas the communication specialists of UNDA/WACC caution against niche thinking. Another important issue is media education and media regulation for the sake of community, diversity, integration and democracy. Comunication should also have a curriculum of its own and be part of all fields of theology. Challenges and priorities differ according to the main focus of each statement. They vary from skills in personal communication, democratization and empowerment, pastoral planning, public presence and participation, grass root communication as a space for dialogue, communication justice and theological reflection. The need for a theology of communication is mentioned, however, without further explanation. The identification of the contribution to the survival of print media as a priority by the German churches is striking.

An inventory of the main problems in the statements refers to five related issues.

1. the outlook in media, communication context and culture
2. the outlook on the audience and related audience research concepts
3. communication models and theological presuppositions
4. ecclesiological identity
5. theory related to praxis.

A general underlying problem is the absence and inaccuracy in defining terms frequently used. Related problems include coherence in outlook, repetition, and the status, goal and addressees of statements. Repetition questions whether new media cultural developments and their impact are judged on their merits, and whether they are contextually applied.

An accurate understanding of the relationship between communication technology, media culture and religion is of vital importance and one of the major underlying problems in church documents.

With respect to the outlook on media, communication context, and culture, the emphasis on media power and effects is problematic, resulting in instrumental and traditional concepts of media use and a contradiction to the recognition of media being cultural transformers. It is striking that barely any media theory is given to ground views and positions taken.

A second related problem involves new media developments, patterns of information traffic, and the concept of interactivity. The question rises whether an instrumental, moral and institutional preoccupation hinders an adequate outlook about the way media and communication context are developing, resulting in moral and ethical claims to media, the emphasis of media education and stands regarding media regulation. The vital contribution that could be made by churches to initiate and be part of societal debate on the development of the information society, when letting go of inner ecclesial survival and power strategies, is not fully acknowledged. Patterns of information traffic are not distinguished, nor pursued in their implications. This results in non-adequate typologies of the audience that can no longer be based on center-peripheral forms of communication. The uncritical muddling up of terminologies like communication, proclamation etc. are problematic, as well as the inclusion of new media in the same outlooks and policies that are held with regard to traditional media.

This also applies to interactivity which is focused on internal networking and reaching the young and traditional church functions and information. With respect to the social cultural role of media and its religious implications, we may identify problems as well. The focus on sociability and disintegration brings up the position of the church itself within the social cultural realm. The churches' attitude towards and relationship with rationalist knowledge, capitalist production, technology, bureaucratic governance, the state, democracy and non territorial communities, for example, is to be questioned, and no longer holds true in an era of globalization.

The outlook on the religious implications allows for contradictions. Definitions about religion, spirituality, secularization, meaning, tradition, truth, church etc. appear to be self evident, which they no longer are. This questions whether the profoundness of the religious implications is acknowledged and accounted for. They force the church to rethink its identity, societal position, the meaning of faith, tradition, concepts of rationality and the incorporation of a concept of interactivity, etc., as does the media use by people as part of their symbolic social interaction and religious identity and expression. It is also vital to rethink ethical challenges in an era in which communication is problematic and processes of 'othering', religious fundamentalism and hatred is increasing.

With respect to the outlook on the audience and audience research concepts, one of the main problems is that 'the audience'', based on historical mass typologies, is taken for granted. References are undefined and sometimes contradictory. Views of the audience are not included and the shift in patterns of information traffic are overlooked. This results in overlooking the need to differentiate audience concepts. Features of two main paradigms given in 3.3. are intermingled in the statements. They tend, however, to be closer to the (dominant) first, than the last position.

The problem of communication models grounded in theological presuppositions is that the latter are treated as autonomous categories, apart from any communication context or praxis. The theological models are not tested against communication or media studies, communication praxis, or audience use. This provides methodological problems. Different communication models each carry their own outlook on communication, on the role of the audience and on messages, and accentuate different positions in which they are related. Churches' clarification of their communication models, therefore, is of extreme importance. It will necessarily involve their societal position, their outlook on the audience and culture, their view of theology, tradition, scriptures, and communication scientific stands. Whether a communication theology is feasible or needed, is not an issue discussed in the documents.

Regarding ecclesiological identity, the positions differ accordingly to denominations and, again, overlapping and sometimes contradictory positions, as well as the lack of definitions, aggravate clear cut generalizations. Identities appear to be non-problematic to themselves. This questions whether churches are aware of the crucial role and impact of changes in the structures of mediated communication. The social and cosmopological view which provided meaning to Christian words and rituals has disappeared. Moreover, different models of church result in different communication outlooks (and the other way around) and therefore are not 'merely' a choice of paradigm.

The last problem we identified is the problem of implementation and praxis. Communication and media issues neither have become an integral part of theological reflection.

In my paper, *Mainline Religion and Global Media Culture: Kairos or Curtain Line* (2004), I have argued: 'To what extent she [mainline religion] will be able to deal with the challenges of the digital media culture, will turn out to be the *kairos*[45] or the curtain line, for the public communication and presence of mainline Christianity'. Intrinsically related to society as God's world, not only the public presence of the Christian stories is at stake - so is our communicational environment.

---

[45] The Greek term *kairos* means not only the right place, the right time and a good opportunity, but also: the *critical* moment, referring to the urgent necessity of serious theological reflection on media culture. *Kairos* also has a connotation of the amazing and the unexpected, which may be the lead to openness in examining post-modern, digital media culture.

Four

The Art of Dialogue

How self-confident is that wisdom which perceives a closed compartment in things, reserved for the initiate and manipulated only with the key. O secrecy without a secret! O accumulation of information! It, always It!

Martin Buber[1]

Simon Blackburn, professor of philosophy at the University of Cambridge and guest of honor on the fifth *night of the philosophy* on the theme of *truth* in Amsterdam (April 8, 2006) told the following anecdote:
'A friend of mine went to a forum on ethics. In the panel representatives of all world religions were present. First a Buddhist told about illumination and ways to settle one's desires. 'Wow', the other panel members reacted, 'great, if this works for you that way, it's good'. Then the Hindu spoke on reincarnation. And all said: 'great, if this works for you that way, it's good'. It went on like this, as a priest came to speak about Jesus, redemption and eternal life. And again everybody said: 'great, if this works for you that way, it's good'. The priest however banged on the table, shouting: 'No, this is not about whether it works for me! It is the true word of the living God and if you don't believe in it, you will all be condemned to hell'. And all of them said: 'wow, great, if this works for you that way, that is good'[2].

This anecdote shortly summarizes what Underwood (2006:65) terms the 'Gordian knot - the tension between people with different views of absolute truth – that is at the core of many of our greatest political, social and international challenges'.

Hamelink (2002) argues that the debate, the predominant conversational form in the media, is inadequate to express reality. Dialogue is much more suitable. In our modern society, however, this appears to be a 'very difficult form of communication'. It takes more time, involves moments of silence, etc. Moreover, the partners involved really listen to one another and are prepared to suspend their judgments. Dialogue therefore, according to Hamelink, calls for communicative skills which must be learned and should be taught in all fields of education.

In this chapter the *art of dialogue* will be the central theme. Since dialogue may entail many different concepts, we will first clarify the perspective we would like to suggest related to (religious) communication.
We will then argue for public space as a condition *sine qua non* for dialogical communication. Media ethics and social responsibilities fit within this scope.
Subsequently, we will relate the art of dialogue to (respectively) media culture, the position of audiences, identity and theology. Thus we will refer to all preceding chapters, including our findings on the policy documents. In this way, we will be able to draw

---

[1] *I and Thou*, (1937: 5).
[2] Source: 'Zoeken naar waarheid en ware liefde' (searching for truth and true love') in *Trouw*, 10-04-2006, p. 6-7.

some final conclusions and recommendations with respect to the relationship between mainstream Christianity, communication and media culture.

The term 'final' used here does not imply definite claims. This is not to say that I will not take a stand on the issues discussed so far. I already did and will continue to do so. The methodology by which I come to a stand, however, on principle will be dialogic in nature. This chapter then in essence, will bear the hallmarks of a *dialogue interieur* that is aimed at arriving at the key questions. In doing so, I hope to invite the reader to take part in dialogue as well.

4.1   The concept of dialogue

Peters (1999:33-62) contrasts two basic concepts in communication theory -dialogue and dissemination- by comparing the communicative styles of Socrates and Jesus as described by their 'canonical disciples', Plato *(Phaedrus)* and the synoptic evangelists *(synoptic gospels according to Matthew, Mark, Luke and John)*.
'In staging a debate between the greatest proponent of dialogue, Socrates, and the most enduring voice for dissemination, Jesus, (sic) I aim to rediscover both the subtleties of what can count as dialogue and the blessedness of nondialogic forms, including dissemination' (1999:34-35).

In Peters' opinion dialogue is often 'uncritically celebrated'. 'Socrates' model of the proper and pathological forms of communication resounds to this day. We are still prone to think of true communication as personal, free, live, and interactive' (1999:50). 'Much of culture is not necessarily dyadic, mutual or interactive. Dialogue is only one communicative script among many. The lament over the end of conversation and the call for refreshed dialogue alike miss the virtues inherent in nonreciprocal forms of action and culture. Life with others is as often a ritual performance as a dialogue. Dialogue is a bad model for the variety of shrugs, grunts, and moans that people emit (among other signs and gestures) in face-to-face-settings. It is an even worse normative model for the extended, even distended, kinds of talk and discourse necessary in large-scale democracy. Much of culture consists of signs in general dispersion, and felicitous communication -in the sense of creating just community between two or more creatures- depends more basically on imagination, liberty and solidarity among the participants than on equal time in conversation' (1999:34).

With respect to this last argument, it might be questioned whether dialogue, in this way, appears to be minimized to more of a quantitative issue than a qualitative one?
Peters describes Socrates' ideal of communication as 'souls intertwined in reciprocity' (1999:43). Soul and word are to be matched, implying selection of the (elite) receiver and disapproval of dissemination. According to Peters, even mass communication to Socrates is 'a dialogue writ large: no stray messages, furtive listeners, or unintended effects are allowed' (1999:46). This is also the reason why Socrates objects to writing. Audience and speech must be closely correlated. Socrates, 'almost thinks in the demographic terms of modern media marketing' (1999:45/46).

Whereas Socrates favors dialogue, according to Peters, Jesus favors dissemination.
Based on a different view of love (*agape* instead of *eros*), of communication (dissemination instead of dialogue) and of reciprocity (undifferentiated scattering as opposed to tight coupling), Peters opposes the communication of Jesus as described in the Synoptic Gospels of Matthew, Mark and Luke to the one favored by Socrates in the Phaedrus.

Peters' argumentation is based mainly on the parables[3] - especially the parable of the sower (Matthew 13, Mark 4, and Luke 8), the 'parable about parables'. 'It is a parable about the diversity of audience interpretations in settings that lack direct interaction (…) the parable of the sower celebrates broadcasting as an equitable mode of communication that leaves the harvest of meaning to the will and capacity of the recipient (1999:51/52).

Summarizing the differences as signaled by Peters, Socrates holds a private and esoteric mode of communication that includes a reciprocal relationship in the intimate setting of dialectic. Love, or *eros*, is attracted by beauty, type of soul and longing for oneness.
In opposition, Jesus' communication is radically public, exoteric, and includes the dispersing of meanings and asymmetrical relationships. Love or *agape* is attracted by need and compassion for otherness. 'Love is supposed to be universal and indifferent to personalities. *Agape* – or Christian love – is supposed to be mass communicated' (1999:56).

In search of forms of communication most fit for democratic polity and ethical life, Peters prefers 'loosely coupled dissemination over tightly coupled dialogue' (1999:35). However, he recognizes both dissemination and dialogue cannot do completely without one another (dissemination without dialogue can become scattered, dialogue without dissemination can become tyranny). Nevertheless, according to his opinion, the motto of communication theory ought to be: 'Dialogue with the self, dissemination with the other' (1999:57).

The 'Christian doctrine of communication', says Peters, is a 'doctrine of broadcasting'. 'There is, in sum, no indignity or paradox in one-way-communication. The marriage of true minds via dialogue is not the only option; in fact, lofty expectations about communication may blind us to the more subtle splendors of dissemination or suspended dialogue' (1999:62).

However thought provoking this volume, -both on theological as communication theoretical grounds-, this chapter on dialogue and dissemination raises questions.
It is said that the Synoptic Gospels evaluate dissemination quite positively, based on a different vision of love and communication. And that Jesus is the 'most enduring voice for dissemination'. If we take biblical theology as point of departure, it is, however, not that clear which view of communication is favored. Next to the parables (which are not always directed to the public at large, nor restricted to the communicative conduct of dissemination), the gospels tell various stories which can be characterized as dialogues. Examples are to be found in the healings -of the one possessed, the daughter of Jairus, (Mark 5, Luke 8), the Syrophenician woman and the deaf-mute (Marc 7), the blind of Bethsaida (Marc 8)- in the dialogue with the rich young man and the healing of Bartimeus (Marc 10, Luke 18) in the story of the twelve year old Jesus in the temple (Luke 2), in the the healing of the leper and the paralytic (Luke 5), in the story of Jesus anointed by the sinner (Luke 7), the confession of Peter (Luke 9), the visit with Zacheus (Luke 19) the story of the men on the road to Emmaus, the dialogue with the Samaritan woman at the well (John 4), with the adulteress (John 8) and the Canaanite woman (Matthew 15) etc.

---

[3] The word *parable* stems from the Greek *paraballein* which means: *parabole*. Next to the parable of the sower, Peters points to the parable of the laborers (Matthew 20) and the three parables on the lost coin, the lost sheep, and the lost son (Luke 15) in order to base the issue of the suspension of reciprocity.

The parables are part of the New Testament, which also includes other volumes, based on other forms of communication, like the letters of Paul, the Acts and the Revelation of John. Moreover, they originated and are embedded in a *liturgical* tradition of the early congregations. Likewise is the larger part of the First (Old) Testament, embedded in the liturgical tradition of the emerging Synagogue

But probably the main objective, next to the fact that Peters' view is based on only a few of the parables singled out of their context, is that the New Testament cannot be detached from the first, Jewish, Testament. Jesus was a Jew, who lived in the Jewish tradition that was based on Jewish Scriptures. The Old Testament shows a variety of conducts of communication varying from stories, drama, ethics and law, prophetical texts, to proverbs, personal wisdom, poetry, songs of lamentation, psalms and even direct dialogue with God (for example Abraham, Mozes, Job etc.). It can be argued that Hebrew tradition, (as is shown even by the gospels, since they cannot be understood without the Old testament) is at least a tradition as much of dialogue as of dissemination. Searching together for religious wisdom and interpretation is an important feature of Judaism. Theological study groups, (the Jewish *leerhuis*), up until today, are a main form of teaching and learning in which dialoguing is predominant.

Peters argues felicitous communication, meaning: creating just community, depends more basically on imagination, liberty and solidarity (1999:34). Obviously he finds these conditions better guaranteed in Jesus' dissemination than in Socrates' dialogue.

This raises problems of both theological and communication theoretical nature. It might be questioned whether dissemination truly is a better guarantee for imagination, liberty and solidarity. This brings to the fore the crucial underlying issue of what is exactly meant by Peters by *dialogue* and by *dissemination*. If dissemination means free accessibility for all through dispersion, indifferent to equal relationship, and dialogue is for the happy few, reciprocal, dialectic, excluding liberty and real solidarity - both meanings appear to include features of a *contradictio in terminis*.
On the subject of free accessibility within dissemination, it might be asked: to what and on who's terms? A message that is determined by the sender? Then why would Jesus allow himself to be persuaded by the Canaanite and Syrofenician woman even in such a way that this might be looked upon as a conversion and turning point towards his own mission? Dissemination can also be free of commitment. Moreover, it is questionable from a biblical theological point of view whether Jesus (and God) is indifferent to equal relationship. It might be argued that in the creative action of God (man created in His image) and in Jesus' term 'Son of man' when designating himself, the divine relationship with man contends both features of symmetry and asymmetry rather than God and humanity as 'radically asymmetrical', as Peters states. Other examples given by him include Christ and the leper and the Samaritan and the wounded man (1999:61), in which, we however on exegetical grounds can not discover any assymetry.

One final theological point concerns Peters' statement that Platonic *eros* passes through the particular to arrive to the general, whereas Christian *agape* passes through the general to the particular (sic) (1999:61). In biblical theology it is the other way around: the love from God passes through his people and his son towards the *koinonia* - the whole living world. God's love for and meaning with man and creation is exampled in his very close relationship with *the one* (his people, his son), but not exclusively bound to them. In and through this one it extends to all, as the dialogue with the Canaanite woman shows. This is the *pars-pro-toto* principle of the Bible[4].

---

[4] See, for example the work of Miskotte, Breukelman, Deurloo, ter Schegget and Zuurmond.

The communication theoretical drawback in Peters' argument about the Christian doctrine of broadcasting and non-paradoxy of one way communication is in his assumptions attributed to its model. One way communication, by definition, is sender based. Peters, however, refers to Socrates' dialogue as 'sender oriented' in contrast to Jesus' 'receiver-oriented model' (1999:35). In section 3.3.5 and 3.4.3 we showed that the choice of a communication model implies views about the audience, message and identity. The attribution of dissemination to Jesus' communication then has consequences. These consequences, on theological grounds, cannot be held.

It is questionable, therefore, whether both Jesus as well as Socrates are given their due in Peters' view of their communicative conduct. Forrester (1993: 67-78), arrives at a very different conclusion: 'Kierkegaard found key, and very similar, clues to the proper relationship of truth and communication in the lives of Socrates and Jesus. Socrates attacked the sophists, and Jesus attacked the Pharisees, in both cases objecting to a radically distorted understanding of the relation of truth, the message, and communication, the medium. The sophists, according to Socrates, regarded themselves as free to manipulate the message, so as to their own objectives and goals. It was something they could manipulate and possess, apportion, sell or use to get their own way. The teacher, the communicator, conveyed information to the recipient. Socrates and Jesus, on the other hand, believed in dialogue, in probing and searching together for the truth. For Socrates, any attempt at manipulation, or foreclosing the discussion, or determining its conclusion in advance, destroys authentic dialogue. Truth cannot be imposed by power; it must be freely sought and freely appropriated. Socrates taught and practiced a self-involving, probing and practically orientated kind of dialogue which always involved respect for the participants as people. (...) Both men encouraged people to probe, to question, to enter into open dialogue. And this in itself was seen as a direct threat to existing powers. Power, Kierkegaard suggests, always seeks to control communication and regards, open, dialogical communication as a threat' (1993:70-71).

Jesus conversations with the Pharisees, the rich young man, to mention but a few examples, confirm this image of dialogical conduct.

It is necessary, therefore, to take a closer look at the concept of dialogue. In search of a grounding theory of what we provisionally will term *relational communication*, we will draw on the work of the Jewish philosopher of religion Martin Buber (1878-1965). In his famous work, *Ich und Du (1923)* - translated in English *I and Thou* in 1937, he develops a dialogical principle as an ontological category[5]. In doing so we hope to overcome the, in our opinion unfruitful discussion on dialogue *or* dissemination.

'Primary words do not signify things, but they intimate relations' (Buber:1958[6]:3).
This is probably the shortest summary given by Buber himself of his dialogical concept.
He distinguishes two primary words, which are always combinations, never isolated words. *I-Thou* and *I-It (*the it can also be replaced by he or she). There is no *I* in itself. It either refers to Thou or *It*.

The basis of the realm of It is different from the realm of Thou, which establishes the world of relation.
'If I face a human being as my *Thou*, and say the primary word *I-Thou* to him, he is not a thing among things, and does not consist of things. Thus human being is not *He* or *She*,

---

[5] In his later work *Between Man and Man* (1929 in German - translated in English in 1947), Buber illustrates his basic concept as developed in *I and Thou*.
[6] The edition referred to is the second edition that was published in 1958.

bounded from every other *He* and *She*, a specific point in space and time within the net of the world; nor is he a nature able to be experienced and described, a loose bundle of named qualities. But with no neighbor, and whole in himself, he is *Thou* and fills the heavens. This does not mean that nothing exists except himself. But all else lives in *his* light. (...) I do not experience the man to whom I say *Thou*. But I take my stand in relation to him, in the sanctity of the primary word. Only when I step out of it do I experience him once more. In the act of experience *Thou* is far away' (ibidem, 1958:8,9).

I-Thou, says Buber, can only be spoken with the whole being. Something which *I-It*, never can.
'The *Thou* meets me through grace - it is not found by seeking. But my speaking of the primary word to it is an act of my being, is indeed *the* act of my being. The *Thou* meets me. But I step into direct relation with it. (...) The primary word I-Thou can be spoken only with the whole being. Concentration and fusion into the whole being can never take place through my agency, nor can it ever take place without me. I become through my relation to the *Thou*; as I become *I*, I say *Thou*. All real living is meeting' (ibidem, 1958:11).

The relation to the Thou is a direct one. No system of ideas, foreknowledge, aim or anticipation intervenes. Thou appears in its relation of mutual and simultaneous action with the I. It cannot be grasped in space nor time, neither can it be defined but by the intensity of what happens in the relation.

This relational aspect cannot be extracted from its social dimension. Buber, in this respect, distinguishes between a world that is ordered and the world-order.
'There are moments of silent depth in which you look on the world-order fully present. Then in its very flight the note will be heard; but the ordered world is its indistinguishable score. These moments are immortal, and most transitory of all; no content may be secured from them, but their power invades creation and the knowledge of man, beams of their power stream into the ordered world and dissolve it again and again' (ibidem, 1958:31).

Spirit is thus defined by Buber as that which is between the *I* and *Thou*. Entering with one's whole being into relation is living in the spirit. Every particular *Thou* is then 'a glimpse through to the eternal *Thou*' (ibidem, 1958:75). In this sense, God -says Buber- is the 'wholly Other' but also the 'wholly Same', who 'properly may only be addressed, not expressed'.
To Buber there is 'divine meaning' in the life of the world and man. 'He who truly goes out to meet the world goes out also to God' (ibidem, 1958:95). 'But again and again, man brings about, instead of realization, a reflexion to Him who reveals: he wishes to concern himself with God instead of with the world. Only, in such a reflexion, he is no longer confronted by a *Thou*, he can do nothing but establish an It-God in the realm of things, believe that he knows of God as of an *It*, and so speak about Him' (ibidem, 1958:115). Structures of communal life 'draw their living quality from the riches of the power to enter into relation' (ibidem, 1958:49).

In the history of the individual and of humanity, however, Buber observes a 'progressive augmentation of the world of it' (ibidem 1958:37). The development of experiencing and using (making spirit into a means of personal enjoyment) is due to the decrease of power to enter into relationship. This undermines, in Buber's words, 'solidarity of connexion'. In this respect, Buber differentiates between person and individual. The latter differentiates himself from others, and thus from his true being. The former, by sharing in relational events, becomes aware of his being. However, Buber underlines there are not 'two kinds of man, but two poles of humanity'. Everybody lives in this 'twofold I' (ibidem 1958:65). But the stronger the I of the *I-Thou* in the twofold I, the more personal one is.

Interestingly, Buber gives three illustrations of 'lively and impressive' *I's* bound up in relation. The first is Socrates: 'This I lived continually in the relation with man which is bodied forth in dialogue' (...) 'went out to meet them' (...) and 'took its stand with them in reality' (ibidem, 1958:66).
The second is Goethe: 'The *I* of the pure intercourse with nature'. The third one is the *I* by Jesus[7], the '*I* of unconditional relation', who 'calls his *Thou* Father'. 'If separation ever touches him, his solidarity of relation is the greater; he speaks to others only out of this solidarity' (Ibidem, 1958:66, 67).

Summarizing, the need for dialogue is fundamental to identity, social life and humanity for Buber. It is *Thou* which makes me to an *I*, a person able to relate to the other in connected solidarity, and therefore related to the Eternal.
Dialogue, to him, is being in a living mutual relation with another. *Genuine dialogue*, therefore, is not identical to conversation or debate, as he explains in *Between Man and Man* (1947). Neither is it a privilege for 'spiritual' people, as some kind of spiritual luxury, or an intellectual activity like dialectic or discourse (argue). The aim of the debate is to make a direct hit. The one spoken to is not regarded present as a person. In a conversation (a chat or a talk) the aim is not communication or connection, nor to learn from or influence someone, but confirming one's own self reliance (1947:37,38).

Genuine dialogue is related to genuine community by Buber, which is neither individualism, nor collectivism. 'The individual is a fact of existence in so far as he steps into a living relation with other individuals. The aggregate is a fact of existence in so far as it is built up of living units of relation. The fundamental fact of human existence is man with man (...) It is rooted in one being turning to another as another, as this particular other being, in order to communicate with it in a sphere which is common to them but which reaches out beyond the special sphere of each (...) This is the sphere of 'between'. (ibidem, 1947:244).

We would like to suggest this perspective of dialogue (both as term and process) as an adequate point of departure with respect to (religious) communication. It means another person is respected as a subject in his or her own right and not to be made into an object, as a 'target' of communication[8]. This includes taking one's communication rights

---

[7] A similar argument is given by Kierkegaard in *Training in Christianity* as shown by Forrester 1993. 'Kierkegaard found key, and very similar, clues to the proper relationship of truth and communication in the lives of Socrates and Jesus. Socrates attacked the sophists, and Jesus attacked the Pharisees, in both cases objecting to a radically distorted understanding of the relation of truth, the message, and communication, the medium'. Forrester, Duncan B. 1993. 'The media and theology: some reflections' in Arthur, Chris 1993 *Religion and the media*. Cardiff, University of Wales Press.
[8] Dialogue stems from two Greek words: *dia*, meaning 'between' or 'through' and *logos* which means 'word'. *Dialogos* thus refers to: 'in consultation' 'by mutual word'. It is a prominent word in the Bible. In Genesis as well as in the Gospel according to John it is used in the first sentences. 'And God said, let there be light: and there was light' (Genesis 1:3, King James version) and 'In the beginning was the Word, and the Word was with God, and the Word was God' (The Gospel according to John 1:1, King James version).
The Greek term *logos* is related to the Hebrew *dabar*, which is best to be translated by *word-and-act-in-one* (God said an it was). Interestingly, Buber and Rosenzweig, in their German translation of the *Thora* (the five books of Moses) use the German word *Treu*, which means as much as loyalty, fidelity. It stems from the Hebrew *emeth*.

seriously. Communication rights cannot be exercised without the existence of a public sphere. The latter is a prerequisite for deliberative and dialogical communication, and is strongly related to media ethics. We therefore will first discuss those issues -in the next section- before relating the concept of dialogue to media culture, the audience, identity and theology.

4.2   Public space: a condition sine qua non

When arguing for other forms of communication, such as dialogue, public space is a prerequisite. It is also one of the pillars of democracy. Public space grounds the freedom of democratic rights, among which communication rights, such as the right to be properly informed and the freedom of speech. Especially when it comes to matters of public interest, the right to be properly informed is the normative basic principle. This principle cannot be adhered to without the existence of public space.

Public broadcasting is a very important ingredient of public space. Specifically with respect to the right of being properly informed -which the European court by jurisprudence has acknowledged- free press and public broadcasting are crucial. Being properly informed intrinsically implies plurality and the existence of a variety of channels. They are a precondition for dialogue as well. Public broadcasting has been the only public mass medium that has never been commercialized. If, however, the public space, the *agora* -by privatization- is turned into a shopping mall, a *market*, it is in danger. Moreover, genuine public communication runs the risk of becoming obstructed. Consequently, public dialogue is impacted as well. Dialogue needs space -to go into issues in depth- and is based on thrust, not on (central) control.

One of the most prominent authors on the issue of the 'representative public sphere' is Jürgen Habermas[9]. His main point, with respect to the transformation of the public sphere into 'representative publicity' that is exercised by economic and political powers. Scientific and administrative 'rationalization', ideologically legitimated, absorb public life - including free communication. This impacts the sense of community and obstructs communication in the public sphere (issues of legitimacy, for example, are not raised). Consequently, the emancipation and social integration of society are likewise blocked.

Van den Heuvel (1999:2) points to contemporary 'far-reaching marketability' of the public domain. By public domain, he refers to 'that societal space in which authorities and organized civilians give shape to our society, in which culture takes its shape, in which the public debate on the quality of life takes place, where people confess their faith, gain their education and put on trial their interests to one another'. Marketability refers to the 'dominant role of the economy, next to and sometimes exceeding governmental authority' (ibidem). The public domain, partly due to economical globalization, has become 'one large market'. Media, once the contributors to the origin and development of the public domain, are deeply involved in this process. The informational and technological developments even boosted the power of the commercial establishment. Alternative visions, turning clients into civilians again and consumers into electorate are marginal if not lacking, states Van den Heuvel. The public domain is seriously weakened. In his opinion the 'bargain market must become an *Agora* again' (ibidem: 7), through the restoration of the public domain.

---

[9] Habermas, Jürgen. 1989 1962. *The Structural Transformation of the Public Sphere: An Inquiry into a Category of Bourgeois Society*. Translation: by Thomas Burger of: 1962 *Strukturwandel der Öffentlichkeit*. Cambridge, Polity Press. Habermas, Jürgen. 1984, 1987. *The Theory of Communicative Action*. Volume one and two. Boston, Beacon Press. Translation of 1981 *Theorie des Kommunikativen Handelns*, Frankfurt am Main.

One of the central questions in our mediatized, visualized society, thus, is whether and what role media (can) play in this respect?

Bauman (2000) -regarding the same question with a specific focus on politics- appears to be rather pessimistic. Television, according to his opinion, blends in perfectly with the attitudes and skills of what George Steiner has termed 'casino-culture'. By this he refers to the demand for cultural products to be sharp, shocking, obsolescent and of maximum impact, in order to be noticed. This instant and episodic casino culture bodes the end of 'politics as we know it'. In this respect, television, according to Bauman, assisted a cultural revolution. The line between private and public has blurred; a language has developed which allows the public sharing and comparing of personal emotions (creating a public and a public space of its own); and, finally, talk shows refer to human life as an accumulation of individual problems to be solved by individual solutions. Societal problems are thus transformed in individual biographies, and the issue of what *good* society is, or is desired - is not considered anymore. This is devastating to politics, which, due to this development, is replaced by what Bauman terms *life-politics*. Life politics is focused on individuality and self referential; it therefore needs *idols*. Authenticity is 'not another form of morality, but a denial of the relevance of ethics. Morality is a feature of interpersonal relations, not of the person's relation to oneself: stretching oneself towards the Other, 'being *for*' the Other and endowing the Other's needs with causal power over one's own endeavors is the constitutive trait of the moral self and moral conduct (…) (Bauman: 2000:11).

In line with this development of life politics, says Bauman, policy is substituted by a succession of (media) events and spectacles, turning citizens into a viewing public of short-lasting *peg communities* that are centered on common individual concerns instead of acting participants. It takes over the integrating function that politics used to have. Political institutions, like governments of nation states, calling for more flexibility and obedience to the mechanisms of the market, do not offer an alternative. They have not been able to keep up with economical globalization. Power in global space, which is economical, is uncontrolled and not institutionalized and far beyond the reach of politics remaining local and territorial. Asking what has to be done about the media, Bauman concludes, is 'asking what has to be done about the world in which they operate' (ibidem 200:12).

Katz (2000:8) shares Bauman's outlook, however his focus is on the relationship between media and national integration. To his opinion the nation state is a necessity for public broadcasting. By this he refers to: '(..) a media system (1) based on a society of shareholders – a citizenry that owns, and feels that it owns the system. It is (2) administered by a board of trusted, civic-minded, and creative people who protect it jealously against the infringements of government and commerce. It is (3) staffed by professionals whose motto is that the customer – that is, the citizen – is not always right, but needs to be well served. Its programming is guided (4) by criteria of quality and relevance, with an eye to the continuity of cultures of the nation and of the groups that constitute it, (5) by concern for diversity of expression – even competing news programs are thinkable, for example, and (6) by a commitment to broadcast news and public affairs in prime time. Its hallmark is (7) that the plurality of groups and interests that make up the society see and hear each other in the *same arena* – on matters of civics and of culture – along with the professional voices of broadcasters and experts. From which it follows (8) that it is viewed by everybody, more or less'.

It is questionable, however, whether Katz's focus, both against the background of new technological communication developments[10] as well as the unification process of Europe, is realistic or merely wishful thinking. Not only the plausibility of the 'restoration of the nation'[11] is questionable in this respect, but also the existence of a 'European public sphere', which is a prerequisite to discuss the position of (public) broadcasting anyway.

Hoffmann (2005), scrutinizing EU policy-making and case law in the realm of media and communications, argues the deregulation and liberalization of the media and telecommunications sectors caused a power shift in favor of the corporate interests that restricted the maneuverability for the nation state.

The crux of her thesis is that the democratic deficit of the EU and the political apathy of its citizens are due to three interrelated aspects: the lack of public deliberation, a deep detachment of European citizens from the EU decision making process and the absence of a European-wide public sphere[12].

At the base of such a public sphere enhancing public deliberation are mass mediated communication processes. Since mass media within the European sphere (pressurized by world wide trends as described in chapter one) have been valued merely in their economic opportunities and international competitiveness, and information has become a commodity, their potential for civil participation is superseded. Moreover, this policy has increasingly eroded the position of public broadcasting.

---

[10] Katz e.g. does not mention the possible integrating function in a nation by other media than public broadcasting. On May, 16, 2006 the Social and Cultural Planning Office of the Netherlands in co-production with the Rathenau Institute (an independent Dutch organization, which from a public perspective, researches issues at the interface of science, technology and society) and the Netherlands Organization for Scientific Research NWO presented *The Digital Generation* (Yearbook ICT and Society 2006). One of the striking conclusions of their research on the virtual world of young people is that the internet can be a uniting means between young of different ethnical backgrounds. Internet appeared to support integration. Foreign and native youth, discussing on internet-fora, gained more understanding for each other's point of view. This is at odds with current convictions of the internet promoting segregation, in which foreign young were assumed to merely meet at their own sites. Moroccan for a, for example, appeared to be a meeting place for both Moroccan and Dutch young, who were discussing opinions on homosexuality, religion and men-women relations, subjects they often cannot discuss with their parents.
Over 80% of the Turkish, Moroccan, Antillean and Surinamese youth on the internet communicate mainly with people of a different ethnical background. 10 to 20% remains in their own group; here community feelings will be strengthened since foreigners are excluded (both in native xenophobic fora as in foreign fora).
Another striking conclusion is that Antillean youth chat more than native youth and foreign girls surf the internet more than native girls. http://www.scp.nl/english/
http://www.rathenau.nl/showpage.asp?steID=2 (Both in English). Retrieved 16-05-2006. See also: de Haan, Jos en van 't Hof, Christine 2006. *Jaarboek ICT en samenleving De digitale Generatie.* Amsterdam, Boom.
[11] It might be even undesirable, historically seen, when related to communication. The positive assumption towards the nation-state (if we understand Katz well) in relation to broadcasting has historically proved to be a dangerous one and runs the risk of becoming related to forms of communication like propaganda – e.g. such as before and during World War II, with horrible outcomes.
[12] Drawing on Capella & Jamieson 1997, as cited in Bennet & Entmann (eds.) 2001 *Mediated Politics. Communication in the Future of Democracy* Cambridge University Press, the public sphere is described as 'any and all location, physical or virtual, where ideas and feelings relevant to politics are transmitted or exchanged openly'.

Due to these and technological developments, nation states that exceed national borders and national (outdated) media policies are not able to tackle the legislative and juridical issues involved. Media regulation has increasingly become a topic with an international dimension.

Hoffmann therefore underlines the extreme importance of supranational instruments for media policy. The core of the media policy, she advocates, is to be the democratizing potential of mass communication needs. This can only be fully reached by the protection and promotion of communicative spaces - both existing and new ones. Crucial, therefore, is the implementation of communication rights[13]. Only then can deliberation become a subject of all European citizens and meet their deliberative needs. Moreover, it is the only way to facilitate the emergence of a truly inclusive free European public sphere, which might help promote a common, civic, European identity, civil competence and solidarity, says Hoffmann.

'(...) the major challenge to the European project is posed by the lack of commonly shared ideas about what it means to be European that flow from a lack of democratic legitimacy and accountability of the European institutions. Those institutions are perceived as 'remote' from everyday life by its citizens, who feel inadequately informed about European issues and are generally rather uninvolved as mirrored in traditionally low turn outs for European elections. This apathy can only be tackled by facilitating broader citizen participation through the creation of a European-wide communicative space as the precondition for deliberative elements that can legitimately elevate democracy beyond the limits of the nation-state. The basis of such development must be created through the regulatory framework of the Union, ensuring the emergence of a public sphere, protecting the diversity of available communicative platforms and securing every citizen's free and equal participation in communication processes'. (Hoffmann: 2005:6).

Communication is understood by Hoffman not as 'transmission of information', but as a 'fundamentally identity-building process that has the power to shape common meanings between groups and individuals' (ibidem:45).

Therefore, communication rights, including the four key principles of freedom, inclusiveness, diversity and participation[14], are to be implemented at the heart of EU media regulation, constituting the foundation of the European public sphere. This also applies to freedom from interference with privacy. 'Once privacy rights are eroded, so are personal communicative freedoms and ultimately the public sphere will become the victim of (self-) censorship and distortion' (ibidem: 49).

Evaluating European media governance and human rights legislation and jurisdiction, Hoffmann pictures a complex jumble of institutions (European Union, Council of Europe, European Court of Justice, Court of Human Rights, the European Commission, the Council of Ministers, the European Parliament and the Committee of Independent Experts) with overlapping and sometimes contradictory competences. In the case of audiovisual policy - the main competence of the Directorate General for Education and Culture, six other directorates come in through responsibilities with respect to communication. Next to these there is the special committee from the European Parliament that has a portfolio on media and information. The decision making process, based on the principle of subsidiarity and including the nation-state level, is complex due

---

[13] By this Hoffman 2005:6 means human rights relating to communication. The normative framework in her analysis of EU policy-making and case law is the Universal Declaration of Human Rights (1948), 'being one of the key ethical cornerstones of European tradition' (European Convention on the Protection of Human Rights and Fundamental Freedoms 1950.

[14] Derived from the *Statement on Communication Rights*, presented by Hamelink, C.J. at the World Forum on Communication Rights, Geneva, 2003.

to 'the multi-layered structure of parallel governance processes'[15] (ibidem:51). With respect to human rights, the odd situation occurs that all member states signed the Council's Convention, except for.... The European Union itself (and thus is not legally bound by it).

Hoffmann correctly argues that communication rights, - access, deliberation and participation in the public sphere on a European level, can only be exercised by guaranteeing participation in the media system, -being the main agent of the public sphere-. 'A communicative platform must be provided for the non-commercial, state-independent exchange of opinions and ideas that can ideally claim to reflect the full range of plurality in a society. This can only be achieved through strong, protected public service media' (ibidem:62). She takes this a step further, however, by stating that 'In order to reach its citizens and involve them actively in deliberation on issues of public concern, however, the European Union must create a favourable regulatory environment in order to meet the basic conditions for an institutionalized public sphere' (ibidem:63).

Nevertheless, the market driven EU policy of liberalization and deregulation that pushes media, -even in a dual system- increasingly into a commercial direction is alarming with respect to the public sphere as well as the pubic service media and diversity.
The ample overview of EU initiatives and regulation and court decisions regarding those issues from 1982 - 2005, as given by Hoffmann, illustrates the failure to establish a public sphere on a European level while concurrently the public service paradigm drifted off the policy agenda. The interests of commercial broadcasters are even furthered by their opposition to public service funding appropriated to online services, web activities and the acquisition of sport rights as 'dishonest competition' that results in formal investigations by the EU Competition Commissioner. The already uncertain future of public service broadcasters is severed. Regarding the birth of a European public sphere, the baby is thrown out with the bathwater.
The situation with respect to communicative freedom rights is not issued by clearer rules and policy -as the extensive case law by the European Court of Human Rights, summarized by Hoffmann- shows. Included are freedom of expression, freedom of information and freedom from interference with private life. With respect to the latter in 2000 the EU-US 'Safe Harbour Arrangement' was agreed upon, and guaranteed that companies would be allowed to continue receiving data. In order to be granted this 'privilege', companies have to agree to privacy principles set by the US Department of Commerce and the Internal Market Directorate of the European Commission. In doing so, they meet 'adequate' privacy protection standards. 'While there are little enforcement or monitoring mechanisms and no individual right for EU citizens to appeal or to claim compensation for infringements, the European Union has trusted its citizens' privacy protection in the hands of a third country's commercial companies' promises' (ibidem: 126). In 2002 a new Directive on Privacy and Electronic Communications was adopted that allowed member states the retention of communication for the sake of 'national security' or the 'prevention, investigation and prosecution of criminal offences'.

Besides these measures at the European level, individual countries have also proposed regulation in the same direction. During the EU chairmanship of the UK in the second half of 2005, the British strongly pushed for data retention (both telephone and internet). The interception of communication between civilians and possible 'terrorists', as such, was not the issue; most EU countries shared the view of its necessity. The only

---

[15] Quoted from the concept of 'network-state' coined by Castells M. 2000. *The Information Age: Economy, Society and Culture. Volume III: End of Millennium*. Blackwell Publishing Ltd.

question to be answered was whether the measure would be given under the terms of enabling legislation or a directive[16].

Next to the political authorities, private interests also have considerable power in steering informational and related privacy matters. An example of this is the search engine Google. Dutch companies, using methods to make their homepage appear higher in the Google result list, were exposed. In no time sites were adjusted according to the wishes by Google, whereas national governments have a lot of trouble forcing companies to operate within the law. In this way Google can also privilege companies based on commercial grounds: the one who pays most will appear higher on the list of 'sponsored results' that precedes the list of hits. The European Union also fears Google since Google's hit list is so much oriented to American companies, that the danger of reduced accessibility to European information, is not unreal. But an even more important issue is that personal data are easy to retrieve. The German internet news site Cnet, reacting on a saying by Google's senior executive that his search engine 'can tell you more on yourself than you even know', 'googled' the senior executives name, retrieved his financial data and his private address and posted the information online. Upon which Google refused to talk to Cnet. Taking into account Google's standing as the main source on the web, this might be annoying for a news website, however, not insuperable. But, if we take this one step further, Google deciding to exclude Cnet from its hit list, this explicitly exhibits the already implicit power of Google to direct information supply, including personal data[17].

Hoffmann's final conclusion is that erosion of public service broadcasting and weakened fundamental communicative freedom rights, like freedom of expression and privacy and data protection, 'constitute a major threat to a viable public sphere and the firm implementation of human rights in general'. 'New ways will have to be found to balance different rights and freedoms under novel circumstances with specific attention to the preservation and enhancement of human rights, democracy and the rule of law in Europe'. (ibidem: 138). '(...) the most fundamental challenge is the protection of the PSB system' (...) 'Therefore, a pan-European public sphere firmly rooted in communication rights and the principles of participation, freedom, diversity and inclusion should become the focus of the policy agenda again' (ibidem 145).

There is a lot at stake, then, regarding public sphere, public broadcasting, communication rights and policies. There is even more to it than we discussed so far. We might broaden our scope to the future of communication in general and include the possibilities of the new technologies, such as disembodied communication, neural intelligent networks, or the humanization of robots.   Will, for example, the right to be properly informed, which was identified as the basic principle with respect to the public interest, be sufficient in the 'digital' future? What normative principles will be guiding? What will be their grounding base? What principles do we actually need in cyberspace? Who will decide on them? These are huge issues with far reaching consequences, for the character and the importance of dialogue, as well as far beyond. Many ethical, theological issues are involved, which questions the position and the contribution of churches in this respect.

---

[16] In the case of the latter, the EU parliament is allowed to participate in the decision making process. In the case of the former, even parliamentary participation is excluded. Governments, in this procedure, take decisions by mutual agreement as part of EU cooperation in the realm of police and justice.

[17] Source: 'Big Brother Google' in *Trouw*, 13-08-2005 p.17.

4.2.1   Social responsibility and media ethics

Placing the right focus on the policy agenda -whether national, European or international- however, is not merely a political affair, even though that is important. The future of our societies, mutually interlinked in so many ways with information and communication technologies, should be a broad concern. Citizens, scholars, people involved in communication, consumer's organizations, NGO's , one issue organizations, educational practitioners, grass roots organizations, human rights organizations, religious institutions, churches, etc. need to join forces in order to tackle the profound challenges.

Hamelink (1995, 1999, 2002) notes the moral challenges in what is popularly known as the 'information society'. This concept, however, is based on assumptions with a nearly mythical status in common parlance. Many of them are related to a misunderstanding of the relationship between technology, information, social processes and moral progress as one of direct impact and linearity. Accumulation of information would effect more knowledge, power, understanding, proper action and the prevention of conflict. This deterministic view veils key sociological questions of benefit, decision, participation and accountability. The same applies to the myth of the 'perfection' of innovations in ICTs leading humanity (or finally, humanoid robots) to a society beyond risks. Critical questions whether we want this development, how 'risk free' risk free actually is, or who is accountable in the end when things go wrong are covered up or simply do not emerge. The equation of technological innovation with moral progress leading to harmony and peace is neither under discussion. Stressing the term *information society* over and over again causes the urgent need for communication, in complex global societies, to disappear from view. The increase of information -to an extent that people are overwhelmed by it while others are deprived of information- and the decrease of capabilities to communicate with one another are inversely proportional.

'To solve the world's most pressing problems, people do not need more volumes of information and knowledge, they need to acquire the capacity to talk to each other across boundaries of culture, religion and language. Dialogue is absolutely essential and critical to the encounter between civilizations. Globalisation without dialogue becomes homogenization and hegemony. Localisation without dialogue becomes fragmentation and isolation. In both cases the sustainability of our common future is seriously at stake' (Hamelink 2002:42). Dialogue is not within easy reach and mass media's content such as 'babbling, hate speech, advertising blurbs, sound bites or polemical debate' is not particularly helpful, according to Hamelink. The first step to be taken is internal dialogue, including three difficult prerequisites: critically questioning one's own assumptions, suspending one's judgments and listening receptively and silently.

The last issue Hamelink brings up is the urgency to adopt a universal declaration on the right to communicate. Current human rights law, in this respect, is inadequate since it does not 'deal with communication as an interactive process'. The right to communicate includes information rights, cultural rights, and protection rights, rights for communities and participation rights[18].

---

[18] Examples of *information rights* given are: the right to freedom of thought, conscience and religion; the right to express opinions without interference by public or private parties, the right of people to be properly informed about and have access to matters of public interest, and the right to access public means of distributing information, ideas and opinions; *cultural rights* refer to, for example, the right to promote and preserve cultural diversity, the right to freely participate in the cultural life of one's community, the right to artistic, literary and academic creativity and independence, the right to use one's own language, the right of minorities and indigenous people

The challenges deduced by Hamelink (ibidem) are to (1) openly discuss the key sociological issues with respect to the information society; (2) identify a realistic view of the possibilities and importance of information and of (3) moral progress due to scientific and technological innovations, - inclusive of facing risks (4) realize the urgent need for 'communication societies' instead of 'information or knowledge societies'; the (5) learning of dialogue and the (6) adoption and codification by the international community of the human right to communicate.

The key issue, then, is how to arrive at genuine social dialogue and which media ethics of public communication are needed accordingly.

White (2003) states the paradigms of social responsibility and public service no longer provide an adequate foundation when it comes to normativeness of public communication. These paradigms, rooted in the libertarian tradition, which -since the printing press- has been the foundation of democratic communication and free flow of public opinion, are now outdated.
Instead, a 'communitarian' ethics emerges.

Several developments allow for this, according to White. Among them are the political independence of the new nations and the rise of a multicultural worldview; new public philosophies by scholars like Buber and Habermas; new community media and group communication aimed at 'conscious raising' such as the pedagogy of Paulo Freire; the development of movements on alternative communication and public journalism; and the increasing importance of normative theory (academic and professional).

Likewise, developments in communication studies made their contribution. The linear concept of communication with its focus on author and media/message was criticized in the mid 1970's and shifted the paradigm. White perceives the particular importance of three shifts:
'(1) The convergence model of communication, which owes much to social interaction approaches to social science. (2) The ritual, communion model of mass communication proposed by James Carey and the forum model put forward by Horace Newcomb. (3) The continued development of the critical-democratic approaches in communication theory with the emphasis on reception theory, audience reception networks, the new semiotic approaches to the complexity of the text, the importance of alternative construction of meaning of fan networks and other perspectives that have an origin in French and British Marxist cultural studies.
The critical tradition has also provided a foundation for developing qualitative methods of research which emphasise subjective meaning' (2003:289/290).

---

to education and to establish their own media; *protection rights* include, for example, the right to be protected against interference with their privacy by mass media or by public and private agencies involved with data collections, the protection of people's private communications, the right of protection against forms of communication that are discriminatory in terms of race, color, sex, language, religion or social origin, the right to be protected against misleading and distorted information, the right of protection against the systematic and intentional propagation of the belief that individuals and/or social groups deserve to be eliminated; *rights for communities* encompass the right of access to public communication, the right of recognition that knowledge resources are often a common good owned by a collective and the right of their protection against private appropriation by knowledge industries; *participation rights* vary from the right to acquire the skills necessary to participate fully in public communication to the right to people's participation in public decision making on the provision of information, the production of culture and knowledge, and the choice, development and application of communication technology.

The development of communitarian communication, says White, is part of a 'much broader trend toward a new foundation of civil society'. The active subject of human relations has become more prominent, whereas overarching ideologies and nationalism have fainted. Moreover, institutional volunteer-based organizations, including churches, have lost their appeal and appear to be unable to provide functional forms of social identity. Mobility, in this respect, is not merely a geographical notion, but also applies to social cultural areas including belief systems. Open, flexible communities (both geographically as well as virtual), easy to enter as well as to leave, are most easy to identify with, says White.

Communitarian ethics thus appears to provide a more adequate basis in contemporary society. However, communitarian ethics and community communication approaches are flawed by the fact that they do not tackle what White identifies as 'the major problem of the colonization of our human life' (ibidem: 291). By this he refers to the demands placed on human interaction by the productive system -that is centered on profit- and, to a large extent, by media.

On the neglected victims of the 'communication revolution' in Europe (women, minority racial and ethnic groups, elderly, the less educated and well to do), Van den Heuvel (1997), in his address to the executive and standing committee of WACC Europe, refers to the Hungarian economist Zsuzsa Ferge. She gave the 1996 *Joop den Uyl* lecture in Amsterdam about the impact of economic developments in Middle and Eastern Europe. 'Faith in the free market and especially in the holy notion of the need for ever increasing growth, she says, rips the social fabric of society, plays down the importance of solidarity, the cement of any human community, endangers peace and overburdens the national environment. She is afraid that the three historical allies for the preservation of community: the state, the civil society and the market are losing their mutual cohesion. 'The world as we know it is falling apart'. Her hopes are built (again!) on the strengthening of the civil society' (Van den Heuvel 1997:5).

Communication is a key concept in this reinforcement process. Trends in world communication (as identified in the first chapter) converge towards disempowerment. Communication, however, is capable of empowering people as well - despite its limits such as the lack of a global dimension and the danger to create new forms of dependency (Hamelink 1995:121-150). He includes various complementary approaches in this respect, at the regulatory level (legislation, self-regulation, access, the right of reply in mainstream media), at the educational level (critical awareness of the organization, functioning, and content analysis of media), at the level of alternative communication next to mainstream mass communication (forms, contents, structures, processes), at the level of access and participation (both in means, management and production), and, finally, at the technical assistance level (development of communication facilities).

Because of the limits and the shortcomings of the application of empowering strategies, however, Hamelink prefers an understanding of empowerment as 'self-empowerment' - despite of flaws such as financial sustainability or lack of infrastructures, as well-. In this strategy, people empower themselves through participation in their own (community) media and networks, that create a public sphere in 'cyber space'.

A matching paradigm for self-empowerment communication, says Hamelink, can either have the state or the market as its center. Its inspirational source is civil democracy. A notion of civil society[19] that is adherent to the nation-state is outdated. Solutions to global problems, as well as the future of the world society, are beyond its reach. The development of a global, civil society which 'should give the concern about the quality of the "secondary environment" priority on its agenda' is needed (ibidem, 1995:147). As it is also necessary to develop major, global, civil initiatives in the realm of world communication. An example of this is the *People's Communication Charter* (appendix four).

Next to communitarian and global ethics, Christians (2000, 2003) adds the concept of 'cross-cultural ethics'. Theoretical models, in his opinion, must be 'explicitly cross-cultural', in order for media ethics to 'respond to the simultaneous globalization of communication and the reaffirmation of local identities' (2000:3). The key challenge, he observes, is the substitution of the 'Eurocentric axis' of communication ethics by a comparative model. Crucial, in this respect, is the development of a 'believable concept of truth' since there are many complex and polemical debates in theoretical discourses about communication ethics. These debates, due to the input of social and feminist ethicists, for example, concern social ethics (holistic, gender inclusive and culturally constituted) that replace individualistic autonomy (based on canonical morality). Another issue centers on narrative ethics and the relationship between contextual values and normative guidelines. Two other topics of discussion involve the possibility and credibility of universals in cross cultural ethics and a legitimate version of distributive justice (now defined by terms of the private market instead of social needs). A final issue concerns the 'politics of recognition'. What is meant by this is whether democracies, based on equal representation for all, have to take account of and grant explicit recognition of cultural and social identities (race, gender, religion). This is not only vital with respect to the challenges of multiculturalism, but essential for the long term vitality of democracy, according to Christians.

The concept of truth is essential in a comparative ethical communication model. 'The central question as we develop a cross cultural ethics is whether scholars of communication and culture can recover the idea of truth. As the norm of healing is to medicine, justice to politics, and critical thinking to education, so truth telling is the occupational norm of the media professions. Without articulating a sophisticated notion of truth, any new model of comparative ethics will have an empty center' (ibidem: 2003:295).

Christians himself opts for a concept of 'truth as disclosure'. Interestingly, he considers a theological framework to be 'inescapable' for the development of this concept. 'In that sense, this essay on the state of communication ethics at present challenges philosophical and sociological perspectives to match theological ones on the question of truth. Clearly the theistic worldview represented here must meet the standard of religious diversity to be credible, as communication ethics becomes international in scope'[20] (ibidem: 295).

'Truth as disclosure' is an alternative to historical 'correspondence perspectives' of truth by both mainstream media and philosophies. Central in these views are objectivism, human rationality, neutrality and impartiality. These perspectives are increasingly

---

[19] By civil society, Hamelink refers to 'all social transactions in the public and private sphere that are not interfered with by the state'. Its defense is legally arranged for in, for example, civil rights and constitutions. Hamelink stresses it also needs protection against corporations controlling economies and global cultural production. 1995:146.

[20] Christians also presented a non-theological perspective of the concept of truth in 'Social Dialogue and Media Ethics' in *Ethical Perspectives* 7:2-3 (September 2000), pp. 182-93).

controversial and attacked, and Christians' plea is to relocate truth in the moral sphere. 'Truth is a problem of axiology rather than epistemology. With the dominant scheme no longer tenable, truth should become the province of communication ethicists who can reconstruct it as the news media's contribution to public discourse' (ibidem: 296).

The moral framework that grounds truth is expressed by Christians through the Hebrew *emeth* and the Greek *aletheia*. The former means trustworthy, genuine, authentic - the latter openness and disclosure. Truth has to do with essence - the heart of the matter[21]. Christians exemplifies such a non-correspondence view of truth as expressed by Augustine's[22] rhetorical theory. Knowledge or opinion are not central in rhetoric, but 'truth-producing'. '*Aletheia*, in Augustine, 'tends to be more relational than propositional, a dialogically, interpersonal, sacramental act rather than a statement... taking into account and being motivated by [the cardinal virtues] faith, hope and charity' (ibidem: 297)[23]. Truth as *aletheia* is related to moral discernment and is contrary to contemporary views of truth, which -instrumentally- look upon truth as facticity.

Related to the concepts of *emeth* and *aletheia*, the other theological root of truth that is given by Christians is creation. The created order founds the worldview of the Kingdom and structures all created existence[24]. It also affirms truth as knowable. It is not autonomous or abstract, nor is it about static qualities of objects, but about the human act of knowing. In that sense, it is inherently personal: knowing and acting accordingly. Thus Jesus can speak of 'doing or living the truth'. '*Aletheia* is not the correspondence of intellectual knowledge and facts. It must be done[25] (...) Truth as disclosure and authenticity is rooted in our creatureliness' (ibidem: 299). Its intrinsic universal value is derived from this being grounded in creational truth, or with the 'primal sacredness of life as a protonorm', (...) 'which establishes mutual respect as a basis for cross cultural collaboration in ethics' (Christians: 2000:2,3).

By personal, Christians does not refer to some kind of individuality, but to a 'deeply meaningful, even religious concern'. Truth is not to be separated from humanity as a whole. It is an integral part of human existence and social formation. In this sense it is an ontological category. 'Human existence is impossible without an overriding commitment to truth. As a primary agent of the lingual world in which we live, the news media[26] have

---

[21] This moral reading of truth has been reflected by many, as Christians shows, among whom Bonhoeffer, Kierkegaard, Buber, Levinas, Gandhi and Hammarskjöld can be counted. But it can also be found in Buddhism, the Talmud and the Truth and Reconciliation Commission in South Africa, for exaple.

[22] Before taking up his office as bishop of Hippo, Augustine (AD 354-430) was professor of rhetoric in Milan.

[23] Christians draws in this quote on Glenn Settle, 'Faith, Hope and Charity: Rhetoric as Aletheiac Act in *On Christian Doctrine, Journal of Communication and Religion* 17:2 (September 1994) p 49.

[24] In this respect, the first words of the creation story, In the beginning', deserve to be considered more closely. Many translations associate the word with a temporal connotation, as if it were some point in history to trace back to the 'origins' of the world. However, the Bible is not a history book, or a book about physics. The book of Genesis was written at the time the people of Israel were deported into Babylonian Exile and started reflecting on how it had come to this and on their existential roots. This is *after* the story of Exodus. In Hebrew it says: *Beresjiet*; in Greek: *En Arche*. Most intriguing is the translation into Latin by: *In principio*. This translation opens up the opportunity to understand the creation story as the fundamental *principle* of God regarding creation and humanity, which is to provide for a created order, which structures all existence. A space to live for the entire creation, under the protection of heaven, and room for humanity to blossom with mankind in relationship to God and his neighbour.

[25] Note, in this respect, the inherent relationship to the Hebrew word *dabar* that is prominent in the story of creation, as explained in footnote 7.

[26] Christians focus, for the sake of specificity, is on news. However, he explicitly includes communications institutions, technologies and practices 2003:295.

no choice but to honor this norm as obligatory for their mission and rationale' (ibidem 2003: 299).

Applied in media praxis, this means there is no need for objectivism and correspondence, but for 'precision in *aletheia*': getting to the heart of the matter. In terms of authenticity and disclosure, Christians suggests 'interpretive sufficiency'. 'Interpretive sufficiency seeks to open up public life in all its dynamic dimensions. Ethnographic accounts have the 'depth, detail, emotionality, nuance, and coherence' that permit 'a critical consciousness to be formed' by readers and viewers. Rather than reducing social issues to the financial and administrative problems defined by politicians, the news media disclose and lay open to enable people to judge authenticity themselves' (ibidem: 300). According to Christians, 'sensitised concepts', in this respect, are vital. They are integrating and give insights from within the data. They relate theory and praxis dialectically and not in a linear manner.

Truth understood in creational, cross-cultural terms then should be the 'media's defining feature', and the 'master principle of communications' (both as a scholarly field and professional practice), concludes Christians. It grounds the public resources for solidarity, social dialogue and peace. Recovering truth telling and developing credible general normative values for cross cultural, comparative communication ethics, however difficult to achieve, are a foundational task, that must be supported by many, including religious communities and institutions.

Concluding this paragraph about public space, social dialogue and media ethics, we will return to our findings in chapter one about the media context, and to the policy statements with respect to church involvement, and social and ethical responsibilities regarding media and communications (as summarized at the end of 3.3.8). This is a realm which is extensively covered in the documents. Nevertheless, it is also problematic in some ways as we discussed in section 3.4.

Relating these problems to the concept of dialogue, public sphere and media ethics, it may be concluded that they are even more pregnant. This raises critical questions, for example, what concept of dialogue is referred to by the church statements? Do they really understand and acknowledge the fundamental need and significance of dialogue to identity, social life and humanity? Regardless even of what the churches themselves understand to be their mission or their needs within the realm of communication?
Do they truly opt for dialogue, including its corresponding consequences? The constant mingling of views about communication and media (in general) with church communicational goals poses difficulties. They become evident in the unclear position with respect to the relationship between dialogue and dissemination.

A similar problem is to be identified in the social/ethical realm where engagement in communication issues for the sake of society and communication -in its own right- interferes with ecclesial communication. Responsibilities are recognized, but appear to be directed outward without becoming a real concern taken on in church praxis. The focus is on a moral evaluation of media and ICT developments, human dignity, access for all, -giving voice to the voiceless-, media education, pornography, diversity, etc. These are commendable issues, however, we rather opt for facilitating people to raise their own voice, rather than giving voice to the voiceless. But they end after being put on paper - as long as they are not incorporated within all church policies and, in this respect, also act as a force for internal transformation.

Moreover, an underlying profound mapping of both social and technological communication developments and processes in relation to one another -including a critical evaluation- is lacking. This means that the conditions for grounding vision, taking a stand, and action remain vacuous. Important issues, in this respect, are the gravity of erosion of the public space and the global commons as a public resource, as well as the issue of media regulation. Opinions expressed in the statements regarding these subjects might have been more helpful if they would have clarified these underlying processes, which remain out of sight in current frames and discourses.

Furthermore, they are often either formulated in terms of responsibilities by others or in terms of demands, which do not interfere with the ecclesial agenda. Properly grounded solutions or suggestions are not made, nor are there proposals for action.

It is to be questioned, in this respect, why broad ecumenical and (inter)religious cooperation, however mentioned, is not sought for. The same applies to concerted action with initiatives by (civil) organizations working towards similar options in the field of communication, ICT, communication rights and the development of the information society. An example of this is the incomprehensible absence by official representatives or delegations of the churches in the CRIS (Communication Rights in the Information Society)[27] campaign. To my knowledge, churches have neither officially joined initiatives like the People's Communication Charter.

One last issue is the lack of a paradigmatic account in the field of communication ethics. An elaborated, well grounded contribution to the development of an ethical framework is also not given. This is more surprising since Christians, who is a communication scholar, opts for a theologically founded paradigm, showing the importance of contributions that could be made by the churches (or religions).

But even when a theological paradigm would not be an option, it might still be questioned whether churches should prioritize communication issues for the sake of the sustainability of a common future for humanity. Given the complexity, radicalness and plurality of information and communication problems in global societies that impact nearly every other area of life, the answer should be yes. Commitment to the whole of creation and the dignity of every human being belongs to the essence of Christianity. Dialogical communication, which is a defining feature of personhood and the basis for relationships and community, does likewise. Of this dialogical communication, churches might become authentic and inspiring examples themselves, concurrently arriving more closely to their destination. Moreover, it is a prerequisite for their public communication in terms of credibility, ethics and community.

---

[27] The CRIS campaign was launched by the *Platform for Communication Rights,* a group of international media and communication NGO's (including WACC and Cameco) in November 2001. It's goal is to create a space for civil society organizations to reflect, act and network on the information society by raising awareness, stimulating debate, facilitating mobilization, sharing information and lobbying and advocacy. The campaign wants to help build an information society based on the right to communicate, principles of transparency, diversity, social and economic justice and equitable gender, cultural and regional perspectives. Themes and actions include: strengthening the public domain, ensuring affordable access and use of electronic networks, securing the global commons as a public resource, instituting democratic and transparent governance, tackling information surveillance and censorship and support community and people centered media. The CRIS Campaign wants to broaden the agenda of the UN World Summit on the Information Society (WSIS) that was held in Geneva in 2003 and in Tunis in 2005 and encourage the participation of civil society groups. Source: *Media Development*, Vol. XLX 4/2002. London, WACC. See also http://cris.comunica.org/ http://www.comunica.org/ , http://wsis.itu.int , http://sos.comunica.org/ and http://www.comunica.org/v21/ . On the issue of gender and media in relationship to the campaign see: www.genderwsis.org and 'Women reclaiming Media' special issue of *Media Development* no. 3, 2005.

4.3   The art of dialogue and media culture

In this section, the social cultural role of media, the religious dimensions of media culture, and the implications for mainstream Christianity, -as given in the first chapter- will be our point of departure[28]. This implies a certain outlook on media and culture.
If we recall the remarks on both in the policy statements, we might differentiate several positions. With respect to media and communication, these positions vary from instruments, neutral tools, amplifiers, or powerful effective forces to views which focus on media as societal fora and popular culture. Throughout history these attitudes have characterized ecclesiastical views on media, from writing and print to cyberspace[29].

Relating the articulated concept of dialogue to what we have identified as media culture (and the position of the audience and audience research), it is obvious that our outlook is not compatible with an instrumental, neutral or powerful effect stand. We also do not look upon media and popular media culture as by definition negative. However - continuous critical observation and evaluation remains a vital need, especially in the realm of global trends, public space, ethics and communication rights for all. But like it or not, media are a dominant factor in the cultural realm, the reconstitution processes of society, as well as in many peoples' lives - not only in terms of leisure, but also in terms of exploring and negotiating (religious) values, meaning and identity, and communication opportunities.
If we are to take people seriously as communication partners, as our concept of dialogue posits, this implies including their media use and use of popular culture, as well as being willing not only to listen to them, but also to be challenged in ecclesiastical communication, identity and being. Moreover, it implies empowering people in their communicational efforts and fully acknowledging their unconditional communication rights, in and outside the church.

Looking for a grounding theory with respect to media culture -as we did before in the realm of communication- we opt for a cultural perspective on media and religion[30] as a meaningful lead. Next to popular culture, this option facilitates the inclusion of two (in our opinion) main issues. One of them is the ecclesiastical (theological) notion of culture. This involves the outlook on the relationship between church and culture in general and engaging mass mediated culture, in particular. The other is the vital issue of cultural pluralism.

The diversity of Christian theological views of the relationship between church/religion and culture have been mainly influenced by both Niebuhr and Tillich[31].

---

[28] Although the communication with media culture cannot be treated apart from the position of the audience, for the sake of clarity we will relate our findings about audience reception in media studies -as given in chapter two- to the next section (4.4) which focuses on the art of dialogue and the audience. The issues discussed here cannot be separated from the outlook on church identity. For the same reasons, that will be our subject in section 4.5. This, in its turn, is related to theological issues, which we will turn to in 4.6.

[29] See for example Fiske (1989), Goethals (1989, 1996), Koole (1986, 1993), Carey 1989, Babin 1991, Gräb 2002, Horsfield 2003.

[30] As in line with the outlooks by Carey 1992 and Tanner 1997 and with the critical social cultural paradigm we identified in 2.4. that also includes issues of power and inequality and therefore also leaves room for the inclusion of ethical issues.

[31] Niebuhr, H. Richard. 1951. *Christ and Culture*. New York, Harper & Row.
Tillich , Paul. 1956. 'The Church and Contemporary Culture' in *World Christian Communication*, second quarter, 1956, pp. 41-43. Also available on www.religion-online.org (retrieved 13-9-2004). Ibidem 1964 *Theology of Culture*. New York, Oxford University Press. Ibidem, 1969. 'On the Idea of a Theology of Culture', in *What is Religion?*, James Luther Adams (ed.) New York: Harper & Row.

Niebuhr defines culture as the "artificial, secondary environment" that man superimposes on the natural. It comprises language, habits, ideas, beliefs, customs, social organization, inherited artifacts, technical processes, and values'[32]. Culture is equated with the 'world' and is to be judged by and distinguished from Christianity. He discerns five historical competing claims: 1. Christ against culture 2. Christ of culture 3. Christ above culture 4. Christ and culture in paradox and 5. Christ the transformer of culture.

Schreiter (1985), -more recently discussing similar issues- in his volume on local theologies related to cultural contexts, discerns three broad categories: *translation* models, *adaptation* models and *contextual* models. Each of them includes basic principles and methods -and weaknesses-. The translation model departs from church tradition and adapts it to a local cultural setting. Adaptation models take local culture and its tradition more seriously, while respecting the integrity of the apostolic tradition. Contextual models are closely related to adaptation models. However, there is a difference. Adaptation models remain focused on the 'received' faith, whereas contextual models acknowledge the cultural context as the locus where Christianity becomes rooted and starts to express itself. Contextual models thus depart from the needs of the people. When related to social factors, contextual models can be further distinguished into two approaches. *Ethnographic* approaches are concerned with identity -starting with the questions of the peoples themselves-, whereas *liberation* approaches concentrate on oppression and the need for social change. They depart from the lived experience of the people, amid oppression, struggle, violence and power. To Schreiter's opinion -in the long run- contextual models are the most important. He also includes the role of the community, which to him is a key source in the development of theology. He concludes that 'it takes the dynamic interaction of all three of these roots – gospel, church, culture– with all they entail about identity and change, to have the makings of local theology. Both living spirit and the network of traditions that make up living communities need to be taken into account' (Schreiter 1985:21). Schreiter's outlook thus appears to differ from Niebuhr's opinion and to come closer to Tillich's view.

Tillich's existential concept of religion 'being ultimately concerned about that which is and should be our ultimate concern' led him to a vision of a non dualistic relationship between religion and culture. Religion gives substance to culture, and culture is the sum of forms in which religion expresses its basic concern. All religious acts -which are not confined to organized religion, just as Christianity is not confined to the church- are culturally formed. Likewise, all cultural creations express the ultimate concern of their culture.

For Tillich, contemporary culture expressed the spirit of the industrial society. Led by methodological investigation and technical transformation (of both world and man), man not only becomes estranged from reality, but even disregards the estrangement process itself. Possessing and relying on his own creative power, he ignores destructive powers, structures and dangers in both personal and communal life. Education is merely an adjustment to the system of production and consumption that is built by man as a second nature. Science and technique, submitting space and time, are assumed to reunite mankind and bring peace and justice. Actually, however, man has become an

---

[32] Quoted from Menuge, Angus J.L. 1999. 'Niebuhr's Christ and Culture reexamined' in *Christ and Culture in Dialogue*. St. Louis, Concordia Publishing House. Retrieved from http://www.mtio.com/articles/bissar26.htm 03-06- 2006.

object in the universal reality that he created and in which there is no ultimate end nor escape. Meaninglessness, dehumanization, emptiness, estrangement, anxiety and despair are the consequences.

In Tillich's opinion, the churches dealt contradictory and inadequately in relating to this culture. Neither adjustment, nor withdrawal in tradition and the past offer a solution. Existentialism in his opinion, offers a lead. The church must actualize itself in cultural forms (language, religious art and 'the need for a symbol relating Christianity's ultimate message of Jesus as the Christ, and the human predicament as rediscovered in contemporaneous culture'). She must also influence contemporary culture. The function of the church is to answer man's existential questions.
'But it must understand that the average kind of preaching cannot reach the people of our time. They must feel that Christianity is not a set of doctrinal, or ritual, or moral laws. (...) They must feel, too, that the Christian symbols are not absurdities, unacceptable to the mind of our period, but that they point to what alone is of ultimate concern – the ground and meaning of our existence and of existence generally'[33].
Transforming or attacking the spirit of industrial society, says Tillich, is not an option. Cultures only change by their inner dynamics. Churches can, however, participate in those. And if they are to take the lead, they are always a cultural force beside others. Taking up their prophetic role, churches can reveal demonic structures whether in society or in the church itself. In order to do so, they must also listen to external prophetic voices (the 'latent church') that are critical of culture or of manifest churches. At the same time, it must also guard the 'right content of ultimate concern' in other movements in order to protect them from becoming demonic. 'Judging means to see both sides. The church judges culture, including its own forms of life. For its forms are created by culture, as it substances makes culture possible. The church and culture are within, not alongside each other. And the Kingdom of God includes both while transcending both'[34].

Tillich's existential outlook on religion and culture, in our opinion -and goal- offers a far more adequate lead than Niebuhr's. However, Tillich's views are based on a different historical period (modernity) featuring industrial society and lack an explicit consideration of the impact of media and mediation. Theological analysis often overviews mediation as a significant factor, as various authors have argued[35]. Reconceptualization, therefore, is needed in terms of contemporary computer mediated culture, in which the notions of modernity, nation and institutional religion are flawed.

Searching for grounding perspectives which do justice to both issues of digital, interactive culture and cultural pluralism, as well as the concept of dialogue, we will discuss three (in our opinion) helpful volumes in this respect, by Tanner (1997), Gräb (2002) and Vink (2004).

In *Theories of Culture, a New Agenda for Theology*, Tanner argues for an anthropological notion of culture. By making this notion explicit, she bares the unselfconscious use of it in theology. Furthermore, she argues an overall profit of a cultural approach towards topics in theology, especially after its postmodern modification in the 1970's and 80's.

---

[33] Tillich, Paul. 1956. 'The Church and Contemporary Culture' on www.religion-online.org p 4 (retrieved 13-9-2004).
[34] Tillich, Paul. 1956. 'The Church and Contemporary Culture' on www.religion-online.org p 5 (retrieved 13-9-2004).
[35] Among others Babin 1991 Schofield Clark (1997, 2004) Horsfield (1997, 2004) Lundby and Hoover 1997).

Historical notions of anthropological culture, in vogue since the 1920's, include many different, geographically-bound definitions. Its core hinges upon the idea of society as a human, plural construction. Cultural differences are not to be explained biologically or naturally, but are differences in customs, values, beliefs and individual principles of interpretation. They are sustained by repetition, habit and conditioned by concepts of a particular culture.

Culture eventually became the dominant paradigm within anthropology, at least until the 1960's. The modern meaning of culture, as reflected by Tanner, includes nine basic elements.

1.   Culture is a human universal
2.   The anthropological use highlights human diversity (cultures)
3.   Culture varies with a social group
4.   Culture with respect to a group is looked upon as an entire way of life (the total body of belief, behaviors, knowledge, sanctions, values and goals),
5.   Group specific cultures are associated with social consensus
6.   Culture constitutes or constructs human nature (and does not regulate or repress it)
7.   Cultures as human constructions are conventions (transmissible accumulations of the past)
8.   Cultures are contingent and
9.   Society shapes the character of its members (social determinism).

These basic elements privilege certain ways of analysis of culture, which -in their turn- further impact key features of the notion of the modern, anthropological idea of culture. The elements, for example, of a group's way of living are considered as a whole (holistic). Analysis is done in relation to social behaviors (of which culture is an ordering principle and direction for action). It integrates the interrelation of cultural elements and is related to the rest of culture (contextual focus). This implies disengagement of individual cultural specific standards. Finally, cultural context is understood synchronically, which also holds for cross cultural analysis. The anthropological notion of culture discourages ethnocentrism.

Tanner shows how the modern anthropological understanding of culture, also due to interdisciplinary input, becomes criticized. 'It seems less and less plausible to presume that cultures are self-contained and clearly bounded units, internally consistent and unified wholes of beliefs and values simply transmitted to every member of their respective groups as principles of social order. What we might call a postmodern stress on interactive process and negotiation, indeterminacy, fragmentation, conflict, and porosity replaces these aspects of the modern, post-1920s understanding of culture, or, more properly as we will see, forms a new basis for their reinterpretation' (Tanner: 1997:38).

The modern vision overlooks various aspects among which are historical processes (in which cultures emerge); social interactions and interrelations (overthrowing the assumed internal coherence and consistency); fragmentation and diversity (outdating the idea of consensus); socio-political variables (culture is not a principle of social order, but (re)created in social interactions of which it is a part); inherent contradictions, changes and conflicts (outdating assumed social stability since social interactions are never apart from cultural interpretations); the 'unification' of the world by means of electronic media and migration (outdating sharp boundaries and assumed homogeneity in self contained units).

'On a postmodern understanding, cultural elements may cross such boundaries without jeopardizing the distinctiveness of different cultures. What establishes the distinctive identities of cultures in that case is the way in which such common elements are used, how they are handled and transformed. The distinctiveness of cultural identity is therefore not a product of isolation; it is not a matter of a culture's being simply self-generated, pure and unmixed; it is not a matter of "us" vs. "them". Cultural identity becomes instead, a hybrid, relational affair, something that lives between as much as within cultures. What is important for cultural identity is the novel way cultural elements from elsewhere are now put to work, by means of such complex and ad hoc relational processes as resistance, appropriation, subversion, and compromise'[36] (ibidem: 1997: 57-58).

This understanding obviously disqualifies presuppositions about culture as made by Niebuhr. Nevertheless, as Tanner states, many theologians and churches still hold a modern, anthropological understanding of culture. As a duality of, one the one hand, 'the world' and, on the other, a historical particularity of Christianity itself[37]. An assumed commonality over time and place as 'some sort of social transmission of heritage, characteristic spiritual affinity, or ruled patterns of behavior' (ibidem 62) and with two poles to be correlated: the Christian pole and the pole of the human situation. Tanner argues that the anthropological notion of cultures, with its differences, is thereby not acknowledged. There is no culture 'in general' - as some sort of human universal.

In her opinion, theology is a culture-specific, contextual activity since the cultural context is the primary framework for interpretation. Moreover, the postmodern understanding of culture questions the idea of a given worldview as a vital feature of communal practice. 'For both religious and anthropological reasons it seems illegitimate for a theologian to give a Christian perspective on life the benefit of the doubt and simply work from there. Focusing exclusively in that way on a single, admittedly human tradition of religious discussion shows undue arrogance and threatens to make an absolute out of historically and culturally conditioned categories and concepts. Knowing that what Christians say about God cannot do full justice to the finally mysterious character of ultimate reality and knowing that Christianity is just one attempt among others to orient life, the theologian should resist the temptation to operate solely from within a Christian context and rise instead to a more expansive, holistic and global outlook' (ibidem: 68).

Tanner's outlook on theology is not one of an 'academic highly specialized intellectual activity' irrelevant to the concerns of most people, but of being embedded in the cultural context of daily life. That is: the meaning dimension of Christian praxis. This comes down to the removal of the distinction between high and low culture as described in chapter one. Theology becomes more of a continuum. This means specialized investigation that is organically connected to Christian practice as theological activity in its own right and with its own theoretical dimension. This disqualifies turning praxis into an object of study of specialized theology in which methodology is based on coherence and completeness. Praxis is not an already existing coherent whole; it is fragmentary and conflicting. Beliefs and values as part of social practices are pushed and pulled by situation specific forces. They are loosely defined, differently interpretable, and contextual.
Meaning is established by the context of usage. New practice, of symbols, therefore, always adds, alters or questions pre-established meanings. This is a continuous, kind of experimental process.

---

[36] We will elaborate upon this inter-relational notion of identity in section 4.5
[37] The notion of Christianity as a 'particular culture' or 'way of life' will be discussed in section 4.4 under the heading of the art of dialogue and identity.

To be relevant, the primary locus of beliefs, symbols and values in everyday Christian practice, in specialized, academic theology, must relate -somehow or another- to what Tanner terms 'everyday theology'[38]. That is: the theological questions that arise in everyday life (often in -however not restricted to- situations of conflict and crisis). 'Specialized theology cannot, however, realistically hope to influence everyday Christian life if it sticks simply to the values specific to its own field. It offers a way of life that is systematically principled and organized according to clear and logically consistent ideas. But to the extent that academic theology abides by values that make the specificities of audience and situation irrelevant, it is not clear how this offer meets the immediate needs of everyday practice. Because of its interest in generalities and in abstract claims with a multicontextual pertinence, its offer may not obviously speak to such situation-specific, practical needs at all –to the shock of world war or genocide, to emerging religious conflict, or attacks on the viability of Christian norms of neighbour-love that spring from economic or political developments' (ibidem: 84).

By necessity, this influence must be based on consent, because institutions, as well as specialized theology, lack both monopoly and authority on the theological activity of ordinary -and generally voluntarily active- Christians.   'From the very start, then, academic theology has to be engaged in negotiations with popular theologies. (…) it must attend to what people already think, meeting at least some of their theological concerns, talking in much the same terms, correcting popular theological opinion where necessary (…) In the process, academic theology will have to compete with theologies of everyday life in great part on those theologies' own terms. In this way, the practical requirements for an effective theology on the level of everyday life (…) become part of specialized theology's own field-specific norms' (ibidem 85-86).

A broad diversity of materials, thus, is available to theology in order to interpret: all beliefs and values in Christian social practice (e.g. in Scripture, ritual activity or other engagements), both contemporary and historical. Neither are they, as Tanner states, limited to 'explicit religious' ones. They include 'the meaning dimension of social practices that Christians pursue in virtue of their other social commitments' (ibidem: 87) as well as Christian practices themselves.

Tanners' theories of culture and cultural pluralism provide us with the first general grounding contours that correlate with our concept of dialogue, pluralism and the religious implications of and in media culture.

To further our line of thought, we will turn to Gräb's volume, *Sinn fürs Unendliche, Religion in der Mediengesellschaft*, [Sense for the Infinite, Religion in the media society] that -in line with Tanner's views- explicitly considers the issues of culture, pluralism, religion and (practical) theology within the context of media society.

Our world, says Gräb, stands in a related multiplicity of mediated meaning. All forms of communication are impacted by and linked up with mediated communication. Moreover, mass media have become a society defining system that determines the symbolic ordering of dealing with our self and the world. Media provide the symbolic representations of views of reality and orientations of values and meaning that constitute society and form the cognitive, moral and religious meaning of everyday life in the general symbolic sphere. Their stories and images stipulate socialization much more drastically than symbolic communication by churches, schools and academies. They are important factors of both religious-cultural pluralism and individualism.

---

[38] See e.g. Goizueta, Roberto S. 2004. 'Because God is Near, God is Real: Symbolic Realism in US Latino Popular Catholicism and Medieval Christianity'.

Religious pluralism, in Gräb's understanding, is not some sort of variety of churches or religions. Media themselves, in their stories, images, commercials, etc., arouse and carry people's longing for meaning, myths, spiritual dimensions, narratives and interpretations of life and self. In sum: for 'sense and taste for the infinite'. This religion in media society deeply challenges and goes to the heart of both churches and theology. It is not sufficient, for example, to simply adjust liturgical forms. 'Es ist das theologische *Verständnis für die Religion* als einer Weise unseres menschlichen Verhaltens zu einer transzendenten, letzten, ebenso abgründigen wie sinngewährenden Realität noch sehr viel stärker (wieder) zu entwickeln. Und es sind die zentralen *Inhalte des christlichen Glaubens* in ihre unter den Bedingungen der religionsproduktiven Mediengesellschaft kommunikable, symbolische Form zu bringen. Im Durchgang durch präzisere Wahrnehmungen der Mediengesellschaft geht es hier deshalb darum, den Weg einer kulturhermeneutisch verfahren >Praktischen Theologie gelebter Religion< weiter auszubauen' (Gräb:2002:14)[39].

Churches, according to Gräb, dramatically lose the power to represent and mediate the symbolic order, the structuring of meaning, the moral orientation, and the basic understanding of being in the everyday life of large 'masses'. Symbolic forms of meaning are manifold exactly due to the representation by media. People are subjects that build culture themselves in a lively process of appropriation of mediated symbolic worlds and forms of meaning[40]. Religious meaning, in this respect, is not outside this process. This leads Gräb to examine religious-cultural transformations (especially in the field of art and popular 'experience' culture) and to set out on the cultural- hermeneutic disclosure of media society. Symbolic representation is a vital issue in his argument. His point of departure is not the issue of how churches could 'use' media, to communicate the gospel as the 'glad tidings', but how they (and other forms of explicit religion) can also be religion-forming spaces of meaning in media society. Since people use media for religious meaning in daily life, this implies church communication, in and outside the media, must associate with the religious building potential of the media in order to be relevant to people.

In contemporary 'knowledge' 'risk', and 'media' society and 'experience' culture, according to Gräb, religion (and art) are indispensable factors. People mistrust the ability of politics to intervene in scientific and economic systems. The evolution of knowledge cannot provide meaning of life or narrations about its sense. Religion(s) can, if they are capable of gearing up for the spirit of the age, by esthetically staging their myths, stories and images of meaning, and by serving and orienting people's needs in this respect. This implies the exclusion of missionary intrusiveness and being ready to support people who are searching for ultimate meaning themselves.

---

[39] This special understanding of practical theology as theology for the praxis and its implications for all other theological fields will be discussed in section 4.6.

[40] Gräb (2002:164) explicitly notes the commonalities in the historical developments of media and religion. 'Schon die Durchsetzung der *Schriftmedien* entwertete den Opfer-Kult. Sie *spiritualisierten* die Religion. Die Durchsetzung der *Druckmedien* entwertete die Autorität der Schriftgelehrten, der Prediger und Theologen. Sie *demokratisierten* die Religion. Die Durchsetzung der elektronischen *AV-Medien* entwertete die öffentliche Darstellung und Kommunikation der Religion. Radio und Fernsehen *individualisierten* und *privatisierten* die Religion – gerade auch bei Übertragung von Gottesdiensten (...) Die neuen digitalen Medien schließlich, das Internet, entwerten die institutionalisierten Angebote für die individuelle und private Religionsausübung. Sie führen zur radikalen *Deregulierung* des religiösen Marktes. (...) die neuen interaktiven und digitalen Medien, die durch den Personal-Computer möglich wurden, bringen eine wiederum durch Medientechnik ausgelöste, entscheidende kulturelle Veränderung: Das Internet hebt Information, Kommunikation, und Interaktion auf eine globale Ebene. Es ersetzt das bisherige Sender-Empfänger-Schema durch dezentralisierte, prinzipiell reziproke, globale Kommunikationsbeziehungen'.

Gräb identifies a trend towards dogmatically unconditioned religiosity that is oriented to personal, biographical, ultimate meaning interests and needs. People no longer accept truth because the church says so. This means symbols and rituals from religious traditions must be arranged according to religiously relevant themes in people's lives instead of their traditional religious belonging.

Popular culture, in this respect, matters. Soaps, movies, popular literature and popular religious images, for example, engage issues of life and death, identity, guilt, health and sickness, fictional worlds, etc. amid everyday life.
'Wir müssen von einer gesellschaftlich durch die *Medien* vermittelten Pluralität, besser Gemengelage von symbolischen Lebensdeutungen sprechen, von einer sehr diffusen >Medienreligion<, von einer vieldeutigen Religiosität. Wir haben jedenfalls Veranlassung genug, uns die Zeitgenossen als Subjekte vorzustellen, die durch den Einfluß der Medien ihr Leben immer schon in Deutungszusammenhänge hineingestellt finden (...) (ibidem: 92-93).
In this scattered religious and cultural pluralism situation, religions, including Christianity and the churches, can no longer set the conditional terms for culture as way of life, or for societal functional systems. Now it is the other way around. Religions are judged on their significance and achievement for contemporary media culture in which they are present. Do they contribute to the meaning of life, tolerance of different cultures, and world peace? Whether or not churches are able to contribute to culture in this way, according to Gräb, is vital for their future capacity within modern society. Their opportunity is in attending to those potentials of their own tradition that allow themselves to be meaningfully inserted in the orientation needs of secular modern society. This will also help prevent fundamentalism and religious fanaticism.

Gräb discerns three crucial assignments for the churches' proclamation and religious education: 1) 'das religiöse Bewußtsein der Menschen pluralismusfähig' zu machen'
2) 'zu der Einsicht verhelfen dass wir, obwohl wir in einer Stadt der vielen Götter leben, gleichwohl eine säkulare Gesellschaft sind, in der nicht die Religionen , sondern die Wissenschaften, die Medien, das Recht Weltwissen vermitteln und die Gesellschaft zusammenhalten'
3) dazu positiv verhalten, dass es nicht so sehr die Religionen sind, auch nicht das kirchliche Christentum, sondern dass es die (Christentums-)Kultur ist, die Kunst und das Kino, wo die Menschen ebenfalls Sinn für ihr Leben finden' (ibidem: 97).

Concretely this means to stand by deepening the search for meaning of life and opening up the stories and language of the Christian tradition in their life orienting meaning, especially with respect to cultural and religious plurality and its related complexness and conflicts.
Moreover, in the increasing dynamics, acceleration and wane of media society, says Gräb, churches have nothing 'new'[41] and surprising to offer - no 'information value'. However, creativity in symbolic forms, as commercials show, can remind one of what is already known. The opportunities, then, are not in 'proclamation as information'. 'Verkündigung als Information, als Ausrichtung einer Botschaft ist der falsche Ansatz, wie überhaupt das Konzept von *Verkündigung* in der Mediengesellschaft nicht mehr greift' (ibidem: 172). It is important to open up the '*Sinn-Wahrheit*' that is preserved in the old tradition through changing times and to construct images in words, forms and

---

[41] One could argue that increasingly less people (especially young) 'know', for example, biblical stories. This is not a valid reason however, to disagree with Gräb's outlook on proclamation as invalid, since it does not match contemporary media culture, nor the trends in communication traffic patterns, nor the insights about the role of the audience., and the media use of young people.

colors that 'invite to sojourn, think thoroughly and feel deeply'. Churches, in this respect, could become places to 'slow-down', offering depth and profoundness and where the experience of time and place is disclosed[42]. Religious communication within the church must also symbolize the final horizons of existential orientation. Fundamentalism as some sort of 'contra' culture or world is also not an option. It would imply the loss of compatibility to societal consciousness, experiences and communication. Churches, in this respect, should not only focus on a meaning disclosing explanation of tradition, but also of contemporary cultural epoch. This involves a 'double hermeneutics' and thus the need of theology. Theology should consciously reflect on media society. 'Worum es gerade nicht gehen kann, das ist der zum Scheitern verurteilte Versuch, (...) an die Flut der Nachrichten auch noch die >Gute Nachricht< von Gott anzuhängen. In die vielen Geschichten vom Leben, die das Fernsehen erzählt, auch noch die Geschichte von Jesus einzubringen. Neben die verlockenden Botschaften der Werbung auch noch die Einladung in die Kirche zu plazieren.

Sehr viel eher ist es die *Aufgabe*, die explizit religiöser Kommunikation gestellt ist, die Wirklichkeit, die uns die Medien vermitteln, *aufzunehmen*, zu *transformieren*, zu *verfremden*, *kritisch* zu *reflektieren*, zu *interpretieren*, zu *deuten*, die Perspektive zu verschieben. Gefragt ist der *religiöse Kommentar zur Zeit* (...) durch Profilierung der *religiösen Deutungsperspektive*. Und das ist eine solche, die nicht mit neuen, sondern mit ganz alten, aber immer noch eindrücklichen *Geschichten* und immer noch nachdenkenswerten *Bildern* imponiert. (...) Die existentiellen Sinn-Fragen (...) können aufgenommen werden (ibidem: 174).

Entertainment, in this respect, fulfils a religious, societal function in providing symbolic and narrative elements of meaning for personal identity building, social competence, life design, recognition of (spiritual) experiences, coping with love, life and death. Media religion, then, is religion of individual self-interpretation and meaning, as Gräbs analysis of the movies *Titanic* (USA, 1997) and *Lola Rennt* (Germany, 1998) shows.

The same applies to the internet, which multiplies the opportunities to experiment with different identities and self interpretations. Institutional control and hierarchy are absent. What is meaningful is decided upon by communicating subjects themselves, who design identity and meaning constructions. For churches' praxis this means an intensified challenge. They have to reform from sender and offer oriented messages to question oriented ones. They can learn from the internet if they, according to Gräb, 'closely watch the religious-cultural markets in the net'; 'observe the needs of contemporary religious-ethical orientation' and if they 'perform the hermeneutics of privatised systems of interpretation' (ibidem: 241).

One of the vital assignments for the churches mentioned by Gräb is to capacitate people's religious consciousness for pluralism and the contribution by churches to tolerance and world peace. This implies tolerance towards the variety within Christianity itself -including media religion- and towards different cultures and religions. One of the main prerequisites to arrive at the latter (and the former, as we will see) is intercultural communication.

Vink (2004), in his volume *Grenzeloos communiceren, Een nieuwe benadering van interculturele communicatie* [*Communicating without Borders, a New Approach to*

---

[42] See, in this respect, the eloquent essay *Werelden van tijd* [Worlds of Time] by the Dutch philosopher and theologian Hans Achterhuis (2003). Achterhuis shows the connection between the process of globalization, which forces us to a continuous acceleration of life and the experience of (life) time.

Intercultural Communication][43], develops a new theory in this respect and disqualifies outdated presuppositions and paradigm's.

Prevailing (Dutch) explanatory models about intercultural communication are methodologically based on comparing national cultures. The concept of national cultures, however, is problematic to Vink because of its presumed homogeneity and its neglect of the dynamism of culture. Other objections include its cerebral character (culture as 'programming of the spirit', excluding its common sense features) and its blindness to differences of power[44]. The term *multiculture* or multicultural society, in this respect veils cultural contrasts, according to Vink. The tense relationship between individuals, groups, society, homogeneity and pluriformity can lead to different views and strategies (e.g. assimilation, integration etc.). These contradictions should be openly discussed and ground real choices.

The concept of national culture is also inadequate to understand processes of globalization and the global context of communication. Global cultural exchange needs a concept of culture that exceeds national culture. In an anthropological sense, culture is a struggle for meaning within groups. Culture, in this respect, is not some sort of group belonging or unchangeable tradition, but a construction that is continuously changing due to the struggle for meaning. Nationality and ethnicity are not univocal concepts, but constructed differences to contrast identities.

Handling cultural differences is of increasing importance in the contemporary world. All cultural communication is intercultural communication, says Vink. He therefore offers an alternative approach to culture and communication and redefines the term intercultural. He terms his model *glocal scanning* after its main elements.

His point of departure is the unicity of the conversation partners, the recognition of the other as different *and* equal, and the empowering abilities of communication (to be or become who you are).

Because the micro and macro and the psychological and the social level in communication cannot be separated, Vink compares communicating with *scanning*. This means to 'feel out the right wavelength' and 'sound out the relationships'. Important in this scanning process are social position and distance, power relations and identity.

For a long time the 'dominant' model in communication studies has been the transfer of information (sender, encoding, message, decoding, receiver, feedback). Daily conversations, however, do not inform, says Vink, but confirm relationships. They have a ritual function. He argues that conversation partners position themselves towards each other and in social space. Both of them have two fundamental needs: the longing for autonomy and, at the same time, for recognition and respect. This implies tact, both towards the other and towards oneself. The former is the prevention of the other's loss of face. The latter is self presentation (which is impossible without recognizing the others' right in this respect). Tact and self presentation are vital mechanisms to build and maintain relationships. Nevertheless, the denial of this relational aspect of a message is often denied and leads to miscommunication.

Self presentation, position finding, and recognition by the environment determine one's identity, which is increasingly cross-border and plural. Identity has two dimensions: a social image (e.g. stigmatization, stereotyping) and a self image. Identities are socially constructed as basic categories of identification. They facilitate understanding as well as

---

[43] Also published in English: Vink, Nico. 2005. *Dealing with differences. How to increase our intercultural competence?* Amsterdam, Royal Tropical Institute.

[44] This implies a view of reality as an independent variable, objectively to be known and detached from the viewer's position and in contrast with holistic understanding.

misconceptions. Differences in social status and power are inherent in communication - both verbal and non-verbal. Communicative abilities, says Vink, have less to do with technical issues than with one's social, cultural, and symbolic resources. They also include gender and physical aspects: women, for example, are said to emphasize connections, compliments and apologies in their communication whereas men stress status, directness and interruptions. Physical aspects involve gestures, attitude, distance or closeness and look or touch.

The vital elements of the scanning process as identified by Vink to understand personal communication are: determining position, tact, self representation, language, power and non-verbal communication. Just as Tanner and Gräb identified historical developments in the understanding of culture and communication, Vink does likewise[45]. In traditional societies communication was determined by tradition. In modernity, people became *inner directed,* building on their conscience as an inner lead also in communicational matters. In postmodern times, people are *outer directed.* They are like radars that explore the environment and react and continuously adjust themselves to it. Self monitoring and -contextual- scanning are of increasing importance in communication. Information and content are of relative minor importance.

The importance of relationships in communication is even greater when cultural differences are involved. To understand this interaction, Vink argues the social context (social differences and different positions) of their communication is crucial. He points to the role of distinctions that are made such as: foreign or alien (and ethnocentrism on both sides); civilized or primitive; black or white (and the racism involved); (im)migrants or natives (inclusion and exclusion, we and they); Christians or Muslims (and the identification of religion, culture and lifestyle); and lays or experts, men or women.

Social differences impact communication. Vink argues that we need to be aware of the impact of (common) language in this respect: e.g, economic refugee, asylum seeker, third world countries, the Dark Continent, the poor, the weaker sex, primitive society, etc.

The concept of the nation-state is also inadequate as a framework for contemporary, global, intercultural communication. Vink argues that it is not the nation-state but the interaction between global and local that determines this framework. Examples of this are the production, circulation and consumption of cultural goods, such as music, religion, tourism and food.

Vink identifies two simultaneous and, at the same time, contradictory trends. *Globalization* or 'reduction of the world' and *localization*: greater attention to locality and local knowledge as a perspective to interpret changes. He summarizes the two in the term *glocalization*. Relating these processes to intercultural communication, two issues are important: the extent of a global culture and the future of face to face communication as a main feature of communication.

Vink does not agree on the, in his opinion, outdated theory of cultural imperialism. He endorses theories of mingled cultures and transculturalization[46]. With respect to the debates on a global culture, Vink supports the view by De Swaan[47] of 'local heterogeneousness' along with 'global homogeneousness. The global consumption

---

[45] Based on Riesman, David. 1956. *The Lonely Crowd.* New haven, Yale University Press.

[46] Since the concept of the nation is not adequate for the analysis of communication both on the micro (national borders do not determine the context of communication) and the macro level (the impact of global changes and developments), Vink coins the notion of *transcultural fields.* This notion points to transnational cultural exchange. Transnational fields unite global and local dimensions and create a common language (local variations of a global idiom).

[47] De Swaan, Abram de. 1995. 'De sociologische studie van de transnationale samenleving' in Heilbron en Wilterdink (eds.) *Mondialisering.* Groningen, Wolters-Noordhoff.

society is not by definition the same as a global culture, says Vink. 'Consuming is the contemporary form of presenting the self (…). The importance of lifestyles in marketing and media suggest that social classes and social distance disappear. This is wishful thinking and certainly no reality. (…) Worldwide a uniform pattern of consumption is growing, but this does not necessarily lead to uniformity' (Vink:2004:99). The active consumption of (cultural) goods is meant to express one's identity/(ies), status and meaning of life. This means people communicate through consumption and lifestyle. Vink, in this respect, concludes that the consumption and the global information society are two sides of the same picture.

The issue of the survival of face to face communication amid new information and communication technologies does not lead Vink to pessimism. Physical proximity, in his opinion, will remain the base of all communication. This even applies to modern technology, since people are physical beings. Of greater importance, however, is the feeling and flexibility of people with respect to increasing cultural differences and the challenges to communication capabilities - especially within complex societies, which include *glocal* interactions, cultural differences and plural identities.
'Even the recent forms of communication require insight into the social position of the conversation partner. Scanning positions remains necessary. The increasing multiplicity of identities on the internet in fact demand an even greater precision in scanning the position of the conversation partner in the social field' (ibidem: 122).

At the end of chapter one we concluded that the challenges by the digital media culture to mainline Christianity are unprecedented. We questioned whether the churches analyzed this culture and these challenges thoroughly enough. In our findings regarding the outlook on media and media culture in the policy statements we concluded churches do not consequently define terms and theories, have a partial view of media culture (more outward bound than inward bound as an opportunity), and do not deduce consequences which result in structural reforms.

In closing this section we will summarize our main points. We indicated:

- a relational concept of both dialogue and culture
- the understanding of cultural pluralism between and within cultures[48]
- the importance of popular theology and popular media culture as a source of religious understanding and meaning of people, and as a source for church and theological renewal
- the vital need to scrutinize this media culture as point of departure for understanding the position of the church; to contribute to this culture by opening up meaning resources that connect to people's need for identity and meaning; and the vital need to help people reach their communication rights and develop communicational and dialogical abilities (*glocal scanning*) for the sake of human empowerment, peace and a common truly global future
- the vital need to develop adequate concepts of church communication away from the 'transportation of information' view, in which both the internal and external communication are closely connected.

---

[48] See also: Welsch, Wolfgang. 1999. 'Transculturality: the puzzling form of cultures today. In: Featherstone, Mike and Lash Scott (eds.) 1999 *Spaces of culture; city, nation, world.* London, Sage. Welsch argues the concept of transculturality relates cultures not by isolation or conflict, but intermixing and commonness. It promotes exchange and interaction. In Welsch' opinion future tasks in -amongst others- political, social and scientific and educational respect can only be solved by 'a decisive turn towards transculturality'.

4.4   The art of dialogue and the audience

One of the main problems identified in the policy statements (section 3.4) concerns the outlook on the audience. Summarizing the inadequacies (section 3.5), we concluded: 'With respect to the outlook on the audience and audience research concepts, one of the main problems is that 'the audience', based on historical mass typologies, is taken for granted. References are undefined and sometimes contradictory. Views of the audience are not included and the shift in patterns of information traffic is overlooked. This results in overlooking the need to differentiate audience concepts. Features of both two main paradigms given in 3.3. are intermingled in the statements. They tend, however, to be closer to the first than the last position. Resulting in an unclear and inadequate concept of the audience, due to the partial understanding of the religious implications of media culture and to the implications of the concept of interactivity. Another reason is the focus on an instrumental vision on media and effects, which prohibit emphasis on the audience. Moreover no references are made towards insights of audience research, which would be helpful to arouse awareness on the complexity of pronouncements on either media, communication processes and the audience' .

In the previous section, the audience has implicitly been highlighted. In this section we will discus the benefits of the insights of audience research for the churches and their communication[49].

In 2006 the Dutch public broadcaster, VPRO, televised a series of documentaries called 'The Future', in which a glimpse of the future was given through a broad variety of fields. One of the programs dealt with the virtual worlds of the online role-playing games, and focused on the game 'Second Life'[50]. This game was -according to the broadcaster's website's information- developed by a company in San Francisco. More than one hundred thousand players are already active in it. They enter this virtual world with their 'avatar', -an idealized character- that allows the player to build a second life in the game. He/she can assume the looks wished for, experiment with different identities, meet friends, buy grounds, build houses, marry, shop, date, have sex, or whatever one can do in real life.
The program shows an Amsterdam couple that is involved many hours of the day in the game. It gives a good insight into the game and also shows how deeply emotional the players can get involved. One of them is going to meet his second life girlfriend (or maybe one should say partner - due to the intensity of their virtual relationship) in Boston.
The broadcaster -again on the website where the program also can be viewed- further comments: 'Our desire for online social contact appears to make good business. The own currency of 'Second Life', the 'Linden dollar', is exchangeable to real 'hard' dollars. There are people who get rich in the game by selling clothing or houses. Anshe Chung is the virtual name of Alilin Graef (33), a Chinese woman living in Frankfurt. She is also

---

[49] The benefits for theology will be discussed in section 4.6.
[50] See: http://www.vpro.nl/programma/detoekomst/afleveringen/ The program about Second Life was aired at 27/02/2006. Other interesting documentaries in this series with respect to media and future developments involve: *The Latest News* (on the impact of freelance producers overtaking the role of the editorial staff), *Searching for Paradise* (on spirituality as a growing sector), *The Greatest Show on Earth* (on mega-stores and fun-shopping), *Robolove* (on robots in the social service sector taking care of elderly people), *Game Over&Over* (on computer gaming as addiction number one, Olympic game, therapeutic instrument and indispensable educational tool), *Living in the Second World* (on cyberspace, where all information on everybody can be found) and *Prevention is better than cure* (on the continuous monitoring of children from the minute they are born). Retrieved 21-06-2006.

called the 'virtual Rockefeller': her income is assessed at 150.000 to 200.000 dollar a year, all earned by designing, renting and selling virtual land. Her bureau employs ten people, who designed 10 to 12% of all the land in the game. It is expected that the online economy of 'Second Life' will grow to two million players in 2010. An increasing amount of people will be able to earn a living from these games. (...)To what extent does this world resembles ours? How virtual is a world in which money *and* emotions are staggeringly real'?

This documentary shows the importance of experience in engaging in media[51]. This goes beyond the traditional views of 'activity' by the audience varying from accepting, negotiating, or opposing a dominant position, to silent critique or resistance (see section 2.2.3 and 2.2.3.1).

This concept of activity does not suffice for contemporary state of affairs. As Glorianna Davenport (1997),-active in developing prototypes and narrative models for interactive media and involved in the multimedia translations project of the American Bible Society-states:

'Why should I want to become involved in an interactive story? Certainly not in order to click buttons, select icons, read menus or scroll bars. Rather, I choose to participate in an interactive story to have an experience' (1997: 298).

In the opinion of Gentikow (2005), research on media use will have to move beyond the 'reading of texts' or the 'ethnographics of media use in the context of everyday life'. She proposes a new approach to reception theory and empirical studies by conceiving of media in terms of media experiences[52]. She discerns six overlapping dimensions of media experiences (appropriate to all media): 1. consumer experiences, 2. experience of media as technologies, 3. perceptual experiences, 4.the aesthetic experiences of media and media texts, 5. cognitive and emotional experiences and 6. communicative experiences. Departing from those user activities would also allow a more precise definition of 'audience-activity' and 'interactivity'[53].

Mullins (1997), on the new literacy and electronic hermeneutic, speaks about a multimedia-experience in which the roles of writer and reader merge: the 'reader as writer'. Hypertext not only challenges us to rethink literacy, the meaning of text, the notion of canon, the place of authority and the concept of knowledge, but also the notion of a 'center', in terms of an ongoing process of re-centering.

Thinking about meaning making and its performances is also shifting in the computer mediated culture that is no longer dominated by print. In the latter, meaning could be objectified and thought of as external. In the electronic context, the reader 'generates

---

[51] It would be a serious misunderstanding to restrict the issue of engagement to virtual reality media. It applies to all media. Examples include: 'flash mobs', 'pod-casting', 'VOD-casting', making your own radio, video movie, pictures and films made and sent by mobile telephone, chatting, etc. even the astonishing (and in our opinion disgusting) 'happy slapping'.

[52] Gentikow, Barbara. 2005. *Exploring media experiences. A new approach to Reception theory and empirical studies*. Paper presented at the First European Communication Conference, Amsterdam, November 2005.

[53] See, in this respect, the volume by Schrøder Kim, Drotner Kirsten, Kline Stephen and Murray Catherine (2003) Throughout the book interdisciplinary and methodological pluralism is argued for and practiced, and grounded in the concept of *discursive realism* which' meta-theoretical foundations are outlined. Due to the convergence of media, the authors also stress the importance of a new sense of 'audience' understanding and the methodological challenges of exploring increasingly interactive audiences. '(...) the phenomenon of audience is changing, as the age of the *recipient* of print and broadcast media is being superseded by the age of the *user* of converged media, requiring an increasing measure of user interactivity.' (...) 'quantitative and qualitative methods are indeed complementary' (Preface: viii).

whatever is to be negotiated and identified as meaningful' (Mullins 1997:328). Meaning is fluid; it can not be thought of as absolute. In computer mediated communication (CMC) dualities such as objective/subjective and internal/external as frameworks of meaning do not apply. The objects of CMC are constructions and, at the same time, discoveries.

All of this impacts the appropriation of religious meaning and sacred texts. Print, fixed and externalized texts. The meaning in sacred text and historical consciousness was an important issue in print culture. In a hypermedia context and culture, it will no longer be central says Mullins. 'At the least, electronic alternatives to the book will make less plausible a narrow sort of historicism. Those socialized in an electronic writing environment find a pluralistic orientation toward meaning normal. A critical self-consciousness about the meaning-making process (...) insists upon the recognition that a text, even a sacred one, is more than simply the presence of an author. At the least, there is awareness that the reader's own imagination and interests are present and important in meaning-making' (ibidem: 329).

Mullins also identifies a number of factors that resist the 'objectification of textual hierarchies or canons' that are so prominent in book culture. Meaning making in CMC constantly brings together materials that have no independent standing. There is an infinitely re-centering; texts are related horizontally instead of hierarchically. 'A culture more deeply shaped by integrated, interactive digitized media is one in which inhabitants will acquire more relational, participative, and performative tacit suppositions that inform meaning-making. It seems likely that such an environment will need to develop new way to think about authority, truth and reality. It must clarify how these matters bear upon communicative artifacts that function to provide religious meaning' (ibidem: 331). Religious authority in the age of print involved three poles: powerful religious institutions enlightened (reasoning) individuals and a sacred text. In computer mediated culture, according to Mullins, people will hesitate to be 'decreed' unless it fits within meaning making as a process. Truth and the real are to be rediscovered and understood, and how to speak about those, must be learned anew since they are an important support for discerning (religious) meaning.

Researching the negotiation of meaning in religious television, Grant (2003) -next to the selection, organizing and interpreting of messages by audiences- points to their resistance to linear hierarchical communication. People find meaning in affective experiences (narrative, metaphor, symbol and imagination) and in root paradigms (primordial tales and mythology).

Next to Grant's exploration of meaning making in religious television, a variety of research about religious meaning making through and in different media has been explored[54].
It would be beyond the scope of this volume to discuss them all. However, in briefly mentioning three of them, we might point to some further conclusions, with regard to the benefits from this type of research for the churches - as mentioned in the outset of this chapter[55].

---

[54] Among others: Lynch, Gordon. 2004. Suckfüll, Monika. 2005. Lövheim,Mia and Sjöborg Anders 2004 Henríquez, Juan Carlos, SJ 2004. Nolan,Steve 2003. Schofield Clark, Lynn 2003. Rey, Germán 2004. Morgan, David 2004. Lindlof, Thomas R 1996. Gooch, Cheryl René, 1996. Mitchell, Jolyon 2004. Koole, Wim.1993.
[55] The choice of those three is made because they show the close relationship of 'enlarging contexts', which is comparable to the circles that appear in the water, after a little stone has been thrown into it.

Hoover (2003) notices the importance of the context of lived lives and practices, where the worlds of religion and media increasingly come together. This interaction involves issues of symbolism and the construction of meaning and identity. 'Religious identity is today oriented toward the 'self'. It is not *absolutely* one of these, but tends to be more *private*, *subjective*, *implicit*, and *reflexive* than in the past. It is increasingly oriented towards symbols. Autonomous selves tend to pick and choose from among traditions, and this has the effect of making the symbols of those traditions more *horizontal*, less embedded in their received histories, and it makes the symbols the most prominent aspect. Religious *identities* are then increasingly mapped with reference to these symbols' (2003:12).

Building on an analysis of field material Hoover discerns three different modes of engagement with media: experiences in the media and interactions about the media and accounts of the media. These engagements are complex and include both negotiations and struggles, resistance and solidarity and autonomy and issues of social location. Interrelated accounts, discourses, behaviors, saliencies and practices all play their part in this process.

Campbell (2003), relates the findings of her ethnographic investigation of online community relationships[56] to religious research in computer-mediated communication. Two of her key findings are of special interest to our above stated goal.

'People join online communities primarily for relationships, not information; relationships are often noted as lacking in the offline church, and: Descriptions given by members of online communities, stating their reasons for online involvement and benefits they receive, provide critiques of the real world church. The characteristics of online communities highlighted offer a picture of what individuals envision and hope a church or Christian community would be like' (2003:223-225).

Campbell concludes that the religious community can benefit 'from asking how this engagement may shape people's views and involvement with the religious community' and 'evaluate contemporary church culture'.

Finally, Myer Valenti and Stout (1996) analyzed the impact of institutional views on media, religious and cultural values, on the media use by their members and the effect of institutional communication to these members.

They examined media uses, attitudes, and behaviors among Mormon women. (The authors state that the Mormon church is critical of media, which 'undermine religious values'; moreover, it supports traditional roles for women and families). Myer Valenti and Stout critique traditional audience (demographically based) research. 'Our goal is to add to the understanding of audience individuality, what we are calling diversity within audiences, and to prevent communication ineffectiveness resulting from presumed homogeneity of media use within a group' (1996:187).

Some of the findings in the study are striking: 79% of the respondents were considered heavy (5 hours a day, 5 or more days) or medium users (4 hours a day, 4 or more days) of TV. Their favorite programs were: sitcoms and drama (33%), and news shows (31%). (2% listed religious programs)[57].

Although the institution urged the restriction of media use, this study confirmed diverse patterns of media use in this conservative, religious research population. It also reflected a diversity of opinions towards both media and the institutional views on the role of

---

[56] Campbell, Heidi. 2001. *An Investigation of the Nature of the Church Through an Analysis of selected Email-based Christian Online Communities* (unpublished PhD thesis, University of Edinburgh).
[57] The study shows similar outcomes regarding radio listening, newspaper and magazine reading.

media. Media even appeared to encourage individual diversity (1996:193). Therefore, religious membership, as the authors state, does not always accurately foretell media use. Content centered assumptions, ignoring the audience, are inadequate. Moreover, it wrecks effective communication.

This overemphasis on content not only prevails in the Mormon institutional circles. It might be questioned whether the disregard of the need of differentiating audiences in the policy statements is due also to content centered assumptions. Our conclusion -they are to be accounted for by the instrumental vision of media and communication- is confirmed even more. Moreover, it is refined by pointing to the need for further conceptualizations, including 'diversity from within' (the title of the piece by Myer Valenti and Stout).

The insights from the audience research and its shifts (given in chapter two) and our conclusions with respect to the poor and problematic understanding of the concepts of audience (3.3.3 and 3.4.2) already showed the importance of audience research to religious communication.
From this section, we might derive some additional conclusions about the benefits in terms of challenges to church communication.

Churches may need to reconsider their attitude and views with respect to both media and the audience. The following propositions derived from this section may be helpful towards a fruitful dialogue about media and audience issues:
Restriction, or a focus on content only, are not options; be aware of and respect people's diverse opinions about and use of media and be willing to learn from people's lived media experiences, audiences' religious lives (both in and outside the church), and initiate member audience-research in this respect.
People do not want to be overloaded by information, they want relationships. Are churches prepared to revise their communication to meet them?
Are churches prepared to evaluate their 'church culture' in respect of people's engagement with media and media culture?
Are churches aware of the importance of (multi) media experiences and interactivity and are they willing to explore the new electronic hermeneutic?
Do they acknowledge the resistance to linear communication and are they willing to give up the transmission view of media and communication?
Do they feel the need to reorient their (digital) communication towards a new understanding of interactivity and a plural orientation serving people in their search for ultimate meaning and identity?
Are they prepared to be partners with people in their relational, participative and performative communicational religious needs?
Are they willing to incorporate the position of audiences (and the variety within them) in their communication policies and acknowledge the complexity of their media experiences, praxis, accounts, behaviors, discourses and interactions by which one-dimensional conceptions are no longer valid?
If religious identities in the media culture are mapped to symbols, how can the churches become meaningful public 'symbolists' to contemporary people?

These are not easy questions for the churches, nor can simple solutions be expected. Dialogue about these issues is needed and cannot remain without implications about authority and identity.

4.5   The art of dialogue and identity

'How to become iconifiers in a technological society?' - Goethals (1989:77) asks, concluding her piece on the church and mass media as competing architects of the dominant symbols, rituals and myths. This, indeed, is a pivotal question. However, to answer it one must clarify what the church (as iconifier, or any other concept) is.

The policy statements show a variety of overlapping, poorly defined and contradictory views in this respect, as discussed in chapter three.
Our research aim was to identify the perception of 'self/Christian' identity. We focused on the institutional position related to issues of authority, the style in relating to the audience and media culture, plurality, tradition and cultural materials in social practice as being a subject for theology. We also discussed some models of church as related to communication.

According to Chappuis (1981), choosing ecclesiology as the theological setting for communication is not an option. It would mean running the risk of adopting -as a starting point- the 'fatal dichotomy' between church and world. On a Christological base -genuinely accepting the world- communication, to Chappuis, is not a 'crushing problem to be solved', but 'a vital, perhaps even liberating process'. Communication involves identity, and identity involves the possibility of mutual communication. The gospel, in this respect, is not merely a message, but in fact *is* communication (emphasis added). It carries the promise of communion 'in the plenitude of interpersonal encounter, in the joy of life giving relationships, in the fulfillment of love' (ibidem:27). Communion is both promise and mission, gift and responsibility. Communication then is not 'about something', but needs to be interpreted as a gift leading to sharing.

However much we agree on the unfruitfulness of the dichotomy between church and world -as has become clear in section 4.3- the problem of identity is not completely solved by exchanging ecclesiology for Christology. A Christological base might be problematic as a setting for communication as well, but even endorsing Chappuis' view on communication - we still need to sort out what Christian identity or self identity by the church means.

Throughout Christian history there has always been a variety of organization, ecclesiology and images of the church[58]. Depending on historical context, one or more models managed to become dominant. Those varied from a 'communion of communities' to the church as 'hierarchy' featured by jurisdiction and obedience, and the church as the 'holy' subculture (with its own 'good' media versus sinful society and bad media) and the church as the 'people of God' and 'communion of believers'.

It is important to notice that all these models are interdependent with historical, cultural dominant styles of communication, in general, and within the church. Because of this close relationship, it is an inherent necessity to further examine the relationship between identity and contemporary interactive mediated culture. Based on the premises of dialogue, culture and the audience as given in the first sections of this chapter, this implies we also have to include the issue of a Christian 'culture' and praxis.

---

[58] The focus is on the 'official' -institutional, mainstream- church. However, there have always been currents of popular faith, theology and alignments both within and outside the 'official' organization.

Pottmeyer (2001) suggests dialogue as 'the key to the ecclesiology of communion'. In his opinion, Vatican II continued the tradition of the early church by defining church as the people of God and the communion of believers. Dialogue (for the first time, according to Pottmeyer) was included in this vision. Preconciliar ecclesiology prioritized the universal church over the local church, the ordained over the congregation, the monarchial over the collegial structure of office and unity over plurality. Corresponding communication was one-way and top-down and based on strict subordination. In the ecclesiology of communion, the communion of believers is structured as the communion of churches. It is based on an organic connection between universal and local church, cooperation between ordained and lay, primacy and collegiality and unity within plurality. The corresponding communication model is dialogical. This was exercised in the early church by mutual exchange of information and reception, facilitating judgment, and consent. Pottmeyer considers a return to one-way communication, out of line with Vatican II, as dangerous since it is not in line with the position of the majority of the faithful, nor with the dignity of the human person. Ecclesial authority should be exercised in dialogue. The difference made between the 'teaching' and 'listening' church, he states, is based on a preconciliar ecclesiology. In the search for truth, it does not apply. But even more important to him, Vatican II posed that the dialogical model also applies to communication with other denominations and religions, non-Christians and the entire world. The goal then must be global dialogue, 'on which the future of humanity depends'.

Heinrichs (1981), reflecting on a 'Christian approach' with respect to theory of practical communication, posits an 'extremely close connection between communication (as the very essence of real life in society) and religion'. He interprets Christianity as a religion of communication and *metacommunication*. By this he means 'that what makes communication possible', some sort of preceding, ultimate or normative communication that becomes historically explicit only in a community or culture, just as meaning becomes explicit in language.
The Christian communicative view of freedom has, as its original consequence, ideological pluralism. This pluralism is to be evaluated positively and on the indispensable basis of the principle of communication without constraint. 'The Christian can and must recognize this principle as 'anonymously Christian'. Theology thereby finds itself fully connected up with philosophical reflections on 'Communicative Society and Human Values. (…) From the very beginning, therefore, the achievement of human values in a communicative society is an original concern of Christianity. (…) the communicative society is not something to be merely tolerated theologically but must be worked for energetically, including a technology which is not merely 'intellectual' but 'intelligent' in a humanistic, communicative, and therefore Christian sense'. (ibidem: 7-9).

With respect to identity and truth, this means that the entire content of Christian faith - which according to Heinrichs is 'nothing other than the development of the dialogical principle itself' can contribute to dialogue within the pluralist communicative society through the principle of love. Christian faith has no need of a special status. It is either outside or above formal, pluralist, societal dialogue. Nor does it need to ignore the laws of social communication in order to put forward its principle of love. 'On the contrary, Christians have to convince themselves and others of the truth that society only achieves truth and happiness when these remain entirely outside our control and are not expropriated by any social group' (ibidem:8).
Together with other religions and forms of humanism, Christianity should counter the danger of a social system that is merely 'celebrating' its 'ultimately empty functioning' by establishing love as the norm and essence of all human values. Christianity must, on top of that, 'transcend' the market principle of 'giving in order to get'. To become capable

of that 'for nothing' (risking the danger of futility), it must establish the truth that human love draws upon the creative love of God. (In Buber's terms: relationships intersect in the eternal You).

This again raises the issue of identity in a wider sense. Can or should we speak about a specific Christian way of life or practice constituting a particular 'culture'? Tanner (1997), argues that contemporary theological reflection on Christian identity departs from a modern understanding of culture. 'Like a culture according to the usual account of it in modern anthropology, Christian social practices are often taken to be a group-specific, unified whole, sharply bounded to form, at least initially, some sort of self-contained unit. These presumptions are not only contested by postmodern developments in cultural studies; as we will see, they sit uneasily with a number of common claims in Christian theology, and entail, often without adequate theological argument, a judgment in favor of a particular position on substantive theological matters-for example, matters of sin and grace' (ibidem:95).

Tanner (1997) shows that the three usual theological definitions given of Christian identity, -referring to social terms, cultural boundaries, and intrinsic continuities in Christian belief and action-, are inadequate.
Christianity, since its early history, participated in wider society. Social relations were formed beyond the Christian association that implied outside infiltration due to external activities. From a postmodern position, the view of Christianity as a distinct group does not apply either. Social groups interact and are divided. Moreover, there is no simple correspondence between a social group and a way of life. Elements of a way of life cross social boundaries.
There are also theological objections. The Christian view of a new identity in Christ and a Christian fellowship cannot be aligned with identity by one social group. Moreover, the Christian understanding of free grace, human creation to fellowship with God, and the universality of sin conflicts with a distinction of social practices between non Christians and Christians. There is no difference on social grounds. Living with or without God (a difference often made by theologians) depends only on the new relationship and the new orientation of standards and values through the grace of God in Christ, not on the community - let alone its maintenance. Such Christian self-concern -in terms of superiority or distinctiveness- is downright 'idolatrous' says Tanner. Moreover, the threat of idolatry is even increased by exchanging the 'Christian society' for another one and in special Western society. In this case, Christian and European identity are so connected that a critical Christian potential is extinguished.

The alternative Tanner suggests, is to define Christian identity as an 'action transforming association'. She bases her view theologically on the assumption that God is the God of the whole world. This implies that all social relations, also outside the interactions which constitute the association, are within the scope of being affected by the conformed standards and values. In this way, this action transforming association brings about a Christian way of life, albeit there is no corresponding, localizable society. Moreover, it has both a social dimension and is capable of critiquing wider society. It has features of a new social movement that aims to change people's ways and social practices without, however, idolizing its own practices or the wider society's practices.

Defining Christian identity by referring to cultural boundaries is also not an option. In this theological modern and post liberal based view, a Christian way of life is discerned from other religions and wider society. Christian life, however, is not self-originating, but influenced, mixed up, modified and reformulated by other cultures' particulars. Even doctrines have become reformulated due to changing cultural scenes in wider society. To say that external influences are irrelevant because they take a new sense in a Christian context, as liberal theologians do, is not conclusive, neither is claiming that Christian theology is never essentially dependent on outside disciplines. Tanner objects to those sayings from both a theological as well as a post modern view. She also tackles post liberal views which recognize that a Christian way of life may be altered, but hold on to Christian identity as self-contained and self-originating. Which, moreover, implies that translating it into 'non-Christian terms' - in this respect is considered a threat.

Tanner argues that there are no sharp nor fixed cultural boundaries. They, therefore, cannot secure Christian identity, nor are they necessary to establish distinctiveness. The postmodern view shows that cultures share a great deal. Shaping -or holding cultural identity- is a subtle process. Exclusion is not necessary in this process. Early Christianity incorporated Greco-Roman codes, for example by changing their goal. This does not simply imply resocialization into a Christian way of life as is suggested by post liberal views. People bring other identities from outside the Christian context. They are not simply 'left behind', since social practices do not form some sort of other independent society. According to Tanner, the post liberal view has an unrealistic account of cultural integration, as historical studies of Christianity show. There are also theological objections to resocialization. It is not in line with the claim of justification by faith.

Moreover, grounding one's view in boundaries and opposition (which never is pure), is, by definition is relational. Simply distinguishing identity is not possible without taking the other way(s) of life into account. This implies that boundaries depend on Christian identity among alternatives, and when these shift, Christian identity shifts as well. Contradictory to being self defining, establishing Christian identity is a complicated, tense process of appropriation and struggle over cultural materials. This applies to all ways of life, not only the Christian. Due to postmodern trends, this complexity is generalized. Moreover, the cultural materials are much the same. Then it becomes the difference in use of which establishes identity. This applies especially for Christian social practices, according to Tanner. In this respect, she identifies a similarity with practices of the socially marginalized. They both are dependent on relations with other ways of life in order to become one themselves, by transferring the materials thus acquired. Identity then is hybrid and emerges in cultural processes. Not *by* boundaries, but *at* boundaries, as Tanner puts it; Christian identity is 'essentially relational'. It can not be explained internally, but in the relational and gradual process of back and forth and contrast and comparison. Moreover, relations with the wider culture are not optional, secondary, or merely a matter of application. They are 'part and parcel of the fundamental theological project (...) necessary to determine the plausibility and intelligibility of the Christian message (...) the 'crucial determinant of Christian identity itself' (ibidem:116), showing the willingness to be guided by the Spirit.

The third and last theological definition of Christian identity is based on intrinsic continuities in Christian practices. Tanner defines (and objects to) three versions of this strategy. The identification of continuity in practice with (1) common beliefs and values, (2) tradition and (3) rules.

Tanner stresses that it is important to notice that this strategy, in general, is often combined with the arguments of viewing Christian identity as a matter of cultural boundaries. The cultural materials that make up for the latter, then, are what Christian practices have in common. However, agreement of claims by Christians used for symbolizing opposition to the wider culture does not, by definition, match internal agreement. There might be struggles over interpretation or implications. Tanner argues that even this is a prerequisite for social solidarity that necessarily must be based on a weak consensus to include the broad diversity of membership. Ambiguity, in this sense, facilitates social solidarity, which is ensured by vague symbolic forms and acts. Diversity of interpretation, however, holds a potential for divisive conflict. Enforcing uniformity by hierarchy is not a solution, both on historical grounds as post modern theories of culture, as well as new insights by audience research. Recipients are not passive. The early church did not discourage diversity of interpretation. It prevented division by encouraging Christian social practices to become, in Tanner's words, 'a genuine community of argument', based on commitment to mutual correction, solidarity, and humility instead of superiority. Common beliefs, values, practices and organization, which' interpretations differ, thus, are not the crucial determinant of Christian identity. What makes up for Christian identity, says Tanner, is exactly the investigation being crucial, not agreement on its outcomes. As conclusions vary and conflict, so do social practices and are thereby altered and come closer or diverge. This requires a community of solidarity and hope and willingness to listen and accept correction. Others are worth listening to. Participants must remain committed to an open debate. Therefore Christian identity of social practices involves a community of argument. Theologically this prevents making a human accounting of God as the center of one's life instead of God. It preserves the divine from being confused with the human, which would turn a Christian way of life into an idol. Thus the issue of ongoing argument is also theologically supported and strengthened. No accounting or Christian conception is final[59].

The claim of tradition as being the ground of Christian identity is objected to by Tanner because of being rooted in modern anthropological understandings of culture. As explained above, claims of distinct social groups, strict cultural boundaries or shared beliefs are inadequate and, therefore, cannot be based on self identical tradition. Tanner refers to tradition as both what is transmitted (cultural materials) and the process by which it is transmitted. In contemporary theological claims on identity of tradition[60], it is almost commonsense to count tradition as transmission. Apart from postmodern cultural critique of this view, Tanner identifies problematic, underlying assumptions. Cultural continuity is only the temporary outcome of historical struggle (cf. Vink's concept of culture). In the theological accounts of tradition, however, continuity is a presumption, isolated from history. Continuity of tradition, in this respect, is guaranteed by a 'timeless deposit' of true propositions. This deposit makes up for the continuous, universal, Christian culture and is irrespective of time or place. This view amounts to the idea of 'high culture', which, as we discussed earlier, cannot be held in media culture. Postmodern theorists of culture even try to get rid of this concept. Presuming continuity in the process of transformation is exactly a-historical as well. Another objection raised by Tanner is identity as viewed as approximation. This means traditional materials and processes of transmission already incorporate future 'new' perspectives, since every step in this process approximates the former one. This again presumes traditional materials are just received and found, not constructed. Insights by audience research contradict this claim. People are active and constructive. Postmodern cultural theory, moreover, claims traditions are invented and are always products of human decision. Tradition, then, is always a selection of many more materials, and a matter of human attribution by acknowledging normative status. A third problem for Tanner, regarding this view of tradition, is the results of transmission are not challenged by each other. The only thing that matters is justice to the materials passed down and the circumstance. Not the fact they may be contradictory. From a postmodern point of view, this hides cultural conflict in the same context. Interpretations do not 'naturally' result but are actively articulated and filtered through political conflict.

---

[59] In this respect, the statement of Pope John Paul II on the absolute exclusion of women to ministry for once and for all is a claim beyond the bounds of the possible.
[60] According to Tanner, these theological views of tradition are influenced by the work of philosopher Hans-Georg Gadamer.

There are also theological arguments to criticize the concept of identity in terms of tradition. What unifies all the different practices is not some intrinsic feature contained by Christian practice, but a 'centre' which -in Karl Barth's terms- must remain open[61]. It is God's freedom and consistency of grace - working in unexpected new ways, times and places and not identifiable with Christian sayings and doings. Christian practices are only held together by their reference to God. It is, therefore, a *unity of task* in discipleship, through respectful, mutual hearing -also to attempts of discipleship before and elsewhere-. But free to obey a free God.

Tanner's third and last critique is of the postliberal theological identification of identity and unification of practices by rules. Again, she brings forward postmodern and theological objections. Rules are historical productions and thus framed. Doctrines, in this respect, are less 'clear definitions of rules' than 'resolved disagreements'. They show features of ambiguities and loose expression, while at the same time carrying the seeds for new controversies. Doctrines, therefore, are closer to Tanner's view of focusing the idea of identity in ongoing debate. Because human actors are involved, rules do not -by definition- guarantee stability as assumed by the post liberal view. There is always struggle over their application.
In line with her view of *identity at the border*, and the way materials are used, Tanner considers rules to be too inflexible and, therefore, prefers to speak about style. This is also in line with postmodern views, in which style refers to the 'specific way a practice is performed when there are other possible options' (ibidem: 144). This unifies Christian practices that respect diversity. Since there are no similarities, Tanner characterizes Christian style by the fact all things are referred to God and thus relativized. This makes up for the difference between Christian and other understandings of the world. The pattern that weaves practices together may change constantly due to God's free grace. Therefore, one cannot make generalizations outside a particular time and place. General characterization, however, does not prove Christian identity. It is only in the weave of practices themselves that one can discover something about Christian identity. Trying to come to generalizations of similarities is futile in this respect, as the word style denotes.

Postliberal theologies suggest the Christian use of materials is only to be maintained by Christianity controlling the process. This is impossible when understanding Christian identity at the border. There is always infiltration, which implies the lack of some sort of pure Christianity to direct this process. Moreover, using the materials also implies the risk of being reversed by them. Tanner tackles post liberal theologians for their want to rule out ambiguities by subordinating borrowed materials and the want to guarantee Christian dominance, as well in contacts with the world as other religions. Translating the Christian message into contemporary terms then is not a priority. Neither is the defense of Christianity which runs the risk of non Christian standards becoming the point of reference for meaningfulness or plausibility. 'Thus postliberals are no fans of the idea that God's purposes are evident in the world of nature or in the structures of human life generally. Certainly, where knowledge of God is concerned, the particularities of this unsubstitutable person, Jesus, always outweigh discussions of a universal Logos or the possibly far-flung peregrinations of the Holy Spirit; and that preference is backed up by a weighty pessimism about the effects of sin' (ibidem:149).
Tanner stresses Christian identity hinges on openness to direction by God's free grace in Christ, which is the organizing principle for the use of borrowed materials and centers the arrangement of theological claims. Borrowed materials should not be subordinated,

---

[61] Cf. Witvliet, Theo. 2003. *Het geheim van het lege midden*. Zoetermeer, Boekencentrum. In this volume [The secret of the empty centre] Witvliet argues identity is not solidified tradition, but a vow that has to take shape over and over again.

but be allowed to shake up Christian claims. Obedience to the Word should not be mistaken for obedience to a human word, which explains the 'fear of a more level playing field between Christianity and the cultural worlds with which it interacts' (ibidem: 151).

Summarizing Tanner's view of Christian identity as a task, group specificity, strict cultural boundaries and homogeneity of practices no longer apply. Christianity becomes a subculture, like all cultures in contemporary world and essentially dependent on relations with others. Departing from both postmodern theories of culture and the universal grace of Christ, she identifies three further conclusions: (1) Christian communities are not self contained and self sufficient. (2) Christian identity is hybrid, transforming borrowed materials at the boundary. Christian practices, thus, are situated in the wider field of cultural life, and can only as such be understood. (3) What unites Christian practices is not an intrinsic element. Therefore, there is no need for protection nor conformity. Unity has to do with concern for true discipleship and a shared sense of the importance to figure that out. Materials to refer to are vague and loose. The diversity of Christian practices is united in a task. Christian community is a community of argument in a continuous relationship of mutual accounting and responding.
Christianity's identity is in the task of looking for one. Theology, based upon diversity and creativity, thereby needs to remind people of the need for openness to a free Word.

4.6   The art of dialogue and theology

In the development of this -and preceding- chapters, theology has already been under discussion. Both views of media that prevail in academic theological circles -as either trivializing the holy, faith, truth and human values or as a powerful neutral instrument to be used to get across an unchanging Gospel- no longer apply, as we have discussed. Concepts of homogeneity of culture, community, Christian identity, continuity, tradition as transmission, a passive audience, and the representation of (religious) meaning also do not apply.

In this section, we will focus on further implications for theology and dialogical communication as contribution to theological renewal. In addition, we will discuss the (un)advisability of the concept of a 'communication theology' (4.6.1).

Forrester (1993) argues that mass media do not raise completely new issues for theology, but help recover long neglected insights, and thus challenge 'comfortable orthodoxies' that academic theology held (and to a certain extent still holds) for a long time. The really important -and academically and scientifically respectable- task was the establishment of the eternal message. Dealing with unhistorical truths and the search for original meaning, its communication was secondary and to be placed within practical theology as some sort of second rate 'applied' 'implementation' theology. This accounted for a narrow based view of theology as theory. Communication, in such a view, became accommodation to modernity. At the heart was an objective, universal truth or message (information). It could be transmitted, exchanged, possessed or even packaged, commodified, sold or 'banked' (in Freire's terms for inauthentic education). It was passed on by theological elite (often in academic jargon) to the masses, which led to a catechetical method.
In the life of Jesus, however, truth and communication cannot be separated, nor in God's creational and liberating acts. Moreover, divine communication stresses that truth cannot be imposed by power. It must be freely sought and appropriated. Building on Kierkegaard, Forrester claims this implies a 'self involving, probing and practically

oriented kind of dialogue, always involving respect for participants as people' (Forrester 1993:70). Truth cannot be possessed; it possesses you. It interacts, questions, challenges, disturbs certainties, calls for decisions and action and draws people into community. It does not control, it allows people space to engage or not.

Forrester, therefore, argues authentic Christian communication, in this respect, can be expressed in drama, documentaries, news, etc. Moreover, the media can play a liberating role in restoring the centrality of narrative and image in communication and safeguard theological reductionism, which assumes that the Word, the message and the truth can be captured in words. (…) 'media can trigger and strongly assist important styles of theological renewal, deepening the understanding of the Gospel and the Church, and presenting opportunities of Christian communication[62] in the modern age which are in fact given by God' (Forrester 1993:77).

Since the later 20th century theological reflection on communication, according to Soukup (2004)[63], can be classified under seven general categories: '(1) pastoral theology, communicating the Christian message or supporting communication among believers; (2) applied theology, answering questions about communication using theological categories (for example should churches use television?); (3) applying theological categories (trinity, incarnation) to communication in an effort to understand communication; (4) using communication tools to analyze religious texts; (5) examining communication as a context for theology; (6) using communication content (film, television, music) to prompt religious reflection; and (7) using communication constructs to inform theological reflection' (2004:3).

He concludes that communication remains a minor part of contemporary theology. Moreover, an interpersonal communication model dominates theological reflection. Mass communication studies are not used. Much of the writing about communication and theology still holds an instrumental view when regarding communication. He suggests that theologians should start by exploring theology done in forms other than printed statements, sermons or theological journals. Throughout history Christians have expressed their theology in art, music and ritual. Contemporary theologians, therefore, should be found working in film, television and graphic novels - for example.

What is to be gained from a mass media cultural perspective for theological renewal? We will return to Gräb (2002) -as promised in section 4.3- to explain his methodological understanding of a 'culture hermeneutic of practical theology as lived religion'.

'Die Praktische Theologie ist eine verstehende Theorie der kirchlichen Religionspraxis im Kontext ihrer kulturell-gesellschaftlichen Bedingungen (…) Die Kultur[64] wird nicht mehr von der Religion dominiert, sondern die Religion wird von ihrem Beitrag zur Kultur her beurteilt' (2002:39).

---

[62] An example of theological insights and practical guidelines is given by Jolyon Mitchell 1999 in his volume, *Visually Speaking, radio and the renaissance of preaching,* that develops a theological understanding of pictorial and multi-sensory orality (building on the concept of orality by Ong). This understanding includes the 'theological centrality of the translation principle, the need for a renewed approach to orality and grappling wit the mulit-sensory revelation of God'. Mitchell makes a plea to 'break out of the 'silent' print culture of the text' (1999:213).

[63] Soukup defines theology 'as the systematic reflection on belief or faith practices, seeking understanding of both individual commitments and corporate actions' (2004:1).

[64] Building on Clifford Geertz, culture is defined by Gräb as 'die von der menschlichen Gattung in ihrer Geschichte hervorgebrachte, gestaltete, erkannte und bezeichnete Welt' (ibidem: 2002: 53). In sum, this means: culture as the world produced by men. However, this is a meaning intended self- and world producing process. Culture hermeneutic then is defined as *'Lehre vom Verstehen der durch sinnbestimmtes menschliche Handeln hervorgebrachten symbolischen Welten'* (ibidem: 57).

To Gräb churches are societal intermediary institutions for meaning and value. However, Christianity and Christian life have multiplied in general culture beyond the church and are symbolically represented by media. Normative, deductive methods no longer measure up. The religious, practical, life-orienting changes in the contemporary history of Christianity, church and society impel a phenomenological and culture-hermeneutical approach of practical theology. 'Die praktische Theologie muß die empirische Wahrnehmung und hermeneutischen Durchdringung der symbolischen Repräsentanzen von Religion und Christentum nicht nur in der Kirche, sondern in allen Bereiche der Kultur, heute insbesondere in den Medien zu ihrem grundlegenden Thema machen' (ibidem: 41-42). Vital issues, in this respect, are the crisis of the reform of Christianity and the presence of religion amid a variety of symbolic representations in culture. These imply a shift from traditional biblical and dogmatic issues towards practical meaning dimensions of personal identity, coping, social relationships, responsibility for others, ethical orientation and interpretation of meaning related to biography. Christianity and church can become of general interest as far as they relate to these existential issues. Theological ethics and practical theology as praxis of lived religion[65] (existential issues), then, are central theological disciplines[66].

In the plurality of religions and cultures, the abundance of religion in media culture and individuality, practical theology must abandon absolutism of truth and learn religious tolerance and plurality by praxis, while -at the same time- revealing final foundations, transcendent meaning, existential hope and unconditional human self interpretation.
It must also help to reform churches by orientation towards a communicative and open observing attitude in a society in which she is a minority, instead of a defensive-apologetic or missionary-truth absolutism attitude. The goal is a church that observes, clarifies and leads into conversation that departs from social and self competences of people, including the implicit religious or 'non' religious. Dialogue, free communication (without claiming a priori truths or closed meaning systems), ability to judge for oneself and convincing others by lived praxis are central in such a church. Lived religion also implies being involved in symbolic forms and rituals that orient meaning to communities and individuals, and empower them.
'Die Praktische Religionstheologie muß zu diesem Zweck mit einem formalen Begriff der Religion arbeiten. Religion versteht sie als Lebensdeutung im Unbedingtheitshorizont, als die Symbolisierung der transpragmatischen, unverfügbaren Sinnbedingungen menschlichen Daseins. Die Praktische Theologie reichert (...) diesen formalen Begriff der Religion jedoch mit elementaren Konturen der *christlichen Rede von Gott* inhaltlich an (ibidem:50). Practical theology, says Gräb, must help religious practice to connect the message of God and the symbolic language of the Christian faith in general, to the ethical, religious life orientation of individual freedom. This freedom is inherent in the Christian message itself.

Building on Clifford Geertz and Schleiermacher's philosophical ethics, culture -according to Gräb- is to be understood in both an anthropological and semiotic sense. Cultural hermeneutics are defined as human made symbolic worlds. (See definitions on both in note 61).

---

[65] Religion, to Gräb -building on Emanuel Hirsch, (History of Theology)- is to be distinguished from theology. Since enlightenment theology (and especially since Schleiermacher who brought enlightenment and pietism together, religion is '*Sinneinstellung und Lebensform* (und deren theologische Symbolisierung)' (Gräb, 2002:46). In short this means both mentality, attitude and way of life together.
[66] See also: Ganzevoort, Ruard. 2006. *De hand van God en andere verhalen. Over veelkleurige vroomheid en botsende beelden*. Zoetermeer, Meinema. Pp. 145-162.

Therefore culture is an organized and symbolized world. This symbolizing handling is significant. It provides meaning through sensory perceptions. Speech, myths, religion, and art and science are the grounding function of meaning for all other culture that is differentiated in cultural systems. Religion to Schleiermacher and contemporary cultural anthropologists, says Gräb, belongs to the human cultural world. To them religion is essentially 'all symbolic building, meaning conscious interpretation of the relationship of people to an ultimate reality' (ibidem: 61). The religious meaning dimension can only be communicated symbolically. It uses myth, while giving it a new meaning - not as imaging reality, but in pointing to (religious, ultimate) meaning. Understanding culture is always mediated symbolic understanding that is carried by producing and receiving individuals. Contextuality makes up for differences in the realm of individuality, sociality, historicity and locality. There is a multiplicity of 'meaning webs'. In this understanding cultural hermeneutic is media-hermeneutic. It is the theory and reflection of understanding meaning that is expressed in cultural media. It must be specified in relation to theoretical, practical, esthetical, economic-social, mythical-religious meaning spheres. It is better therefore to use the term culture hermeneutics. A religious-theological, cultural hermeneutic is thus defined by Gräb as the hermeneutic of culture and its media, related to their inherent, unconditional dimension of meaning value. In contemporary days, cultural media are mainly materialized in electronic mass media. Practical theology must include historical origins and systematic referring coherences in the symbolic worlds of contemporary religious culture. It is its special task to relate the hermeneutic of biblical and Christian traditions with mass mediated cultural hermeneutics. Its goal is to contribute to the opening up and communication of the symbolic world of Christianity in the multiplicity of symbolic worlds in contemporary media society.

To Gräb the crisis of the church and religion in modern society is a 'plausibility crisis'. Religious symbols' systems, focusing on the totality of reality and truth, are deviant with the differentiating functional systems of organized society. The latter are focused merely on economic, functional meaning. It is questionable whether an all enclosing religious understanding of reality is plausible at all in a functionally differentiated society. The religious reality outlook conflicts with reality experiences, appearing to shape another realm and not meaningful to everyday life, life experiences, or questions.
Christianity had already lost its societal integration power. The new outlook of the world, however, is based on the manageability by technique, economy and politics. In general, this means the decline of the plausibility of traditional theology that is not capable of satisfying people's existential needs. Instead, there is the functional logic of differing systems that are without ultimate meaning or moral norms - except for its functionality. In the search for existential meaning giving interpretations, Christian answers are not adequate. Moreover, they are unintelligible to many. The plural 'new religious' meanings, such as new age, for the lack of community or new social forms are also not adequate.

Theological axioms lost the objective truth of ontological meaning. In the bookshop, academic theology is in the same department as the esoteric, astrology and psychotherapy. Nevertheless, religious questions have remained. Religion never disappeared. But she does not find her way into the church and is not interested in traditional theology. Therefore, according to Gräb, both church and theology have to reorganize. The vital thing to do first is to prepare themselves for the existential questions of the people, and render account of the how and where religion is searched for nowadays. It is the task of religion to keep 'the meaning of the question for meaning' awake - i.e. stories, images, symbolic forms that make the indescribable describable. Religion is to be found especially in popular culture and media. This should be explicit in theology. People put together variable, fragmented answers to ultimate questions. This might stimulate a new entrance into the existential religious meaning potential of biblical tradition and faith teachings. In the bible people tell about their life experiences, anxieties, longing, being bound and liberation. These are inviting and identifiable life stories and patterns of life on issues of life and death, love and hatred, righteous and violence, and justice and injustice. Cultural industries and advertising freely 'use' this symbolic reservoir already by trying to address feelings, anxieties, ideals, etc. by biblical motives. Church and theology, reciprocally, might question what messages advertising and storytelling cinema's put forward, which, in existential meaning and orientation, 'make one think'.

Issues of life orientation, then, are the challenge for theology. They are religious in as far as they are related to the ultimate. Theology should recognize being fundamentally related to life. This means connecting to people's questions. Theology emerges in life because we are self-related creatures. In questioning ourselves about who we are, we do 'Religions-Theologie' as Gräb terms it (ibidem: 246). This religious theology is not the same as theology of religions. Practical religious theology departs from the broadening of religion into 'the religious'. Therefore, religious questions are looked upon in the cultural-anthropological and subjective-theoretical connections within the contours of modern plural and individual society. Theology is the reflective and speech competence in religious questions of life. It reads experienced reality, reflects existential questions of faith, and sees to symbolic forms. It must find a language which enables answers that people can experience and take part in. Traditional theology lost contact with the religious life questions of this time and is in a deep credibility crisis. Institutional religion and churches are not adjusted to think about -and from within- people's religion in a media society. It needs, says Gräb, to do away with 'dogmatic lumber'. On the *agora* of media society, it needs new accomplishments in the realm of theological-content, organizational-structural and technical-financial issues. The church should become a religious service center that is open to society, and understands itself and its communication by taking its departure from people. A retreat in institutional security and dogmatic and obtrusive missionary campaigns is not an option. Churches do not hold the 'revelation truth' to be proclaimed. Religion is present where it becomes alive in people. Such religion announces itself where people feel involved in symbolic meaning, ritual forms, liturgical praxis, etc. The symbolic-ritual performance of the religious that is related to society in a qualitatively high and attractive way is vital in this respect. 'Die religiöse Profession muβ sich von ihren Leistungen für die ethisch-religiöse Bildung und Selbstbildung der Menschen her begreifen. Es sind ethisch-religiöse Bildungsziele zu entwickeln und Organisationsstrukturen, die deren Realisierung möglich machen. Hierarchische Verhältnisse, das Denken von Aufträgen und Ämtern her waren demgegenüber möglichst abzubauen. Von Aufgaben und Ämtern wäre umzustellen auf *Ziele und Leistungen*. Die kirchlichen Angebote und Dienstleistungen sind von den Interessen und Erwartungen der Mitglieder her neu zu strukturieren. Und die >Gemeinde< sollte als ein sozialer Raum erfahren werden können, in dem nicht eine Burgmentalität dominiert, nicht >Besitzverhältnisse< verteidigt werden, sondern eine offene Boulevard-Atmosphäre herrscht, in der vieles möglich ist und auf Eigeninitiative hin ausprobiert werden kann' (ibidem: 255/256).

The vital issues, according to Gräb, with respect to church work include the symbolic and ritual multi-sensorial communication of the gospel as a life service meaning offer, without authoritative a priori's. Ecclesial office holders or synod theologians do not define the being and assignments of church - these are found in communication between all, including (distanced) members. Next to communicative competence, such management needs hermeneutic theological competences. Related to forms of living in contemporary society, the church acts as a social space and crossroads - offering high quality meetings, dialogues, readings, educational programs etc. in cooperation with people's self organizations. It does not do this hierarchically, but *pneumatologically*, building partnership and dialogue. Thus it becomes a societal sphere of exemplary praxis of mutual recognition and questioning as basis for further development.

Thus the theme of theology is lived religion - which is beyond philosophical-theological 'final grounds' thinking. Individual religion, as well as the symbolic worlds of church and media culture need an empirical, cultural-hermeneutic, socio cultural-mediated and praxis-near *religion-theology*. The focus of such theology cannot be restricted to a practical discipline.

(...) daβ die >gelebte Religion der Individuen< *den* Gegenstand der Theologie als *Religionstheologie* bildet, während es die Sache der *Religionsphilosophie* ist, den Gedanken des Absoluten zu *denken*. (...) die empirische, historische, soziologische und psychologische Wahrnehmung der Religion sowie ihre kritische, theoriegeleitete Reflexion und Begründung *die* Aufgabe einer kultur- und kirchenpraktischen Religionstheologie in allen ihren historischen, systematischen und praktischen Verzweigungen sein muβ – sonst ware Theologie überhaupt nur als kritische Religionsphilosophie möglich' (ibidem:263).

Both professional praxis and theological studies, says Gräb, need urgent reform. After World War I the 'new-evangelical Word-of-God' theology became dominant and, since 1945, also church-walled-in. Bible and revelation became central and disconnected from historical, social cultural contexts. It focused on dogmatic and normative church proclamation and faith. Theology thus became an issue of professional theologians and their core-communities. It lost contact with lived religion, the theme of theology, which became the theme of religion sociology and cultural sciences. It deprived theology from its power to enter into issues which did not rise explicitly as being theological, but very much as religious issues in the ethical-political, economic and esthetic meaning dimensions of culture and society, says Gräb. God's autonomous self disclosure went beyond all historical and societal ambivalences and church-religious praxis. This theology forced the church into a de-contextualized proclamation assignment. It was out of touch with the individual religious interests and ethical orientation needs within the complex of social relationships. Now is the time for the churches and theology, Gräb states, to again resume the interrupted modern reformation. That should especially be the task of practical and systematic theology. They should not go further into dogmatic supra-naturalistic themes of theology, Christology and ecclesiology, which do not resonate beyond professional theologians and core communities. What is needed in today's crisis, according to Gräb, is a reformulation of themes in the interest of the -symbolic and rhetorical- mediation of meaning-of-life and ethical orientation-needs of contemporary people. This reform also includes a shift from 'ecclesiological, theologians' theology' to 'religious led theology', as well as a reform of theological faculties towards social interest in everyday religious praxis of people[67]. 'Danach wäre von der Theologie eine weite, interdisziplinäre, religions- und kulturtheoretische Fundierung mit einem breiten, die biblischen, systematisch- und praktisch-theologischen Disziplinen umgreifenden, christentumsgeschichtlichen Aufbau verlangt' (ibidem:266).

The concept of everyday praxis-based religious theology is, as Gräb shows, historically connected to the notion of (people's) piety. The meaning of piety for theology shows itself only if it is looked upon as carried by subjects. Piety is concrete lived religion.

---

[67] See, in this respect: Soukup, Paul, A.J. 1989. Peter G. 1989. Thomas, Pradip N. 1989. Fore, William F. 1989. London, WACC. Mary Hess and Franz-Josef Eilers. E.g. Hess, Mary E. 2004. Horsfield, Peter, Hess, Mary E. and Medrano, Adán M. (eds.) 2004. Eilers, Franz-Josef. 2003. London, T&T Clark.

Theology, therefore, cannot reflect only on an official church model of faith expression. It must try to understand lived religion that is located in the plurality of symbolic worlds, cultural self expressions and practical forms. Piety today shows that concrete Christian faith, meaning and forms of life, has become an individual matter, which is multiplied especially in (popular) culture[68] and becomes manifest in symbolic worlds. These have been partially driven out in churches' symbolic and ritual praxis. Theology and church do not, however, control these processes. The religious has become a free floating, mass mediated, meaning potential.

'Gemeinsam ist allen diesen Phänomenen neu- und pseudoreligiöser Bewegungen und Gemeinschaftsbildungen, daβ sie nicht von verfaβten Religionen, nicht von den Kirchen, nicht durch die Hierarchie, nicht von oben, nicht durch Lehre und Theologie gesteuert, sondern Bestandteil allgemeiner, dezentrierter und deregulierter gesellschaftlicher Kommunikation sind' (ibidem:272).

The challenge of theology, as theology of and for praxis, thus, is to reformulate Christian tradition. She tries to manifest the contours of Christian meaning of life and its form in the multiplicity of contemporary meaning offers that can be acquired freely. In such a way that biblical and Christian historical hermeneutic are constructively confronted with the hermeneutic of multiple, cultural expressions of religious meanings and interpretations in media society.

Churches, according to Gräb, remain an important factor of ritual-societal communication, even if they are a minority, and a minority accepts its ritual offers. The vital question is whether they, in their symbolic and ritual communication, are capable of rendering the content of Christian faith in the plausibility horizons of contemporary people and recognize and support them as subjects in their religious meaning-making.

4.6.1   The concept of communication theology

The concept of practical theology as theology of praxis and hermeneutics of lived religion in a mediated communication society like ours straightforwardly relates theology and communication. The question of how these fields are exactly connected to one another in contemporary times, however, has been under continuous debate for more than 25 years now[69]. In 1981 the WACC published a complete issue of *Media Development* (4/1981) about theology and communication that ranged from theological theories of practical communication and biblical key terms on communication to universal solidarity and communicational freedom as goals of communication[70]. The same was done by the *Catholic International* in November 2001 (vol. 12 no. 4). Both volumes considered the issue of communication-theology, however, it must be recognized that the Roman Catholic thinking in this specific field has been elaborated much more widely than in Protestant circles. This has to do with the underlying thought of the felt need to develop a communication-theology (alike liberation-theology or feminist-theology) in order to acquire full recognition both in the field of theology as well as in the organizational and hierarchical structures.

The debate about the relationship between theology and communication has taken various directions, (often including unclearly defined concepts). Felton (1989) discerns

---

[68] See, on this issue, also: Knoblauch, Hubert. 2003. 'Europe and Invisible Religion' in *Social Compass* 50(3), 2003, pp. 267-274. And: Luckmann, Thomas. 2003. 'Transformations of Religion and Morality in Modern Europe' in *Social Compass* 50(3), 2003, pp. 275-285.

[69] For an extensive bibliography on theology and communication, see: Soukup, Paul. 1983, 1989, 2001, 2004.

[70] In the special congress issue of *Media Development* on communication and theological education (October 1989) the interfaces between theology and communication also received a chance.

five, in his opinion, 'compatible and complementary key relationships', each with its own concepts, categories, terms and horizons.

- The first is 'theology and communication', which means theology borrows theories, models and methods from communication science to reflect upon religion
- The second is 'communicative theology', which means a communication-centered and -oriented theology. Theology is viewed from within the field of communication. It values culture, communicative human beings, and theology being formed by and using communication.
- The third interface is 'systematic theology of communication'. Communication is studied from within the theory and praxis of theology to arrive at a theoretical systematic, theological view. Often biblical frameworks or theologies of revelation, Trinity, Incarnation and doctrinal development are involved (as is the case in many of the church policy statements that are discussed). A 'conversionist' understanding of Christ and culture is presumed
- The fourth relationship is a 'pastoral theology of communication' that studies communication from within pastoral theology. Both Latin American Bishops' documents of Medellin (1968) and Puebla (1979) can be considered to be based on this outlook, as well as *Communio et Progressio* (1971). This outlook emphasizes popular communication and local communities
- The fifth interface given by Felton is a 'Christian moral vision of communication'. Communication is studied from within moral theology, and chiefly focuses on communication practice and policy making. This field involves ethical issues of media and communication, such as social justice, participatory and democratic communication, and responsibility for the media environment. Its central point is communication as a basic human right.

Forde Plude (2001) defines communication theology within the Catholic perspective, conditioned by Vatican II, as 'doing theology from a position within today's culture which is defined by communication emphases, with a perspective that seeks to understand the divine Presence and action in the varied dimensions of this communication culture'. Its methodology 'focuses on communication modalities as experienced and understood within today's electronic-culture'.
In her essay 'Moving Toward Communicative Theology'[71], she argues communication studies can play a central role as a systematic, hermeneutic principle to theology. Theology is defined as 'faith, seeking understanding'. Theologians involved in communicative theology may attend to the communicative dimension of their discipline, focus on communicating effectively to today's public in electronic culture, or elaborate a theology that arises from a communication/culture base. She notes theologians have not systematically reconceptualized theology in the light of communication studies, including structural and functional theories, cognitive and behavioral theories, interpretive theories, critical theories and interactional theories of communication. It is Forde Plude's conviction that '*until we have integrated facets of communication studies into theology* (2001: 6) the rich resources of communication studies will not be valued and utilized by congregations, leadership, seminaries or the academy. This integration, as was the case with liberation theology and feminist theology, prohibits ignoring the field whose contribution is vital to the revision of fundamentals and methods of theology.

Van der Meiden (1980, 1981, 1999) appeals for a more 'communicative theology' as well, although in a different way. He discerns four basic elements in the relationship

---

[71] Forde Plude prefers this term and concept because 'from this view theology is systematically informed by communication both in its process and its content' (2001:13).

between communication-theory and theology: theology as a fruit of communication (reflecting systematically on what people experienced as revelation); communication as an object of theology (sending out information and systematically structuring the contents of human faith); communication as an instrument for theology (preaching, teaching, translating, prophesying); and theology that is aimed at communication (theology being an instrument to bring people to God, and to one another). Looking at contemporary theology on communication, Van der Meiden (1981) observes three attitudes. The first states that theology has nothing to do with 'normal channels and instruments of communication' since the Holy Spirit has its own channels. The second view emphasizes the 'scandalous' character of the gospel; the church must translate and propagate it without 'betraying the untranslatable secret and mystery of the cross'. The third attitude states that theology is the systematic ordering of experiences of communication with God and of the religious community with believers. Theology only has to 'do with this side, the receivable part of the truth'. Van der Meiden argues theology should protect itself from being lifted out of the normal communication systems by calling upon the Holy Spirit. To Van der Meiden the Spirit is not a mysterious other communicator, but the translator of Acts 2. A 'pluralistic distributor who makes people conscious of their own communicative possibilities. (…) The Gospel was preached in languages (*gloossa)* but understood in dialects (*dialektos)*. The message of Pentecost is a message of hearers. (…) Theology can never arise above this fact, that hearers decide what they hear and believe' (1981:44).

By a 'communicative theology', Van der Meiden does not mean a 'genitive-theology' - a theology *of* communication. It is a 'communication centered and oriented theology, being built up around the very heart of theology'. Communication, to Van der Meiden, is included in the term *theology*. A communicative theology should not be subject to human communication science. However, it should carefully look at communication research to understand why and how people believe, what they say they hear, what they select, resist etc. It also should be involved in media-knowledge. And finally it should prophetically criticize the economic power of the cultural industry.

Hinze (2006) researching the practices and efforts of dialogue within the Roman Catholic Church, holds the view that a 'hybrid method of phenomenology, hermeneutics, and a postmodern approach to culture can be understood as combining historical theology and practical theology in the service of fundamental and systematic theology' (Hinze 2006:17). There is however an 'unfinished theological agenda for a dialogical church' (ibidem:240).

Hinze is critical of Cardinal Dulles' model of dialogue based on Platonic, Augustinian and personalist theory of dialogue, representative of Catholic doctrine, which rejects a 'modern liberal approach'. This line of thinking and argumentation, says Hinze, (ibidem:260) is also held by Cardinal Ratzinger (Pope Benedictus XVI). Hinze feels Dulles' approach underestimates the importance of changing historical circumstances as well as the differences of cultures. He demonstrates the need for more sustained theoretical and theological attention. He suggests to more profoundly explore what he describes as the 'three trajectories of dialogical thought' (ibidem: 262): the modern personalist approach (associated with Buber); the hermeneutical approach, which goes into the dialogue-like relationship between readers and texts (associated with Gadamer) and social theoretical approaches to communication (in the line of Habermas and Mead. The difference in those views compared to Dulles' view is that the former attend phenomenologically to concrete historical practices of dialogue, whereas Dulles departs from an idealist character from dialogue, informed by the phenomenological tradition (e.g. Heidegger) which then is concretized by personalist, hermeneutic and social theorists.

Hinze is aware of the critics of dialogue (we will get back to this issue in chapter five). He suggests these criticisms and the older hierarchical models of authority and tradition (as given by Dulles) must be 'matched by an alternative theology of the church's identity and mission equal in scope and depth and spiritual richness'. Hinze does not deny the 'crucial roles of papal, episcopal, and clerical authority' but pleas to reformulate the theology of ordination and offices, towards a dialogical understanding of church and world. This implies a repositioning of theology and exercise of officeholders, to the benefit of people's participation and co-responsibility, contrary to Dulles' position of consultation only, which is a clause in the new Code of Canon Law in the Roman Catholic church. Hinze also explicitly relates his alternative theology of the church within a Trinitarian ecclesiology. 'Ultimately, an alternative theology of the church that advocates dialogical discernment and decision making will be based on a more comprehensive understanding of the communicative character of revelation, liturgy, and he church; on a revised understanding off all of the baptized faithful, and he ministries and offices of the laity and ordained; and on a theology of the Catholic Church in relation to other Christian communions and a theology of the people of God that can illuminate the relations between all God's people in the world. Most importantly, the identity and mission of the church draw their inspiration and justification from Christian convictions about the identity and mission of the Triune God' (ibidem: 2006. 266).

However we appreciate Hinze's effort to research -and depart from- dialogical praxis, which implies attending to historical and cultural context, as well as his plea for changes in theology and responsibilities, there are also critical questions to be raised. One of them is whether Hinze's views of dialogue and of authority are consistent -both on communication scientific as well as theological grounds-. It appears, if we may put it that way, as if he wants to run with the hare and hunt with the hounds. Another question is whether basing his view of dialogue in a Trinitarian ecclesiology, is that unproblematic as he appears to assume. Returning to our sections on theological groundings of communication (3.3.6, 3.4), it might not be that plain. Overall, his vision appears to uphold an inward ecclesiastical position, in claiming the most important is church identity and mission being justified by Christian convictions of the triune God. The problem with that statement is whether the Christian convictions of the triune God are that univocal as presumed. Moreover, whether the concept and process of dialogue, which inherently leaves scope for dissent and offers no guarantee with respect to consensus, is given its full due.

Soukup (2001, 2002), who has most extensively authored materials about theology and communication in terms of bibliographies (1983, 1989, 2001, 2004), makes a plea for a cross disciplinary reflection without handing over one discipline to another. According to Soukup, communication can address various branches of theology from within. Examples given by him include systematic theology and Christology, revelation, ecclesiology and moral theology. They all offer a different methodology that makes Soukup conclude that communication can be the basis for broad theological formation. Most fundamentally, Soukup argues, 'communication is a moral act, thus binding people to an integrity of action' (2001:31).

Eilers (2003, 2006) holds another view. He distinguishes three different historical approaches to theology and communication: theology of communication, communicative theology and communication theology.
Theology of communication is, in Eilers' words, to 'baptize' the media, or to 'theologize' communication. Communicative theology aims at making theology more understandable. Recently this concept is also in vogue in German speaking countries and

focuses on a theology that grows from spiritual experiences of communities. In this respect, it is related to liberation theology.

Communication theology does not begin with the instruments or with community experiences, but with the self communication of God. Building on Karl Rahner and Avery Dulles, this self communication is the key concept for the whole of theology. Communication theology, therefore, cannot be a genitive theology. Since God is a communicating God, theology is inherently concerned with communication. The main elements of communication theology are Trinity, revelation, Incarnation and the church.

'The Trinitarian self-communication of God in revelation and incarnation is continued till the end of time through the Church. It is her mission to continue God's communication into the here and now of the present time (...) under the guidance of the Holy Spirit, whom Jesus promises to the Church. It is to be lived especially in *Kerygma, Koinonia* and *Diakonia'* (2006:13).

In line with the German theologian, Gisbert Greshake, who -according to Eilers-, has convincingly proved that the expression and concept of communication is, from its origin and roots, theological, Eilers' outlook on communication is one of 'a theological principle under which the whole of theology is considered and studied' (2006:5). Communication is an 'essential dimension of any theology' (2004:21). From this principle, Eilers infers the need for 'a communication based ecclesiology' (including new ICT). Communication is at the root of Christianity, not some activity beside others and 'far beyond instrumentalization'.

By way of conclusion we will relate the different concepts of communication theology to the insights about theological implications that we discussed throughout the book and in section 4.6. Summarizing the outlooks (staccato), we might consider them under five headings:

1. Theology and communication; Soukup: cross disciplinary study of theology and communication
2. Communicative theology; Plude: theology from within culture and with the perspective of finding Gods presence in it. Van der Meiden: communication centered theology, more from a public relations principle (which is his professional background). Hinze (partly)
3. Systematic theology of communication; communication studied within theology (Hinze, partly)
4. Pastoral theology of communication; communication studied from within pastoral theology
5. Communication Theology; Eilers: communication as the central theological principle

The difficulties with these artificial discernments are twofold. For example: Van der Meiden's view of communicative theology in its elaboration appears to have much in common with Eilers' view of communication theology. On the other hand, they differ in their grounding point of departure. For Eilers this is God's self communication, whereas for Van der Meiden it is the position of the 'hearer'. Moreover, he also appears to have the view that theological studies should not be the subject of communication science in common with Soukup.

This underlines the necessity for a more careful clarification of terms and positions taken.

A second problem is more content based. In section 3.4.3 we outlined the problem of theological presuppositions as a point of departure. However, we agree theology has an inherent communication aspect; the problem with communication theology is that communication risks the danger of not being given its due because it is a priori based in theology. Moreover, if it is such a vital principle within theology, one might ask whether this is a matter of tautologism. Or pushing it even further, whether it would not be sufficient to just hold on to the term *theology*.

A difficulty with both interpretations of a communicative theology grounded in culture is not so much its position taken -on that we agree- as it is with its goals in elaborating this outlook. If the goal is to strengthen a position within theology and church, it might be asked whether media culture and communication are given their due as vitally reforming all fields of theology, as well as church structural and organizational forms. They might risk the danger of somehow being 'incorporated' and lose their reforming and critical potential. If the goal in the end is to make better public relations or marketing by the church, a similar problem arises. Moreover, it is questionable whether a public relations or marketing principle[72] is compatible with the principal of dialogical, relational and empowering outlook of communication that we proposed. This outlook is inviting, open ended, non-manipulative, confronting and it takes account of human dignity, human freedom and personal responsibility. I t is a form of communication which is biblically grounded in the narrative parable as mutual 'communication-action'. The parable, used by Jesus as a very significant form of communication -according to Traber (1987: 323)- was a 'public relations disaster'. The parable view of communication is diametrically opposed to any propagation form.

The most attractive solution, then, seems to be the one Soukup argues for: let both theology and communication studies have their due and study them in relationship. However, we would like to add cross disciplinary exchange in the field of culture to this. As already argued in the introduction.

Building on Tanner and Gräb, however, we would propose a change of terms. An interdisciplinary exchange between *theology, theories of culture and communication*. Theology is defined as religious theology, as argued for by Gräb; culture in a postmodern sense, as argued for by Tanner; and communication replaces the term *media*, which is not only a too narrow based concept in contemporary circumstances, but also connoting a 'neutral' instrumental outlook.

What is gained from this tripartite undertaking of culture-communication-theology? First of all, that all three fields are given full due. Second, their relationship is built on what they have in common instead of what discerns them. Mediation is a vital core of both culture and society, as well as of theology. The input of communication theory, especially with respect to audience research, relates to both the contemporary 'individual' state of religious meaning making as well as communicating. Moreover, the critical potential of all fields is included. The postmodern culture outlook challenges not only the concepts of culture, but also those of theology and communication - including intercultural and interreligious communication, as discussed by Vink in his concept of communication as glocal scanning. Communication and theological ethics challenge contemporary culture and individual as well as societal, global communication. Finally, the unfruitful disunion between Christian culture and society, and academic theology and people's religious praxis is overcome and the development of a multicolored diversity and plurality is guaranteed.

In this way, each field can be given its due, as well as profit from the challenges offered by other fields. It also underlines the vital necessity of theology to be concerned and involved with the global communication environmental issues. This necessity is often overlooked by theology or restricted to moral considerations, which do not go beyond issues of harmful web or other media content. Important as this may be, the issue of

---

[72] See, in this respect, Traber, Michael. 1987. 'The Illusion of "Mission as Marketing"'. In *The Ecumenical Review*. Vol. 39, no. 3, July 1987. pp. 318-326.

human communication rights such as the right to be properly informed or secured in terms of privacy rights, and the concern for public sphere/discourse are essential in a twofold way. Both issues are violated in contemporary communication structures and policies. A church or any other religious organization that is merely interested in religious communication should realize the necessity of a public space to communicate in. Moreover, being concerned with people, human community, creation and peace, it simply cannot withdraw from the huge threats that the world is facing. Communication is a vital common ground in all political, economic, social, cultural and religious problems that humanity is forced to cope with. It is also vital in the search for solutions. Therefore, it might be questioned whether or not religious organizations in this state of world affairs should be engaged far more deeply in communication ethics. Not in the way of reproving media or its content, but on the level of building just structures and facilitating real dialogue between people. This could be a very important contribution to human society and community, to trustworthiness, and to the communication of the gospel. It would be a great service to the world if churches or religious organizations could be exemplary spaces of dialogue, not merely internally, but in cooperation with other (religious and non-religious) organizations that share the same concern for communication and humanity. Trustworthiness, as the churches claim for themselves with respect to Jesus' way of communicating, is simply living it. In a way there is no gap between 'sayings' and 'doings' (dabar). Since the assent of faith is not merely an intellectual matter, but mainly intuition, imagination of ultimate meaning, religious symbolism, mystery and -above all- experience, it might be a good way of communicating the gospel by linking up people's life histories with biblical symbols, narratives and parables. This invites them to dialogue and partnership, in a free, respecting way, which is simply based on their humanity and creational being, which can never be made merely into an object, not even of (religious) communication.

Ganzevoort (2006) underlines how practical theology as a hermeneutic of lived religion, next to hermeneutics of religious sources and of professing religion, will -moreover-elevate the distinction between theology and religious studies. In his opinion, this distinction will become increasingly impossible, unnecessary and unfruitful. Both religious studies as well as theology cannot withdraw in 'neutrality'. In a plural-religious world the interaction of religious perspectives in his opinion, is vital. Metaphysical truth claims are problematic in scientific discourse. Theologians must make sure they develop a discourse which is understandable in both different religious and non-religious contexts and capable of dialoguing with different disciplines. This causes him to appeal for a theology which is determined more by religious studies than confession. Moreover, this outlook about practical theology will also help the field to develop a new integrating identity. If it stays closely bound up with ministry, church or the mediation of Christian faith in general, says Ganzevoort, it runs the risk of becoming marginalized in scientific and societal issues.
'Rather the inter religious context must be allowed for, next to a shift from the focus on the ordained to lay. This type of (public) practical theology, which emphasizes lived religion in all its appearances, and hermeneutically reflects on them with a view of mutual understanding and improved coexisting, to my opinion is highly relevant' (ibidem:151-152).

4.7   Conclusion

In this chapter we discussed the unfruitful distinction between dialogue and dissemination and between Christianity and culture. We explained the concept of dialogue as being ontological and relational, and proposed it (both as term and process) as an adequate point of departure for (religious) communication. This is impossible without a public space and sphere. Since both public sphere as well as communication increasingly become a matter of global private interests, and political policies instead of countering these developments, encourage them for the sake of neo-liberal market pressures, media ethics, and social responsibilities in the realm of communications are vital to human coexistence and survival. To cope with the challenges of the so called 'information society', communitarian, cross cultural and global media ethics are essential. Churches and religious organizations could and should play a far more greater key role in this, for the sake of humanity and creation - in cooperation with ecumenical, interreligious and civil organizations. Churches should no longer hold a separate vision between Christianity and culture. They could, in many ways, benefit from the anthropological notion of culture and a cultural approach to theology, as proposed by Tanner. Everyday practice, popular theology and religious pluralism are closely related to the concept of dialogue. Moreover, it bridges the gap to media symbolic, religious functions and meaning making processes in this realm by people, oriented to personal biographies (Gräb). As well as it facilitates inter-religious and intercultural communication as 'glocal scanning' (Vink).

The concept of dialogue related to both concepts of audience and identity could also be a highly profitable source of inspiration for churches and religious organizations. Audience research challenges the outlook of the church, which overlooks the position of the audience as a partner in dialogue. This is one of the reasons that church communication is not adequate. There is not only a need to differentiate audiences, but also to take into account a range of related challenges, as discussed in section 4.4. On of them is the outlook on church identity. Theological definitions in terms of cultural boundaries, intrinsic continuities in Christian belief and action, or in social terms are inadequate. Instead Tanner appeals for a more hybrid outlook on identity as action transforming associations and communities of argument.

All of this also deeply impacts theology. In modern history the view of theology was narrow and elite based and accommodated to modernity. A mass media cultural perspective could provide a beneficial input in theological renewal. Gräb pointed out such a benefit in the concept of a cultural hermeneutic of practical theology as lived religion. This would be helpful in the plausibility crisis of theology in general. But it would also help relate to the issues of people's lives and their search for ethical and religious orientation. This demands a serving church as a free social space, a symbolic multi sensorial communication and a reform towards an interdisciplinary religious-led theology. Whether the different options to relate theology and communication in one concept are helpful, in this respect, remains questionable. The discernments are artificial and sometimes confusing because of partly overlapping features. We propose an interdisciplinary exchange between culture-communication-theology in order to give each field it's full due to the benefit of all. Culture (as defined by Tanner in the post-modern sense), communication (related to the concept of -intercultural and interreligious- dialogue and public space) and theology (as defined by Gräb as religions-theology) in their exchange, moreover, underline what they have in common in terms of mediation, plurality and critical potential.

Five

Dialogue, the Art of Thinking Together

The object of a dialogue is not to analyze things, or to win an argument, or to exchange opinions. Rather, it is to suspend your opinions and to look at the opinions – to listen to everybody's opinions, to suspend them, and to see what all that means. If we can see what all of our opinions mean, then we are sharing a common content, even if we don't agree entirely. It may turn out that the opinions are not really very important – they are all assumptions. And if we can see them all, we may then move more creatively in a different direction. We can just simply share the appreciation of the meanings; and out of this whole thing, truth emerges unannounced – not that we have chosen it'.

(...)

'I think, then, that there is the possibility of the transformation of consciousness, both individually and collectively. It's important that it happen together – it's got to be both. And therefore this whole question – of communication and the ability to dialogue, the ability to participate in communication – is crucial.

David Bohm[1]

Retrospective Considerations

Throughout this volume, we opted for communication as dialogue. Foremost, because it is an essential ontological feature and the heart of human and divine existence, as Buber explained, and -thus also- of Christianity and churches. But also because of its relational aspects - of vital importance with respect to the intercultural and inter-religious conflicts, global living together, and both religious and non-religious fundamentalism. This chapter offers retrospective considerations on dialogue and, by listing some of the issues that merit further reflection, is also an invitation to further dialogue.

Genuine dialogue involves dissemination as sharing, inviting, openness. It is a stubborn misunderstanding to equate dialogue with endless relativity - getting nowhere. On the contrary, in genuine dialogue we share our points of view. However, we do take our partners in communication seriously. First of all by respecting them as human beings. This is a very important essential condition *sine qua non*. It is not someone's religion or philosophy of life, but his/her being human that deserves respect. As soon as that prerequisite is detracted from, even in the slightest way, humanity runs a devastating risk. When people's inherent humanity is 'taken away' and their alleged 'inhumanity' is propagated in (mass) communication, all of the world's humanity is diminished -if not destroyed- as recent history proves, i.e. the Holocaust, the Chinese and Russian penal colonies, the genocide in Rwanda, Abu Graib and Guantanamo Bay, Tjetseni, and Lebanon. However, the silence of the non-reporting, for example with respect to the global arms trade, the neglect of children's rights, the raping and trade of women for the sex industry, or the violation of their human rights on religious grounds, the non implementation of certain UN resolutions, and the appropriation of public sources and patents for commercial goals, is part of the reverse side of the same medal. As is the

---

[1] *On Dialogue* (2004, 1996). London, Routledge. p. 30 and p. 109.

deliberate manipulation of information by authorities and the inequality in communication and information rights and powers. Genuine dialogue and imparity of the dialogue partners do not go together. It aims at self empowerment. If not, it runs the risk of becoming amoral.
Respecting people as human beings implies respecting them as fellow neighbors, the *Thous* through which I become *I*. Respecting them, by not making them into an object of our 'truths', but being prepared to listen without a priori prejudices. It also means being aware of one's assumptions. As it means taking time to try to really understand the meaning of the other's communication. Finally it implies to share and to question - as we are willing to be questioned ourselves. This is dialogue as the art of thinking together to arrive at possible new understandings, points of view, and practices.

It is also a persistent misunderstanding that the goal of dialogue is in consensus. Dialogue also explicitly includes the possibility of 'radical disagreement'. The goal of dialogue is in the process of dialoguing itself. That is not at all easy to arrive at, as Bohm (2004, 1996) shows; neither should we naïvely nor optimistically presume that proposing dialogue is some sort of 'easy' solution to the many, very complex problems we are confronted with. Power struggles, contemporary structural systems, technological developments and historical and contextual backgrounds interwoven with social cultural, economic and political features and myths are complexities of a huge order. Let alone the issue of the (un) willingness to take part in dialogue.

Moreover, we are living in a time of transition, trying to cope with a process of globalization which -up until now- is merely economic. There is nothing wrong with economy, but when market-growth becomes the only dominant factor and criterion for all other fields, including communication, to an extent that people, public goods, and public space are sacrificed, our environment, both natural and otherwise, is in great trouble. That is one of the main reasons why gaps are increasing and tensions are speeded up - whether or not under the veil of religion. People are made insecure because of collapsing expectations of democracy, economy, technology and politics, because of continuous wars, assumed terrorist dangers, depersonalized 'other's religions', the lack of natural sources, of community, decency, etc. As they feel frustrated because of the impossibility to really interfere with global, national or even local economic and political policy making. The only human role seems to be consuming - for which commercial media bombard us with 24 hours a day commercial messages and sound bites, whether through television, radio, the internet, our phones or bill boards all over[2]. Even virtual space is commercialized. People are also frustrated because of the lack of respect, being treated inhumanely, or not recognized in their core identity, (outside and within the church, meeting of religions. In this respect, it might be asked what role media exactly play in the complexity and needs of today's world and what their contribution is with respect to dialogue and communication. For mutual thrust is a prerequisite for dialogue.

The complexities and struggles related to dialogue also apply within churches. Learning to dialogue is not easy, as Hinze (2006) shows in his volume on practices of dialogue in the Roman Catholic Church with the subtitle: '*Aims and Obstacles, Lessons and Laments*'. The laments are about the criticasters, who feel that dialogue undermines tradition and authority. The advocates, on the other hand, state dialogical practices are restricted and subverted. There is also the problem of exclusion of certain people and taboo topics from dialogue (certain schools of theology, lay theologians, controversial

---

[2] In the Netherlands, in early 2006, there was a law suit whether it was allowed to use cows in pastures as billboards, by painting them with commercials.

topics as married clergy, women's ordination, using condoms to fight aids, sexual abuse by clergy, etc.). 'If conflict avoidance is the operative motive, the community is not being well served in the dialogical process' says Hinze (ibidem: 251). 'The development of the skills of dialogical discernment and decision making is one of the defining lessons of this postconciliar period' (ibidem: 255). Moreover, he points to the importance of dialogue to foster self-examination, reform, repentance and reconciliation.

It is another persistent misunderstanding that the concept of genuine dialogue would not be compatible with communicating the gospel. If that were true, the core of the genuine concept of communication, which is mutual sharing would not be given its full due. The same applies to the core of the genuine concept of dialogue - mutual enrichment while suspending judgments. In this respect, one of the most beautiful stories in my opinion, is that of Abraham haggling with God (*sachar* in Hebrew, from which the Dutch word '*sjacheren*' is derived, which means as much as *chaffer* that has the same connotation and sound) to protect the people in the city of Sodom (Genesis 18:20-33). The story of the Samaritan woman at the well dialoguing with Jesus represents this as well. Both stories show how people really meet God and one another and engage in encounter. How they listen, share their own meaning and -in the end- are in a way, both impacted fundamentally by this meeting. They somehow think together, with both familiar as non familiar conversation partners, even if it appears to be a dialogue including misunderstandings - as in the story of Jesus and the Samaritan woman. That, however, does not matter. What does matter is the opening up of truth and humanity, which is discovered in the process of dialoguing.
Moreover, if we take Tanner's and Gräb's notions of culture and theology seriously, religious communication cannot do without dialogue, as theology cannot do without people's religious beliefs and practices.

Throughout this volume it also became clear that opting for dialogue involves a whole range of implications. From societal and ethical contributions in the development towards a genuine global communication society that respects and guarantees human communication rights; to striving after a healthy communication environment and protection of global space and public broadcasting; to educational engagement in dialogue and (intercultural and inter-religious) communication throughout society and religious organizations; to re(de)fining concepts of media, communication, culture, the audience and theology; and to reforming both institutional identity and structures - including the composition of staff and its capabilities, policy priorities (actively put into praxis) and finances-[3].

---

[3] These outlooks diametrically oppose the conclusions drawn by Lehikoinen (2003) in his thesis, *Religious Media Theory, Understanding Mediated Faith and Christian Applications of Modern Media* (University of Jyväskylä, Studies in Humanities). 'Utilization of media is one of the main strategies of Christianity in its battle to re-establish its universality in the wake of the challenges of modernity and postmodernity. Christianity aspires to use media technology to enhance its performance in postmodern society and culture. In this sense, the medialization, brandification and the technologization of religion seems to be inevitable' (2003:293). He adds to that the importance of a hegemonic position in society which 'ensures that the communications dynamics of a given community can have as much influence as possible on the surrounding society and culture as well as the individuals. In this position, its communications dynamics can be actualized to a large extent, simply because of previous privileges' (ibidem: 293). These quotes reveal not only an instrumental view of media ('tools to challenge secularization') and a restriction of communication to dissemination, but also an inadequate analysis and conceptualization of both separate (media) culture and religion as well as an outdated view of effect theories in media studies. Moreover, assumed regained hegemony and privileges for Christian institutes simply fall short of reality. The latter also applies to the -outdated- concept of secularization. Similar views, unfortunately, are still held among church leadership and in academic theological circles. As long as these views -based on

In our opinion it is of vital importance, when reflecting on religion, communication and culture, to interdisciplinary depart from the concept of dialogue -including its implications- based on the reality of contemporary media culture. Communication and cultural studies in this respect make a good dialogue partner to theology and vice versa.

A worldwide genuine communication society at all levels cannot be reached without a broad, society wide conversation about what future we actually want. Not only for ourselves, but for our children, grandchildren and generations to come. Churches have an important contribution to make in this respect. Besides cooperating with others, they could broaden their ethical agenda beyond the 'usual' (however important) issues of pornography, church access etc. They could also be more active in public discourse. Religion is not merely a 'private matter'. Both on theological as well as anthropological grounds, this statement cannot be held.

Moreover, there is a larger societal interest involved, as White (2006) shows, since human existence is impossible without basing itself on some kind of definition of both personal and cultural identity.

'The Enlightenment solution to religious conflict by making it a matter of private opinion and admitting as valid in the public sphere only an analytic, univocal, means-end has not been a solution because it excludes religious values and religious people from the public sphere, prevents personal morality and religious values from making an explicit contribution to societal development and tends to push religion toward a fideistic or fundamentalistic expression that increases religious strife. Without collective, communitarian symbols to motivate toward development many societies moved toward a disastrous nationalism, imperialism or even racist totalitarianism as a public religion'. White opts for another solution which emerged with a dialogical culture and communicative society based on recognized diversity, acceptance of conflicts -which are creative-, on cultural values moved out of the realm of power to the realm of communication, on societal cooperation away from rational planning and social engineering and on the acceptance of all rationality as construction. He argues strongly for a dialogical, communicative society based on a symbolic mode of discourse (emphasis by White). Contributing to dialogue as well as conflict resolution. Symbols enable different identifications, are based on community experiences from different communal backgrounds, enable incorporations of new meanings, are part of narrative on communal value conflict and resolution and are not forcing. Dialogue to forge common multi-vocal symbols enabling multiple identifications, according to White, 'produces a supra-cultural set of symbols that act as a common "civil religion"'. (White: 2006).

Potentially religions can contribute much for the sake of living together, humanity and creation. However, this can only be credible and trustworthy when religious institutions and believers make their faith visible while doing justice. With respect to dialogue and communication, this implies being an example of dialogue and honesty themselves, providing people with historical and religious backgrounds of world affairs, connecting with people's lives and languages and helping people reach dialogical capacities. It also means to improve living together and to dialogue on issues of culture and religion, so that people themselves are able to find and decide about ultimate meaning and identity.

---

outdated premises- are maintained, churches will widen the gap to people, and further loose their relevance in society. Transformation of theological reflection about media and communication is indispensable.

Being there for people implies being present in the *agora* - to receive and offer and to be enriched and enrich. It also implies protecting and reconstituting the *agora*, public space and the commons from being turned further into a market and merchandise.

This volume, as we said before, is not 'a guide to'. It is supposed to stimulate and help one understand the crucial need and the profoundness and the implications of genuine dialogue. Not as an easy idealistic idea, but as a profound and critical challenge, for Christianity and its care for God's world of which it is part, for inter-religious and intercultural communication, for theological reflection and for the interdisciplinary exchange of media-, religion, and cultural studies.

There are many other issues related to our research which merit attention, such as:

* the implications of further dialogue with cultural studies for theology (Brown, Greeve Davaney and Tanner: 2001)
* the 'holistic' communication formation of church leaders (Eilers:2003)
* the rescription of religious education in media culture (Hess:2004, 2002, 1999)
* media education (*Media* Development, 2/1995)
* material religious visual culture (Morgan: 2005, 1999, 1998)
* virtual religion (Lövheim and Sjöborg:2004)
* gender and women reclaiming media (*Media Development*: 3/2000 and 3/2005).
* the influence of audience-images on constructing religion and spirituality in media-productions (Hardy:2004)
* sacred visual communities in the media age (Sumiala-Seppänen:2004)
* ethics of the audience (Mitchell:2003)
* the framing of violence in the news (Mitchell:2004)

Likewise, the theoretical, methodological and practical research and expertise in this field within the continents of Latin America, Africa and Asia deserve far more attention.

This volume, then, leaves many issues and questions unanswered.
Concluding, I would like to share two of the issues which kept puzzling me along this research as an invitation to further dialogue. They involve the concepts of Christian fundamentalism, secularization and religion in relationship to global media and media culture.

Thomas (2005) notes a massive rise of Christian fundamentalism[4] over the last two decades that increasingly use media to support aggressive, Christian crusades. This media-based 'marketing of God', especially through broadcasting and web-based information strategies, is inherently related to the political right wing and their (media) policies, as Thomas shows. Fundamentalists have an explicit political agenda. Probably the best known example is the US based, globally acting televangelists[5]. Slowly, but increasingly, research is developing about the impact of Christian fundamentalists' media

use in the 'developing' world[6]. De Witte (2005), for example, in her research 'The Holy

---

[4] There is more research and writing being done on other types of religious fundamentalism, like in Islam, Hinduism and Judaism (the latter two being related to the religious right as well). Christian fundamentalism, however, suffers from a lack of critical, research and reflection from within Christianity.
[5] See e.g. http://religiousbroadcasting.lib.virginia.edu/televangelists.html .
[6] See e.g. Smith, Dennis A. 2005 'Moving beyond modernity in Latin America'. J. Kwabena Asamoah-Gyadu 2005, 'Reshaping Sub-Saharan African Christianity'. De la Torre, Renée, 2005,

Spirit on air in Ghana' speaks about the 'pentecostalisation' of the public sphere in Ghana.

The impact of fundamentalist media activities are correlated to a number of negative outcomes, as summarized by Thomas. These are: tensions and breakdowns in interfaith relationships, identity crises among converts, unraveling local cultural consensus, animosity against minority Christians, threats against the social gospel witness of mainstream churches and their projects, anti-Christian lobbies and activities and the fuel for inter-religious conflict. Nevertheless, Christian mainstream churches do not explore Christian fundamentalism, nor challenge their approach of mission. They are probably not in a position to do so, due to their decline and multiple crises, lack in resources, as well as in innovative and creative policies. Instead, however, they make a similar maneuver as public broadcasting did (in a way) to private broadcasting: 'if you can't beat them join them'. This implies: going with the successful and offer more of the same, says Thomas. 'The mainstream church neither has the political will nor the resources to challenge the ultra-Conservatives. Fundamentalist positions are tolerated because in an increasingly divided world across religious lines, a world in which religious identities are at stake, there are implicit moves to stand by one's faith, warts and all (2005:6).

Through their control of vast media empires and networks, they impact the way people experience religion (e.g. Pat Robertson's Christian Broadcasting Cable Network, one of the largest cable providers in the USA, is linked with media mogul Rupert Murdoch through the sale of Robertson's International Family Entertainment, which was then merged by Murdoch with Fox Kids Worldwide - while Robertson is still co-chairman of the board). Moreover, they legitimate (on a global scale) both conservative political views and aggressive forms of Christianity. These global 'evangelism' networks are multi-billion dollar businesses, and similar to commercial media, profit and audience maximization are key objectives.

Instrumentalism is *par excellence* the underlying view of media use by fundamentalists. Basing themselves on media as 'a gift of God' and tool for the dissemination of 'God's truth', they are in media for different reasons: the global 'marketing of paradise as big business' (God sells) and the furthering of their political agenda. Family, community and nation are the targets. And the message is simple: guaranteeing the promise of individual (material) prosperity and salvation.

These alarming developments, added by contemporary issues of the use and role of media in sacrilege and sacredness, add to my plea for the inevitable, crucial engagement in media and communication issues as a vital and central core by what we still (can) term mainstream Christianity and mainstream theology. One of the vital questions, in this respect, for which we really need an interdisciplinary dialogue as thinking together is how to develop a conceptual framework of (religious and non-religious) fundamentalism(s)? And how this framework is related to both human communication rights and media ethics, and to pluralism and public social values as well as to people's ultimate meaning making?

Another puzzling theme is the concept of secularization and the theoretical construct of religion in relation to media (-culture) and communication.
In the first chapter we quoted Hoover, who conceptualizes religion as 'religious practice (experience, participation) that inhabits the religious-symbolic marketplace'. The base of

'Campañas para moralizar a los medios en México. Ihejirika, Walter, 2005, 'Media and fundamentalism in Nigeria' all in *Media Development* 2/2005, pp. 13-21 and 30-44.

this 'transitional religion' is the praxis of popular, material and commodity based religiosity that is centered on the symbolic resources of the public sphere. It dominates and changes traditional religious practice.

In chapter four we built on Tillich's existential concept of religion as 'being ultimately concerned about that which is and should be our ultimate concern'.

Then there is Luckmann's newly refined functional theory about 'invisible religion' in which he stresses the experiences of (different levels of) transcendences[7] as the core of religion (Knoblauch: 2003:267). To Luckmann (2003), religion -as well as morality, is a universal aspect of the *conditio humana* and not a passing phase in evolution (as has been the dominant paradigm). The process of becoming a historical being with a personal identity of its own is considered, by Luckmann (2003:276), as 'being essentially religious'[8]. The way the religious core of worldviews is embedded in social structure is called a social form of religion by Luckmann (ibidem: 278). He discerns different social forms, of which the institutional specialization of religion and monopolization of its functions in the Christian churches that were allied to the state was one. The social transformations during the late 18th and 19th century undermined this social form, - conventionally looked upon as secularization-. In fact, according to Luckmann, it was the emergence of a new, privatized, social form of religion. This form came to prevail in the last decades. By redefining the general social structural and cultural framework, in which churches co-exist with individualized forms, rather than by replacing institutionalized religion. A market of world views, supplied by a variety of sources, including New Age, became available. 'Finally there are the mass media which select and transmit collective representations produced elsewhere but which also started of as independent producers in recent years' (ibidem:281). This resulted in 'institutional de-specialization' of religion and immediate accessibility of collective representations referring to transcendences. The main feature of 'privatized syncretism' as contemporary social form of religion is termed by Luckmann, is the absence of prevailing social models for universal experiences of transcendence and the search for meaning - which both remained. The appearing decline of religion, especially in Western Europe, as summarized in the theory of secularization, however, is to be explained otherwise, says Luckmann. Religion 'underwent an epoch-making change of the social form of religion'. A broad range of alternative religiosity in Europe, based on subjective experiences, thus parallels the re-sacralization in other parts of the world. Traditional ecclesiastic orthodoxies, without institutional power, now are 'islands surrounded by a sea of a religion that leaves little to be venerated but the self-indulgent quasi-autonomous Self' (ibidem: 283). The same applies to morality, 'submerged in a (...) nearly solipsistic morality of self-fulfillment' (ibidem). Likewise, there is a shift of transcendences from the great to minor ones. Religion and morality, then, are 'still alive in one form or another', Luckmann concludes.

Finally, there is Hjarvard's concept of 'banal religion'. Building on Billig's concept of 'banal nationalism' as being familiar symbols of aspects of culture and society that are not necessarily seen as expressions of national culture, Hjarvard (2006:6) states the study of religion must consider *banal religious representations*. They maintain individual faith and collective religious imagination, but are not related to institutional religion and are excluded as marginal or 'superstition'. They include elements of folk religion (vampires), items taken from institutionalized religion (the cross) and non-religious representations (thunder and lightning). Banal does not imply unimportance or inferior. On the contrary, banal elements illuminate supernatural and intentional forces beyond the

---

[7] Minor transcendences are set by the boundaries of time and space; intermediate transcendences are defined by the otherness of fellow beings and great transcendences by the boundaries of everyday life itself. Collective representations of coping with the latter were conventionally considered to be 'properly' religious (Luckmann 2003:277).

[8] Cf. White: 2006, above.

representations of religious imagination. Hjarvard suggests it might be more illuminating (theoretically and analytically) to consider the banal elements of religion as 'constitutive for religious imagination' and institutional religious texts and symbols as 'secondary rationalization'. The increasing role of media, according to Hjarvard, gives room to an increase of banal religious interpretations. New religious movements and religions reflect a return of magical elements from pre-modern world, while also providing self-reflexive individuals a source of identity and meaningfulness. 'It should be noted, however, that neither old nor newer kinds of religion necessarily imply a reenchantment of the modern world'. (...) The media (...) have become 'society's main purveyor of enchanting experiences' (ibidem: 7, 8). One might question whether and how this view of secularization differs from Luckmann's theory.

Comparing the above concepts of both religion and secularization related to media culture, added by more 'restrictive' definitions of religion in the sense of the 'large world religions', it appears difficult to find a common denominator to define both religion and secularization. This justifies the view of the necessity to deeply think through, and probably differentiate, both concepts. They seem to vary along a continuum of very broad interpretations that nearly include everything to be potentially religious, to narrow ones, which may not be adequate in media culture. In the research, the conversations and the conferences on Media Religion and Culture -thus far- these terms (as well as culture) often seem to be taken for granted, whereas connotations differ. Again, interdisciplinary dialogue as thinking together might be helpful.

As every chapter started with a quote, I would like to finish with one. It pretty much summarizes a motto of this volume and of the continuous dialogue within myself throughout this research. (Including the unpleasant frustrations and joys of dialogue, and the attempt to critically question my own presumptions, opinions, and understandings).

'This is a message in a bottle, launched with no future destination, heaven knows where it will end up. In 2004, the ideologists, the fanatics and the trade merchants enjoyed a bumper year. They fuelled the flames in the Middle East, in the United States and even in my small homeland, the Netherlands. Here, we were confronted with a nasty mix of political issues: a lingering problem surrounding the integration of certain Muslim groups, an underlying identity crisis amongst the Dutch people, a shocking murder[9] which puts these questions in a radical religious perspective, a rising right-wing nationalist movement which is using the killing as a pretext to rush through its own agenda.

This ongoing radicalisation must be stopped if we don't want to lose ourselves for ever in fictions, false emotions, discrimination and downright hostility. But how?

First there is fear. (...) Feelings of fear can be whipped up into a permanent state of mind which can then be exploited for political ends. This can all easily culminate in a self-fulfilling prophecy: the fear does not avert the situation which frightens us, but actually creates it. History is littered with examples.

For what are the facts? As a result of wars, climate change, famines, politics and religious fanaticism, large new groups, many millions of migrants, will be swept adrift for decades to come. At the same time, the population growth in Europe will come to a sharp halt. (...) In any favourable future scenario, therefore, migrants have a role to play. (...).

---

[9] The author refers to the killing of Theo van Gogh, Dutch filmmaker, by a Dutch-Moroccan 'Muslim-extremist' on November the 2nd, 2004.

We have no choice but to prepare ourselves and our children for this new world. The key to accompany this is so-called intercultural competency, the ability to recognise people from a different background and to understand their words and actions to some extent. On no account does this mean there can be no internal differences. The point is that people know enough about each other to negotiate, to find a way to work together, to reach a compromise. In this country, there's always been a pretty high level of such intercultural competency. That wasn't 'weak' or 'cowardly', it was our hope and our strength. Throughout these months this attitude to life is in danger of being overshadowed by a new trend: confrontation. (...) where discrimination and racism are elevated to new fundamental values. (...) Karen Armstrong, one of the great minds to consider the relationship between Islam and modernity, describes this process as a shift in the paradigm from logos – reason – with its forever curious, visionary orientation, to mythos, a supernatural, emotional way of thinking chiefly focussed inwards, which seeks its guide for this bewildering world mainly in the past. This is happening amongst Christians and Muslims, but also amongst ourselves, children of the Enlightenment. Here, too, conviction can turn to fundamentalism.

Those wishing to remodel the Netherlands into a cultural fortress will reduce the complex age we live in to one great internal fantasy of fear. It is a way of thinking which suits demagogues and some politicians, but shoots wide of the real problems. We, in our modern western corner of Europe, will have to consult ourselves on all kinds of fixed truths. We will have to be unyielding against those who want to destroy our common foundations, but this demands precision and care. We will have to hold onto our constitutional state and defend our fellow citizens, not forgetting the very weakest individuals: minorities, immigrant women and children. We will sometimes have to accept painful measures in order to save rare, important qualities: our pacification and its by-product, our renowned tolerance. We will have to resist intolerant Islam, and embrace at the same time the humanist forces within Islam. And ultimately we will have to return to the source: uprooting, humiliation, the ever increasing anger of the non-western world. This is a huge European problem. We can no longer afford this national navel-gazing. The real challenges and dangers of the twenty-first century are too great for that.

We are doomed to vulnerability'.

Geert Mak[10]

These words were written several months after the Netherlands was in turmoil because of the murder of Dutch filmmaker, Theo van Gogh, on the 2nd of November 2004. Geert Mak, a well known and award winning writer, titled his pamphlet, *Doomed to vulnerability*. It was followed by a supplement on the 5th of May, the day that The Netherlands commemorates its liberation from the occupation in World War II. It is called, *Subsequent Message in a Bottle*, and its final words are: 'There is only one possibility: the dynamics of hope. We have no alternative'.

Vulnerability and hope, dynamics relating religion and dialogue.

---

[10] In 2005 Dutch writer Geert Mak published a pamphlet called: *Doomed to vulnerability*. It was published by Atlas (Amsterdam, Antwerp). The above quotation, -from an English translation by courtesy of Atlas- is part of the last 5 pages of the booklet (89-95) and cited with permission of the publisher. See also: http://www.geertmak.nl and http://www.ndcvbk.nl .

Annexes

Appendix One: Global Reach of the Largest Media Players

Time Warner, the largest producer of media content in the world and the largest owner of brand names, is the number one cable broadcasting system operator in the US and holds controlling interests in cable TV channels CNN, Headline News, Cartoon Network and HBO. CNN International is the dominant global TV news channel that reaches 200 nations in different languages. Time Warner also owns Warner Bros film studios (one of the six that dominate the global market) and Warner Bros television production studios (one of the largest TV show production companies in the world); as well as the largest US magazine publishing group including Time; and Warner music group (one of the five firms dominating the global recorded music industry. Moreover the company is the leading book publisher with 42% of sales outside the US; has a 10% stake in France's Canal satellite (digital TV service); 100% of Citereseau and 49% of Rhone Cable Vision, two French cable television system companies; 90 % of Time Warner Telecom; 37% stake in Road Runner, the cable Internet Access service. It is also one of the largest worldwide movie-theater-owning companies (over 1000 screens outside the US); has a 20% stake in Midi Television, the first private South African television network; over 40% stake in Towani, a joint venture with Toshiba and Japan's Nippon Television, which produces movies and TV programs for the Japanese market and export and has a 4.5% stake in Enic. It is owner of four European football teams; has a 23% stake in Atari, 14% in Hasbro; minority stakes in non US broadcasting joint ventures: Germany's N-TV, European music channel VIVA and Asian music channel Classic V; stakes in US satellite TV company Primestar (31%), Japanese cable company Titus (25%) and Chofu (19%) and 50% stake in Columbia house record club. It owns Hanna-Barbera animation studios; 150 retail stores and a 50% joint venture in the worldwide chain of Warner Bros restaurants.

Disney's list is no less impressive. Its name is related to a.o. ESPN international, the world leader in televised sports; InfoSeek, an Internet portal service; major film studios such as Miramax; major music recording labels; 50% stake in Super RTL, joint venture with Bertelsmann; stakes in Eurosport TV network, Spanish Tesauro, German terrestrial and cable channels RTL2 and TM3, Brazilian pay TV company TVA and Argentine Patagonic Film; the world's largest theme parks and resorts; Club Disney (a chain of children's restaurants); Disney cruise line; Disney Quest, a chain of high tech arcade game stores; sports teams and 660 stores worldwide.

News Corporation's holdings include Fox television network; Fox Sports Net; Fox Kids Worldwide; Family Channel; Golf TV Channel; film studio, Twentieth Century Fox; over 130 daily newspapers (controlling 70% of Australia's newspaper circulation), including the Times of London and the New York Post; British Sky Broadcasting (BskyB), satellite TV service; Sky TV channels and Sky News; Latin American TV holdings; German Vox TV network; European radio interests (Sky Radio); Eastern European telecommunication companies, PLD Telekom and PeterStar; Asian Star TV satellite; pan Asian TV channels, ESPN and Star Sports; Indian TV channels, Zee TV, El TV and Zee Cinema; Indian Cable TV Company; Indonesian pay TV; Japan SkyPerfectTV broadcasting satellite; Star Chinese Channel (Taiwan); Phoenix Chinese Channel; Australian FoxTel; 52% control of New Zealand's newspaper circulation and numerous stakes in sports leagues and professional sports-teams (baseball, hockey, rugby, soccer). News Corporation is aggressively expanding around the world. Looking at the subscribers worldwide[1], it is striking how extensive its presence is through Star TV in nearly every country of Asia, -ranging from China, India, Hong Kong and Taiwan to Bangladesh, Nepal, Guam and Macau-. In Europe, News Corporation has most heavily penetrated Italy, Germany, Spain and France.

Those media giants also have strongly entered into web activities and web related strategic alliances.

Time Warner, owner of 200 websites including the CNN and the World Cup website, allied with Bell telephony, with AT&T (which acquired cable giant TCI for $ 48 billion and has links with the Yahoo! portal), and with Oracle.

Disney, owner of ESPN, with its own portal, the Go Network, (a joint venture with Info Seek) and its own children's website Daily Blast (available exclusively by Microsoft Network), allied with major US Telco companies and America Online (one of the largest portals, which purchased the leading web browser Netscape and allied itself with Sun Microsystems.

News Corporation allied with Yahoo!, with WorldCom (MCI) and with British Telecom.

---

[1] *The Guardian*, April 10, 2003. www.MediaGuardian.co.uk offers an extensive file on Rupert Murdoch's News Corp.

Appendix Two: Facts and Figures on Internet and WWW

European Internet Usage, interactive advertising, online interactive sport coverage and paid online content.

European Internet usage is the highest in Iceland (79% of the population is online) and Sweden (68%), Denmark (63%), the Netherlands (61%), Norway (59%), UK (57%), Switzerland (53%) and Finland (52%). The lowest percentages are to be found in Albania, Armenia, Bosnia-Herzegovina, Georgia, Moldova (all 1%) and Ukraine (2%). The total figure for Europe is 29%. The UK has the leading number of ISP's -nearly 400- followed by 300 in the Czech Republic, 260 (!) in Ukraine, 200 in Bulgaria and in Germany. (For the sake of comparison, Andorra: (36%) has only one). By 2008, it is predicted that 48% of all European households will have broadband[2].

The majority of the sites on the Internet are commercial. Internet advertising is growing and taking new formats. It is becoming subtler at the same time. In the first half of 2003, US advertising industry revenue accounted for $ 3.3 billion (10.5% higher than the same period in 2002). 'Interactive advertising' or 'paid search' or 'keyword advertising' is the booming category and is driven by high-speed broadband. This is followed by classified advertising, at the expense of display advertising or ad-banners (still leading category) and sponsorships. The top ten advertising industries accounted for 70% of total revenues and the top 50 for 95% (2003).
Consumer advertisers spend most online, followed by retailers and automotive companies, entertainment and travel companies, hotels, computer- and financial services, advertisers, media companies and business services firms. All through performance-based deals (cost-per-click, cost-per-action, or straight revenue share). US total advertising spending is expected to grow to $ 293 billion by 2006 of which $ 8.1 billion will consist of online advertising. By 2007, online advertising spending is forecasted to reach $ 9.3 billion[3].

But online advertising (by itself) will not be sufficient to capture the audience of Internet users. Since simultaneous usage of Internet and television is increasing, a mixture of advertising strategies and multi channel marketing remains necessary. Research among 7000 consumers in France, Germany, Italy, Spain, the Netherlands and the UK demonstrates that 25-34 year old use both media at the same time and surf (16 hours per week) while watching television (more than 5 hours a day); especially during commercials, or watching television while online or reading mail[4]. With new digital

---

[2] Source: Greenspan, Robyn, 'Europe poised for High-Speed Surge' on CyberAtlas, May, 23, 2003, www.nua.ie. CyberAtlas provides information, data and updates of figures on Internet Surveys in Europe and elsewhere. E.g. data on personal video penetration, top parent companies of internet sites at home, online advertising, mobile industries and subscribers, online population, leading e-mail sites, internet usage, data collection awareness, information society index, broadband subscriptions, TV watching and web surfing, online sports revenues, users resistance to paid content, surfing habits, digital TV households etc. See also the Information Society Project Office (ISPO) of the European Union: http://europa.eu.int/information_society which publishes IS newsletters (Information Society Trends) on world developments in the info society and Eurostatistics at: http://europa.eu.int/comm/eurostat and Kelly, Mazzoleni and McQuail, (2004), The Media in Europe (3rd edition). London, Sage.
[3] Sources: Parker, Pamela, 'Slowly, Surely, Internet Advertising Climbs' on CyberAtlas, November, 11, 2003, www.nua.ie , Greenspan, Robyn, 'U.S. Online Ad Growth Underway' on CyberAtlas, July, 15, 2003 based on the reports of the Interactive Advertising Bureau (IAB) and PricewaterhouseCoopers.
[4] Source: Greenspan, Robyn, 'Many Channels Surfers Are Web Surfers' on CyberAtlas, April 29, 2003, www.nua.ie .

technology developing, like the interactive personal video recorder (PVR) that will search out people's favorite programs to record and allows people to customize their viewing experiences -including the elimination of commercials-, advertisers will have to invent new and more sophisticated ways to reach the audience. Offering interactive content during a television program is but one of the options.

Next to interactive advertising, online interactive sport coverage through broadband channels provides another new lucrative revenue stream, especially for broadcasters who own sports rights. Immediate stats and scores are combined with real-time content and the market of interested sport fans is huge[5]. By the end of 2002 the sport broadband services market (led by the U.S., China, Japan, Germany and South Korea) accounted for $ 344 million. By the end of 2005, it was expected that there would be 113 million sports broadband users globally. By the end of 2008, 309 million are expected resulting in estimated revenues of $ 6.4 billion. Online entertainment (sports, games, filmed entertainment and music) in the US -alone- is expected to reach $ 15.7 billion by 2007. Online ticketing and paid digital content are still the moneymakers, but research shows that (U.S.) internet users are willing to pay for fantasy leagues, where they can form their own fantasy teams and make sports bets. Statistics, analysis and predictions might become another tremendous money-spinner.

Paid online content revenues in Western Europe are expected to grow to € 2.36 billion in 2007. This is generated (mostly) by online games (589 million) and digital music (550 million), followed by audio/video entertainment (424), adult entertainment (422), other content (horoscope, sports, health, kids, 183), financial and business news (121) and general news and archives (78)[6].
According to Regan (2000:16), 82% of the 3.6 million sites on the WWW[7] (of which 2.2. are publicly accessible) are in English. Favorite online activities are surfing -to a very restricted number of favorite sites- and sending e-mail. Yahoo!, MSN Microsoft, AOL Time Warner, Ebay, Google, Lycos, About/Primedia, Amazon, Viacom and Walt Disney Internet Group are the most visited sites. MSN Hotmail and Yahoo! Mail are, with distance, the leading e-mail services. Outside the US, MSN Hotmail has a market share at nearly 70% in the UK, New Zealand and Australia and over 40% in Hong Kong and Singapore[8].

[5] Figures in this section stem from Greenspan, Robyn, 'Sports Content Revenue Soars, Scores' on CyberAtlas, retrieved April 21, 2003, www.nua.ie .
[6] Source: CyberAtlas staff, 'Users still Resistant to Paid Content' on CyberAtlas, retrieved April 11, 2003, www.nua.ie based on the Jupiter analysis of Europe including Germany, Austria, Switzerland, UK, Ireland, Sweden, Denmark, Norway, Finland, Netherlands, Belgium, Luxembourg, France, Italy, Spain, Portugal and Greece.
[7] Data on the amount of websites are but a random indication due to the enormous increase of sites put on the net; in 2003 e.g. there was reported a total amount of websites of three billion. '200 miljoen keer per dag effe Googlen' in Trouw 25-10-2003, p. 7.
[8] Source:CyberAtlas staff, 'Global usage and Popularity, June 2003', on CyberAtlas July 28, 2003 and August 22, 2003, www.nua.ie.

Appendix Three: Initial Inventory of the Main Basic Policy Statements

The documents are listed by church/institute:

1. Vaticaan/Pontifical Commission for Social Communications,
2. World Council of Churches (WCC),
3. Lutheran World Federation (LWF),
4. World Association for Christian Communication (WACC),
5. Working Party UNDA/WACC Europe
6. UNDA/WACC Working group Comite Episcopal Europeen pour les Medias (CEEM)
7. Commission of the Bishops' Conferences of the European Community (COMECE)
8. Church of England/Communication Office
9. Catholic Bishop's Conference of England and Wales
10. Central Religious Advisory Committee, UK
11. Evangelische Kirche Deutschland (EKD)/ Gemeinschaftswerk der Evangelischen Publizistik/ Evangelische Pressedienst
12. Deutscher Bischofskonferenz/ Zentralstelle Medien
13. Svenska Kirkan/ Communication Office Swedish Church
14. Evangelical Lutheran Church of Finland/Information Office
15. Den Norske Kirke/ Norwegian Church Information Office
16. Roman Catholic, Protestant and Old Catholic Churches in Switzerland

1. The Vatican[1]

Inter Mirifica, Vatican II Decree, 1963
Church and Social Communication: Pontifical Message First World Communication Day, 1967
Social Communications and the Development of Nations, Pontifical Message World Communication Day, 1968
Social Communications and Family, Pontifical Message World Communications Day, 1969
Social Communications and youth, Pontifical Message World Communications Day, 1970
Social Communications at the Service of the Unity of Mankind, Pontifical Message World Communications Day, 1971
Communio et Progressio, Pastoral Instruction 1971
Social Communications at the Service of Truth, Pontifical Message World Communications Day, 1972
The Mass Media and the Affirmation and Promotion of Spiritual Values, Pontifical Message World Communications Day 1973
Social Communications and Evangelization in Today's World, Pontifical Message World Communications Day, 1974
Social Communications and Reconciliation, Pontifical Message World Communications Day, 1975
Social Communications and the Fundamental Rights and Duties of Man, Pontifical Message World Communication Day, 1976

---

[1] The enumeration of Vatican documents basically draws upon Franz-Josef Eilers, SVD, Church and Social Communication, Basic Documents, Manila, Logos Publications, 1997 and Church and Social Communication, Supplement 1, Basic Documents 1998-2002 by the same author, 2002.

Advertising in the Mass Media: Benefits, Dangers, Responsibilities, Pontifical Message World Communications Day , 1977

Rights and Duties of the Recipients in Social Communication, Pontifical Message World Communication Day, 1978

Social Communications for the Protection and Development of Childhood in Family and Society, Pontifical Message World Communication Day, 1979

Social Communications and Family, Pontifical Message World Communications Day, 1980

Social Communications and Responsible Human Freedom, Pontifical Message World Communications Day, 1981

Social Communications and the Problems of the Elderly, Pontifical Message World Communication Day, 1982

Social Communications and the Promotion of Peace, Pontifical Message World Communications Day, 1983

Social Communication: Instruments of Encounter Between Faith and Culture, Pontifical Message World Communications Day, 1984

Social Communications for a Christian Promotion of Youth, Pontifical Message World Communication Day, 1985

Guide to the Training of Future Priests Concerning the Instruments of Social Communication, 1986

Social Communications and the Christian Formation of Public Opinion, Pontifical Message World Communications Day, 1986

Social Communications at the Service of Justice and Peace, Pontifical Message World Communications Day, 1987

Social Communications and the Promotion of Solidarity and Fraternity Between Peoples and Nations, Pontifical Message World Communications Day, 1988

Religion in the Mass Media, Pontifical Message World Communications Day, 1989

Pornography and Violence, Pastoral Response, 1989

Criteria for Ecumenical and Inter-religious Cooperation in Communications, 1989

The Christian Message in a Computer Culture, Pontifical Message World Communications Day, 1990

Communication Media and the Unity and Progress of the Human Family, Pontifical Message World Communications Day, 1991

The Proclamation of Christ's Message in the Communications Media, Pontifical Message World Communications Day, 1992

Instruction on Some Aspects of the Use of the Instruments of Social Communication in Promoting the Doctrine of the Faith, 1992

Aetatis Novae, Pastoral Instruction, 1992

Videocassettes and Audiocassettes in the Formation of Culture and of Conscience, Pontifical Message World Communications Day, 1993

Television and the Family: Guidelines For Good Viewing, Pontifical Message World Communications Day, 1994

Cinema: Communicator of Culture and of Values, Pontifical Message World Communications Day, 1995

Media: Forum for Promoting Women's Role, Pontifical Message World Communications Day, 1996

Communicating Jesus: The Way, The Truth and The Life, Pontifical Message World Communications Day, 1997

Ethics in Advertising, 1997

Sustained by the Spirit, communicate hope, Pontifical Message World Communications Day, 1998

Mass Media: a friendly companion for those in search of the Father, Pontifical Message World Communications Day, 1999

Ethics in Communication, 2000
Proclaiming Christ in the Media at the Dawn of the New Millennium, Pontifical Message World Communications Day, 2000
Preach from the housetops: The Gospel in the Age of Global Communication, Pontifical Message World Communications Day, 2001
Ethics in Internet, 20002
Church and Internet, 2002
Internet: A New Forum for Proclaiming the Gospel, Pontifical Message World Communications Day, 2002
The Communications Media at the Service of Authentic Peace in the Light of 'Pacem in Terris', Pontifical Message World Communications Day, 2003
The Media and the Family: A Risk and a Richness, Pontifical Message World Communications Day, 2004
The Communications Media: At the Service of Understanding Among Peoples, Pontifical Message World Communications Day, 2005
The Rapid Development, Apostolic letter of the Holy Father John Paul II to those responsible for Communications, 2005
The media – a Network for Communication, Community and Cooperation, Pontifical Message World Communications Day, 2006.

Communication in other Pontifical Documents:

Evangelii Nuntiandi, 1975
Catechesi Tradendae, 1979
Familiaris Consortio, 1981
Christifideles Laici, 1988
Redemptoris Missio, 1990
Ecclessia in Africa, 1995
Vita Consecrata, 1996
Ecclesia in America, 1999
Ecclesia in Asia, 1999
Ecclesia in Oceania, 2001

Communication in other Church Documents:

On Social Communication in Latin America, Puebla, 1979
On Books and Reading, Germany, 1980
Local Church and Communication, Manila 1979
Film Makers, Film Viewers: Their Challenges and Opportunities, Los Angeles, 1992
Church and Social Communication in Asia, 1999

2.   The World Council of Churches[2]

The Bossey Consultation, 1965 (followed up by Bossey II in 1967)
Study on the Church and Mass Communication, 1966
The Church and the Media of Mass Communication, The Uppsala Assembly Report, Appendix XI, 1968
Beyond Neutrality. A Christian critique of the media. John Bluck. WCC 1978. No. 3 in the Risk Book Series.
The New International Information Order, what is it and what has it got to do with the Churches? 1979
Communicating Credibly, Statement Vancouver Assembly WCC, 1983
Opening Eyes and ears. Kathy Lowe. World Council of Churches, in association with the Lutheran World Federation and the World Association for Christian Communication, 1983
Beyond Technology. Contexts for Christian Communication. With contributions from the WCC's Sixth Assembly. John Bluck. Wolrd Council of Churches, 1984. No 20 in the Risk Book Series.
Christian Communication Reconsidered. John Bluck. WCC Publications, 1989
Global Communication. Is there a Place for Human Dignity? Dafne Sabanes Plou. World Council of Churches Publications, 1996. No 71 in the Risk Book Series
Shifting Realities, Information Technology and the Church. David Lochhead. World Council of Churches Publications, 1997. No 75 in the Risk Book Series
The Globalization of Communications. Some religious implications. Chris Arthur. 1998. WCC-WACC.

3.   The Lutheran World Federation[3]

Joint report of the task force on mass communication and the task force on publication strategy. Agenda, Commission on studies 1972, Appendix 1. Geneva LWF, April 1972
Perspectives for Public Communication. Cees Hamelink. 1975
The Churches and New Communications Technologies – progress report, Vancouver, 1982
Strategy report, 1982
Relating to the Information Age, Budapest Assembly 1984
Christian Communication Today, LWF Commission on communication, 1984
Value, Power and the Information Society, Assembly Hong Kong, 1997
The LWF: a communicative communion. Guiding Principles for Comprehensive Communication within the LWF, 2002

---

[2] Listed are the main basic policy documents and books published by WCC on the subject. Not included are the minutes of the central committees, the reports of the central committees to the assemblies, the assembly reports (except for separate appendices on media and communication), the minutes of the committees on communication and reports on the sub unit / department of communication. The enumeration is based upon the doctoral dissertation of Raine Haikarainen, Informaatiosta Kommunikaatioon, Ekumeeninen keskustelu viestinnästä 1948-2000, Suomalainen Teologinen Kirjallisuusseura, Helsinki, 2002. For a detailed overview of literature and church documents on media and communication by the World Council of Churches and the Lutheran World Federation see pp 289-304, 364-365 in this volume.
[3] See note 2.

4.   The World Association for Christian Communication[4]

Statement on Communication and Development, 1985
Christian Principles of Communication, 1986
Communication in Theological Education The Seoul Manifesto, 1989
Communication and Community: The Manila Declaration, 1989
Statement on Ecumenical Relationships, 1991
Women Empowering Communication: The Bangkok Declaration, 1994
Communication for Human Dignity The Mexican Declaration, 1995
Film in Christian Communication. Theme issue of Media Development, 2/1980.
Theological reflections on communication. Media Development 4/1981
Book and Religion, Media development 3/1982
Church Statements on Communication, Media Development 1/1984
Communication for All. The Church and the New World Information and Communication Order. Philip Lee (editor). New York Orbis Books, 1986
Communication and theological education. Special Congress Issue October 1989. WACC London, 1989
Ethno-religious conflict and media, Media development 3/1992
Media education... the state of the art... Special issue on Media education 2/1995.
Renewing communication and mission. World Association for Christian Communication, 1996.
Churches and Faith Organisations on the Internet. Report by Heinz Hunke, Secretary General of IDOC, Rome, and prepared for the international workshop on "Globalisation and Electronic Communication", Seoul, Korea, 9-14 June 1997. World Association for Christian Communication. 1997
Communication: from Confrontation to Reconciliation, Congress Issue Media Development 4/2001
The Campaign for Communication Rights in the Information Society, Media Development 4/2002
The church and communication, Michael Traber, WACC, undated

5.   Working Party UNDA/WACC Europe

Audiovisual Media Education an urgent pastoral and social concern. Memorandum addressed to authorities of European Churches. 1995.
Identities and Communities: What Kind of Communication? Media, Culture and Society European Ecumenical Working Group UNDA-WACC, 1999

6.   Comite Episcopal Europeen pour les Medias (CEEM)

L'importance du travail médiatique de l' Eglise, Appel du Comité épiscopal européen des médias (CEEM) aux conferences épiscopales en Europe. *CEEM, 1995. Also in English:* The

---

[4] WACC - in its present form inaugurated in 1975 - contributes in many ways to the ecumenical discussion on media and communication. Especially its publications Media Development (the former WACC Journal), Action, (the electronic news and information magazine), and the Media and Gender Monitor can be considered having a continuous impact. Listing the many separate articles and special themes referring to policy views is beyond the scope of this study. For an overview of issues see WACC's website www.wacc.org.uk . Our listing is restricted to the declarations of the international congresses, of which the first was held in Manila in 1989 and to issues of Media Development directly related to our subject. It is by no means an exhausted overview.

importance of church media work. *Appeal by the Committee of European bishops in charge of the media (CEEM) to the bishops' conferences in Europe, 1995.*
Evangelio, Iglesia y sociedad de la información. Congreso de obispos europeos de medios de comunicación social, Monserrat/España, April 1999. Recomendaciones dirigidas a las conferencias episcopales. Also in English: Recommendations to the National Bishops' Conferences. Includes: 'Briefing Paper for the Synod of Europe', Monserrat, April 1999.

7. Commission of the Bishops' Conferences of the European Community (COMECE)

Comments of the Secretary General of ComECE on the Green Paper of the European Commission concerning the Convergence of the Telecommunications, Media and Information Technology Sectors and their Effects on Regulatory Policy A step towards the Information Society. Compiled by the Media Policy Working Group of ComECE. Brussels, April 1998
A call for Media Education. Rome, 30 March, 2001
The future of EU Media Policy in the Information Society, 2001
Television without frontiers, Public Consultation, 2003

8. Church of England

A Christian Approach to television. Published by the Church Information Office on behalf of the Archbishops' Advisers on Radio and Television. 1968
Communication within the Church. A report of Six Regional Conferences for Diocesan Representatives, conducted by the Church Information Office. 1972.
Broadcasting Society and the Church, Report of the Broadcasting Commission of the General Synod of the Church of England, 1973
General Synod: *The Responsibility of the Church in Communication.* A report by the Church Information Committee. Church House, London, 4th January 1978.
General Synod: *Financing the BBC.* A submission from the Church of England Committee for Communications. 1985.
General Synod: Response to the Home Office Green Paper. *Radio: Choices and Opportunities.* A submission from the Church of England Committee for Communications. 29 June 1987.
General Synod: *Communications: A Policy for The Church of England.* A Paper from the Church of England Committee for Communications. October 1988.
General Synod: A Matter of Respect. *Reflections on Government Broadcasting Policy.* A Paper from the Church of England Committee for Communications. Church of England Committee for Communications, January 1989.
The Portrayal of Sex and Violence and Standards of Taste and Decency in Broadcasting, Cable and Video Works. Submission to the Broadcasting Standards Council from the Board for Social Responsibility and the Church of England Committee for Communications. January 1989.
General Synod of the Church of England: *A Response by the Church of England Committee for Communications to the Government's White Paper.* March 1989.
General Synod: *A Report on the Findings from the Communications Committee Questionnaire.* Church of England Committee for Communications. October 1989.
General Synod: *Regulation of the Press. The Church of England's views.* Church House London, January 1993.
The Future of the BBC. Church House, London, January 1993.

The Future of the BBC. Response to the Government Green Paper by the Church of England Communications Committee. April 1993.
Paying the Piper. Advertising & the Church. A Report of the Working Party established by the Communications Committee of the Church of England. Communications Unit of the General Synod of the Church of England by Church House Publishing. 1994.
Cybernauts Awake! Ethical and Spiritual Implications of Computers, Information Technology and the Internet. Board for Social Responsibility of the Church of England. Church House Publishing. 1999.

9.   Catholic Bishops' Conference of England and Wales

Submission to the BBC Charter Review, 2004

10. Central Religious Advisory Committee

Religion in Religious Broadcasting. Report of the CRAC Working Party November 1996

11. Evangelische Kirche Deutschland (EKD)/ Gemeinschaftswerk der Evangelischen Publizistik/ Evangelische Pressedienst

Publizistischer Gesamtplan der Evangelischen Kirche in Deutschland, 1979
Kirche in der Öffentlichkeit, Programme und Probleme ihrer publizistischen Repräsentanz. Hans Joachim Dörger. Verlag W. Kohlhammer, 1979.
Kommunikative Kirche. Bericht von Landesbischof D. Dr. Johannes Hanselmann bei der Tagung der Landessynode der Evangelisch-Lutherischen Kirche in Bayern in Bayreuth am 25 November 1980. Evang. Presseverband für Bayern München. Claudius Verlag, München
Medienbericht Evangelische Medienarbeit und die neuen Informations- und Kommunikationstechniken. GEP 1984
Die neuen Informations- und Kommunikationstechniken, Studie der EKD 1985
Jahrbuch Mission 1989. Verband evangelischer Missionskonferenzen, Hamburg, 1989
Bildung, Information, Medien, Die Denkschriften der Evangelischen Kirche in Deutschland (Band 4/3). Kirchenamt der EKD 1991.
Von Gutenberg bis Internet, Kirchen und soziale Kommunikation, Evangelisches Missionswerk, 1997
Chancen und Risiken der Mediengesellschaft. Gemeinsame Erklärung der Deutschen Bischofskonferenz und des Rates der Evangelischen Kirche in Deutschland. Hannover/Bonn, April 1997.
Mandat und Markt. Perspektiven evangelischer Publizistik. Publizistisches Gesamtkonzept 1997. Herausgegeben vom Kirchenamt der Evangelischen Kirche in Deutschland. GEP Buch. Gemeinschafstwerk der Evangelischen Publizistik, Hannover, Juli 1997.
Begrenzte grenzenlose Kommunikation. Im globalen Dorf lebt der Süden noch an der Peripherie. Br. 254.4 J176b. Urs A. Jaeggi. Brot für Alle, 1999.
Das Evangelium unter die Leute bringen. Zum missionarischen Dienst der Kirche in unserem Land. Kirchenamt der Evangelischen Kirche in Deutschland, Hannover April 2001.

12. Deutsche Bischofskonferenz, Zentralstelle Medien

Church and audiovisual communication; prospective study for the Catholic Church in Germany. U.M. Krüger. In: "The church and communication research". Multimedia International, 1972
Die Neuen Medien – Informationen, Fragen und Anregungen im Blick auf den Menschen und die Gesellschaft. Materialien zur Medienpolitik nr. 4. Herausgegeben von der Zentralstelle Medien der Deutschen Bischofskonferenz. Bonn, 1982.
Medienpolitische Grundpositionen. Materialien zur Medienpolitik nr. 5. Herausgegeben vond der Zentralstelle Medien der Deutschen Bischofskonferenz. Bonn, 1985.
Kirche und Kommunikation. Zur bleibenden Aktualität von Communio et Progressio.. Sonderheft zum Welttag der Sozialen Kommunikationsmittel 1991. Medien Praxis Grundlagen nr. 6. Herausgegeben von der Zentralstelle der Deutschen Bischofskonferenz, Bonn, 1991.
Vom Reichtum der Medien. Theologische Überlegungen Praktische Folgerungen. Matthias Wörther. Echter Verlag Würzburg, 1993.
Multimedia, Der Wandel zur Informationsgesellschaft. Eine Studie zu Konzepten und Diskussionen im Feld der Katholischen Kirche in Deutschland. 1995.
Struktur und Organisation kirchlicher Kommunikation. Eine Arbeitshilfe für die Gestaltung der Kommunikationsarbeit im Bistum. MDG Medien-Dienstleistung GmbH, München und Zentralstelle Medien der Deutschen Bischofskonferenz, Bonn, Juli 1998.
Medien und Kommunikationskompetenz. Die zukunft der AV-Medienstellen in der Informationsgesellschaft. Erarbeitet vom Sachausschuss Medien- und Kommunikationspädagogik der AG der diözesanen AV-Medienstellen. Herausgegeben von der Zentralstelle Medien der Deutschen Bischofskonferenz. Bonn, 2. Auflage, April 2000.

13. Svenska Kirkan/ Communication Office Swedish Church

Svenska Kyrkans Medie strategi. Svenska kyrkan, Uppsala, 1997.
Kommunicera mera – med flera! Svenska kyrkans mediutredning 1998-2000. Svenska Kyrkan, Uppsala, 2000.

14. Evangelical Lutheran Church of Finland/Information Office

News Mediation and Ethics. Address at the Finnish News Agency's Centenary Celebrations on 1 November 1987. Archbishop John Vikström, 1987.
Kirkko Ja Viestimet Seurakunta ja sähköiset viestimet paikallistasolla. Kirkon tiedotuskeskus – KT 1990
Vakuuttavaa kristillistä viestintää. "Credible Christian Communication", Kirkkojen maailmanneuvosto 1983, 2. pianos 1988. Kirkon tiedotuskeskus, Helsinki 1991.
Kirkon Suunta 2000 Alhaalta kasvava kirkko. Suomen evankelis-luterilaisen kirkon piispainkokouksen 14.9.1988 asettama Kirkko 2000 –prosessin seurantaryhmä. Suomen Ev.-Lut.Kirkon Keskushallinto Sarja B 1992:2, 17-01-1992.
Avoimeen Tiedottamiseen Julkisuusperiaate Seurakuntien Tiedotuksessa , Kirkon tiedotuskeskus 1992
Kommunikoivaan Kirkkoon Kirkolissen viestinnän periaate- ja ideaohjelma. Suomen EV–LUT. Kirkon Keskushallinto Sarja B 1992:8, 1992 (also in Swedish: *Kommunicerande Kyrka* Princip- och idéprogram för kyrklig kommunikation. Den Ev.-Luth. Kyrkans i Finland Centralförvaltning Serie B 1992:8.

Förslag til Kommuniationsplan för Kyrkan. Betänkande utarbetat av en arbetsgruppp tillsatt 14.2.1990 av biskopsmötet i den evangelisk-lutherska kyrkan i Finland. Finlands Ev.Luth. Kyrkas Centralförvaltning serie B 1992:3. 03-01-1992.
The Communicative Church, the Church's Communication Strategy 2004-2010, Helsinki, 2004

15. Den Norske Kirke/ Norwegian Church Information Office

Kirkens Informasjonsarbeid et Forsøk På En Helhetsvurdering. Church Council of Norway, 1973
Information Service Church of Norway. Report on a survey of information services within the Church of Norway, by the Secretary for Regional Development Lutheran World Federation, Office of Communication. On request of the Church Council of the Norvegian Church. 1975.
Utredning om arbeid med Kommunikasjons - Spørsmål I Kirkerådet. Commission pointed out by the Church Council of the Church of Norway. 1982.
Informasjon i Den norske kirke. En plan for informasjon i sentrale, regionale og lokale ledd i kirken. Kirkens Informasjonstjeneste. 1989.

16. Roman Catholic, Protestant and Old Catholic Churches in Switzerland

Zur Entwicklung der Massenmedien, Thesen der Kirchen. Freiburg, Bern, Luzern. Vorstand des Schweizerischen Evangelische Kirchenbundes, Konferenz der Römisch-Katholischen Bischöfe der Schweiz und vom Bischof und Synodalrat der Christkatholischen Kirche der Schweiz. 1983.

Appendix 4: People's Communication Charter

We, the Signatories of this Charter, recognize that:

Communication is basic to the life of all individuals and their communities. All people are entitled to participate in communication, and in making decisions about communication within and between societies. The majority of the world's peoples lack minimal technological resources for survival and communication. Over half of them have not yet made a single telephone call. Commercialization of media and concentration of media ownership erode the public sphere and fail to provide for cultural and information needs, including the plurality of opinions and the diversity of cultural expressions and languages necessary for democracy. Massive and pervasive media violence polarizes societies, exacerbates conflict, and cultivates fear and mistrust, making people vulnerable and dependent. Stereotypical portrayals misrepresent all of us and stigmatize those who are the most vulnerable. Therefore, we ratify this Charter defining communication rights and responsibilities to be observed in democratic countries and in international law.

Article 1 Respect
All people are entitled to be treated with respect, according to the basic human rights standards of dignity, integrity, identity, and non- discrimination.

Article 2 Freedom
All people have the right of access to communication channels independent of governmental or commercial control.

Article 3 Access
In order to exercise their rights, people should have fair and equitable access to local and global resources and facilities for conventional and advanced channels of communication; to receive opinions, information and ideas in a language they normally use and understand; to receive a range of cultural products designed for a wide variety of tastes and interests; and to have easy access to facts about ownership of media and sources of information. Restrictions on access to information should be permissible only for good and compelling reason, as when prescribed by international human rights standards or necessary for the protection of a democratic society or the basic rights of others.

Article 4 Independence
The realization of people's right to participate in, contribute to and benefit from the development of self-reliant communication structures requires international assistance to the development of independent media; training programs for professional media workers; the establishment of independent, representative associations, syndicates or trade unions of journalists and associations of editors and publishers; and the adoption of international standards.

Article 5 Literacy
All people have the right to acquire information and skills necessary to participate fully in public deliberation and communication. This requires facility in reading, writing, and storytelling; critical media awareness; computer literacy; and education about the role of communication in society.

Article 6 Protection of journalists
Journalists must be accorded full protection of the law, including international humanitarian law, especially in areas of armed conflict. They must have safe, unrestricted access to sources of information, and must be able to seek remedy, when required, through an international body.

Article 7 Right of reply and redress
All people have the right of reply and to demand penalties for damage from media misinformation. Individuals concerned should have an opportunity to correct, without undue delay, statements relating to them which they have a justified interest in having corrected. Such corrections should be given the same prominence as the original expression. States should impose penalties for proven damage, or require corrections, where a court of law has determined that an information provider has willfully disseminated inaccurate or misleading and damaging information, or has facilitated the dissemination of such information.

Article 8 Cultural identity
All people have the right to protect their cultural identity. This includes the respect for people's pursuit of their cultural development and the right to free expression in languages they understand. People's right to the protection of their cultural space and heritage should not violate other human rights or provisions of this Charter.

Article 9 Diversity of Languages
All people have the right to a diversity of languages. This includes the right to express themselves and have access to information in their own language, the right to use their own languages in educational institutions funded by the state, and the right to have adequate provisions created for the use of minority languages where needed.

Article 10 Participation in policy making
All people have the right to participate in public decision-making about the provision of information; the development and utilization of knowledge; the preservation, protection and development of culture; the choice and application of communication technologies; and the structure and policies of media industries.

Article 11 Children's Rights
Children have the right to mass media products that are designed to meet their needs and interests and foster their healthy physical, mental and emotional development.. They should be protected from harmful media products and from commercial and other exploitation at home, in school and at places of play, work, or business. Nations should take steps to produce and distribute widely high quality cultural and entertainment materials created for children in their own languages.

Article 12 Cyberspace
All people have a right to universal access to and equitable use of cyberspace. Their rights to free and open communities in cyberspace, their freedom of electronic expression, and their freedom from electronic surveillance and intrusion should be protected.

Article 13 Privacy
All people have the right to be protected from the publication of allegations irrelevant to the public interest, or of private photographs or other private communication without authorization, or of personal information given or received in confidence. Databases derived from personal or workplace communications or transactions should not be used

for unauthorized commercial or general surveillance purposes. However, nations should take care that the protection of privacy does not unduly interfere with the freedom of expression or the administration of justice.

Article 14 Harm
People have the right to demand that media actively counter incitement to hate, prejudice, violence, and war. Violence should not be presented as normal, "manly", or entertaining, and true consequences of and alternatives to violence should be shown. Other violations of human dignity and integrity to be avoided include stereotypic images that distort the realities and complexities of people's lives. Media should not ridicule, stigmatize, or demonize people on the basis of gender, race, class, ethnicity, language, sexual orientation, and physical or mental condition.

Article 15 Justice
People have the right to demand that media respect standards of due process in the coverage of trials. This implies that the media should not presume guilt before a verdict of guilt, invade the privacy of defendants, and should not televise criminal trials in real time, while the trial is in progress.

Article 16 Consumption
People have the right to useful and factual consumer information and to be protected against misleading and distorted information. Media should avoid and, if necessary, expose promotion disguised as news and entertainment (infomercials, product placement, children's programs that use franchised characters and toys, etc), and the creation of wasteful, unnecessary, harmful or ecologically damaging needs, wants, products and activities. Advertising directed at children should receive special scrutiny.

Article 17 Accountability
People have the right to hold media accountable to the general public and their adherence to the standards established in this Charter. For that purpose, media should establish mechanisms, including self- regulatory bodies that monitor and account for measures taken to achieve compliance.

Article 18 Implementation
In consultation with the Signatories, national and international mechanisms will be organized to publicize this Charter; to implement it in as many countries as possible and in international law; monitor and assess the performance of countries and media in light of these Standards; receive complaints about violations; advise on adequate remedial measures; and to establish procedures for periodic review, development and modification of this Charter.

Supporting International Treaties
The text of the People's Communication Charter is based on a wide variety of international treaties and conventions. There is currently a website compiled by Prof. Cees Hamelink, which collects the most important treaties in a single site. You can go to this website by typing in the following url:
http://www.unesco.org/webworld/com/compendium/sub_content.html.

Bibliography

Abelman Robert and Hoover Stewart M. (eds)
  1990. *Religious Television Controversies and Conclusions.* Norwood, Ablex
  Publishing Corporation.
Achterhuis, Hans
  2003. *Werelden van tijd.* Stichting Maand van de Filosofie en Hans Achterhuis.
Alasuutari, Pertti
  1999. Introduction: 'Three Phases of Reception Studies' and 'Cultural Images of
  the Media' in Alasuutari, Pertti (ed). *Rethinking the Media Audience.* London,
  Thousand Oaks, New Delhi, Sage Publications. 1-21. 86-104.
Alexander, Bobby C.
  1997. 'Televangelism: Redressive Ritual Within a Larger Social Drama' in
  Hoover, Stewart M. and Lundby, Knut *Rethinking Media, Religion and Culture.*
  Thousand Oaks, Sage, 194-208.
Ang, Ien.
  1991. *Desperately Seeking the* Audience. London, Routledge.
Ang, Ien
  1995. 'The Nature of the Audience' in Downing John, Mohammadi Ali and
  Sreberny-Mohammadi Annabelle (ed) *Questioning the Media, a critical
  introduction.* (2nd edition). Thousand Oaks, Sage Publications.
Ang, Ien
  1996. 'Dallas between reality and fiction' in Cobley, Paul (ed.) *The
  Communication Theory Reader.* London, New York, Routledge. 466-478.
Anyimadu-Bona, Gabriel
  1993. *The evolution of the World Council of Churches' (WCC) thinking on
  communication as portrayed in its official statements from 1948 to 1991.*
  Unpublished Masters Thesis in Social Communication. Roma, Universita'
  Pontificia Salesiana, Instituto di scienze della Communicazione Sociale (ISCOS).
Arthur, Chris
  1989. 'Learning to be responsible for the media environment' in *Media
  Development*, Special Congress Issue, October 1989, 10-12.
Arthur, Chris
  1993. (ed.). *Religion and the Media, an introductory reader.* Cardiff, University
  of Wales Press and London, WACC.
Arthur, Chris
  1997. 'Media, Meaning, and Method in Religious Studies' in Hoover, Stewart
  M. and Lundby, Knut *Rethinking Media, Religion and Culture.* Thousand Oaks,
  Sage, 184-193.
Arthur, Chris
  1998. *The Globalization of Communications, Some Religious Implications.*
  Geneva World Council of Churches, London, World Association for Christian
  Communication.
Baan, Peter A.
  Kerk op het net, over kerkelijke communicatie via internet. Unpublished
  Masters thesis University of Amsterdam.
Babin, Pierre
  1990. 'Communication and participation in an electronic age' in *Media
  Development*, Post Congres Issue, April 1990. 6-9.
Babin, Pierre, Iannone, Mercedes.
  1991. *The New Era in Religious Communication.* Minneapolis, Augsburg
  Fortress Press.

Babrow A.S.
    1988. 'Theory and method in research on audience motives' in *Journal of Broadcasting and Electronic Media*, 32 (4), 471-87.
Badaracco, Claire
    2004. *Non Christian media Ethics & Constructed Religious Image and Identity.* Paper presented at the 4th International Conference on Media, Religion and Culture. Louisville, September 2004.
Bahr, Hans-Eckehard
    1968. *Verkündigung als Information, Zur öffentlichen Kommunikation in der demokratischen Gesellschaft.* Hamburg, Furche Verlag.
Bailey, Edward I.
    1997. *Implicit Religion in Contemporary Society.* Kampen, Kok Pharos
Bailey, Edward I.
    2002. The secular Quest for Meaning in Life. Lewiston, New York, Mellen
Bar-Haim, Gabriel
    1997. 'The Dispersed Sacred: Anomie and the Crisis of Ritual' in Hoover, Stewart M. and Lundby, Knut *Rethinking Media, Religion and Culture.* Thousand Oaks, Sage, 133-145.
Bartolini, Bartolino, Rev. Fr. S.D.B.
    1977. *Audiovisual and Theology.* Lecture World Congress Audiovisual Media and Evangelization Munich 1977. Città del Vaticano, SM-OCIC.
Baum, Gregory
    1993. 'The Church and the Mass Media' in *Concilium*, 1993/6, 63-70.
Bauman Zygmunt
    2000. *As Seen on TV.* Politeia Conference May 2000. Leuven, European Centre for Ethics, Catholic University of Leuven.
Becker, Jörg.
    1996. 'The Internet, structural violence and non-communication' in *Media Development* 4/1996, 10-12.
Beker, E.J., Deurloo, K.A.
    1978. *Het beleid over ons bestaan, vragen en verwijzingen rondom de voorzienigheid.* Baarn, Ten Have.
Bernward, Frank
    1974. 'Bundesrepublik Deutschland: Sehverhalten und Interesse der Fernsehzuschauer gegenüber kirchlichen Sendungen' in: *WACC Journal* 3/1974, 44-47.
Bettig, Ronald V.
    2003. 'Copyright and the commodification of culture' in *Media Development*, vol XIX, no. 1/2003. 3-9.
Bieger, Eckhardt.
    'Religion im digitalen Fernsehen. Technische Entwickelungen und Kriterien für kirchliche Entscheidungen' In *Communicatio Socialis*, 2006, Heft 2, 133-143.
Biernatzki, William E.
    1993. 'Internationalization of the Media' in *Concilium* 1993/6, 39-46.
Biernatzki W.E., S.J.
    1991. 'Televangelism and the religious uses of television', in *Communication Research Trends* Vol. 11 (1991) No.1, 1-30.
Biernatzki, W.E., S.J.
    1995. 'Religion in the Mass Media', in *Communication Research Trends* Vol 15 (1995) No. 2, 1-37.

Biernatzki, William E. S.J.
  1997. 'Globalization of Communication' special issue of *Communication Research Trends* vol. 17 (1997) no.1. Centre for the Study of Communication and Culture, Saint Louis University.
Blom, J.C.H. Wieten, J. Wijfjes, H.B.M. (red).
  1996. *Van geloof, hoop en liefde, vijftig jaar interkerkelijke omroep in Nederland, 1946-1996.* Kampen, Kok, Amsterdam, uitgeverij Otto Cramwinckel.
Bluck, John
  1984. *Beyond Technology, contexts for Christian communication.* Geneva, World Council of Churches.
Bluck John
  1989. 'On the rejuvenating power of communication studies' in *Communication Development,* Special Congress Issue, October 1989. 15-16.
Bluck, John
  1989. *Christian Communication Reconsidered.* Geneva, World Council of Churches Publications.
Bohm, David
  2006 (1996). Edited by Lee Nichol. London, New York, Routledge Classics.
Bolter, Jay David
  1999. 'Typographic Writing: Hypertext and the Electronic Writing Space' in Mayer Paul A. (ed)
  Computer Media and Communication. New York, Oxford University Press Inc. 294-306.
Bordewijk J.L. and van Kaam, Ben
  1982. *Allocutie, enkele gedachten over communicatievrijheid in een bekabeld land.* Baarn, Bosch&Keuning.
Boomershine. Thomas E.
  1989. 'Christian Community and Technologies of the Word' in McDonnell James, Trampiets, Frances, (eds.). 1989. *Communicating Faith in a Technological Age.* Middlegreen, St. Paul Publications. 84-103.
Boomershine, Thomas E.
  2001. 'Toward a Biblical Communication Theology' in *Catholic International,* Vol. 12 no. 4, November 2001. 27-31.
Boomershine, Thomas, E.
  2004. *The Religions of the Book and Religious Warfare in Digital Culture.* Paper presented at the 4th International Conference on Media, Religion and Culture, Louisville, US.
Bouhuijs, Nico, Deurloo, Karel
  1973 (1967). *Taalwegen en dwaalwegen, Bijbelse trefwoorden.* Baarn, Ten Have.
Bouhuijs, Nico, Deurloo, Karel
  1974 (1968). *Dichter bij de profeten.* Baarn, Ten Have.
Bouhuijs, Nico, Deurloo, Karel
  1977 (1967). *Dichter bij Genesis.* Baarn, Ten Have.
Bouhuijs, Nico, Deurloo, Karel
  1980. *Een vreemdeling in ons midden, dichter bij verhalen over de naam van God.* Baarn, Ten Have.
Bouhuijs, Nico, Deurloo, Karel
  1980. *Vechten voor vrede, dichter bij verhalen over vriend en vijand.* Baarn, Ten Have.

Bouhuijs, Nico, Deurloo, Karel
    1988 (1981) . *Gegroeide geschriften, dichter bij het ontstaan van de
    bijbelboeken.*Baarn, Ten Have.
Brandon Scott, Bernard
    1999. 'A New Voice in the Amphitheater: Full Fidelity in Translating' in Soukup,
    Paul A. and Hodgson, Robert (eds.) 1999. *Fidelity and Translation,
    Communicating the Bible in New Media.* Franclin Wisconsin, Sheed & Ward and
    New York, American Bible Society. 101-118.
Brants, Kees and Siune, Karen
    2002 (1998). 'Politicization in Decline?' in McQuail, Denis and Siune, Karen
    (eds. for the Euromedia Research Group) *Media Policy, Convergence,
    Concentration & Commerce*, London, Sage Publications, 128-143.
Brasher, Brenda E.
    1996. 'Thoughts on the Status of the Cyborg: On technological Socialization
    and Its Link to the Religious Function of Popular Culture' in *Journal of the
    American Academy of Religion* 64:4, (1996) 809-830. See also: www.religion-
    online.org retrieved September 7, 2004.
Brown, Delwin; Greeve Davaney Sheila; Tanner, Kathryn ed).
    2001. *Converging on Culture, Theologians in Dialogue with Cultural Analysis
    and Criticism.* New York, The American Academy of Religion and Oxford
    University Press.
Brunsdon C. and Morley D.
    1978. *Every Day Television: Nationwide.* London: BFI.
Buber, Martin
    1958. 2nd edition. *I and Thou.* New York, Charles Scribner's Sons.
Buber, Martin
    1964 (1944). *Werke, Zweiter Band, Schriften zur Bibel.* München, Kösel-Verlag,
    Heidelberg, Verlag Lambert Schneider.
Buddenbaum, Judith M. and Stout, Daniel A.
    1996. 'Religion and Mass Media Use: A Review of the Mass Communication
    and Sociology Literature' and 'Mainline Protestants and the Media' in Stout,
    Daniel A. and Buddenbaum, Judith M. (eds.). 1996. *Religion and Mass Media
    Audiences and Adaptations.* Thousand Oaks London New Delhi, Sage
    Publications. 12-34 and 51-60.
Buddenbaum, Judith. M.
    2002. 'Social Science and the Study of Media and Religion: Going Forward by
    Looking Backward' in *Journal of Media and Religion*, vol. 1, no. 1, 2002. 13-24.
Bühler, Karl-Werner,
    1972. 'Katholische Pastoralinstruktion und protestantische Uppsala-Erklärung
    zur Massenkommunikation', in *Communicatio Socialis*, 5. Jahrgang 1972,
    no. 1, 1-6.
Castells M.
    2000. *The Information Age: Economy, Society and Culture. Volume III: End of
    Millennium.* Blackwell Publishing Ltd
Campbell, Heidi.
    2001. *An Investigation of the Nature of the Church Through an Analysis of
    selected Email-based Christian Online Communities* (unpublished PhD thesis,
    University of Edinburgh)
Campbell, Heidi
    2003. 'Approaches to Religious Research in Computer-Mediated
    Communication' in Mitchell, Jolyon and Marriage, Sophia (eds.) 2003.
    Mediating Religion, Conversations in Media, Religion and Culture. London, New
    York, T&T Clark. 213-228.

Campbell, Heidi
        2004. 'Challenges Created by Online Religious Networks' in *Journal of Media and Religion* Vol. 3 No. 2, 2004. 81-99.
Campbell, Heidi
        2006. 'Religion and the Internet' in *Communication Research Trends* Vol. 25 (2006) No.1
Carey, James W.
        1992 (1989). *Communication As Culture*. London, Routledge.
Centre for the Study of Communication and Culture.
        1982. *Theology and Communication a Bibliography compiled by the Centre for the Study of Communication and Culture. London, CSCC.*
Chappuis, M.
        1981. 'Christology based communication' in *Media Development* 4/1981. London, WACC
Chidester, David
        2000. 'The Church of Baseball, the Fetish of Coca-Cola, and the Potlach of Rock 'N' Roll, in Forbes, Bruce David and Mahan, Jeffrey H. (eds.) *Religion and Popular Culture in America*. Berkeley and Los Angeles, University of California Press, 219-238.
Christians, Clifford G.
        1997. 'Technology and Triadic Theories of Mediation' in Hoover, Stewart M. and Lundby, Knut 1997 *Rethinking Media, Religion and Culture*. Thousand Oaks, Sage, 65-82.
Christians, Clifford G.
        1999. 'Ethics, economics and innovation: The future of accountability' in *Media development* 2/1999. 12-15
Christians, Clifford G.
        2000. *Social Dialogue and Media Ethics*. Politeia Conference May 2000. Leuven, European Centre for Ethics, Catholic University of Leuven.
Christians, Clifford G.
        2002. 'Religious Perspectives on Communication Technology' in *Journal of Media and Religion*, vol. 1, no. 1, 2002. 37-47.
Christians, Clifford G.
        2003. 'Cross-Cultural Ethics and Truth' in Mitchell, Jolyon and Marriage, Sophia (eds.) 2003 *Mediating Religion*. London, T&T Clark, pp 293-303.
Cobb, Jennifer
        1998. *Cybergrace the Search for God in the Digital World.* New York, Crown Publishers, Inc. Christians, Clifford.
        2006. 'Truth at the frontiers of science' in *Media Development*, 2/2006. 6-10.
Cobb, Jennifer
        1998. *Cybergrace, The Search for God in the Digital World*. New York, Crown Publishers.
Cobley, Paul (ed).
        1996. *The Communication Theory Reader*. London, New York, Routledge. Coleman, John A. 1993. 'The sociology of the Media' in *Concilium* 1993/6, 3-11.
Communication Commission National Council of the Churches of Christ in the USA,
        1997. *The Church and Media Statements from the National Council of the Churches of Christ in the USA*. New York, NCC.
Consultation Statement on the Role of Media in Evangelism.
        Undated. Seattle, International Christian Media Commission.
Cooper Ramo Chama, Joshua.
        1996. 'Finding God on the Web' in *Time*, December 16, 1996, 44-53.

Corea, Ash. 1995. 'Racism and the American Way of Media' in Downing John, Mohammadi Ali and Sreberny-Mohammadi Annabelle (eds.) *Questioning the Media, a critical introduction*. (2nd edition). Thousand Oaks, Sage Publications. 345-361.

Davenport, Gloriana
1997. 'Stories as dynamic Adaptive Environments' in Soukup, Paul A., Hodgson, Robert (eds.) *From one medium to another Communicating the Bible Through Multimedia*. Kansas City, Sheed & Ward.

Deacon David, Pickering Michael, Golding Peter, Murdock Graham
1999. *Researching Communications, a Practical Guide to Methods in Media and Cultural Analysis*. London, Arnold, New York Oxford University Press Inc.

De Bens, Els and Østbye, Helge
2002 (1998). 'The European Newspaper Market' in McQuail, Denis and Siune, Karen (eds for the Euromedia Research Group) *Media Policy, Convergence, Concentration & Commerce*, London, Sage Publications, 7-22.

De Bens, Els and Mazzoleni, Gianpietro
2002 (1998). 'The Media in the Age of Digital Communication' in McQuail, Denis and Siune, Karen (eds. for the Euromedia Research Group) *Media Policy, Convergence, Concentration & Commerce*, London, Sage Publications, 165-179.

De Boer, Connie en Brennecke, Swantje
2004 (5th revised version 2003, 1995). *Media en Publiek, Theorieën over media-impact*. Amsterdam, Boom.

De Dijn, H. and Van Herck, W. (eds.)
2002. *Heilige plaatsen; Jeruzalem, Lourdes en shopping malls*. Kappellen. Pelckmans.

De Feijter, Ineke
1992. *Comunicacion popular in Argentinië, aanknopingspunten voor kerkelijk mediawerk*. Unpublished Masters Thesis, Theological Faculty University of Amsterdam. Also in Spanish: *Comunicación popular en Argentina: puntos de referencia para el trabajo eclesiástico de medios*.

De Feijter, Ineke
1993. *Verkondiging op radio en tv: de positie van kerkdienstuitzendingen*. Unpublished thesis for church exams Theological Faculty, University of Amsterdam.

De Feijter, Ineke
1996. 'Kerk en Media: haat of liefde? In *De Open Poort, 76/5 mei 1996*.

De Feijter, Ineke
2000. *Van Babel tot Areopagus, over geloof en moderne communicatietechnologie*. Unpublished lecture for churches in Arnhem.

De Feijter, Ineke
2001. 'Geloof en communicatietechnologie' in *De Open poort*, 81/5 mei 2001, 8-10.

De Feijter, Ineke
2004. *Mainline Religion and Global Media Culture: Kairos or Curtain Line*. Paper presented at the 4th International Conference on Media Religion and Culture. University of Louisville Kentucky.

De Haan, Jos en van 't Hof, Christian. (eds).
2006. *Jaarboek ICT en Samenleving: De digitale Generatie*. Amsterdam, Boom.

Demac, Donna A. and Downing, John.
1995. 'The Tug-of-War Over the First Amendment' in Downing John, Mohammadi Ali and Sreberny-Mohammadi Annabelle (eds.) *Questioning the*

Media, a critical introduction. (2nd edition). Thousand Oaks, Sage Publications. 112-127.

Demac, Donna A. with Sung, Liching
1995. 'New Communication Technologies and Deregulation' in Downing John, Mohammadi Ali and Sreberny-Mohammadi Annabelle (eds.) *Questioning the Media, a critical introduction*. (2nd edition). Thousand Oaks, Sage Publications. 277-292.

De Saussure, F.
1974. (1915). *Course in General Linguistics*. Translation W. Baskin, London, Fontana.

Desjardins, Mary
1995. 'Cinema and Communication' in Downing John, Mohammadi Ali and Sreberny-Mohammadi Annabelle (eds.). *Questioning the Media, a critical introduction*. (2nd edition). Thousand Oaks, Sage Publications. 394-412.

De Swaan, Abram de.
1995. 'De sociologische studie van de transnationale samenleving' in Heilbron en Wilterdink (eds.) *Mondialisering*. Groningen, Wolters-Noordhoff.

Deurloo, Karel
1984 (1981). *Waar Gebeurd, over het onhistorisch karakter van bijbelse verhalen*. Baarn, Ten Have.

Deurloo, Karel
1983. *Om het recht lief te hebben verhalen over de boerenprofeet MICHA*. Baarn, Ten Have.

Deurloo, Karel
1988. *De mens als raadsel en geheim, verhalende antropologie in Genesis 2-4*. Baarn, Ten Have.

Dewey, John
1925. *Experience and Nature*. Chapter five: 'Nature, Communication and Meaning'. Jo Ann Boydston (ed.). *John Dewey, The Later Works, 1925-1953. Volume 1:1925. Experience and Nature*. Carbondale and Edwardsville, Southern Illinois University Press.

Dörger, Hans Joachim
1979. *Kirche in der Öffentlichkeit Programme und Probleme ihrer publizistischen Repräsentanz*. Stuttgart, Berlin, Köln, Mainz, Verlag W. Kohlhammer.

Downing, John, Mohammadi, Ali, Sreberny-Mohammadi, Annabelle (eds.).
1995 (2nd ed.) *Questioning the Media, a critical introduction*. Thousand Oaks London New Delhi, Sage Publications.

Downing, John
1995. 'Media, Dictatorship, and the Reemergence of "Civil Society" and 'Alternative Media and the Boston Tea Party' in Downing John, Mohammadi Ali and Sreberny-Mohammadi Annabelle (eds.) *Questioning the Media, a critical introduction*. (2nd edition). Thousand Oaks, Sage Publications. 184-204. 238-252.

Dulles, Avery, S.J.
2001. 'The Travails of Dialogue' in *Catholic International*, Vol. 12 no. 4, November 2001. 36-40.

Economic Concentration of the Media and Social Responsibility.
2000. Workshop Politeia Conference 25-26 May 2000, Discussietekst, Nederlandstalige versie. Leuven, European Centre for Ethics, Catholic University Leuven.

Ediger, Max
2006. 'The Jolly IT Giant' in *Media Development*, 2/2006. 46-51.

Eilers, Franz-Josef SVD. Ein langer Weg der Annäherung, Katholische Kirche,
        Kommunikation und Mission'
        1989. 'in *Jahrbuch Mission* 1989, 107-117.
Eilers, Franz-Josef, SVD.
        1997. (1993). *Church and Social Communication, Basic Documents.* Manila,
        Logos (Divine Word) Publications.
Eilers, Franz-Josef, SVD.
        2002. (1994) (3rd revised and enlarged edition). *Communicating in Community,
        an Introduction to Social Communication.* Manila, Logos (Divine Word)
        Publications, Inc.
Eilers, Franz-Josef, SVD. (ed.).
        2002. *Social Communication Formation in Priestly Ministry.* Manila, Logos
        (Divine Word) Publications.
Eilers, Franz-Josef, SVD.
        2002. *Church and Social Communication in Asia, Documents, Analysis,
        Experiences.* Manila, Logos (Divine Word) Publications.
Eilers, Franz-Josef, SVD.
        2003. 'The Communication Formation of Church Leaders as a Holistic Concern'
        in Mitchell, Jolyon and Marriage, Sophia (eds.) 2003, *Mediating Religion,
        Conversations in Media, Religion and Culture.* London, New York, T&T Clark.
        pp. 159-166.
Eilers, Franz-Josef SVD. (ed.)
        2003 *E-generation, The Communication of Young People in Asia – A Concern
        of the Church.* Manila, Logos (Divine Word) Publications.
Eilers, Franz-Josef SVD.
        2004 (2003). *Communicating in Ministry and Mission An Introduction to
        Pastoral and Evangelizing Communication.* Manila, Logos (Divine Word)
        Publications.
Eilers, Franz-Josef, SVD.
        2006. *Some Reflections on Communication Theology.* Paper presented at the
        5th International Conference on Media, Religion and Culture. July 2006.
        Sigtuna, Sweden.
Emmanuel, Dominic, SVD.
        1999. *Challenges of Christian Communication and Broadcasting, Monologue or
        Dialogue?* London, Macmillan Press LTD.
Ethiek in de informatiesamenleving.
        2002. Maart. Openbaar debat, VU podium, Amsterdam, Vrije Universiteit.
Farrell, Thomas J. and Soukup Paul A. (eds.).
        1993. *Communication and Lonergan Common Ground for Forging the New
        Age.* Kansas City, Sheed & Ward.
Felton, Daniel J.
        1989. 'The unavoidable dialogue: five interfaces between theology and
        communication' in *Media Development*, Special Congress Issue, 1989. 17-23.
Fernback, Jan.
        2002. 'Internet Ritual: A Case Study of the Construction of Computer-Mediated
        Neopagan Religious Meaning' in Hoover, Stewart M. and Schofield Clark, Lynn
        (eds.). 2002. *Practicing Religion in the Age of the Media.* New York, Columbia
        University Press.
Ferré, John
        2003. 'The Media of Popular Piety' in Mitchell, Jolyon and Marriage, Sophia
        (eds) *Mediating Religion, Conversations in Media, Religion and Culture.*
        London, T&T Clark. pp. 83-92.

Finnemann, Niels Ole
    1999. 'Modernity Modernised: The Cultural Impact of Computerisation' in
    Mayer Paul A. (ed) *Computer Media and Communication*. New York, Oxford
    University Press Inc. 141-159.
Firet, J.
    1971. 'Evangelische informatie via de media' in Hamelink (ed) *Kerk en
    Massamedia*. Baarn, Bosch & Keuning.
Fischer, Ulrich
    2006. 'Was senden die eigentlich? Kirchliche Fernsehsender in Deutschland' in
    *Communicatio Socialis, Internationale Zeitschrift für Kommunikation in Religion,
    Kirche und Gesellschaft*. 2006, Heft 2. 144-155.
Fiske, John
    1989 (1982). *Introduction to Communication Studies*. London and New York,
    Routledge.
Fiske, John and Hartley, John.
    1992. *Reading Television*. London and New York: Routledge
Fombad, Charles Manga
    2001. 'Service providers and liability for digital defamation: Finding the right
    balance' in *Media Development*, 2/2001. 59-64.
Forbes, Bruce David and Mahan, Jeffrey H. (ed).
    2000. *Religion and Popular Culture in America*. Berkeley, Los Angeles, London,
    University of California Press.
Forde Plude, Francis
    1994. 'Interactive Communications in the Church' in Granfield, Patrick (ed.) .
    The Church and Communication. Kansas City, Sheed and Ward.
    179-195.
Forde Plude, Frances
    2001. 'Moving Toward Communicative Theology', unpublished article.
Forde Plude, Frances
    2001. 'Interactive Communication in the Church'. In *Catholic International*,
    Vol. 12 No. 4, November 2001. pp 44-50.
Fore, William. F.
    1970. *Image and Impact how man comes through in the Mass media*. New
    York, Friendship Press.
Fore, William. F.
    1987. *Television and Religion The shaping of faith, values, and culture*.
    Minneapolis, Augsburg Publishing House.
Fore, William.
    1989. 'Eine Lernerfahrung für die alten Kirchen' in *Jahrbuch Mission* 1989,
    118-132. (Translation: Karin Willms).
Fore, William.
    1989. 'Communities of faith must relate to contemporary culture' in
    Communication Development, Special Congress Issue, October 1989. 26-28.
Fore, William.
    1993. 'The religious relevance of television' in Arthur, Chris (ed.). 1993.
    Religion and the Media, an introductory reader. Cardiff, University of Wales
    Press and London, WACC.
Fore William
    1996. 'Cultural and Spiritual Values in a World of Commercial Media' in
    Renewing Communication and Mission. London, Wacc.
Fore, William F.
    1997 (1990). *Mythmakers Gospel Culture and the Media*. New York,
    Friendship Press.

Forrester, Duncan B.
    1993. 'The media and theology: some reflections' in Arthur Chris (ed.) *Religion and the Media*. London/Cardiff WACC and University of Wales Press. Pp 67-78.
Franklin, Robert M.
    1998. 'The Church and Mass Media Communication in the Twenty-First Century' in *International Review of Mission* Vol. 87 no. 346, July 1998, 410-416.
Freire, Paulo.
    1970. *Pedagogia do Oprimido. Pedagogy of the Oppressed.* Translation: M.B. Ramos. 1974 New York, Seabury Press.*Pedagogy of the Oppressed.*
Fuchs, Ottmar.
    1993. 'How the Churches Deal with the Media' in *Concilium* 1993/6, 80-90.
Galtung, Johan and Ruge, Marie
    1965. 'The structure of foreign news' in the *Journal of Peace Research*. No. 2:64-91. Oslo, Peace Research Institute.
Gandy, Jr, Oscar H.
    1995. 'Tracking the Audience: Personal Information and Privacy' in Downing John, Mohammadi Ali and Sreberny-Mohammadi Annabelle (ed) *Questioning the Media, a critical introduction.* (2nd edition). Thousand Oaks, Sage Publications.
Gans, Herbert J.
    1980. *Deciding What's News.* New York. Vintage/Random House.
Ganzevoort, Ruard
    2006. *De hand van God en andere verhalen, Over veelkleurige vroomheid en botsende beelden.* Zoetermeer, Meinema.
Gentikow, Barbara
    2005. *Exploring media experiences. A new approach to reception theory and empirical studies.* Paper to the 1st European Communication Conference. Amsterdam, November 2005.
Gerbner, G.
    1973 Cultural indicators – the third voice' in Gerbner G., Gross L. and Melody. W. (eds.) *Communications Technology and Social Policy.* New York: Wiley
Giles D.
    2003. *Media psychology.* Mahwah, NJ: Lawrence Erlbaum Associates.
Goethals, Gregor
    1981. *The TV Ritual, Worship at the Video Altar.* Boston, Beacon Press.
Goethals, Gregor
    1989. 'The Church and the Mass Media: Competing Architects of Our Dominant Symbols, Rituals and Myths' in McDonnell, James and Trampiets, Frances, *Communicating Faith in a Technological Age.* Middlegreen, St Paul Publications, 56-77.
Goethals, Gregor
    1990. *The Electronic Golden Calf, Images, Religion and the Making of Meaning.* Cambridge, Massachusetts, Cowley Publications.
Goethals, Gregor
    1993. 'Media Mythologies' in Arthur, Chris (ed.) *Religion and the Media, an introductory reader.* Cardiff, University of Wales Press and London, WACC.
Goethals. Gregor
    1996. 'Visible Image and Invisible Faith' in Soukup, Paul A. *Media, Culture and Catholicism.* Kansas City, Sheed & Ward. 37-54.

Goethals, Gregor
    1997. 'Escape from Time: Ritual Dimensions of Popular Culture' in Hoover,
    Stewart M. and Lundby, Knut *Rethinking Media, Religion and Culture*.
    Thousand Oaks, Sage, 117-132.
Goethals, Gregor
    1997. 'Multimedia Images: Plato's Cave Revisited' in Soukup, Paul, Hodgson,
    Robert (eds.) 1997, *From one Medium to Another: Communicating The Bible
    Through Multimedia*. Kansas City, Sheed & Ward. 229-248.
Goethals, Gregor
    1999. 'Aesthetics, Fidelity, and New Media Translations' in Soukup, Paul A. and
    Hodgson, Robert (eds.) 1999. *Fidelity and Translation, Communicating the Bible
    in New Media*. Franclin Wisconsin, Sheed & Ward and New York, American
    Bible Society. 133-172.
Goethals, Gregor
    2000. 'The Electronic Golden Calf, Transforming Ritual and Icon' in Forbes,
    Bruce David and Mahan, Jeffrey H. (eds.) *Religion and Popular Culture in
    America*. Berkeley and Los Angeles, University of California Press, 125-144.
Goethals, Gregor
    2003. 'Myth and Ritual in Cyberspace' in Mitchell, Jolyon and Marriage, Sophia
    (eds.) 2003. *Mediating Religion, Conversations in Media, Religion and Culture*.
    London, New York, T&T Clark. pp. 257-269.
Golan, Guy
    2002. 'Religiosity and the Third-Person Effect' in *Journal of Media and Religion*,
    1 (2), 105-120.
Gräb, Wilhelm
    2002. *Sinn fürs Unendliche, Religion in der Mediengesellschaft*. Gütersloh, Chr.
    Kaiser Gütersloher Verlaghaus.
Granfield, Patrick (ed.).
    1994. *The Church and Communication*. Kansas City, Sheed and Ward.
Grant. Myrna R.
    2003. 'Christ and the Media: Considerations on the Negotiation of Meaning in
    Religious Television' in Mitchell, Jolyon and Marriage, Sophia (eds) 2003.
    Mediating Religion, Conversations in Media, Religion and Culture. London, New
    York, T&T Clark. pp. 121-130.
Gray, Ann
    1999. 'Audience and Reception Research in Retrospect: The Trouble with
    Audiences' in P. Alasuutari (ed.) *Rethinking the Media Audience*. London,
    Sage. 22-37.
Grimes, Ronald L.
    2002. 'Ritual and the Media' in Hoover, Stewart M. and Schofield Clark, Lynn
    (eds.). 2002. *Practicing Religion in the Age of the Media*. New York, Columbia
    University Press.
Habermas J.
    1962. Darmstadt: Hermann Luchterhand Verlag. English translation by Burger
    T. and Lawrence F. 1989. *The Structural Transformation of the Public Sphere:
    An Inquiry into a Category of Bourgeois Society*. Cambridge, Mass.: MIT Press.
Habermas, J.
    1968. *Technik und Wissenschaft als Ideologie*. Frankfurt: Suhrkamp Verlag.
Habermas, Jürgen.
    1989 1962.*The Structural Transformation of the Public Sphere: An Inquiry into
    a Category of Bourgeois Society*. Translation: by Thomas Burger of: 1962
    Strukturwandel der Öffentlichkeit. Cambridge, Polity Press.

Habermas, Jürgen.
    1984, 1987. *The Theory of Communicative Action*. Volume one and two.
    Boston, Beacon Press. Translation of 1981 *Theorie des Kommunikativen
    Handelns*, Frankfurt am MainHagen,
Hagen, Ingunn
    1999. 'Slaves of the Ratings Tyranny? Media Images of the Audience'in P.
    Alasuutari (ed) *Rethinking the Media Audience*. London Sage. 130-150
Hahn, Johan G.
    1988. *Het zout in de pap: Levensbeschouwing en Televisie*. Hilversum, Gooi en
    Sticht.
Hahn, Johan, G. and Tillmans, Frits (eds.)
    1989. *Kijken naar Levensbeschouwing*. Hilversum, Gooi&Sticht.
Haikarainen, Raine
    2002. *Informaatiosta Kommunikaatioon, Ekumeeninen keskustelu, viestinnästä
    1948-2000*. Doctoral dissertation. Helsinki, Suomalaisen Teologisen
    Kirjallisuusseuran Julkasuja 234.
Hamelink, Cees J.
    1971. 'Kerken en kolonels' in Hamelink (ed) *Kerk en Massamedia*. Baarn, Bosch
    & Keuning.
Hamelink, Cees J.
    1973. 'Mass Media Alienation and Emancipation' in *WACC Journal* 1/73, 5-11.
Hamelink, Cees J.
    1975. *Perspectives for public communication a study of the churches'
    participation in public communication*. Baarn, Ten Have.
Hamelink, Cees J.
    1995. 'Information Imbalance Across the Globe' in Downing John, Mohammadi
    Ali and Sreberny-Mohammadi Annabelle (eds.) *Questioning the Media, a critical
    introduction*. (2nd edition). Thousand Oaks, Sage Publications. 293-307.
Hamelink, Cees J.
    1995. *World Communication, Disempowerment & Self-Empowerment*. London,
    New Jersey, Zed Books.
Hamelink, Cees J.
    1997. *New Information and Communication Technologies, Social Development
    and Cultural Change*. Geneva, United Nations Research Institute for Social
    Development.
Hamelink, Cees J.
    1999. *Digitaal fatsoen, mensenrechten in cyberspace*. Amsterdam, Boom.
Hamelink, Cees J.
    'Confronting Cultural Rights' in *Media Development* 4/2001, 44-47.
Hamelink, Cees J.
    'Communication may not build peace, but it can certainly contribute to war' in
    Media Development 2/2002, 36-37.
Hamelink, Cees J.
    2002. *De leugen regeert. Over leugen en bedrog in de informatiesamenleving*.
    Rede in verkorte vorm uitgesproken bij de aanvaarding van het ambt van
    hoogleraar Theologie en Communicatie bij de faculteit der Godgeleerdheid van
    de Vrije Universiteit te Amsterdam op 24 mei 2002. Amsterdam, Vrije
    Universiteit.
Hamelink, Cees J.
    2002. 'Theologie en Communicatie: de uitdagingen van een nieuwe leerstoel'
    in *Gereformeerd Theologisch Tijdschrift*.

Hamelink, Cees J.
    2002. 'Moral challenges in the information society' in *Media Development*,
    4/2002, pp 40-43. London, World Association for Christian Communication.
Hamelink, Cees J.
    2003. 'The Decent Society and Cyberspace' in Mitchell, Jolyon and Marriage,
    Sophia (eds) 2003. *Mediating Religion, Conversations in Media, Religion and
    Culture.* London, New York, T&T Clark. pp. 241-256.
Hamelink, Cees J.
    2004. *Regeert de Leugen? Mediaplichtigheid aan leugen en bedrog.*
    Amsterdam, Boom.
Hamelink, Cees J.
    2004. *Human Rights for Communicators.* Cresskill, New Jersey, Hampton Press
    Inc.
Hamelink, Cees J.
    2006 'Human Communication and the convergence agenda' in *Media
    Development*, vol. LIII 2/2006, 3-6.
Hardy, Ann
    2003. *The Influence of Audience-Images on Constructions of Religion and
    Spirituality: A Production Study.* Paper presented to the Sacred Media
    Conference, Jyvaskyla, Finland, July 2003.
't Hart, Harm, van Dijk, Jan, de Goede, Martijn, Jansen, Wim, Teunissen, Joop
    1997 (1996). *Onderzoeksmethoden.* Amsterdam, Boom.
Heinrichs, Johannes
    1981. 'Theory of practical communication: a Christian approach', in *Media
    Development,* 4/1981. 3-9.
Heinz, Gérard
    1981. *Radiodiffusion et Télévision, Approches Théologiques.* Unpublished
    doctoral thesis, Protestant University of Strasbourg.
Heinz, Gérard
    1981. 'God's revelation is not by words alone' in *Media Development,* 4/1981.
    34-38.
Hellman, Heikki.
    1999. 'Legitimations of Television Programme Policies: Patterns of
    Argumentation and Discursive Convergencies in a Multichannel Age' in P.
    Alasuutari (ed.) *Rethinking the Media Audience.* London, Sage. 105-129.
Hemels, Joan , Hoekstra, Henk (red).
    1985. *Media en religieuze communicatie, een uitdaging aan de christelijke
    geloofsgemeenschap.* Hilversum, Gooi en Sticht.
Hemels, Joan
    1993. 'Democratization and Control of the Media: The Issues and the Debate'
    in *Concilium*, 1993/6, 21-38.
Hemels, Joan
    1999. *Journalistiek en religie in de actuele cultuurbeleving.* Amsterdam, Otto
    Cramwinckel Uitgever.
Henau, Ernest
    1993. *God op de buis, over religieuze uitzendingen in de openbare omroep.*
    Leuven, Davidsfonds.
Henau, Ernest
    De Bleeckere, Sylvain, Elchardus, Mark, Goossens, Cas, Huypens, Jos, Ter Steeg,
    Louis, Van de Voorde, Mark. 1996. *Media & Spiritualiteit.* Leuven, Davidsfonds.

Hess, Mary
> 2003. 'Practising Attention in Media Culture' in Mitchell, Jolyon and Marriage, Sophia (eds.) 2003. *Mediating Religion, Conversations in Media, Religion and Culture*. London, New York, T&T Clark. pp. 133-142.

Henze, Arnd
> 1993. 'Young Man, Come Down from the Pulpit! The Experiences of a Theologian in Secular Political Journalism' in *Concilium* 1993/6, 111-118?

Herman, Edward
> 1995. 'Media in the U.S. Political Economy' in Downing John, Mohammadi Ali and Sreberny-Mohammadi Annabelle (ed) *Questioning the Media, a critical introduction*. (2nd edition). Thousand Oaks, Sage Publications.

Herrmann, Jörg
> 2003. 'From Popular to Arthouse: An Analysis of Love and Nature as Religious Motifs in Recent Cinema' in Mitchell, Jolyon and Marriage, Sophia (eds) 2003. *Mediating Religion, Conversations in Media, Religion and Culture*. London, New York, T&T Clark. pp189-199.

Hermes, J.
> 1995. *Reading Women's Magazines*. Cambridge: Polity

Hermes, Joke
> 1999. 'Media Figures in Identity Construction' in P. Alasuutari (ed) *Rethinking the Media Audience*. London, Sage. 69-85.

Herring, Susan
> 1999. 'Posting in a Different Voice: Gender and Ethics in Computer-Mediated Communication' in Mayer Paul A. (ed) *Computer Media and Communication*. New York, Oxford University Press Inc. 241265.

Hinze, Bradford E.
> 2006. *Practices of Dialogue in the Roman Catholic Church, Aims and Obstacles, Lessons and Laments*. New York, London, Continuum.

Hirsch, Mario and Petersen Vibeke G.
> 2002 (1998). 'European Policy Initiatives' in McQuail, Denis and Siune, Karen (eds. for the Euromedia Research Group) *Media Policy, Convergence, Concentration & Commerce*, London, Sage Publications, 207-217.

Hjarvard, Stig
> 2006. *The Mediatization of Religion, A Theory of the Media as an Agent of Religious Change*. Paper presented at the 5th International Conference on Media, Religion and Culture: 'Mediating Religion in the Context of Multicultural Tension'. Sigtuna, Uppsala, Sweden.

Hoertz Badaracco, Claire
> 1997. 'A Utopian on Main Street' in Hoover, Stewart M. and Lundby, Knut *Rethinking Media, Religion and Culture*. Thousand Oaks, Sage, 246-262.

Hoffmann, Julia
> 2005. *Re-thinking Democratic Legitimacy Communication Rights and Deliberation in a European Public Sphere*. Unpublished Master Thesis, Faculty of Communication Science, University of Amsterdam.

Höhns, Martina
> 1993. *Die "Neue Weltinformations- und Kommunikationsordnung" Eine Analyse der Diskussionen im Ökumenischen Rat der Kirchen*. Studien zur Politikwissenschaft Bd. 81. Hamburg, LIT Verlag.

Hohstadt, Thomas
> 1999. *Dying to live, The 21st Century Church*. Odessa, Damah Media.

Höijer, Birgitta
> 1999. 'To be an audience' in P. Alasuutari (ed.) *Rethinking the Media Audience*. London, Sage. 179-194.

Höller, Karl
        1969. 'Kommentar zu einem Kommentar über "Inter mirifica"', in
        Communication Socialis, 2/1969, 25-35.
Hoover, Stewart M. and Lundby, Knut (eds.).
        1997. *Rethinking Media, Religion and Culture*. Thousand Oaks, London, New
        Delhi, Sage Publications.
Hoover, Stewart M.
        1997. *Religion in a Media Age*. Public Lecture at the University of Edinburgh.
Hoover, Stewart M.
        1997. 'Media and the Construction of the Religious Public Sphere' in Hoover,
        Stewart M. and Lundby, Knut (eds.) *Rethinking Media, Religion and Culture*.
        Thousand Oaks, Sage, 283-297.
Hoover, Stewart M.
        1998. *Media Scholarship and the Question of Religion: Evolving Theory and
        Method*. Presentation to The International Communication Association,
        Jerusalem, 1998.
Hoover, Stewart, M.
        1998. *Religion, Media, and the Cultural Center of Gravity*. Address to the
        Trustees of the Foundation for United Methodist Communications, Nashville,
        1998.
Hoover, Stewart M.
        2000. 'The Cross at Willow Creek, Seeker Religion and the Contemporary
        Marketplace' in Forbes, Bruce David and Mahan, Jeffrey H. (eds) *Religion and
        Popular Culture in America*. Berkeley and Los Angeles, University of California
        Press, 145-159.
Hoover, Stewart M.
        2001. 'Religion in the media Age'. Draft, prepared for submission to *Expository
        Times.*
Hoover, Stewart M. and Schofield Clark, Lynn (eds.).
        2002. *Practicing Religion in the Age of the Media*. New York, Columbia
        University Press.
Hoover, Stewart M.
        2002. 'The Culturalist Turn in Scholarship on Media and Religion' in *Journal of
        Media and Religion*, vol. 1, no. 1, 2002. 25-36.
Hoover, Stewart M.
        2003. 'Religion, Media and identity: Theory and Method in Audience Research
        on Religion and Media' in Mitchell, Jolyon and Marriage, Sophia (eds) 2003.
        Mediating Religion, Conversations in Media, Religion and Culture. London, New
        York, T&T Clark. pp. 9-19.
Hoover, Stewart M.
        2006. *Religion in the Media Age*. London, New York, Routledge
Horsfield, Peter
        (undated). *The impact of electronic media on the culture we live in and some
        major implications for churches and Christian faith*. And: 1997 *The media: the
        major source and centre of religious activity and ritual in contemporary society*.
        Melbourne, Electronic Culture Research Project, Uniting Church Commission for
        Mission.
Horsfield, Peter
        (undated). *The Church and Electronic Culture*. www.religion-online.org
        retrieved 7-9-2004.
Horsfield, Peter
        1989. 'Teaching theology in a new cultural environment' in *Media
        Development,* Special Congress Issue, October 1989. 6-9.

Horsfield, Peter
    1993. 'Teaching theology in a new cultural environment' in Arthur, Chris (ed.).
    Religion and the Media, an introductory reader. Cardiff, University of Wales
    Press and London, WACC.
Horsfield, Peter G.
    1996. 'Theology and the new Cultural Environment' in *Renewing
    Communication and Mission.* London, Wacc.
Horsfield, Peter G.
    1997. 'Changes in Religion in Periods of Media Convergence' in Hoover,
    Stewart M. and Lundby, Knut *Rethinking Media, Religion and Culture.*
    Thousand Oaks, Sage, 167-183.
Horsfield, Peter
    2002. *The Mediated Spirit.* CD Rom. Melbourne, The Commission for Mission,
    Uniting Church in Australia.
Horsfield, Peter
    2003. 'Electronic Media and the Past-Future of Christianity' in Mitchell, Jolyon
    and Marriage, Sophia (eds) *Mediating Religion, Conversations in Media,
    Religion and Culture.* London, New York, T&T Clark. Pp. 271-282.
Horsfield, Peter G.
    2003. 'The ethics of virtual reality: The digital and its predecessors' in *Media
    Development* vol. XLX 2/2003, 48-60. Also presented as paper at the
    Conference on 'Virtual reality and communication ethics', Urbana-Champaign,
    2002.
Horsfield, Peter, Hess, Mary E. and Medrano, Adán (eds.).
    2004. *Belief in Media, Cultural Perspectives on Media and Christianity.*
    Aldershot (UK), Burlington (USA), Ashgate.
Horsfield, Peter
    2004. 'Theology, Church and Media - Contours in a Changing Cultural Terrain'
    in Horsfield, Peter Hess, Mary E. and Medrano, Adán M. (eds.) 2004. *Belief in
    Media, Cultural Perspectives on Media and Christianity.* Aldershot, Burlington,
    Ashgate. 23-32.
Hulsether, Mark D.
    2000. 'Like a Sermon, Popular Religion in Madonna Videos' in Forbes, Bruce
    David and Mahan, Jeffrey H. (eds.) *Religion and Popular Culture in America.*
    Berkeley and Los Angeles, University of California Press, 77-100.
Hunke, Heinz
    1997. *Churches and Faith Organisations on the Internet, A general overview.*
    London, WACC.
Is Internet Outside the Reach of Regulation, Moral Responsibility and Social Control?
    2000. Workshop Politeia Conference May 2000, Discussietekst,
    Nederlandstalige versie. Leuven, European Centre for Ethics, Catholic University
    of Leuven.
Ingunn
    1999. 'Slaves of the Ratings Tyranny? Media Images of the Audience' in P.
    Alasuutari (ed) *Rethinking the Media Audience.* London, Sage. 130-150.
Jaeggi, Urs A.
    1999. *Begrenzte grenzenlose Kommunikation, Im Globalen Dorf lebt der Süden
    noch an der Peripherie.* Bern, Brot für Alle.
Jager, Okke
    1988. *De verbeelding aan het word, pleidooi voor een dichterlijker en zakelijker
    spreken over God.* Baarn, Ten Have.
Jakobson, R. and Halle, M.
    1956. *The Fundamentals of Language.* The Hague: Mouton.

Jakobson, R.
1960. 'Closing statement: linguistics and poetics' in Sebeok, T. (ed.) *Style and Language*. Cambridge, MIT Press. Also in de George, R. and de George F. (eds.) 1972. *The Structuralists from Marx to Levi-Strauss*. New York, Doubleday, Anchor Books.

Jakubowicz, Andrew
1995. 'Media in Multicultural Nations: Some Comparisons' in Downing John, Mohammadi Ali and Sreberny-Mohammadi Annabelle (eds.) *Questioning the Media, a critical introduction*. (2nd edition). Thousand Oaks, Sage Publications. 165-183.

Jakubowicz, Karol.
1999. 'Public Service Broadcasting: Proud past, interesting future?' in *Media Development* 1/1999 32-36 and 'Public Service Broadcasting in the Information Society' in *Media Development* 2/1999, 45-49.

Jelen, Ted G.
1996. 'Catholicism, Conscience, and Censorship' in Stout, Daniel A. and Buddenbaum, Judith M. (eds.). 1996. *Religion and Mass Media Audiences and Adaptations*. Thousand Oaks London New Delhi, Sage Publications. 39-50.

Jensen, Jens F.
1999. 'Interactivity' – Tracking a New Concept in Media and Communication Studies' in Mayer Paul A. (ed) *Computer Media and Communication*. New York, Oxford University Press Inc. 160-187

Jensen, Klaus Bruhn
1999. 'One Person, One Computer: The Social Construction of the Personal Computer' in Mayer Paul A. (ed) *Computer Media and Communication*. New York, Oxford University Press Inc. 188-206

Jewett, Robert
2000. 'The disguise of vengeance in Pale Rider' in Forbes, Bruce David and Mahan, Jeffrey H. (eds.) *Religion and Popular Culture in America*. Berkeley and Los Angeles, University of California Press, 243-257.

Jindra, Michael
'It's about Faith in our Future, Star Trek Fandom as Cultural Religion' in Forbes, Bruce David and Mahan, Jeffrey H. (eds.) *Religion and Popular Culture in America*. Berkeley and Los Angeles, University of California Press, 165-179.

Jones, Steven G.
1999. 'Understanding Community in the Information Age' in Mayer Paul (ed) *Computer Media and Communication*. New York, Oxford University Press Inc. 219-240.

Jørgensen, Knud
1981. 'God's incarnation: the centre of communication' in *Media Development*, 4/1981. 27-30.

Katz E. and Lazarsfeld P.F.
1955. Personal Influence: The Part Played by People in the Flow of Mass Communication. Glencoe, Free Press 1970.

Katz, Elihu
2000. *Media Multiplication and Social Segmentation*. Politeia Conference May 2000. Leuven, European Centre for Ethics, Catholic University of Leuven.

Kappenberg, Barbara
1981. *Kommunikationstheorie und Kirche, Grundlagen einer kommunikationstheoretischen Ekklesiologie*. Frankfurt am Main, Verlag Peter D. Lang GmbH.

Kay, Allen and Goldberg, Adele
1999. 'Personal Dynamic Media' in Mayer, Paul A. *Computer Media and Communication*. New York, Oxford University Press. 111-119.
Kellner, Douglas
1995. 'Advertising and Consumer Culture' in Downing John, Mohammadi Ali and Sreberny-Mohammadi Annabelle (eds.) *Questioning the Media, a critical introduction*. (2nd edition). Thousand Oaks, Sage Publications. 329-344.
Kelly, Mary J.
2002 (1998). 'Media Use in the European Household' in McQuail, Denis and Siune, Karen (eds. for the Euromedia Research Group) *Media Policy, Convergence, Concentration & Commerce*, London, Sage Publications, 144-164.
Kelly, Mary, Mazzoleni, Gianpietro, McQuail, Denis (eds.).
2004. *The Media in Europe*. London, Sage Publications.
Klapper J.
1960. The Effects of Mass Communication. New York: Free Press.
Klaus, Bernhard
1969. *Massenmedien im Dienst der Kirche. Tehologie und Praxis*. Berlin, Verlag Walter de Gruyter & Co.
Kleinsteuber, Hans J.
2002 (1998). 'The Digital Future' in McQuail, Denis and Siune, Karen (eds. for the Euromedia Research Group) *Media Policy, Convergence, Concentration & Commerce*, London, Sage Publications, 60-74.
Knoblauch, Hubert
2003. 'Europe and Invisible religion' in *Social Compass*, 50/3, 2003, 267-274.
Koelega Dick G. A. en Drees Willem B. (red.) .
2000. *God & co? Geloven in een technologische cultuur*. Kampen, Kok.
Koole, Wim
1971. 'Kleine Katechismus voor Kritische Kerkelijke Kijkers' in Hamelink (ed) *Kerk en Massamedia*. Baarn, Bosch & Keuning.
Koole, Wim
1986. *Ons dagelijks beeld, over geloof en televisie*. Baarn, Ten Have.
Koole, Wim
1987. 'Inspiratie in een televisiecultuur' in *Geloof & Esthetiek, Artikelen over een vergeten hoofdstuk in de theologie*. Nijkerk, Callenbach.
Koole, Wim
1993. *De Troost van Televisie, ervaringen van kijkers en makers*. Kampen, Kok.
Koole, Wim
1996. *Een spoor van emoties, een fragment televisiegeschiedenis*. Kampen, Kok.
Koole, Wim en Van den Heuvel, Albert
1999. 'Kerk en media' (special issue) in *Allerwegen* no. 34, 1999.
Kopp, Mathiass
2006. 'Das Gewissen der Menschen bilden. Papst Bendeikt XVI. und seine Sicht der Medien' in *Communicatio Socialis, Internationale Zeitschrift für Kommunikantion in Religion, Kirche und Gesellschaft,* 187-192.
Kwabena Asamoah-Gyadu, J.
2004. 'Pentecostal Media Images and Religious Globalization in Sub-Saharan Africa' in Horsfield, Peter, Hess, Mary E. and Medrano, Adán M. (eds.) 2004. *Belief in Media, Cultural Perspectives on Media and Christianity*. Aldershot, Burlington, Ashgate. 65-80.

Larsen, E.
    2000. *Wired churches, wired temples: Taking congregations and missions into cyberspace.* http:www.pewinternet.org.
Laswell H.
    1948. 'The structure and function of communication in society' in L. Bryson (ed.), *The communication of Ideas*, New York, Harper, pp. 32-51.
Lawrence, Bruce B.
    2002. 'Allah On-Line: The Practice of Global Islam in the Information Age' in Hoover, Stewart M. and Schofield Clark, Lynn (eds.). 2002. *Practicing Religion in the Age of the Media.* New York, Columbia University Press.
Lee, Philip (ed.).
    1986. *Communication for All, The Church and the New World Information and Communication Order.* Madhya Pradesh India, Satprakashan Sanchar Kendra, New York Orbis Books, Ibadan Nigeria, Daystar Press.
Lee, Philip
    2000. A Labour of Love, *The World Association for Christian Communication 1975 – 2000.* London, WACC.
Lee, Philip
    2006. 'Convergent technologies: Future perfect or imperfect?' in *Media Development*, 2/2006. 17-23.
Lent, John A.
    2001. 'Cartooning and democratization world-wide' in *Media development*, 2/2001. 54-58.
Liebes T. and Katz E.
    1990. *The Export of Meaning: Cross-Cultural Readings of 'Dallas'.* Oxford: Oxford University Press.
Licklider, J.C.R. and Taylor, Robert W.
    1999. 'The Computer as a Communication Device' in Mayer, Paul A. *Computer Media and Communication.* New York, Oxford University Press. 97-110.
Linden, Ank
    1996. 'Communication and human rights: a challenge we cannot refuse' in *Media Development* 4/1996, 20-24.
Linderman, Alf
    1997. 'Making Sense of Religion in Television' in Hoover, Stewart M. and Lundby, Knut *Rethinking Media, Religion and Culture.* Thousand Oaks, Sage, 263-282.
Lindijer, Coert H.
    1998. *Postmodern Bestaan, menszijn en geloven in een na-moderne cultuur.* Zoetermeer, Boekencentrum.
Lindlof, Thomas R.
    1996. 'The Passionate Audience, Community Inscriptions of *The Last Temptation of Christ*' in Stout, Daniel A. and Buddenbaum, Judith M. (eds.). 1996. *Religion and Mass Media Audiences and Adaptations.* Thousand Oaks London New Delhi, Sage Publications. 148-167.
Lindlof, Thomas R.
    2002. 'Interpretive Community: An Approach to Media and Religion' in *Journal of Media and Religion*, vol. 1, no. 1, 2002. 61-74.
Lochhead, David
    1988. *Theology in a Digital World.* The United Church Publishing House, The United Church of Canada.
Lochhead, David
    1997. *Shifting Realities, Information Technology and the Church.* Geneva, World Council of Churches Publications.

Lorey, Elmar Maria
    1970. *Mechanismen religiöser Information, Kirche im Prozeß der Massenkommunikation*. München/Mainz, Kaiser - Grünewald Verlag.
Lövheim, Mia and Sjöborg, Anders
    2004. *Seekers in Cyberspace: Youth Maintaining and Challenging Religion Online*. Paper presented to the 4th International Conference on Media, Religion and Culture. Louisville, 2004.
Lowe, Kathy
    1983. *Opening eyes and ears, new connections for Christian communication*. Geneva, World Council of Churches, the Lutheran World Federation, London, the World Association for Christian Communication.
Luckmann, Thomas
    2003. 'Transformations of religion and morality in modern Europe' in *Social Compass* 50/3, 275-285.
Lundby, Knut
    1997. 'The Web of Collective Representations' in Hoover, Stewart M. and Lundby, Knut *Rethinking Media, Religion and Culture*. Thousand Oaks, Sage, 146-164.
Lundby, Knut
    1997. 'Summary Remarks: Mediated Religion' in Hoover, Stewart M. and Lundby, Knut *Rethinking Media, Religion and Culture*. Thousand Oaks, Sage, 298-309.
Lynch, Gordon
    2004. *The dreams of the autonomous and reflexive self: exploring the religious significance of contemporary lifestyle media*. Paper presented at the 4th international Conference on Media Religion and Culture. Louisville, September 2004.
Mahan, Jeffrey H.
    2000. 'Establishing a Dialogue about Religion and Popular Culture' in Forbes, Bruce David and Mahan, Jeffrey H. (eds.) *Religion and Popular Culture in America*. Berkeley and Los Angeles, University of California Press, 292-299.
Mak, Geert
    2005. *Gedoemd tot kwetsbaarheid*. Amsterdam/Antwerpen, Atlas.
Mak, Geert
    2005. *Nagekomen Flessenpost*. Amsterdam/Antwerpen, Atlas.
Martín Barbero, Jésus
    (1985). *De los medios a las mediaciones, Comunicación, cultura y hegemona* . México, Ediciones G. Gilli, S.A. de C.V. Also published in English (1993) as *Communication,Culture and Hegemony: From the Media to Mediations*. London, Sage.
Martín Barbero, Jésus
    1997. 'Mass Media as a Site of Resacralization of Contemporary Cultures' in Hoover, Stewart M. and Lundby, Knut (eds.) *Rethinking Media, Religion and Culture*. Thousand Oaks, Sage, 102-116.
Martini, Carlo Maria.
    1996 (1994). *Communicating Christ to the World*. Translated by Thomas M. Lucas, S.J. Quezon City Philippines, Claretian Communications. First published by Sheed and Ward, Kansas City.
Mattelart, Armand and Michèle
    (1998) (1995). *Theories of Communication a Short Introduction*. London, Sage. Originally published as *Histoire des théories de la communication*. Paris, Éditions La Découverte.

Mattelart, Armand
    1999. 'Against global inevitability' in *Media Development*, 2/1999, 3-6.
Mayer, Paul A.
    1999. 'From Logic Machines to the Dynabook: An Overview of the Conceptual
    Development of Computer Media' and 'Computer Media Studies: An Emerging
    Field' in Mayer Paul A. (ed) *Computer Media and Communication, A Reader*.
    New York, Oxford University Press Inc. 3-22. 320-336.
Marcuse, Herbert.
    1964. *One Dimensional Man*. Boston: Beacon Press.
McCombs, M.E. and Shaw, D.L.
    1972. 'The agenda-setting function of the press' in *Public Opinion Quarterly*,
    36:176-87.
McDonagh, Enda
    1994. 'Moral Theology as Communication' in Rossi Philip J. & Soukup Paul A.
    (eds.). 1994. *Mass Media and the Moral Imagination*. Kansas City, Sheed &
    Ward. 281-288.
McChesney, Robert W.
    1998. 'The political economy of global media' in *Media Development* 4/1998,
    3-8.
McChesney, Robert W.
    2000 (1999). *Rich Media, Poor Democracy, Communication Politics in Dubious
    Times*. New York, The New Press.
McDonnell, James
    'Bibliography on communication and theology' in *Media Development*, 4/1981,
    51-54.
McDonnell, James
    1982. *Theology and Communication A Bibliography Compiled by the Centre for
    the Study of Communication and Culture*. London, CSCC.
McDonnell James
    Trampiets, Frances, (eds.). 1989. *Communicating Faith in a Technological Age*.
    Middlegreen, St. Paul Publications.
McDonnell, James
    1989. 'Communicating the Gospel in a technological age: rediscovering the
    contemplative spirit' in McDonnell James, Trampiets, Frances, (eds.). 1989.
    Communicating Faith in a Technological Age. Middlegreen, St. Paul
    Publications.
McDonnell, Jim
    2003. 'Desperately Seeking Credibility: English Catholics, the News Media and
    the Church' in Mitchell, Jolyon and Marriage, Sophia (eds.) 2003. *Mediating
    Religion, Conversations in Media, Religion and Culture*. London, New York, T&T
    Clark. pp. 33-43.
McLuhan, Marshall
    1966 (1964). *Understanding Media: the Extensions of Man*. New York, Signet
    Books., The New American Library, Inc.
McQuail D., Blumler J.G., & Brown, J. W.
    1972. 'The television audience, a revised perspective' in D. McQuail (ed.),
    Sociology of mass communications. Harmondsworth, UK: Penguin, 135 1 64.
McQuail, Denis
    1995. 'Western European Media: The Mixed Model Under Threat' in Downing
    John, Mohammadi Ali and Sreberny-Mohammadi Annabelle (eds.) *Questioning
    the Media, a critical introduction*. (2nd edition). Thousand Oaks, Sage
    Publications. 147-164.

McQuail, Denis
    1997. *Audience Analysis.* Thousand Oaks, London, New Delhi, Sage
    Publications.
McQuail, Denis
    2000, 4th edition (1983). *McQuail's Mass Communication Theory.* London,
    Thousand Oaks, New Delhi, Sage Publications.
McQuail, Denis
    2002 (1998). 'Commercialization and Beyond' and 'Looking to the Future' in
    McQuail, Denis and Siune, Karen (eds. for the Euromedia Research Group)
    Media Policy, Convergence, Concentration & Commerce, London, Sage
    Publications, 107-127. 218-224.
McQuire, W.J.
    1974. 'Psychological motives and communication gratifications' in J.G. Blumler
    & E. Katz (eds.) *The uses of Mass Communications.* Beverly Hills, CA: Sage,
    167 - 196.
Meier, Werner A. and Trappel, Josef
    2002 (1998). 'Media Concentration and The Public Interest' in McQuail, Denis
    and Siune, Karen (eds. for the Euromedia Research Group) *Media Policy,
    Convergence, Concentration & Commerce*, London, Sage Publications, 38-59.
Meyer, Birgit and Moors, Annelies (eds.)
    2006. *Religion, Media and the Public Sphere.* Bloomington and Indianapolis,
    Indiana University Press.
Meyer, Birgit
    2006. *Religious Sensations, Why Media, Aesthetics and Power Matter in the
    Study of Contemporary Religion.* Rede in verkorte vorm uitgesproken bij de
    aanvaarding van het ambt van hoogleraar Culturele Antropologie, in het
    bijzonder de studie van identiteit en religie bij de faculteit der Sociale
    Wetenschappen van de Vrije Universiteit Amsterdam op 6 oktober 2006.
Melzer, Heinz
    1968. 'Publizistik im Spiegel von Konzilsdekret und Uppsala-Erklärung' in
    Communicatio Socialis, (1968) no. 1, 289-295.
Metz, Johann Baptist
    1993. 'The Electronic Trap. Theological Remarks on Televised Worship' in
    Concilium 1993/6, 57-62.
Meyrowitz, Joshua
    1995. 'Mediating Communication: What Happens?' in Downing John,
    Mohammadi Ali and Sreberny-Mohammadi Annabelle (eds.) 1995, *Questioning
    the Media, a critical introduction.* (2nd edition). Thousand Oaks, Sage
    Publications. 39-53.
Miguez-Bonino, José
    1990. 'Communication and liberation: changing sides' in *Media Development*,
    Post-Congress Issue, 1990.
Miles, David
    1999. 'The CD-ROM Novel *Myst* and McLuhan's Fourth Law of Media: *Myst*
    and Its 'Retrievals' in Mayer Paul A. (ed) *Computer Media and Communication.*
    New York, Oxford University Press Inc. 307-319.
Mills, C. Wright.
    1956. *The Power Elite.* New York: Oxford University Press
Miskotte, K.H.
    1980 (1946) *Bijbels ABC.* Baarn, Ten Have.
Mitchell, Jolyon P.
    1999. *Visually Speaking, Radio and the Renaissance of Preaching.* Edinburgh,
    T&T Clark, Ltd. Louisville Westminster John Knox Press.

Mitchell, Jolyon and Marriage, Sophia (eds).
       2003. *Mediating Religion, Conversations in Media, Religion and Culture*.
       London, New York, T&T Clark.
Mitchell, Jolyon and Marriage, Sophia (eds.)
       2003. *Mediating Religion, Conversations in Media, Religion and Culture*.
       London, New York, T&T Clark. pp. 107-120.
Mohammadi, Ali
       1995. 'Cultural Imperialism and Cultural Identity' in Downing John,
       Mohammadi Ali and Sreberny-Mohammadi Annabelle (eds.) *Questioning the
       Media, a critical introduction*. (2nd edition). Thousand Oaks, Sage Publications.
       362-378.
Morgan, D.
       1998. *Visual Piety: A History and Theory of Popular Religious Images*. Berkeley,
       CA, University of California Press.
Morgan, David
       2002. 'Protestant Visual Practice and American Mass Culture' in Hoover,
       Stewart M. and Schofield Clark, Lynn (eds.). 2002. *Practicing Religion in the
       Age of the Media*. New York, Columbia University Press.
Morgan, David
       2003. 'Protestant Visual Piety and the Aesthetics of American Mass Culture' in
       Mitchell, Jolyon and Marriage, Sophia (eds.) 2003. *Mediating Religion,
       Conversations in Media, Religion and Culture*. London, New York, T&T Clark.
       pp.107-120.
Morgan, D.
       2005. *The Sacred Gaze: Religious Visual Culture in Theory and Practice*.
       Berkeley, CA, University of California Press.
Morley, D.
       1980. *The Nationwide Audience: Structure and Decoding*. London: British Film
       Institute
Morley, David
       1986. *Family television: Cultural Power and Domestic Leisure*. London, Comedia
Morley D.
       1997. 'Theoretical orthodoxies: textualism, constructivism and the "new
       ethnography" in cultural studies' in Ferguson M. and Golding P. (eds.) *Cultural
       Studies in Question*. London, Sage
Morley, David
       1999. 'To Boldly Go…: The Third Generation of Reception Studies' in Alasuutari
       P. (ed.) *Rethinking the Media Audience*. London, Sage. 195-205.
Mowlana, Hamid
       2003. 'Foundation of Communication in Islamic Societies' in Mitchell, Jolyon
       and Marriage, Sophia (eds.) 2003. *Mediating Religion, Conversations in Media,
       Religion and Culture*. London, New York, T&T Clark.
Mullins, Phil
       1997. 'Media Ecology and the New Literacy, Notes on an Electronic
       Hermeneutic' in Soukup, Paul and Hodgson, Robert (eds.), *From One Medium
       to Another, Communicating the Bible through Multimedia*. Kansas City, Sheed
       & Ward, 301-333.
Mulvey L.
       1975. 'Visual Pleasure and Narrative Cinema' in *Screen*, vol. 16, no. 3.
Murdock, Graham
       1997. 'The Re-Enchantment of the World: Religion and the Transformations of
       Modernity' in Hoover, Stewart M. and Lundby, Knut *Rethinking Media, Religion
       and Culture*. Thousand Oaks, Sage, 85-101.

Myer Valenti and Stout
    1996. 'Diversity from within' in Daniel A. and Buddenbaum, Judith M. (eds.).
    1996. *Religion and Mass Media Audiences and Adaptations.* Thousand Oaks
    London New Delhi, Sage Publications.
National Council of the Churches of Christ in the USA.
    The Church and Media, Statements from the National Council of the Churches
    of Christ in the USA. Br 254.3 N213c. NCC Communication Commission, New
    York, 1998
Negus, Keith
    1995. 'Popular Music: Between Celebration and Despair' in Downing John,
    Mohammadi Ali and Sreberny-Mohammadi Annabelle (eds.) *Questioning the
    Media, a critical introduction.* (2nd edition). Thousand Oaks, Sage Publications.
    379-393.
Nelson, Ted
    1999. 'A New Home for the Mind' in Mayer, Paul A. *Computer Media and
    Communication.* New York, Oxford University Press. 120-128.
'New Perspectives on Media and Culture' special issue of *Communication Research
    Trends* Vol. 8 (1987), no.2. London, Centre for the Study of Communication
    and Culture.
Newcomb T.
    1953. 'An approach to the study of communication acts' in Psychological
    Review, 60, pp 393-40 and in Smith A.G. (ed.) 1966 Communication and
    Culture. New York, Holt, Rinehart & Winston.
Newman, Jay
    1996. *Religion vs. Television Competitors in Cultural Context.* Westport,
    Connecticut, London, Praeger Publishers.
Niebuhr, H.R.
    1951. *Christ and Culture.* New York, Harper & Row
Noble, David F.
    1999 (1997). *The Religion of Technology the Divinity of Man and the Spirit of
    Invention.* New York, Penguin Group.
Noelle-Neumann, E.
    1984. *The Spiral of Silence.* Chicago, University of Chicago Press. In 1974 she
    published a first article on this subject: 'The spiral of Silence: a theory of public
    opinion' in: *Journal of Communication,* 24:24-51.
Nolan, Steve
    2003. 'Towards a New Religious Film Criticism: Using Film to Understand
    Religious identity Rather than Locate Cinematic Analogue' in Mitchell, Jolyon
    and Marriage, Sophia (eds.) 2003. *Mediating Religion, Conversations in Media,
    Religion and Culture.* London, New York, T&T Clark. pp. 169-178.
O'Connor, Alan and Downing, John
    1995. 'Culture and Communication' in Downing John, Mohammadi Ali and
    Sreberny-Mohammadi Annabelle (eds.) *Questioning the Media, a critical
    introduction.* (2nd edition). Thousand Oaks, Sage Publications. 3-22.
'Okinawa Charter on Global Information Society' in *Media Development* 4/2000.
Ong, Walter, J. s.j.
    1996 (1969). 'Communications Media and the State of Theology' in Soukup,
    Paul A. 1996. *Media, Culture and Catholicism.* Kansas City, Sheed & Ward.
    3-20. Originally published in *Cross Currents,* 19 (1969), 462-480.
Ortiz, Gaye
    2003. 'The Catholic Church and its Attitude to Film as an Arbiter of Cultural
    Meaning' in Mitchell, Jolyon and Marriage, Sophia (eds.) *Mediating Religion,*

Conversations in Media, Religion and Culture. London, New York, T&T Clark.
pp. 179-188.

Osgood C.
1967. *The measurement of Meaning.* Illinois, University of Illinois Press.

Ó Siochrú, Seán and Girard, Bruce, with Mahan, Amy
2002. *Global Media Governance, a Beginner's Guide.* Lanham, Boulder, New
York, Oxford, Rowman and Littlefield.

Østergaard, Bernt Stubbe
2002 (1998). 'Convergence: Legislative Dilemmas' in McQuail, Denis and Siune,
Karen (eds. for the Euromedia Research Group) *Media Policy, Convergence,
Concentration & Commerce*, London, Sage Publications, 95-106.

Palakeel, Joseph
2006. *Engaging Communication in Easing Cultural and Commmunal Tension
and Conflict: A Communication Theology Perspective.* Paper presented at the
5th International Conference on Media, Religion and Culture, Sigtuna, Sweden,
July 2006.

Palakeel, Joseph
2006. 'Communication theology in priestly formation' in Srampickal, Jacob,
Mazz, Giuseppe and Baugh, Lloyd (eds.) 2006 *Cross Connections,
Interdisciplinary communiton studies at the Gregorian University*, Rome, Editrice
Pontificia Uniersità Gregoriana.

Palmen, Connie
2004. *Iets wat niet bloeden kan.* Stichting maand van de Filosofie en Connie
Palmen

Park, Jin Kyu
2004. *Locating the Study of Media, Religion, and Culture Within the Debate
between "Culturalist" and "Structuralist" Perspectives.* Paper presented at the
4th International Conference on Media, Religion and Culture, Louisville, UK,
2004.

Peck, Janice
1997. 'Psychologized Religion in a Mediated World' in Hoover, Stewart M. and
Lundby, Knut *Rethinking Media, Religion and Culture.* Thousand Oaks, Sage,
227-245.

Peters, John Durham
1999. *Speaking into the Air, a history of the idea of communication.* Chicago,
The University of Chicago Press.

Pinn, Anthony
2000. 'Rap Music and its Message, On Interpreting the Contact between
Religion and Popular Culture' in Forbes, Bruce David and Mahan, Jeffrey H.
(eds.) *Religion and Popular Culture in America.* Berkeley and Los Angeles,
University of California Press, 258-275.

Podesta, Anthony T and Kurtzke, James S.
1990. 'Conflict Between the Electronic Church and State: The Religious Ritgh's
Crusade Against Pluralism' in Abelman Robert and Hoover Stewart M. Editors,
1990. *Religious Television Controversies and Conclusions.* Norwood, Ablex
Publishing Corporation. 207-226.

Politeia Conferentie.
2000. 25 en 26 mei. Leuven, Overlegcentrum voor Ethiek KU Leuven en The
European Ethics Network.

Politics and Propaganda: The Media in Eastern Europe Before and After the Fall of the Berlin Wall.
2000. Workshop Politeia Conference May 2000, Discussietekst, Nederlandstalige versie. Leuven, European Centre for Ethics, Katholieke Universiteit Leuven.

Pottmeyer, Hermann
'Dialogue as a Model for Communication in the Church' in *Catholic International*, Vol. 12 No. 4, November 2001, pp. 41-44 This article is a reprint from Granfield, Patrick (ed.)1994. *The Church and Communication.* pp. 97-103. Kansas City, Sheed and Ward.

Price, Joseph L.
2000. 'An American Apotheosis, Sports as Popular Religion' in Forbes, Bruce David and Mahan, Jeffrey H. (eds.) *Religion and Popular Culture in America.* Berkeley and Los Angeles, University of California Press, 201-218.

Radway, Janice A.
1996. 'Reading the Romance' in Cobley, Paul (ed.) 1996 *The Communication Theory Reader.* London New York Routledge. 448-465.

Real, Michael
1995. 'Sport and the Spectacle' in Downing John, Mohammadi Ali and Sreberny-Mohammadi Annabelle (eds.) *Questioning the Media, a critical introduction.* (2nd edition). Thousand Oaks, Sage Publications. 460-475.

Rebel, Henk Jan
2000. *Communicatiebeleid en Communicatiestrategie.* Amsterdam, Boom.

Regan, Jane
2000. 'From French revolution to information revolution' in *Media Development* 1/2000. London, WACC, 14-19.

Reijnders, Stijn, Rooijakkers, Gerard and van Zoonen, Liesbet
2005. *Community Spirit and Competition in Idols. Ritual Meanings of a TV Talent Quest.* Paper presented at the First European Communication Conference. November 2005. Amsterdam.

Rey, Germán
2004. 'Identities, Religion and Melodrama: A View from the Cultural Dimension of the Latin American Telenovela' in Horsfield, Peter, Hess, Mary E. and Medrano, Adán M. (eds.). *Belief in Media, Cultural Perspectives on Media and Christianity.* Aldershot, Burlington, Ashgate. 81-90.

Robinson, Cedric J.
1995. 'Mass Media and the U.S. Presidency' in Downing John, Mohammadi Ali and Sreberny-Mohammadi Annabelle (ed) *Questioning the Media, a critical introduction.* (2nd edition). Thousand Oaks, Sage Publications.

Rodríguez, América
1995. 'Control Mechanisms of National News Making: Britain, Canada, Mexico and the United States' in Downing John, Mohammadi Ali and Sreberny-Mohammadi Annabelle (ed) *Questioning the Media, a critical introduction.* (2nd edition). Thousand Oaks, Sage Publications.

Rolfes, Helmut
2004. 'Gibt es eine kirchenamtliche Lehre der sozialen Kommunikation? Ein Rückblick 40 Jahre nach ‚Inter Mirifica" in *Communicatio Socialis*, Internationale Zeitschrift für Kommunikation in Religion, Kirche und Gesellschaft, 37. Jahrgang, 2004, Heft 3, 219-244.

Roman, Anthony G.
2006. *Texting God: Religion & SMS in the Philippines.* Paper presented at the 5th International Conference on Media, Religion and Culture. July 2006. Sigtuna, Sweden.

Romanowski, William D.
    2000. 'Evangelicals and Popular Music, The Contemporary Christian Music
    Industry' in Forbes, Bruce David and Mahan, Jeffrey H. (eds) *Religion and
    Popular Culture in America*. Berkeley and Los Angeles, University of California
    Press, 105-124.
Rosengren, Karl Erik
    2000. *Communication, an introduction*. London, Thousand Oaks, New Delhi,
    Sage Publications.
Rosenthal, Michele
    2002. "Turn It Off": TV Criticism in the *Christian Century* Magazine, 1946-
    1960.
Rossi Philip J. & Soukup Paul A. (eds.).
    1994. *Mass Media and the Moral Imagination*. Kansas City, Sheed & Ward.
Russo, Michael A.
    1993. 'The Bishops and Abortion: A Case Study in Reporting Church News' in
    Concilium 1993/6, 91-98?
Ryan, John and Wentworth, William M.
    1999. *Media and Society, the Production of Culture in the Mass Media*.
    Needham Heights, Allyn & Bacon.
Sabanes Plou, Dafne
    1996. *Global Communication, is There a Place for Human Dignity?* Geneva,
    World Council of Churches Publications.
Schillebeeckx, E. O.P.
    1964. *Openbaring en Theologie*. Bilthoven, uitgeverij H. Nelissen.
Schiller H.
    1969. *Mass Communications and American Empire*. Boston: Beacon Press.
Schleifer, S.A.
    1993. 'An Islamic Perspective on the News' in in Arthur, Chris (ed.). 1993.
    Religion and the Media, an introductory reader. Cardiff, University of Wales
    Press and London, WACC. 163-175.
Schmidt, Joachim
    1980. *Rundfunkmission Ein Massenmedium wird Instrument*. Erlanger
    Taschenbücher Bd. 44. Erlangen, Verlag der Ev.-Luth. Mission.
Schofield Clark, Lynn and Hoover, Stewart M.
    1997. 'At the Intersection of Media, Culture, and Religion: A Bibliographic
    Essay' in Hoover, Stewart M. and Lundby, Knut *Rethinking Media, Religion and
    Culture*. Thousand Oaks, Sage, 15-36.
Schofield Clark, Lynn and Hoover, Stewart M.
    1997. 'At the Intersection of Media, Culture, and Religion: A Bibliographic
    Essay' in Hoover, Stewart M. and Lundby, Knut, 1997 *Rethinking Media,
    Religion and Culture*, Thousand Oaks, London, New Delhi, Sage. 15-36.
Schofield Clark, Lynn
    1998. *Building Bridges between Theology and media Studies*. Presentation to
    the Catholic Theological Society of America. June, 12, 1998.
Schofield Clark, Lynn
    2002. 'The "Protestantization" of Research into Media, Religion, and Culture'
    in Hoover, Stewart M. and Schofield Clark, Lynn (eds.). 2002. *Practicing
    Religion in the Age of the Media*. New York, Columbia University Press.
Schofield Clark, Lynn
    2002. *From Angels to Aliens, Teenagers, The Media, and The Supernatural*.
    New York, Oxford University Press.

Schofield Clark, Lynn
    2003 'The 'Funky' Side of Religion: An Ethnographic Study of Adolescent
    Religious Identity and the Media' in Mitchell, Jolyon and Marriage, Sophia (eds.)
    Mediating Religion, Conversations in Media, Religion and Culture. London, New
    York, T&T Clark. pp. 21-32.
Schofield Clark, Lynn
    2004. 'Reconceptualizing Religion and Media in a Post-National, Postmodern
    World: A Critical Historical Introduction' in Horsfield, Peter, Hess, Mary E. and
    Medrano, Adán M. (eds.) 2004. *Belief in Media, Cultural Perspectives on Media
    and Christianity*. Aldershot, Burlington, Ashgate. 7-22.
Schofield Clark, Lynn (ed.)
    2006. *Religion, Media, and the Marketplace*. Rutgers University
Schofield Clark, Lynn (ed.)
    2006. *Religion, Media, and the Marketplace*. Rutgers University Press.
    Piscataway, NJ, Rutgers University Press.
Scholte, Jan Aart
    2000. *Globalization, a critical introduction*. Basingstoke, Hampshire and New
    York, Palgrave.
Schreiter, Robert, J.
    1985. *Constructing Local Theologies*. London, SCM Press
Schrøder, Kim Christian
    1999. 'The best of both Worlds? Media Audience Research between Rival
    Paradigms' in P. Alasuutari (ed.) *Rethinking the Media Audience*. London, Sage.
    38-68.
Schrøder, Jim, Drotner, Kirsten, Kline, Stephen and Murray, Catherine
    2003. *Researching Audiences*. London, Arnold.
Schultze, Quentin J.
    1989. 'Religious Belief in a Technological World: The Implications of the
    Electronic Church' in McDonnell James, Trampiets, Frances, (eds.). 1989.
    Communicating Faith in a Technological Age. Middlegreen, St. Paul
    Publications. 112-132.
Schultze, Quentin J.
    1990, 'Defining the Electronic Church' in Abelman Robert and Hoover Stewart
    M. Editors, 1990. *Religious Television Controversies and Conclusions*.
    Norwood, Ablex Publishing Corporation.
Schultze, Quentin J.
    1996. 'Evangelicals' Uneasy Alliance With the Media' in Stout, Daniel A. and
    Buddenbaum, Judith M. (eds.). 1996. *Religion and Mass Media Audiences and
    Adaptations*. Thousand Oaks London New Delhi, Sage Publications. 61-73.
Schultze, Quentin J.
    2000. *Communicating for Life Christian Stewardship in Community and Media*.
    Grand Rapids, Baker Academic.
Self, Rebecca L.
    Mickey Made Me: Walt Disney Productions as Civil Religion for a Global Order.
    Paper presented at the Media, Religion and Culture Conference, Sigtuna,
    Sweden, July 2006.
Servaes, Jan and Lie, Rico
    2001. 'Media versus globalisation and localisation' in *Media Development*,
    3/2001, 19-24.
Settle, 'Faith, Hope and Charity:
    Rhetoric as Aletheiac Act in *On Christian Doctrine, Journal of Communication
    and Religion* 17:2 (September 1994) p. 49.

Shanks, Thomas E.
    1994. 'Power, Truth, and the Flow of Information' in Rossi Philip J. & Soukup,
    Paul A. (eds.). *Mass Media and the Moral Imagination*. Kansas City, Sheed
    Ward.
Sherry, J.L.
    2001. 'The effects of violent video games on aggression' in *Human
    Communication Research* 27 (3), 409-431
Shields, Richard
    2004. 'Moral Discourse within the Church, an Essential Dimension of Social
    Communication' in *Communicatio Socialis*, Internationale Zeitschrift für
    Kommunikation in Religion, Kirche und Gesellschaft, 37. Jahrgang, 2004, Heft
    3. 245-260.
Sinha, Nikhil and Stone, Allucquére
    1995. 'Computers and Communication' in Downing John, Mohammadi Ali and
    Sreberny-Mohammadi Annabelle (eds.) *Questioning the Media, a critical
    introduction*. (2nd edition). Thousand Oaks, Sage Publications. 255-276.
Sisley, Joy
    1999. 'Power and Interpretative Authority in Multimedia Translation' in Soukup,
    Paul A. and Hodgson, Robert (eds.) 1999. *Fidelity and Translation,
    Communicating the Bible in New Media*. Franclin Wisconsin, Sheed & Ward and
    New York, American Bible Society.203-217.
Siune, Karen and Hultén, Olof
    2002 (1998). 'Does Public Broadcasting Have a Future?' in McQuail, Denis and
    Siune, Karen (eds. for the Euromedia Research Group) *Media Policy,
    Convergence, Concentration & Commerce*, London, Sage Publications, 23-37.
Slinger, Peg
    1993, 'Television commercials : mirror and symbol of societal values' in Arthur,
    Chris (ed.). 1993. *Religion and the Media, an introductory reader*. Cardiff,
    University of Wales Press and London, WACC. 199-207.
Smythe, D.W.
    1977. 'Communications: blind spot of Western Marxism' in *Canadian Journal
    of Political and Social Theory* I: 120-7.
Søgaard, Viggo
    1993. *Media in Church and Mission, Communicating the Gospel*. Pasadena,
    William Carey Library.
Sorbets, Claude
    2002 (1998). 'Debating National Policy' in McQuail, Denis and Siune, Karen
    (eds. for the Euromedia Research Group) *Media Policy, Convergence,
    Concentration & Commerce*, London, Sage Publications, 180-190.
Soukup, Paul A. s.j.
    1983. *Communication and Theology Introduction and Review of the Literature*.
    London, The World Association for Christian Communication in cooperation
    with the Centre for the Study of Communication and Culture.
Soukup, Paul A. s.j.
    1985. 'Interweaving theology and communication' in *Media Development,*
    1/1985, 30-33.
Soukup, Paul A. s.j.
    1989. 'Changing the way communication is taught in seminaries' in *Media
    Development,* Special Congress Issue October 1989. 2-5.
Soukup, Paul A. s.j.
    1989. *Christian Communication A Bibliographical Survey*. New York, London,
    Greenwood Press.

Soukup, Paul A. s.j.
  1993. 'Church Documents and the Media' in *Concilium* 1993/6, 71-79.
Soukup, Paul A. s.j.
  1996. *Media, Culture and Catholicism.* Kansas City, Sheed & Ward.
Soukup Paul A. s.j. Hodgson Robert (eds.).
  1997. *From one Medium to Another Communicating the Bible Through
  Multimedia.* Kansas City, Sheed & Ward.
Soukup Paul A. s.j. and Hodgson, Robert (eds.).
  1999. *Fidelity and Translation, Communicating the Bible in New Media.* New
  York, American Bible Society and Franklin, Sheed and Ward.
Soukup, Paul A. s.j.
  1999. 'Communication Models, Translation, and Fidelity' in Soukup, Paul A.
  and Hodgson, Robert (eds.) 1999. *Fidelity and Translation, Communicating the
  Bible in New Media.* Franclin Wisconsin, Sheed & Ward and New York,
  American Bible Society. 219-231.
Soukup, Paul A. s.j.
  2001. 'What Does the Bible Have to Do with Mass Media, Anyway?' and
  'Communication Theology as a Basis for Social Communication Formation' in
  Catholic International, Vol. 12 no. 4, November 2001. 12-17 and 31-35. The
  latter also in: Eilers, Franz-Josef, svd. (ed.). 2002. *Social Communication
  Formation in Priestly Ministry.* Manila, Logos (Divine Word) Publications. 45-64.
Soukup, Paul A. s.j.
  2004. *Recent Work in Communication and Theology: A Report.* Paper
  presented at the 4th international Conference of media, Religion and Culture.
  Louisville, US.
Soukup, Paul A. s.j.
  2004. 'Transforming the Sacred: The American Bible Society New Media
  Translation Project' in *Journal of Media and Religion*, vol. 3 no.2, 2004.
  101-118.
Splichal, Slavko
  1999. 'Using the principle of publicity to create public service media' in *Media
  Development* 3/1999, 3-8.
Sreberny-Mohammadi, Annabelle
  1995. 'Forms of Media as Ways of Knowing' and 'Global News Media Cover
  the World' in Downing John, Mohammadi Ali and Sreberny-Mohammadi
  Annabelle (eds.) *Questioning the Media, a critical introduction.* (2nd edition).
  Thousand Oaks, Sage Publications. 23-38. 428-443.
Sreberny-Mohammadi, Annabelle
  1995. 'Global News Media Cover the World' in Downing John, Mohammadi Ali
  and Sreberny-Mohammadi Annabelle (eds.) *Questioning the Media, a critical
  introduction.* (2nd edition). Thousand Oaks, Sage Publications.
Staudenmaier, John M.
  1989. 'Moving at the Speed of Light: the Influence of Communication
  Technologies on Modern American Culture' in McDonnell, James and
  Trampiets, Frances (eds.) *Communicating Faith in a Technological Age.*
  Middlegreen, St Paul Publications, 28-48.
Staudenmaier, John M.
  1993. 'The Media: Technique and Culture' in *Concilium* 1993/6, 12-20.
Stoffels, Hijme
  2002. *Geen wonder?! Geloven in de postmoderne samenleving.* Inaugurele
  Rede, 22-02-2002, Amsterdam, Vrije Universiteit.

Stone, Allucquere Rosanne
    1999. 'Will the Real Body Please Stand Up? Boundary Stories about Virtual
    Cultures' in Mayer Paul A. (ed) *Computer Media and Communication*. New
    York, Oxford University Press Inc. 266-293.
Stout, Daniel A. and Buddenbaum, Judith M. (eds.).
    1996. *Religion and Mass Media Audiences and Adaptations.* Thousand Oaks
    London New Delhi, Sage Publications.
Stout, Daniel and Buddenbaum, Judith
    1996. 'Toward a Synthesis of Mass Communication Research and the Sociology
    of Religion' in Stout, Daniel A. and Buddenbaum, Judith M. (eds.). 1996.
    Religion and Mass Media Audiences and Adaptations. Thousand Oaks London
    New Delhi, Sage Publications. 3-11.
Stout, Daniel A. and Buddenbaum, Judith M.
    2002. 'Genealogy of an Emerging Field: Foundations for the Study of Media
    and Religion' in *Journal of Media and Religion*, vol. 1, no. 1, 2002. 5-12.
Stout, Daniel A.
    2002. 'Religious Media Literacy: Towards a Research Agenda' in *Journal of
    Media and Religion*, vol. 1, no. 1, 2002. 49-60.
Sturgill, Amanda
    2004. 'Scope and Purposes of Church Web Sites' in *Journal of Media and
    Religion*, Vol. 3, no. 3, 2004.165-176.
Sumiala-Seppänen
    2004. *Communio Sanctorum, Sacred Visual Communities in the Media Age.*
    Keynote lecture at the 4th International Conference on Media Religion and
    Culture, 2004, Louisville, US.
Sumiala-Seppänen, Johanna, Lundby, Knut & Salokangas, Raimo (eds.)
    2006. *Implications of the Sacred in (Post)Modern Media*. Göteborg, Nordicom,
    Göteborg University.
Sunderaj, Victor (ed.).
    1998. *Pastoral Planning for Social Communication*. Montreal, Paulines.
Sutinen, Erkko
    1994. 'Computers and Change in Mission' in *International Review of Mission*,
    vol. 83, no. 331, October 94, 585-594.
Tanner, Kathryn
    1997. *Theories of Culture, a New Agenda for Theology*. Minneapolis, Augsburg
    Fortress Press.
Ter Borg, Meerten, B.
    1991. *Een uitgewaaierde eeuwigheid, het menselijk tekort in de moderne
    cultuur*. Baarn, Ten Have.
The Task of a Public Broadcasting System
    2000. Workshop Politeia Conference May 2000, Discussietekst,
    Nederlandstalige versie. Leuven, European Centre for Ethics, Catholic University
    of Leuven.
'The Seoul Statement of the MacBride Round Table on Communication' in *Media
    Development* 4/1996, 24-26.
Thomas, Pradip
    2003. 'Intellectual Property Rights and communication: A glossary of terms' in
    Media Development 1/2003, 34-38.
Thomas, Pradip N.
    2003. 'Digital cohabitations: The social consequences of convergent
    technologies' in *Media Development*, 2/2003, 3-12.

Thomas, Pradip
    2005. 'Christian Fundamentalism and the media' in *Media Development*
    2/2005, 3-9.
Thomas, Pradip
    2006. 'Understanding the new sciences in the pursuit of life' in *Media*
    Development, 2/2006. 51-56.
Thomas, Sari
    1995. 'Myths In and About Television: Entertainers and Economics' in Downing
    John, Mohammadi Ali and Sreberny-Mohammadi Annabelle (eds.) *Questioning*
    the Media, a critical introduction. (2nd edition). Thousand Oaks, Sage
    Publications. 444-459.
Thompson, Robert J.
    2000. 'Consecrating Consumer Culture, Christmas Television Specials' in
    Forbes, Bruce David and Mahan, Jeffrey H. (eds.) *Religion and Popular Culture*
    in America. Berkeley and Los Angeles, University of California Press, 44-55.
Thorn, William
    1996. 'Models of Church and Communication' in Soukup, Paul A. 1996.
    Media, Culture and Catholicism. Kansas City, Sheed & Ward. 82-106.
Tillich, Paul
    1952. *The Courage to be.* Yale, University Press.
Tillich, Paul
    1955. *Biblical Religion and the Search for Ultimate Reality.* The University of
    Chicago Press.
Tillich, Paul
    1956. 'The Church and Contemporary Culture' in *World Christian Education,*
    second quarter, 1956, 41-43. www.religion-online.org, retrieved, 13-9-2004.
Tillich, Paul
    1959. *Theology of Culture.* New York, Oxford University Press.
Tillich, Paul.
    1959. *Frühe Hauptwerke.* Stuttgart, Evangelisches Verlagswerk.
Tomaselli, Keyan G. and Shepperson, Arnold
    1997. 'Resistance Through Mediated Orality' in Hoover, Stewart M. and
    Lundby, Knut *Rethinking Media, Religion and Culture.* Thousand Oaks, Sage,
    209-226.
Tomka, Miklós
    1993. 'Eastern Europe: The Media in Transition' in *Concilium,* 1993/6, 47-54.
Traber, Michael
    1987. 'The Illusion of "Mission as Marketing"' in *The Ecumenical Review* vol.
    39 no. 3, July 1987, 318-326.
Traber, Michael
    1990. 'The Holy Spirit and Communication' in *The Ecumenical Review* vol. 42,
    no. 3-4, July-October 1990, 207-215.
Traber Michel & Nordenstreng, Kaarle
    1992. *Few Voices, Many Worlds, towards a Media Reform Movement.* London,
    World Association for Christian Communication.
Trappel, Josef and Meier, Werner A.
    2002 (1998). 'Media Concentration: Options for Policy' in McQuail, Denis and
    Siune, Karen (eds. for the Euromedia Research Group) *Media Policy,*
    Convergence, Concentration & Commerce, London, Sage Publications,
    191-206.

Truetzschler, Wolfgang
    2002 (1998). 'The internet: A New Mass Medium?' in McQuail, Denis and
    Siune, Karen (eds. for the Euromedia Research Group) *Media Policy,
    Convergence, Concentration & Commerce*, London, Sage Publications, 75-94.
Tulloch, John
    1999. 'The Implied Audience in Soap Opera Production: Everyday Rhetorical
    Strategies among Television Professionals' in P. Alasuutari (ed.) *Rethinking the
    Media Audience*. London, Sage. 151-178.
Underwood, Doug
    2006. Book review of Peters, John Durham. 2005. *Courting the Abyss: Free
    Speech and the Liberal Tradition* in *Journal of Media and Religion*, volume 5,
    number 1, 2006, pp 63-66.
Underwood, Meredith
    2000. 'Lost in Cyberspace? Gender, Difference and the Internet "Utopia" in
    Forbes, Bruce David and Mahan, Jeffrey H. (eds.) *Religion and Popular Culture
    in America*. Berkeley and Los Angeles, University of California Press, 276-291.
Valle, Carlos
    1989. 'Kommunikation und Gemeinschaft, Biblisch-theologische Reflexionen' in
    Jahrbuch Mission, 1989. 70-81. (Translation: Karin Willms).
Valle, Carlos
    1995. *Challenges of Communication*. Delhi, Indian Society for Promoting
    Christian Knowledge.
Valle, Carlos
    1996. 'Communication and Mission' in *Renewing Communication and Mission*.
    London, Wacc.
Van Beeck, Jozef S.J.
    1991. 'Divine Revelation: Intervention Or Self-Communication?' in *Theological
    Studies,* no. 52:2, June 1991. 199-226.
Van den Bulck, H. and Beyers, H.
    2005. *Media Studies Coming to Terms With the Contemporary European Media
    Scene*. Paper presented at the First European Communication Conference,
    Amsterdam, November 2005.
Van den Heuvel, Albert H.
    1967. 'A Meditation about Theology, Communication and the Mass Media', in
    The Christian Broadcaster, XIV, Vol. 9. pp 5-17
Van den Heuvel, Albert H.
    1997. *In or out? The neglected victims of the Communications revolution in
    Europe'*. Address at the Executive and Standing Committee of European
    Regional Association of the World Association for Christian Communication,
    7-9 February, 1997, Malaga, Spain.
Van den Heuvel, Albert
    1999. *Uitverkoop van het Publiek Domein?* Lecture at the conference 'Het
    Informatieparadijs' at the Thomas More Academy in Nijmegen (20-11-1999).
Van den Heuvel, Albert
    2001. *Values for a Global Society*. London, World Association for Christian
    Communication.
Van den Heuvel, Albert
    2006. 'Faith, hope, love and new technologies" in *Media Development* 2/2006.
    11-17.
Van der Meiden, Anne
    1980. *Alleen van horen zeggen... bouwstenen voor een communicatieve
    theologie*. Baarn, Ten Have.

Van der Meiden, Anne
    1981. 'Appeal for a more communicative theology' in *Media Development*.
    4/1981. 43-45.
Van der Meiden, Anne
    2000 (1999). *De markt van geloven*. Baarn, Ten Have.
Van Dijk, Teun A. (ed.)
    1985. *Handbook of Discourse Analysis*. London, Academic press.
Van Dijk, Teun A.
    1991. 'The discourse analytical approach' in *Racism and the Press*. London,
    Routledge
Van Gennep, F.O., Leertouwer L., Doorman S.J.
    1987. *Soms gebeurt het zomaar, over de mogelijkheid van geloofsverkondiging
    door een kerkelijke omroep*. Baarn, Ten Have/ IKON.
Van Ginneken, Jaap
    1999 (1998). *Understanding Global News, A Critical Introduction*. London,
    Thousand Oaks, New Delhi, SAGE Publications. Also in Dutch, *De Schepping
    van de wereld in het nieuws, de 101 vertekeningen die elk 1 procent verschil
    maken*. 2002 (Second actualized edition) (1996). Alphen aan de Rijn, Kluwer.
Van Ginneken, Jaap
    2000. *Verborgen Verleiders, hoe de media je sturen*. Amsterdam, Boom,
    Teleac/NOT.
Van Ruler, Betteke
    1996. *Communicatiemanagement in Nederland. Een verkenning naar de visie
    van communicatiemanagers op de inhoud van hun beroep*. Houten/Diegem,
    Bohn Stafleu Van Loghem.
Van Zoonen, Liesbet
    1995. 'Gender, Representation, and the Media' in Downing John, Mohammadi
    Ali and Sreberny-Mohammadi Annabelle (eds.) *Questioning the Media, a critical
    introduction*. (2nd edition). Thousand Oaks, Sage Publications. 311-328.
Vink, Nico.
    1990. *The telenovela and emancipation*, a study on tv and social change in
    Brasil. Amsterdam, Royal Tropical Institute.
Vink, Nico
    2004 (2001). *Grenzeloos Communiceren, een nieuwe benadering van
    interculturele communicatie*. Amsterdam, KIT Publishers.
Vink, Nico
    2005. (ed.) 'Religion and identity in a globalizing world', reader *International
    Development studies 2005*. C.M. Kan Institute, University of Amsterdam.
Vink, Nico
    2005. *Dealing with Differences. How to increase our intercultural competence?*
    Amsterdam, Royal Tropical Institute.
Walker, Andrew
    1996. *Telling the Story, Gospel, Mission and Culture*. London, Society for
    Promoting Christian Knowledge.
Ward, David
    With Oliver Carsten Fueg and Alessandro D'Armo. 2004. *A Mapping Study of
    Media Concentration and Ownership in Ten European Countries*. Hilversum,
    Commissariaat voor de Media and David ward.
Warren, Michael
    1997 (1992). *Seeing through the Media, A Religious View of Communications
    and Cultural Analysis*. Harrisburg, Trinity press International.

Welsch, Wolfgang.
    1999. 'Transculturality: the puzzling form of cultures today. In: Featherstone,
    Mike and Lash Scott (eds.) 1999 *Spaces of culture; city, nation, world*. London,
    Sage.
Werkman, H.N.
    1985. *Hasidic Legends*, A Suite by H.N. Werkman. Groningen, Wolters-
    Noordhoff Bouma's Boekhuis.
Westley, B. and MacLean M.
    1957. 'A conceptual model for communication research' in Journalism
    Quarterly, 34, pp. 31-80.
White, Robert A. s.j.
    1992. 'Twenty years of evolution in the Church's thinking about
    communication' in *Communicatio Socialis, no. 25 – 1992/3, 248-259*.
White, Robert A. s.j.
    1994. 'Communication: Meaning and Modalities' in Granfield, Patrick (ed.)
    1994. *The Church and Communication*. Kansas City, Sheed and Ward. 19-39.
White, Robert A. s.j.
    1997. 'Religion and Media in the Construction of Cultures' in Hoover, Stewart
    M. and Lundby, Knut *Rethinking Media, Religion and Culture*. Thousand Oaks,
    Sage, 37-64.
White, Robert A. s.j.
    1998. 'Communication Planning for Church Renewal' in Sunderaj, Victor (ed.).
    1998. *Pastoral Planning for Social Communication*. Montreal, Paulines. 17-40.
White, Robert A. s.j.
    2001. 'The New Communication Emerging in the Church' in *Catholic
    International* Vol. 12 No. 4, November 2001, 18-25.
White, Robert A. s.j.
    2003. 'The Emerging 'Communitarian' Ethics of Public Communication' in
    Mitchell, Jolyon and Marriage, Sophia (eds.)
    2003 *Mediating Religion*. London, T&T Clark, 285-292.
White, Robert A. s.j.
    2004. 'Major Issues in the Study of Media, Religion and Culture' in Horsfield,
    Peter, Hess, Mary and Medrano, Adán (eds.) *Belief in Media, Cultural
    Perspectives on Media and Christianity*. Aldershot, UK, Burlington, US, Ashgate.
    197-217.
White, Robert A. s.j.
    2006. *Harmonizing Pluralism, Freedom of belief, and Public Social Values: The
    Conundrun of Contemporary Cultural Globalization, The role of symbolic
    discourse in conflict resolution*. Paper presented at the 5th International
    Conference on Media, Religion and Culture: 'Mediating Religion in the Context
    of Multicultural Tension'. Sigtuna, Uppsala, Sweden.
White, Robert A. s.j.
    2006. 'The "Media, Religion and Culture" perspective: discovering a theory and
    methodology for studying media and religion' in Srampickal, Jacob, Mazza,
    Giuseppe and Baugh, Lloyd (eds.), 2006, *Cross Connections, Interdisciplinary
    communications studies at the Gregorian University*. Rome, CICS, Editrice
    Pontifica Università Gregoriana. 313-342.
Wiersinga, Herman
    2004. *De vitale vragen van Bonhoeffer*. Zoetermeer, Meinema.
Williams, Kevin and Miller, David
    1995. 'AIDS News and News Cultures' in Downing John, Mohammadi Ali and
    Sreberny-Mohammadi Annabelle (eds.) *Questioning the Media, a critical
    introduction*. (2nd edition). Thousand Oaks, Sage Publications. 413-427.

Windahl, Sven, Signitzer, Benno with Olson Jean T.
    1998 (1992). *Using Communication Theory. An Introduction to Planned
    Communication.* London, Sage Publications.
Winner, Langdon
    1999. 'Who Will We Be in Cyberspace?' in Mayer Paul (ed) *Computer Media
    and Communication.* New York, Oxford University Press. 207-218.
Winston, Brian
    1995. 'How Are Media Born and Developed?' in Downing John, Mohammadi
    Ali and Sreberny-Mohammadi Annabelle (eds.) *Questioning the Media, a critical
    introduction.* (2nd edition). Thousand Oaks, Sage Publications. 54-74.
Witvliet, Theo.
    2003. *Het geheim van het lege midden.* Zoetermeer, Boekencentrum
Woodward, Kenneth L.
    1993. 'Religion Observed: The Impact of the Medium on the Message' in
    Concilium 1993/6, 99-110.
World Association for Christian Communication
    1984. 'Communication for peace and justice' in *Challenge and Change, Review
    1983, plans 1984. London, WACC.*
Wörther, Matthias
    1993. *Vom Reichtum der Medien Theologische Überlegungen Praktische
    Folgerungen.* Würzburg, Echter Verlag.
Zagano, Phyllis
    1996. 'The Presentation of Religious Information via Media' in Soukup, Paul A.
    1996. *Media, Culture and Catholicism.* Kansas City, Sheed & Ward. 27-33.

Index

Subject Index

About the author

Ineke de Feijter is Assistant Professor in the masters program on Media, Religion and Culture at the Faculty of Theology and Religion of the *Vrije Universiteit* Amsterdam.

Her areas of research and teaching include the religious dimensions in and of global media culture and the implications for mainline religions; media and religious conflict; media, religion and the public sphere; media ethics; mediation, religious identity and communities; and media and inter cultural communication.

She is a member of the international research team on 'Blasphemy, Sacrilege and the Sacred, Conflicts Around the Presence and Representation of Islam and Christianity in the Public Spheres of the Netherlands, Germany and the United Kingdom', -anticipated-part of the Norface Research Program on the Re-emergence of Religion as a Social Force in Europe (forthcoming 2007).

She studied theology in Amsterdam and Buenos Aires (Comunicaión Popular) and took her master's degree at the University of Amsterdam and her doctoral degree at the *Vrije Universiteit* Amsterdam. Her professional career includes both communication (journalism and public relations) and theology. She was head of the communication department of IKON, the ecumenical national public broadcaster in the Netherlands, and served the United Protestant Church of Belgium as a minister.

She authored several articles and papers on the relationship between churches and media culture among which *Mainline Religion and Global Media Culture: Curtain Line or Kairos? Some Theological Reflections*. Louisville, Kentucky, 4th International Conference on Media, Religion and Culture, 2004.

Religion und Biographie/
Religion and Biography

hrsg. von
Prof. Dr. Detlev Dormeyer (Dortmund),
Prof. Dr. Ruard Ganzevoort
(Amsterdam),
Prof. Dr. Linus Hauser (Gießen), und
Prof. Dr. Friedhelm Munzel (Dortmund)

Detlev Dormeyer; Herbert Mölle;
Thomas Ruster (Hg.)
Lebenswege und Religion
Biographie in Bibel, Dogmatik und
Religionspädagogik
Die Theologen der Universität Dortmund
haben seit längerem an dem Zusammenhang
von Religion und Lebensgeschichte
gemeinsam gearbeitet. Sie beleuchten in dem
vorliegenden Sammelband die These, daß
Religion nur in Verbindung mit individueller
und kollektiver Lebensgeschichte ihre
Überzeugungskraft und Plausibilität
gewinnt, von drei Seiten aus, von der
religiösen Literatur, von theologisch-
philosophischem Denken, von den heutigen
Rahmenbedingungen. In die biographische
Dimension der religiösen Literatur führt
Wolfgang Esser ein mit dem Thema:
"Religiöse Selbsterneuerung in den
Lebensgeschichten der Volksmärchen".
Roland Kollmann stellt die heutigen
Möglichkeiten und Rahmenbedingungen
einer religiösen Biographie mit dem Thema:
"Religion als Risiko" vor. Es folgt der
Teil "Biographie und religiöse Literatur"
mit Überlegungen zu biographischen
Elementen in der Bibliotherapie (Munzel),
in den Josef-Geschichten (Wied), in
Geschichtsdarstellungen Israels (Mölle), im
Markus-Evangelium (Dormeyer), in Plutarchs
antiker Biographie Cato (Wördemann),
im lukanischen Doppelwerk (Riesner), in
Erzählungen über Engel (Friederich).
Der Teil "Biographie und theologisches
und philosophisches Denken" führt ein
in Johannes vom Kreuz (Ruster), in Edith
Stein (Petermeier) und in biographisch
veranlaßte Brüche theologischen Denkens

(Maurer). Der religionspädagogische
Teil nennt die gegenwärtigen Risiken,
überhaupt eine Lebenschance zu erhalten
(Grewel), den lebenslangen Wandel
des Glaubensbewußtseins (Englert,
Uni Essen), Hinderungsfaktoren sowie
Möglichkeiten religiöser Entwicklung
(Scheipers), Sektenstrukturen (Rustemeyer),
Wertentscheidungen in der Berufswahl
(Krämer), ethisches Lernen (Reis),
Religiosität bei Schülern mit geistiger
Behinderung (Arenhövel). Das breite
Spektrum der lebensgeschichtlich gelebten
und lebbaren christlichen Religiosität wird
umfassend und exemplarisch aufgezeigt.
Bd. 1, 2000, 320 S., 20,90 €, br.,
ISBN 3-8258 4226-6

Christa Zöller
Rockmusik als jugendliche
Weltanschauung und Mythologie
Weltanschauliche Elemente in der Rock-
und Popmusikkultur haben neomythischen
Charakter und sind eine Erscheinungsform
jugendlicher Identitätsfindung. Religiöse
Gefühle zu leben und der Wunsch, sie
auszudrücken, sind bei Jugendlichen
vorhanden und finden zunehmend individuell
und erlebnisorientiert in Jugendkulturen
ihren Ausdruck. Wichtigstes Medium dafür
ist Rockmusik. Die damit verbundenen
Gefühle und religiösen Praktiken müssen
ernst genommen und wertgeschätzt werden,
denn sie sind sowohl Ausdruck der Suche
auf dem Weg zu Identität als auch eine
jugendliche Antwort auf die Frage nach
eigener Weltanschauung, Religiosität und
Religion.
Bd. 2, 2000, 224 S., 20,90 €, br.,
ISBN 3-8258-4517-6

Detlev Dormeyer; Herbert Ulonska
Christologie in der Lebenspraxis
Elementare christologische Grundfragen
und ihr Transfer in die Bibelarbeit
Biographie und Religion gehören bei einem
so elementaren Thema wie der Christologie
eng zusammen; denn es wird konfessorisch
geglaubt, geredet und geschrieben, auch
durch die Autoren selbst. Diese Subjektivität

LIT Verlag Münster – Berlin – Hamburg – London – Wien
Fresnostr. 2 48159 Münster
Tel.: 0251 – 62 032 22 – Fax: 0251 – 23 19 72
e-Mail: vertrieb@lit-verlag.de – http://www.lit-verlag.de

ist gewollt, weil der Interpret und seine Interpretation durch die eigene Glaubens- und Lebenspraxis verbunden sind. Die einzelnen Beiträge sind aus einem lebendigen Dialog zwischen den Autoren und ihren Adressaten, Studierenden des Lehramts und Religionslehrer/inn/en erwachsen und wollen wieder in die Lebenswirklichkeit der Unterrichtenden und ihrer Schülerinnen und Schüler zurückgeführt werden.

Bd. 3, 2000, 168 S., 15,90 €, br.,
ISBN 3-8258-4569-9

Jörg Bade
Depression und Segen
Zur seelsorgerlichen Begegnung mit depressiven Menschen
"Eine Frau, ein Mann ist appetitlos, lustlos, kraftlos, das bisherige Leben durch eine Depression los-geworden. Wird das zugesprochene seelsorgerliche Wort, wird das Einfühlen der pastoralen Gesprächstherapeutin, wird das übliche Verhalten einer Seelsorgerin oder eines Seelsorgers angesichts des depressiven Gegenübers ausreichen? Mut zur seelsorgerlichen Ohnmacht, so eine These dieser Arbeit, darf als Voraussetzung für einen hilfreichen Umgang mit Menschen in einer Depression betrachtet werden. Der Segen allerdings entwirft und spendet ein positives Gegenbild zur depressiven Losigkeit. Er stellt geheiltes Leben in Aussicht."

Bd. 5, 2000, 360 S., 25,90 €, br.,
ISBN 3-8258 4607 5

Thomas Körbel
Hermeneutik der Esoterik
Eine Phänomenologie des Kartenspiels Tarot als Beitrag zum Verständnis von Parareligiosität
Esoterik ist heute ein Teil der religiösen Landschaft und bezeichnet ein dynamisches, "religiös" erscheinendes Geschehen. Doch die formale und inhaltliche, wie auch die terminologische und historische Bestimmung von "Esoterik" ist selten klar. Das führt oft zu Missverständnissen. Am Beispiel der Tarot-Karten wird die "esoterische" Weltanschauung reflektiert,

Unter verschiedenen Perspektiven wird das Begriffsfeld Esoterik systematisch erschlossen. Die jahrhundertealte Tradition ist Hintergrund vieler Praktiken zur Lebensbewältigung. Diese sind für suchende Menschen biographisch bedeutsam, Der Autor wirft Fragen an die Esoterik und an die Kirche auf und stellt sich ihnen. Er verfolgt damit den diakonischen Auftrag der Kirche, Menschen zu dienen und ihnen in ihrer Not und ihrer Suche nach Heil beizustehen, indem er einen Weg zu einem inneren und dialogischen Verstehen eröffnet.

Bd. 6, 2001, 456 S., 25,90 €, br.,
ISBN 3-8258-5378-0

Stefan von Hoyningen-Huene
Religiosität bei rechtsextrem orientierten Jugendlichen
Religiosität und Rechtsextremismus scheinen auf den ersten Blick wenig miteinander gemein zu haben. Politische und religiöse Orientierungen besitzen jedoch im Jugendalter bei der Identitätskonstitution eine zentrale Funktion. Der Frage, welche Rolle Religion bei der Sinnfindung rechtsextrem orientierter Jugendlichen spielt, geht Stefan v. Hoyningen-Huene in seiner Untersuchung nach. Anhand von Analysen von Interviews mit rechtsextremen Jugendlichen und von Texten aus rechtsextremen jugendkulturellen Szenen zeigt er die vielfältigen Verbindungen von Religion und Rechtsextremismus auf.

Bd. 7, 2003, 336 S., 24,90 €, br.,
ISBN 3-8258-6327-1

Corinna Cornelius
Harry Potter – geretteter Retter im Kampf gegen dunkle Mächte?
Religionspädagogischer Blick auf religiöse Implikationen, archaisch-mythologische Motive und supranaturale Elemente
Der grandiose Erfolg J. K. Rowlings mit ihrer „Harry-Potter"-Serie hat viele Fragen sowohl nach dem Wert als auch nach den Problemen dieses Werkes ausgelöst. Die vorliegende Arbeit nimmt zunächst eine literarische Bestimmung des Phänomens „Harry Potter" vor. Religiöse Implikationen (Weihnachten,

LIT Verlag Münster – Berlin – Hamburg – London – Wien
Fresnostr. 2 48159 Münster
Tel.: 0251 – 62 032 22 – Fax: 0251 – 23 19 72
e-Mail: vertrieb@lit-verlag.de – http://www.lit-verlag.de

Pate, Halloween) werden jeweils aus theologischer Sicht, werkimmanent und unter religionspädagogischen Aspekten transparent gemacht und kritisch hinterfragt. Es folgt die Darstellung archaisch-mythologischer und supranaturaler Elemente (z. B. göttliches Kind, Schöpfung/Inkarnation), an die sich eine Auseinandersetzung mit den „Schlüsselwörtern" der „Harry-Potter"-Rezeption (Magie und Zauberei) anschließt. Die alt- und neutestamentlichen, kirchengeschichtlichen wie auch religionswissenschaftlichen und -geschichtlichen Bezüge erhellen Anlage und Aussage des Werkes und führen gezielt in religionspädagogische Überlegungen. Für den Religionsunterricht und für die Gemeindearbeit bieten sich mit diesem Buch viele Möglichkeiten, auf das „Harry-Potter"-Phänomen zu reagieren oder – vom Werk J. K. Rowlings ausgehend – religiöse Motive und Vorstellungen zu thematisieren und zu erarbeiten bzw. zu ordnen.
Bd. 8, 2003, 112 S., 14,90 €, br., ISBN 3-8258-6830-3

Cordula Langner
Pro-Existenz Jesu
Das Jesus-Bild Heinz Schürmanns: Glaubenszeugnis der exegetischen Reflexion und Ausdruck seiner Jesus-Beziehung
Vor dem Horizont der „Leben-Jesu"-Forschung, im Rahmen der „Neuen Frage" nach Jesus thematisiert Heinz Schürmann in zahlreichen wissenschaftlichen Artikeln und spirituellen Schriften unterschiedliche Aspekte seines Jesus-Bildes, die hier erstmals systematisch als konsistentes Gesamtbild der theologischen Diskussion vorgestellt werden. H. Schürmanns Jesus-Bild gründet in seinem Glaubens-Leben und in der exegetischen Forschung. Als Glaubenszeugnis eröffnet es theologisch-wissenschaftlich und spirituell vielfältige Möglichkeiten einer Jesus-Beziehung und lädt zu ähnlichen Glaubenserfahrungen ein.
Bd. 9, 2003, 384 S., 29,90 €, br., ISBN 3-8258-7009-x

Heye Heyen
Biographie-Faktor Höllenglaube
Eine qualitativ-empirische Studie aus religionspädagogischer Perspektive
„Nach dem Tod droht die (ewige) Hölle" – das glaubt nach eigenen Angaben etwa jeder fünfte Westdeutsche. Auch heute noch wird – besonders in fundamentalistischen Kreisen – Kindern gezielt Höllenglaube vermittelt. Das hat Auswirkungen auf das spätere Leben und Erleben der betroffenen Menschen. In dieser Studie werden daraufhin die biographischen Erzählungen von vier betroffenen Personen mit qualitativen Methoden untersucht. Die Ergebnisse werden in einer Zusammenschau der Perspektiven von Theologie, Psychotherapie, Sozialisation und Bildung auf ihre Voraussetzungen und Konsequenzen hin reflektiert.
Bd. 10, 2003, 464 S., 34,90 €, br., ISBN 3-8258-7059-6

Ruard Ganzevoort; Heye K. Heyen (eds.)
Weal and Woe
Practical-Theological Explorations of Salvation and Evil in Biography
This book explores the connections between salvation and evil in their Christian, religious, and non-religious shapes. How are our biographies embedded in the Christian tradition and the surrounding culture? How do we deal with experiences of evil and how do we yearn for or enact shalom? The Kampen research group in practical theology and ethics explores these concepts and argues for a multidimensional understanding.
Bd. 11, 2004, 168 S., 17,90 €, br., ISBN 3-8258-8065-6

Dominique Hardy
Warum glauben die Deutschen anders als die Franzosen?
Eine vergleichende religionspädagogische Studie zur Erziehung der Großeltern
Fragen Sie einen deutschen Christ der heutigen Großeltern-Generation, welche Erinnerungen er oder sie von der religiösen Erziehung behalten hat. Sehr oft

LIT Verlag Münster – Berlin – Hamburg – London – Wien
Fresnostr. 2 48159 Münster
Tel.: 0251 – 62 032 22 – Fax: 0251 – 23 19 72
e-Mail: vertrieb@lit-verlag.de – http://www.lit-verlag.de

werden Sie auf offene Wunden, ja sogar auf Empörung stoßen: „Unter welcher Bevormundung, welchen Ängsten und welcher Unfreiheit haben wir gelitten!". Stellen Sie dieselbe Frage in Frankreich. Sie werden wahrscheinlich von der Antwort der dortigen Großeltern überrascht sein: „Ja, es gab einige unangenehme Dinge, aber im ganzen war es schön". Keine große Empörung, keine schlimme offenen Wunden. Die Umfrage von Dominique Hardy bestätigt, dass es effektiv einen Unterschied zwischen den beiden Ländern gibt und versucht ihn zu erklären.

Bd. 12, 2005, 168 S., 17,90 €, br., ISBN 3-8258-8764-2

Ilse Flöter
Gott in Kinderköpfen und Kinderherzen
Welche Rolle spielt Gott im Alltagsleben zehnjähriger Kinder am Anfang des 21. Jahrhunderts? Eine qualitativ-empirische Untersuchung
Ausgehend von der Frage nach der Rolle Gottes im Alltagsleben 10 jähriger Kinder am Anfang des 21. Jahrhunderts bietet diese qualitativ-empirische Untersuchung tiefe Einblicke in die religiöse Vorstellungswelt von Kindern deutscher und muslimischer Herkunft. Durch eine Fülle von Original-Zitaten ergeben sich Erkenntnisse über die religiöse Sozialisation in der Postmoderne, sowie über die Gottesvorstellungen und Gottesbeziehungen der Jungen und Mädchen. In diesem Buch wird anschaulich dargestellt, dass Kindertheologie im Sinne von Theologie von Kindern kein leerer Begriff ist.

Bd. 13, 2006, 440 S., 39,90 €, br., ISBN 3-8258-9244-1

Mathis-Christian Holzbach
Plutarch: *Galba-Otho* und die Apostelgeschichte – ein Gattungsvergleich
Plutarchs fragmentarisches Werk „Galba-Otho" und die Apostelgeschichte des Lukas werden auf gattungsspezifische Gemeinsamkeiten hin untersucht. Es wird nachgewiesen, dass „Galba-Otho" und die Apostelgeschichte als zweites Buch des lukanischen Doppelwerkes zu dem Überrest der untergegangenen hellenistischen, biographischen, pathetischen Geschichtsschreibung gehören. Es ist zu beobachten, dass beide Werke, die nahezu in derselben Zeit verfasst worden sind, mit den gleichen Wirkungsmechanismen arbeiten, um den Leser ethisch zu beeinflussen. Diese Intention wird sowohl bei Plutarch als auch bei Lukas an individuellen, handelnden Personen greifbar gemacht – ein Merkmal, das für die biographische Geschichtsschreibung typisch ist.

Bd. 14, 2006, 328 S., 29,90 €, br., ISBN 3-8258-9603-X

Wissenschaftliche Paperbacks
Theologie

Michael J. Rainer (Red.)
"Dominus Iesus" – Anstößige Wahrheit oder anstößige Kirche?
Dokumente, Hintergründe, Standpunkte und Folgerungen

Bd. 9, 2. Aufl. 2001, 350 S., 20,90 €, br., ISBN 3-8258-5203-2

Rainer Bendel (Hg.)
Die katholische Schuld?
Katholizismus im Dritten Reich zwischen Arrangement und Widerstand
Die Frage nach der „Katholischen Schuld" ist spätestens seit Hochhuths „Stellvertreter" ein öffentliches Thema. Nun wird es von Goldhagen neu aufgeworfen, aufgeworfen als moralische Frage – ohne fundierte Antwort. Wer sich über den Zusammenhang von Katholizismus und Nationalsozialismus fundiert informieren will, wird zu diesem Band greifen müssen: mit Beiträgen u. a. von Gerhard Besier, E. W. Böckenförde, Heinz Hürten, Joachim Köhler, Johann Baptist Metz, Rudolf Morsey, Ludwig Volk, Ottmar Fuchs und Stephan Leimgruber.

Bd. 14, 2., durchges. Aufl. 2004, 400 S., 19,90 €, br., ISBN 3-8258-6334-4

LIT Verlag Münster – Berlin – Hamburg – London – Wien
Fresnostr. 2 48159 Münster
Tel.: 0251 – 62 032 22 – Fax: 0251 – 23 19 72
e-Mail: vertrieb@lit-verlag.de – http://www.lit-verlag.de

Theologie: Forschung und Wissenschaft

Karl Matthäus Woschitz
Parabiblica
Studien zur jüdischen Literatur in der hellenistisch-römischen Epoche.
Tradierung – Vermittlung – Wandlung
Bd. 16, 2005, 928 S., 69,90 €, gb.,
ISBN 3-8258-8667-0

Tilman Beyrich (Hg.)
Unerwartete Theologie
Festschrift für Bernd Hildebrandt
Bd. 17, 2005, 296 S., 24,90 €, br.,
ISBN 3-8258-8811-8

Ulrich Feeser-Lichterfeld;
Reinhard Feiter in Verbindung
mit Thomas Kroll, Michael
Lohausen, Burkard Severin und
Andreas Wittrahm (Hg.)
Dem Glauben Gestalt geben
Festschrift für Walter Fürst
Dem Glauben Gestalt zu geben, ist das
zentrale Anliegen von Walter Fürst, geb.
1940 in Stuttgart, von 1985 bis 2006
Professor für Pastoraltheologie in Bonn.
Viele seiner Themen hat er dabei im Dialog
mit Frauen und Männern in der pastoralen
Praxis entdeckt, viele seiner Gedanken
im Austausch mit Kollegen, Schülern
und Freunden entwickelt. Die Festschrift
führt dieses Gespräch fort. Ausgehend von
Impulsen Walter Fürsts diskutieren Kollegen
und Mitarbeiterinnen und Mitarbeiter die
Ausrichtung der Pastoraltheologie im Dienst
einer glaubwürdigen pastoralen Praxis.
Bd. 19, 2006, 384 S., 34,90 €, br.,
ISBN 3-8258-8783-9

Andreas Klein; Matthias Geist (Hg.)
„Bonhoeffer weiterdenken … "
Zur theologischen Relevanz Dietrich
Bonhoeffers (1906–1945) für die
Gegenwart. Mit einem Exposé von
Ulrich H.J. Körtner
Der vorliegende Band versammelt Beiträge
jüngerer WissenschafterInnen der Theologie,
die sich zum Ziel gesetzt haben, die
vielschichtigen Herausforderungen des
Denkens Bonhoeffers aufzunehmen und in
unterschiedlichste Richtungen kritisch und
produktiv fortzuführen. Der Bogen spannt
sich dabei von ethischen über systematisch-
und praktisch-theologischen Fragen bis hin
zu Gender Studies. Durch diese Studien wird
auch deutlich, daß Bonhoeffers Leben und
Werk Impulse freizulegen vermögen, die
noch lange nicht erschöpft sind und jeder
Generation Anlaß geben können, Neues aus
Altem zu gewinnen.
Bd. 21, 2006, 200 S., 19,90 €, br.,
ISBN 3-8258-9279-4

Ottmar John;
Matthias Möhring-Hesse (Hg.)
Heil – Gerechtigkeit – Wahrheit
Eine Trias der christlichen Gottesrede.
Mit Beiträgen von Ottmar John, Matthias
Möhring-Hesse, Klaus Müller, Hans-
Joachim Sander, Magnus Striet, Saskia
Wendel und Knut Wenzel
Dieser Sammelband nimmt die
Monotheismusdebatte zum Anlass, neu über
die Eigenschaften Gottes nachzudenken.
Er geht von der Grundannahme aus, dass
der einzige Gott durch die Trias von
Heil-Gerechtigkeit-Wahrheit ausgesagt
werden muss. Die Beiträge suchen aus der
Perspektive verschiedener theologischer
Disziplinen und von unterschiedlichen
theologischen Ansätzen die Trias von Heil,
Gerechtigkeit und Wahrheit auszuleuchten.
Sie machen deutlich, dass die moderne
Monotheismuskritik vor allem dann
Plausibilität erheischen konnte, wenn die
Einheit von Glaube, Praxis und Vernunft aus
dem Blick gerät.
Bd. 22, 2006, 200 S., 19,90 €, br.,
ISBN 3-8258-5588-0

LIT Verlag Münster – Berlin – Hamburg – London – Wien
Fresnostr. 2 48159 Münster
Tel.: 0251 – 62 032 22 – Fax: 0251 – 23 19 72
e-Mail: vertrieb@lit-verlag.de – http://www.lit-verlag.de